Feeling Our
FEELINGS

*What Philosophers Think
and People Know*

by Eva Brann

PAUL DRY BOOKS

Philadelphia   2008

First Paul Dry Books Edition, 2008

Paul Dry Books, Inc.
Philadelphia, Pennsylvania
www.pauldrybooks.com

Text type: Minion
Display type: Bembo
Designed and composed by P. M. Gordon Associates

1 3 5 7 9 8 6 4 2
Printed in the United States of America

Library of Congress Cataloging-in-Publication Data
Brann, Eva T. H.
 Feeling our feelings : what philosophers think and people know / Eva Brann.
 — 1st Paul Dry Books ed.
     p.   cm.
 Includes bibliographical references and index.
 ISBN 978-1-58988-046-7 (alk. paper)
 1. Emotions (Philosophy) I. Title.
 B105.E46B73 2008
 128'.37—dc22

                                                    2008030369

Frontispiece: Sappho turns to Alcaeus, two poets singing to each other. It is commonly thought that this early red-figure vase-painting illustrates the poem, perhaps by Sappho, cited on page 5. From a spouted cylindrical mixing bowl for wine. Height: 20.4 in. Date: 480/470 B.C.E. Painter: Brygos or his circle. Inscription: "Alkaios, Sapho, Dama [masc.] is beautiful."

Feeling Our
FEELINGS

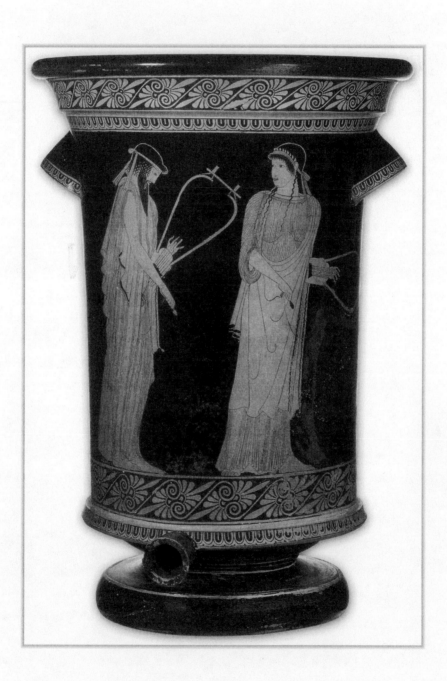

To Beate Ruhm von Oppen
1918–2004

Brief Contents

Contents

By Way of a Preface

On the Title

The phrase "Feeling Our Feelings" comes from the words a little boy called Zeke said to me some thirty years ago when he was four. I was swinging him in a park in Cambridge, Massachusetts, and I wasn't doing it right. "Swing me higher," he said. "I want to feel my feelings." The phrase stuck with me; you might say it festered in my mind; it agitated questions. Why do we all want to feel our feelings so generally that people "not in touch" with them are thought to be in need of therapy? What feeling did swinging high induce? Was it an exultation of the body or an exhilaration of the soul? When Zeke wanted to feel his feelings, was there a difference between the general feeling, the mere consciousness of being affected, and his particular feelings, the distinguishable affects?—as, when you sing a song, there is a difference between the singing done and the song sung. Or is there?

> O body swayed to music, O brightening glance,
> How can we know the dancer from the dance?[1]

When a dancer is dancing a dance or a singer singing a song, the grammarian *names* the occasion of Yeats's question, calling the dance or song an "internal accusative." He means that the verb's object is not outside its action, that it makes the object as it acts. A philosopher, however, actually *engages* the question; Aristotle tells how we can know the dancer from the dance: A capable dancer precedes and survives the dance; even asleep he is, somehow, a dancer.[2] Hence you may be singing "Swing low, sweet chariot," putting all of yourself into it, and yet remain also a singer in general.

Do we find here a usable analogy to the particular feeling of "swinging high" and feeling one's feelings more diffusely? Do these feelings the boy wanted to call on precede and survive the thrill of swinging? Are we somehow feeling-ready, in the sense of being ever and always, perhaps sub-liminally, feeling-fraught? Does that perhaps mean that our inner cosmos is thrumming with an affective background murmur, a feeling which is not *a* feeling—of love, of pride, of hate, of shame? And further, is there love, pride, hate, shame that is not *for* an object or *about* a situation? This turns out to be what philosophers call the question of intentionality, by which they mean "aboutness": Do robust feelings always tend toward, focus on, weave themselves about an objective cause? Yet the very verb "to feel" seems to take as its grammatical and intentional objects most naturally the affects themselves—as if it awaited them—and only more attenuatedly what they are about: We feel the fear acutely, but sense the causal danger diffusely; we can feel sharp fright though we only vaguely surmise that a bear is nosing around the tent.

Of course, once you are in the question-raising mode, swarms of them come from all directions yet always tethered to one central question: What *are* we, as—perhaps ultimately—passive, reactive beings? What are we that being affected is the great voucher for our being actively alive? And there are showers of subsidiary questions as well: Is feeling sleepy or hungry the same or very different in kind from feeling love or anger? Why do we nowadays often say "I feel that . . ." when perhaps we ought to say "I think that . . ."? Why do we speak of "feelings" not of "felts" when, after all, we speak not of "thinkings" but of "thoughts"?[3] Is it that we "have" feelings as progressions, but thoughts are completions? And these are only a few of the questions raised by *one* affect-term, the one in the title.

In this book I try, when I am able—which is usually when I find help—to answer questions like these, and when I'm not, at least to clarify them, for I think that while straight answers are best if you can come by them honestly, the next best thing is to be very clear about the problems. Here I am assum-ing that questions about feeling, once they have been put in words, will cast their spell on any reader, either because of their novelty or, more often and better, because of the opposite—because we recognize that they've always been with us, though suppressed and postponed. Are there human beings who have not sometimes felt anything from plain puzzlement to real agony about the feelings they are feeling? Aren't many—perhaps most—people natural experts on feeling feelings but perhaps lifelong novices at articulat-ing that experience?

And so there is also a subtitle: "What philosophers think and people know" about feelings. Sometimes these two are one and the same, since some philosophers mean merely to put solid ground under ordinary peo-ple's ordinary opinions, or to use what is probably a happier figure, they mean to uncover the deep roots of normal human life—not to pull and then hold them up to withering criticism, but to inspect and carefully replant them. There are some philosophers, however, who, in searching for the basis of human feeling, are drawn to be more radical, to go to the roots in such a way as to uproot common opinions, so that human life may never look quite the same again (though even these, read charitably, will probably turn out to have illuminated what we all know). There are, moreover, yet other philosophers and scientists, especially contemporary ones, who use a derogatory term, "folk psychology," for what ordinary people think they know, and these non-folks make it their mission to correct popular misapprehensions, mostly for their fellow scientists. Though I am wary of them, they also must be attended to because they are bound to be often right—in their own counterintuitive terms.

But why write a book in which philosophical theories play a central role? Why not just think about human feeling and report the results of my inquiry?

The reason ought to be pretty obvious. It has to do with our—my—limited capacity for originality, understood not in the sense, so inappropriate to philosophy (which ought to be truth-telling) of making up novel conceptual devices, but in a good sense of finding the ageless origins of our being. Many of us who have longed to get to the bottom of a matter—here human feeling—have learned that we are not, ourselves, able to devise the deep-rooted and comprehensive, the "original," theory that might satisfy that longing. So we study what others have written to help us think. This task, however, is also a temptation. The philosophic text won't help us unless we immerse ourselves in it as it is written—never mind its "background." Yet even, or especially, if we don't get sidetracked by circumstantial considerations, we can get so involved in construing an author's meaning that we lose the impetus of the inquiry; we understand the text and lose the question. Then we end up with a series of meticulously clued-out accounts, and too often this investment of scholarly labor is out of proportion to the reader's profit or ours, since the theses we have understood are not truths we any longer care about.

I would if I could avoid that damping of the life of the quest, but here's the rub: It seems to me that the philosophers who have something persuasive or at least beguiling to say are those who think *as* philosophers about human feeling. They embed their understanding of the feeling soul in a natural and hyper-natural, that is, a physical or metaphysical inquiry, or conversely, they derive their theory of nature and what is beyond nature from thinking through what it means for human beings to feel.

Hence to get the good of their thinking about feeling and what it means to feel our feelings, it is necessary to consider the supra-human frame of their thought, be it prior to or consequent on their psychology, to capture in a reasonable number of pages the relevant elements of their whole philosophy. Anyone can see the dangers and difficulties of that: To avoid becoming unprofitably prolix one might become scandalously superficial; for example, to convey succinctly the characteristic insights, one may find oneself resorting to compressed schematisms, thus traducing the depth of a design whose validation comes from the cohesion of its details.

If, moreover, the approaches are troublesome, so are the results. For though the very point of studying a number of philosophical works is to see the subject from that many perspectives, the outcome may be that one's head is filled with incoherently alternative opinions, since anyone who has undertaken a reading course on human feelings will hardly end up thinking that there is solid progress here. Indeed, as the terms of the enigma are continually reconceived, the soul may become progressively disengaged—it has all but disappeared from current emotion studies.

Nonetheless I have chosen, even in the face of these misgivings, to call on certain philosophers for help because they wrote substantially on human feelings and embedded their treatments in—or derived them from—comprehensive designs that had depth: Plato, Aristotle, Cicero (for the Stoics), Aquinas, Descartes, Spinoza, Hume, Kierkegaard, Heidegger. Since these philosophers preserve, for the most part, their personal humanity as they write of the most human propensity, what they think does not diverge so very far from what we readers know; on the contrary, it illumines, as I said, common understandings and dignifies them by showing from what point of view they make sense.

It might help readers to list the approaches to which I have in fact had occasional recourse, especially in the last chapter, but which I have *forgone* as organizing principles of inquiry. I don't pretend to offer:

1. *Continuous history*—the Herculean task, which I would be quite incompetent to attempt and few readers would wish to face, of giving a connected account, epoch by epoch, document by document, of the prevailing opinions people have had about feeling and of all the writings that articulated or influenced those views. Moreover, such an account would have to be given not only for the traditions of our West, but for the whole human world. It isn't even clear that the library-filling result would make much sense. For while it is reasonable to think that opinions which follow upon others in time—supposing it didn't (to my surprise) turn out that human beings in fact thought every sort of thing about human matters simultaneously at all times—are causally connected, that is not the same as discovering a rational descent, a coherent directed development toward something. Even biological evolutionists, who generally eschew final cause, actually have in the principle of adaptation an engine if not of a goal-directed progress at least of a cause-driven process. But what would serve similarly in tracing the evolution of the passions, which are so frequently anti-adaptive as hell?

2. *Thematic treatments*—the directly opposite approach, in which the passions are taken up in monographs one by one: love, shame, disgust, and "mood," to give especially rich examples. This approach is full of interest, but though it has been tried, it is probably not possible to reach the nature of feeling itself through the study of this or that particular affect.

3. *Philosophical schools*—the approaches to human affectivity that have exercised so wide an influence and have been so often formulated that they may be considered as theories in abstraction from particular authors: Epicureanism, Stoicism, Associationism, Existentialism, Phenomenology, Neostoicism, Cognitivism, as well as physiological and neuroscientific accounts. This approach has the virtue of imposing on the expositor the obligation to get the generalized gist of the theory, which is sometimes simultaneously the vice of effacing the powerfully singular ground of thought on which stood the originators of the school. (As the reader will discover, I have not wholly avoided dealing in schools of thought, and in the last chapter Cognitivism is indeed taken up as the predominant contemporary trend.)

4. *Taxonomy*—the discerning, listening, enumerating, ranking, categorizing, and defining of human feeling. This is more difficult to do than it is engaging to read, for who can love a list, though the main labor is in it? We tend to inherit and borrow these catalogues without asking how they were first made. Did we discern them within ourselves and then recognize them in language or the other way around? We have all asked ourselves— I imagine—at some helpless moment, "What is this that I am feeling?" It is the arch-question of lyric poets: What, my heart, are you up to? How do we so inexactly, how do they so precisely, find the words? In short, how do I discern *that* I am feeling, *what* I am feeling, *whether* I have felt all the feelings there are to feel or at least that most others feel, what feelings come in opposing pairs or in related complexes, which are primary and which derivative? And, having somehow coupled my feelings with familiar names or, conversely, being presented with such a name, summoning within me a sample of an affect answering to it, how do I devise what is more than a descriptive heap of pertinent adjectives, how do I compose a definition of essential properties? All the philosophers, some crucially, some incidentally, engage in this list- and definition-making, and that is why it will turn up in this book without being my main pursuit.

5. *Conceptual history*—the tracing of the terms denoting human affect, in so far as these come into and go out of use or appear to change their meanings subtly or abruptly. This is the deeply engaging speculative inquiry into the way the ground shifts under or with terminology when "words change their meanings," and the way these shifts indicate revolutions in

human consciousness.[4] It is an approach requiring much intellectual sensitivity to the way old meanings are buried—"sedimented"—in new uses.
No one writing about human matters as they appear over time can avoid
giving some attention to this approach; the originator is Husserl. I will use
it occasionally rather than systematically.

6. *Linguistic analysis*—the fine discrimination of usage. One might call
this the positivistic counterpart of conceptual history, meaning a more time-
restricted, fact-directed inquiry into what people mean as revealed when
they speak (in our case, English) in ordinary life. This approach depends
crucially on the analyst's ear for language, which is not guaranteed; moreover, its philosophical results are narrow.

7. *Moral connection*—the passions' relation to virtue and vice or the
emotions' relation to morality. Almost all considerations of the passions
eventually lead to the problem of their control or, at least, their management in individuals and thence to their social consequences. All the major
treatments of the passions that I have read culminate in ethical, that is to say,
virtue-directed or in moral, that is to say, rule-directed reflections and in the
positing of the best human type. And so the most dispassionate beginnings
tend to have more or less fervent endings, which I will report incidentally,
as they bear on the nature of passion.

8. *Psychological theories*—the points of view that base their observations
concerning the passions on natural theories of the soul (or the converse)
and often only implicitly on metaphysics (or its denial): The pre-Freud-
ian theories have been largely eclipsed by psychoanalysis, where "soul" and
its parts turn into "psyche" and its depths. Perhaps the neglect of these
approaches—which will be frequently though sporadically called in—is
most in need of some justification. Mine is, to be sure, a speculation: I
think that psychological theories that are discredited, or are in the course
of being discredited, either disappear or wander over to literature as handy
tropes for human depths, or enter folk psychology as ready-made accounts
for human peculiarity, whence too they fade in time. Philosophical systems,
on the other hand, only go into short temporary oblivion, often less than a
millennium, whence they emerge refurbished with sophisticated embellish-
ments, redone in neoteric form. I am thinking of the periodic revivals of the
Platonic, Aristotelian, Stoic, Thomistic, Cartesian, Kantian, and Hegelian
approaches.

What is to be found in psychological writing that is of uneclipsable
interest are researches into the pathology of the passions and their social
effects. That means that even those psychologists who are by profession

most strictly scientific, the physician-psychiatrists, cannot help but concern themselves with the moral questions that occupy lay thinkers about human affectivity: Are people whose emotions are out of control sick or bad; are they victims or instigators of evil?

I need hardly excuse the fact that the multitude of therapies devised yearly for the relief of the emotional miseries of the modern condition are, more or less respectfully, set aside here.

9. *Emotions in the arts*—especially in literature and music. What work of language from Homer's epics onward, what composition of notes beginning with the Greek modes, is not an enterprise in expounding or expressing particular passions and the passionate life in general? This activity is not a field of inquiry, but the reflective remaking of the world itself. "The Emotions in the Arts" seems to me an absurd title, precisely because one could hardly write a book about feelings without constant recourse to their artful expression, be it poetic, narrative, tonal, visual. I shall, in fact, begin with some pretty wild lyric poetry by some of those supposedly rationalistic Greeks.

10. *Physiology*—last, but the opposite of least, the somatic or bodily approach to the passions and emotions, which have always been felt in the body and thought of as somehow somatic. This question has been a perennial preoccupation: Are the bodily "feels" in the breast or groin or skin of the passionate essence or are they mere epiphenomena of human feeling? The school that went for the body as the locus of emotions, initiated by Darwin and made explicit by William James, set the course for what is now the liveliest and most influential approach to the emotions: their physiological origins in the states of the body and their neurological reflections in the neural patterns of the brain. I will recur to these theories (insofar as I grasp them) when they bear on our conscious experience of feeling our feelings—which is just where the explanatory power of neuroscience becomes most fascinatingly questionable.

You might now think of my approach—that by way of picked philosophers—as a kind of spot check on the state of reflection on human affectivity or, in the way I do, as a hitting of the high points that will best help me to make sense of myself—and of the world, natural and human-made, then and now, passing and perennial, the world that impinges on me by instilling or eliciting feelings in me. The final recourse has, of course, to be what I know of myself, and what you know of yourself—"what people know." "What philosophers think" could not even so much as raise the question for us unless it already were a sleeping passion of our soul waiting to be roused.

But then the articulation of the questions can initiate the multiple clarifications that are the prerequisites for forming those stable views we can live with and, when push comes to shove, live by.

Finally, a note on terms: I have begun with "feeling" and put the whole book under that title, but in the review of various approaches other terms necessarily appear and take center stage. So I will sketch out some first distinctions among the most common words, which should become more precise as the philosophers speak for themselves. The first and oldest term is "passion" (Greek *pathos*): a strong, natural affect, under which we are passive rather than active, which we suffer in both senses of being pained and being victimized; "pathology" is a revealing related term. Therefore passion traditionally implies a soul capable of being subjected, even abjectly so, to feeling—and yet strong enough to be masterfully ascendant through thinking. Love and pride are thus the prime passions.

At a certain time "passion" yields to "emotion" in English. "Emotion" comes from *ex-movere*, Latin for "moving out [of its place]," "stirring up," and the emphasis on passivity under external influence yields, correspondingly, to an interest in the internal motive force and its artful expression. These multifarious psychic displacements and their objects become the focus of psychology, while their poignant description becomes consciously the province of art.

"Feeling" tends to be used in English in the most general sense I began with, as sensitivity to, or awareness of, our physical or psychic state—though sometimes it has a harder edge, denoting the "feels" that are closest to the body and have the least articulate definition, particularly pleasure and pain.

"Affect" is, if anything, even more general, referring to any excitation the human constitution undergoes, usually as opposed to cognitive activity, but in at least one great case, Spinoza's, including it. "Sentiment" tends to carry a sense of diffuseness, often of flabby mildness. Its derivative, "sentimentality," has long denoted degraded feeling—emotional schmaltz and artistic schlock. Heartfelt insincerity and lax impassionedness are deeply puzzling human modes, but bypassed here, as being just one thing too many.

At last, "mood"—which becomes, so it seems to me, the most interesting affect of modernity—comes to be defined as a feeling without an object: We fear a bear (not every bear, of course, not a teddy bear, but the scary sort of bear that turns up in a lot of the literature on fear), but we have anxiety about nothing in particular. It might be said, speaking roughly, that when philosophy is metaphysical, love is the moving passion; when it becomes existential, anxiety is the revealing mood. Consequently what certain philosophers think about this affect, and how that does indeed differ from what people know, will be taken up toward the end.

Usage Note: The reader will, I hope, forgive my shifting use of the pronouns "I," "you," "we," "one," a practice for which I persecute my students. I am sometimes giving my own opinions, sometimes appealing to the reader's experience, sometimes relying on our common humanity, and now and then playing the impersonal spectator.

Westport, Mass., May 2005
Annapolis, Md., June 2008

Note on Citations

This book is not intended as a work of scholarship for scholars but rather as an effort at inquiry for amateurs of the topic—our feelings.

The endnotes are meant to serve a triple purpose. The first is to direct readers to the main texts I wrote about; I have made an effort to cite these as independently of specific editions as possible. The second is to help readers disposed to check the grounds of my interpretation. The third purpose is to credit commentaries and expositions that I have used with profit.

In those chapters that deal in part or in whole with contemporary studies, I have given a short bibliography right in the endnotes, wishing to avoid the appearance of giving *the* bibliography for that author or subject. For in our time the emotion literature has grown beyond the bounds of one layperson's mastery. I have looked at only a minuscule part of it and cited only a part of that part. It lies in the way these studies have been developing that my sources here are more often "secondary" than "primary," meaning that they are specialized detailings on the basis of received categories rather than large-gauged foundational works; the citational practice reflects these facts.

In order to keep the text uncluttered, I have refrained from internal cross-referencing; the reader can follow terms or themes by using the very ample Index.

Note of Thanks

This book first took shape in the course of the Schmidt Study Group on Emotion held at my college in the fall of 2004. In attendance were my colleagues Joseph Cohen, Michael Dink, George Doskow, Deborah Renaut, and John Verdi. I learned from each of them, but my special thanks go to Joe Cohen for pushing us into studying Spinoza's *Ethics,* a book which, once discovered, became the center of reference for me.

I am grateful to Ann Martin, the producer and first critical reader of the manuscript, and to Lucy Martin for the figures.

Many thanks to my publisher, Paul Dry, who watched this book grow and grow and never said, "No more!"

Finally, I am deeply obliged to my colleague Eric Salem, who gave this manuscript as attentively critical a reading as an author could wish for, not only catching numerous flaws, but contributing many thoughts and formulations.

St. John's College, Annapolis
June 2008

Feeling Our
FEELINGS

chapter I

Passion Itself

Poetry

Emotion: Reason, Heart: Mind, Feeling: Understanding, Passion: Thought—these and similar pairs are stock couples of our thinking and talking. More often than not the pairing-up is a pitting-against: destroying Passion vs. edifying Thought, warm Heart vs. cold Mind, rich Emotion vs. anemic Reason, vague Feeling vs. clear Understanding (or permutations thereof). The couples are thought of as oppositions, and people (of whom philosophers do form a subclass) take sides. They might seem to be endorsing the storms of spring or proscribing the squalls of fall, except that we do indeed appear to be so made, our psychic economy seems to be so arranged, that we often feel ourselves rent in two, riven by hostile powers answering to some one or other of these terms, and so we must make choices.

Philosophers, who like to think and hate to be disturbed, tend to favor the side whose rubric-heading is Reason. But of course there are among them also dyed-in-the-wool dissenters from their native party, though I know of no ancient writer of any school who praises Passion passionately; even the ancient hedonists, indeed they particularly, teach *a-patheia*, passionlessness.

It is the moderns who make it a project to rehabilitate the emotions, as these human experiences are by then termed. They call on the emotions as indefeasible facts to be acceded to, as guides to the body's health, as devices for survival and well-being, as psychotherapeutic escape-valves, as antidotes for arid rationalism, as access routes to deeper layers of being.

The most spectacular, sophisticated, and revealing case of the modern call to feeling I know is Nietzsche's youthful work (he was twenty-eight), *The Birth of Tragedy from the Spirit of Music* (1872). It is couched in terms of hyper-human forces—though not Eros but Dionysus—and of human ritual—though not the rites of love but of Tragedy. Dionysus, the god of tragedy, stands for the call on the human capacity to accept suffering, to welcome the dissolution of individuality, to undergo the "glory of passivity"[1] in an ecstasy of surrender to the blindly musical, aboriginally potent abyss of the world that knows no logical distinctions or paradoxes. Tragedy is presented as the communal Greek ritual during which the faceless force is transformed into a shower of lucidly lit Apollonian visions.

But in Nietzsche's work, tragedy "commits suicide," and the culprit that urges her on is a newly-born god-superseding demon: Socrates.[2] Socrates is the destroyer of the tragic worldview, who reduces Apollonian clarity to dialectical sophisms, who is intolerant of potent paradox, who is a purveyor of optimistic levity—in short a rationalist and the father of every rational enlightenment—"enshallowment," to coin a Marx-like phrase—be it ancient or modern.

From the first, *The Birth of Tragedy* was censured for being totally ahistorical.[3] But that is nothing to the point. Nietzsche is bemoaning a human loss, and Socrates is the name for the avatar of this self-contented graying of the modern world, the ancestor of all that rational philosophizing of the West.

Yet there is a mistake here, one that matters to our self-understanding. It is not a philological or historical factual error, but a deliberate misreading of the philosophical tradition: Socrates, the very "type of the *theoretical man*,"[4] sat among the spectators of Old Tragedy, Nietzsche says, and *failed to understand* it.

Did he fail to understand it? Is that famous battle between the poets and philosophers—an *old* battle to Socrates[5]—based on obtuse misapprehension, and is the Western trust in thinking founded from its inception on a psychic inability to feel deeply? Surely not. For it seems to me that we may look past the Dionysiac-Apollonian-Socratic/force-ritual-dialectic frame of Nietzsche's young work to a less mystical, more natural dualism: the opposition of passion as expressed in imaginative poetry, and thought as recorded in dialectical discussion. In those terms Socrates is a man experienced, indeed expert, in passion—as is his Plato and all the philosophers and scholars, and for that matter pot-painters (Frontispiece) of antiquity, who heard and read and painted, and in their works preserved the poets who would otherwise be lost to us. Here I mean not the tragedians but the lyric poets who sing of themselves as seized by one passion in particular.

With that passion, for which love is too limp a term, they themselves had a love-hate relation. One of the earliest of them, Alcman, says, presumably of Eros: "An ache (*achos*) takes hold of me, you destructive spirit (*daimon*)." But he also says of Aphrodite's Eros: "Once again"—this is these poets' continual refrain: "yet once more"—"by Cyprian Aphrodite's order, sweet Eros suffuses me and melts my heart."[6] (The difference between Aphrodite and Eros as the gods of love is a lovely puzzle.) The philosophers go both ways too. They both fear and shun and love and honor these divinities, as they honor their poets. Socrates is made to speak of "the old wise men and women" who knew all about love, for instance "noble Sappho and clever Anacreon,"[7] and Plato in his own voice wrote this epigram for Sappho:

Some say there are nine Muses.— How careless!
Look at Sappho from Lesbos: She's the tenth.

The whole point of this prologue is to support the claim that so-called Greek rationalism is so immediately up against the passions as to know whereof it speaks—that when Socrates calls Eros a "tyrant"—the tyrant being the worst human type he knows because it is self-enslavement incarnate[8]—he is experienced in and mindful of passion alive then and there at its most passionate; he is not, as may be true of some later rationalists, beating a long-dead horse; he is fully, though novelly, erotic.

I want to make certain here that I don't give the impression of going overboard the other way by crediting the Greeks with being the first articulate initiates into human feeling. No one who has read of the foul, destructive lust that Ishtar, goddess of love, displays for Gilgamesh, king of Uruk, and the wild grief of Gilgamesh for the friend of his heart Enkidu, as it is described in the great epic that preceded these poets by, possibly, two millennia, no one who has experienced the Hebrew Bible with its tempestuous God and his temperamental people, could possibly think that.

That said, let me bring passion itself on the scene here. This is passion felt here and now, recognized from the past, appropriated as one's own, feared and hoped for, reflected on with double-edged expressiveness—the love-hate for Love.

Here, then, are some poems or parts of poems by several Greek lyric poets. Most of them lived in the sixth century B.C.E. Alcaeus and Sappho were fellow islanders from Lesbos, and they seem to have been friends or something more; there is a part of a tart poem by Sappho, quoted by Aristotle in his *Rhetoric,* in which she tells Alcaeus to stop beating around the bush if he has something honest in mind.[9] Anacreon lived a generation or more later on the island Samos—most of the lyric poets came from the eastern Aegean islands. Let Anacreon go first, for his brutal candor:

Once again, Eros, like a blacksmith, has whacked me
With his huge axe and doused me in a wintry ditch.

We owe the survival of this distich or "two-liner" to a late handbook on meter, where it is, with hilarious deafness to import, cited as an example of a meter invented by Anacreon.[10] (Much of the surviving early lyric poetry, which was read throughout antiquity, comes to us from latter-day scholarly works that mined it, with touching care and comical myopia, for examples of grammatical and prosodic usage.) Anacreon's meter was, incidentally, "bradycataleptic tetrameter." Should there be a reader who wonders what that is, here is the scansion of the Greek, transliterated to show how beautifully the intricate meter offsets the brutal meaning:

⌣ ⌣ −   − / ⌣   ⌣ − // ⌣ − / ⌣ − / ⌣   − −
Megaloi deute m'Eros ekopse hoste chalkeus

⌣ ⌣ −   − / ⌣ ⌣ ⌣− // ⌣ − / ⌣ − / ⌣ − −
pelekei, cheimeriei d'elousen en charadrei.[11]

Sappho had already said that "Eros, like a down-rushing squall falling on the oaks, whipped round my heart," and, again from that handbook, comes this Sapphic fragment:

Eros, once again, the limb-loosener churns me—
A bittersweet, intractable, creeping thing.[12]

Here is Archilochus from the Aegean island Paros, of the seventh century, so Sappho's predecessor:

But, O my comrade, the limb-loosener breaks me: Longing (*pothos*).[13]

And her countryman Alcaeus speaks of Eros as

... the most terrible of gods:
Iris, the beautifully-sandaled, bore you,
Mingling with Zephyr, the golden-haired.[14]

No old god is of such uncertain parentage as Eros, though so much that is of importance to human beings hangs on his ancestry; Socrates will show how much the parentage of Love matters in the dialogue *Phaedrus*. Plutarch, who quotes the fragment, also cites a grammarian's explanation of what appears to be Alcaeus's own myth-making: This parental fiction—Iris being the rainbow, Zephyr the west wind—is intended to point up "the many-splendored (*poikilon*) and flowery nature of the passions." But before it is charmingly springlike, love is a terrible god to the archaic poets. (I call them "archaic" because their time is often called that by historians; it means both "being at the originating beginning" and "acting as the ruling principle" of what is to come.)

Then, again and finally, here are two more of Sappho's poems, the first all that we have, the second just the first stanza of a seven-stanza whole:

To me he seems to be a man equal to the gods—that one, who sits facing you and listens to your sweet talking close by and your lovely laughing. Oh yes, it makes my heart in my breast beat wildly. For when I glance at you even briefly my voice no longer obeys me but my tongue is broken, and straightway a light fire runs under my skin, and I see nothing with my eyes, and my ears are buzzing, and sweat runs down me, and a trembling seizes the whole of me, and I am greener than grass, and you would think that I was all but dead.[15]

You of the many-splendored throne, deathless Aphrodite, wile-weaving child of Zeus, I beg of you: Lady, don't break my spirit with suffering and sorrow.[16]

I've put the poems into prose because, this being one of those point-making misuses of poetry for other purposes that I've scorned above, I'm more after the sense than the sound. I think, however, that the cunning simplicity, the artful immediacy, the sovereign candor, survive.

My point is not only to document the unabashed personal directness of this passion in these Greek poets (or, to say it in a fancy way, the devastatingly accurate phenomenology of erotic seizure), but also to remind the reader that there are two divinities associated with love, Eros and Aphrodite. As I've noted, something more will be said about their interesting relation in the next chapter, on Plato.

Here is a pedantic yet effective way to appreciate this moment in the history of love. In the Homeric epics, "eros" is named only three times. He, or rather, it, is twice said to "'cover round' the knowing heart" (*amphikalypse*);[17] it can't help but remind us of Calypso, the "Coverer" who holds a less and less willing Odysseus to her bed for seven years. Once, eros "enchants the spirit."[18] Homeric *eros* is, I think, quite lower-case, no divinity but a passion only. But then, in a curious reversal of the usual direction, which is toward the de-divinization of human affects, *eros* becomes capitalized: *Eros* the god. Perhaps a generation after Homer, Hesiod fixed the family relations of the Greek pantheon in his *Theogony,* the "Birth (or Coming-to-be) of the Gods," and made Eros a—parentless because primeval—god. He says that "first of all Chaos came to be and then wide-bosomed Earth" and the Underworld, and "Eros who is most beautiful among all deathless gods, the limb-loosener, who breaks the thought in the breast and its sensible counsel."[19] He does not come into the world as a son of Aphrodite but as her companion, together with "beautiful Yearning" (*Himeros*).

Aphrodite herself was "foam-born," from *aphros,* "foam," a wonderful but false etymology;[20] another one, also false, was from *a-phron,* "senseless." That foam was the effervescence from the private parts of *Ouranos* ("Heaven"); he was castrated with a jagged-toothed sickle by his son *Kronos* (interpreted by the Greeks as *Chronos,* "Time") as he "was covering Earth, stretched all over her." These members Kronos tossed into the sea off the southernmost tip of the east coast of Cythera, where I have myself seen them. So neither Aphrodite nor Eros has, as do other gods, a clear, legitimate parentage; Aphrodite, however, made it into the Olympian pantheon; not so Eros.

It is the same in the initiating epic poem of Parmenides, the first philosopher, who came on Being, philosophy's first and last concern, in the
blazing passion of an unprecedented encounter. He says that the nameless
female spirit (*daimon*) who "pilots all things" "contrived Eros, the first of
all the gods."[21] Eros is a god not born but devised, "contrived" (*metisato*).
Parmenides, who traveled from his Italian home in the West to visit Athens
and possibly to talk to a very young Socrates,[22] might well have known the
eastern Island poetry—the western Eros too is a "limb-loosener," and, like
his associate Aphrodite, an aboriginal being that has come-to-be but was
not properly born.

These considerations throw a little light on the power of this poetic *eros:*
It is upper-case and lower-case at once. It is Eros, a god, who, like a horse-
tamer, "breaks" the heart and the spirit and the mind and overpowers the
body and loosens the limbs and confounds the senses and confuses good
sense. It is also *eros,* an affect assented to proudly and abjectly and, as a realized capability, a proof of being all there. That is what "passion" means: *chosen suffering,* receptivity for the god—*enthusiasmos,* which means literally
"having the god within."

This is the all-too-human god whom the philosophers of the next two
chapters know very well from life and in poetry, the breaker of hearts they
try to break by reason and the tyrant of the soul they try to tame to our service. I have meant to leave the impression that Eros dominates the discourse
on the passions in the high time of antiquity, the archaic and classical period
in Greece. It is a lopsided judgment in view of the powerful part anger and
shame and fear have in Greek literature. Nonetheless, these writers, especially the lyric poets and the philosophers, are the experts of experts in love-
matters (*ta erotika*)—love, longing, yearning, desire, and appetite (all words
that will turn up in the next three chapters). Modern authors, on the other
hand, for whom the passions have turned into emotions, bring a new kind
of affect to the fore: mood. Moreover, they designate a signature mood for
our age: anxiety. But that affect lies far in the future, and the beginning is
with love.

chapter II

Eros, Spirit, Pleasure

Plato's Beginning

W hy is the beginning so often the high point of a tradition? Some treatments of human preoccupations seem to lose grandeur and depth as they gain shrewdness and sophistication. To figure out the way of that is to have learned something about what it means to live through time and off a tradition, to have understood how we exist—with or without recognition and acknowledgment—as heirs, who are borne up and borne under by those who came before us and are behind us. The Greeks already spoke of "epigones," the lesser late-born successors of heroes, smarter and shallower. Our latter-dayness in human wisdom is, happily, not the problem of this book—though the preoccupation of plenty of others, for it engenders, along with aggressive forgetfulness, anxiety, the theme-mood of modernity.[1] I avert to it here as a justification for the somewhat bottom-heavy account of older passion studies in this book, a necessary apology, as it were, in view of the enormous quantity of contemporary work on the affects, done often in willful oblivion of the forerunners' artful depth.

1. Eros as Go-Between and Passion as Soul-Horse

To wit, Sappho and Socrates on love: I wonder how it is that this passion, which has, I imagine, attracted more words than any other, has never again, in my reading, received treatment so accurate symptomatically and so true psychologically.

To be sure, we are dealing with experts here. Sappho was thought of as a kind of high priestess of love in the little band about her, and Socrates, who as I said, acknowledged beautiful Sappho as a source of knowledge along with wise Anacreon,[1] declared himself "to know nothing else than love matters" and to be "formidable" (that is, expert: *deinos*) only in these.[2] This is the very Socrates who says of himself that he knows only that he knows nothing,[3] and who has generally a pretty low opinion of self-declared experts, for they tend to be sophists.

The two dialogues in which Socrates especially reveals himself as the triumphant practitioner and theorist of love are the *Symposium* and the *Phaedrus.* He can show himself (or rather Plato can display him) in both capacities at once, because for him Eros (*eros*) and Speech (*logos*) are closely related. Hence a dialogue can reveal him literally in the act of love which *is* his discourse, in the act of speech that is aroused and arousing, raptly rational for himself and thought-stirring for us. In both dialogues Socrates presents himself as not only erotic but also as spirited, for in both, he tacitly and intentionally outdoes his companions in the experience as well as the understanding of love—the hands-down victor in what the Greeks called an *agonia,* a competitive struggle. For, it bears repeating, this Socrates, who is always claiming to know only that he knows nothing and to whom knowl-edge-experts—never artisans—are figures of fun, this very Socrates claims, as I said, to understand only one thing: love-matters, *erotics.*

It is not my plan to give interpretations of those two great dialogues on love in all their artful complexity, but to concentrate my account on Socrates' love expertise—and that not as reporting one of the many things that were said once long ago, but, to the best of my ability, as current truth worth absorbing.

A. Daimonic Love: The Symposium

The story of the night on which Agathon, the tragic poet, hosted a drinking party to celebrate his winning of a prize had assumed mythic standing by the time it was narrated, once again and at second remove, though the tell-ing had been checked out by Socrates himself. This time round it had just been told to Glaucon, probably the Glaucon who is Plato's brother, the one who will appear in the *Republic,* and now, a couple of days later, it is being told to a "companion."

Socrates turns up late and alone at this party of lovers' pairs. He had retreated—something similar has happened before—to a neighbor's porch, absorbed in thought. He comes got up for a festivity; in particular he is freshly bathed and wearing light sandals, which is unusual for him, for he normally goes barefoot. Not to prolong the suspense: The special party-dress is intended to draw attention to his ordinary, everyday persona, which is that of Eros on earth; he will be a dressed-up guest at a party for himself. The center of the dialogue will reveal just that.

The company of guests decides to forgo compulsory drinking and music at this party of parties in order to repair in all sobriety what they claim is a great omission in all poetry until now: Eros, Love, is a god without praise songs, without *encomia.* (There have, of course, been plenty of animadver-sions as the poetry of the first chapter showed; Eros inspired more appalled wariness than suave praise.) Many speeches are made, of which only five of those preceding Socrates' are reported. There will be a seventh, by a gate-crasher, Alcibiades, who simply substitutes Socrates for Eros in his uninhibited, half-drunken panegyric.

The first five speeches have this in common: They present the god, quite naturally, as the object of worship and awe. Thus he is either himself lovable, that is, he has the features of an object of love, a beautiful beloved, or he is a powerful force, an irresistible divinity, now cosmic, now personal. Among them the five give a pretty complete survey, Greek in dress but universal in experience, of the affect of love—that is, before one really thinks about it. I will give the gist of each speech. I resist the temptation to point out the art of it—the way Plato's craft details the gifts of each speaker in this brilliant band of rhetoricians, tragedians, and comic poets. This is a bare-bones account for a purpose: to show how Socrates, who begins his presentation pretty near the numerical center of the text, rebuts and corrects each in turn—implicitly and graciously.

1. Phaedrus goes first. He is otherwise unknown but seems to be around whenever Socrates talks of love; Socrates will address his own speech to him particularly.[4] Phaedrus presents Eros as one of the oldest gods, so old that nothing is ever said about his parentage, either privately or poetically. This Love, being venerable, induces an old-fashioned affect: shame, which is the source of nobility, honor, and bravery—Homeric heroism. This shame is a major passion, then and now (to be taken up by Aristotle). The role of love is that it puts us under observation by someone about whose esteem we care above anything.[5] That is exactly how shame will be analyzed: feeling oneself seen as deficient by those who matter, or fearing to be thus seen. Phaedrus's, the most dignified speech, is refuted not by Socrates but by Alcibiades, who is himself an example of a futile sort of shame caused by love.

2. Pausanias doubles Eros: He is a companion of Aphrodite who herself comes in two forms, Vulgar and Heavenly, namely Lust and Love. Eros mirrors this duplicity. There is a lofty love between the older lover and the beloved boy (the ideal but not the actual relation in this elegant company, who are in fact bound by more mature love involvements). And there is a base, exploitative one. Pausanias is interested in the different city-states' different conventions guarding against abuses. So he adds the seamy side and makes Aphrodite the divinity responsible for both kinds of love.

3. Eryximachus is a scientist, a physician who despite his unlikely name—"Belch-Battler"—was evidently as real as the others present. For him Eros is a cosmic, we would say a natural, force. He adopts Pausanias's double Eros, the sound desire of healthy bodies and the sick desire of sick bodies.

The science of medicine consists of replacing bad by good desires in bodies and then harmonizing the good ones. In fact, all of nature is under the
double Eros, from pestilences to fertility. All the sciences, astronomy, divina-
tion, music, are in effect versions of medicine that battle the disorderly love
and aid the harmonious one. Love, the all-powerful force relating bodies, is
what the physician is really always dealing with.

4. Aristophanes, the great poet of Old Comedy, picks up the doctor's
view of the physicality of cosmic love and in those terms gives a hilarious
account of individual love. His speech, perhaps the funniest thing in philosophic literature, displays the comic poet's most characteristic concerns, his
physicality and his conservatism. His comic trumping of the more decorous
previous praises of Eros is both boisterously lusty and reverent—reverent,
that is, toward the natural fact of human incompleteness.[6] The phrase "original nature" (*archaia physis*)[7] dominates his speech. In his comic origina-
tion myth of Eros, this is what happened: Originally humans were globes
with eight wriggling limbs, a double-faced head on a columnar neck, and
private parts on each side below; they procreated by seeding the earth. Some
spheres were male, some female, some hermaphroditic. They rolled up and
down the cosmos so rambunctiously—intending even to invade Olym-
pus—as to infuriate the gods. Therefore Zeus sliced them all in half, pulled
the skin inwards and tied it at the belly button, twisted the face of the half-
head to the new front and eventually, out of pity, the private parts as well. So
we go around seeking our unique partner—and making do with whoever of
the right sex comes along, male with male, female with female, while those
true hermaphrodites, the two-sex couples, engage in a mixed mating. This
somatic view of human longing turns out to be psychically the most acute,
since it provides an origin for our sense that we have one uniquely fitting
partner in the world, our *symbolon*,[8] the shaped tally that locks into the half
that we are—while the other pairings are making-do. And this is the one
account—that love longs to repair humans by reconstituting us one out
of two when Zeus had split us into two out of one—that Socrates attacks
directly, for it is the most powerful.

5. Agathon the tragedian, the last speaker before Socrates, is as flighty as
the comedian was forceful. He gives a description of Eros as a lovable, soft,
graceful, delicate, supple boy, the youngest of the gods—as simple Phaedrus
made him the oldest. This artificial composition degenerates into a false
ecstasy of jingling juxtapositions.

Socrates' turn has come. He begins, with permission, to question Agathon. Within minutes he has the tragedian reversing himself: Love can't be
beautiful.

In this short dialectical interlude Plato has laid the foundations for the analytic of desire that will be repeated through the millennia, with or without direct reference. I will pull it together in a separate section (3) because it makes an amazing connection only implicit in the *Symposium* yet I think, intended to be pondered: The actual *structure* of desire or love *is similar to that of a question*—as is, purely fortuitously, the Greek *word* for loving and for questioning. Word-play abounds in the dialogue.

Then Socrates goes into the speech mode. As I said, at the beginning of the dialogue, the man who always claims to have only a "meager wisdom . . . like a dream" and who thinks experts are faintly funny declares himself "to understand nothing but love matters."[9] Now we learn who taught him and what he learned. His teacher was a priestess, Diotima ("Honor-of-Zeus") from Mantinea ("Oracle-town"), and he claims to be the mere reporter of her speech to him. Of course, he can't, in all modesty, depict a god who is his own spitting image—as she can and will.

Diotima, as Socrates tells it, had once made him admit what he has just elicited from Agathon: that Eros is neither beautiful nor good. For love is desire, and what is desired are things of beauty, and good things are beautiful, and what is desired is what is *lacked*—which all adds up to saying that this god is needy, ugly, and even bad.

This is shocking enough as mythopoetic invention—Socrates wants us to conclude that Eros can't be a god. But philosophically it is simply revolutionary. It revalues Love in turning attention from Eros as an external force or an embodiment of the objects of love to eros as a human condition. The word [E]ros had always been the name both for the god and for human passion, but this new kind of god is passion incarnate and desire deified, a divinity who *is* what he is called, a cause of what he himself exemplifies.

Of course, he is no Olympian. Diotima appeals to a peculiarly Socratic interest, a middle realm of knowledge. Between wisdom and ignorance there is something called right opinion, an ignorant knowledge. It is our chief cognitive region, in which we know truths but can't explain them. (These are what Spinoza will call "inadequate ideas.") The new god is in an analogous position: He is a being *in between* (*metaxy*) the mortal and the immortal. Such a divinity is called a *daimon,* sometimes rendered "spirit." (I write *daimon* even in English because the degradation to "demon," meaning an evil spirit, is later and mainly Christian.) All that is daimonic operates between gods and mortals.[10] It is the power of the go-between, the interpreter and transporter of prayers to the gods and orders to men. There are many *daimones,* many agents of the "in-between" who connect heaven and earth. Thus Eryximachus is tacitly refuted. Love is not a horizontal force connecting bodies with bodies but a vertical power, connecting gods and men.

Now, for the first time, Eros gets a parentage. Soon Aristophanes would also give Eros a birth in his *Birds.*[11] It is hilarious enough: "Blackwinged night dropped a wind-egg whence, as the seasons came round, burst forth Love the longed-for." But Aristophanes' image is not the bold Olympico-philosophic mythmaking of Socrates: On Aphrodite's day of birth the gods made a feast. "Ways and Means" (*Poros*), son of "Wile" (*Metis*), was invited. But Poverty (*Penia*), uninvited, skulked at the edges, and when Poros came out to sleep off his drunk, Penia crept in with him, and they begot Eros, Aphrodite's younger companion (nine months younger, I suppose, though who knows a goddess's gestation period). So he is neither a very old god, as Phaedrus supposed, nor a very young one, as Agathon claimed, but rather of Olympian age though not parentage. He is conceived of opposites on Aphrodite's day, and that fixes his character: As her attendant he loves beauty; as maternally poor, however, he is untender, tough, dried out, goes about as if homeless but is at home with need and with *a-poria,* waylessness, perplexity—Socrates' famous starting point of inquiry. This picture is the opposite of the beautiful, soft Erotic form of divinity presented by Agathon, but it is identical with the ugly, rough-and-tough, barefoot Socratic constitution of body that Alcibiades will describe.

Yet as the son of Poros, Eros has his ways and means. He is a schemer after "beautiful and good" things and people, "courageous, go-getting, taut, a terrific hunter, ever weaving wiles, a desirer of mindfulness and with the means for it, engaged in philosophy through all his life, a terrific enchanter (*goes*), drug-dispenser (*pharmakeus*), and sophist (*sophistes*)."[12]

Again this is the Socratic cast of mind as delineated in the Platonic dialogues: philosophic from boyhood,[13] enthralling to his companions,[14] knowledgeable in drugs and spells,[15] at times indistinguishable from a sophist (such as he himself accuses Diotima, his invention, of being[16]), full of reflective self-knowledge—and in untiring pursuit of the handsome and promising young.

So here we have it: This *daimon,* Love, is a philo-sopher, a lover of wisdom, that is, one who is neither quite "aporetic" nor so very well provided, who is between ignorance and wisdom—and yet somewhat more on the latter side; some Greek listeners would surely have heard in *daimon* its homonym, a participle that means "skillful." The gods don't pursue wisdom since they *are* wise, nor do those humans who are so ignorant that they don't feel the lack. Desire (*epithymia*) comes from knowing oneself needy. This is the philosopher[17] who knows himself as neither wise nor ignorant. His understanding of philosophy as in its nature incomplete will ring on in various modes and even supersede itself. Thus Hegel will make it his aim to turn philosophy into an absolute science, when it will lay aside the name "*love of knowledge*" and be called "*actual knowledge.*"[18]

But these daimonic philosophers are "the In-betweens," and Eros in particular is one of them, for wisdom is concerned with the most beautiful things, and so is Love. I think Diotima is bringing out here the fundamental axiom of Platonic philosophy, that the end and aim of thinking is both what is estimably good, and what is attractively beautiful: To think is to pursue *the* good, and the good *is* beautiful. It is thus that philosophy is understood as more than an ascetic passion, a bare need for truth, be it lovable or fearful; it is rather an aroused *eros,* a directed longing for prospective beauty. This, I would venture to say, is the reason that myths are admitted into the dialectical effort: They present the visualizable prospect of ultimate beauty. One might object that an erotic search for truth is not an entirely unbiased inquiry, since it is directed by hopes and expectations—longing and faith, one might say. That is undeniable, though to admit the directedness of Socratic inquiry is not meant to mount a critique but to pose a problem—not within my scope here.

Before they turn to desire directly, there is a conversation, a dialectical passage, which begins with Diotima summarizing for Socrates how he, and hence of course, even more, all the present speakers, had hitherto been mistaken. They supposed that Love was the beloved, not the lover.[19] Indeed, our usage too is ambiguous: A "love" can be either a passion or its object. Socrates wants to know what use this newly-conceived lover-god is to humans.

Well, this isn't what Socrates will be told, but—to interject a prospective note—this very lover-god is put to use as the human divinity of lovestruck Romanticism. In *Death in Venice,* Thomas Mann will present this sentiment as coming from the *Phaedrus* (the dialogue that furnishes the mythical background of his story) and as spoken by Socrates: "And then he expressed the most delectable thought, the cunning wooer—this, that the lover is more divine than the beloved, because the god is in the former but not in the latter." It is in fact Phaedrus who says this in the *Symposium:* "The lover is more divine than the beloved. For he has god within."[20] To "have a god within," to be *en-theos* or *enthous,* is to be "enthusiastic," to be divinely inspired. Diotima's erotic Eros will be used by a Romantic master to divinize lovers.

Back to the soberly dialectic interlude of the dialogue. To answer Socrates' question Diotima helps him investigate what exactly it means to desire beautiful things. Let me abbreviate: It means to want good things, and that in turn means to desire happiness. That's the end—what we want is, finally, to be happy. Love "in sum is the desire for happiness and for being happy."[21] What happiness is, will be left to Aristotle to say.

Here Diotima tacitly criticizes Aristophanes, for retelling an old and a false myth: The story about people in love seeking their other half must be wrong. Love is not about halves or wholes, but about wanting the good. By the same token, Pausanias's doubling of love into high and low is shown to be false. What is worse, although he has grasped that Love is not only a divinity but also a human passion, Pausanias burdens its object, the beloved boy, with the ignobility of a false response, as if the object of love was responsible for the baseness of the relation.[22] For Diotima love is in all cases, always, of the good—though Alcibiades will soon exemplify the way a good object can be wrongly loved and how love, although of the good, can be bad.

At this point no previous speech, neither Pausanias's nor Eryximachus's nor Aristophanes' nor Agathon's, is left unrefuted, except perhaps Phaedrus's. His speech needs explanation more than rebuttal: How does love indeed give rise to valor and to the thirst for honor? Diotima will be coming to that.

But first, what is the meaning of loving or desiring the good? It means wanting to possess it and to keep it forever. "Love is, in sum, love of the good to be one's own forever."[23] So that's the good of love to humans. But what is the work, the effort, the strain involved?

It turns out that, as it was wrong that Love himself *is* beautiful, so it is even wrong that love is *of* the beautiful. Here is what Socrates came to Diotima for—the wisdom he finds amazing in her and means to learn: Love is not of the beautiful but of giving "birth in the beautiful" (*tokos en kaloi*) in both body and soul.[24] Note this, surely intentional, ambiguity: "In the beautiful" might be neuter, but it could well be masculine singular. What Diotima is saying and keeps explaining is, amazingly, just this: *All* human beings are pregnant, and at a certain age they long to give birth; but they need to do it "in" or "upon" the beautiful. To answer to this need, Diotima has invented a strange, almost weird figure. At a certain age "our nature desires to give birth,"[25] whatever the sex. Thus pregnancy is both male and female. (I must say here that depending on one's disposition toward Plato, Diotima's image can be read as denigrating women by reassigning even their one productive function in Greek life to the male, or as elevating them by celebrating a female element in productive men.)

Now male pregnancy, as evidenced in birthing, is not unheard of, though exotic. (Recall the primitive's couvade, male labor pains, much beloved by anthropologists.) But it gets stranger. The male too gives birth, but his pregnancy *precedes* the act of impregnation, for, strangest of all, his delivery is in the very act of inseminating another: The pregnant male can't bear in the presence of ugliness, so "he goes around seeking that beautiful thing in which he might beget."[26] Diotima is playing here with two verbs, *tiktein* and *gennan,* which both have a double sense: giving birth for women and begetting for men.

Of course, it is the soul's conception she is talking about, and the confusions she insinuates into her figure represent the human conditions for beginning to philosophize: being big with unborn conceptions and finding a human being who will be both the venue of the birth and the receptacle of the seed—meaning someone who makes us articulate by wanting to learn with us.

Socrates reports that in one of the several other conversations with him she had told him what an expert in love-matters particularly needs to know: what the cause of desire is, as distinct from its object. *Why* all that longing to beget, to give birth? The answer is in the "to be one's own for ever" part of the definition of love. The cause of love, or better, the root longing expressed in love is that for *immortality*. By procreation animals last beyond their present existence; in mere living we humans become ever new, continually leaving behind and *losing* our old selves, but in true learning we *replace* lost memories—if learning is indeed recollection—and thus ourselves, the content of our souls. So love circumvents death: "By this device, you, Socrates, a mortal, partake of immortality."[27] Diotima means that in this life we change constantly; it is by loving, by giving new birth in beauty that we go beyond our changing selves. That is always Socrates' Diotiman wisdom: that through genuine inquiry we can seize moments of being, rise above change, lay hold of immortality, enter the life after death—in *this* life, now. It is what he means when he tells his young friends on the day of his death that philosophy is the devotion to dying and being dead.[28] Philosophy means being absorbed in time-transcending conversation or, perhaps, being rapt here and now in atemporal visions that leave the body behind.

This longing for some sort of immortality also accounts for the love of honor (*philotimia*)[29] that Pausanias had associated with love. For him the love of immortal fame and a good name forever is behind all human love—of children, husbands, lovers, so that for him too all love is the desire for some sort of immortality. Socrates does respect this other-dependent desire to escape the depredations of time, though it is not the veritable delivery from death.

So far Socrates might be well initiated into the erotic mysteries, but whether he can follow the ultimate rites and visions that come next, Diotima says she does not know—nor are we ever told. What does come next and last is the famous "ladder of love."

It begins with loving one beautiful boy and engendering there beautiful reasonings (*logous*). In other words, living human beauty is at the beginning of the philosophical way. As is always the case in Socratic ascents, the lowest rung is left behind but it is also all-determining. For example, in the *Republic*, knowledge ascends from mere image to genuine being, yet imaging is the connecting principle of all the cognitive stages.[30] So here visible individual beauty, though soon to be despised in view of the higher-order beauty that is common to bodies, to souls, to civic institutions, to knowledge, nevertheless impassions the whole upward way and makes the ultimate vision of invisible beauty plausible. Bodily Eros both primes and pervades the philosophic ascent.

No sooner has Socrates' Diotima taken the company up to the gods than all hell breaks loose. Alcibiades, the most beautiful, brilliant, sought-after, and corrupt young man of antiquity, bursts in, drunk. He is got up as Dionysus, the god of drink, leaning on his crowd of attendant revelers acting the parts of sileni and satyrs, those genial beast-men. He calls for wine all round for the hitherto sober company and agrees to join in making a speech in praise—not of Eros but of Socrates; it will be a speech in figures. His figure for Socrates is a flute-playing satyr, one of those little clay figurines that come apart and reveal tiny statuettes of gods within. Like a satyr (the physical Socrates evidently has some silenic features—a snub nose, bulging forehead, and protruding eyes) he enthralls by his music. He, Alcibiades, has experienced something under his spell that he thought himself incapable of: shame, shame for his inability to follow Socrates' advice.[31] That is, of course, a self-indulgently defeatist version of the effect Eros is said to have in Phaedrus's speech, the ability to make those under his rule reluctant to behave shamefully before each other.

In the same equivocal vein he now reduces the image of Socrates-Eros, intimated in Diotima's great mystic *daimon*-guide, to a small silenic attendant, to be opened up by Alcibiades himself. His whole speech is shot through with a sort of shameless candor, composed of the self-assertive desire to subjugate and seduce Socrates and a generous wish to praise him with loving accuracy, all compounded by a sense of his own hopeless inadequacy—a would-be insider's encomium with an undertone of dissonant pathos. Socrates' novel notion for hymning of the god was to sing him as a lover rather than as beloved. Alcibiades had missed that momentous account of a mythical women's love-wisdom, so he reverts to the old mode of praising the god as beloved. But he does it in pretty bizarre form: He, the handsome youth, is the scheming lover, the *erastes,* and Socrates-Eros, certainly ugly and quite old (in his fifties or so, depending on how long ago that night of attempted seduction which Alcibiades is here revealing occurred)—this Socrates is here, as it were, one of Alcibiades's "boy-loves" (*paidikois*).[32]

What happened that night might be called the glorious scandal of pedagogy: Socrates serenely refuses and shows himself the true pupil of Diotima and any teacher's model for all time. Alcibiades' praise—and with it the articulate part of that sober drinking party as well—comes pretty much to its end with an account of Socrates' courage and hardiness, in particular with an incident like the one that opens the dialogue. Once, when in camp on campaign, Socrates stood from dawn to dawn absorbed in thought pursuing some question, searching, and kept standing there because he couldn't figure it out. That, at least, is what Alcibiades infers—that Socrates was in unresolved perplexity, thinking hard. But he and we don't know that; it might, for all we know, have been some fulfilling rapture of the intellect, an ascent and sojourn among the forms such as Diotima has described. Soon after, the party is swamped by a second wave of revelers.

B. Ascending Love: The Phaedrus

Now to passion as soul-horse in the *Phaedrus*. Passionate love *seems* to be the main subject of the dialogue *Phaedrus*—at its center is the grandest figure of the soul in love known to me—but it is really about rhetoric. In his sober way Aristotle will follow the same path: His consideration of the passions, the first systematic one we have in the West, is presented in his treatise on rhetoric, the art of persuasion. The general reason is not obscure. Great persuasive speaking is driven by and arouses the passion of speaker and audience respectively.

The dialogue is a triptych, a composition of three panels.[33] Its first panel consists of two speech exercises. One, by the orator Lysis, is read off a scroll that Phaedrus has brought along. The other is Socrates' *extempore* reprise—a rhetorical game of can-you-top-this that any reader will readily concede to Socrates, the amateur who is more skillful than the professional. The almost incidental topic in this competition is the debater's question, "Resolved, that a beloved (boy) should give in to the non-lover, that is, to the unimpassioned suitor, rather than to the lover." Lysis's speech is a humanly mingy affair, Socrates' is more artful, but these local love-problems of Greek pairs with their slyly deceitful argumentation—for the "non-lover" is probably meant to be shamming—excite, at least in me, no particular conviction. They are competitive exercises incited by Phaedrus's artless admiration of Lysis's speech. Socrates himself is made uneasy by his own disengaged debater's performance.

The middle panel consists of his "palinode," his counter-song, a retraction to placate "Aphrodite's Eros," whom these speeches have insulted. Since my subject is passion, that is the part of the dialogue I will want to tell about briefly in a moment.

The last part of the dialogue takes up the question of what it means to speak and write well, what is the true art of rhetoric. Rhetoric turns out to be, for Socrates, a "soul-leading" (*psychagogia*) that requires the skill of distinguishing and collecting kinds of beings and also kinds of souls. This true rhetoric is not practiced in unresponsive writing but in live speech addressed to individual souls. That is, of course, a description of Socrates' own philosophizing.[34]

So back to the center. To get the aroma of Socrates' palinode, one must savor the setting. This Socratic dialogue is the only one set in the country outside the city walls of Athens. The *Symposium* is recounted on the way up from Phaleron, Athens's old harbor. The *Republic* begins on the way down to Piraeus, Athens's new harbor. But both settings are technically within the city, being enclosed by the long walls that connected the harbors to the city several miles inland. The *Phaedrus,* however, takes place on the grassy banks of the Ilissos, the river flowing without and around the city. Socrates doesn't usually go there, because he is a lover of learning, and the country and the trees don't wish to teach him anything as people in the city do.[35] Nonetheless, it turns out that he is better acquainted with the local deities than is Phaedrus. In fact it is he who offers a final prayer to the nature-haunting god Pan ("the All"), whose shrine is evidently in the vicinity. Socrates takes advantage of the unique pastoral setting to bring his speech under the aegis not only of the Olympians, but of water, wind, and grove deities. Moreover the time of the idyll is high noon, the "panic" time, the time of horror and ecstasy. This is a Socrates gloriously out-of-bounds. And while they speak, the cicadas strum away musically in the background, giving to the conversation a sort of cosmic background noise, the thrumming of love.

Nevertheless, as in the *Symposium,* Socrates does not appropriate his own speech but here attributes it to Stesichorus, a real poet who really hails, serendipitously, from Himera ("Yearning-town"). And as in the *Symposium,* he addresses his speech to Phaedrus. It is a speech of seduction, but it is as candid in its aim as the earlier ones were surreptitious. For Socrates is not after sexual favors from his "beautiful boy," but wants to convert him, so that "he might make a life devoted to Eros by means of philosophical conversations" (*logous*).[36]

In the *Symposium* the nature of Eros the god was revealed; in the *Phaedrus* the soul-in-love is shown. There is, to be sure, much more in this speech of speeches than that. In the very center both of the dialogue and its central speech (again, as so often, central by the numbers) Zeus appears[37]— incidentally throwing light on Diotima's name, "Honor-of-Zeus." For he, the god of gods, is the deity of those who look for a philosophical and ruling nature to love, that is to say, for a future philosopher-king (who, incidentally, first appears in the exact middle of the *Republic*).[38] Latter-day writers on philosophy may eat their hearts out at such interweaving of compositional cunning, visual imagination, and philosophical signifying.

Those lovers of lovers of wisdom are borne up in the company of their god, who dwells on the outside, the convex side of Heaven. There they see true Being, colorless, shapeless, intangible;[39] it is the realm of Platonic forms. The recollection of these invisible sights is the preoccupation of those who philosophize on earth. And the fact that *eidos,* Socrates' word for what we call the non-sensory "form" or "idea," means, primarily and paradoxically, a visible aspect, a look, a sight is the lexical warrant for the *Phaedrus's* figurative philosophy.

A winged two-horse chariot conveys the human being upward. Or rather that chariot as a whole *is* the human being in a figure. It is a figure twice composite: once implicitly in its material constitution, because in its fall to earth—how that happens I will tell in a moment—the soul assumes progressively more of a body and a body's weight, and again explicitly in its tripartite composition, insofar as it consists of two horses and a charioteer.

Wingedness is of the essence here, in this human takeoff toward the realm of Being that philosophers seek. Where are the wings on this two-horse chariot? Is it the horses that are, Pegasus-like, winged, or the charioteer or the chariot's wheels? It is impossible to tell, because, as happens time and again in grand word-visions, they are not fully visualizable: Words may construct what space, given to univocal patency, cannot contain. To give two examples: The grand cosmic myth in which the *Republic* culminates is visually incoherent, and so is the vision that ends Dante's *Paradiso*. The divine circularity of the latter will not geometrically accommodate the human figure: "But for that I had no proper wings. . . . For this high fantasy the power failed."[40]

Moreover, Plato has conflated two figures. One is of the soul's sprouting of feathers, a tumescent irritation irrigated by the effluence of beauty. No reader can miss what is being described here; in fact there are representations of winged erect male members on Greek artifacts.[41]

Here is a conjecture about Socrates' intrusion of a picture of the soul as "mono-pteric," as having—no, *being*—a single, sprouting wing, into the multipartite chariot figure. He means to signify what had probably never been said before—that all the parts of the analyzed soul are one in desire, that from rational top to passionate bottom, the soul is our actual erectile member, that true eroticism is psychic, that *real* arousal may be through the body but is never for the body.

The other figure, then, is that of the chariot. Its parts are amply described in the *Phaedrus,* but their psychological explication comes from the *Republic.* Since the *Phaedrus* was probably written after the *Republic,*[42] one might think of the former as illustrating the latter, which I will do in naming the parts of the figure.

First the part unassigned in terms of the scheme of the *Republic,* the chariot itself. I take that to be interpretable as putting the human soul in a body, though I cannot point to any explicit support in the text. It is, however, pretty clear that the chariot-figure as a whole is not that of the totally pure disembodied soul but of a soul that has strong sensations. Thus it must be, contrary to one's first impression, a body-related soul that is figured here; in its fall it is, as I said, an increasingly embodied, a heavy, soul. It is a representation of the tradition (whose counter is to be found from the Stoics through Descartes to William James into contemporary times) that assigns the passions primarily to the soul and only their occasioning to the body—all the passions, that is, but the love aroused by hyper-physical beings, which is purely a-somatic. Every human soul is born as a body's soul, and that circumstance is both its burden and the beginning of its release, which is through physical beauty. Indeed, that is the soul's function among us humans: to make the body "ensouled" (*empsychon*)[43] and to impart to the body something of its own ungenerated and indestructible self-motion. Perhaps what I am trying to convey might be put like this: Here, bound to earth, the body is ensouled; there, on the way to hyper-heaven, the soul is embodied; at least it has senses. Or once again: As the soul rises on the wings of Eros, its relation to the body is transfigured and finally becomes a mere figure. That is why "a living being is called both mortal and immortal."[44]

In accordance with the partite plan of the *Republic,* the description presents a team and a driver, to both of which together the soul is likened in its "composite capacity" (*symphytōi dynamei*).[45] Of the human soul-horses, one is beautiful and good, *kalos te kai agathos,* the term for a man of good breeding, a gentleman. The other is the opposite, and it makes the driving difficult.

Here Socrates breaks off to speak of "the wing"[46] mentioned above and its power to soar to the gods and to say how the bad horse can pull the winged chariot down. The chariot must have two wings, but this section is about a single winged soul that is feathered all over and gazes upward "like a bird" about to extend its wings.[47] The bird is evidently everywhere a phallic figure.[48] This part of the speech ends with the erection of the wing-soul at the sight of beauty, with the divine madness that enthralls it, and with a precise description of what it feels like (for either sex) to be in love—the glory and the slavery. Finally the ecstatically kaleidoscopic vision of the soul turns into one of Eros himself, Eros the Winged: "Winged" in Greek is *pteros*; Socrates hears this as pt-Eros.[49]

Then Socrates turns back to the soul-chariot.[50] The charioteer's function is to fight the bad horse, to pull back on the reins, eventually to subdue it. The work is hard and sweaty, and the whip is needed. Who can doubt that this human driver-figure represents what in the *Republic* was called the reasoning part of the soul? But what about the bad horse, the dark horse? It is the "crooked, bulky, poorly slung together, stiff-necked comrade of wantonness and hybris . . ." and displays all kinds of ugliness.[51] When the soul is ignited because the charioteer has looked into his beloved's eyes this horse goes wild and wants to jump him and drags the whole team toward the boy with sex in mind.

This horse clearly represents the part of the soul that was called desire (*epithymia*) in the *Republic,* where, as in the *Phaedrus,* the soul is said to be divided into three "kinds" (*eide*),[52] except that in the latter, two of the three are "horseshaped" (*hippomorpho*).

Here is how the language of the *Phaedrus* places desire: Love is a desire; "that is clear to all"; it is one of many desires, each of which is subject to "hybris," overpowering excess; thus desire is a *pathos*, a condition as opposed to an action, and this condition is fraught with a sense of displacement (*atopiai*) and of perplexity[53] and madness. Here *pathos*, once meaning any affect, is sliding into passion as an affliction, a "yearning" (*himeron*—recall that it is the speech of the poet from Himera) that can only be relieved by the sight of the object of love.

But what of the second horse of the soul-team? It is the bright and beautiful horse: erect, high-necked, governable—ruled by the command of *logos* alone. It is a "lover of honor together with moderation and shame, the comrade of true opinion" (or glory: *doxa*).[54] In its high-bred, proud submission to thought, it helps the reasonable charioteer to control the passionate dark horse. This steed, the lover of honor, is clearly an image of the middle part of the soul in the *Republic*. It might well be called Socrates' greatest contribution to psychology, to the constitution of the soul. Its Greek name is *thymos*. In the *Phaedrus* it helped us to turn debasing desire into elevating *eros*, to feel our feelings nobly. Now *thymos* will be shown as our very center, where we feel our feelings of self—vehemently.

2. Spirit as Soul-Center and Desire as Soul-Base: The *Republic*

Thymos is known to us in English from the herb thyme which exudes a strong aroma. "Fume" is the cognate in Latin. (*Th* and *f* go back to the same Indo-European consonant.) Thus the original meaning is "breath" (of life), exhalation, ebullition, smoke, vapor. "Spirit," which comes from the word for breath in Latin, *spiritus*, is a good translation for *thymos*. In the Homeric epics it is often used for the vital principle, breathing life, as is *psyche*, "soul," which means literally "a cold breath." But there is in it also another sense, that of "fuming," of tempestuously roused spirit and of desire, appetite, and finally even friendliness (*to philetikon*), "for spirit is the capacity of the soul by which we are friendly, namely to those we know and rough to those we don't know," says Aristotle, agreeing with Plato.[1] For this second set of meanings, spiritedness is probably the better term. A rival word for breath, *pneuma*, is softer. It doesn't have that sense of expressive boiling-up; in a Christian context it comes to mean "spirituality."

Socrates has given over a part of the soul to this thymotic spiritedness. It is one of the soul's three "kinds" (*eidē*), the middle—and the central—part. The general notion of the soul as analogous to a political constitution, a complex topography with territorial power relations, is the chief device of the *Republic*.[2] It is novel enough, but the concentration of *thymos* into just one part, compensated for by its elevation to the central and mediating part, is an innovation that will dominate, acknowledged or not, passion discourse through the ages into our time.

Thomas Aquinas, for example, will incorporate the two passionate parts—the parts that are "horse-shaped" in the *Phaedrus*—into his "Treatise on the Passions." Although both kinds of passion will be, for him, sensory appetites (not, to be sure, understood as Platonic possessive *epithymia*, but rather as Aristotelian directed *orexis*), yet he will not entirely lose the thymotic element: There are some passions which are always about what is desirable or repellent as just pleasant or unpleasant, and others that are indeed directed to the same sought or avoided objects, but when acquisition or evasion of these objects is arduous, demanding, difficult. The pursuit of these gets up one's back, so to speak, arouses one's indignation, one's ire; hence these latter passions are called "irascible." These latter passions preserve the Platonic version of spiritedness, which is a disposition to be ardent for honor, indignant at wrongs, righteously angry with others and ashamed with oneself—in sum, proud even in one's wants.

Thus what was once the respiration that evidences vitality itself is concentrated into one third of the soul. But what it loses in generality it gains in force and function. As Eros the *daimon* mediated between heaven and earth in the *Symposium*, so spiritedness is the psychic "in-between," connecting the soul's high and low parts.[3]

Here is how Socrates presents *thymos*, or as he will say "the *thymos*-kind" (*to thymoeides*) in the *Republic*.[4] First of all, as I said, the soul-forms are derived from the political community that Socrates and his conversational partners—Glaucon and Adeimantos, Plato's brothers—have built "in words."[5] It is constituted of three castes. Socrates presents first the caste of those who are spirited, aggressive, courageous: the *warriors*; then those who love learning and have the knowledge and wisdom: the *governors*; and finally those who make, acquire, and consume things: the *producers*. The psychic constitution is said to be analogous to the political constitution in being tripartite, and as in cities, one part is predominant in each single citizen's make-up, though each soul has all parts. Thus the set of the defining characteristics of some one caste dominates each individual soul. Of course, what makes this so is ultimately the converse: The collection of each individual's defining characteristic makes the caste what it is.[6] Justice is then defined similarly for politics and for people: "doing one's own business" according to the duties of one's caste and the bent of one's soul.[7] The same three castes and human types, each severely held to its own duty, will be present in the *Bhagavad Gita* (third or second century B.C.E.); perhaps these are basic psycho-political types.

The claim that the soul is constituted of different parts is not made without an argument, one that rests on a psychological application of an ontological axiom about opposites: The denial "that the same thing can do, suffer, or be opposite things in the same part at the same time toward the same thing"[8] is a forerunner of the Law of (Non-) Contradiction in its onto-logical form, that is, the version in which it applies not only to speech but also to things; Aristotle will state it formally.[9] We do indeed experience opposite motions of the soul simultaneously, as is illustrated by the story of one Leontius who, walking by some corpses, desired to look at them, but at the same time felt indignantly angry with himself, turned away and covered his eyes until desire finally overcame him. "Then, pulling his eyes open, he ran up to the corpses and said: 'There, you accursed eyes, fill yourselves with the beautiful sight.'"[10]

The desire Leontius succumbs to arises from a sort of natural perversity, the pleasure people feel at excruciating sights (the sort catered to by Roman circuses, Gothic novels, and modern slasher movies), a pleasure proud people are indignant at feeling and ashamed to indulge. Even before telling the story, Socrates had already concluded that by his axiom the soul must have different parts which are involved when its desires force it into doing what is contrary to sound reason and make it feel ashamed. In fact it must have three parts.

This time, in the *Republic*, Socrates keeps the thymotic part for last. It is, as it were, a mean called forth by the extremes. He begins with a dual soul, composed of the part with which the soul reasons, called the *logistikon*, that is, the part given to *logos*, and another part given to erotic love, hunger and thirst, and other appetites. This second part is "fluttered" by all sorts of desires and is "a-rational (*alogon*) and desire-devoted (*epithymetikon*), the companion of certain repletions and pleasures."[11]

I might say here that since the soul is like a political constitution, it is a hierarchy in which there is low and high valuation but no suppression. Desire has its place. In fact in the ideal polity Socrates has constructed, the caste dominated by acquisition and consumption has more freedom to indulge in pleasures than the two others, who are under a severe discipline. This constitutional or topographical nature of the soul, so strongly asserted by Socrates, has staying power; it survives into Freud's writings. But there will also arise a counter-claim: that the soul is unitary and works as a whole. That claim does indeed run into the "inner-conflict" problem that was Socrates' point of departure: How is it that we can entertain two affects simultaneously?

Glaucon first thinks that spirit must be identical with this a-rational desire,[12] but the Leontius story convinces him of the opposite, that the spirited part is *always* allied with the rational part in something like a civil war between reason and desire. So it is a distinct third part—in fact, children display spiritedness even before they are fully rational[13]—though eventually it comes under the command of reason in the battle to discipline the desires.[14] To settle the matter, Socrates quotes Homer: "He struck his chest and had a word with his heart."[15] In Socrates' interpretation the poet makes the part that can reason about better or worse rebuke the a-rationally fuming part (*toi alogistos thymoumenoi*).[16] Here the spirited part is, inconveniently but significantly, called a-rational. It is simply both—and neither.[17]

So what really is this soul-part, this Socratic novelty? It is first of all the upshot of a recognition that our whole passionate life has two very different constituents. One of these is basic but also humanly low; as so often in the dialogues these valuations are acknowledged to coincide so that the least respectable element has the saving grace of being the most necessary. This, I want to say, is the happy effect of hierarchy-making: The nether parts receive acknowledgment as the pervasively acting principles of the superstructure.

Thus beyond the basic desire for things necessary to biological life (food, drink, and sex), there is the desire for "commodious living," for the acquisition of goods and their enjoyable consumption. This further developed material desire is the defining function of the desire-devoted soul-part in the *Republic,* and it is the defining attribute of that caste of the ideal city which, taken by itself, is very like our own "commercial republic," that society of producers and consumers delineated by Alexander Hamilton in the *Federalist.*[18] If, however, in the political context of the *Republic,* desire is a prosperity-seeking and -providing passion, in the philosophical settings of all three dialogues here discussed it turns up in a higher role as well: the love of wisdom.

But again, basic and pervasive though desire be, it is not central. Its very name proclaims that. *Epi-thymia* is *thymos* plus a preposition: life-energy insofar as it is directed "upon" (*epi*) an object; thus the dictionary defines the verb *epithymein* as "to set one's heart upon a thing." *Epithymia* is *thymos* outward-directed. In the dialogue *Cratylus,* which is devoted to etymologies, Socrates himself recognizes that *epithymia* is piggy-backed on central *thymos,* which he connects, evidently correctly, with *thysis,* "stormy rage."[19]

And that brings out the meaning of *thymos.* It is passionate *self-respect,* which boils up not over the *possession of objects* as primarily *valued for themselves* but over the *acknowledgment of one's worth* as manifested in *respect from other people.* That is why pride and shame belong in its complex and why a warrior's courage is its first civic manifestation. Valor, steadfastness under danger, is the inner sense of value, a passion that shades delicately into a virtue; in Plato's city it is the defining virtue of the warriors, and it makes them friendly to their own and roughly recalcitrant toward outsiders.[20] It is because *thymos* is amenable to reason, somehow thought-prone, but not independently thoughtful that it is so sensitive to the according and withholding of respect by other human beings. Recall that "respect" means literally a directed look, an appraising regard. Hence spiritedness is as vulnerable to shame as it is prone to pride. Socrates' continual effort is to transform such unreliably other-dependent passion-virtues into true self-respect: self-knowledge and deep thoughtfulness about what is good.

So *thymos* effects a distinction of the self-regarding from the object-seeking passionateness. Thus the former passions, which can boil over with heated life, are put at the center, while topographically low and high desires surround it. Herewith is posed a question that will remain active in clear or cloudy versions through the millennia: What is our ultimate, our master affect—love or pride? It is a question that reaches into heaven. There is an angel who renounces love for pride and falls: Lucifer turns into Satan. The psychology of this choice is superbly set out by Milton in *Paradise Lost*. The question also reaches into contemporary thinking about gender: Are women, perhaps under societal influence, more given to the connections of care and love and men to the isolation of principle and pride?[21] Or are some human beings of either sex congenitally more dominantly endowed with one or the other capacity of the soul? All these questions the dialogues raise but do not definitively answer, *except one*: What is the ultimately—not commonly, but ultimately—noblest capacity? It is not "heart," courage, in the sense of spirit, but love as the desire to know Being. That is unequivocal: There is, or ought to be, a human master passion—philosophy.

3. Desire and Questions as Analogues

This philosophy—not as practiced by professionals but by amateurs and dilettantes (that is, by lovers and delighters) such as Socrates—is a matter of many simple questions and rare, unsimple answers. Questions are the motive power of the love of wisdom.

I think that both the *Symposium* and the *Phaedrus*, without any explicit indication, intimate the formal relation between the *desire* to know and the *asking* of questions. As so often in the dialogues it is by wordplay.[1] The punning is, however, more explicit in the *Phaedrus*—not that the speaker himself intends his double meaning. Lysis ends his speech against the lover with the words: "[If you] think that anything has been left out, do ask (*erota*)!" "Ask" is homonymous with "love," both in the imperative.[2] Lysis is unintentionally contravening his own debating thesis. He can be heard as saying: "If you are still unsatisfied, considering the argument [favoring the non-lover] insufficient, just love!"

Recall that Socrates had elicited the formal characteristics of desire—of which love is the leading case—as intentionality, open negativity, and futurity, though not in these terms. "Intentionality" means that desire intends—tends toward—an object which is something articulably desirable. "Open negativity" means that desire is a sort of unfulfilled outline, a negatively delineated receptivity which assumes the shape of a vision, the image of the absent object. "Futurity" means that desire is expectantly directed to what is yet absent but is to be attained in the future. Indeed, long-breathed desire shades into hope, a vitalized kind of patient, attentive waiting.[3] Aristotle will say, to be sure, that "desire is for the 'right now.'"[4] And so it is; what we want we *want* now, but we haven't yet *got* it.

Questions are point by point analogous: A question asks about something, a quest has an object; thus a question has intentionality, perhaps very general. A question also has open negativity, a more directed receptivity that shapes itself about the absent answer, sometimes as a prefiguring image, sometimes as a suggestive concavity. And finally futurity is built into *bona fide* questions, which are expectancies, patient hopes for satisfaction to come by effort. Thus it is that philosophy has more perplexities than resolutions—not because it has a woolly preference for the quest over the quarry but because of the very condition that its questions be focused but open, directed but not jigged. Jig-questions are simply requests that preconceptions be precisely responded to; examples are the questions so unhappily but not incorrectly called "teacher's questions": "Does Plato's theory of erotic passion endorse Platonic love?" A merely industrious student would know just what was wanted; a thoughtful one wouldn't know where to begin with such erotetic wrongheadedness.

In sum: Philosophy, Socratic philosophizing at least, proceeds by dialectic, by conversational question-asking. But question-asking and desiring are formally similar. Why not believe that they are sometimes humanly identical? That seems to me to be *a* way to see why Socrates can appear as Eros.

4. The Word "Passion"

Since in Plato's work on pleasure, which I am about to consider, both the use of the word "passion" and the relation of the passions to pleasure remain unfixed, while Aristotle will soon settle both, this is a good moment to offer at least a sketch of the word for the affect this book is about—at least until the eighteenth century, when "passion" was largely replaced by "emotion."

Our "passion" is derived from the Latin past participle *passus* of the verb *pati*, "to suffer, to submit," as in "suffer harm," or "submit to fate," usually used for something bad that afflicts people. It comes to us through medieval Latin, particularly through references to the Passion of Christ. The etymology of the Latin "passion" words is only uncertainly related to Greek *pathos,* but various Latin usages were heavily influenced by Greek passion-terms; *pathicus,* in fact, became a Latin word. The interesting developments occur in Greek terms. "Pathos" is, of course, an English word too.

The Greek word *pathos* similarly comes from a verb *paschein*, "to suffer," whose past infinitive is *pathein.* It has a conjectured etymological relation to *penthos,* "sorrow" (there is a restaurant in Big Sur in California called "Nepenthe," "Sorrowless"), and more remotely to Indogermanic *bhend* "bind."[1] So from the beginning *pathos* was loaded with a sense of suffering and subjection, as is indeed the German word for passion, *Leidenschaft*; *Leiden* means both suffering and sickness.

Nonetheless, the Greek usage of the verb *paschein* can be quite general: It means "to undergo, have happen to one" and is paired with its opposite, "to do" (and various verbs connected with *ergon,* "deed"). So Odysseus says of a bard that he sings truly of the Greeks, telling "all they did (*erxan*) and underwent (*epathon*)."[2] Since, however, what just befalls us is frequently not good, the verb and the condition do often refer, as I said, to suffering in the bad sense. *Pathei mathos,* "by suffering comes learning" . . . to the unwilling, says Aeschylus.[3] But since, again, what happens is sometimes indifferent as well, *pathos*-words may also mean just a property, predication, condition, situation, experience—anything that affects a human being or a thing. So in the *Philebus,* Socrates calls certain "properties inherent in motions of the body" produced by music, *pathe* (plural of *pathos*),[4] and Aristotle, going back to a Pythagorean usage, speaks of "the properties (*pathe*) and parts of the heavens."[5] However, since a *pathos* is often a changeable property, the emphasis is usually on the injurious direction, say from white to black or sweet to bitter.

The use of *pathos* for human affects is concurrent (though the group of passions now called emotions is not really established until Aristotle's treatment in the *Rhetoric*). Democritus, for example, an early atomist born a long generation before Plato, said: "Medicine cures the body of sickness, wisdom relieves the soul of passions."[6] Plato himself certainly speaks of passions in the psychic sense, as a condition of the soul, for example in the *Phaedrus:* "the erotic passion" (*to erotikon pathos*).[7] But in the *Philebus,* about to be discussed, there is, as my example above shows, no such fixed meaning. There is, however, a related word, *pathema,* used several times in the sense of a "feel"[8]—"feels" being a term often used nowadays for pre-emotions, not very distinct, hardly articulable bodily affects.[9]

Finally, Aristotle brings out definitively what was always in the term: its passivity. Doing and suffering (*poiein* and *paschein*) are together one of his "categories," meaning the universal questions that can be asked of any thing; one of these is: doing or done to?[10] The English verb "suffer" has, as it happens, a built-in passive sense; it is from Latin *sub-ferre,* "to bear [up] under, to support." When passion is, in our epoch, transmogrified into emotion, an implicit intention is to get out from under the "suffering" implied in the old term.[11]

And yet—something is lost in the transition. There is a long disquisition on "pathos" in Hegel's *Aesthetics.*[12] In it he recalls a less subjectively demeaning, an objectively grander sense.

Pathos, then, constitutes the true center, the genuine domain of art. . . . For pathos touches a string that resonates in every human breast; everyone knows what is valuable and rational in the content of true pathos and acknowledges it. Pathos moves because it is what is powerful in human existence.

By *pathos* Hegel means a high capacity for being moved in the soul—that contradiction in term, a passive power for masterful suffering, which distinguishes passionateness from emotionality.

5. The Perplexities of Pleasure

An older Socrates is about to lead the oldest and most searching inquiry into pleasure known to me. Pleasure and pain are the most pervasive of affects but also the most elusive of notions.

Yet why start with difficulties? It is, after all, the expositor's business to explain, not to complain. Well, to begin with, the two ancients who have the most extensive and most influential things to say about pleasure both change their minds, or, more cautiously, they differ from themselves—and each other—in their writings. Indeed, it does not necessarily follow, as scholars do often tend to assume, that if authors say different things in different places or even in the same place, they have changed their minds or even that they have contradicted themselves. For they might be of two minds about the same matter in one work because the matter itself is paradoxical or in different works because they have taken a different perspective. Be that as it may, such disagreements burden our own thinking with perplexities. These, however, turn out, when marshalled, to be just what we want to think about, because the complexities are native to the topic; they form the knot we need to untie, and sometimes even to cut. Here are the questions about pleasure I have found knotted together in the works about to be considered.

The topic is pleasure, and no one argues that *human* pleasure is not a feeling, a condition of which we are aware and which we, moreover, remember and thus *re*-cognize, so that it is both conscious and *self*-conscious (not that anyone knows what "conscious" or "self-conscious" really means). But is it a passion, that is, an affect or feeling having a certain structure, having say a distinctive inciting object or image and observable bodily concomitants? It might be just the satisfaction of some primitive somatic craving. There are old experiments on rats in whose hypothalamus (an emotion-triggering brain site) stimulation-delivering devices were implanted. The animals could activate these by pressing a lever. This they did at the rate of several thousand times an hour for ten hours. The inference was that the animals were rewarding themselves for a slight effort with an intense pleasure, aroused directly without intervening desire-arousing object—sheer, brute desirability without an intervening desideratum. So perhaps living beings can have pleasure without a mediating emotion—a direct, merely neuro-physiological, simple reaction of "again and again."[1] The experiment *seems* to support the ancient suggestion that pleasure is a pre- or proto-passion, or not a passion proper at all but an unmediated affect belonging among the somatic "feels" and distinct from psychic "feelings." Here is a first framing of the questions concerning pleasure: Is it a passion? It is a helpful framing because we come thereby to look for common—or missing—marks.

But why ask? No one, to be sure, is not interested in pleasure, though probably somewhat more people are interested in getting it than in under-standing it. For the former, "I know it when I feel it" is good enough, and even for those for whom getting it isn't enough, having felt pleasure is, as I said, obviously a necessary beginning to reflection. That is true for all inter-nal affects: The word has to call up an experience, otherwise what is there to talk about? Yet it seems even less imaginable of pleasure that a being who has never felt it should care or discourse about it.

What the word pleasure calls up is—I was about to say, inevitably—something desirable, hence good. The "good" part is the crux of all ancient treatments, which turn on the question: Is pleasure good, a good, the good, indifferent, or bad for the soul? Modern approaches tend to be much more sanguine about the fundamental beneficence of pleasure, though they dis-tinguish those that are medically dangerous. The "desirable" part develops almost oppositely: The ancient pagans know pleasure simply as what is always sought after (except under strong counter-motivations), because it is the desirable *par excellence,* and they regard pain as correspondingly to be avoided. The post-pagans, ourselves included, know of the rival voluptuous-ness of pain, both the feeling of it for oneself (masochism) and the inflicting of it on others (sadism). This is not pain exultantly borne for a purpose, as Prometheus suffers, bound on a rock with a raven pecking at his liver, defy-ing the tyrant-god, Zeus, who inflicts the torture on the Titan to extract his secret.[2] This is pain inflicted and undergone for pleasure. Socrates, in this an exemplar of antiquity, seems to be as incapable of conceiving the thought that one might choose pain, horror, disgust *for its own sake* as of the thought that one might want the bad; his companions seem always to find his view immediately plausible. It is, to my mind, one of those marks that distinguishes—exceptions being admitted—antiquity from modernity, and behind it is a long story, the story—largely Christian—of the perverse will. It is a tale not for this book, but perhaps the next one. The ancients, it appears, well understood pleasure-*from*-pain but not pleasure-*in*-pain.

Let me now present a list of the perplexities regarding pleasure, a veri-table geyser of problems and complaints. It will, I promise, be faster to read than it was to compose.

First heading: What is pleasure, and its contrary, pain?

1. Is pleasure a passion, something that attends passion, a supervening effect? More generally, is it a condition, a disposition, or something *sui generis*?
2. Is pleasure one or many? Do enjoyment, pleasure, delight (mentioned together in the *Philebus*)[3] have something in common that is *the* pleasure? Are there fundamental types of pleasure?
3. Is there mere pleasure from direct stimulation (as the rats suggest), or is human pleasure always pleasure *at* something, caused *by* something, by an object having more independent value than as a mere stimulant? In contemporary terms: Is pleasure an independent affect or merely the "valence" of an affect?
4. Is pleasure always linked to desire? Is it a direct circular process: desire is of pleasure and pleasure fulfills the desire for pleasure? Or is the desire always for an object whose obtaining gives pleasure? Do we ultimately desire pleasure or its object? Is pleasure simply and only what we seek, and pain what we avoid?
5. Is desire fulfilled desire ended, so that pleasure comes just when the longing is gone—and so always comes past its time? Or is desire itself pleasurable and its fulfillment the pleasure of contentment?
6. Is pleasure self-exhausting or self-maintaining?
7. Can pleasure be directly induced, or must it be a spontaneous by-product? Can we actively and directly live for pleasure?
8. Is pleasure some positive internal condition we project upon a world that then appears pleasurable, or does the world induce pleasure by showing itself accommodating our natures? Do we take pleasure, or does the world give pleasure?
9. Is pleasure infinite in the sense of a conceivable "more and more," or is there a perfected state, when "it doesn't get any better than this"? Are there limits to our own nature's capacity for pleasure, even thresholds where it flips into pain?
10. What are the analytical and experiential relations of pleasure to its contrary, pain, and its contradictory, feelinglessness? (A contrary is as black to white, a contradictory as black to non-black.)
11. Is its essence definable or even describable?

Second heading: How are pleasure and good related?

1. Is pleasure the good, a good, no good, indifferent, bad?
2. Is pleasure what makes life happy, or does happiness incidentally give pleasure, or does it go both ways? (Is happiness a feeling? Is it passive or active?)

3. Is pleasure simply what we want? Is "want" here to be construed as "lack" or "wish"? Can we lack what we feel no want of, or want what we have not lacked, or lack what we do not need? In sum, how is pleasure related to natural and psychic demands?

4. Is what we ultimately want pleasure or happiness? In particular are all human beings the same in this respect? Can we desire pain absolutely, that is, not as an intermediary to a consequent pleasure?

5. If we say that either pleasure or happiness is what we finally want, all else being means, is that merely by definition or does it illuminate the nature of either?

6. Is something good-for-us, absent pleasure now or later, imaginable?

7. Are there bad and false pleasures? Are they nonetheless pleasures? Is their badness in their effects or in their intrinsic qualities? Is the falseness in a mistaken object or a misconstrued affect? Can we in fact misconstrue our own affects?

8. Are pleasures only of the body, of mind alone, of body and mind together? How is the last relation to be construed? What are the pleasures assignable to each class, if it exists?

9. Is there truly gratuitous pleasure, not based in want and not paid for over time?

10. Is pleasure best understood as either a metaphysical or an evolutionary indicator of well-being and power, and is pain to be construed as a deficit in organic integrity?

Almost all these questions, some inchoate, all intertwined, most explicit, will be taken up in the *Philebus*.

6. Socrates on Pleasure: Before the *Philebus*

I've used the dialogue *Philebus* to head this section because in it an older Socrates, presented by an older Plato, saying as much about pleasure as ever had or would be said, has changed his mind, or better, his perspective. The dialogues on which I actually report in this section, the *Gorgias* and the *Republic*, are generally considered to belong to the early and middle time of Plato's writing. This would not be of consequence except that the Socrates of these works seems to be younger than the one of the *Philebus*, not in age—in fact he dies in a presumably early dialogue—but in spirit. In any case, in the two dialogues here discussed he is spiritedly and uncompromisingly hostile to pleasure; in the late dialogue he is soberly and sensibly accepting of it.

In almost all the ancient discussions, the issue is the worth of this basic affect more than its nature. It is the life-issue about which philosophers (and ascetics) will ever after most differ from the public, and the preachment they will most ardently and least successfully labor over. So Socrates' head-on opposition is meant as shock therapy, the first such. I will be correspondingly terse.

A. *The Infinity of Pleasure: The* Gorgias

In the *Gorgias*[1] an aggressively self-confident young man, Callicles, asserts against Socrates that the happy—and virtuous—life is that of the strongest desire most amply satisfied: "Luxury, licentiousness, and liberty, if they are well-supported by power and intelligence are virtue and happiness." Socrates seizes on the contradiction: When we are well filled up, desire goes dead and so does pleasure; hence the life of pleasure must be one of continual inflow and outflow. Socrates tells the famous fable of the pleasure-lovers' leaky body-jar and running soul-sieve; neither the dribbling body nor the perforated memory can hold onto pleasure. Callicles is uncowed. That's just the point: To be fully satisfied is indeed death; pleasure depends on the continual alternation of desire and satisfaction. In other words, not desire fulfilled, but the cycle of satisfaction and want is pleasure. Socrates compares it to itching and scratching, to erotic excitation and relief. Oddly enough, Socrates does not press the logical case, the inherent self-annihilation of pleasure, but rather its vulgarity. Callicles waffles for a moment but recovers his assertiveness: Pleasure really is *that* shameful, *and* it is happiness.

Now Socrates engages in some familiar dialectic. He gets Callicles to admit that being in a good condition is incompatible with being in a bad one. And he gets him to say separately that pleasure as Callicles understands it always does involve pain—the pain of the desire, the need itself. Then he puts these two concessions together to reveal that pleasures can't be the same as good. Next he argues that the wise and the brave feel enjoyment and pain much as do the foolish and the craven, from which it follows that pleasure does not make anyone good or pain bad. Callicles blows up at these quibbles. Of course, he now says, some pleasures are and make one better than others. Socrates quickly seizes the advantage: Then some pleasures are better than others, and there is a skill for choosing between them—which is not Gorgias's sophistical rhetoric. Instead, what we do must have the good as its aim and pleasure as a possible means, not the other way around. Thus there are two lives—one the rhetorical and political life directed ultimately to producing and having pleasure, the other the philosophical life directed toward the good. Callicles gives in, unconvinced.

These issues, the curiously limitless yet self-canceling structure of pleasure and the choice of lives, "which any human being, even of little intellect, would take extremely seriously," are taken up more penetratingly in the *Philebus*. There, however, a more compromising Socrates will allow for a third life which gives pleasure its due as a good.

B. The Worth of Pleasure: The Republic

In the *Republic*[2] the discussion of pleasure occurs as Socrates compares three kinds of life and their characteristic pleasures, that of making money, of acquiring honor, and of getting wisdom. The lover of wisdom, the philosopher, tastes all three pleasures, the honor-lover two of them, and the wealth-lover only his own. But really it is only the thoughtful person whose pleasure is true; the others are just painted illusionistically (*eskiagraphemenes*, "achieving a look of solidity by shading"). For pain is the contrary of pleasure, and in between is a sort of peace of soul. Those in bad pain praise as a pleasure not enjoyment but peace, but they would also find the cessation of positive pleasure painful. So there's nothing solid about these affects; they exist merely as relative to other states. To be sure, there are some sudden terrific pleasures that just come and go on their own, like pleasures of smell. But for most people most pleasures, the ones that enter the soul through the body, are of the former, relative kind: relief pleasures. That is because most people have no experience of positive pleasure. They want to fill up on what has no full being, like drink and other things only suited to the body. Thus they spend all their lives just getting back to what we would call the base line, and, like cattle, always look downward. That is true with respect both to the desire- and the spirit-dominated people, the money-lovers and the honor-lovers.

The purpose of the whole conversation was to answer the question: Is it true that the most unjust man makes for himself a better life than the just?[3] Socrates is now ready to claim that the most unjust of men, the tyrant, who is also most lust- and pleasure-ridden—he indulges in erotic greed, the counterpart of money-loving—is indeed also the most miserable. In fact, he is, in point of true pleasure, distant from the oligarch (the money-lover) in the ratio of one to three, who is in turn distant from the philosopher as one to three. Thus arises the proportion 1:3::3:9. To make that figure solid, not a mere "illusionistic shading," Socrates cubes 9. $9^3 = 729$, and that is the distance in pleasure that separates the miserable tyrant from the philosopher in point of "true pleasure." With that *jeu d'esprit*, the point about justice is about made, for "true pleasure" here seems to mean happiness. Both the logic and the language of the *Republic* imply this. The tyrant has at once the means and the desire for feeling pleasure, for acquiring riches and indulging his lust, and yet his life is the farthest from the best, the happiest life. "Happiness" (*eudaimonia*) is the word used a number of times of that condition from which the tyrant's life and that of the city he rules are most distant.[4] The difference between pleasure and happiness, the illusoriness of the one and the solidity of the other, is here merely figured by the third dimension of the tyrant's distance. Aristotle will be the one to give a sober account of the criteria by which happiness and pleasure are to be at once distinguished and combined; it is one of his high moments. As for the Socrates of the *Repub-*

lic, he has so far had too youthful a spirit to legitimize pleasure as part of a distinct "life." That is about to happen.

7. Plato on Pleasure: The *Philebus*

Would you trust an inquiry into pleasure that was very pleasurable to read? The *Philebus,* Plato's dialogue subtitled *On Pleasure* (hedone): *Ethical* (not, apparently, by Plato himself but accepted by the tradition) fulfills the evident requirement of maintaining a certain distance from the subject; it is, in fact, a little crabbed—no one's warmly favorite dialogue. That delimited *subject* is the relation of pleasure to good, whence the "ethical" of the subtitle. But there is no askable *question* about pleasure that I can think of that is not explicit or implicit in the dialogue. Usually Socrates won't allow a conversation about the goodness, purpose, or manner of acquisition of any subject to go on long without insisting that we should first inquire into its very nature. The question "What is pleasure?" is, however, not explicitly raised in the *Philebus,* though elements of possible answers are introduced incidentally. On the matter of its goodness Socrates offers a perfectly explicit though nuanced answer.

Plato says in one of his letters that "there neither is nor will be any written composition by Plato, but the ones now so called belong to a Socrates become beautiful and young."[1] Setting aside the intriguing idea that the Socrates well known never to have written anything is the author of the Platonic writings that Plato says he never wrote or would write, what does "beautiful and young" mean? I think "beautiful" means what it does in the *Symposium,* infinitely, seductively attractive from within. And "young" means—for Socrates is really young only in one dialogue, the *Parmenides*—ever-fresh, full of spirit, radical, ironic, agile. Well, the Socrates of the *Philebus* is not thus beautiful or young. This dialogue is thought to be a late work of Plato, and Socrates has grown old along with his author—a little professorial. His young conversational partner, Protarchus, who may be real or invented, thanks him for granting this "conference" (*synousia*);[2] there is also a larger silent audience of whom Socrates is quite as aware as a lecturer would be.[3] The dialogue is just an excerpt from an extended conversation. Its debating point has been stated before the beginning by Philebus, a fiction with a shamelessly obvious "speaking name": "Youth-lover" (*philos, hebe*); he is a devotee both of youth and of youths—the two young men like to be called "boys." Although Socrates has promised more conversation tomorrow, since it's getting near midnight,[4] as the written dialogue ends Protarchus wants to squeeze yet a little more out of Socrates. He wants to go, being, my guess is, tired after his lecture—as the old tend to be and as the "young" Socrates never was, at least not of conversation. The *Philebus* seems to be at the start of the tradition that serious inquiry into the

human root-affects is peculiarly endless, characteristically dry—and irresistible.

Socrates starts the lesson by summarizing Philebus's claim, which Protarchus has inherited but may not agree with: "That enjoyment, pleasure
(*hedone*), delight, and all things in accord with them are good for living
beings," and immediately recapitulates also his own: "That mindfulness
(*phronesis*), thought, memory, and all that is related to these, right opinion
and true reasoning, are better than and superior to pleasure—for all those
beings who are capable of taking part in them"[5]

Philebus wisely doesn't speak for himself. He turns the argument over
to his friend, and in fact his fewer and fewer interventions are merely self-
assertive. He is a self-consistent first exponent of a long consequent tradition most explicitly represented by the Epicureans (who in fact talked a lot,
though at their best in verse, as did Lucretius, crabbed Epicurus's poetic
expositor): "[Epicurus] denies that there is any need of reason or argument
[to prove] that pleasure (*voluptas*) should be sought out and pain (*dolor*)
avoided. These things are sensed just as that fire is hot and snow white. . . ."[6]
Besides, Philebus is—probably quite insouciantly—moderate: Pleasure is
good, not *the* good, as Socrates will put the more absolute position. Moreover he may not be one of "those beings capable" of the intellectual life. Even
his friend says, don't ask him questions, don't stir him up when he's well
asleep;[7] so Socrates, who is eager enough to involve Protarchus as respon-
dent, is very willing to let Philebus lie. (I must say here that though the
"young" Socrates often makes such distinctions of capability in theory, in
life he'll talk to anybody, anytime.)

For this dialogue, Philebus embodies the truth that if pleasure-lovers
aren't allowed to have the last *word* in the literal sense, yet they *feel* unrebut-
table, and their silence is in effect the last word. Socrates acknowledges that
fact in a sentence which, while it concedes the taciturn youth's demand to be
left to his inertial pleasure, does so precisely in order to defeat his purpose.
He says that the prime issue of philosophy is the way reason identifies one
and many, a problem that courses through all speech, "always and from way
back and now," (a phrase Aristotle borrows almost exactly for his own prime
topic, Being.[8]) Presently that unlikely, apparently pallid piece of Socratic
ontology will become crucial to all thinking about pleasure in the dialogue.
This issue of the one-and-many is so stirring that, "as it seems to me, there
is a deathless and ageless passion (*pathos*) for these accounts (*logōn*) in us.
And whenever a young man first gets a taste of it, he feels pleasure as if he
had discovered a treasure of wisdom, and enthused by pleasure in his joy of
account-giving, he stirs up everything."[9] So Philebus in his inert disdain is
depriving himself of what he claims to live for: pleasure.

To summarize Socrates' complex subsequent development in a sentence:
He argues first, moderately, that the good life consists of neither pleasure nor

intellect (*nous*) alone, but of their mixture; he radicalizes his compromise, however, by then arguing that for us humans, within our particular cosmic setting, thought is far better than pleasure. But he has said what he has said: that thinking itself gives acute pleasure. Indeed, if it didn't, how would the life of the mind ever "mix" with the life of pleasure? Wouldn't it be just an alternation of possibly quite refined sensory and even psychic delights with dour mentation? I think Socrates must implicitly concede to tacit Philebus, who is reposing in pleasure, that the activity which stirs talkative Protarchus provides pleasure as well—that the life of the mind is not incidentally but inherently pleasurable and that the stark opposition between pleasure and thoughtfulness as human capacities is no more tenable than their separation as ways of life. Aristotle will pick up this subtle but defining difficulty.

It may, however, be that Socrates' terms are partly set by current events, events that occurred long after his death, at the time the dialogue was being written. Plato was then presiding over a swirling debate about pleasure. Eudoxus had come to the Academy, Plato's school. He was a mathematician and astronomer responsible for much that was future-fraught in the mathematics of his day—for example, the theory of proportion that underlies modern equations and the method of exhaustion that prefigures the calculus. But he also had a new theory of pleasure: that pleasure is *the* good.

When a great mathematician says something like that, it signifies, but what? Aristotle says that Eudoxus argued that all beings, rational and arational, go for pleasure, whatever that might in particular be, and that, since what is chosen is good, what is chosen by all must be best, and that is *the* good.[10] Evidently Eudoxus, whose own particular notion of pleasure must have been sufficiently intellectual even for Plato, is reasoning here from quantity to quality, which can't, on the other hand, have been acceptable either to Plato himself or to the long-dead Socrates. There were probably people like the inert Philebus who meant nothing much by saying that pleasure is good, or, if you like, *the* good, except that they intended to live for it. There was Speusippus, Plato's successor-to-be as head of the Academy, who reacted by arguing that pleasure is not good, nor of course is pain, so that the remaining third, *a-patheia,* "passionlessness," the contradictory of pleasure, must be *the* good.[11] And way back there had been the old "young" Socrates who had said boldly that pleasure is contemptible. The present Socrates has—or perhaps poses as having—a damped spirit and expresses what seems to be Plato's desire to compose these factions: Pleasure is good but not best. This Socrates, without forgetting his old devotion to those forms, the "invisible looks" located in a hyper-heaven, adopts Plato's more recent preoccupations, the intellectual sources and causes specifically of the visible cosmos.

They begin by citing Aphrodite, an Olympian and a cosmic force. She is clearly the goddess of "Philebus the handsome," who is also Philebus the inertial, having turned the argument over to Protarchus. Socrates fusses about calling the goddess by a name agreeable to her—I have no doubt because her name sounds like "Mindlessness"; *A-phro-dite : a-phro-nesis* (*phronesis* : mindfulness)—and names her "Pleasure." She has, Socrates says, many shapes, and so is Pleasure a "many-colored" thing. There is a fool's pleasure in excess and a wise man's pleasure in restraint; they are all one as pleasures, but they are many insofar as some are good, some bad. Here is a first reason for Socrates to raise that natural "marvel" of the one-and-many introduced above.[12]

Socrates says he isn't talking about current and easily soluble logical quibbles concerning the multiplicity and unity of perishable things, but about the timeless unities, the "monads" such as "man" and "beauty," that is, the forms, about which there are serious disputes. He then gives a thumbnail sketch of the familiar problems raised by these Socratic-Platonic forms: whether they exist, how their ungenerated and indestructible being is to be understood, and how these eternal monads enter into the infinities of perishable things. These are the matters that are said to give such pleasure to the young in the passage quoted before. They do, of course, give the greatest pleasure to Socrates. For him they are the very best way, "of which I am forever the lover, though it has often deserted me, leaving me bereft and perplexed"[13]—a poignant confession. This way they must now follow. Thus pleasure will be implicated in a Platonic "ontology," in an "account of Being."

Socrates, however, begins in a curious way. The way he wants to take was a divine gift to the ancients who lived closer to the gods. I have no doubt that Socrates means the Pythagoreans to whom Plato had evidently turned as the problem of the activity of the forms *within* the visible world, the cosmos, became more acute to him. To give the tersest account of this late-Platonic Pythagoreanism: The "one-and-many" complex, which comes into being from the ungenerated forms informing the generated world, is now embedded within two larger cosmic principles or sources con-natural (*symphyton*) with them, "the Limit and Non-Limit" (*peras : apeiria,* often rendered as "the finite and the infinite"—not quite accurately, because these terms ought not so much to name the generated domains or realms—which the field-like terms imply—as the principles from which they arise). Between these two sources there comes into being that well-ordered world of one-and-many for which the Greek word is *kosmos.*

This cosmology is arithmological. I mean that the ordering of the world proceeds—not as a process in time but in thought—by the generation of definite, delimited numbers from the interaction of the two source-principles; these specific numbers underlie the variety of ordered experience contained in our world, somewhat as in modern science the general formulas of physics are thought of as doing. The first, outermost principle is a delimiting or determining factor. It acts *by means* of the monads (or ones) over the field of multiplicity (or many). This field, receptive to discriminating action, is inherently unlimited and indeterminate, and that is the effect of the second, negative principle. Thus the extreme opposing principles interact over the inner cosmic field so as to number, sort, and order it:

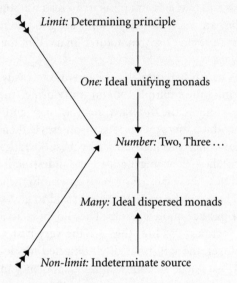

Limit: Determining principle

One: Ideal unifying monads

Number: Two, Three . . .

Many: Ideal dispersed monads

Non-limit: Indeterminate source

Socrates explains the thought-stages:

> This being the way in which things are made into a cosmos (*diakekosmenon*) we must always assume one form (*idea*) and search for it . . . and after that two . . . and three or some other number, and each of these in the same way until one can see that the first one, in accordance with the source-principles (*kat' archas*) is not only one-and-many and unlimited, but also *how many.* And one must not bring the idea of the Non-Limit to bear on the multitude until one has an overview of its every number between the infinite and one.[14]

Protarchus doesn't quite understand this all too compact capsule of Pythagoreanism; in fact, docile as he is, he nearly rebels at being thrown into more perplexity (*aporia*). It is, to be sure, an arcane presentation of the cosmology of the one-and-many, and philosophically more imaginatively suggestive than rationally worked out. I've only made a stab at schematizing it. At the opposing extremes function the two greatest and least determinate source-principles, those of bounding and exceeding. These generate, each on its side but under the remote influence of the other, the two somewhat more determinate principles of singularity and multiplicity, and those in turn come together in the middle to generate the numerically constituted cosmos; it is an intellectual dual descent converging from the extremes toward an increasing concreteness, our real world. Socrates' "overview of every number" then seems to refer to our understanding of the genesis of the natural number system.

Arcane as this cosmology is, its motive becomes clear enough: It is meant to offer a basis for the explanation of pleasure within the constitution of a rational cosmos—the knowledge of which Socrates will offer as the better half of human happiness, better in fact than the "worldly" pleasure for which this cosmos is the ground. Cosmology rather than the cosmos is what is finally fulfilling.

The problem to which this cosmology is germane is the fact that worldly pleasure, with its one name and one goddess, is yet many-colored, "dappled." Socrates has already named some of its kinds: enjoyment, delight. He will also want to review its worth—good, bad; that is, after all, the central issue. He will assign its location: body, soul, intellect. He will distinguish characteristics: the pleasures of restoration after depletion, of "settling down" (*katastasis*[15]) after agitation, pleasures that depend on something having previously gone awry. The term *katastasis* is, incidentally, picked up by Aristotle for one of his definitions of pleasure, the more downbeat one.[16] Moreover it becomes one side of a chief distinction made by the Epicureans, that between "kinetic" and "katastematic" pleasures, those that are but a tickling of the flesh and those that *are* a deep equilibrium of the body—"*are*," not "arise from," in the Epicurean case, which does not distinguish between the pleasure felt and its bodily condition.[17] To ask how all these multiplicities are possible is an everlasting delight for the Platonic Socrates, though to answer is a perennial perplexity. The answer cannot be superficially logical but must be deeply ontological. That is what the *Philebus* keeps reaffirming—which is why it must be so prominent in the project of this book, which is to view our feelings in various philosophical frameworks.

I think that the chief reason why Socrates drags down the two *principles,* Limit and Non-Limit, whose *domains* are the Finite and the Infinite, is that pleasure and pain, most of all human things in the world, seem to have them in their constitution. Recall what Socrates set out in the *Gorgias,* that the pleasant is a kind of embodied infinity, the "more-and-more" incarnate, while *the* good is, they agree, finite in the sense of finished: sufficient, complete, perfect.[18]

At this point Socrates comes down from the heavens to begin to look at "lives." A "life" (*bios*) is a span of human existence considered as a whole in the process of being accomplished. Its mode is close to what people now mean (if they mean anything) by "existential," concerned with the way we are in the here and now. Imagine, then, a life of pleasure without thoughtfulness. Socrates shows easily that a life of enjoyment without memory or mindfulness is not livable, is indeed unlived—just as long ago, shortly before he died as an embodied man, he had said that the unexamined life was in effect unlivable and so unlived.[19] It would be the life of a mollusk!

Protarchus is left speechless. But now, Socrates says, go on to imagine a life of intellect without pleasure, a life entirely without affect (*apathes*)!

So they agree that the life that is a *mixture* of pleasure and thought is best. Philebus's divinity, Pleasure, cannot be the Good. Philebus pipes up, impertinently: "Neither is your Mind the Good. . . ." Socrates turns the pun to use: Not *my* mind, perhaps, but true Divine Mind.[20] This intervention brings him to an extended and hard stretch of argument, with a new "device." The assignment of all that is to the two sources, the Limited and the Non-limited, had just been revealed by the divinity to Socrates. He now takes up not these ultimate principles, but the intra-cosmic domains derived from them, the Finite and the Infinite. From these he gets a third realm: their Mixture. It is clearly the cosmological ground of the mixed life, corresponding to the inner, the concretely numerical, part of the diagram of principles above, just as the life of the mind and of pleasure correspond respectively to the first two realms, the Finite and the Infinite. To these three Socrates adds a fourth factor, an agent, the Cause of the Mixture (*symmixis*).[21] Protarchus, being funny, suggests a fifth, the power of separation. Not yet, says Socrates.

In the Infinite domain he puts all things that admit of more or less, such as "fierce-*and*-gentle," the spectrum of feeling-intensity—an example of the unifying collection Socrates' way calls for. Mix with that the kind that "has its birth" from the Limit, meaning the Finite, and the result is a harmonizing of opposites, commensurate and concordant, because, in effect, articulating number has been introduced, just as the diagram shows.[22]

Here is one of Socrates' cases. Take sound, which is, to begin with, infinitely continuous in pitch and in volume. (In fact, that continuum is the ancient musicians' mark of the speaking voice as opposed to music, though here it stands, oddly enough, for inarticulate pleasure.) Introduce delimitations and with them discontinuities. Thus tones arise, and from these come consonances—the double or the 2:1 ratio that, when realized in plucked strings, makes the octave, the largest interval of the diatonic scale, then the 3:2 ratio that is the interval of the fifth, and so on. Thus pleasing music, well-adapted to our auditory discrimination, comes about through rational number-relations, so-called "ratios," as do many other "cosmic," that is, well-ordered structures. They obviously represent the "mixed" life.[23] For here we see mind at work to introduce measure into inarticulate continuity, thereby producing moderated pleasure; thus intellect is already at work in the pleasure hedonists think of as mindless. Of the cause of the mixture, that which brings the disparate domains together, Socrates says little, except that, as it is mind (or intellect, *nous*) in humans, so it is Mind, "king of heaven and earth," in the Cosmos.[24] Philebus has to make one last helpful remark: "Socrates, you're worshiping your own god." "And you, my companion, yours." Then he's out of it.

Having come from the heavens down to human life, Socrates now goes upward again from the human situation: Our feeble human body is constituted of the four elements that are also found in, and are indeed derived in us from, the cosmos: fire, water, earth, air. Moreover, our body has a soul. So mustn't we believe, reasoning from us to the constituting cosmos, that the world that much the more has soul *and* mind? Thus we have confirmed, though pretty cursorily, the ancient saying that Mind, as the fourth class called the Cause,[25] rules the world. In sum, our mind belongs to the class of Cause and pleasure belongs to that of the Infinite.

Now a new question. How do pleasure, and also pain, come into being *in us*—"through what feeling"?[26] Here is what I think Socrates is after: Pleasure has been reaffirmed as being in the class of the Infinite, but that is notional Pleasure, pleasure as it is thought about. The pleasure-and-pain we actually feel is describable in terms of the class in which finite and infinite are combined; here arise harmony, health, and equilibrium as well as their opposites. Thus hunger is a kind of "breaking and aching" (*lysis* and *lype*), while eating is a restoration, and *that* is pleasure. Filling up, reintegration, those, or rather the feel of them, are the bodily events that *are* the pleasure—not the re-achieved equilibrium itself, but the process of attaining it.[27] This is an explanation that comes very close to the currently influential James-Lange theory, which says that the bodily processes are *identical* with the pleasures.

But there are also pleasures and pains of the soul by itself, separately—the anticipation (*prosdokima*) of pleasures, the pleasing hope of pleasures to come. Such pleasure or pain derives from remembered or imagined pleasure or pain. We live

> not only with the sense
> Of present pleasure, but with pleasing thoughts
> That in this moment there is life and food
> For future years.[28]

Then the first, bodily, pleasure is the present body-feel of a physical process, while the consequent psychical pleasure is an expectant memory-image of a sensory pleasure to be repeated or even of a memory to be revived. Plato's phenomenology of pleasure is pretty refined.

Having given the physical conditions for both pleasure and pain, Socrates sees a third, middle possibility. In a state of equilibrium an organism would be without feelings of pleasure and pain—a-pathetic, though not in the sense of "inert." This would indeed be the life of the mind and of thoughtfulness, a divine life, for the gods feel neither joy nor pain.[29]

It is easy to read past Plato's noting of Speusippus's theory of *apatheia*. But the theory is notable not only as a forerunner of the damped hedonism of Epicurean humanism, but also as a premonition of the passionless joy of the divinity of Aristotle's, Thomas's, and Spinoza's theologies. Plato's passage is, first, an admission that pleasure needs a body to come about and, second, an intimation that the completely homeostatic body is an organic self-contradiction.[30] Socrates will soon return to this "middle" case as a human possibility—a sort of abrogation of the law of the excluded middle for human feeling.

When Socrates now comes to speak of the kind of pleasures belonging to the soul itself, he must consider sensation and memory. There may be, Socrates says, affects that never reach the soul (such as are now ascribed to the autonomic nervous system), but what is more interesting is that kind of sensation (*aisthesis*) "which comes about when the soul and the body have in common one affection (*pathei*) and are moved in common."[31] We tend to forget our sensations, but we sometimes do have memory, which is just "the saving of sensation." When the recall of the affection the soul has shared with the body is not spontaneous but is an effort by the soul alone, it is called "recollection," *the* Socratic way of inquiry—which in his earlier days was into much deeper matters than pleasure, into Being itself.[32]

Thus prepared, we can understand better the pleasure that belongs purely to the soul. The body is, finally, still behind the remembered or recollected pleasures of the soul. As has been intimated, this recollected pleasure is the temporal complement of the expected pleasure mentioned before; the memory gives expectation its material, its pre-visions, just as it gives remembrance its stuff, its re-visions.

And now comes an analysis of the function of desire (*epithymia*), an ingenious proof that desire, unlike pleasure belongs to the soul alone. Pleasure is of body and soul; desire is of the soul by itself. An illuminating moment!

The argument, in brief, is this (using an example): A man is thirsty. But it is not, strictly speaking, *drink* or a drink he wants; it is rather *to be filled* with drink. He desires the opposite of how he *now* feels, namely empty; he wants *soon* to feel full. Thus it is not the body's feeling that is the desire, but the soul's memory of fullness: "This argument tells us that *there is no desire of the body.*"[33]

Another consequence of the role of memory and expectation is that we can feel pain and pleasure simultaneously, for instance, the somatic pain of thirst and the psychic pleasure of having once been replete or being about to fill up.[34]

These observed phenomena now help in a new turn of the inquiry: Can pleasure and pain be said to be true or false? That question has various meanings: 1. Can we think that we really feel pleasure or feel real pleasure when we don't? Socrates drops that question, perhaps because it boggles the mind. But he does ask: 2. Must pleasures always be true, that is, always be just *what* we feel them to be? Can we *be wrong* in the basic identification of our feelings? Why could not our pleasures *be false*, that is, *mistaken*? Socrates says that pleasures have other qualities, such as intensity; why should they not have the logical quality of falseness? 3. Would such *falseness*, such confusion, be the same as *badness* in a pleasure? Socrates tacitly makes that identification. 4. Is a pleasure's falseness located in a *mistaken cause*? Is it the quality of the cause that makes a pleasure "correct or beneficial"?[35] Socrates intimates that it is.

At last Protarchus demurs: "In such a case, Socrates, we call the opinion false, but no one would call the pleasure itself false."[36] So Socrates must show Protarchus how pleasures themselves can be false, and perhaps show us how that makes them bad. He sketches a theory of cognition, of the relation of internal language to mental images, which is still current and still embattled. We form opinions, and these can be true and false. Protarchus agrees that our judgments *are* true or false. When we utter them they are rational speech (*logos*).[37] Thus the soul is like a book: "Memory, falling in with sensations and those feelings connected with them, seems almost, as it were, to write such speeches in our souls." At the same time there is also another workman within, one who paints images in our souls that illustrate memory's narrative; these are true or false as the opinions are true or mistaken. Both of these affections of the soul, the writing and the depicting, can belong to the present, past, and particularly to the future, just as did the psychic pleasures of experience, memory, and above all expectation. Hence internal speech, mental images, and expectant pleasures can come together, as when a man calculates on a golden future, envisioning a lot of gold in painted fantasies (*phantasmata*), and thereupon feels much pleasure.

Now both good and bad people have such writings and paintings and consequent feelings within, but the pleasures felt by the good—because they are god-friendly (*theophileis*)—are true and those of the bad false, presumably because their badness vitiates the whole internal complex. But just as false opinions, those not based on what truly is, was, or will be, are still opinions, so the false pleasures are still pleasures. And their falsity is what makes them bad, just as opinions are bad by reason of being false.

The argument therefore seems to be from character: Bad people devise mistaken or fraudulent inner narratives and images. (Recall that for Socrates ignorance is "the lie in the soul."[38]) Thus their pleasures are derivatively wrong—hence bad—not just in having a tainted tone, but in thus bearing witness to the spurious causes that arouse them. Here is an early, perhaps the earliest understanding of affects as appraisals, judgment-like events that can be true or false, a theory that will gain currency through the Stoics and Neostoics.

What would be an example? Perhaps it would be the case of someone who was engaging in "th' expense of spirit in a waste of shame" and finding the pleasure acute if somehow hollow, then deluded himself about the quality of its inciting object, telling himself justificatory tales that went against reality. Socrates also maintains, however, that there are also simply wicked, worthless pleasures, not so much mistaken in their cause as corrupt in themselves.[39] These pleasures, which are attributable to a simple depravity of soul, are of interest because they are the most acute, and best exemplify the infinite nature of pleasure.[40]

The varying intensities of such depraved or sick pleasures, pleasures of physical fillings and depletions, growths and wanings, combinations and dissolutions, show Socrates that pleasures are false not only by false judgments of their cause, but also by their intrinsic indeterminacy. Just as in visual cognition the true size of an object is calculated by its relative distance from the observer, so pleasures appear to be gaugeable by comparison with their distance from their relative pains. But that measure is quite indeterminable, in fact, self-interfering. Thus whereas before, opinions imbued pleasures with their quality of truth or falsity, so now the pleasures themselves cause errors with respect to their intensity.[41] Socrates is making the strangely plausible point that corrupt pleasures have no fixed measure: They feel more pleasant than they are!

That consideration of relative intensity leads Socrates back to the "middle life,"[42] the life of painlessness and pleasurelessness, what I—not Socrates—will call the Speusippus solution. Socrates raises a problem about this middle condition. Is painlessness actually pleasant? If that is what the promoters of passionlessness mean, they are surely contradicting themselves: They do believe in pleasure, only they call it lack of pain. But that's not what these "expert speakers on nature" mean: They mean to say that Philebus's pleasure is just an escape from pain and that there "simply is no pleasure."[43] Socrates concedes that their "irritation" with pleasure is in some way noble. But, we are now reminded, Socrates himself thinks they are wrong: There *are* positive pleasures.

Where the "enemies of Philebus"[44] are helpful is in the way they denigrate pleasure, by attributing the greatest intensity to the lowest pleasures, those arising from the body's relief. Socrates mentions an itching disease and its relief, scratching:[45] Such pleasures, however, tend to befall not those moderate people who follow the advice of "nothing too much," but the dissolute livers.

So the two partners come to consider a type of pleasure already mentioned, the mixed pleasure. All sorts of mixture are reviewed: mixed bodily pleasures, mixed psychic pleasures, mixed body-soul pleasures. Again Socrates uses, derisively, the itch as example. Itching (*gargarlizein*) is a mixture of slight pain and an acute pleasure of relief that drives people wild with delight; in some of them it causes "total discombobulation (*ekplexis*) and shrieks with mindlessness (*aphrosynes*)."[46] Socrates clearly isn't speaking just of primitive itch relief here with his allusion to Aphrodite; the verb from *ekplexis* is used of being love-struck.

Reading this account of the most acute pain-pleasures, we can't help but notice that Socrates entirely omits, perhaps knows nothing of, the evidently overwhelmingly pleasant—or frightful—states caused in the *psyche* by mind-altering substances. To him the pleasures of the soul, the pleasures of memory, anticipation, imagination, and, finally, of thought, are all moderate, not in the sense of being damped—they go very deep and last very long—but in the sense of not being excruciating, of literally not being acute, not sharp, not pointed. Of course, Bacchic and other substance-caused transports were well known and also ritually induced in antiquity, but in the Athens of the dialogues they don't figure as a type of pleasure. It is something of a puzzle to me that the very ancients who had the most vivid imaginations had so little interest in the wilder pleasures, the "artificial paradises" specific to the imaginative soul—but perhaps the explanation is right there: in the natural freshness of their mental imagery. Moreover, they had, as I see it, no emotion-fraught phantasies, such as captivated the German romantics, of Dionysian or Apollonian epiphanies.[47] For they had seen the seamy, even horrific side of the former,[48] and they lived close up to the marble realizations of the latter.

Back to the *Philebus,* to the mixed pleasures of the soul alone. Here we come to what are now usually called the emotions; Socrates names in particular those later described as the "vehement passions," anger, fear, yearning, grief, love, jealousy, envy, and such.[49] These affects are filled, saturated (*mestas*), with pleasure mixed with pain. Socrates' comments start on their way two notions continued by later writers: that the emotions are allied with, but separable from, pleasure-and-pain, and that the strong ones are "mixed" in that respect.

Socrates now gives a brief analysis of tragic and comic pleasure, the enjoyable weeping at grievousness that characterizes the one and the pained laughter at ridiculousness that marks the other.[50] Such ridiculousness, such inadvertent comicality, is a vice stemming from lack of self-knowledge, a lack of regard for the inscription on the temple at Delphi, "Know thyself"; within a few pages Protarchus has now quoted both famous precepts inscribed on Apollo's sanctuary: "Nothing too much" and "Know thyself." They are drifting from pleasure via the passions to vice: The analysis of comic laughter involves taking pleasure in the complacent self-ignorance of others, and in that pleasure there is said to be a trace of envy, be it in life or in the theater—envy, I imagine, at others' blissfully ignorant, clueless conceit of themselves.

It is now not far from midnight, and Socrates doesn't much want to go through all the possible combinations of pleasure and pain.[51] So they turn to the unmixed pleasures, which are pure and positive.

First among these are what we call the esthetic pleasures, the delights that Kant will term "disinterested":[52] "those arising from what are called beautiful colors or shapes, and most that come from fragrances and sounds, all the ones that come with no sensed (*anaisthetous*) need attached but furnish painless sensed (*aisthetas*) satisfactions and pleasures purified of pain."[53] This description of sensations free from sensed need, devoid of desire, is surely the beginning of all estheticism—desireless delight. Moreover, Socrates immediately establishes what might be called the philosopher's esthetic: Pure pleasure comes not from paintings, but from canonical geometric shapes such as are turned out by straight edges and lathes, compasses and draftsmen's triangles; their beauty is not relative, and their distinctive pleasure is as unlike itching and scratching as possible. The influence of this notion of a pure esthetic pleasure most purely experienced in the simplest ruler-and-compass figures was tremendous. Even at the beginning of modern astronomy it was still a subject of debate whether the beauty of the perfect heavens permitted the substitution of the mechanically produced, double-focused, non-self-congruent Keplerian ellipse for the simply drawn, single-centered, perfectly self-congruent Ptolemaic circle and epicycle.[54]

Having separated pure from impure pleasures, Socrates reiterates that the intense—and bad—pleasures are measureless and belong to the class of the Infinite, and the pure ones are measured, moderate, and belong to the Finite.[55] The next question is the relation of either class to truth. Of course, the uncontaminated, unmixed class is truer, that is, more truly pleasure. Socrates adds one more criterion to the judgment of pleasure. We had the related elements of mixture vs. purity and intensity vs. measuredness; now he adds means vs. ends. Pleasures, especially those of the process toward repletion, the bodily pleasures, are means; those who enjoy them are in fact enjoying the pain of thirst and its cure; they live to be thirsty so they may drink.[56] To say that certain pleasures are means is to say that they are endless: They have no completion, only a cessation; you may be full, but you're not fulfilled.

So it is as absurd to call those bodily pleasures actually good as it is to call the psychic pleasures all bad, especially to say that virtues like self-control are not pleasant. Nor does it make sense to say that someone who feels pleasure is the more virtuous, that is, the better, the more intense are his pleasures. All such claims are absurd.

Here the consideration of pleasure peters out; Socrates doesn't want to subject it to every test to the neglect of the factors he favors, mind and knowledge.[57] Those not being to the immediate point of this book, I condense the ensuing long discussion into two sentences: The best arts and sciences are those depending on ordinary arithmetic and measurement.

But even above these there is the knowledge of a yet higher kind of counting and measure, namely dialectic, not an art of mere persuasion—such as Protarchus's teacher, the sophist Gorgias, taught—but the philosophers' knowledge of Being and beings and self-sameness and difference;[58] in these truth is located.

This knowledge is the province of mind, of intellect, whose advocate Socrates is in this "trial" (*krisis*) between Philebus's claim that wisdom and pleasure are identical and his own claim that they are different and that wisdom is better than pleasure.[59] For, Socrates says once more in conclusion, no one would want pleasure without knowledge or memory of it; neither would anyone want wisdom without the appropriate pleasures. Thus the perfect, the altogether good life we would all choose is that of neither of these alone, but the life mixed from both.

So they set off once more on Socrates' way, the way to the Good; they look for the best manner of mixing the "fount of honey," pleasure, with "the fount of pure, healthy water," wisdom, calling on Dionysus, the god of wine, or on Hephaestus, the god of crafts, for help.[60]

Now comes a surprise: This best life needs knowledge not only of the pure geometry but also the "false rule" of the embodied circle and all the other impure applied arts, such as sensory music. So also for pleasures; the experience of all those at all compatible with wisdom is included, which means of all but the most intense ones. This old Socrates has devised a fairly permissive, humanly sensible, "bodiless cosmos ruling over the ensouled body."[61] That conclusion now brings us to the "forecourt of the Good" and its dwelling.

There follows an irritatingly concise presentation of "the capability (*dynamis*) of the Good." It has taken refuge in the "nature of the beautiful," in measure and symmetry, which always go together with beauty and virtue.[62] Of course, truth is also in this "blend" (*krasis*).

The judgment is at hand: Protarchus concedes that much pleasure, especially the *aphrodisia,* the pleasures of love, are mindless, unmeasured and unbeautiful. So pleasure is not our greatest good; instead "eternal nature" has chosen and ordered our "acquisitions" as follows:

First, *measure and fitness*—Socrates is recapitulating the principles that shape the cosmos.

Second, *symmetry and beauty*—the esthetic effects of the mathematical contents of the cosmos so shaped.

Third, *mind and wisdom*—our way of apprehending first principles.

Fourth, *the knowledges, arts and true opinions*—the rational products of mind and wisdom.

Fifth, and last, *the pure pleasures*—the beneficial affects of our embodied souls.

Here the long dialogue, which had no proper beginning, ceases without reaching a real end; it is, for all its final stipulations, composed in the image of the limitlessness that marks common pleasure and the indeterminacy that afflicts its analysis.[63] Old Socrates asks to be let go, although Protarchus thinks there is a "little bit left" to discuss. It is quite a little bit: Aristotle will now carry on.

8. Aristotle on Pleasure and Happiness: After the *Philebus*

Aristotle's writing about pleasure tracks the *Philebus* so closely in a certain respect that it makes sense to consider it now. The respect in which Aristotle refers to the Platonic dialogue is the valuation of pleasure: the question of whether pleasure is a good, the good, or no good—where good, real and apparent, turns out to be construed simply as the desired, the "appetible" (*orekton*).[1] The question, which is in fact surely a prime preoccupation of reflective human beings, would, however, be idle—would indeed remain unasked—were an alternative not suggested. This possibility, that there is something other than pleasure that is recognizably desirable—it is, of course, *happiness*—in turn helps to delineate the nature of pleasure, which is surprisingly elusive. Indeed, we live with or without it so intimately that it is even harder to turn on pleasure in thought than it is to reflect on the passions proper. For it is, as Aristotle will present it, a feeling but not an object-directed passion: We get pleasure *from* something, but our pleasure does not go *to* it, as love goes to the beloved. To pre-formulate Aristotle's understanding: Pleasure is what I think of as a *concomitant-feeling*, an affect that, by its very nature, comes upon us in the course of an action or passion. I think this is a penetrating discovery, and it levers all the pleasure-perplexities of Section 5 into a new mode.

To throw Aristotle's view into relief, I might, losing a lot of nuance and overlooking problems, put the main Platonic notion this way: Pleasure comes primarily as the filling of a present need. But for Aristotle it is primarily a sort of bonus for doing both right and well over time. Since it seems to me that Aristotle improves upon Plato in this instance, I want to report that my current freshmen, upon reading the *Nicomachean Ethics,* Aristotle's chief consideration of pleasure, were more inclined toward Plato's *Gorgias:* that pleasure arises in the course of an ever-necessary process of replenishment. So it's an open question, to which the response is perhaps somewhat age-determined.

A. Definitions of Pleasure

Definitions of pleasure are to be found in three of Aristotle's works: the *Nicomachean Ethics,* the *Rhetoric,* and *On the Soul.* I will begin with recording the following ones.

1. Pleasure is not correctly spoken of as being a sensory coming-to-be (*aistheten genesin*), but rather it should be called the activity (*energeian*) of a continuous state (*hexeos*) in accordance with nature, where what matters is not so much that pleasure is sensory as that it is "unimpeded."[2]
2. Pleasure perfects (*teleoi*) an activity not as an already present continuous state, but as a certain supervening perfection (*telos*), as the moment of bloom (*hora*) on things at their prime (*akmaiois*).[3]
3. Let us assume that pleasure is a certain movement (*kinesis*) of the soul and an all-at-once (*athroan*), perceptible settling-down (or restoration: *katastasin*) into one's already-present nature—and pain is the opposite.[4]
4. Taking pleasure (*to hedesthai*) consists in the sensing (*to aisthanesthai*) of a certain passion.[5] The passions are what pleasure and pain follow upon.[6]
5. Taking pleasure or being pained is to be active (*to energein*) with respect to good and bad by the discerning standard of sensation (*aisthetikei mesoteti*).[7]

There is no getting around the fact that these five definitions—or descriptions—don't all say the same thing. That is exactly what makes me trust Aristotle's guidance. Pleasure looks different to him as he thinks about it again or in a different context.

The first two definitions, which come from Books VII and X of the *Nicomachean Ethics* respectively, are certainly almost contradictory. In the first, pleasure is an activity of an ongoing continuous state (meaning that it *is* the state in its actuality), in the second it attends, perfects, completes an activity but *is not* the state itself.

I should say here what this "activity," this *energeia* (Aristotle's own coinage), is. It means literally "being (fully) at work," being fulfilled. "Work" (*ergon*) doesn't necessarily mean labor, striving effort, for Aristotle. In its high sense, in which it pertains to the living soul, an activity is an end in itself, a fulfilling absorption in an object of worth, say of love or knowledge; I think of it as a *vibrant stasis*. (In a lesser sense, it can also mean something more "kinetic," a work in progress like a deed being done in the world of action or even the production of things in the world of artifacts.) For any being it is the state of being fully what it was meant to be. Its complementary antecedent is *dynamis*, "capability," potency, the latent power that emerges into activity when the right conditions are present.[8] These are ultimate terms in Aristotle's universe of development, that is, of becoming and culmination under the aegis of a desirable end.

In Definition 1, then, pleasure is not a process (as it is, in the main, in the *Philebus*), but a completion of our natural condition that results not from a *development,* but from the *fruition* of our powers.[9] In Definition 2, pleasure has gone beyond both directed process and fulfilled activity to mark a supervening finality for which there is—this is the crux—no word in Aristotle's ontology. Thus pleasure is a gratuitous accompaniment, a super-erogatory grace, upon the most desirable condition: to be in the active state in the right way.

B. Understanding Happiness

This is the moment to introduce happiness, *eudaimonia,* literally "being under a good *daimon"* and therefore living with a good personal fate. Both "fortunate" and "happy" in their original sense of "by a (good) chance" are close to the basic Greek meaning, although most of us now would say that happiness was a good *feeling* that arises within us rather than good fortune which happens to us—even if the former is often induced by the latter. Aristotle certainly means by it a human condition, but neither something that just "happens" to us, that we passively undergo, nor a mere feeling. On the contrary, it is an activity. Here is what Aristotle thinks goes into happiness and how he then defines it.

First, it is generally agreed that happiness is the very best thing, and that it is final. "Final" *(teleion)* means both complete and sufficient in itself, a condition to be chosen for its own sake. People have many subsidiary desirable *goods,* but they always really want happiness. It is the ultimate good. Aristotle takes this as a fact not in need of argument. Yet it is clear that for him this only locates happiness in common discourse but does not define it. Happiness is not *merely* the *desideratum* that everyone wants and therefore calls "good."

Thus there is in fact argument about what happiness—understood as "the good life" and "doing well"—really is. Ordinary people, Aristotle says, think of this good life as consisting of obvious, visible goods (though they admire those who make a big, obscure thing of it). They think it consists in private pleasure and enjoyment; more refined people and men of action think the good is honor and is to be found in a public life. But since people want honor to assure themselves of their own excellence (*arete*), what they really desire is just this excellence or virtue. Even the life of virtue can't be the final good, however, because experience tells us—I love Aristotle for having noticed—that one can be quite miserable while practicing virtue.[10]

What, then, is a more detailed account of that final good, said to be happiness? Aristotle posits that just as a man as craftsman has his particular work (*ergon*) to do, so a human being as human must have its distinct work. And the highest good for a human being must be fulfillment in that work.[11] Thus for Aristotle doing—not being—is primary; here starts the modern West. We are what we do. No, it goes deeper: Our very being *is* activity.

This distinctive "work of any human being is the activity ("being-at-work," *energeia*) of the soul in accordance with reason (*logos*)."[12] A good man will be thus at work in the best way, in accordance with human excellence ("virtue," *arete*). The definition of happiness immediately follows: "The human good is the activity of the soul in accordance with excellence."[13] It will be a rational activity; moreover, it has to last through a complete lifetime.

To recapitulate the distinctive features of Aristotelian happiness: It is not a feeling but an activity, not a passion that comes and goes but a lifelong condition, not a supine affect but an exertion of the soul in the humanly most characteristic way, namely intelligently and excellently. For excellence or virtue (either translates *aretē*) requires the exercise of reason, as we will see in the next chapter. It will deal with Aristotle's treatment of the passions, some of which are identified with virtues.

Perhaps a way to appreciate the energetic nature of Aristotelian happiness is to distinguish it from beatitude, which is the glory that rewards goodness and faith, or from bliss, which is the enjoyment of one's mere being, or from ecstasy, which is going out of oneself into a higher state. Aristotelian happiness is like none of these; it is, simply, completely realized humanity, which is identical with lifelong, right-minded activity. I wonder whether Aristotle even gave very much attention to the affective felicities just mentioned.

This might be the occasion to supply a typology of happiness, taken from Stephan Strasser's *Phenomenology of Feeling* (1956).[14] He discerns six types of happiness in life: 1. *Contentment*—a peaceful, accommodating, moderate life, desiring only the possible (really a Stoic life); 2. *Luck*—a confident, adventuring life of successful acquisition quantitatively evaluated; 3. *Harmony*—a fully developed, self-congruent life; 4. *Rapture*—a life breaking out of mundanity by natural or artificial means; 5. *Release*—a life of dying to the world and its suffering; 6. *Transcendence*—a life in anticipation of eternal beatitude. I report these types because it seems hard to think of a way of living happily that cannot be ranged under one or several of them; Aristotelian happiness seems to fit into the middle, the third type, active "harmony."

I have delineated happiness here because of its relation to, or rather, its distinction from, pleasure. But before I come to the topic of pleasure, an interjection on the future: It can be fairly said that in the beginning of the twenty-first century the study of happiness is right where it was in Aristotle's time, and all the questions his treatment must raise are still current. Is it obvious that happiness is *the* human end? Is happiness a stable state or a restless pursuit, as says our Declaration of Independence (quoting Locke)?[15] Is it the satisfaction of all desires, whatever they may be, the positive feeling of contentment (as distinct from lethargic repletion)? Is it a proto-passion, a passion, or an indefinable affect? Is it a type of life or a transient episode? Is it achieved or adventitious? Is it obtainable by gaining possessions or by finding meaning? And a novel, very modern project: Is it subject to expert management and evaluation?[16]

For Aristotle, though distinct from the life of pleasure, the happy life is indeed pleasant.[17] In fact "most people say that happiness comes with pleasure, and that is why enjoyment (*to chairein*) is named from blessedness (*to makarion*)." The etymology is false but it is a passing acknowledgment that people know other types of well-being; *makaria* is the word for the bliss enjoyed by the gods.[18] The preceding quotation is from Book VII of the *Nicomachean Ethics*. (I have mentioned that Aristotle has several divergent discussions of pleasure and pain even in the same work; the second one in the *Ethics* occurs in Book X, the last of that work.)

The discussion in Book VII is mostly concerned with refutations of those preoccupying arguments, familiar from the *Philebus,* against pleasure as a supreme good, or a good at all. Definition 1 above comes from this book. In terming pleasure an activity Aristotle seems to assimilate it to happiness, though, on the other hand, he distinguishes it by referring it to what is a natural and ordinary state for us rather than our highest activity. To be sure, at the culmination of his philosophy in Book XII of the *Metaphysics*[19] he says not that pleasure is an activity, but that God's activity is pleasure. What else can he say to praise the life of the Divine Intellect? For God cannot be *happy* in the sense that happiness requires the soul to be at work in accordance with human reason, since he is in a state of already-perfect fulfillment and his pleasure is unconditioned. I think he speaks of *human* pleasure as an activity in Book VII of the *Ethics* from the perspective of facilitating his sidelining of the process- or replenishment-notion of pleasures, since he regards those as pleasures, to be sure, but as incidental, as less than truly desirable ends.

In this perspective on pleasure, pain becomes a subject because it figures in the replenishment theory of pleasure; there pain is the feel of that neediness the ongoing relief of which is pleasure. There is a divergent modern analysis of physical pain by Elaine Scarry that sees it as exceptional among human affects: It is almost beyond conceiving and imaging; in fact it is only objectifiable in similes like burning, stabbing, drilling. The reason she gives is that pain alone of all affects is objectless, non-intentional. This is, in effect, pain absolute, divorced from pleasure. I don't believe such a notion was current among the ancients.[20] (Moods, the preoccupation of Chapter IX, will, however, be also analyzed in just that way as objectless.) Aristotle's view of pain, insofar as he considers it, is more like that of the *Philebus*: Pain is a negative desire, the desire for relief. Perhaps one difference between these treatments is that the modern author is thinking mostly not of the natural pain of living but of the inflicted pain of torture. Here is an observation which I think has some truth and, if so, much significance: The ancient philosophers tend to bypass in thought what they wish to avoid in life—and tend to think it sound to do so. The tragedians do the opposite; they dwell on extreme affliction.

I will omit Aristotle's acute arguments against the misconceptions of those who deny that pleasure is a good, even the greatest good. But the final pages of Book VII are not to be missed.

Aristotle is explaining why sharp bodily pleasures appear to be more choiceworthy than other kinds. They mask pain, they are intense, and they are the only kind of enjoyment some people are capable of. There are many people to whom a state apparently neutral between pleasure and pain is actually painful; the students of nature (*physiologoi*) in fact claim that *any* animal finds mere living laborious; even seeing and hearing give pain, though we have gotten used to it. This pessimism will resonate in modern times. The young, to be sure, live as if drunk with wine because they are growing, and in its stirrings "youth is sweet."[21] Sensitive, excitable people (*melangcholikoi*), on the other hand, need medicating continually because they are continually being gnawed at and hungry, and though these people are degraded by excessive feeling, they apparently crave strong pleasure-relief.

There are, however, pleasures that are not the response to pain but are rather incidental to nature. "Those things are pleasant by nature which put that particular nature into practice" (*poiei praxin*).[22] That type of pleasure does not necessarily imply unrest. Though "Change in all things is pleasant," according to the poet Euripides, that is only because of a certain baseness in us. In our better mode,

> there is activity (*energeia*) not only in motion (*kineseos*) but also in motionlessness (*akinesias*), and pleasure is more in rest than in motion.[23]

The activity here distinguished from motion is activity in the main and highest sense, the "vibrant stasis" described before. Aristotle is alluding to the highest pleasure he knows, the pleasure which accompanies the happiness of that contemplative activity in which the *Nicomachean Ethics* culminates. It is indeed a pleasure not of motion but of rest, rest not in the sense of stagnation but of fulfillment.

The first consideration of pleasure, in Book VII of the *Nicomachean Ethics,* was undertaken by Aristotle in behalf of someone philosophizing about politics, for such a one is the *architekton,* the master-craftsman who is responsible for establishing what in the public world "we call good and bad simply."[24] So the discussion in that book was a review, particularly in the light of people who have no self-control, of opinions about the meaning and function of pleasure, without reference to true happiness. Thus it contained only a final mention of the truest pleasure, even though happiness had in fact already been on the scene. Aristotle had defined it in Book I and had there said that the vulgar identify it with pleasure.[25]

In Book X he reconsiders pleasure, but this time in a more private, or at least more personal, setting, not only in its function in the bringing up of children, but also with respect to mature human virtue and happiness. The arguments concerning pleasure as a good are not so different from those of Book VII.[26] But a deeper view begins to emerge, one more concerned with what pleasure actually is, the ultimate question. Some of the answer is embedded in Aristotle's refutation of arguments against pleasure coming from Plato's Academy and given in the *Philebus*. In the course of his critique, Aristotle asserts that pleasure is neither a quality nor a motion. That much only being assumed, he starts with his own analysis "from the beginning."[27]

Pleasure is perfect and whole at any moment. As when we open our eyes we see perfectly then and there, so pleasure is all there, fully, at once. Thus it is a-temporal; it does not come to be or display itself as might a quality, with passing time. It involves no process such as, for example, does the building of a temple, during which, as the stones are being fitted together, the building is imperfect. While things that move come to their completion over a certain spatial and temporal trajectory, pleasure isn't the kind of thing that moves "out of" a place or "through" a time. This is Aristotle's well-considered conclusion: Pleasure is *not*—whatever the *Philebus* may have claimed—a becoming or a motion. It is immediately believable to me that pleasure does not involve the coming-into-being of *a something*. But it would be more interesting to make it experientially plausible that pleasure therefore has no development, does not reveal its qualities in time. At first it seems counterintuitive. But perhaps Aristotle is delineating the "perfect moment" sense of high pleasure and its "timeless instant" feel, the strangely familiar rarity of life-stopping fruition.

So Definition 1 of Book VII is superseded not insofar as pleasure was said not to be a genesis, but insofar as it *was* said to be an activity—though perhaps sometimes in the sense mentioned, in which a locomotion or a change is in some lesser sense an activity. For as I have noted, any being-at-work, insofar as it is still *on the way to* that fulfilled being Aristotle calls *energeia* proper, shares that name. But now the notion of pleasure will be revised *beyond* either genesis or activity.

In Definition 2 of Book X pleasure is not only not a becoming or motion, but it is not even an activity at all, because—and I think that this is Aristotle's most original and loveliest contribution—it is a *bloom upon an activity*. Or in more learned language, it is a supervenient non-quality, a true *je ne sais quoi*, the moment-by-moment sense of perfection I have just described in relation to the atemporality of pleasure. Aristotle is good at giving categorical terms for the elements of being, but I don't think this epi-sensation, this second-order affect, distinct but delicate, sturdy but not forceable, has any such a name. Yet I know of no descriptive definition of pleasure that strikes home more than this one: Isn't it a persistent experience that pleasure pursued is pleasure uncaught, but pleasure unsought in pursuit of good work is pleasure gratuitously received?

The definition also has the bonus of setting the terms for clearly distinguishing pleasure from happiness, which *is* an activity. I cannot think of a distinction that is more important to the ethical life than that between pleasure, the gratuitous moment which happens to us incidentally as we subject ourselves to experiences worthy or even unworthy, and happiness, the good life-span that we bring about in being at work in the ways of excellence.

Indeed the consideration of happiness and its concomitant but distinguishable pleasures follows immediately: They are not, of course, to be found in fun and games (*ta paidia*) but in the activities of serious leisure, among which there is one that surpasses even the life of virtuous action. This activity is an end in itself, self-sufficient, yet enhanced by friendship. It is the activity that engages what is divine in us: the life of the intellect (*nous*), the life of "intellectual vision" (*theoretike*), which, for men as for god, coincides with pleasure.[28] It is unfortunately not the business of this book.

The *Rhetoric* is the source of Definitions 3 and 4, and its context determines them. Definition 3 seems to cling to the motion-view of pleasure but combines with it a moment-view: The coming into being of the pleasure in the soul is followed by a sudden and total settling-down, a reclining, into a natural state, a *katastasis*, felt as such. Definition 4 says that pleasures and pains are passions perceived or, what seems about the same, that passions are inseparably attended by pleasures and pains. That is to say, to be aware of a passion is normally to feel it as pleasant or painful, to assign it a "valence" to use a modern term. Of course, passions are precisely not actions or activities, so that description too seems to be—in fact *is*—at odds with the chief definition of the *Ethics*.[29] However, it has staying power: That pleasure and pain are passion-concomitants is the common understanding through time.

These latter two definitions are unmistakably crafted for their rhetorical purpose, which is largely to obtain a favorable verdict from assemblies. Let us assume them, Aristotle says, so as to make the art of persuasion plausible and learnable. Aristotle has much to say about the psychology of pleasure from this aspect: The pleasant is what is uncompelled, unpressured, unimpeded, such as passing the time, fun-and-games, breaks, and sleep.[30] This is a different view of pleasure than the one in the nobler setting of the *Ethics*, where it is a bloom on activity. In the *Rhetoric* we are said to desire these unforced experiences, and everything we desire is pleasant to us. But the desires here meant are natural desires, those of the senses.

They are a-rational (*alogoi*); they need and have no understanding behind them. There are, however, also desires that are aroused in us with the help of speech (*meta logon*), by which we are persuaded that certain objects are indeed desirable and therefore pleasant. So the orator has to understand how to arouse pleasure by speech, and that turns out to be by arousing the passions: Pleasure can be generated via the passions. While the pleasures of the present are associated with natural desire and come through the primary, the bodily, senses, the pleasures of hopes for the future and memory of the past are derivatively sensed by the imagination.[31] By arousing pleasures or pains indirectly through deliberately raising specific passions, pleasures that are to be now enjoyed or suffered, but even more to be hoped for or feared, the speaker induces people to change their judgments, for an audience's decisions depend on hopes and fears.

Aristotle never makes the connection explicit, but I think that both definitions of the *Rhetoric* (3 and 4) are specifically intended to serve, and do well serve, the purpose of persuasive speech. As the speaker arouses the requisite passion, pleasure begins to arise, and soon and suddenly, as with a click, the soul is home free as it were, settled in a condition that feels natural. This is the moment when the audience has been captured for the speaker's cause.

We see that for rhetoric to work in this way, Aristotle has had to acknowledge a feeling that is different from the activity-pleasure of the ethical context: There is a passion-pleasure too. And why shouldn't there be? That pleasure consists, as Definition 4 says, "in the sensing of a certain passion," meaning in the feel of it as we sense an inclination or aversion for its object and experience the gratification of whatever desire, positive or negative, arises with the passion—that is, as I noted, about the most commonsensical thing to say about such pleasures.

There remains Definition 5 from *On the Soul*, which is devised with respect to the powers of the soul. It says more explicitly what I supplied for Definition 4, but in terms of the faculty of sensation as an active judging agency, a standard (*mesotes*) that can sense "good and bad" as an articulable state rather than as a mere feel. That sensation is thus able to discern or judge (*krinei*) is an Aristotelian notion; it is a difficult theory which I need not go into here,[32] where the point is that pleasure or pain can be thought of—somewhat metaphorically—as the approval or disapproval of our sensory part. That too rings true: From the point of view of our psychic activity, sense perception seems to "say yes and no" by way of the feeling of pleasure or pain. That is indeed analogous to a judgment. It will remain murky, once "appraisal theories" of the passions come on the scene, whether affirmations and refusals are being attributed superveniently to feelings or feelings are being contracted into qualified propositions. (In logic, the "quality" of a proposition refers to its affirmative or negative character.)

It is scarcely believable that the great poets, epic, lyric, tragic, comic, who lived long before or in Socrates' time and who sang of desire and passion, pleasure, and pain, didn't also think deeply about them, or that the first inquirers into Being and Nature, known, significantly, as Presocratics, did not delve into human affect as well, or that the Sophists, whom Socrates bedeviled because their business was persuasion rather than truth, didn't know a good deal about these matters, too. But we have very little surviving from any of them by way of reflective writing on these themes—if there ever was very much. For us, therefore, Plato and Aristotle begin the inquiries that are pursued in this book, and their terms, distinctions, and evaluations will pervade the tradition. Those who, like myself, do not trust themselves to begin thinking all on their own should, I think, begin instead with the beginning of their tradition, and that is my apology for this long chapter.

9. Pleasure and Desire Long After

This tradition of inquiry that begins with Plato and Aristotle goes on, elaborated, revised, or revoked in different explicit or implicit philosophical frameworks to our day. Pleasure and desire will turn up incidentally in all the chapters to follow—passion is of course the focus, and where there is passion there is pleasure or pain (especially in Kant, Schopenhauer, and Nietzsche)—but I want to end this chapter with a coda on a *work* of the early and some *research* of the late last century that deals thematically with pleasure and desire respectively.

A. Beyond Pleasure: Freud

The work is Freud's *Beyond the Pleasure Principle.*[1] It belongs here because its theory of pleasure is recognizably that of Aristotle in the *Rhetoric* and its concluding reference is to Plato's *Symposium.* Its charm is in its speculative mode:

> It may be asked whether and how far I am myself convinced of the truth of the hypotheses set out in these pages. My answer would be that I am not convinced myself and that I do not seek to persuade other people to believe in them. Or, more precisely, that I do not know how far I believe in them. There is no reason, as it seems to me, why the emotional factor of conviction should enter into this question at all. It is surely possible to throw oneself into a line of thought and follow it wherever it leads out of simple scientific curiosity, or, if the reader prefers, as an *advocatus diaboli,* who has not on that account sold himself to the devil.[2]

I enter this long quotation because Freud's spirit of inquiry, not so far from one I would myself wish to adhere to, shows that something more than a literary oeuvre survives from a system seriously discredited as science.[3]

Here is the hypothesis of the pleasure principle: Since "unpleasure (*Un-lust*) corresponds to an *increase* in the quantity of excitation and pleasure to a *diminution*," the mental apparatus endeavors to keep the quantity of excitation present in it as low as possible or at least to keep it constant. "Anything that is calculated to increase that quantity is bound to be felt as adverse to the functioning of the apparatus, that is as unpleasurable." Freud quotes G. T. Fechner's formulation as equivalent: "... every psycho-physical movement crossing the threshold of consciousness is attended by pleasure as, beyond a certain limit, it approximates to complete stability"—and for unpleasure the opposite.[4] This is recognizably the *katastasis*, the settling down, of Aristotle's Definition 3, which was taken up by the Epicureans. Of course, for Freud the soul has been replaced by the mental apparatus (actually *seelische Apparat*), and the context is psycho-physical, which implies primarily quantitative rather than qualitative assignments of the "energies" involved, while for Aristotle the sensory judgment is of "good and bad," as in Definition 5.

There is a more telling difference: For Aristotle pleasure is a *concomitant*, following upon the soul's activity, while for Freud it is a *principle*, an original source in the psychic economy, deeply embedded in the psyche. (*Psyche*, the Greek word for soul, has been borrowed by psychologists to circumvent the too spiritual-sounding English "soul." Freud himself was not so squeamish; he used, as noted above, "*seelisch*," but that adjective doesn't go into English.)[5] Pleasure and Unpleasure (*Unlust*)—the latter, dis-ease, is wider than positive physical pain—are feelings that come from "the most obscure and inaccessible region of the mind." This much, however, Freud insists upon, first to last:

> The dominating tendency of mental life, and perhaps of nervous life in general, is the effort to reduce, to keep constant or to remove internal tension due to stimuli (the "Nirvana principle," to borrow a term from Barbara Low)—a tendency which finds expression in the pleasure principle.[6]

Then the passage continues: "and our recognition of that fact is one of our strongest reasons for believing in the existence of death instincts." These are the instincts "beyond the pleasure principle" that gives Freud's work its name.

The chief manifestation of these further instincts is a compulsion to repetition, for which Freud has found much evidence in children and adults; in the latter it often has the aspect of a "malignant fate",[7] which, however, looks self-arranged to the psychoanalyst. One among many examples is the lover whose affairs with women always pass through the same sorry phases. This compulsion to repeat even unpleasant experiences often overrides the pleasure principle. (Freud observes that the tendency to take pleasure in *exact* repetition belongs only to childhood; children demand, for instance, that the same story be retold frequently and in exactly the same way.)

He interprets this repetition compulsion as a strange, newly discovered instinct, an instinct that does not, as seems usual to us, impel change and development but is an "expression of the *conservative* nature of living substance." He now interprets all repetition and recapitulation in organic, living beings as a tendency to return to, to restore, an earlier state of things, an "*old* state of things, an initial state from which the living entity has at one time or other departed." If we accept as a truth without exception that everything that lives "dies from *internal* reasons—becomes inorganic once again—then we shall be compelled to say that 'the goal of all life is death.'"[8] Freud seems to be describing pleasure as demise.

Freud's problem now becomes the unifying reduction of a "*dualistic*" theory of instincts, those of life and death, for he had always recognized a sexual instinct as well, namely Eros, the preserver of life. "The libido of our sexual instincts would coincide with the Eros of poets and philosophers which binds all things together."[9] This libidinal instinct Freud eventually lodged in the ego (as well as in other parts of the "topographically" conceived soul), where it shows itself as narcissism and may become destructive in the form of sadism, which is, in turn, interpretable as a displaced manifestation of the death instinct.

Freud's particular problem is to relate the two "polarities" of sexual and ego instincts, love and selfishness for short, to the evidently deeper polarity, life and death, so as to advantage the latter. The interpretation of narcissism as a death instinct establishes that desired relation. In the ego, even the life-preserving libido displays a death-drivenness. At least that is the intention I discern in the confusing welter of cross-related instincts, an intention driven here mostly by a speculative need for a unifying reduction.

What is left is the task of relating a remaining—namely the non-ego-related, object-directed—part of the sexual instinct to the death instinct. Science gives Freud no help, but the hypothesis of a "poet-philosopher" does: Aristophanes in Plato's *Symposium*. Freud interprets the comic dramatist's fable in this germane way: "Living substance at the time of its coming to life was torn apart into small particles, which have ever since endeavored to reunite through the sexual instincts."[10] So that, amazingly, *sexual union is a return to our inorganic, that is, unindividuated, dead, past.*

It is noteworthy that this instinct has been, acceptably to Freud, called the Nirvana-instinct. Thus he has a footnote to his *Symposium* citation pointing out that it has an avatar in the oldest of the *Upanishads,* in which Atman, the Self or Ego, being lonely, divides himself into man and wife: We two are thus, he says, each of us "like half a shell."[11]

To me it seems that the net result of *Beyond the Pleasure Principle* is this: First the relatively innocuous pleasure principle of the title has receded, gotten lost in favor of an instinctual pair: life and death. But ultimately, so has the life member of that pair. The death instinct has taken over the sexual instinct. The pleasure principle, the tendency to the reduction of excitation so as to achieve stability, seems to have been superseded by the super-principle of a more ultimate stability beyond it, the stasis of a return to the inorganic. In a final section, however, Freud returns to pleasure.[12]

There is a question whether the function of keeping excitation constant or even extinguishing it, as exemplified most acutely in the discharge of tension in the sexual act, is best served by the pleasure principle as a "bound" or "unbound" instinctual impulse. Binding—the technical word is *cathexis* ("holding down")—is the concentration of psychic energy in an object, self or other. Freud contends that in children, in whom the pleasure feelings are more diffuse, they are also more intense, but that in adults the dominance of the pleasure principle is, though tamer, more secure. The exact relations of cathexis to pleasure remain to be worked out, he says. But it is a fact that the life instincts (which here briefly reemerge) are unpeaceful and tension-producing, "while the death instincts seem to work unobtrusively." So, finally, and as one would expect: "*The pleasure principle seems actually to serve the death instincts.*"[13] I cannot help wondering: What is there in our past and particularly in our present world to support Freud's notion that the human species tends to seek a *reduction* of excitation? But then, his materialist quietism might be construed as a recognition that the frantic external business and the willful internal restlessness of modernity are underlain by a different finality.

Aristotle's inquiries into pleasure then relate to Freud's essay in two ways. The first is in that understanding of pleasure which makes it a "settling down" into the organism's most natural state; that happens to be life for the Greek and death for the Austrian. The second is in Aristotle's view that pleasure is a concomitant and enhancer of activity, while for Freud the energy of the psyche wants damping. For Aristotle the *energeia* of the soul has on it pleasure as its bloom; for Freud, the pleasure instinct of the psyche serves its dissolution. Progress!

Finally, philosophical theories about the nature of pleasure in the later last century can be marshalled (with certain misgivings about each) under three headings: 1. Pleasure is a non-localized physical sensation (like fatigue only, well, more pleasant); thus it accompanies the pleasure-giving activities or objects, but the connection is elusive. 2. Pleasure is a quality that may belong to any conscious state whatever; it is, however, hard to isolate the single feature that makes different states pleasant, nor can the specific causes of the pleasurable effect be pinpointed under this theory. 3. Pleasure is the consequence of the satisfaction of desire, so that appetition and its object figure in this theory; but then, what of the pleasures that arise spontaneously without prior desire or object?[14] These are old quandaries, now drily but logically developed.

B. The Study of Desire: Research

The research on desire I want to refer to finally comes, as does most of con-temporary work, more from narrowly focused articles in the academic mode than from grandly conceived books of philosophical inquiry. Hence it is normally based on trend-establishing conceptual frameworks distinguished from each other by expert-addressed differences presented in technical terms.

It is by no means the case—how could it be?—that desire was not treated in grand style after Plato and Aristotle. All the philosophers considered in this book will think about desire within the setting of their own encompass-ing frameworks. But so will many others, here set aside. A particularly deep view of desire, not to be ignored because it is so pervasive in his system and so original in its conception, is that of Hegel.[15]

Hegel's treatment of desire is the culmination of that modern approach which means to deflect attention from the object to the subject, just as the-ories of knowledge now focus not on the thing known but on the knower. Classical theories direct our interest to the object desired; the intentional-ity, the "for-ness," is the point of departure in devising a structure of desire. Indeed for Plato and Aristotle, that is the all-important question: What should the desire be *for*? Now this interest and the locus of value is shifted to the faculty itself. Aristotle says unequivocally that we approve the object and consequently want it rather than the converse,[16] but Spinoza will say that it is our desire which makes the object good. Hobbes will pick up the infinity ascribed to pleasure in the *Philebus* to conclude that there is no highest good, only "a perpetuall and restlesse desire of Power after power, that ceaseth only in Death."[17] In the literature of modern times, to paint with an unconscionably broad brush, the transfer of the desiring intention from objects in the world to ideas in the imagination and the consequent illimitability of self-affection and self-assertion are all pervasive and promi-nent themes.[18] They are most prominent in Romanticism, which will be a topic of Chapter IX.

Hegel drives the subjective approach to its ultimate realization. I am thinking here less of the fact that the *Phenomenology of Spirit*, his most psy-chologically expressive work, is dominated from first to last by desire, the desire of the subject (that which is an "I") to develop into identity with sub-stance (that which is an "it"). The desire I am thinking of has a more precise relevance to this book. It presides over a particular moment in this dialecti-cal development. A dialectical development is a conceptual progression in which each concept reveals itself as its own opposite, with which it is then reconciled, composed, so as to attain a next "moment" in the development. The moment of desire is that in which a human being ceases to be merely a conscious living being and turns on itself to become a *self*-conscious being, one that is fully an "I." That happens when human desire is directed not to a merely natural other, a thinglike good, but toward another being who is capable of a reciprocal desire. This is a desire that desires desire, as when in love we *want* the other's love. To desire desire means, whatever else is involved, to seek recognition, to strive self-assertively. What is desired is a value, and to desire desire is to seek to be valued, to be recognized as a self in one's own right by another self who desires the same on its part; this desire is willful, prideful. Self-consciousness, then, comes about between two desiring beings, each of whom can see *itself* in the other. Hegel has not only transmuted the intentional *object* of desire into *desire itself* but he has done what to my knowledge no other philosopher has succeeded in doing: He has explained philosophically *why* human beings are social. Our distinctive humanity, our assertive self-consciousness, can arise only *between* conscious human beings. Humanity comes about as mutuality of desire, as the composition of confronting affects.

The labors I want to report on last belong to a field that was demarcated in the last quarter of the last century: "desire theory." I take it up here because it might pique the reader's interest to see contemporary work on desire juxtaposed to the initial ancient thinking, and because the current approach to desire gives a foretaste of what has happened to the passions as they are taken up in emotion studies nowadays (Ch. X). Generally speaking, the approach of this book, to consider the passions as they appear in a grand philosophical framework, is no longer operative. All the approaches are, of course, recognizably influenced by schools of thought. Thus they are usually built around a thesis about the functions of the emotions, such as cognitivism, which treats them as forms of knowledge, or around a choice of styles and techniques, notably analytic and ordinary language philosophy, which emphasizes analysis of meanings and logical argumentation; other examples are phenomenology, which insists on a careful description of the way the phenomenon in question is experienced; psychoanalysis, which frames the account of the emotions in terms of a specific psychic economy or topography; philosophy of mind, which examines mental capacities; and neuroscience, which studies emotions as brain events. When a field such as desire theory is broached, there is of course an implicit hope that some consensus, some "conceptual shakedown," that could be called 'the current state of knowledge" will emerge since the work is framed, whatever its approach, as research—that is, as part of a common task which builds progressively on discoveries made.

What actually results is a mass of acutely discerned distinctions that often cut across each other, of refutations of positions that then rear up again in amended form, of new terminology and counter-terminology. Often the human import of desire shrinks under the pressure of these results. The examples of desire are usually deliberately pedestrian: going out to buy some milk, to cite an example. The research is interesting if you are already interested, but the reason it doesn't add up is its very virtue, its particularity and its minimal groundedness: It is by its own terms not bound into or derived from a fully realized philosophical—I mean ontological—texture. Since, once the problems to be researched are framed, anyone can figure out solutions, simple or ingenious, I will here rest content with giving a set of questions, as I did for pleasure. They are simply borrowed from the scholarly literature.[19]

Here then are the questions discerned by scholars in the twenty-fourth century after Plato and Aristotle wrote on desire.

But first, an overview of the disciplines in which desire has been studied: In "theory of action," desire, as one of the "motivational states," is more or less reduced to its observable effects; in "theory of emotion," which has tended to be cognitivist, desire as a feeling has yielded to the more cognitive "belief" as a motivator of emotion. In "person theory" emphasis has been on "secondary desires," desires aimed at desires, such as the wish not to want to smoke. In "philosophy of mind" emphasis has been on intentional states as a hallmark of the mental, basic among which are desire and belief, though these concepts have in turn been criticized as "folk psychology," as being naïve. In "value theory" desire has been considered as a ground of value, that is, the claim that what is an object of desire is *ipso facto* good; here the question of the inevitable egoism of desire is addressed: Is it a confusion to conflate the fact that I will get satisfaction from having my desire fulfilled with the altruistic object of that desire? If I want you to be happy, I will, to be sure, be happy if you are, but that wasn't supposed to be my direct object, but only the *incidental* satisfaction of getting my object, which was your happiness. In other words, is it possible to construe desire as unselfish even though when fulfilled it carries a piggy-backed satisfaction? Does "I got what I wanted" have a legitimate double meaning: I wanted your happiness and mine came along? (I dwell on this because young students tend to get caught up in the conundrum of altruistic desire.) In "decision theory," finally, a calculus for desire, construed as preference, is sought. This is a sampling of research perspectives.

Here, then, is a conspectus of problems (and implied frameworks) of desire: How is desire caused? There seems to be a multitude of origins, some non-intentional, such as biology, heredity, physical situation, and some intentional, that is, having a particular objective cause, such as a material object or even others' beliefs and desires. How does desire in turn become a cause? When the onset of a belief (such as that a bear is nearby) engages a standing desire (to stay safe), which is the cause of running? A similar question concerns so-called "dispositional" and "occurrent" desires (such as the latent readiness to fall in love and the occasion given by a particular person). How are these related? How are desires for things for their own sake related to desires for means? Should desire be said to be satisfied when we actually have got what we wanted or when we merely believe that we have? What are the criteria for strength of desire: intensity, persistence, pervasiveness in one's life? Is it possible to articulate parameters for possible ends of desire, since they seem to range from world peace to physically touching someone? Can only future states be desired and only what is believed to be good? Should desire be construed as going directedly to the object: "I want that object, the beloved," or as terminating in a proposition: "I want that this beloved be mine"? (To that one I know—instructed by an expert, Jane Austen—an answer of wider application: Upon her engagement to Fitzwilliam Darcy, Elizabeth Bennet "agitated and confused, rather *knew* that she was happy, than *felt* herself to be so."[20] That is to say, generalizing: Feelings can be apprehended propositionally *or* directly, depending on one's frame of mind.) Several of these questions had been explicitly considered in the ancient texts.

Next, what *is* desire? There being a multiplicity of current answers, should we look for one of these senses proposed to be desire proper? Perhaps desire is no "unified thing" and has nothing such as used to be called an "essence" at all? In any case, should the inquiry begin by distinguishing between the concept and the phenomenon of desire, between the verbal, notional and the empirical, experiential aspects?

Is it profitable to distinguish types of desire, such as self-regarding, unconscious, assertive, competitive, higher-order, practical, pleasure-seeking, sexual, aversive desire? (If so, here's a type of my own: Is there a kind of self-surviving desire, one that outlasts its satisfaction, as when we pig out way past appetite?)

What is the relation between desire and belief? Is desire separable from belief or *is* it belief? If there is a distinction, is it a simple or complex one? Are these the right differentiating characteristics: that desire is directed at good, belief at truth; that desire is just for the future while belief ranges over past, present, and future; that a desire usually implies a distinct belief but not the converse (for example, if I want to run away it must be because I believe that a bear is present, but not every such belief implies that desire)? Is it true that desires often have a vaguer content than does belief? Are desires about what might be, and beliefs about what is, so that desires seek to fit the world to the affect, while beliefs intend to fit the cognition to the world?[21]

And finally, how do desire and belief interact? Must they do so rationally, which would be to say that reasoning cognition is their common ground? Does cognitive belief normally control affective desire (don't we wish!)? For example, could I nonetheless want to overeat even though I wanted to be thin and truly believed that overeating made me fat? If not, would that mean that genuine belief is immediately translated into desire (as for Socrates truly to know and to act, really to understand and to do are immediately connected)? When I want to run away because I believe there is that bear around, why does the desire cease—"blink out by conceptual necessity"—the moment I realize that the belief is false, cease instantaneously not by a conscious change of mind but in one fell swoop? Are desires then possibly just "desirability judgments," so that to want something is nothing but to opine, to believe that it will yield pleasure or prevent pain? With that final question, transformed into a claim, desire disappears and leaves us humans, as pleasure-cognizing beings, defined by the poles of excitation and rationality. That describes a nightmarish type of denizen of the modern world—a quondam human being in whom the imaginatively passionate mean between arousal and rationality has atrophied.

chapter III

The Passions as Extremes

Aristotle as the Founder of Passion Studies

The poets wrote lyrics, Plato wrote dialogues, and now Aristotle writes treatises. The poets, appalled and enchanted, sang of Eros as god; Socrates, bending the erotic power to his purpose, speaks of him as a *daimon*; Aristotle, soberly putting the passion in its place, says simply that eros is a *pathos alogiston*, "an arational passion,"[1] with pleasure as its aim. Logical placement, classification, is Aristotle's primary device for mastering the nature of the passions. The way divine Eros—scarcely ever mentioned by Aristotle—is cut down to size as pleasuring eros is an instructive example: Every desire is for pleasure; eros is a desire. Q.E.D.[2] Pleasure (or pain) are, moreover, associated with every passion.[3] *Eros* (love) and *philia* (friendship) are in fact nearly the same, both being the desire to be together, although, since bodily congress is also involved in love, it is more specific than friendship and so included as a subclass.[4] Here is its class-descent:

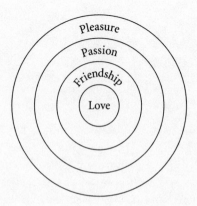

Aristotle is the founder of all methodical emotion research, the first to mount an accuracy-demanding inquiry not into this or that particular passion but into passion in general, not with a this-or-that possible "aporetic," that is, terminally perplexed, outcome, but with results delivered professionally, with authority. In the course of this new approach, he sets out a theory of the soul more complex than that of Socrates in the *Republic* (Secs. 2–3), he makes lists and establishes oppositions of passions (Sec. 4), he devises a theory of passion-virtue (Sec. 5), he connects the passions systematically with the moral virtues and vices (Sec. 6), and he exploits them for forensic persuasion (Sec. 7). And he starts on its way the study of *the* socially central passion, Shame (Sec. 8).

1. Why Aristotle Studies the Passions: Ethics and Persuasion

Heidegger, wanting to co-opt Aristotle for the analysis of social human existence, says in *Being and Time,* "It is no accident that the first systematically conducted interpretation of the affects that has come down to us is not treated within the frame of 'psychology,'" but rather in Aristotle's *Rhetoric,* where it is the first methodical hermeneutic, that is, the first interpretative theory, of the "mundanity of Being-together" as mere people, of everyday "publicness" (*Oeffentlichkeit*). This mode, he says, needs and "makes" a mood for itself, into which and out of which the orator speaks. Heidegger goes on to say that it has remained unnoticed that the treatment of affects has not advanced a step worth mentioning, but on the contrary, the affects have sunk down into mere satellite phenomena.[1]

There are three cavils to be registered: 1. Aristotle's interest in the passions is in fact fundamentally psychological and ethical, as I will show in the following five sections. 2. The passions as moods are both eminently individuating and metaphysical, as Heidegger himself understood very deeply— and Aristotle before him; I doubt that the latter would have wished to have attributed to him the notion that the passions are fundamentally social and thus bar the way to a psychic ontology, as they do for Heidegger. 3. As Chapter VII is devoted to showing, Spinoza considered human affect as coextensive with human being and thus anticipated Heidegger by some three centuries. Nonetheless the closer we come to our time the more Heidegger's charge rings to some extent true. We know a lot more but not much better than old Aristotle.

There seems to be general agreement that of the three main sources for the passions according to Aristotle, the *Eudemian Ethics* is the earliest, though clearly he had been talking about the passions from way back; the text itself mentions the "classification of passions, capabilities, and conditions made in previous discussions."[2] It seems that the *Nicomachean Ethics* and the *Rhetoric* belong to a period when Aristotle, after a long absence including a time in Macedonia as the tutor of young Alexander (later "the

Great"), had returned to Athens in the thirties of the fourth century B.C.E. to found his school, named "Peripatetic" after a covered walk (*peripatos*) in its precincts. The *Politics* seems to have been in progress about the same time as the *Rhetoric*. Since the *Nicomachean Ethics* is a sort of introduction to the *Politics*, it may be that these lectures on ethics, which were either dedicated to or edited by his son Nicomachus, were given somewhat earlier than those that make up the *Rhetoric*. But since all of Aristotle's major works seem to be later editions of lecture courses, hard dates are almost impossible to determine. I am relating this uncertain chronology because it seems to indicate that the treatment of the passions and their psychology was probably antecedent to their exploitation as proposed in the rhetorical handbook.[3]

Basic notions from his metaphysics, in particular "capability" and "being-fully-at-work" (*dynamis* and *energeia*), will have a role in Aristotle's study of the passions, since all beings live or function between these two terms. But primarily his interest in the passions is ethical and consequently psychological, insofar as the constitution of the soul, above all its—our—appetites, must be thoroughly understood if the passions are to be regulated.

2. The Appetitive Reach of Human Beings: Rational, Reason-Amenable, Natural

"All human beings by nature reach for knowing," or less strainedly but also less accurately, "All men desire to know"—so begins Aristotle's central work, the *Metaphysics*, the text that gave its name to philosophy's very own effort, the search for being. The verb is *oregontai*, to which "reaching" and "directing toward," are etymologically related. The noun is *orexis*. It is Aristotle's own introduction of a common word into philosophy. Plato does on occasion say that the soul "reaches for being" (*oregetai tou ontos*),[1] but he doesn't use the noun *orexis* for this hunger, which both philosophers believe in. "Appetite" is not a bad rendering since it comes from Latin *ad-petere*, "to seek after." Some translators say "desire," but then they have no term left for *epithymia*, which is a subclass of *orexis*. Besides, "desire" does not carry the meaning of physical outreach, albeit it appears to be a wonderful word, coming as it may, by an attractive though uncertain hypothesis, from augury, star-gazing—when the star (*sidus*, gen. *sideris*) you seek is invisible you de*sidera*te it, wish it down.

That the first verb of the *Metaphysics* should be "to reach for," "stretch after," "hunger for" is as it should be, since the pervasive theme and grand climax of the work is the reaching of beings toward their own fulfillment and their stretching toward the divinity. Moreover, the beginning states an all-important fact known to any nursery-school teacher's aide (like myself): that there is a time in each life when every human being does reach for knowledge.

Accordingly, the soul is through and through appetitive. By "soul" Aristotle does not mean, as does Plato, a separable being with parts, the true human being, as it were, that has a problematic relation to the body in which it goes about. For Aristotle the soul is rather in inseparable union with the organic body; it is that body's "abiding-condition-of attaining-its-end" (*entelecheia,* the condition of "holding fast," *echein,* in a state that is "finished, accomplished," *enteles*). This perfect condition is that its organs (from *ergon,* "work")—literally, its working or instrumental parts—should be working as they are meant to work. It is, in other words, the principle of life, that which makes a living body function as such.[2] When I say that the soul is inseparable from, that it can be regarded as an aspect of, its body, I am speaking of it in the respect in which it has passions. Aristotle intimates that there is a certain function which *is* separable: Our intellect (*nous*) alone can separate itself—occasionally—from the body and thus from sensation, imagination, and appetite.[3] But that intellect which is not merely separable but is actually separate no longer has appetite, being fulfilled within itself. Thus while in its grandest version—as the divinity that, moving others, is itself unmoved—the intellect itself turns out to be the object of the hunger for knowledge, it is beyond being humanly appetitive.

Since the soul is conceived as one animating principle, its "parts" (*moria*), so definitely distinguished by Plato as "kinds," become much more problematic. Thus Aristotle says:

> Whether these two parts [the part "having reason" (*logon* echon) and that which is arational (*alogon*)] are really to be bounded off, as are the parts of the body and all that is divisible into parts, or whether they are two in reason but inseparable in nature, just as are "convex" and "concave" in a curve, doesn't at present make any difference.[4]

Of course, for the study of the human soul it makes all the difference ultimately, and is, indeed, still a contemporary preoccupation.

How Aristotle sees the soul that can be impassioned is best shown in a diagram and its exposition (Fig. III-A). It is a lopsided figure since the passions are only a subclass of appetite in general, and the part pertaining to the rational appetite, which reaches neither for pleasure nor vindication, is here left blank. A similar diagram drawn for the even denser psychology of Thomas Aquinas fills in the blank, more or less in Aristotle's spirit.[5] The main division of this blank right-hand side is between a knowledge-related part and a calculating part; the first is for contemplating invariable first principles, the second for deliberation about things we can change.[6]

I should say here that to speak of the soul thus schematized as "impassioned" is a convenient inaccuracy. Aristotle is very clear: Since the soul is a *principle,* that is to say, a beginning (and a termination) of motion, it cannot

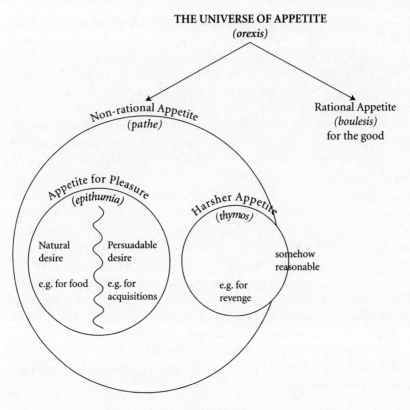

Figure III-A

be itself moved or affected, either in or by itself; it is neither a thing nor a worker. We shouldn't, therefore, say that the soul grieves or rejoices or pities, any more than we say that it builds a house. What is moved, affected, impassioned is the human being composed of a body animated by a soul. The movement is not *in* but *by* the soul as a small unmoved mover.[7] What *is* moved and affected is the whole human being, the ensouled, soul-activated body, the embodied soul.

But then, where in the psychic economy is the left-hand side of the diagram located, and what is its name? It must be a region of the soul that is more closely involved with the body than the intellect and not as immovable as the soul seen from a higher vantage point. The answer is not absolutely necessary to the project of this chapter and, moreover, so abstrusely speculative that I relegate it to the merest sketch of a note.[8]

With these cautions, I turn to the functions of the soul displayed in Figure III-A, which are, for working purposes, shown as "parts" topographically interpreted. The relations of these parts are culled and collected from different places in Aristotle's texts.[9] They are therefore speculative, though, I believe, not too far off from what Aristotle would approve.[10]

A. Object-Directed Appetite: The Good

The delineation of appetite (*orexis*) and its analysis is not so different from that of desire. Above all, it has an object that it tends toward—"intends," as later writers will say. Different kinds of appetites are, to be sure, distinguished by the "parts" of the soul from which they originate, but appetite as such is distinguished by the fact that it is "directed at" (*orekton*) an object: "Every appetite is *for* something."[11]

Because it tends toward its object, appetite is that which causes motion (*to kinoun*); it is the only mover in the soul. Neither the imagination nor even the intellect could move anything had they—and thus we—not appetite. Thus, insofar as they do move us, they are appetite-like; as purely cognitive powers they are "receptive to" but do not "tend toward," or rather, make us tend toward their object. Therefore it is appetite that is the source of the soul's practical actions; it is the object of appetite that moves the thinking that moves the action.

The general object of appetite, "the appetible," the *orekton*, is the good. But it may be either the merely apparent or the genuine good. For appetite by itself, being in itself neutral with respect to rational judgment (as is the imagination as well), can be right or wrong in its desire, while intellect is always right. The good that human beings can be literally, sensorily moved by is called the practical good, a good that is not stably given but might be this or that.[12] There is also a good which moves the contemplative soul only—for all cognition has, as I said, an appetitive constituent: "We hunger to know." Intellectual appetite is, however, off my map of the passionate soul. Its final object is a more remote, a purer, a more intellectual good, is in fact god himself, who incites motion as a final cause—an end that attracts by being desired without itself reciprocating. Yet even then what moves us is still appetite, albeit not passionate, reasonless desire. And it moves not only us but the heavens and all within them:[13]

> Ma giù volgeva il mio desirio e il velle
> si come rota ch'egualemente è mossa,
> l'amor che move il sole e l'altre stelle.

> But already the Love that moves the sun
> and the other stars was turning my desire
> and will as if they were a wheel that has uniform motion.[14]

I am citing Dante's *Divine Comedy* here not because Aristotle does not speak clearly—and rapturously—for himself,[15] but because the Christian writer, though an Aristotelian, shows so clearly by contrast what is remarkable and hard to bear about the pagan divinity: his unmovedly self-sufficient felicity. In calling God Love, the Christian poet implies that we are drawn both by the *love of God* in the sense of God's being the object of our love (objective genitive), and also by the *love of God* in the sense of our being the objects of His subjective love (subjective genitive).[16] Dante's God too is an Aristotelian unmoved mover, but as a Creator—the pagan god did not make the world, which is eternal—He has a reciprocal relation to his Creation.

The love God has for his creatures is not, however, a passion any more than the love that draws the pagan philosopher to his god. It is not a *need*, or so theologians wish to argue. Thus Thomas, Dante's teacher, devotes effort to explicating the love an immutable being can in fact have.[17] Briefly, such love is understood as nothing but the willing of another's good.[18]

In this respect too the quotation from the *Divine Comedy* is illuminating, because it mentions will along with desire. If you look at Figure III-A, you will see that rational desire, the highest employment of which is contemplation, is attributable to *boulesis*. This word is often rendered as "will," but that is misleading. *Boulesis* is not a forcefully independent faculty of the soul whose weakness is a human disaster and whose surplus potency is incipient sin. Pagan *boulesis* is rather purposeful wishing, as its verb, *bouleuein*, means rational choice-making, deliberate planning—quite secular and not theologically fraught; it can be mistaken or flabby, but not sinful, not set against God. Clearly, when willing supersedes deliberating, the passions are going to have a harsher master and will in turn be more refractory. For Aristotle the soul is still in a pretty unstrained relation to itself: "'I must drink,' desire says. 'This is potable,' says sense or imagination or intellect. Straightway one drinks"—unless something external interferes.[19]

I now return to the definition of appetite after this anticipatory digression about its own transmutation and that of its object in the Christian adaptation of Aristotle's *orexis*. It is a given that appetite is the ultimate source of motion and action because it is *par excellence* what is directed at an object. Thus on a lower level it initiates the motion of practical thinking if the object desired belongs to the variable world of place and time, while by a higher appetite the activity of the theoretical intellect that views timeless beings is "motivated."[20] In any case, appetite moves toward the good, apparent or genuine.

There are, however, intermediate powers and movements involved in appetitive motion. Aristotle uses the phrase "prepares x for service" (*paraskeuazei epitedeios*), which I'll abbreviate to "preps." Then the chain goes:

Intellect or sensation preps imagination;
imagination preps appetite;
appetite preps passions;
passions prep bodily organs.

He adds that this process is "all-at-once and quick because active (*poietikon*) and passive (*pathetikon*) are related by nature."[21] I think he means that the intermediate faculties, those between intellect and bodily organs, in turn quickly activate and are activated. What is remarkable about the motive chain is 1. that it can begin, as in my chain, at the very top with intellect (*nous*), but that it may also start at the psychic bottom with sensation (*aisthesis*), for both can influence the imagination, and 2. that appetite, though the extreme cause of locomotion, is a mean when it comes to being activated, that is, put to work. For imagination must present an object to the passive appetite, and the appetite must act in turn on the passive passions, which are then, for all their passivity, nonetheless the immediate causes of putting the body in motion.

In sum, appetite is a stretching toward good which puts into play, as informed or informing, all the capacities of the soul and of the body whose life it is.

B. Non-rational Appetite: The Passions

As I said, the figure concentrates on the class of non-rational appetite, for which the generic term seems to be "passion."[22] The rational appetite, the intellectual reaching for the good, which involves thoughtful choice,[23] is thus left here looking like the mere negative of the passions, just everything outside the class-circle—though for Aristotle it is the primary human direction. It is, once more, the ultimate stretching toward a divinity, called *Nous*, the Intellect that moves while remaining unmoved, the unmoved mover who stirs the world by his—that is the grammatical gendering—attraction without the need for reciprocation.[24] Indeed, in Greek it is always the passionate part of the soul that is negatively expressed: *a-logon* or *a-logiston*. These negatives are not, however, to be translated as "ir-rational," since to be reason-less is not to be unreasonable. Human beings are distinguished by Aristotle as "the only animal that has *logos*,"[25] but that does not make the other animals *ir*rational; the perversion of reason expressed by that negative can only belong to a naturally rational being who talks or acts mindlessly or crazily. (Those offended by the exclusion of animals from the intelligent class might recall that "having *logos*" means in the first instance "having rational *speech*";[26] whether or not animals have speechless reason was already a matter of argument in antiquity.)

As—inevitably—allied with the thinking faculty (*dianoia*), rational appetite articulates itself in yea- and nay-saying propositions; non-rational appetite expresses itself practically, as pursuit and its opposite, aversion.[27] For as in the realm of discourse affirmation involves the possible denial of the claim made, so in the universe of appetite "stretching toward" goes with a possible "recoiling from" the object fixed on. Why this is so, why our human world is inescapably polar both under thought and feeling, is one of those ever-preoccupying questions touched on only sporadically in this book, as the customary positive-to-negative pairing of the passions comes to the fore. Aristotle helps by saying that the appetitive and the avoiding capacity are not actually (*kat' energeian*) different from each other with regard to their thought-structure—nor really distinct from the sense for pleasure and pain. They differ, of course, in their real-life effect, and that makes all the difference to us.[28] Seeking and avoiding are two directions of import on one road of affect.

C. Pleasure- and Spirit-Passions

Now I invite the reader to inspect Figure III-A more closely, particularly the left-hand side, non-rational appetite, that is, the passions.

Aristotle distinguishes two classes of passionate appetites: those of desire (*epithymia*), which are after sweet pleasure, and those of the spirit (*thymos*), which pursue a harsher satisfaction. I think it is left indefinite whether these two classes between them exhaust all the passions. So I have drawn the diagram as if there might be other types in the largest circle. In fact, as the following pages will show, it isn't easy to say either how the pleasure-passions and the spirit-passions are logically related to each other—not quite as contradictories (because they aren't mutually exclusive), perhaps more as contraries—or how they are each and both related to rationality.

Look next, then, at the smallest circle on the right side of the large passion-circle. These are the passions of the spirited class; they are the rousingly temperamental, harshly tumultuous or insinuatingly simmering, though on occasion also gentling feelings. Let it be said right away that they too have a "sweet" aspect. Take, for example, a harsh, apparently unsweet passion such as anger. To contemplate revenge, which is the solace of anger, is sweet. Recall that in Greek *hedus*, "sweet," is the word for "pleasant"; Homer says that "anger (*cholos*), much sweeter than trickling honey, expands like smoke in the breasts of men"; a few lines later this smoke boiling up is called *thymos,* spirit.[29]

But although the harsh desire-passions are sometimes also sweet, Aristotle classifies them separately, under spirit (*thymos*). Here he is clearly correcting Plato, who in the *Republic* sharply separates desire from spirit. He couldn't be plainer. Criticising Socrates' warrior guardians in the *Republic,* who are, to be sure, supposed to be friendly to their own but, more characteristically, fierce to outsiders, he says:

> It is the spirit that makes the element of friendliness (*to philetikon*). For *spirit* is the capacity of the soul by which we *feel friendly* [my italics]. A sign of this is that the spirit is more roused toward companions and friends when it deems itself slighted than toward those unknown.[30]

Now friendliness or affection is a kind of love and so a desire, albeit non-erotic—the desire to be with each other. Then, since spirit has been shown to be desirous, it follows that all the human affects Aristotle specifies are "orectic." He has in his support not only the fact that anger and revenge *are* sweet and so somehow desired pleasures, but also the fact of language itself. For anger, the most characteristic of the spirit-passions, is *orge* in Greek, and *orge* is etymologically related to *orexis*. Indeed, looking at the diagram one might argue that he precedes Spinoza in conceiving the human being as altogether appetitive, but this is not something he dwells on explicitly. All he insists on several times is that "appetite is divided into three: into purpose, into spirit, and into desire."[31] Since even contemplative activity is drawn by appetite for the good, this scheme draws in the whole soul—clearly and even explicitly: "If the soul is divided into three, appetite will be found in each."[32] Yet the question of questions about the passions, whether we human beings are then ultimately affective, is, as I said, not explicitly addressed by Aristotle. I will guess at an answer he might approve: As for Socrates inquiry was desire-like and beholding a possession of what is loved, so for Aristotle learning is appetite-like, and knowing is appetite not stilled but steadied. So here my question becomes moot. Affectivity is what animates us, first and last.

The absorption of the spirit into appetite, its reclassification, so to speak, and that of those motions and conditions of the soul that are characteristic of it—anger and gentleness, pride and shame, and the virtue of courage and vice of cowardice—starts a long tradition. Thomas will divide the passions, ranged under appetite, quite confidently into "concupiscent" (pleasure-seeking) and "irascible" (temperamental). But I can see difficulties.

To begin with, it's not, on introspection, so clear that the inner boiling, the smoke that *thymos* generates, be it ever so sweet along with its harshness, has much of an appetitive stretching toward an object. *Thymos* fumes within and explodes outward; in the thymotic mode, we may long for revenge, but what exactly do we want? Not, it seems to me, a graspable, possessable, enjoyable object; in fact a good explosion can dissipate the pressure of need pretty speedily. That spirit engenders passions is clear, and that they are not precisely passions for pleasure seems right, but that they are always appetitive doesn't seem quite so true. Here Aristotle's classification seems to be top-down, that is, derived from a decision that *all* of the soul, starting with the embodied intellect, is indeed appetitive, rather than bottom-up, from introspective experience.

Here is another problem, then. Just as the harsher, "thymotic" passions derive some taste from the sweet ones, so they take a tincture of reason from the side of the rational appetite, figured in the circle that invades the right side. Aristotle, here following Socrates, says, "Spirit somehow (*pos*) follows reason but desire doesn't."[33] Aristotle infers from this that, while they are baser than spirit, yet "it is more excusable to follow natural appetites" insofar as these are natural desires common to us all.

Regarding these natural appetites, the physiologically basic, low but healthy desires, like hunger and sex, Aristotle hasn't got much to say in the context of humans. They are shown at the very left of the diagram, sharing the circle of pleasure-passions with those affects which are central to the work that is generally regarded as his main study of the passions, the *Rhetoric*.

These latter are the passions that can be reached by persuasive speech because they are what we would call "discretionary." They are desires which are mainly for objects that are not physically assimilated like nourishment but that can be won, acquired, possessed, used—sensed and enjoyed as objects, such as the passion to possess jewelry. The reason these pleasure-passions are at once *a-loga,* non-rational, *and* subject to *logoi,* rhetorical language, is that words have the—curious—ability not only to express thought but to arouse or allay passions.[34] Even Aristotle, who tries hard in the *Rhetoric,* cannot quite explain this wonder: that reason *can* speak to desire. It happens, but Aristotle, no more than Plato, tells how. (Here the neuroscientists claim to have some answers—interacting brain circuitry)

These pleasure-passions might well be said to be central to *human* beings because they are not, like the natural desires, shared with animals—so at least Aristotle thought[35]—and because, unlike the more heroic spirit-passions, they are so humanly and ordinarily sweet when satisfied and so very sour or bitter when rebuffed. In fact they are not only accompanied by pleasure, they are preceded and followed by it, pleasure-enveloped as it were, for people expect or remember the pleasure that will come or has come with the satisfaction of the desire. Aristotle cites people in love who are constantly preoccupied by the expected or remembered presence of the beloved, as if they were having the sensation of it, for "imagination is weak sensation."[36] That holds true also for unpleasant situations escaped. Aristotle cites Euripides:

Once safe, it is sweet to remember troubles[37]

and four centuries later Virgil will say of trials endured:

Once past, perhaps even this will be a joy to remember.[38]

Thus—Socrates had made a point of this—any pleasure-passion, though it seems to belong primarily to the sensed present, has an extended life in time through the expectant and reminiscent imagination.

The figure for this section classified passions in their relation to appetite, but there is another way of approaching them.

3. The Qualities of the Human Soul: Conditions, Powers, Passions

Here then is the way Aristotle captures the passions by means of a distinction, almost incidentally. His intention is to delineate virtue: Virtues are not passions (*pathe*), as betokened by the fact that, while we are praised for our virtues, we are not praised or blamed for just being afraid or angry but for being thus affected "in a certain way." There is, moreover, no choice about having passionate experiences like anger or fear, while virtues do involve provident choice (*prohairesis*). Elsewhere, to be sure, Aristotle seems to say the opposite, "Purpose and spirit and desire are all appetite, and choice is common to thinking and appetite,"[1] but I think he means the (sometime) choice of "what," not "whether" or "how," that is, of the object, not of the affective fact. Nor are the virtues powers (*dynameis*), because we are not praised for being *capable* of being "moved" (*kineisthai*) to feel. (Any post-romantic will claim to know otherwise). It follows that the virtues are conditions (*hexeis*).

So we learn indirectly that the passions can be viewed as one of three modifications of the soul—as distinct from parts: conditions, powers, passions.[2]

Elsewhere Aristotle sets out these three qualities more formally.[3] There is, first, the stable "condition" acquired by thoughtful habituation, the way we consistently "carry" ourselves (the term is *hexis*, a noun from the future of the verb "to hold" or "keep"; thus *hexis* is an achieved state, not a mere capability. The German noun *Verhalten*, "comportment," comes close). Virtues are *hexeis*.[4] Next comes natural "ability" or "power" (*dynamis*). This term covers talents and strengths such as athletic prowess and active health.

And finally there are the "passive qualities" (*pathetikai poiotetes*), and there is "passion" (*pathos*). Aristotle treats these two passivities together, though the first is not applied, as we would say, "subjectively." When we call honey sweet we don't mean that honey, like "the summer's flower to itself is sweet," that it is affected sweetly by itself, but that it is the cause of sweet sensation in others. Yet the sweetness is to be called a passive quality in the sense that it qualifies, that is to say, affects its honey-substance.

Passions, affects, though here so classified, are not *bona fide* qualities. For they are supervenient, thus usually easily dissolved and quickly broken off, while qualities proper are intrinsic and persistent. The soul has both passive qualities and passions. The first are, then, more permanent and hard-to-remove, "such as madness and irascibility [the propensity for anger]" and similar unnatural "out-of-mind conditions (*ekstaseis*)." These are affective qualities that modify the soul. A passion is said to occur when, for example, someone who has been hurt is "rather angry" (*orgiloteros*). For whoever is somewhat angry is not said to be prone to anger (*orgilos*) but rather "to suffer a certain affect (*peponthai ti*),"[5] in the sense of being subjected to a quasi-quality, one not deep in his nature but a passing perturbation.

What comes out here is not only how close the meaning of passion still is in Aristotle's mind to suffering passively, but—and this will be important—how definitely he distinguishes between a settled passionate disposition (*diathesis*)[6] and the flare-up of passion.

Finally, all the terms come together through an odd kind of pseudo-syllogism—an enthymeme to boot, that is, a composite syllogism, two merged trains of thought in which one or more premises go unstated; here they are supplied in brackets. It is set out in the early *Eudemian Ethics,* as follows:[7]

[Virtues are related to the powers and conditions of the soul.]
These powers and conditions are related to the passions.
Passions are related to pleasure and pain.
∴ Virtues are related to pleasure and pain.

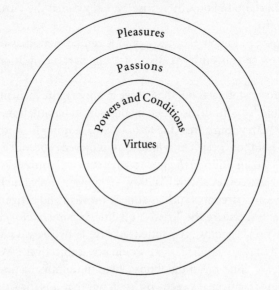

Figure III-B

These embeddings are neither real deductions nor even wholly logical, but they show Aristotle working through the relation of virtue to pleasure via passion which will become important in Section 6.

Having located the passions 1. in the universe of appetite, 2. among the quasi-qualities of the soul, and 3. as links between ethics and enjoyment, it is time to name them in some order.

4. The Lists of Passions:
Eudemian Ethics, Nicomachean Ethics, Rhetoric

We—at least I—read over lists of passions with minimal engagement. Yet if you stop to think, they are remarkable productions. After a while authors get and modify them from each other (as scholars get bibliographies). But Aristotle's is the first we have; how did he make an inventory—from intro-spection, observation, speech-usage, literature, or by some—unarticulated—principle? Looked at seriously, the problem is deep. How do we even begin to learn that this inward feeling is correctly called by that audible sound, that that outward expression really betokens this inward affect? Are we poets who can give public names to unheard-of, intensely private feelings? How do we learn to control or deregulate our own features, subdue or inflate our words, and generally camouflage, expose, or even feign our own passions, and—probably consequently—to recognize the passionate life of others? Surely all such experiences and arts are necessary to make a list, especially an ordered list or "taxonomy" of passions.

I will concentrate here on Aristotle's three lists. They must surely be presented under the assumption that when people hear or see the listed word a separable, discernible affect will come to mind. Hence they must have been made in a universe in which the passionate life and its language had been well and commonly elaborated. I leave here unasked the question: Does the fact that with a little attention they are perfectly familiar to us betoken that we happen to live in an unbroken tradition with a specifically Greek self-understanding or that the lists are humanly common and universally recognizable, immediately or upon a little exegesis? Probably some of both.

The *lists* are presented here with two particular motives in mind: as the premises of Aristotle's ethics of virtue (Sections 5 and 6) and as the preparation for his art of persuasion; detailed *descriptions* of passions selected from the lists are in fact presented in the *Art of Rhetoric* (Section 7).

Here are the three lists Aristotle offers.[1] The first is from the *Eudemian Ethics,* usually thought to be an early work; the second is from the *Nicomachean Ethics,* his central writing on individual human nature; and the third is from the *Rhetoric,* which includes, as I said, his analysis of the individual passions. He offers no completeness proof for any of them.

1. Eudemian Ethics

The list includes fourteen triples, from which I have made a selection.

1.	Anger-proneness (*orgilotes*)	anger-devoidness (*aorgesia*)	gentleness (*praotes*)
2.	Rashness (*thrasytes*)	cowardice (*deilia*)	courage (*andreia*)
3.	Shamelessness (*anaischyntia*)	confusion (*kataplexis*)	modesty (*aidos*)
4.	Uncontrolledness (*akolasia*)	insensibility (*anaesthesia*)	sound-mindedness (*sophrosyne*)
5.	Envy (*pthonos*)	nameless (*anonymon*)	indignation (*nemesis*)
6–7.	———	———	———
8.	Boasting (*alazonia*)	self-denigration (*eironeia*)	truthfulness (*aletheia*)

| 9–13. ——— | ——— | ——— |
| 14. Operating (*panourgia*) | naiveté (*euetheia*) | mindfulness (*phronesis*) |

This outline (*hypographe*), the earliest such surviving, is *very* interesting. Right below the listing Aristotle says, "These and such are the *passions* [my italics] that happen to the soul." But anyone can see that the items are as much virtues and vices as passions. In fact, the very last item on the right-hand side, mindfulness or practical wisdom or judgment, is Aristotle's chief of the intellectual virtues, the virtues that are distinguished from the ethical virtues as being more excellences of thinking than virtues of character.[2] And among the right-hand items I've omitted there is Aristotle's most vivid virtue, "greatness of soul." (If, incidentally, you look at the Greek names, you will see—I think—a swipe at Socrates, for *eironeia*, "irony," claiming to know nothing, which is Socrates' way of inciting truth-seeking inquiry, is there opposed as a vice to truth, namely to truthfulness about oneself.)

What we have here is, I think, Aristotle beginning to work out his famous theory: that virtue is the mean between two vices understood as extremes (Section 5). In the *Eudemian* table, extremes and means are together called passions, but the mean itself, which is not listed in the middle but at the right, as if to show it as an outcome, is also referred to as "ethical virtue" which is "about certain middles and some mean (*mesoteta*)."

Now why are the passion- and virtue-denominations thus mixed up? One way to put the answer is that this outline is not about passions at all but about the *propensities* called passionate qualities in the last section, that is to say, the list names natural temperaments or "emotional dispositions" as distinguished from "occurrent emotions," passionate flare-ups.[3] The first two items, the two that will ever after be (or perhaps always were) regarded as the most vehement human affects, show what I mean. *Orgilotes* and *thrasytes,* the disposition to fly off the handle and to rush into danger, respectively, are not the same as *orge* and *thrasos,* the consequent passing accesses of anger or over-confidence. Aristotle's mean here arises as a condition (*hexis*) between two *powers* or *passion qualities,* the very ones, as I said, set out above, namely the natural abilities and passion-propensities of the soul. The effort is clearly to bring the stable virtues into some relation to the passionate yet stable psychic nature human beings evince. Then Aristotle's discovery is that virtue is some sort of middle between opposed inborn temperamental excesses and deficiencies. Presumably all human beings are born more to one or the other side of each pair of discernible propensities; some might even lean now this way, now that, depending on age and situation. In any case, we know what to do to achieve ethical virtue: Pressure yourself to oppose the excess or deficiency natural to you, graft, as it were, a second nature onto your inborn tendency. Moreover, behind the passionate life there are always pleasures sought and pains avoided,[4] so we know where to start with our self-reform. The scheme here is eminently practical, and indeed Aristotle will say that the real point of ethical theory is not to know but to act.[5]

I might add here that Aristotle's incidental notion of passion-virtue reverberates through time. Four and a half centuries later, Quintilian, the great Roman teacher of rhetoric, will say that the Greeks distinguish two species in the genus of that which "one is moved by" (*commotus*); one is *pathos,* which he renders as *adfectus,* "affect," and the other *ethos,* which has, he says, no current Latin name, but which he calls *mores.* The affects are vehemently felt, brief, and lead to upset; the *mores* are gentle, persistent, and tend to benevolence;[6] these latter are clearly Aristotle's virtue-passions or passion-virtues. I wondered why the Romans left this class unnamed, until I recalled that Aristotle himself, being without a term for "moral virtue," appropriated for the purpose *ēthos* (from *ethos,* "habit"),[7] and that we ourselves have no word for the conjunction of passion and goodness.

Now the other two lists:

2. *Nicomachean Ethics* and *Rhetoric*

The lists are presented together for comparison.

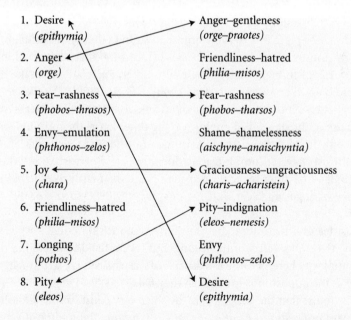

1. Desire
   (*epithymia*)

2. Anger
   (*orge*)

3. Fear–rashness
   (*phobos–thrasos*)

4. Envy–emulation
   (*phthonos–zelos*)

5. Joy
   (*chara*)

6. Friendliness–hatred
   (*philia–misos*)

7. Longing
   (*pothos*)

8. Pity
   (*eleos*)

Anger–gentleness
(*orge–praotes*)

Friendliness–hatred
(*philia–misos*)

Fear–rashness
(*phobos–tharsos*)

Shame–shamelessness
(*aischyne–anaischyntia*)

Graciousness–ungraciousness
(*charis–acharistein*)

Pity–indignation
(*eleos–nemesis*)

Envy
(*phthonos–zelos*)

Desire
(*epithymia*)

The list in the *Ethics*[8] is a "for example" selection—he continues it with the words "and generally whatever pleasure and pain follow on." It is a little haphazard; the opposing passions aren't given or are given out of line. Truth to tell, the passions recede in the *Ethics* because, I think, Aristotle has worked it out that his mean-extreme spectrum requires that the extremes be of the same *kind* as the virtuous mean, namely vices; he now sees that you can't mix passions and virtues any more than a color spectrum can have a sound in the middle. Still, the passions are uncircumventably behind human virtue because they are the instigators of pleasure, and pleasure is the mark of virtuousness (Section 6).[9]

The *Ethics* list begins, interestingly, with desire, which is not, strictly, a passion but a *characteristic feature* of a *subclass* of appetite, namely the class of pleasure-passions (Fig. III-B). This ambiguity about the place of desire among the passions will dog its history. In the *Rhetoric* list,[10] on the other hand, desire comes last, because it is actually the beginning of a new topic useful in the art of persuasion, the characters of people as they change with age:

> The young are, by character, full of desire and ready to do what they desire, and they are apt to pursue the desires of the body, especially those of sexual love (*ta aphrodisia*), and that's the one they can't control. They are fickle as well as very particular in their desires, and now they desire impetuously and now they are suddenly through with it.[11]

Who can doubt it? This passage gives a taste of the way Aristotle will flesh out his mere listings (Section 7).

There is one passion, joy (*chara*), in the *Ethics* list which, although it occupies the same place as a passion similar in sound (*charis*) but different in sense (graciousness) does in the *Rhetoric* list, is somewhat on its own in this grave array of human affects; one philosopher, Spinoza, will make it basic. There is another, shame (*aeschyne*), which occurs only in the *Rhetoric*, rightly, because it is the most social of affects, and the *Rhetoric* treats of the public use of the passions. Longing, on the other hand, the most lonely passion, is only in the *Ethics* list; it is Aristotle's rare gesture toward *eros*.

What the lists have in common are, aside from some perturbations, the order, the bulk of passions recognized as major, and their fairly fixed names, the primacy of anger and fear, and the positive-negative pairing of most passions.

This last feature turns out to be central in Aristotle's thinking, for he is considering the ethical effect of the feeling. But I want to add some dimensions of complexity here, because few aspects of the passions are so thought-provoking as the oppositions into which they fall.

It seems to me that the passions are, by their very constitution, subject to a duality of oppositions: As *affective* they can modify the soul positively or negatively, and as *intentional* they are similarly modified by their object. Thus love has as its negative affect hate, but also love in itself, popularly thought of as good for us and directed to the goodness of its object, can be wrackingly ensnared in a bad object. So also longing desires self-abolition, and its object can be assuaging or torturing; hate is now an ugly, now a sweet feeling, and its object might be hateful for its excellence or for its vileness; joy can be elevating or demeaning (as in *Schadenfreude,* "joy-in-injury"), and its object can be holy or unholy; envy is disparaged as a negative passion, yet its object is a good—another's good.

To this dual source of a positive or negative assignment add a third dimension, intensity. Flabby, carping hate is dingy; strong, pure hate incandescent. So the polarity of the passions is by no means simple. But Aristotle is just laying foundations.

5. The Bracketing Effect: Extreme-Mean-Extreme

Aristotle's best known ethical notion is that virtue is a mean or middle (*mesotes*) between extremes. He applies it as well—in fact first—to the passions, or rather, to our propensity for a passion. How did he come by it? What does he mean by it?

I imagine it came to him from all quarters at once. It was, if not folk wisdom, at least the wisdom of the wise; one of the Seven Wise Men, who belonged to archaic Greece, Cleobulus of Lindos, said "The mean is best" (*metron ariston*), and Plato says that this wisdom junta assembled and dedicated its pithy sayings at Delphi, and that is how "Nothing too much" came to be inscribed on Apollo's temple; Aristotle himself begins with the observation that excess and deficiency is generally harmful.[1] Interest in means must have been spurred by current mathematics, for Eudoxus, whose theory of pleasure was extensively critiqued by Aristotle, was primarily a great mathematician who discovered the general theory of proportion which is much concerned with means. Aristotle, who is no mathematician at heart, likes nonetheless to borrow its devices; thus his explication of justice relies quite technically on the theory of proportion and its different kinds of mean.[2]

This theory of the mean, which locates the mean—in variable positions—between two terms called extremes, has a feature very seriously serviceable to Aristotle. It is his explicit way of philosophizing concerning the deepest principles not to attempt to do what people tend to think of as the proper business of such inquiry: to define.[3] He prefers to show what a notion, at least a very basic notion, means by zeroing in through usage and circumscription, and to let the meaning show itself by indirection through various approaches. We saw something of that sort in his treatment of pleasure, and it holds for his main terms, such as *energeia.*[4]

Readers of the *Ethics* cannot help but be shaken up by the discovery that the virtues are delineated from the outside in, captured by what they are *not,* by vices. It is the notion of extremes and means, where the passion-propensities play the role of extremes at least early on, that allows Aristotle to zero in on, to *bracket,* the moderate middle, which is the virtue. Just so is the target of an artillery attack said to be "bracketed" by short and long shots—except that here the final hit is a happier event.

Still, first and last in the development of the extremes-mean theory must have been Aristotle's own observation that, in matters temperamental and ethical, going overboard is not good, but that going overboard in one direction is usually less bad than in the other.

Of course, behind the notion of a mean is the idea that the temperamental capacities and the affects that arise from them tend to come on a sort of continuum or spectrum that can be represented on a (straight) line, and that figure seems to be what Aristotle has in mind.[5] I think this usage makes sense, because the passions, which underlie the virtues, are, as Aristotle says when observing the powerful educational effects of music on passionate people, "motions of the soul"[6]—as we say "e-motions." Our soul is moved. Movement, however, is continuous and its spatial track may be a straight line.

This passion-spectrum can, however, be seen in two ways:

1. It represents intensity, for example from the excess (*hyperbole*) of anger-proneness (*orgilotes*) and real anger down to the deficiency (*elleipsis*) of anger which is lack of temperament and actual non-anger (*a-orgesia*); the latter two are the "privatives" of the former with respect to language and their "contradictories" in logic. Somewhere between these passion-propensities (and their effect) sits the well-calibrated *feeling that appears as the virtue,* here gentleness: "For virtue is about passions and actions."[7] Just where the mean (*to meson*) is located depends on us and on the passions involved. It depends on us because our feelings of fright or confidence, desire, anger, pity, and generally of pleasure and pain, are either too much or too little for the situation and

> neither are well, but it is needful to [feel rightly] *when* and on *what* occasions and toward *whom* and for *what* service and *as* is called for—that is the mean and the best thing, which belongs to virtue.[8]

So the mean is tailored to the person and the occasion, and also to the passion, to its perceived siting on the spectrum.

> It happens, however, that the oppositions (*antitheseis*) are now more evident on the side of excess and then of deficiency. The cause of this contrariety (*enantioseos*) is that ... sometimes the transition is made more quickly from excess to the middle condition, sometimes from deficiency. ...[9]

Aristotle exemplifies this observation in his several complex discussions of courage. The first of civic if not the chief of personal virtues, courage is in some respects close to fearfulness because it is in the face of fear that courage shows itself. But under another perspective, courage is closer to confidence, because the lack of that makes for cowardice.[10] Nevertheless the happy mean hit on in a given class of cases *is* determinate and unique, while the ways of missing the moral aim and its satisfactions are multifarious and even infinite. As Tolstoy so unforgettably says, "All happy families are alike; each unhappy family is unhappy in its own way."[11] Aristotle claims that these felicitous middle states are almost nameless. I think what he means is that the moderated passion has no name. Again, that makes sense: Passions don't bear moderation well; they turn into virtues which have their own names, here *praotes,* gentleness. To be sure, Aristotle says, "There are means even in passionate matters (*pathemasi*) and concerning the passions." That would seem to contradict my notion of the missing passion-mean, but then he circuitously confirms it. He takes the example of shame: The person who has too much is covered in confusion (*kataplex*), the one who has too little is shameless, while the middling one is modest. And then he says that though modesty is not a virtue it is praised.[12] But in the *Eudemian* list it *is* a virtue, and Aristotle has distinguished passions from virtues by the former *not* being praised. So I'll stick with the notion that in the intensity spectrum the middling passions are practically indistinguishable from the stable condition called virtue. It makes experiential sense.

2. The intensity spectrum is presented as a quantitative figure, and who hasn't experienced the rise and fall of passion-strength—which, to be sure, finally transforms the passion? But there is another, a more directly qualitative way to capture human virtue and vice and their underlying passions.[13] The tamed passion-virtues are not the *means* but the *antitheses* of the extreme passion-vices: "All of these somehow lie opposite (*antikeintai*) to all." More precisely, while "in its meaning and verbal account virtue is a mean, in respect to what is best and right it is an extreme" (*akrotes*).[14] Here is the figure to show the difference between the two means.

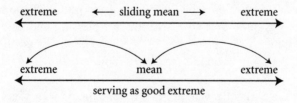

Figure III-C

What the second figure has in its favor is what it makes clear: that virtue is neither mere mediocrity nor passionlessness (*apatheia*). Aristotle warns against defining virtues simply as passion subdued—though we readily do just that, because we do see people go bad through either pleasure or pain of any excessive degree. Instead he wants passional control to be properly qualified, as described in the passage quoted; courage is not fear suppressed but fear *rightly* felt.[15] When extremes and mean are seen in this perspective, as outside-in opposites, virtue is no longer passion moderated; it is an acme, an eminence, underlain by a strongly controlled strong passion. Similarly there is no longer a sliding mean that, by approaching it, mitigates the excess, say, of cowardice.[16] Instead of having a quantitative position on a spectrum that slides gently across the right degree of apprehensiveness into rashness, cowardice on one side now faces courage as its abrupt opposite, as does mindless rashness on the other.

We can meld these two means structures to get an ethics wonderfully true to experience: The approved virtuous mean lies discernibly between two repudiated extremes; these therefore oppose *both* each other *and* their mean; the theory of the mean has room for the mean as an extreme and as a middle—which is, I think, according to life. Goodness lies in *both* moderation *and* excellence. One of the two colorable meanings of the word for virtue, *arete*, is "serviceableness," the other "outstandingness." Aristotle calls this latter extreme "virtue as the best thing";[17] it is, I think, where his heart lies.

Observe that this description emphasizes a polarity in the human passionate and ethical constitution. Tables of such polar opposites were made from early times, for instance by that early philosophical band the Pythagoreans.[18] I surmise that the impetus came from the basic human impulses of pleasure and pain with the accompanying reactions of internal inclination and aversion and of external pursuit and avoidance, together with the basic rational activity of positing and negating and its articulate utterance by asserting and denying. And so the passions, which are circumstantial specifications of pleasure and pain, would indeed be polar in feel and in expression.

Moreover, Aristotle will, in the light of these oppositions, make a consequence-laden claim: "Whenever something is pleasant or painful, the soul pursues or avoids it *as affirming or denying*" (my italics).[19] Plato saw desires as analogous to questions; now Aristotle sees pleasure-and-pain as analogous to judgments. Successive schools, *ancient and modern,* will base their theories of the passions on this insight: Passions are somehow analogous to cognitions.

I think that Aristotle, who appears to take these mean-suggesting passion-polarities as given, has in fact a deep theory about them. The passion-propensities *are mere capabilities* (*dynameis*), while the passion-passivities (*pathe*) *are not yet* activities (*energeiai*). That is to say, the passions are in their very being on-the-way, unstable movements, capabilities being exercised ("potentialities being realized," to use current Aristotle-derived jargon), and they are also like material to be worked into a steady, active finality (*entelecheia*). For, Aristotle says, material (*hyle*) is by its nature passive and moved; its function is to be receptive to form.[20] So one might say that the passions both point to and shape up about a virtuous mean because they are by nature both on a sliding scale and receptive to a formative discipline. Passions are the psychic material of virtue, but material that is always partly shaped by present character.

6. From Passions to Virtues and Vices

That pretty well marks out how passions are related to virtues through the mean in the two *Ethics*. A figure will display the relation:

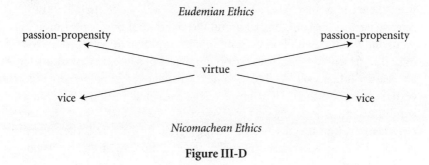

Figure III-D

And so will a brief passage from the earlier work, here somewhat freely rendered since Aristotle's note-taker was almost excessively inelegant, but worth citing because he was clearly in command of the basic terms:

> [T]he soul has two parts, and virtues are divided between them; some, the thoughtful ones (*dianoetikai*), belong to the part having reason and their work is truth . . . and some belong to the arational part and have appetite (*orexin*)— for if the soul is indeed divisible not every part has appetite [this must refer to "arational appetite"; later, at least, the whole soul is appetitive]. Therefore it follows necessarily that the bad and the respectable in moral matters are so by reason of pursuing or avoiding of certain pleasures and pains. This is clear from those divisions [distinctions] that have been made into passions, powers, and conditions. Thus it results from these [divisions] and positions laid down before that every moral virtue is about (*peri*) pleasures and pains, . . . [and] it is clear that [conversely] pleasures and pains arise from the said conditions and passions.[1]

Thomas puts this pithily in his commentary on Aristotle's *Physics*: "For virtue to be engendered there must be a transmutation of the passions."[2] The passage he is writing about naturally approaches the passions from their physical side. Virtues (*aretai*) are perfections or "completions" (*teleio-seis*), vices (*kakiai*) are "departures" (*ekstaseis*—"stepping-outs") from one's proper nature, for virtue makes one "either dispassionate or impassioned as one ought to be," whereas vice is "impassioned or contrarily passionless."[3] I have translated the same word, *apathes,* once "dispassionate" and once "passionless," because Aristotle, as set out above, is very interested in, and of two minds about, the relation of virtue to weak passion: How is it that a passion well and virtuously subdued is not a defect in passion, a passion-deficiency? This is, of course, the millennial problem of "cold rationality," of fatal reason, of which more will be said in the last section.

The transmutations (*alloioseis*) toward virtue are effected on the "passions peculiar" or "proper" (*oikeia pathe*) to each person. For there are desires common and necessary to all people and desires that are private (*idioi*)[4] and adventitious, so that passions are often quite personal. Moreover, the basic change—here I am citing the *Physics*—is attributed to the sensing part of the soul, "for all moral virtue is about bodily pleasures and pains and these are either in present doings, or in remembering, or in hoping." But present pleasure comes from an object of sense, so that ultimately all pleasure—hence all passions—comes from changes wrought by an object on us. The virtues themselves, however, the reformed passions, are steadfast conditions and not changes—not "e-motions," so that we sometimes exercise them even in the absence of feeling—though what underlies them is change.[5] Of course, in other, "meta-physical" contexts Aristotle admits nonsensory appetites.

In his writing on the soul, Aristotle bridges the gap with a thought-provoking formulation.[6] He has just spoken of the "perplexity" (*aporian*) concerning the passions of the soul, whether any of them belong to the soul alone and are thus separable from the body. Most of them do seem to involve the body. But then he gives a physico-mathematical example for thinking about this problem: Let something straight touch a bronze sphere; it will do so at a physical dot (*stigme*), while the straightness separated from the matter will not touch the sphere in that way but in a mathematical point (*semeion*). So also "it would seem" at first that the passions (or perhaps affects would be better here) all involve the body, be it spirit, gentleness, fear, pity, boldness, joy, or loving (a helter-skelter list of feelings with physical involvement). The body seems to act as a sort of filter of feelings: Sometimes, when the body is unresponsive, the external provocation is great but the affect minimal, and sometimes, when the body is sensitive, the reverse occurs.

Still, as the mathematical analogy shows, there *is* a second perspective. We can think of the passions *as* passions yet not involved with the body, as we can think of a straight edge as a mathematical straight line tangent to but having no real contact with the bronze sphere. And since the passions are both psychical and physical, they are related to the body abstractly in thought and somatically in life. For they bring together the directedness of the soul with the receptivity of sense. Therefore Aristotle calls the passions, in a memorable phrase that encapsulates a mystery as much as an insight,

immattered reasons (*enyloi logoi*).[7]

Passions are then *in reason* non-physical but *in effect* embodied; Aristotle has devised a suggestive formula for answering a first question of this book, How can thinking treat of feeling?

The motive behind Aristotle's elaborate group of investigations just briefly set out here was the delineation of *the* human good, happiness, which required, on the one hand, its distinction from pleasure, considered in the previous chapter, and, on the other, its connection with virtue. For virtue is, Aristotle thinks, what makes human beings both good in themselves and well at work. Virtue is not really in the thing done but in the *way* it is done— with self-knowledge, from choice, for its own sake, and from a steadfast condition.[8] All that is what passionate behavior is precisely *not*, and its taming is what ethics is about. For, Aristotle has said, happiness is being fully at work in accordance with virtue.[9]

7. Passion and Persuasion: The *Art of Rhetoric*

If a passion is "immattered reason," then, we may suppose, it can listen to reasonable speech. The diagram of the soul's appetitive world (Fig. III-A) shows that for Aristotle the passions can indeed do so. Some are capable of hearing rational argument—the spirited passions; some are capable of listening to persuasive speech—the desirous passions. There is a rock-bottom remainder of what we might call the want-passions—the natural needs, such as hunger and the other indefeasible needs of the body—that no amount of talk can assuage or divert for long.

Is sex necessarily among these latter? That large part of the contemporary therapeutic establishment and, of course, of the world in general, which thinks so has grand antecedents in Greek tragedy. Perhaps no more terrific indictment of self-chosen male virginity and helpless female desire has ever been staged than Euripides' *Hippolytus*. The hero of that play is the self-consciously chaste and women-despising son of the Amazon Hippolyta, "the [female] Horse-breaker." (Recall that Amazons lived without men except for a yearly encounter for procreation.) Hippolytus blasphemes against Aphrodite, the goddess of love, by his exclusive devotion to chaste Artemis, goddess of the chase, and by scornfully refusing to satisfy the desperate love of Phaedra, the daughter of a mother who mated with a bull to produce the Minotaur. Hippolytus, "the [male] Horse-breaker," is punished by being pounded to death between a tsunami and a sea-bull, as the runaway horses of his chariot finally fail to submit to him. There is, to be sure, no hint that it is suppressed desire that is breaking out. It is rather the objective right of another's sexual passion to be served that is destroying the chaste young man. Here is the tragedian's (anticipatory) reply to the soul-chariot figure of the philosopher, in which the charioteer can and does and is right to rein in and break the black horse of sexual desire. No questions regarding human needs is more religiously and later psychologically fraught than this: Is sex a natural necessity or a spiritual choice?

But to return to the speech-amenable passions, which are the special concern of the *Art of Rhetoric,* especially of Book II.

The second part of Plato's *Phaedrus,* neglected in my earlier exposition, sets out the requirements for a genuine future "art" (*techne*) of rhetoric. Handbooks of tricks and devices for persuasive speaking evidently abounded,[1] but these left rhetoric in the cookbook stage, not an "art" in the sense of *techne* (whence our term "technique"), that is, a worked-out, teachable kind of know-how, a craft. Socrates asks of genuine rhetoric that it deliver truth, especially about right and wrong as found by dialectic, and that it be organically constructed, as is a living being. But he also calls rhetoric a "soul-guidance" (*psychagogia*), and demands that the rhetorician should know the soul's parts.[2] For as Lincoln, the incarnation of the Socratic rhetorician, will put it in the terms of his day, it is "a drop of honey that catches [the listener's] heart, which . . . is the great high road to the reason. . . ."[3]

One might say that Aristotle, in his down-to-earth way, fulfills all of Socrates' requirements and especially the demand for a soul-craft. The divisions of the soul in the *Rhetoric* are the same as those already set out; what is new is the extensive phenomenology, that is, the interpretative account, of the emotions as observed experiences and expressions. Aristotle needs such descriptions because for him rhetoric is primarily the "technique-informed method concerning [various kinds of] persuasion" (*he entechnos methodos peri tas pisteis*).[4] But such persuasion requires proofs. Now there are three conviction- or persuasion-producing proofs (*pistis* means both the persuasion attempted and the conviction produced). They are: from the moral character of the speaker, from the art of speech itself, and from the disposition, one way or another, of the hearer.[5] To make that last, the disposition, favorable, however, the speaker must know the passions of the soul, for by manipulating them he can make people change their verdicts. So while, he says, in public deliberations the speaker's character counts most, in lawsuits the hearers' passionate disposition matters most. To the ways in which these dispositions are to be exploited and passions are to be roused or allayed is devoted the long section analyzing the passions under three heads: by what propensity the passion arises, by whom it is aroused, and on what occasion it occurs.[6] There follows the first comprehensive phenomenology of the passions surviving in the Western tradition.

A. Love

Love. I have to start with what *isn't* there: *eros.* To be sure, the kind of love that includes being-in-love as opposed to friendship isn't totally unregarded in the *Rhetoric.* Aristotle says that

> those in love rejoice in talking and writing to or [just] doing something about the beloved because they think that by remembering him in all these ways they are, as it were, bringing him before the senses.[7]

But that is said peripherally. One might explain the absence of love as a topic in the *Art of Rhetoric* by the fact that it isn't the kind of passion apt to be the subject of *public* persuasion. That, however, is not enough of an explanation. The larger question is why erotic love (Socrates' great theme) is present only minimally even elsewhere in Aristotle's work, why he has in fact shrunk its compass in the economy of appetite (Fig. III-A). The narrower question is whether it is even clear that private love *isn't* in fact of great public consequence. (It seems to me that a semi-serious book investigating the effects through the ages of private affairs on public affairs could be at once sagacious and salable, and I can think of several enticing titles.) In any case, the Athenian public thought that Athens owed her freedom to two lovers, the tyrannicides Harmodius and Aristogeiton, who were moved by their love to deliver the city from the oppression of the Pisistratids, and whom their fellow-citizens celebrated in song (both Herodotus and Thucydides notwithstanding, who think it worth their while to debunk that founding myth of Athenian democracy twice in each of their histories).[8] Moreover, anyone who has lived through the American student movement of the last century will remember the slogan "Make Love not War," with its implication that eros is an even better moral equivalent of war than cricket. Anyhow, eros clearly has a public dimension, and it is, I think, more Aristotle's no-non-sense approach than the subject's inherent unimportance that makes him focus on *philia,* friendship, over *eros,* love, as a public rubric. Why, is clear from his political theory, in which friendship, a less "particular," less exclusive relation than sensual eros, is the glue of the whole political community: "Friendship holds the city together."[9]

About friendship (*philia,* which means both the friendly feeling and the accomplished relation) Aristotle says this: It is wanting good things for the other, mutuality of affection, sharing joys and sorrows, holding similar opinions about good and bad—and more such familiar features, for example, having the same sense of humor and the same tastes, and not feeling embarrassed before each other except when there is real cause for shame. In sum, friendship is reciprocality, for which Aristotle has a lovely word: friends are *philophiloi,* "friends' friends."[10] Schiller will echo it in his "Ode to Joy": "*Wem der grosse Wurf gelungen, eines Freundes Freund zu sein.*" It is, like the other descriptions, a very full and recognizable phenomenology of friendly feeling. The opposing member of this passion-pair is hate (*misos*), about which Aristotle makes the acute observation that it applies to whole classes of characters. We usually hate people as members of groups (hence our contemporary notion of "hate crimes"), but with individuals we are instead angry.[11] I have taken friendliness and hate out of their listed order here to contrast them with eros.

B. Anger

Nearly every one of Aristotle's lists begins with anger (*orge*). Why is it first? To begin with, it is *the* "thymotic," the fuming passion, the subject of the first Greek epic, the *Iliad,* which begins, "*The wrath*—sing it, O goddess!"[12] Next, according to the schema of the appetitive soul (Figure III-A), these spirited desires partake of reason and are therefore most amenable to argument. But above all, getting angry in various modes of expression or repression is our most vehement (I would say, if that wasn't proscribed, our most "manly") spur to action, for either sex.

As I have insisted, for Aristotle the whole soul is, as it were, qualified by appetite (though, once again, what will become an explicit primary truth for Spinoza is here just an inferrable fact). Thus anger is accordingly defined: "Let anger then be an appetite, accompanied by pain, for exacting a visible price for a visible slight of the angry man himself or of someone belonging to him, when said slight is inappropriate."[13] Aristotle says "appearing" (*phainomenes*) in both places where I put "visible"; I think he means that both the insult and the revenge (*timoria*) must be both apparent and in full sight of others, so that the slight that produces anger always comes from some identifiable agent. Anger, as appetite, is often accompanied by a certain pleasure; we have, Aristotle says, an image of sweet revenge in our daydreams.

"Slight," literally "belittling" (*oligoria*), is accordingly defined as the [public] enactment (*energeia*) of an opinion about what is visibly of no account. I think Aristotle means that it is the intention, not the matter, that makes the put-down. He then details the modes and occasions of belittling. They seem to have done a lot of that kind of thing in those days, more than we tolerate in our casually egalitarian public civility; the art of *oligoria* does, however, still flourish in Parliament and in the common rooms of English universities.

Ready anger is thus the almost ritualized reaction to being "dissed" in violent yet highly codified settings, like gangs, in which a small slight or even an unintended gesture of disrespect can become fatal. This fact seems to me a keen confirmation that Aristotle is right to emphasize slight as the prime cause of anger. Still, it is curious that of the dozens of reasons why we "get mad" or "lose our temper" in the course of an ordinary modern day, none—

not even their ancient analogues—seem worthy of notice in the *Rhetoric,* not getting mugged, not failing to get one's rights, not being made to wait, not being badly serviced or incorrectly billed.[14] But perhaps these are, from serious to trivial, at bottom all felt more as assaults on our comfort than on our dignity, not as insults but as injuries.

The opposite of anger is *gentleness,* which prevails when the occasions for offence-taking are relaxed, and which, though more desirable to live with, is less interesting to read about.

C. Fear

Friendliness and *hate* have been mentioned above. Next is *fear* (*phobos*), usually high on the list of affects, because it is the only *spirited* passion that other animals give irresistible evidence of sharing with people, because it is humanly universal, because it is civilly instrumental.

Aristotle defines: "Let fear be a certain pain or disturbance coming from the imagination (*phantasias*) of a future bad thing that is destructive or painful."[15] So fear is a *future*-feeling, and here starts the division of passions by their temporality. But apprehension of evils to come takes imagination. In *On the Soul* Aristotle indeed considers that some animals may have imagination.[16]

There too he says that

> when we form the opinion that something is terrible or fearful, straightway we feel the passion that goes along with it (*sympaschomen*), and the same for what inspires boldness. Our condition with respect to imagination, however, is just the same as that of viewers who see terrible or encouraging things in a picture (*en graphei*).[17]

Here Aristotle is making the point that the judgment of danger is spontaneous and that the fear-passion arises immediately along with an inference of danger we cannot help making, while it is in our power not only to call off or to suppress a mental image but even to view it dispassionately. Hence imaginative passions are, to speak in modern terms, aesthetic affects such as a willing spectator (Aristotle uses the word for theater-goers, *theomenoi*) might seek—discretionary, we might say. In the *Rhetoric,* however, it is, in fact, the image which directly inspires the primary, real fear. Here, then, is in summary form a problem that bedevils the psychology of emotions: How is the pictorial power of imaginative vision, *phantasia,* related to the passions—as instigator or as illustrator? Is it cause or epiphenomenon?

Aristotle goes on to say that dangers far off, and presumably imaginatively less distinct, are less fearful, that signs presaging something fearful are themselves frightening, that among these is the evident anger of people able to harm us. Aristotle then gives a list of people to be afraid of, especially those who have power to hurt, "for mostly men do wrong when they can." Of these the most to be feared are not the overtly aggressive ones, but the "gentle, the ironic, and the unprincipled." The rhetorical lesson is that if you plan to scare your audience for some purpose, manage to make it plausible to them that they will indeed suffer somehow by someone so that there *is* reason to be afraid, but remember also that it is necessary for fear to arise that there should remain some hope for safety. I think he means that without such hope fear goes over in blank, imageless despair.

Boldness or confidence is then just the contrary of fear. What is naturally missing in Aristotle's persuasion-directed inventory of these opposite passions is the virtue they flank, so allow me a little digression on it. In the extreme-mean-extreme context, where confidence is construed as rashness, with cowardice at the other end, this mean is *courage,* the first of excellences in the *Nicomachean Ethics.* It is the one most extensively specified there.[18] (Justice is excepted from this scheme in the *Ethics,* because it is the virtue of virtues, "virtue complete," hence not captured between specific vices or passions, being opposed to the whole of vice or passion. Moreover the means that define justice are not in the soul but in the situation.)[19] Among the several kinds of courage that lie between cowardly fear and rash boldness, military courage—facing death—ranks highest for Aristotle, but there is a secondary type I cannot omit mentioning, political or civil courage.[20] For us, citizen-courage, whose failure has proved so devastating in the continental totalitarian states of the last century, is a matter of conscience ("the knowledge we have within"). Such courage is a matter of psychology among the Stoics, of morality among the Romans, and of spirituality among the Christians. For Aristotle, on the other hand, civic courage resembles fighting courage precisely because its motive is not regard for one's own integrity, but for others' high opinion; this regard is expressed as the sense of shame (*aidos*), which affects only those who have some appetite for what is fine or beautiful (*kalon*).[21] Shame can be respected as a virtue, but properly construed it is a passion: the fear of disrepute.[22]

D. Shame

So *shame* is next in the *Rhetoric,*[23] and it is the last of these passions I will take up, except to say out of order how pity and "righteous indignation" (whose name, *nemesis,* is used by us for the agent of just retribution) come to be an opposing pair, though both are signs of a good character. It is simply because, as pity is pain felt for another's undeservedly doing badly, so indignation is pain at another's undeservedly doing well, in other words, at getting away with it.[24] I want to say here that my brief reports hardly do justice to the acuity of Aristotle's observations with respect to the whole register of passions, but here the reporter perforce has the Hobson's choice of just transcribing the text or omitting all the fine detail.

But back to shame. "Let shame (*aischyne*) be a certain pain or disturbance about that mischief (*kakon*), whether present, past, or future, that appears to bring people into disrepute, and shamelessness a certain belittling and lack of feeling (*apatheia*) about the same things." So we are ashamed of misdeeds that seem shameful to those we are mindful of. There follows an inventory of disgraceful doings from fleeing in battle to profiteering from the weak, from flattering those from whom we want a loan to taking credit for others' accomplishments, from shirking labor that older people are willing to do to engaging in certain sexual practices. Whichever of these acts they commit, people are ashamed only before those whom they respect (which might be themselves) and whose admiration they in turn cherish. For "shame is a visual image (*phantasia*) concerned with loss of respect (*adoxia*)." That is to say, shame depends on imagining how we look to someone whose re-gard or re-spect—in the literal sense of a "look returned"—we care about; it is alto-gether bound up with imagining. Not caring, being apathetic about being seen in a disgraceful light is, then, shamelessness.

This is the place for a brief note on the words for this affective sphere. There are four Greek words all of which can somehow be rendered by forms of "shame."

1. *aidos,* a noun, means a shy kind of modesty and physical reticence, in German *Scham*; we might speak of being ashamed to undress. The Greeks thought such conventional shame was typical of the soft, fully garbed barbarians; they, taking pride in their well-trained bodies, contended in the nude, following a Spartan innovation.[25] Aristotle thinks such shyness is a feeling proper only to the young. As such it is the opposite of shamelessness (*anaischyntia*),[26] which means that *aischyne* (below) is partly synonymous with *aidos*. An older, grander meaning of the latter is "reverence, awe, respect." "*Scham* exists wherever there is a 'mysterium,'" says Nietzsche.[27] *Aidos* is etymologically unconnected to the other three, which all belong together.

2. *aischros,* an adjective, means both physically ugly and morally shameful.

3. *aischyne,* a noun, means shame in the same two senses the word has in English: the shame that people bring on themselves from others by disgraceful acts, as in the cry "For shame!" and the shame peo-ple ought to feel within themselves when they have done such acts, as when an indignant lawyer says to a disgraceful senator, "Have you no shame, sir?" Thus "shame" imputed in the first sense con-demns, and aroused in the second sense rehabilitates. Aristotle uses the word in the latter sense.

4. *aischynesthai,* a passive verb, means "to feel ashamed." Aristotle speaks of "those who feel shame" (*hoi aischynontai*). Our English active verb "to shame," that is, to put to shame, to embarrass, seems to have no Greek counterpart, though of course the denigrating activity does.

It must be said that this is a gross account. All the given usages plus others cut across each other.[28] I have made this inventory not for the sake of offering a Greek lesson but because of the very particular interest that the passion of shame has attracted in the century just past. This seems the place to insert a brief account. For whether acknowledged or just appropriated, rediscovered or borrowed, Aristotle's exposition of shame has resonated over a long time.

8. Shame after Aristotle

I mean a *long* time after. Passions have cycles of popularity, and shame has, like desire, recently come into its own as a subject of "systematic research and theory development," mostly in psychology and sociology. The motives for these studies range from the attraction of a newly discerned vacuum (such as I once saw described, with serene inadvertence, as a "much needed gap" in the field) to an urgent moral concern about the perceived loss of shame in our culture.

A. Theories of Shame

Here is a brief sampling of theories. An early study, Dodds's *The Greeks and the Irrational,* dealt in cultural-anthropological terms with Greek epic "shame-culture," in which honor or loss of face is at stake, and with its evolution into a tragic "guilt-culture," in which an inward sense of evil is projected on external punishing divinities. Shame-cultures had been recognized by anthropologists in many communities of the world, tribal and modern.[1] Later Bernard Williams, taking a more historical-conceptual approach in *Shame and Necessity,* found even within shame elements of guilt, so that "the Greek conception that brings (something like) guilt [for which the Greeks had no word] under a wider conception of (something more than) shame" can illuminate our understanding of both; they are, so to speak, simultaneously rather than evolutionarily related, though guilt is only implicit in shame. Shame here is the *aidos* of the previous section, the sense of who one is in the sight of *others.* Williams recognizes a special link of guilt to hearing, to the *internal voice* of judgment; thus one who feels guilt cannot escape its inner call, but one who feels shame can try to hide from *public view*—though I cannot resist entering a poet's demurrer to the very wish.

Not with a Club, the Heart is broken,
Nor with a Stone—
A Whip so small you could not see it
I've known

To lash the Magic Creature
Till it fell,
Yet that Whip's Name
Too noble then to tell.

Magnanimous as Bird
By Boy descried—
Singing unto the Stone
Of which it died—

Shame need not crouch
In such an Earth as Ours—
Shame—stand erect—
The Universe is yours.[2]

Even earlier there was a spate of now neglected existentially—and/or phenomenologically—oriented studies of shame, in which accounts were given of the passion as constitutive of human existence and as significant in human experience respectively. Max Scheler, an early Phenomenologist, wrote a detailed disquisition on *Scham* in the sense of sexual modesty. Its gist is this:

> That "turning back" into the self, the dynamic with which modesty-shame (*Scham*) begins, occurs neither when one regards oneself as "given" in the mode of a general object nor as an individual, but when the other person palpably oscillates between an individualizing and a generalizing intention toward me, while my own intention and the experienced counterintention do not have the same but opposite direction with respect to this distinction.[3]

This (typically) difficult sentence means that modesty-shame does not arise when, for example, we undress, if we think of ourselves as, say, a "case" in the doctor's examination room or as a "model" in the artist's studio. Nor do we feel ashamed of our nakedness where we are purely and naturally ourselves, as with a lover in bed. It does arise when the doctor or painter seems to begin to see us as an individual, or when the lover seems to be making generalizing comparisons. Modesty, then, is a self-protective feeling aroused in an individual faced with a promiscuity of approaches. Hence sexual modesty can be said to express a tension between love and lust; it is the emotional recognition of a dynamic between individualizing qualitative valuation and surrender to an object, on the one hand (love), and generalized sexual drive and selfish pleasure-seeking, on the other (lust). Thus modesty-shame is the "natural soul-clothing" of our sexuality, and actual clothes are only a "crystallization of such shame and its symbol." Its purpose is "the preservation of the powers of individuality and the inhibition of their release."[4] Therefore, one might infer, it adds a tensed significance to sexual encounters. And that is neatly corroborated in a passage from Milan Kundera's novel *Immortality:*

> [T]hat shame, even if it was only an illusion of shame, that shame was present, it was with them in the small hotel room, it intoxicated them with its magic and gave everything meaning.[5]

Kundera, I might say here, belongs to those who think that shame is gone in modern times and had gone much earlier than do those who bemoan its loss in the America of the turn of the twenty-first century: "On Europe's dial another hour had struck; shame had disappeared." That hour, however, seems to strike at any and all times; only read what Epictetus thought at the turn of the second century C.E. of the man, evidently a type, whose "sense of shame and modesty have been completely extirpated."[6]

Scheler goes on to discuss a raft of related self-feelings, from disgust (in German the verb is reflexive, *sich ekeln* [compare *sich ängstigen*]) to reverence (in German, *Ehrfurcht,* honoring and fearing at once). My brief account hardly conveys Scheler's complexity of insight and expression.

Heidegger assigns *aidos* to the moods (which will be the subject of Chapter IX); it betokens not mere shyness but that basic attunement to Being which puts the human being on guard—makes it regard and be in tune with and close to what is highest. He quotes: "For *aidos* sits with Zeus, and thrones over human works."[7] "Reverence" seems to be near the meaning intended.

Riezler distinguishes *aidos* from *aischyne,* as the shame felt before acting, which is awe, from the shame felt after the act, which is dishonor. Out of fragments of habits and traditions, society forms a system of things and acts to be treated with shame. These are the *pudenda,* things to be treated with protective shame (the *pudenda,* like *aidoia,* are ordinarily the "private parts"), and the *veneranda,* things to be treated with awed respect. Riezler observes that these two elements have shifting relations both to society and to each other; for example, shame about bodily privacy is disappearing, and—probably not unrelatedly—so is a sense of reverence. In general, radical enlightenment abjures the secretive, and that itself militates against shame. Yet though shame and awe are historically social phenomena, they are fundamentally natural dispositions: the protection of what is humanly vulnerable. Nonetheless they are themselves also vulnerable; delicacy is easier to dissipate than to recover.

To return to recent treatments of shame: Shame is usually included in the large number of studies on the emotions in general, studies that are pri-

marily reflective on the basis of anecdotal observation rather than empirical on the basis of controlled studies; they usually include shame, shyness,
and modesty. Coming late in the Western history of attention to the subject,
such works say, often in more sophisticated or wordy ways, what has already
been said more fundamentally and succinctly. Thus one of the most weighty
of recent books begins with the observation that emotions are complex
because of "*their great sensitivity to personal and contextual circumstances*"
(a sentence that lacks deniability), and gives, as its first example, the case of
the artist's model's shame at suddenly perceiving herself as being looked at
as a woman. It is the very case Scheler had observed.[8]

Almost all agree that shame has something about it that sets it more particularly apart from the other emotions. Shame is globally self-directed—
we are ashamed not only of our deeds but of our whole self.[9] One might
say that shame is a fall from one's own grace. Jack Katz gives the following
analysis: Whereas other emotions are to be studied through the observer's
perspective of another's overt conduct, the structure of experienced shame
must be investigated from the inside, for shame concerns more one's being
than one's doing; in fact it is a relatively passive self-reflection that inhibits
action. Shame is a "distinctively prismatic experience," which refracts many
shades of feeling, three in particular. It is, first, a way of seeing oneself from
the standpoint of others, "an eerie revelation of self"; it is, next, a form of
impotence, in which one is blocked from taking control of one's identity,
a vulnerability in the face of the inability to escape the shaming circumstance or to turn the clock back on the shaming event; and it is, third, the
wish to escape by disappearing, by being swallowed up by the earth, a chaotic attempt at hiding from a global feeling that sweeps through the self
even if the stigma is minor.[10] Thus it seems that shame can be devastating
because it assumes into its intense self-regarding the scornful gaze of the
whole world.

An etymological reminder that shame is a kind of little death is in the
word "mortification" (from Latin *mors,* "death," and the verb for "make").
An illustration comes from an incident in Jane Austen's *Emma* that no reader
forgets, when the heroine thoughtlessly exercises her wit on a respectable,
fluttery old gentlewoman in reduced circumstances. Emma's mentor, Mr.
Knightley, brings her shameful deed home to her. As a result, her feelings

> were combined only of anger against herself, mortification, and deep concern.
> . . . Never had she felt so agitated, mortified, grieved, at any circumstance in
> her life.[11]

Dying away in shame means, however, being reborn with one flaw the less.
Salutary mortification precedes moral regeneration, as we've all painfully
learned.

In a more recent but similar, if somewhat less elegant, "conceptualization" by Nathanson, shame is

> a mechanism that throws the organism into a painful experience of inner tension by attempting to reduce the possibilities for positive affect in situations when compelling reasons for that positive affect remain.[12]

Such shame "protects an organism from its growing avidity for positive affect."[13] It starts out not as an emotion, which involves memories of experience in Nathanson's terminology, but precisely as an affect, defined as "the strictly biological portion of an emotion."—"Whereas affect is biology, emotion is biography." An example of such a shame affect is a child who has a fervent positive curiosity in a stranger's face, but suddenly senses, "perhaps providentially," the inappropriateness, even risk, of such an intrusive interest. The child averts its gaze and takes refuge behind its mother, thus diminishing its positive interest affect, while yet maintaining it by peeping out. This is, of course, a case of bashful rather than guilty shame.

Another feature of shame is that it is an "aftermath state," a passion that follows other passions such as fear or greed, when an individual experiences the "return to social consciousness" from these "vehement" passions that assert a world in which there is only a single person against all others.[14]

B. Modern Decline

Another approach taken in a group of studies of shame is, as I mentioned, a response to its decline in the world, especially in contemporary America, the sense "that we live in a culture that is becoming shamefully shameless."[15] One, perhaps positive, reason for this fading of shame is that conscience, the attention to an internal authority, is winning out over shame, respect for the regard of others—in tandem, it is said, with individualism over social control, rationalism over cultural psychology, vulgarian over aristocratic sensibilities, in sum, liberated over traditional attitudes.[16]

I want to interject here that these reflections may ring truer and may find more defenders among those who formally study the human world than among those who just somehow live in it. A kind of culminating delegitimization of shame represented by Martha Nussbaum's book *Hiding from Humanity* seems to me a case in point. She considers shame and disgust together: One feels disgust, the other is shamed—that is their complementarity. She explains this relation by viewing disgust as a fear of contamination, presumably by that which is the source of shame for another.

The book contains both analysis and advocacy. With the help of studies from philosophy, cognitive science, empirical, clinical, and psychoanalytic psychology, she details both emotions. Disgust is first and last a phenomenon of vulnerability: We are reminded of our bodily mortality.[17] (There are, as I have recorded, very different ways to see disgust.) Shame "is a painful emotion responding to a sense of failure to attain some ideal state," a sense of inadequacy and incompleteness. Therefore, far from involving diminished self-respect, it implies self-regard as a backdrop; in psychoanalysis shame is thus connected to the "ego-ideal." There are many kinds of shame, but the primitive type, which pervades all later life, is infantile shame that arises from encounters with narcissistic defeats. In these the baby's feeling of omnipotence, its sense of being of sole and unique importance to someone else, is shattered. Thus shame does not depend on public shaming, it can be dyadic; only one other is needed.[18]

The advocacy part is concerned with legal reform and social revisionism. The social aim is—to omit the long inquiry into the role the emotions play in law—to provide a "psychological foundation of liberalism,"[19] which will induce society to admit neediness and vulnerability. Accordingly disgust as a reaction to any sort of defect or taint is critically analyzed as being irrational, socially dangerous rather than helpful, and only limitedly an evolved defense against pollution (the older understanding). The same goes for shame. For example, the category of the normal that seems necessary for discriminating a shameful situation—"natural" is not an operative concept in this book—is criticized because it is used "to stigmatize deviant behavior." Though we must give up the exorbitant infantile demand for complete control, "we retain our nostalgic longing for the bliss of infantile oneness with the womb. . . . The idea of normalcy is like a surrogate womb. . . ." (I must observe that the use of the first person plural in this claim seems to me somewhat exorbitant.) Therefore "normalcy," as a device for marking and stigmatizing certain behavior as shame-inducing, is typically "an aggressive reaction to infantile narcissism and to shame born of our own incompleteness." So the offender is to be regarded as victimized and the observer is infantilized.[20] Consequently shame is here conceived much more as socially oppressive than as personally redemptive. Thus is nullified for the sake of social reconstruction, what the individual sinner seeking salvation is so poignantly ready to observe of himself: *Culpa rubet vultus meus,* "Sin reddens my face."[21]

C. Empirical Studies

As for the more empirically directed investigations, they all reference Darwin, who inventories the physical indices of "shame for some moral delinquency," indices which, he claims, are almost if not completely universal; the main ones are blushing and hiding the face. He says that the object of hiding the face cannot be to conceal the blush because it happens even "under circumstances which exclude any desire to hide shame, as when guilt is fully confessed and repented of." His general explanation of our emotive expressions is that those whose occasion is not purely physiological, like blushing, were once serviceable, purposeful, and voluntary, but have gradually turned into heritable habits by various routes, one of which applies to shame: Primeval man, even before becoming morally sensitive, was highly so about his appearance to the other sex. Since the face is the most regarded part of the body, someone ashamed of his looks would naturally hide that part; hence covering the face is now a habitual reaction, involuntary (though controllable). What is interesting about blushing is that although it is an involuntary nervous, that is, physiological, reaction, it is impossible to induce it by physical means. "It is the mind which must be affected." Thus Darwin seems to explain the two chief and universal signs of shame as coincidentally simultaneous events with different etiologies: Face-hiding, "losing face," is an inherited habit, blushing the physiological effect of a mental affection.

Notice that Darwin does not distinguish shame from embarrassment and shyness. Shyness is now generally regarded as a personality trait, a propensity for withdrawing, rather than as an emotion, but whether shame and embarrassment are the same emotion remains in dispute. But note too that etymologically "embarrassment" is a kind of blockage ("bar" is in the word), and that brings its original sense close to a shame-feature: blocked action.[22] In any case, all three are forms, in Darwin's terms, of self-attention; they are reflexive aftermaths.

Empirical studies of shame have, like those of desire, burgeoned in the last two decades. Shame had been a "sleeper" emotion, partly because over several centuries "the denial of shame has been institutionalized in Western societies"—either as superceded by moral guilt or as obviated by rational candor.[23] It has now become not only "gold to be mined psychotherapeutically" but the subject of much research and theory, no more definitive than that about desire.

As before, a list of issues will be as close as I can come to telling what is being done.

A good deal of effort goes, as always in psycho-social science, into finding impeccable definitions—those that are inclusively general, informatively precise, and plugged into the technical terms of a theory-based research program. For example: Shame interrupts or inhibits special kinds of positive, social relationships, since it is "associated with negative evaluations of the self." Which is what everyone had been saying.[24]

Once past the general methodology- and concept-constructions which tend, in these investigations, to be technically abstruse and speculatively banal, there is a wealth of intriguing observation. It does not lead, on the whole, to conclusive consensus. (For example, it appears that shame has not been satisfactorily "operationalized," meaning that the experimental procedures for determining the presence, kind, and degree of shame are flawed.)[25] But it does lead to these more refined questions for research, among which are these: How does shame, "perhaps the most painful . . . affect," conceived as the adaptive capacity of "conservation-withdrawal," the protective disengagement of an organism from visibility, arise in children as mediated by their developing brain functions?[26] If shame-gestures are interpreted as a kind of appeasement-display following a social transgression, can its components be encoded (tabulated)? Can different response patterns, especially in children, distinguish shame from guilt, "avoiders" from "amenders"?[27] If shame is interpreted as a defensive strategy triggered by an interpersonal threat, can it be seen as an evolved mental mechanism which is not exclusively self-conscious, as it is in humans? If so, is it to be found in other animals as well, serving in them fitness-enhancing biosocial goals, chiefly damage-limitation by signaling submission in socially threatening situations?[28] How and why are "stigmas," publicly visible or internally felt marks of a "spoiled identity," generally perceived as a "shameful difference"?[29] Why are such stigmas causes of a kind of endemic shame not only for the bearers but their families?[30] When does shame become pathological? Is its disclosure therapeutic? Is there shame in the therapeutic relation itself?

I add my own questions: In view of Darwin's theory of the universality of shame, can a particular cultural norm whose transgression arouses it serve to specify types of shame, such as rage-shame, humiliation-shame, mortification-shame, embarrassment-shame? In other words, can shame be differentiated through its local causes? And finally, how is shame related to honor, in view of the fact that both have an inner aspect (the feeling of shame and the sense of honor) and an outer one (the person shamed and the reputation dishonored)? How does the affect of inner shame differ from the sense of honor—as a passion differs from a virtue, that is, a flare-up from a persistent condition? Or is honor something in between these two, a keen yet steady, acute yet sub-surface sentiment, a high sensitivity for a right to respect by reason of a commitment to a personal or cultural code?[31]

I have dwelt so long on shame because it appears to be the morally most potent of passions. Whereas other emotions may explode and wreak havoc on others, shame implodes and blasts the self. Nonetheless, the flight into shamelessness, be it to faux-primitivism or sophisticated liberation, ends up being less escape from a burden than exposure of a folly. Something in us, our humanity, does not take naturally to our divesting ourselves of our "soul-clothes" or kindly to others similarly exposing themselves—if only because when no one is ashamed anymore, be it from levity or ideology, how, in the absence of the fear of the Lord, will anyone resist the impulse to do harm? "For mostly men do wrong when they can."[32]

Primitive desirousness, impassioned love, proud spiritedness, shrinking shame (*epithymia, eros, thymos, aidos*), the hungers, thralldoms, ebulliences, and delicacies dwelling conjointly in the strongly-natured soul as it turns inward and outward—these have been my theme in the first three chapters.

I have told of their linkage and their elevation in ancient philosophy as well as of their isolation and reduction in modern research. What next?

It is, I think, generally supposed that ways of thinking differ in proportion to their distance in time. Well, we now come to a school of thought that is quite close to Aristotle in time and more distant from him in theory than even those modern ones we have just been considering: The Stoics will want not to moderate but to dispel the passions.

chapter IV

The Pathology and Therapy of the Passions

Stoicism through Cicero

The ancients don't seem ever to have talked of "stoicism"; as far as I can tell they spoke only of "the Stoics," "those of the Stoa." When it comes to thinking—and the Stoics thought long and hard—an "ism" betokens a sum that is less than its parts. Every recorded Stoic seems to have thought differently from every other, sometimes by a composable smidgen, sometimes by a nearly devastating margin. When you consider that the Stoics formed both a school and a movement, that they were active over half a millennium in antiquity and that their theories were reactivated from early modernity to post-modern times, that they included Greek philosophers and Roman citizens, an emperor in his capital and on campaign and a slave from the distant provinces and settled in Rome, and that their writings are preserved mostly in fragments often reported by their opponents, you might despair of getting hold of a Stoic gist. Yet the Stoics were, as I said, both a distinct school and a diffused movement with enough tradition and coherence to make it possible to discern a mainstream and its perennial preoccupations. It centered—I think it is no exaggeration to say—on the passions.

1. Why Study Stoicism? Why through Cicero?

Thus it is easier to say what is against such study by the interested layperson than what is in its favor. Whereas the individual authors around whom this book is built open up to any willing reader, to study the Stoics and to glean their common stoicism from them—fragmented as are their texts, kaleidoscopic their opinions, extended over time their development—requires the help of knowledgeable scholarship, of which I make grateful use. Cicero's *Tusculan Disputations* (45 B.C.E.), the longest continuous, and the most accessible, account of the preceding Stoic positions—a third phase was to follow—is insufficient in the very aspect I think necessary for reflecting on the passions: the theory of world and soul in which they are sited. Still, he gives clear accounts of Stoic argumentation concerning the passions, of their taxonomy (that is, their order and enumeration), and of the treatment they require—for whatever wrinkles the Stoics introduced into their accounts, the passions are always pathological. Moreover, his book includes a pretty fair introduction to Epicureanism, which I will take up by the way (Sec. 7).

When I say that Cicero gives accounts of the preceding Stoics, I am referring to two of the three epochs, the three Stoic schools that stretch over five hundred years: The Early Stoa (founded about 300 B.C.E.) was located in Athens. It was named after the venue where the Stoics taught, the Painted Portico (*stoa poikile*) in the Agora, the Athenian marketplace. (The portico was rediscovered by the American excavators of the Agora, among whom I spent a small but indelible part of my youth.) Its founder was Zeno and its codifier Chrysippus. The Early Stoics were still close to Socrates, whose notion that virtue is knowledge will be in one way or another behind the Stoic understanding of the passions. Most of the philosophical underpinnings for the account of the passions are traceable to this phase.

From the Middle Stoa (which lasted to the end of the first century B.C.E.), the name of Posidonius will turn up in my account for introducing, driven by experience, a modification of the Stoic notion that passions simply *are* thoughts.[1] It was in this phase that Stoicism began to become lower-case stoicism, a movement. That is to say, the doctrines ceased to be philosophical schools of thought and, propagated by Roman gentlemen, became the common opinion of the Roman governing and military classes, as Kant's moral teaching would later be for Prussians.

The last phase, the Late Stoa (to roughly 200 C.E.), ceased to be much concerned with theory and became mostly an ethical movement. The slave Epictetus (late first century) and the emperor Marcus Aurelius (second century) wrote in this spirit. As a philosophical school the Stoa began to fade out, but as a movement stoicism went popular—a frame of mind fitted to a cosmopolitan and precarious world. This last phase is not very germane to my account.

The reason is not that late stoicism is unimportant. On the contrary, it is the winning philosophy; when people speak of "being philosophical about it," they mean "taking it stoically." They have in mind a softened version of the life advocated by Epictetus, who was the most famous of the professional Late Stoics.[2] It is a life devised to gain personal control in a large, hazardous world, a way of life strenuously concentrated on subjective, inward control, on determinedly letting go whatever is not "up to us"—which is everything external. I am omitting Epictetus's fiercely practical philosophizing because he is so deliberately untheoretical. Although he uses the terms of the earlier Stoas, he allows their coherent philosophical depths to drop away, and though he appears to have read works by the classical Stoics, he discourages his disciples from such reading or reflection.[3]

For all the extensiveness and fragmentation of Stoic thinking, the reasons for coming to grips with it are compelling. A first, if not a chief, reason is that, for a citizen of a country which expresses in its founding document "a decent respect to the opinions of mankind," it is practically impossible not to be interested in the bases of so large and long-lived a movement-philosophy—"a philosophy" in the broad sense of a set of opinions to live with. Such an interest is, to be sure, always in tension with the Socratic injunction not to care what many people say but only what you and I really think. But the Stoics also give plenty of opportunity for an inquiry not merely into the opinions of mankind, but into the way things are, as I will show in a moment.

A second reason that the Stoics are worth attending to is that they are, so to speak, the moderns of the ancients. A sign of their incipient modernity is how naturally the early modern philosophers absorbed and built on their teachings—to mention only the two that appear in this book, Descartes and Spinoza. In the next-to-last section of this chapter (8), I will list in bare, broad strokes some Stoic features that have shaped our modernity and that will turn up later on in the book. The study of the Stoics helps in thinking about the following rousing enigma: Why didn't the ancients make it through to full-blown modernity? They were on the brink in so many respects—rational astronomical hypotheses, proto-integrals, rudimentary steam engines, to name just a sample each from natural science, mathematics, and technology. Was it by reason of deliberate self-limitation, intellectual abstemiousness, the way Plato denigrates observational astronomy and Aristotle abjures the thought of actual infinity, or was it something less purposeful, more situational? Or was it, perhaps, just this—that modernity never was the necessary destination of antiquity?

The Stoics give further focus to the perplexity. They provide the theory of mind and knowledge—or something even prior, the very readiness to engage in cognitive theory, the acknowledgement of the possibility of a knowledge of knowledge that was specifically and strenuously denied by Socrates in the dialogue *Charmides*[4]—that will be called into service by the seventeenth-century initiators of the revolution in thinking that underlies our modern modes. We know it as epistemology. Particularly in respect to the passions, quite aside from the current Neostoic revival, the Stoics are behind much of modern theory, not least of which is the basic physicalism and its problematic yoking with a thoroughgoing rationalism initiated by Descartes. It ultimately induced a Romantic reaction, a counterrevolution that included a reevaluation of the emotions. It was driven not so much by a rejection of the Stoic notion of the passions for being pathological as by an acceptance of pathology as a heightening of experience. I realize these are very broad-gauged claims, but I only intend to show why Stoicism is, for all the difficulties, worth attending to.

Finally, the main and most substantial reason for studying the Stoics is in the fascination of Stoic theorizing itself. On the one hand it seems rousingly counterintuitive and repellently cold-hearted, though oddly enough, the specific location of the passions in the heart comes from the Stoics.[5] For example, Stoic advice on grief-management—that nothing not up to me need or should touch me—wouldn't work on most of us, for whom a sense of helplessness aggravates rather than lightens "distress," which is Cicero's chief pathology. Take even the irritation of intrusive noise: When it issues from my large neighbor on the right, the Naval Academy, which is unamenable to my control, I get angry, but when it comes from my small neighbor on the left, my college, I take it serenely, since a phone call will end it— probably. Similarly, Cicero reports the Stoic argument against pity, which, though later taken up by Spinoza and though in the context brightly rational, isn't reasonable as the heart goes. On the other hand, some Stoic arguments have an ineluctably sound and self-securing aspect, which it would be wise to get hold of.

What is most engaging in Stoic thinking about the passions is the claim, bold and yet elusive, that the passions *are* modes of thinking and so subject to reason. One of the obstacles to thinking about the affects, which I set out in the beginning and will return to in the end, is that, if they are indefeasibly other than thought, thinking can scarcely get at and certainly not into them. This is the problem the Stoics believe they have boldly solved—with far-reaching consequences. It has been argued that modern psychoanalysis, as the laborious verbalization of affective motivations, owes a debt to cognitive Stoicism.[6] What is elusive is the meaning of the Stoic claim. Just how are such affective movements of the soul thought-like? The Stoics have a brilliant answer, the very theory that underlies psychoanalysis: Passions are not so much *verbalizable* as inherently *verbal,* and are in fact a patho-logy, an—erroneous—account which is not *of* an affect, but which *is* the affect. To understand this claim is to be led into the depths of human being. The elusiveness consists in the fact that it is never quite clear whether human utterance can indeed totally exhaust human affect. In fact Posidonius, of the Middle Stoa, will acknowledge a non-rational residue, and then the question becomes whether he thereby adjusts or undermines Old Stoicism. For it appears that the Stoic claim that the true sage is *a-pathic,* passionless, has then to be complicatedly modified.

All in all, the satisfaction to be gotten from understanding the reflective Stoics is, it seems to me, not dependent on the acceptance, but rather on the apprehension of a deep possibility, an apprehension such as is the delight, the foreplay, so to speak, of thinking.

2. The Stoic Theory of World and Soul

The approach of this book is to locate various understandings of the passions within their philosophical framework. Ancient Stoic philosophy seems to me, together with its—somewhat despised—cognate, Epicureanism (see Sec. 7), to require a kind of study interestingly different from that which fits the thinking of Plato and Aristotle considered in Chapters II and III. For one thing we do not, as I said, have extended works by its first originator, Zeno of Citium, and its greatest elaborator, Chrysippus, but only quoted snippets preserved by later expositors. These are, to be sure, conveniently collected in the four volumes of *Stoicorum Veterum Fragmenta*. However, as the title shows—*Fragments of the Old [or Early] Stoics*—there is also the before-mentioned Middle and Late Stoa, an unbroken tradition of well over half a millennium, incessantly modified and elaborated, and extending its influence, even as it fades, into Neoplatonism and Christianity. Once more, the Stoicism of most interest in my context, namely the philosophical framework, comes to us as an extended school rather than as an integral text, which means that any brief presentation must suppress the incessant polemical differentiations that constitute the life of this tradition.

But there is a second factor that sets the study of Stoicism apart from that of Plato's and Aristotle's work, at least to my mind. In studying the latter we recover the beginnings of reflection both in the sense of what came pretty nearly first in time (in our West) and—this matters far more—what has to be thought before anything else can be thought. With the Stoics we are further on. One way to put it is that they are more sophisticated—which term has even to non-Greek ears a double sound: less naïvely immediate yet more reductively simple, less intellectually complex yet more technically cunning. That description—supposing it has some truth—says: More like us. A biological figure would then convey the relation of the Stoics to early modernity and to us now in particular, and so to Modernity in general. Some biologists of the seventeenth century proposed a theory of *preformation*. They thought that the whole living being is already preformed in the seed or sperm, which is thus a small version of the organism, in the human case a *homunculus*; it matures by expanding in size. The winning theory was, of course, that of *development by cell division and specialization*. One might say that Plato and Aristotle started developments (including Stoicism) that through periods of dormancy and revivification were diversified and elaborated into our current philosophical condition. But the Stoa is a preformation of modernity, modernity writ small. To read Stoic texts is to see us in reduced size. I have, as I mentioned, collected some of these preformations as they touch on the passions in Section 9.

Since expositions are not to be detective novels in which the solution is postponed to the end for the thrill of suspense, I shall begin by saying in gist what the Stoics thought the passions were. The abbreviated summary follows closely one given by Arius, a teacher of philosophy in the first century B.C.E.; the Emperor Augustus was his pupil.[1] This is the Stoic theory of the passions in a nutshell:

Passions are mistakes. Every passion (*pathos*) is an *impulse* (*horme*), which is *excessive* (*pleonazousa*) and *disobedient to approving reason* (*apeithe toi hairounti logoi*). Thus every passion is an upset or *upheaval* (*ptoia*), and conversely, every upset is a passion. Every passion of the soul is a *belief* (*doxa*) and, moreover, a *weak conception* (*asthenes hypolepsis*).

The italicized English words (with their Greek originals) tell what terms must be understood to get hold of the Stoic theory, in all its repellent yet thought-inciting strangeness—repellent because it doesn't only seem to, but actually does, deny human affection, in the double sense of denying the actuality of passion as well as the worth of the human bonds it effects, inciting because of the admirably sovereign life that it sanctions.

A. Order of Inquiry

Stoicism is from the first a hierarchy of theories. It is epistemology and physics, that is, theories of how we *know* and what *exists* in nature, before it is ethics, the theory of how to *live*. Those studies will therefore be the philosophical frame for the passions. What there is none of is meta-physics, the inquiry into what is beyond nature. There is no theory of beings beyond or after physics—no "ontology," no account of Being.

To repeat: The Stoic founders insisted on an order of inquiry. First comes logic, by which they mean not just a technique for thinking validly, but precisely what we mean by epistemology, the account of the human cognitive constitution that explains how and with what criteria of truth the world comes to and into us. Second is physics, the theory of the material constitution of the soul and of the cosmos, the natural world.[2] In that order is encapsulated the revolution through which modernity is preformed in antiquity. It is that hundred-and-eighty-degree turn by which the apprehending human subject is to be investigated *before* the presented and apprehended object.

That order of inquiry has been criticized early and late. In the above-mentioned dialogue *Charmides* of the early fourth century B.C.E., Socrates cannot bring himself to think that there is a knowledge of mere knowledge, a self-reflection void of any intended object. Socrates thinks that knowledge cannot itself be a knowable object, for it is the very concern with knowable objects. In his *Introduction* to the *Phenomenology of Spirit*, written in the early nineteenth century, Hegel again assails the attempted pre-knowledge of knowing, this time because it cannot help but regard knowing as a sort of instrument, a tool that will unavoidably belabor and transform its object. The Stoics appear to have originated a very modern philosophical notion— that it is necessary to devise a theory of knowing to secure inquiry into the knowable.

The Stoics have a problem of this sort in fascinatingly acute form: Their second theory, that of existents, is a physics. They are what is nowadays called "physicalists" or materialists, meaning that they believe that what exists, *including soul*, is body and the motions proper to it. In this view they are at one with their cruder cousins, the Epicureans, except that the Stoics believe that body is continuous, that is to say, indefinitely divisible, while the Epicureans think that it is atomic, meaning that it is constituted of uncuttable [*a-toma*] least bodies.

The Stoics liken logic, in which they include the theory of knowledge and of truth, to a hedge thrown around a fruitful field that is philosophy; physics is the land and ethics the fruit.[3] This image displays the trouble. In general, you have to know the lay of your land before you can enclose, that is, comprehend it; you have to know the "what" of both the knowing soul and the knowable world before you can tell the "how" of their mutual impingement. In particular you have to know whether knower and known are alike or unlike. And indeed, the Stoics had an answer from "common notions," that is, they had a preconception about this: All is body. Thus the soul-subject as well as its world-object is bodily. By the same token, however, the firstness of the theory of knowledge, of epistemology, is a little shaky, since it is in fact preceded by a theory of matter—and this flutter of priorities will reach into the theory of passion.

What, we might now ask, were the Stoic founders and re-founders after? This is always the question of questions, not in the sense that philosophy is allowed to be wishful thinking, but in the sense that no question can be framed except out of a care. What Stoics cared about seems to be the coherence of the world with itself, its cosmic constitution, and the coherence of human beings with this world, their epistemological adequacy. These coherences are established as economically, matter-of-factly, common-sensibly as possible. Here is a recipe for a curiously viable weirdness.

B. Physics

The medium of coherence is, accordingly, physical, a pervasive, continuous substratum functioning to make individual bodies cohesive in themselves and with each other. It is called *pneuma* in Greek, that is, "breath, wind," and *spiritus* in Latin. It is a recognizable forerunner of the ether that seemed the necessary stationary medium for light waves in modern physics until 1881, when Michelson and Morley showed that in fact no detectable ether wind washes over the earth as it travels in its orbit. The *pneuma*, too, was thought of as a continuous medium, a medium for "tension" (*tonos*). It was conceived as the cause of a "tensional motion" (*tonike kinesis*), a to-and-fro self-movement,[4] a wavelike, vibratory contraction and expansion, variously described but always thought of as both permeating the world and acting within the boundaries of individual bodies to determine their physical state.

I shall here say only a little of its macrocosmic properties and problems, only as much as forms a background for the passions; for my purposes it is the soul-*pneuma* (*pneuma psychikon*) that matters.[5] Yet even that little will be laden with future uses.

The Stoics have a god, and that god is identical with the cosmic *pneuma*. This divinity is in one aspect an artificer's fire (*pyr technikon*) that fashions as it pervades matter. From here to Spinoza's God, whose bodily aspect is but one of his modes, it is only a step. As for Christian spirit, whose complex conceptual derivation from the Hebrew Bible and Pagan, particularly Stoic, philosophy is beyond my means, I merely reference it.

What follows is interpretative speculation, for the Stoic texts are unclear and commentaries correspondingly indecisive. The Stoic divinity must be as physical as the matter it fashions by pervading it. To make this plausible, the Stoics interested themselves in theories of mixture, in particular in "total blending" (*krasis di' holon*). This is the sort of blending (Hume will later refer to it in one of his theories of the passions) in which two continuous substances occupy the same space[6] without either losing its own qualities, or—by reason of its elasticity—necessarily increasing the total volume. What the Stoics gained by this problematic cosmic blend was the mutual incorporation into one another of two of their basic principles, "the Active" and "the Passive." The *ultimate grounding* of the passions must, I think, lie in these first principles, albeit I have found no Stoic text that says as much in so many words.[7]

God, then, is the active, pneumatic proto-element that structures the passive material proto-element without being spatially separable from it; between them are articulated the traditional elements of air, fire, water, and earth. This strange but purposeful cosmic scheme is the model for the human soul contained within it. For as in the cosmos the god-*pneuma* is *logos*, "reason," the articulating, disposing cosmic activity, so the human soul-*pneuma* is in rational control of the body which it infuses as its psychic ruler. This control is exercised through a sort of node, a command-center (*hegemonikon*, "ruler's seat").

The Stoic soul-body relation is, however, more complex yet, for there is a scale of living things whose functioning the *pneuma* organizes into different degrees of diversity and responsiveness, from merely material bodies through animals to rational animals. In the higher types, the *pneuma's* tension is more intense and produces these characteristic motions: In merely material bodies, it effects a mere passively movable "state" (*hexis*); in animals it organizes a "nature" (*physis*) which is—albeit merely reactively—self-moving; in rational animals (*logika zoa*), it is responsible for movement-by-choice.[8] This last degree of toned *pneuma* is the soul (*psyche*, Latin: *anima*). Hence the soul, the *anima*, is not, as for Aristotle, the principle responsible for giving biological life to any "animal"—that is now the function of the nature-*pneuma*—but for rational life only. In modern biology books, that Stoic notion, that the animal body is not in need of a soul for its life-functions, is, of course, a given.

The soul-*pneuma* is blended with the animal's whole body, but that does not prevent it from harboring a center whence it is toned, a physical seat, a sort of pulse-source, for the complex tension that is rationality. This is the aforesaid "command-center," usually located at the heart, though there is disagreement about that. The soul-*pneuma* has, in fact, seven functions besides, each originating in the part of the body proper to it: sensing—namely sight, hearing, touch, taste, smell—as well as voice and reproduction.[9] The physics of these disparate functions in one medium is unclear, but it might help to think of waves of different lengths and amplitudes, originating in various regions of the ether—not that I understand that very well either.

The command-center at the heart unifies information received from the senses and transmits instructions to the body (such as for us originate in the brain; the transmitting *pneuma* is indeed comparable to the nervous system). Sometimes the Stoics think of the soul as being what animals and humans share, sometimes as being the rational command-center alone. In the latter case, soul equals mind.[10]

In the former sense, the soul's first function is self-perception (*syneidesis*), the pre-rational, we might say intuitive, familiarity (*oikeiosis*) animals have with their own nature that makes them act it out, together with those naturally developed responses that are expressed in animal behavior. This acting out of one's nature, the self-preserving maintenance of one's being, will become for Spinoza the very essence of any thing.

C. Knowledge

With the soul understood as mind, we come to the Stoic theory of knowledge. It is in itself the most future-fraught theory of antiquity and with respect to the Stoic passions the most immediately important part of Stoicism. We must remind ourselves that all the mind's features, up to a certain startling limit, are those of a bodily medium and are therefore literally physical.

At the center of the theory (though not necessarily of the pneumatic structure) is *phantasia*. Neither "fantasy" nor "imagination" will do to translate the Stoic meaning of the word. It is related to the Greek verb for "making appear" and "bringing to light" (*phainein*), for, as Chrysippus points out, *phantasia* comes, through the verb, from *phaos,* "light."[11] It is for the Stoics not a power or *faculty,* but an *affection,* a *pathos,* of the soul-*pneuma* by which it shows something to itself. *Phantasia* is said both of the individual appearing item and of the general apparitional mode—thus "appearances" and "Appearance." But *what* appears and *how* and *to whom*?

What appears as a *phantasia* is what all the senses, but most typically the sight of the eyes, have delivered to the command-center. But of course they do not deliver the body itself that activates the senses, as a body. What eventuates instead is what we call a *representation.*[12] A re-presentation in the sense that dominates and bedevils modern philosophy (and latter-day cognitive science) is the mental object *par excellence.* Kant says that *representatio* is the very genus of all the cognitive modes.[13] It has these two features: It is before us both as a mental *this,* a presentation which is an object appearing to us who are its subjects, *in its own right,* and as a *re*-presentation which is an image or some indication *of something else.* This is exactly how Chrysippus describes *phantasia,* and why he emphasizes the light etymology: "Just as light shows itself and the other things encompassed by it, so [a] *phantasia* shows both itself and what has made it."[14]

Thus the "what" of a representational *phantasia* is other external bodies, in accordance with the realist, nominalist, and empiricist bent of the Stoics. This heap of "ists" refers respectively to the Stoic beliefs that what is real is body, that universals are only conventional names, and that what is to be known are facts of experience. This attitude to the world will determine the Stoic treatment of the passions.

The "how" of appearances is variously understood, from the simple but problem-loaded imprint (*typosis*) of the body on the soul-*pneuma* to a sophisticated but under-determined "alteration" (*alloiosis*) wrought by the external body on the soul. Zeno the founder seems to have introduced the term *typosis,* which, taken literally as a seal impression, raises the question of how one soul can contain simultaneously a great number of such physical type-impressions. Chrysippus the elaborator proposed *alloiosis,* "alteration," as the mode of impingement. If these are anything like wave disturbances in the air, a medium could support many at once.[15] Except for the huge increase in physiological and neurological specificity, the identical problem is fully alive in our cognitive and brain sciences: Just what is the identity element that brings the outside object reliably inside? Or leaving aside the prejudgment that there is some similarity, what is the criterion for the correctness of our apprehension?

The same holds true of the question *to whom* Appearance appears. It is the totally unsolved question of consciousness and self-consciousness. The Stoics do indeed grapple with this problem, for it is central to their ethical concerns and to the management of the passions in particular.

For the evaluation of appearances—the process we call perception and they call *aisthesis*—is not the end of it for us humans, as it is for animals, which merely perceive. Human beings are not only passively impinged upon, they also have, like god, an active element, *logos*:

> Of appearances some are rational (*logikai*), and some nonrational (*alogoi*); rational are those of rational animals, and nonrational, of animals that are nonrational. The rational appearances are thoughts (*noeseis*), the nonrational ones happen not to have a name.[16]

On the face of it, this sentence may not seem to say much, until the reader fetches up against the notion of a rational appearance, a thought-appearance. It turns out that for human beings perceptions *are* thoughts without ceasing to be bodily affections. This two-in-one character is made plausible by the observation that an appearance is expressible in utterance:

> Appearance takes the lead and then utterable thinking (*dianoia eklaletike*) is present, which expresses "what" has affected it through the appearance.[17]

Although the passage may seem to speak of a cause (an appearance) and an effect (the thought), this is evidently not what is meant. Perception *is* the present thought, which can then be expressed. The notion that a human appearance-affection is a thought will be crucial to the Stoic understanding of passion.

Here is how the Stoics think of Appearance-as-thought: In animals there is just the perception, a simple impression, but in humans it is more complex. Together with the appearance comes a movement they call "assent" (*synkatathesis*, literally "what is simultaneously set down"). Indeed it is said by some to be identical, by others all but identical, with the appearance; Cicero repeats that the Stoics say that "perception itself is assent" (*sensus ipsos adsensus esse*).[18] This *adsensus*—its English transcription "assent" is a little misleading—is the thought-aspect of a human appearance; it is not so much an agreement as a "taking in." To perceive is to have a thought. This actual identity of sensory affect and functioning thought to form the kind of perception characteristic of a rational, a conscious, being comes to full expression in Kant's *Critique of Pure Reason*. It is conveyed in the saying that "thoughts without content are empty, *intuitions without concepts are blind*" (my italics).[19] The rational structure of perception is neither for Kant nor for the Stoics a conscious activity; it is part of our proper, naturally exercised cognitive constitution. (Hence for both the Stoics and for Kant sense and thought are *actually* one, and distinct only *analytically*. It must be said, though, that Cicero here contradicts himself, for he says both that perception *is* assent and that assent is *voluntary*.[20] It will not be the last time that these slight but crucial slippages from identity to close succession in the cognitive process beset the Stoics. Be that as it may, they are the first to face these everlastingly central problems of representational cognition.

For Plato and Aristotle, the warrant for tellable truth came from the degree of being of the object. For the Stoics, there are no degrees of being (though there are, to be sure, degrees of value). Furthermore, truth-telling is entirely subjective, since all we have is our representation, the appearance, but not that which appears.[21] To know is to know what is within, what is re-presented.

What then is the criterion (*kriterion*) of truth by which to judge the assimilation of the inner representation to the outer object, when the latter is inaccessible? Here, for the first time in philosophical inquiry, such a criterion is needed, since truth is not imparted to us by the knowable being itself. This standard for "judgment" (*krisis*) is that the appearance should be clear and distinct (*trane* and *ektypon*, literally "piercing" and "deeply impressed"), which are the very criteria for certainty—the subjective assurance that now replaces the trust emanating from objective being—that will be adopted by Descartes. I might add that this set of Stoic criteria is not satisfactory for modern representationalists (among whom most cognitive and brain scientists are to be counted) because it is too subjective; what is currently preferred is a Darwinian operational reality check: The representation is correct insofar as it is conducive to the well-functioning or at least the survival of the individual.

An appearance that meets these criteria is said to be "graspable" or "grippable" (*kataleptike*). Cicero reports that Zeno himself contributed the figure of "grasping" to our cognitive vocabulary, very much in accord with Stoic materialism, and that he used the figure of a hand to illustrate Stoic knowledge. An outstretched hand stood for an appearance, a slight contraction of the fingers for assent, and a fist for the grasped appearance, the one accepted as veridical.[22] Grasping, *katalepsis,* thus *is* assent, conscious acceptance of the appearance as representing something real. Such belief is expressible by the uttered language referred to before, and what is so expressed, something meaning-like, is "a speakable [thing]" (*lekton*). The Stoics say that "a *lekton* is available (*hyparchein*) as something subsisting (*hyphistamenon*) in accordance with a rational appearance, a rational appearance being one according to which the thing that has been let appear is established in speech."[23] This weasly sentence testifies to that startling limit of Stoic materialism I spoke of above, for the word "subsisting" is used by the Stoics—much to the disgust of Galen the physician who thinks they are quibbling—as distinct from "being" (*to hyphistos* vs. *to on*).[24] A *lekton* is not a body and so it doesn't exist, yet it *subsists*; as the Germans say: *Es gibt es* ("We come across such items")—non-beings that are somehow to hand. I mention this Stoic addition to their inventory of things to come across not merely because Nonbeing is about the most interesting topic there is (except for Being), but because it is an example of the unintended and unacknowledged involvement with negativity that positivists tend to get caught in, an involvement that will have a bearing on the passions.

Have we, at this point, got an answer to the questions: To whom do the appearances appear? Who grasps them? To whom are they real or unreal? To whom does the representation present itself and its content? Is it to the speaker, the utterer of meanings—for meanings, properly hedged, are what *lekta* must be?

No, that is not the answer; nor will there be any other; bodies, inherently extended, simply do not have what it takes to "in-tend" something, to turn within themselves reflectively. Moreover, *lekta* in particular are no solution. They are not the thoughts of a *mind*; they are the contents of *speech*. Furthermore, they do not *convey* the being of the object of which they are said; they rather *correspond* to it in an unspecified way. They are truly nonexistent[25] and, as the Stoics say, our minds are not causally affected "by them" (*hyp' auton*), but only "with a view to them" (*ep' autois*)—an example of what Galen regarded as Stoic quibbling, we might well say. So human speech does not lead us to a receptive intellect *to* whom an appearance might present itself. Here, then, because of their physicalism, the Stoics might seem to have difficulties even beyond those of the idealistic modern representational philosophers. The Stoics, however, would reply that, instead of the passively receptive Aristotelian intellect we might seem to be demanding, they have their actively articulating Stoic reason, which is already functioning in all perception to turn it into self-perception. In other words, they might say that reflexivity, turning in on oneself, which is, it seems, the most articulable feature of consciousness, is already built into the coexistent identity—to coin a necessarily self-contradictory phrase—of *pneuma* and *logos*.

But now, leaving these perplexities, let me pass to another site of nonexistence that brings us ever closer to the passions, for it is also the place of error—and since passions will be mistakes, a theory of error is indispensable.

A "grasped appearance" (*phantasia kataleptike*) is a representation trusted to have a real object, called a *phantaston*, "a thing that can effect a *phantasia*," "such as white or cold, or anything that can move the soul." Note how far subjectivity has advanced. The object, the *phantaston*, is named by its causal relation to perception. But there is also a pseudo-object, so to speak, that produces a *phantasma* rather than *phantasia*, and it is called a *phantastikon*. These new words have meanings not far from their English versions—"phantasm" and "fantastic." A phantasm is a false appearance, an affection of the soul arising from nothing that can effect a "real" appearance. The *lekton* was merely a theoretical nonexistent, the phantasm is an experiential nonbeing: "Something capable of effecting an appearance (*phantaston*) underlies an appearance (*phantasia*); nothing underlies a fantastic presentation (*phantasma*)."[26] Chrysippus says of such a fantastic presentation that it is "dragged in across a vacuum." To appreciate the denigration, recall that the Stoics believe in a continuous plenum of matter.

If anyone were to be tempted to think of Stoic *phantasia* as having some relation to the ordinary imagination, Chrysippus's description of the "fantastic presentation" should correct that. He is speaking of the visions of melancholics and madmen, but I think he would include dreams and, with qualifications, deliberate fictions as well. These latter the ancient poets might credit to the divine Muses, the philosophers to meaningful imaginative production, and the moderns to the imagination in its "creative" function. For Chrysippus such imaginary presentations are pulled in from nothingness—*mere* phantasms. In any case, we see that falsity arises in perception when the object is not a real thing or fact in the physical world, but a vain self-elicitation of the representational function. This understanding will play a great—if perhaps implicit—role in the management of the passions.

We are now ready to see what the terms used above in defining passion mean. Passions occur, to begin with, in the passive aspect of the whole human being, the body; that is why they are rightly called passions. They are inherently a kind of turbulence, anything from hiccup to upheaval; the Greek word is *ptoia*. It has a long history among the passions. Sappho says: "My heart in my breast beats wildly when I look at you," and her word for "trembles, beats wildly, palpitates" is *eptoaise*.[27] The verb, *ptoein,* means "to flutter with excitement, to be agitated," with an underlying sense of fright. Plato, too, uses the word for the arational part of the soul when it is "flustered."[28]

This is, then, the particular emotive impulse the Stoics mean by *ptoia.* The word for any impulse in general, *horme,* is native to their physics-bound world, for there, as in the early modern physics, it signifies a beginning of movement, an initial impulse felt as a "start," as in being startled. Every passion is such a physical "start"; every start is—only in a human being—a *ptoia,* a passion.

The passion-impulse, or upset, is called forth by an appearance, a *phantasia.* For:

Things with soul move by themselves when an appearance comes about in them and calls forth an impulse. And again, in some animals, when appearances come about, and call forth an impulse, their perceptual nature (*physis phantastike*) moves an impulse in an orderly fashion, as, when in a spider there occurs an appearance of web-spinning and an impulse toward spinning follows—and nothing else but its perceptual nature is being obeyed by the animal. . . . rational animal, however, has reason (*logos*) in addition in its perceptual nature, which judges (*krinonta*) appearances, and rejects in its appraisal (*apodokimazonta*) some and accepts others so that the animal is led in accordance with them.

The appraising judgment concerns "noble" and "shameful," and these are the "starting-impulses" (*aphormai*) which it is in the nature of reason to look to (*theoresantas*) and to follow; we choose the noble and avoid the shameful.[29]

From this summary passage by Origen, a Christian Bible commentator of the third century c.e., we learn first what is only reasonable—and traditional—that in ensouled beings which are capable of self-motion, that is, in animals, impulses to such motion are preceded by perceptions, in the Stoic case, representations. Second, we learn that in mere animals such impulses follow the perception without reflection, obedient to "instinct," as we say. Third, in human beings, reason interposes between the perception and the action—"action" being rationally endorsed motion, after a "critical" review of the perception—and the judgment has to do with noble and base, the preservation of the human being's moral nature according to a built-in "theorizing" by reason.

Now back to Arius's definition. Passion-impulses are "excessive," which means that they are disturbances of the body beyond what the perceptual nature of the human being is "at home with." *Oikeiosis* means "making oneself at home with" ("home," *oikos*), "making one's own," appropriation. It is an important Stoic notion for explaining any animal's self-pursuit, one which gives its efforts a naturally reflexive nature—maintaining *itself*, following and expressing its *own* nature, the *syneidesis* mentioned above.

A passion-impulse is beyond what a being's nature requires or can morally support. And thus it is disobedient to reason. "Disobedient to choosing (or approving) reason" is what only a rational being can be. Only a rational soul, the Stoics think, can be *un*reasonable. Here they differ most sharply from Plato, who in various dialogues maintains that it takes a non-rational part of the soul to be unreasonable, though it might be amenable to reason. This difference is really the crux of all thinking and perplexity about the passions, ancient or modern: *Is our psychic constitution composite in that there is a passionate opposed to a rational part of the soul, or are we psychically unitary, so that we are either all emotion or all reason, or a mere potentiality that is activated in either mode?* The Stoics, this is the moment to say, will opt—shakily—for the next-to-last possibility, the all-rational one: The passions are irrationally, that is, erroneously, rational—and so amenable to talk therapy. For, once again, ir-rationality, a—deplorable—lapse in rationality, is not a-rationality, a—natural—lack of rationality.

Thus every passion, whatever else it may be, is a judgment, a belief, an opinion (*doxa*), and, moreover, a "*weak* supposition." Not only will the hypothesis of the opinion (*hypolepsis*) be false, it is flabby, forceless (*asthenes*) in the face of the disturbance effected by a still fresh passion as it moves an "irrational contraction and elation" (*systole, eparsis*) in the soul-*pneuma*. The weakness is in the soul-*pneuma*'s toning; the tension is too relaxed; this flaccidity *is* the weak opinion.

Here begins the labor of figuring out what the Stoics actually mean. And this is the question: Is the passion *ultimately* really a rational (if wrong) thought, opinion, supposition, or is there a tiny bit of something else, perhaps a wrinkle in time that precedes the reasoning? To me the purest Stoics, who take passion as mistaken reason *sans phrase,* are most intriguing. Chrysippus, be sure, distinguishes Zeno's "disobedience" to right reason as well as his own "perversion" (*diastrophe*) from a mere mistake or error. Certainly the "disobedience"—the term is attributed to Zeno by Chrysippus—is no mere slip, it is a serious rational misjudgment, apparently a willful one, where "willful" and "perverted" cannot mean belonging to a command-giving faculty other than reason itself. For willing is nothing but rational choosing, at least before Augustine brought a new notion of free but recalcitrant willfulness into the world.[30] Somehow, in some mode, passion is for these Stoics a serious mis-appraisal carried out by reason, an egregious error—serious as an error, flabby in its reason-toning. The question is whether they can make that stick in the face of human experience. I doubt it. But that much the more valuable for thinking out my and most people's disinclination to let human affect be a mere misguided upset to be damped by reason, is a sophisticated theory of the opposing side, such as the Stoics have worked out. For my sort of derivative philosophizing should indeed consist of getting a clear view of the contrasting possibilities and developing a warm—though correctable—adherence to one of them for carrying on my life.

First, we must keep recalling that all these passion-events are bodily occurrences, that the reason-*pneuma* and the body-*pneuma* are coextensive. Are they, like nature and god, one or finally two? Well, they are at least distinguishable in their functional part; the basic principles of the Passive and the Active are respectively operative here.[31] That is, as I surmised, the reason why there are "passions," affects, to begin with; it is the body-*pneuma* that is upset by an excessive start. On the other hand, it is appearance, a psychic factor, that starts the start. As we have seen, an appearance can be wrong: when it is brought about by no real body, when it is an effect caused by its own nothing, a self-illusion. This happens, recall, when *phantasia* has turned into *phantasma* and the appearing object is "fantastic."

Over and over the Stoics do insist that passions are mistaken beliefs. The condition for this possibility has certainly been laid in just that notion of *phantasma*. The way the ethical Stoicists speak of the therapeutic management of the passions relies strongly on this nothingness of the object. To be sure, they argue chiefly that, object aside, the turbulence of passion is bad in itself[32] and that virtue is "im-passivity" (*a-patheia*).[33] But this argument works because of the "indifference" of all imagined good and evil objects except subjective virtue and vice. When something other, something in itself indifferent, appears as good or bad and is so judged, it is surely—albeit I have not found this connection made explicitly—because there is a *phantasma* at work, not always a mad one, but perhaps a more mildly misleading one.

So the first cognitive source of error is at hand in the aberrations of the *phantasia*. Now where is the critical opinion (*krisis*) actually located? Where does the *logos hairetos,* the appraising and approving reason—*hairetos* is a moral word for an ethical choice—actually function? At the command-center, the *hegemonikon*. Here the *kriterion* is applied and the approving or rejecting judgment, the *krisis,* is made and transmitted via the *logos-pneuma* through the body to start or restrain its members from action-motion. But even before that, the *krisis* acts to permit or to damp the "contractions and raisings" (*systolai* and *eparseis*) of the blood-*pneuma*. (Note that the Stoic vocabulary is still in use for measurements of blood-pressure.)

Thus passion is *entirely voluntary.* It is the consequence of our decision, the decision that it is right and appropriate to reality to sustain this disturbance. Therefore, it is eminently controllable by our appraisal of its acceptableness. However, it never *is* acceptable or appropriate—except, Cicero will point out, in the curiously self-referential case when people are deeply grieved by their own vice, that is, by their "weak suppositions," their own inability to control their passions, by the flabbiness of their rational constitution, of their control-*pneuma*. Cicero says that in this case you must fall back on the ultimate Stoic position—that the passions are bad in themselves, even if reality-based.[34]

As is so characteristic of Stoic thinking, there are some tiny, marginal incongruities here, which allow supposedly congruent notions to be pried apart for questioning. The material *hegemonikon* as control-center sited in the *pneuma* is supposedly identical with the mind. But is the Stoic mind after all—somehow—separable from its transmitting *pneuma* and its passive body? "Appearance" is another case. Is a representation, especially the phantastic one, after all—somehow—distinguishable into a presenting *phantasia* and its causative material substrate? But the possible cleft of most interest to the passions is this: Is there really no slip between the cup and the lip—is passion *altogether* judging thought, or is there a disjunction, however tiny, between affect and thought?

Stoics are implicitly ambivalent and explicitly in mild self-contradiction with each other or themselves, it seems. Putting the last question physically, it's not quite clear whether the upset in the body and the *logos-pneuma*'s rational misjudgment are quite congruent and thus as indistinguishably identical as two superimposed triangles would be, or whether there isn't a slight sequence—first the upset, then the judgment. Some Stoics do in fact admit a pre-passion (*pro-patheia*); Cicero calls it a "mini-contraction," a *contractiuncula*,[35] a little bite that is natural and that even a Stoic sage cannot eliminate. They also distinguish a "well-passion" (*eu-patheia*), a feeling of one's own sound, stably rational equilibrium.

Posidonius of Rhodes, Cicero's teacher, seems, as was mentioned, to have picked up on these difficulties to the point of revisionism. Since we know of his work mostly from Galen's report in his *Precepts of Hippocrates and Plato,* and Galen was advocating a contrary Platonic psychology for the purpose of psychotherapy, it is not clear that the account we have is fair.[36] If it is, it represents a—probably somewhat inadvertent—overturning of Stoicism's main ethical tenet. For Posidonius, at least as Galen sees it, wondered how an "excessive" impulse, being itself a rational movement (since its medium is congruent or identical with the *logos-pneuma*), could exceed reasonable judgment. He thinks that there must be some alternative "psychic energy" involved, some "passionate movements" (*pathetikai kineseis*) that derive from the spirited and desirous parts of Plato's psychology. Thus he corrects the counterintuitive Stoic sense that passions are entirely voluntary: Most people feel that feelings are *ultimately* passions, something that comes over us. Posidonius does evidently think stoically in supposing that in maturity we can disengage ourselves from these affections by rationality. What he blunts is the beautiful radicality of the claim that passions *are* judgments, approving appraisals—affectlessly logical affirmations.

3. Cicero's Rowing and Sailing

The work known as the *Tusculan Disputations* is entitled in one Latin version *Tusculanarum Quaestionum libri quinque,* "Five Books of Tusculanian Questions"—this question-format is a forerunner of the disputation-format used by Thomas for a record of a live debate, when the question-suggestion from the floor casts doubt on the master's thesis and is therefore answered in the negative. Cicero had elicited such questions—really theses inviting rejection—from one of the unnamed friends with whom he is strolling through the grounds of his villa in Tusculum, and he now gives an account of the long ensuing conversation. In Book I (Day 1) the topic has been the fear of death, in Book II (Day 2) whether pain is an evil, and in

Book V (Day 5) it will be the relation of virtue to happiness. Books III and IV are about the passions, and the thesis to be disputed on Day 3 is, "It seems to me that the wise person is subject to distress."[1] The thesis proposed for Book IV (Day 4) is, "I do not think it is possible for the wise person to be free of every passion." These, then, are the assertions to be refuted, the first a particular case of the second.

In both books, Cicero first "rows" for a while "with the oars of dialectic" to get out of the harbor and then "bends on the sails" of rhetoric. That is, first he does a bit of philosophy and philology, and then he uses oratory and poetry to amplify and exhort.

The first question concerns distress or dis-ease (*aegritudo*), which is, together with desire, a harder affliction to bear than any sickness of the body. Nonetheless, Cicero does not translate Greek *pathos* as *morbus*, "sickness." Instead he uses *perturbatio animi*, "disturbance of mind." "Emotion," close as it is to "commotion," is a good but somewhat anachronistic rendering; I will stick with "passion," for Cicero immediately reverts to the language of pathology. The passions are "insane" in the sense that *sanitas*, "health," belongs to the mind that is serene and in agreement with itself.

"Distress" itself, *aegritudo*, though a particular passion—that of grief, sorrow, anguish—is based on the word for being physically ill, *aeger*.[2] Why is *it* the topic-passion here? Because Cicero is writing for his own relief. In the beginning of 45 B.C.E. he lost his only daughter, Tullia; he went into retreat—a withdrawal from civic obligations that laid him open to the charge of unstoic grieving.[3] He was distracting himself by enormously prolific production, of which the *Tusculan Disputations*, written in the summer of that year, were only a part. *Aegritudo* is what he is fighting in himself.

The "rowing" part of the book consists, besides the Latin usage sections, of syllogistic deductions in the manner of the Stoic school, proving in a variety of ways that the wise person is not subject to distress. The futile argumentative exercises, which might at best win assent without producing conviction, don't even have the saving grace of validity or clarity. For example, the sixth syllogism goes as follows:

1. Anyone who feels pity will feel envy [on the unlikely grounds that anyone pained at another's misfortune will also be pained by his good fortune].
2. The wise person feels no envy [surreptitious assumption].
3. Therefore he feels no pity [since by 1. nobody feels pity without envy].
4. But if a wise person were subject to distress he *would* feel pity too [surreptitious assumption].

5. But he doesn't [by 3.].

6. Therefore the wise man is not subject to distress [by *modus tollens*].

Cicero must have been very distracted. So he switches to rhetoric: "For distress is a terrible, sad, hateful thing, something we should avoid by every effort we can—oars and sails together, as the saying goes."[4] It sounds sadly like whistling in the dark.

Book III ends with a review of other theories of passion, particularly the Epicurean, which is presented here in Section 7, and with a review of the remedies for grief, which are outlined in Section 6.

The thesis, that even a wise man is subject to grief, can scarcely be said to have been disproved, but it doesn't matter. For it will now be shown that, contrary to the thesis offered for this Day 4, a wise man can be free of *every* passion.

4. The Foursquare Taxonomy of the Passions

In the preface to Book IV, Cicero declares his eclecticism, but he will actually defend the Stoic line. Here he "rows" again, for the Old Stoics were interested in "thorny bits," like classification and definitions, while being brief in their tranquilizing rhetoric. The theoretical contribution of the Tusculan books lies in accessibly recording this taxonomy, this classification, of the passions, which is usually the most laborious and most revealing aspect of a passion-theory—laborious because it requires a lucid survey of identified passions, revealing because it implies a micro-psychology, a closer look at the soul.

Hence Cicero starts with the soul, and, surely inadvertently—acuteness is not his special gift—makes nonsense of the Stoic position. For, perhaps under his teacher Posidonius's influence, he divides the human soul according to the old Pythagorean-Platonic mode into a rational and an irrational part. The basic Stoic position, sometimes modified but never quite abandoned, is, of course, precisely that the soul is partless and that passions are beliefs, opinions, and judgments, as he himself says.[1] Indeed the soul doesn't even turn up either in Cicero's term for, or in Zeno's definition of, the passions; the word there is not *anima*, "soul," but *animus*, "mind," the governing principle of the human being.

For the definition and classification he goes back to Zeno, the founder of the Old Stoa. A passion is "a movement of mind contrary to nature and turned away from right reason." Others say "a too-vehement impulse" (*horme* in Greek, *adpetitus* in Latin, our "appetite"), that is, one that deviates too far from "the consistency of nature"; of consistency more in a moment. Then comes a four-square tabulation, firm and long-lasting in the taxonony of emotions. It arises from the combination of two values, goods and evils, and two times, present and future. It yields a grid of the genus-passions within which all others are specified:

	Good	Bad
Present	Joy: elation	Distress: contraction
Future	Lust: hunger	Fear: avoidance

Figure IV-A

These are the passions that are inconsistent with nature, that is, with rationality. They are not volitions, for willing as controlled expectation is a function of reason—the way of the Stoic sage. But the non-sage, as soon as he receives an impression of something as good to have, will allow himself to feel an unbridled "hungering" for it (Greek *orexis*), that is, lust (Latin *libido*). If he already has it and allows himself an unreasonable "elation," a swelling of mind, that is joy (Latin *laetitia*; this is the word that Spinoza will use for his root passion, attending, however, more to Christian than Stoic usage); but if a bad thing is seen as in the offing, there will be an effeminate avoidance reaction that is fear; and when the thing is present the avoidance or drawing-in is irrational, a sort of contraction of the mind, called distress (*aegritudo*). This is clearly Cicero's own case, which he is seeking to cure. "Distress," or my own term "dis-ease," are weak words for Cicero's affliction. *Aegritudo* means debilitating psycho-physical sickness. *Aeger* has a root-meaning of "vibration"; "distress" here means a restless, listless, throbbing curling up upon oneself—the dystonia of the soul-*pneuma*.

Besides the genus-passions there are the genus-consistencies. "Consistency" (*constantia*), Cicero's word for Greek *homologia*, "agreement," is the condition of mind in which it is in accord with reason and nature, and thus self-consistent. The earlier Stoics allowed, as was said, for a rational version of each genus-passion, called *eupatheia*, literally, "well-passion." These wise counterparts are:

	Good	Bad
Present	Delight	
Future	Volition	Caution

Figure IV-B

The grid now displays clearly Cicero's previously infirm answer to the question of Book III, whether a wise man feels distress. There is no "well-passion" consistent with reason in the box corresponding to distress among the ill affects.

One reason that there is no rational distress or dis-ease has to do with its time; it would be a particularly un-Stoic response precisely because it was to a *present* bad. For, as Cicero reports, the Stoics privilege the present; that is when our life is fact, is real. It is therefore in the present that the sage nullifies bad affects. (It seems to me that, in general, materialists will be presentists, for while matter may be *always,* we touch it, in perception, only *now.*)

Nonetheless, for future good, that is, for things we hope for, we can exercise rational planning, what the Greeks call *boulesis* and Cicero calls "volition." For future bad we have rational fear or caution. For present good there is delight (*gaudium*), reasonably controlled elation. But for present bad, which distresses the unwise, there is, as I have said, no counterpart in reason, "For present bad the wise man has no affective response" (*adfectio nulla*), but the stupid respond with distress.[2] I cite the Latin because it gives something away, namely, that we are, after all, talking of affects,. The reason that there is no wise response to present bad is not just that it is no longer preventable or that it isn't worth the commotion of mind, the *perturbatio animi* that is Cicero's name for passion-sickness. Although a sage does not in any case allow himself to suffer what by the Stoic definition is a "too vigorous impulse," there is something more fundamental to prevent him from feeling distress. He recognizes no genuine present bad except vitiated reason, and that is just what no sage is affected by.

The four "effects" of the genus-passions (Fig. IV-A) are, it seems, indeed affects: too vehement for wisdom. The "hungering" of lust is too unbridled a longing, since it is not controlled willing. The "avoidance" of fear is too craven a deflection, since it is not consistent with the frightening object. The "elation," the uplift, of joy is an excessive outpouring, since it is not sobered down by a realistic judgment of the causing good. And above all, the "contraction," the reduction of life in distress, is an excessive shrinking from the world, since it is induced by grief uncontrolled by reason. This last, a "very torture chamber" where the mind itself is destroyed,[3] was Cicero's own condition while he wrote the *Tusculan Disputations.* It was a pathology from which, as I said, he was on his own and with his friends' urging trying to extract himself.

It is this personal circumstance that gives the work its own slightly repellent pathos—repellent by its rhetorical drone, poignant in its philosophical ineffectiveness: "Reading and writing do not comfort me, but they do distract me," he wrote to his friend Atticus.[4]

5. The Passions Explained: Perturbations of Mind

The "effects" of the passions, hungering, avoidance, elation, and contraction, are not meant to be their consequences, but further descriptions of them in terms that are recognizably physical and not meant figuratively. The Stoic passions are, after all, as physical as is the mind itself. Therefore all these somatic motions can occur also in a less excessive, better reasoned way, and that, in turn, explains the possibility of Stoic "well-passions" (Fig. IV-B), the *eupatheiai*, the "consistencies."

For on the face of it, if passion is *ipso facto* sick, no passion should be well. Yet as we have seen, there are in Cicero's report three classes of good passions, passions sobered by rational judgment. These are damped motions in the body. In fact they are reduced to a little "bite," a twinge, an entirely natural small perturbation. Cicero does not address—probably did not worry about—what these twinge-affects, comparable to the pre-emotions of more detailed Stoic theory, are. Are they, and are all mentions of affects, evidence that there *are* passions, pre-passions (*propatheiai*) that *precede* and are thus separable from rational judgment? This is one of those modest-seeming problems that indicate a hairline fault in a theory which could break it apart; I have discussed it in Section 2.[1] But I might observe here that if these good passions are indeed accompanied by no affect, if they are, without remainder, only right reason, then although I cannot imagine what they "feel like" (for want of a better phrase), yet I do know of an instantiation: The angels in Thomas's *Summa Theologia* are said to feel no passion and yet to do deeds of compassion, to feel no love or desire and yet to *feel* a love at once natural and purely intellectual.[2] Thomas cites Augustine, who adds that God himself is said in Scripture to be angry yet to feel no perturbation. Augustine actually refers to the good passions of the Stoic sage here, though he clearly thinks that they must be affects, for that is "a part of the infirmity of this life."[3]

What the Stoic sage in the most theoretically pure sense, in whom the passions are identical with thoughts, has in common with the denizens of heaven is the constitution of his soul. Though he is matter and they are spirit, neither have any passionate element but are all intellect; Thomas devotes some pages to this fact. But perhaps this analogy is not best designed to bring the Stoic sage's frame of mind, his passionless passions, closer to us.

Passions, Cicero reports repeatedly, come about "by judgments and opinions"; in fact they *are* appraisals.[4] Of what? Of good and bad. That is to say, they are not cognitive judgments but evaluative ones. They don't answer the question "What is it?" but "What good is it? What purpose does it serve?" For "by nature everyone pursues what he thinks is good and avoids the opposite."[5]

So then good and bad are a matter of opinion. Of course the same putative good or bad thing is involved in the present and the future-directed
passion, in what is had and what is hoped for. Although Cicero does not
argue the metaphysics, he vigorously preaches the teaching. All philosophical schools have the same cure for passion, he says, generalizing very inac-
curately, which is "to speak solely about the passion itself, saying nothing at
all about the status of the things which arouse the passions but addressing
themselves to getting rid of the passion itself."[6] No object is in itself good or
bad; every external thing is indifferent. What is unqualifiedly good is virtue,
"a consistent and harmonious affective state of mind" (*constans conveni-
ensque adfectio animi*), one that makes its possessors worthy of praise and
which is worthy of praise on its own account, even without considering its
utility."[7] Virtue can be called, in short, right reason, *recta ratio*—note the
not-quite-consistent language of affect and reason. Its opposite, vice, is "a
turbid and agitated motion of the mind."

So Cicero thus reports the Stoics as being quite radical subjectivists—not
relativists, but rather moral absolutists of the subjective mind. As such they
are forerunners of Kant, who will begin the main part of his first exposition of morality thus: "Nothing in the world—indeed nothing even beyond
the world—can possibly be conceived which could be called good without
qualification except a *good will.*" "Will" is here, as for the Stoics, reason in its
evaluative mode. There is even in Kantian morality an analogue to a "well-
passion": "the moral feeling," a non-passionate affect which follows on our
rational self-consistency in moral willing—the self-satisfaction of reason.[8]

Passions, then, "come about through judgments and opinions." But the
Stoics say more: Dis-ease, for example, is "an *unexhausted (recens)* opinion
that a bad thing is present in which one thinks it right to lower and contract
the mind."[9] I italicize "unexhausted," fresh, recent (Greek *prosphaton*), which
some Stoics, Posidonius in particular, inject into the definition because of a
certain trouble they have with time.[10] Time, they admit, tends to cure grief,
but how can mere temporal passage do anything to passion unless it is the
emotion of a passive psychic part capable of being damped by "exhaustion,"
rather than a rationally grounded, atemporal judgment of a commanding
mind? Our feelings of grief might wear out, but does our judgment of a loss
lessen with time? Is the freshness found in the recency of the objective event
or in the unexhaustedness of the physical affect? "Freshness" seems to be yet
another admission of a non-rational element in the passions, a modification of the Stoic position that passes unnoticed by Cicero; the same happens
to the Neostoics. In the wearing-down of feelings through temporal passage may lie the downfall of the Stoic position, though one might save it by
adopting the complementary adjustment: that our judgment, erroneously
upset when a loss is recent, rights itself with reflection. And that is what
Cicero overlooks in accepting the word "recent" into the definition of the

passions. The pure Stoic position is or ought to be not that the passions—
as affects—are damped but that the judgments, which *are* the passions, are
corrected. For the "fount of all perturbations," they say, is *intemperance*—
one might translate "un-toning"—"a rebellion by the whole mind and by
right reason, which are so turned away from the prescription of reason that
the lusts of the mind can in no way be governed or contained."[11] I think
when Cicero says "lusts" (*appetitiones*), he means "impulses" (*adpetitus* =
appetitus), because that is the Stoic teaching. Impulses are the first motions
once something has made its appearance to us as a stimulus. In a sage, control of these originating impulses can go incredibly far, especially when reason has anticipated the bad event. Then even the death of our children can
be borne with equanimity. Cicero quotes an unknown poet in support: "I
knew when I fathered them, that they must die."[12]

Toward the end of his "rowing" over the shoals, the "reefs of precision"
of Stoic theory, Cicero specifies the genus-emotions. His most exhaustive
example is, again, distress or dis-ease. There are fourteen species enumerated, such as "pity," which is distress over someone else's unjust suffering—
a passion Stoics generally disapprove. The other definitions are similarly
sensibly pedestrian; thus grief is distress over the untimely death of someone dear. Then comes a section on individual character. Cicero chides the
Stoic preoccupation with the body : mind :: sickness : irrationality analogy as
unnecessary talk, not of the essence. But surely in a physicalist philosophy
it is of the essence that irrationality should be viewable as physical sickness.
He himself cites, once more, the chief mental infirmity of the mind, that is,
"a vigorous opining that some object is worthy of pursuit which is in fact
not worthy of pursuit, that opinion being deeply attached and rooted in the
mind." Such firmly infirm opinions will in turn make the body sick. Besides
these actual conditions there are also "proclivities," dispositions of character, just as—Cicero admits the analogy—a body can be prone to certain ill-
nesses. Besides infirmities and proclivities, which are fixed in the mind and
only separable in thought, there is "vitiation," a defect which is a real condition, that of being inconsistent and in "dissent" (*dissensio*) with oneself
over one's whole life.[13] (Recall that "assent" is a Stoic term of art, namely
the commitment to a proposition). So self-dissent is constitutional inconsistency. These various dispositions are not so much passions as tendencies
to be impassioned, to be thoughtless. Cicero soon ends, relieved—as are
we—to be through these *logika*, these rationalities.

He now turns, as in the third book, to the smooth sailing of rhetoric. As
in the previous book, the rhetorical section includes reviews of non-Stoic
doctrines, the defense of the Stoic position, and finally a consideration of
the cures for passion (Section 6).

The Epicureans, the real adversaries, will be treated in Section 7. Cicero,
oddly enough, mildly blames the other school he takes seriously, the Peripa-

tetics, for soothing the mind while avoiding the "thorny parts of classifying and defining."[14] These particular followers of Aristotle (named Peripatetics after the covered walk of Aristotle's school, the Lyceum) whom Cicero cites held a notion of moderate passions as natural and useful. The "limited" passions have only a remote relation to Aristotle's understanding of human excellence—and passion—as articulated through a mean between extremes. Cicero sensibly observes that for a Stoic—and he is here their defender— moderate passion cannot be good or useful or even achievable. How can a moderate amount of a bad thing be good or helpful or even maintain a temperate limit? The Stoics are right in their terms: How can anger, for example, or any other passion be useful when they are all a form of insanity—literally "non-health" or sickness? So, no pruning or clipping—what has its roots in error must be torn out and dragged away.[15]

Thus the fourth book concludes with the therapy of passion, and first of all with what we call in our technicized language "grief-management." It will become a preoccupation of the Late Stoa.

6. The Cure for Dis-ease: Therapeutic Philosophy

The passions are pathological, that is to say, they are accounted for as a sickness, the sickness of letting a *pathos* overcome the *logos*. But since it is an illness of thought, the therapy is in thinking well. So philosophy goes curative.

In the Late Stoa it becomes almost exclusively therapeutic, hortatory, consolatory. Three works are exemplary: Epictetus's *Handbook* (*Enchiridion*), a selection from his long work written during banishment from Rome, the *Discourses* (c. 115 C.E.), and Marcus Aurelius's *Meditations*, written in Greek while on campaign on the Danubian frontier (c. 170–189 C.E.) and actually called *Ta eis heauton*, "Things [said] To Himself" or "Self-Admonishment." The crippled scholar-slave and the chronically ill soldier-emperor clearly belong to one school. Both use the old Stoic philosophical vocabulary but in its "ethical" application, meaning here not so much for use toward becoming excellently virtuous, as for making oneself internally comfortable—and only incidentally kind.

Both works have much personal charm and human wisdom. They have been appreciatively read by the "modern pagans," by Montaigne, who quoted Epictetus over and over, and by Montesquieu, who thought that Marcus Aurelius's *Meditations* was "a masterpiece of antiquity," as well as by later writers of the Enlightenment.[1]

Yet they exist, to my taste, in an unfresh air, a still atmosphere of withdrawal and defense. Gone is the elation of fateful tragedy, gone the zest for deflating the mysteries of Being or even for spinning out the complexities of human cognition. Instead, the school that half a millennium before discovered cognitive subjectivity now preaches, along with exhortations to meticulous self-inspection, the most hard-edged objectivity for the sake of divesting things of their value:

> In everything which pleases the soul . . . or is loved, remember to add this to the description: what is the nature of each thing, beginning from the smallest. If you love an earthen vessel [a thing quite believable to a former archaeologist like myself], say it is an earthen vessel which you love; for when it has been broken, you will not be disturbed.[2]

That is Epictetus's lesson. Marcus Aurelius goes on to apply the lesson to a child. When you are kissing your child, say that it is a human being you are kissing, so that when it dies you "will not be disturbed." The same for a wife. Or

> [m]ake for yourself a definition or description of the thing . . . so as to see distinctly what kind of thing it is in its substance, its nudity . . . and tell yourself the proper name and the names of the things of which it has been compounded and into which it will be resolved.[3]

The emperor regards this procedure (which is a forerunner of Descartes' analytic method as well as to all sorts of reality therapy) as an aid to forming rational opinions. But you have to be in a lowered state of soul, its tensions damped and controlled, to let a naming reduce what seems to most of us so stark a reality to impotence. Consequently imagination, that faculty which expands the time and enhances the world in which we live, is repeatedly proscribed by Marcus Aurelius: "Wipe out your imagination"[4]—because we should live in the present rather than in the past or future. For in the present we see and analyze things just as they are, and in the present we can exercise what is in our power: our own acts of opinion, of impulse, of desire, as opposed to what is not: accidents of body, property, reputation, political power. It is the small tone of materialism shorn of its stark ontology. To be sure, the emperor appears to be an observer of nature and her stages, but it is the beauty of what is off and in decline: over-ripe olives close to enticing rottenness and old ladies—I like this—comely in their maturity.[5]

All the Late Stoa's worldly wisdom is distilled into Epictetus's frequent phrase "not up to us." Test every impression, he advises. "[I]f it has to do with the things that are not up to us, be ready to reply, 'It is nothing to me.'"[6] Is this the heroism of reason or the cowering of the spirit? Is the volitionally dispassionate life splendidly free or abjectly repressed? Perhaps both at once, but latter-day scholars implicitly underwrite the latter view by explaining Stoicism as a movement pervading a Roman imperial world too cosmopolitan and mobile for throwing out local roots while too internally dangerous and externally threatened for sanguine worldly enjoyment. Yet—was the smaller cosmos of the Greek city-state any less appalling? No, only more inspiriting.

How can one get hold of that elusive reciprocity between world and soul that makes a mood and a need spread through a large population and define a historical epoch? To do that would be to write a *history* of the passions (which this book is most designedly not). And who knows whether such a temporal tracing would show any necessary relation of consequence going either way between external circumstances and internal passional life?

Could these latter-day Stoic works console anyone seriously sad, with their main preaching that calls for a forcible application of the reason to the task of denuding—to use the emperor's term—the world of its power to hurt, that is to say, of its signifying resonances? Perhaps some.

This strenuous conflation of will and reason, this willful rationality— which will be resurrected in modern times—was evidently felt to be too intellectually demanding, too much tailored to an educated elite for universal appeal. The Stoics and Christians were natural antagonists: Stoic physicalism versus Christian spiritualism, Stoic presentism versus Christian futurity, Stoic divine immanence versus Christian transcendence, Stoic civic participation versus Christian withdrawal—in a word, reason versus faith. And though the Christians eventually borrowed much Stoic philosophy, including the appraisal of certain passions as evil, it was not with a view to cognition-based passionlessness. How could it be when a Passion, an act of salvific suffering, was at the center of their faith?

I have gone to the final phase of the huge Stoic episode to show that it is, in fact, the therapeutic aspect of Cicero's exposition that comes to fruition. He himself participates in what is now called the Middle Stoa, which means in this context that his "ethics," his precepts for the Stoic life, are still somewhat attached to a theory of the passions, as set out in the previous section. However, both Books III and IV of the *Tusculan Disputations* end, as I said, with practical passion-therapy. For such is the personal point of Cicero's writing—grief-management.

First Cicero considers "pre-meditation (*praemeditatio*) of future evils," that is to say, mental preparedness, a topic broached above. Anaxagoras, the early Greek physicist, is apparently its inventor: "I knew [beforehand that] my child was mortal." It helps because being suddenly overwhelmed aggravates the grief and makes us feel either guilty at not having prevented it, or depressed at its necessity.[7] Yet it is also a valuable consolation—though such rhetoric cannot diminish the sum of bad things—to suggest that these events are indeed a necessary part of life. Thus here, in the rhetorical approach, Cicero allows the "nature of the thing itself" to slip in, although, speaking strictly Stoically, not it but only our dealing with it should matter. For instance, he says, the sufferer might be asked: Why really should poverty be bad? Or leaving aside subtleties of argument, we can produce encouraging examples, as of Socrates despising wealth.

But what really counts is the eradication of the *belief* that it is "becoming" (Greek *prosekon*), that it is "appropriate" for us to be grieving.[8] It follows that grief is cast into the mode of the voluntary. It is a *decision* to be distressed, not a natural reaction. Hence it is our commitment to being distressed, not the event, that causes distress. When we understand its futility it dissipates.

The medicine of consolatory rhetoric must be timely—not administered too soon. For example, if you persuade the recently bereaved that only shameful conduct is really bad, you will have taken away his folly without removing the grief. Now Cicero goes eclectic, his "usual custom": Try all the schools' rhetoric. So much for Book III.

The reprise in Book IV sharpens the advice. The cure is in philosophy, and in Stoic philosophy it is to wash away the emotions altogether by a form of consolation that 1. teaches the indifference of all external, putatively good and bad things and 2. preaches the unnaturalness and non-necessity of all emotions. The first is for the educated, the second for the commonality, because the notion of the indifference of goods demands a deeper grounding than that of the unwholesomeness of passions. Hence one should, to be widely effective, say nothing about the object and everything about the passion, nothing about the thing longed for and everything about an excessive impulse.[9] In aid of this rhetorical task, Cicero quotes much poetry, most of it intended to drive home the shamefulness of passion, whether praised or blamed by the poet himself.

Is all this wise? Does it even work? Modern grief-managers do not agree that denigrating *every* object of loss—the sage's way—is wise. On the contrary, they bid us get in touch with our feelings; the total rationalization of emotion is not, it seems, among our many Stoic legacies. On the other hand, they do also think that after a while grief becomes a willful choice which even an ordinary person can work to reverse, and more generally that rational articulation, talking, is a cure for mental pathology. Modern psychology, especially psychoanalysis, does have some discernible roots in Stoicism.[10]

Yet it is a puzzle to me, not why there was a hunger for such consolations, but why it was sometimes found actually to be consolatory. What was in the Old Stoa a brilliantly crisp new notion—that emotions are thoughts and thus absolutely amenable to thought—is in the *Tusculan Disputations* a somewhat incantatory preachment whose ontological antecedents and cognitive consequences are curtailed in favor of a kind of self-manipulation that didn't work on its author and probably wouldn't work on me. I would put the trouble this way: Thinking things through—irradiating passion with reason—is *the* wise human response to upheavals of the soul; but think-

ing things away—nullifying the independent value of objects and eradi-
cating the stubborn affective residue of passions—takes an intellectually
potent dispassion that Cicero is not up to; perhaps no one is. But writing
books clearly helped, though probably for very un-Stoic reasons: Concentration on work *is* distraction from grief, and hope of recognition is always
a comfort.

7. The Close but Lesser Adversary: The Epicureans

It might seem invidious here to treat the Epicureans as Cicero does in the
third book of the *Tusculan Disputations,* as the mistaken, lesser adversaries of the Stoics.[1] For the followers of Epicurus, who taught in Athens from
306 to 270 B.C.E., were also a school and a movement. Yet one might argue
that while lower-case stoics pretty faithfully represented the ethical side of
the Stoa, lower-case epicureans were known to subvert the actual doctrine
of Epicurus into mere hedonism. Cicero however numbered among his
Roman friends serious Epicureans, who, as we shall see, were anything but
hedonists in our crude sense. Moreover, Epicureanism played a strong part
in the founding of modernity, especially in its most salient feature, natural
science. For example, Newton declares himself in effect an Epicurean, at
least in his understanding of the basic constitution of matter in the universe.
He says in his *Principia*:

> The extension, hardness, impenetrability, mobility and inertia of the whole
> result from the extension, hardness, impenetrability, mobility, and inertia of the
> parts; and hence we conclude the least particles of all bodies to be also extended,
> and hard, and impenetrable, and movable, and endowed with their proper iner-
> tia. And this is the foundation of all philosophy.[2]

This, the fitting basis of Newton's new dynamics, the science of inertially
moving bodies accelerated by the force of mutual attraction or impact, is a
version of ancient atomism, of which the Epicureans were the chief exponents, and a doctrine popular among the anti-Cartesian scientists of Europe
in the seventeenth century. (Indeed one might say that Newton's physics
of Epicurean atomism supersedes Descartes' physics of Stoic continuity.)
How atomism comes to be the basis of philosophical hedonism—how little
hard bodies falling into the abyss account for pleasure as the end of human
life—is to me the most interesting question about Epicureanism.

There are two more attractive aspects of this school. One is that Epicurus
was the first to admit women to his establishment, which makes something
about this second attractive fact a bit of a mystery. The Epicureans were
the only philosophical school I know of whose doctrines were presented,
very faithfully, in a long poem, Lucretius's *On the Nature of Things,* a phil-

osophical epic that is a true work of art, written in ravishing Latin. It is a work as beautiful as Epicurus's own Greek writing is crabbed. It is fiercely anti-religious for the sake of human comfort, and yet its climax is death and destruction.[3] It is dedicated to Venus, "the Pleasure (*voluptas*) of gods and men," and paints—here's the mystery—as ugly a picture of women's love as ever could be.[4] Cicero, incidentally, was Lucretius's contemporary, but, although he had evidently read the poem, he gives no sign of it in the Tusculan books.[5]

Nonetheless it makes a certain sense to think of the Epicureans as the opposing subsidiaries of the Stoics. First, Epicureanism can be conceived as secondary to Stoicism because it shares basic features with the latter and then deviates in a characteristic way. For example, both philosophies are thoroughly physicalist. The soul is material for both, but the *pneuma* of the Stoics is, as I said, a continuum, while the subtle soul-atoms of the Epicureans are, of course, discrete. Guided by their respective theories of knowledge, both schools advocate going slow in judgment. Both preach, ultimately, a kind of *a-patheia,* "passionlessness," but the Stoics conceive it as *eu-patheia,* "well-passion," while the Epicureans opt for *a-taraxia,* "non-disturbedness." (It is, incidentally, fascinating how much negative language is used by the positivist philosophies that give Nothing no share in Becoming.) A rebel angel will advocate this passionless pleasure as a way of living in hell! Nisroch advises:

> Sense of pleasure we may well
> Spare out of life perhaps, and not repine,
> But live content, which is the calmest life.[6]

Second, the Epicureans can be regarded as the lesser school because the two elements of the Epicurean world, atoms and void, are just too minimal to lead to a plausible explanation of psychic phenomena, certainly to one as sophisticated as the Stoic theory.

Curiously these ancient providers of the "primordial" matter of modern dynamics were not even much interested in a realistic physics. Lucretius, following Epicurus's sanction, gives indifferently multiple, even antic explanations of natural phenomena, for example of the phases of the moon. What he cares about is erasing religious spooks from his addressee's mind. Thus the atomic physics is to serve the consolatory purpose of showing that we are local configurations arising from random swerves in a downward rain of particles through a void and in time dissolve into these. It is to be a comfort to us that we live, a composite of void, of vacuum—of nothing, from which, according to the first law of nature, nothing comes—and of somethings which are ultimately discrete, infinite, indestructible, indivisible, impenetrable, and invisible; that the primordial motion underlying our existence is—

inexplicably, since the void is directionally indeterminate—into the abyss; that our free will is but a particular case of the cosmic random swerve; and that our death is a mere decomposition into the primordial constituents, so that any terror of *post mortem* punishment is misplaced.[7]

Lucretius's cosmology could not possibly be in the service of *joyous* pleasure. Indeed some ancients had trouble believing that Epicureans could have pleasure at all, even the joyless sort. Thus Plutarch wrote an essay called "That a Follower of Epicurus Cannot Live Pleasantly." The study of the "outer view and inner law" (*naturae species ratioque*) is, as I said, expected rather to dispel the "terror and gloom of the mind" induced by religion,[8] to produce a negative sort of peace of mind. Nor, as I have intimated, is this account of the natural world designed to give binding explanations of the "nature of things" that comprise it. For its faux-common sense keeps undermining itself in this way: On the one hand Lucretius is a radical sense-empiricist: "What must be held in greater credit than the senses? Or shall reason, sprung from a 'false' sense, have the power to speak against them when it is itself totally sprung from the senses?" On the other hand, Lucretius himself gives a long catalogue of sensory illusions such as the contraction to a vanishing point of a colonnade seen in perspective.[9] Here too the senses tell true; it is the reason that makes too hasty inferences and should wait for more aspects. But how can such a collection of sense-aspects ever converge on a conclusion about the real nature of the thing, the portico, when reason itself is derived from them? Which aspects are privileged, and by what fiat, to present the object as it really is—probably a parallelepipedal solid? There is, moreover, a deeper difficulty: The elements, the *primordia*, of the universe are all below visibility or any sense perception. Neither atoms nor void can be sensed *as such*; they are reached by analogical reasoning. There is no sense-report of the principles of nature.

These, then, are the two questions to be put to Epicurus himself. First, how is atomism a viable philosophical framework for human affects? Second, why and under what description is pleasure the principal affect and end of life?

The answer to the first question lies in the notion of a gradation in atomic size. There is a class of particles—Epicurus kept it "without denomination" (*akatonomaston*)—that is exceedingly fine and mobile. It is stretched all through the configuration of coarser atoms which is our body.[10] This is the sensing and passionate soul. Similar super-fine particle-figures stream off the surfaces of internally vibrating bodies. These hold their shape as they transit to and impinge on the sense organs and move the soul to sense objects and "feel" their qualities.[11]

Second, I will try to say why the Epicureans so highly value pleasure (in Greek *hedone*, hence "hedonism") and what they mean by it. In their writings they call pleasure and its contrary, pain, "passions" (*pathe*). Modern commentators have called them "feelings," so as to distinguish them as diffuse subjective affects from the more focused, object-directed passions or emotions.[12] If we recall that the Stoic passions are *failures of cognition,* it is illuminating to think, in contrast, of the Epicurean passions as actual *feelings.* This is indeed the ultimate difference between the two theories, since Epicurus agrees with the Stoics that the less indefinite affects, the passions, are dependent on the rational soul and therefore corrigible by truer opinions. What characterizes the Epicurean feelings is that they are, irreducibly, just that: feelings. But what those are, Epicurus can't say—hardly anyone can, to be sure—but the body/void frame is particularly not up to affectivity.

No more does he think it is necessary to answer the second question I have addressed to him, for he cannot even "conceive the good, apart from the pleasures of taste, apart from those of sex and those of sounds and those of form," and so the reply as reported by Cicero is that we need no reasons or discussions. As honey just *is* sweet, so is pleasure, and that sweetness just is our good. Note that *hedone* comes from *hedus,* sweet; all we need to do is point that out.[13] And that is that. Compare this Epicurean readiness to leave the master-feeling of their philosophy unelucidated with the complex considerations given pleasure by Plato and Aristotle. Recall that the hedonist's willingness to live with explanatory insufficiency was made dramatically incarnate in Plato's figure of Philebus.

Epicurus and his followers do, on the other hand, have a lot to say about the mode of pleasure that is the beginning and end of living blessedly and that is our "first and most congenial good." All pleasures are indeed good, but not each is, everything considered, choiceworthy. We must engage in a calculus, a balancing of pleasure and pain, which comes to this: pleasure means no pain in the body and no trouble in the soul—the unperturbed state (*ataraxia*) of the unperturbed wise man. The more mobile pleasures of the body are not proscribed, but the wise man prefers the mental ones, the pleasures of psychic "stand-still," (*katastematike*), for they offer relief from the pains of the mind, which are the worst. These pleasures of tranquillity are not idle; happiness comes from being in command of an accurate *physiologia,* a true account of the nature of things. For Epicurus the contemplation of regularly recurring motions, just insofar as they are soberly unamenable to high-flown deifications and simply ascribable to primordial movements, seems to have been the ultimate tranquilizer—an oddly soft use to make of this ultimately hard-edged natural philosophy.[14]

This use of physics may, however, help to answer the question Epicurus suppresses: why (restrained) hedonism and atomism (of all materialisms) found each other complementary. I don't believe anyone knows if Epicurus's physics in fact preceded his ethics or the reverse or neither. I surmise, then, that if the human soul is, to start with the physical framework, conceived as a temporary configuration of fine particles, the milder, integrity-preserving motions of that labile conjunction might be construed as pleasure and its violent disruptions as pain, and these would be interpretable as the respective conditions to be above all desired and avoided. Moreover, in a world devoid of divinity to inspire longing, personal pleasure might well be the ultimate end of life; in a philosophy eschewing dialectic activity and without a metaphysics of intellectual fulfillment, physical pleasure would indeed coincide with happiness; and for a being placed in an infinite void of falling or colliding atoms, inner tranquility, an undisturbed psycho-atomic shape, would be the most desirable and comforting of feelings. Or one may start with ethics, since the doctrine of pleasure is meant to be a doctrine of virtue as well. For "the virtues have grown together with living pleasantly and living pleasantly is inseparable from them."[15] It would make a pleasant exercise to figure out more exactly how a focus on feeling pleasure comes to imply atomic materialism. But I've already said more than I meant to about a serious but to me incomprehensible theory. For how can arrangements of hard massy particles give rise to human affect which is, whatever else it is, some form of internality or consciousness? Where in any configuration of hard massy atoms and the interstitial void could awareness come about? A current answer might be that consciousness is an "emergent" property, but that, I think, is a sophistication not contemplated by Epicurus.[16]

I should end this section by saying what Cicero has against Epicureans as a school in the *Tusculan Disputations,* much as he respects them individually. First of all, they think that "distress" and other passions are just facts of nature, which is precisely what the Stoics deny. Secondly, Cicero thinks their therapeutic advice to distract the mind from pain by directing it to the contemplation of pleasure is unsound, since it precipitates the sufferer, so to speak, from the frying pan into the fire. Pleasure is just another passion, and passion is the problem. To be sure, Epicurus has identified pleasure with virtue, but Cicero is suspicious: In this identity the predicate pleasure, ordinary sensory pleasure, seems to be more forceful than the subject virtue. Indeed, Epicurean virtue seems to me to be just the prudence that keeps pleasure within the bounds of harmlessness, a restraint that might, of course and as Cicero knows, produce a perfectly decent fellow-citizen. But now to return to the main preoccupation of this chapter, the far more consequential Stoics.

8. A List of Some Stoic Preformations of Modernity Relating to the Passions

Here, by way of an introductory transition to the later parts of this book, is a very bare listing of items in the Stoic (and Epicurean) legacy to our modernity.

Found in Descartes:

1. The rational soul is a unity. To be sure, for Descartes this soul is non-physical whereas for the Stoics rationality is physical; in that sense they are opposites. But Descartes' insistence on the oneness of the soul, accompanied with the claim that it is "joined to the whole body" by means of the "animal spirits," bears the marks of the Stoic *hegemonikon* and *pneuma*. Moreover, as do the Stoics, Descartes transfers the traditional animating functions of the soul to the body, though he does it to keep the soul itself purely rational.

2. Two chief Cartesian notions are "innate ideas" and the truth-criteria of "clarity and distinctness." "Inborn" ideas are foreshadowed by the Stoic "preconceptions" and "common notions," which are not congenital ideas, to be sure, but something close—modes of conceiving and concepts developed from aboriginal mental predispositions. The Stoics initiate the characterization of reality-related presentations as "clear" and "distinct," *traneis* and *ektypoi.*

3. Passions are "emotions," commotions of the soul, for Descartes as they are "perturbations of the mind" for the Stoics. The categories of doing, *poioun,* and suffering, *paschon,* are basic for the Stoics, and Descartes also introduces his work on the passions with them.

4. Animals are automata. Descartes, like the Stoics, insists that animals do not share in the kind of cognition necessary for being, albeit mistakenly, passionate.

Found in Spinoza:

1. God and nature are one, a self-structuring whole. That is both Stoic cosmology and Spinozan theology. So also is the notion that human beings are part of this nature-cosmos and therefore partake of its divinity.

2. The natural world is completely determined by its pervading order. Both Stoics and Spinoza enunciate a determinism combined with a—somewhat opaque—requirement for human choice.

3. There is no evil when the whole is considered *sub specie aeternitatis.* For the world is God, and all good; evil is in human intention or perspective; "under the aspect of eternity" it vanishes. Spinoza goes further: There is not even negativity.

4. There is an impulse of self-preservation, *horme* for the Stoics and *conatus* for Spinoza, that is the initial and basic motive moment for living things.

5. Pity, an emotion usually praised as humane, is actually bad. Both Stoics and Spinoza believe this and for broadly similar reasons: It is an infirmity that relies on passion to do what ought to be done by reason.

6. There is in the Epicurean interest in physics something *remarkably* like the blessedness Spinoza finds in the intellectual love of a God who is nature, a love that is identical with the theoretical study of physics. Recall that Epicurus says that the aim of physical account-giving (*physiologia*) is exactitude about the cause of what is most important and that "blessedness depends on such knowledge [as the recurrent motions of atoms] and on the theoretical nature of the heavenly bodies. . . ."[1]

In general:

1. A knowledge of knowledge, what we call epistemology, is possible and necessary. This is what Socrates disputes strenuously in the dialogue *Charmides*. It is a Stoic discovery that will dominate early modern philosophy.

2. Thus philosophy must consist largely of what is now called "philosophy of mind," the study of our cognitive constitution.

3. That entails a new focus on the sort of self-knowledge which turns the human being into a Self, a Subject, an interiority, that reshapes rather than merely receives the world. The locus of truth is now no longer in the *being of objects,* which are directly present to a receptive intellect, but in the *certainty of the subject,* as it reflects on its own conceptual activity. Therefore something quite new, a criterion (*kriterion*) for judging the correspondence of the mental representation to the external objects is needed. In Descartes it is clarity and distinctness that makes idea-presentations credible; later other criteria, perhaps linguistic ones, will be proposed. Consequently ontology, the account of the Being of things external to the soul, fades as truth becomes indirect, being channeled through a theory of knowledge. All these Stoic ideas turn up in, even dominate, modern philosophy, and they become the increasing subject of critique, culminating in postmodernist assaults on the chief cognitive innovation of the Stoics.

4. That innovation is "representationalism," the notion that the mind receives an image—not necessarily an analogue image—of the object, a representation it interprets or, as we say, "processes" by means of its innate rules and functions. Aristotle accepts, to be sure, psychic representation in the imagination and memory, but knowledge itself is not representational. The intellect "takes in" the form of things; it does not present them to itself; it *becomes* them. The Stoic faculty of perception, on the other hand, is something quite new. The *phantasia* is a *cognitive* imagination. In early Stoic accounts it in fact receives "impressions," in analogy to seal impressions. In Hume's epistemology "impression" will be a central term and acceptable to him because of its analogue connotations, that is, its re-presentational and imaginal qualities. For Kant, representation will be the genus-name of all mental presentation (Latin *repraesentatia,* German *Vorstellung*), that is, for

all modifications of the soul.[2] But nowadays, as, to speak broadly, linguistic metaphors replace visual ones, representationalism has come under strong criticism[3] and has receded in philosophy, just as it is in full swing in cognitive science.

5. As a by-product of the Stoic attention to meanings linguistically expressed, which they call "speakables" or "things spoken" (*lekta*), there arises the idea that while physical objects exist, some items, these very meanings, are not present as *existing* in spatio-temporal ways. Yet they are in some way there, namely as *subsisting* (*hyphistamenon*).[4] This theory of the subsistence of ideal items like meanings was a Stoic legacy revived by Alexius Meinong who, at the turn of the twentieth century, thought about the question "What is there and in what way?"[5]

6. Symptomatic of the Stoic shift from Being to *logos* is their achievement of a new logic, one in which the relations of whole propositions to each other is worked out, as distinct from Aristotle's logic in which terms denoting individual and universal beings were connected. Here the Stoics anticipated the modern preoccupation of symbolic logic—a natural Stoic interest because Stoic knowing requires continual judging through inferential linkages.

7. The mind, the rational "command-post," is thus no longer describable as a contemplative receptivity but is rather a trainable, skillful judge of the *phantasiai,* the appearance-perceptions formed by *phantasia,* and an operator connecting propositions about them. This functional mind with its predispositions, a mind that *operates* over its contents—as opposed to a receptive intellect that *becomes* its objects—is, however, at birth a blank slate, a *tabula rasa,* which is filled by perceptual experience: "The Stoics say that when a man is born the command-center part of his soul is just like a paper serviceable for drawn copies."[6] No separate account of the thinking operation need then be given. In Locke's philosophy you will find mind described as a "white paper" to be painted on by "EXPERIENCE" (his caps), but no separate account given of the operations (as distinct from the ideas) of the mind; and there is something more—a hint that the mind might be physical.[7]

8. Influenced by the medical research of their day, the Stoics are throughgoing physicalists; the mind is bodily, including the seat of reason, that is, the *hegemonikon* and the whole control system, the *pneuma.* Contemporary neuroscientists tend to insist on some sort of a mind-brain identity, and to assign to the nervous system a function not unsimilar to that of the *pneuma.*

9. It follows that the Stoics were thorough-going empiricists, since they denied ideal being of the sort that can be reached by thought alone.

By "empiricism" (from *empeiria*, experience), I mean here the notion that knowledge ultimately requires a sort of stacking of similar sense-impression such as of "something white" in memory. "And when many memories formed alike have come about, then we say that [someone] has experience."[8] And that is just what Locke and Hume, the so-called British empiricists, think, though, for that matter, they all get it from Aristotle, albeit with this great difference: For Aristotle experience yields the universal (*to katholon*),[9] which is the *prelude* to knowledge. The Stoics, however, as the aboriginal "nominalists"—people who think that universals, be they ideal or experiential, are only *nomina*, "names"—have, like their modern heritors, no truck with universals. Experience arises as an accumulation of impressions, not as a unifying idea.

10. The sum and consequence of all the foregoing, the result that is possibly the defining feature of modernity, is the close alliance, up to identity, of willfulness with rationality and of thinking with artful manipulating. This willed mastery of reason was meant by Stoics to be exercised in self-control and is used by the moderns in the control of nature. The case might be put this way: The most read of the Late Stoics, Epictetus, preached confining our desire to what is within our control—inner nature. It is a small step to the conclusion: Widen control; learn to control external nature as well.

11. And the condition and consequence of said willfulness is a thoroughgoing subjectivity. Subjectivity is neither solipsism, the idea that "I myself alone" (*solus ipse*) am the world, nor relativism, the idea that what the world is, it is in relation to me. It is, rather, the notion that the world only matters as I interpret or value it. Modernity is shot through with subjectivity—a condition that must be as old as humanity but which it took the Stoics to make into a full-fledged philosophy. In this book the Romantics will be the chief expositors of subjectivism as it plays out in emotion (Ch. IX).

9. The Neostoics of Our Day

Early modern thinkers clearly mined reports of Stoicism, then took off on novel ventures. They absorbed elements of the epistemology, particularly the representationalism, as well as aspects of the ethics, namely the control by reason of the human condition. As far as theories of the passions were concerned, they went off on their own ingenious constructs, which were closely tied to their characteristic philosophical frameworks.

In the welter of emotion-theories of the present day, however, the case seems to be somewhat the reverse. The self-identified Neostoics, chief among whom is Martha Nussbaum,[1] pay less attention to the philosophical framework of the ancient Stoics and more to their analysis of the passions as judgments, more precisely, as evaluative judgments or judgments of appraisal. Neostoicism is, in its contemporary appearance, a form of so-called "cognitivism," the general view that the emotions give information to the organism, but not just purely cognitively, also evaluatively. The best known early proponent, Robert Solomon, describes his intention as follows:

> The thesis of this book is quite simply stated: to return to the passions the central and defining roles in our lives that have so long and persistently been denied, to limit the pretensions of "objectivity" and self-demeaning reason which have exclusively ruled Western philosophy, religion and science since the days of Socrates.[2]

To this characterization of the Western tradition as a whole, whose culminating activity—philosophy—refers in its very name to the human master passion, and whose most poignant historical moment is called "the Passion," I will say nothing, except to refer to the first three chapters of this book and to observe that such self-denunciation is a powerful propensity of Western modernity, an expression of its passionate self-concern.

Solomon himself takes no explicit account of that basic aspect of the ancient Stoic teaching that he is about to reinvent in other respects: that the passions are indeed cognitions—albeit *false* ones. What is intriguing is that in his school of thought the way to save the poor beaten-down passions from dominating reason is by rationalizing them in the sense of making them forms of reason, of human cognition. Yet, on second thought, what else was to happen? It is just about within our powers to apply our articulating reason to passion. When we do it, the thinking will, as is its nature, maintain itself, while the passion may pale and shrivel before it. Even if we think passionately enough to stay in sympathy with the passion we are thinking about (and indeed, it's that or grinding the logic-machine), we can't get our feelings to utter reciprocally, to accept or reject the adequacy of our thinking—unless it be that they too are thoughts. To put it another way, under thinking, everything must respond in the mode of rational thought or be a surd, a deaf-and-dumb object. Even Pascal, who, because he says that the heart has its reasons which the reason does not know, is often cited in behalf of an emotion-logic unfathomable to reason, does not mean that at all. What he is rather saying is that there is a primal thought before thinking, which he is pleased to locate in the heart: the immediate intuition of—*nota bene*—intellectual principles that precedes discursive reasoning.

Thus there must either be an ontology of affect as other than reason—an account of feeling in terms of fundamental categories of arationality, recognized by reason through a kind of self-overleaping, a reaching beyond its own domain, or the affects must be absorbed into thinking—and that is the accomplishment of the Stoics: to unify the human soul and its world on the ground of articulable reason.

But as we have seen, the Stoics have difficulty erasing every vestige of non-thought from the passions. It is a difficulty that carries over into Neostoicism, which works without an elaborate account of first principles but instead with a detailed analysis of the logic and psychology of emotion. Martha Nussbaum's solution is to *impassion reason.*

Accepting the Stoic formulation that a judgment is an "assent to an appearance" and an evaluation, and that judgments are mainly propositions, she insists on this crucial feature: The judgment she is detailing is not a mere registering of the fact of an appearance but is *simultaneously* an appraisal. This appraisal is made in the context of a person's values and life; it is "eudaimonistic," where she takes *eudaimonia* as being the Greek word not for a "feeling" of happiness, but for the worldly and psychic ordering that makes for the individual's "humanistic flourishing." Such evaluative, eudaimonistic judgments are not only the necessary constituents of emotion but they are also sufficient. That is to say, emotion *is made out of such judgments* and nothing additional is needed. If an adversary were to object that there are aspects of emotion and affect that don't look like judgment—pain, tumult, etc.—the answer would be: Reason itself "moves, embraces, refuses. . . ." So why, she argues, would such a dynamic faculty be unable to house, as well, the disorderly notion of grief? That is what I mean by saying that as the emotions are judgments so reason is here emotional, that reason is being impassioned.[3]

Consequently emotions are judgments without remainder; there are no elements of, say, grief that are missing from the evaluative eudaimonistic judgment called grief. The word "feelings," when used of affects which have "rich intentional content," that is to say, are fraught with meaning, are merely terminological variants for the cognitive terms "perception" and "judgment." Affects of the intentionally poor sort, for example, feelings of psychological fatigue or ferment, or more concrete bodily feels like trembling and "boiling" are, none of them, definitively associated with emotion and should not enter into their definition.[4] The same is, all in all, true for the feelings of pleasure and pain.

This Neostoic view of the emotions is far more complex than the original—in any case fragmented—theory because it touches on some of the vast recent research in neuroscience, psychology, and anthropology, and even animal ethology. For example, the Stoics, as Descartes after them, ascribed no passion to animals, but in the face of modern animal studies that view may be untenable; animals certainly behave as if they experienced grief and joy; this calls for a revised Neostoicism.[5] A similar difficulty arises with respect to the imagination, which plays a major role in the emotions because it represents the object in the quasi-sensory form on which the emotions can focus. The ancient Stoics were not strong on the non-cognitive imaginative imagination as it might function positively in passion, since they had preempted *phantasia* for purely cognitive use and saw the *phantaston* simply as a false impression. But Nussbaum means to extend the Stoic line by admitting a shaping of the emotions by the sensory detail of the imaginative texture beyond what "the eudaimonistic thoughts by themselves supply." Yet, finally: "There is no easy way of plugging those [imaginal perceptions] into a general definition of the emotions."[6] In other words, the cognitive theory can't accommodate the whole experience. Here is a left-handed compliment to the ancient Stoa: Its epistemology fits its account of the passions too tightly for tinkering!

The Stoics are thus a good end to the chapters on ancient thinking about the passions: They throw a bridge over into modernity.

From Cicero's *Tusculan Disputations* (45 B.C.E.), composed at the end of the ancient Stoa's philosophical period, to Descartes' *Passions of the Soul* (1649 C.E.), written at the beginning of modern times, lie one thousand and seven hundred years. I shall include from all these centuries only Thomas Aquinas's "Treatise on the Passions." I am far from thinking of it as "representing" those Middle Ages, although it has some title to that standing, since its mother-treatise, the *Summa Theologiae,* is indeed a sort of summary of the then available knowledge. Nonetheless the next chapter will present Thomas's treatise primarily for itself, as a masterful treatment of the psychological siting and descriptive detailing of the passions.

chapter V

The Passions Sited

Thomas Aquinas and the Soul in Sum

What the passions are for Thomas Aquinas may, in the first instance, be inferred from their place in the *Summa Theologiae,* the work from which my account will be primarily taken. A "Summa" is more than a summation; it is an organized totality, a synthesis of knowledge, in this instance, of divine things.

Thomas's *Summa* has three parts. Of these, Part I, which concerns God and his creation—Man in particular—and Part II, which deals with human acts, were written between 1265 and 1271. Part III, which is about Christ as Savior and the sacraments, was written somewhat later; it will not be used in my account except to make the point that, within the order of the whole *Summa,* the passions are to be found in the middle part, in the twenty-six questions known as the "Treatise on the Passions." They are, moreover, located in the first part of Part II, which places them in the very middle of Parts I and II taken together, since they are preceded by 140 questions and followed by 141.

Moreover, the passions themselves are sited in the middle part of the soul, as the diagram on p. 151 illustrates. Their centrality to human life, expressed in Thomas's psychology, is thus echoed in the composition of the work meant both to establish theology as a science and to replace old manuals with a new order of instruction (*ordo disciplinae*) for beginners.[1]

A note: I call the author Thomas rather than, as do Catholic writers, St. Thomas, or as is secular practice, Aquinas (from Aquino, the town in Italy near which he was born); I mean nothing by it, except a preference for real names.

1. Why Read Thomas on the Passions?

It is a question that needs to be answered in the face of the fact that his "Treatise on the Passions" is omitted or drastically cut in published selections.

1. The siting of the passions in the *Summa* and in the soul promises a very expansive view of human affects, relating them at once rigorously and widely to the human, natural, and divine economy.

2. The teaching form of the *Summa* is, at least to me, very inviting. Debate (*disputatio*) was the instructional way of the universities of Thomas's time. He employs a modified version of these fairly formalized events.[1] The initial element is the "question," *quaestio*. It is the indication of a topic, but also a genuine question, that is, an inquiry, articulated in the *Summa* in terms of alternatives: "whether" (*utrum*) or not something is the case. Of course, the question with its articulations presupposes a good deal of learning and reasoning; furthermore, the correct answer is, in the *Summa*, the *positive* response to the question (not so in the records of live disputations). The "or not" is, however, given full scope, for in each article the subquestion is followed by a list of objections, some found in authorities, some devised by Thomas himself. These are fair and succinct statements of the counterarguments that have come to his notice. There follows an "on the other hand," the gist of the answer by an authority or by Thomas (who is, after all, the tradition incarnate), then a lengthy response, setting out his own pronouncements, then replies to each objection. To my taste, the comprehensive openness combined with rational determinateness is intellectually at once fulfilling and arousing—whether or not I can accept the bases of the argument—especially in respect to so confounding a subject as human affect. In sum, to borrow from his own vocabulary, his writing is "complacent," meaning "pleasingly satisfying," in this case to the ordinary intellect. It anticipates our requirements; in that sense one may even see why it isn't totally absurd to think of the *Summa* as a beginner's manual.

3. Thomas's knowledgeableness makes for an overview of psychic powers unmatched in any other writing I know. He has at his command pagan, Christian, Islamic, and Jewish writers—all equally present at once, without any temporal qualification—and in particular, Aristotle, of whose psychological theory he gives a lucid and enhanced version.

The resulting psychic order in all its subtle differentiations does not strike me as just scholastic, that is, as mere book learning. It seems rather to be informed by acute introspection and wide experience. But how would a monk know? Besides a well-absorbed learned legacy, there must have been a capacious imaginative empathy and (who knows?) perhaps some youthful moments? Moreover, the monastic pressure-cooker must have been instructive—think of the incisive human knowledge developed by effectively cloistered women novelists and poets. At any rate, in reading Thomas I am never haunted by the query induced by some—no, much—contemporary scholarly writing on the emotions: Where have you been?

4. There is a certain illumination on peculiarly contemporary issues to be gotten from Thomas's treatment of the passions. For example, as I will have occasion to mention again, neurophysiological accounts, be they from somatic physiology or brain science, rely on introspective reports of affect for their protocols. How would a researcher identify a physical event as emotion-related unless a subject named a feeling? The subtle differentiation of the elements of the soul in the "Treatise on the Passions" would be descriptively helpful, were it but known.

5. Finally, the very central siting of passion—within the divine economy between God and the Savior, within the Creation between the angels and the animals, and within the soul between the intellectual and the merely animating function—provides a thought-provoking counterpart to the purpose most often currently assigned to the passions. For among contemporary explanations the primary one is in evolutionary terms; in those terms the survival value of affect-directed behavior is emphasized, even in the face of the evident species-destructive side of the passions, especially when combined with another evolutionary result, technology—such is the dominance of the evolutionary paradigm. For Thomas too the passions are in one aspect merely natural and pertain to the animal's mere life, but from another they are moral and pertain to human good, that is, to salvation—a function meriting, if not belief, at least consideration.

In sum, Thomas writes on the passions with such capaciousness and specificity, such rationality and humanity, that he stocks the mind even of a nonbeliever with ideas indispensable to thinking about them.

2. The Soul Situated, the Passions Sited

Getting the good out of the *Summa* means, as I said, seeing the passions as sited within the soul and the soul as situated in the *Summa*. For that is Thomas's way of definition—through placing in a structure. Here, omitting what is off my topic, is a schematic look:

Broadly, surveying the whole work:

Part I	God and his Creation
	Spiritual creatures—angels good and bad
	Corporeal creatures—heaven and earth
	Spiritual and corporeal creatures—animals and MAN
Part II	Man and HUMAN ACTS
Part III	Savior and sacraments.

Narrowly, looking at the middle part:

Part II, ɪ   Man's end—beatitude
              Human acts only—will
              Human and animal acts—PASSIONS
              Habits—virtues, vices, sins
Part II, ɪɪ   VIRTUES, graces, ways of life.

The necessary background to Thomas's treatment of the passions as human acts is, therefore, his setting out, in Part I, of the constitution of those creatures in which there is a union of body and soul, man and the animals.[1] Accordingly I begin with a brief overview of the whole human soul in which the passions are sited. It is essentially an explication of Figure V-A, zeroing in on the passions in the middle.

But first a note on the "siting" metaphor: Nearly all the great theories concerning the soul, that is, the organization of our inner life, are topographical in the sense of being expressible in diagrams assigning psychic functions to places located in a figuratively spatial order. How it is possible to spatialize the soul, why we are driven to do it, and whether it is avoidable—these are perennially stirring questions I shy away from in this book, lest it become endless.

I want to repeat that Thomas's combination of inherited distinctions and psychological acuity makes for a view of humanity in which, it seems to

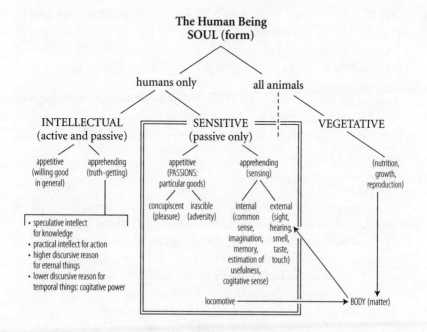

Figure V-A: The Parts of the Soul

me, every element that introspection dredges up and observation draws in finds a place. I might go so far as to say that later treatments proceeded more by economizing on terms, privileging parts, and reinterpreting functions than by expanding the elements of this psychology—at least until there came on the scene the notion that the human soul might have a part, the Unconscious, not directly accessible to human consciousness, the "infernal" home of the passions.

The term "part" is an issue. Thomas speaks of "parts or powers"; Descartes will protest the very idea of a diversified soul.[2] I think that reference to parts is figurative, that is, expressible in a figure, as in my ramified diagram (or in a Freudian topography, Figure IX-A). What is really intended are capacities or powers, but understood as powers "apart," meaning that their functions are discernibly separate and also that certain parts of the soul can exist apart from the others—this apartness of the parts, their "separability," invites spatial depiction. Thus the vegetative part alone exists in plants, the vegetative and sensory parts together in animals, the intellectual part alone in angels. Human beings require the whole gamut. A partite soul is, moreover, a necessary element in a progressive scale of ensouled creation from a tree to an archangel.[3] So I'll use "power" or "part" with the understanding that the soul is, strictly speaking, not divisible in the way a spatially extended body would be, that all its powers are mutually involved, and that the soul is not the efficient mover but the activating form of the body, as Aristotle says.

Another issue is the naming of the parts. Since all translators wrestle with the best English version of Latin terms that are actually extant in English, though there recondite and misleading, terminology gets confusing. I've opted in the diagram to stick with the anglicized Latin terms, adding an explanatory English word below.

Here, then, is the setting out of the elements of the soul shown in the diagram, those needed for locating Thomas's understanding of the passions. A note: His distinctions are *far more* numerous and subtle than those shown.

1. *Union of body and soul.*   Thomas begins with a whole, the human being, a union of body and soul. That is what the human being *is*, a psychosomatic composite. The account of the union is tantamount to a definition of the soul, for body and soul (excepting its immortal part) are not separate substances, but are complementary aspects of the living being, exactly as for Aristotle.[4] The body by itself is mere matter understood as "potentiality," that is, a capability for being informed, activated, made actual, for becoming a fully functioning being. The organic body is, to be sure, not a totally unshaped, un-informed matter, but I make mere reference here to Thomas's difficult and fascinating account of its pre-shaping, a marked, individuated

phase, the *materia signata* ("designated matter"), that brings matter closer to its forms.[5]

The soul is then the activating, actualizing principle. Two parts (or powers) of it are not separable from its body, the vegetative and the sensory. The intellectual soul survives dissolution.

Thus Thomas avoids the "mind-body problem" that will both serve Descartes' purposes and bedevil his schemes; consequent attempts to solve it will, roughly speaking, go first toward assimilating all being, including the human kind, to what is thought-like (idealism) and then, currently, toward the reverse, the reduction of the soul to bodily states and of the mind to physical events in the brain (mind-brain identity)—a return to the materialism of the oldest Western philosophy, that of the Greek "physicists" and later, the Stoics.[6] It can never be said too often that we are caught here between a rock and two hard places—the rock being the brute obtusenesses of mere force-and-matter (materialism), and the hard places being the metaphysical intricacies of soul-informed matter (Thomas) and the sophisticated impossibilities of body versus soul (Descartes); in addition, there are all sorts of in-between conceptions. These quandaries are the subtext for all consideration of the passions, and the best I can do is to consider the options clearly.

2. *The relation of its powers to the soul.*   For Thomas, elaborating on Aristotle, the essence of the soul is, then, that it, the *anima,* is the principle of animation, of life. Animation has two principal aspects in human beings, movement and cognition. The soul activates the body to flourish as a body and to move in space in various ways, but above all, the soul knows its world through the senses which, by way of the imagination, supply the intellect with the bodiless forms it requires to think.[7] Therefore the soul, though certainly a unity, has those aforementioned three major "parts," from the bottom up: vegetative, sensory, intellectual. And this is the place to note that Thomas emphasizes not only that our soul is essentially one in itself, but also that it is, even in its highest reaches, an individual soul. He is opposing the Islamic thinker Averroes, who argues that there is one intellect for all beings.[8] Thomas's interest, in both the separability of the intellect from the body and its individuality, stems from the fact that these are requirements for an afterlife and salvation. The relevance to the locating of the passions is that the purest intellectual "appetite," a pure desire, namely the love of God, must be seated in a separable and individual intellectual soul. This "passion for divine things" is a longing which is "without bodily change." However, such a condition of separation from the body is in any case unattainable and not even helpful for the living human being, and a blessedness not reachable in life.[9] Therefore I will say little about it here, for I want to stick with the middling human condition.

One more preliminary: How are the powers related to the soul? The lower ones obviously belong not to the soul alone but to soul and body together, to the whole human being.[10] How are they distinguished? By their objects, for capacities are recognized by the objects they are concerned with. Thomas does not mean the individual inciting objects (as I think Spinoza will), such as might give, say, each love-passion the inimitable flavor of its "love," its object. He means primarily the very general object-features of a so-called "formal object," such as the degree of universality of the object (from which the powers derive their standing in the soul's hierarchy) and the abilitiy of an object to modify a power (which is determined by the way its relates to that power). For example, an object may act on a power as a moving cause or as a purposed end or through its specific (though not individual) object features; thus friends might help us up when we've fallen, or attract us to seek their company, or move us by their humanity.[11] The more narrowly specified objects will then be coordinated with the more specific passions.

3. *The vegetative soul.*   I will begin with, and get out of the way, the lowest part or power, the one least universal because it is active solely within organic bodies. By it the body is animated to take nourishment, grow, and generate. With this last activity, the soul begins to extend beyond itself in its ascent to universality by producing other humans. Thus it comes closer to the middle part. For Thomas, the psychic hierarchy is not so much a perfect continuum as a graded ascent. Notice this strange consequence: The power of locomotion, by which the human being enters the natural world, is located in the middle part simply because it extends man's scope.

The vegetative functions and locomotion are, then, the psychic functions most immediately active in the organic body and its world; these are the functions humans share with animals.

4. *The intellectual soul.*   I jump next to the highest, most universal power, for between it on one end and the vegetative power on the other the passions are sited. This highest part is the one of most consequence to Thomas, and I will reduce his enormously subtle complex to the element needful for the passions. That would appear to be the "appetitive" sub-power, *will,* intellectual desire. A look at Figure V-A will show that the intellectual soul's double aspect of appetition and knowledge is repeated in the sensory soul: There too is desire and cognition, distinguished as passive and active (insofar as sensory apprehension is somehow cognitively active)—but in very involved ways. Thus the parts *differ* in the universality of their object and *coincide* in having a desirous and a cognitive power. The passions come under *sensory desire.*

I'll begin, however, by sketching the "apprehending" side of the intellectual soul, whose lower counterpart and supplier is the imagination; it is an internal sense located under the apprehending, that is, the knowing part of the sensory soul.[12]

A note on terms, first *appetitive* and *apprehensive*: The former, from Latin *ad-petere*, "to aim at, to desire," has shrunk in English to signify, as "appetite," primarily physical hunger and relish for food, so "desire" is perhaps a better term for the longing part of the upper soul. "Desire" is, however, also the going translation for "concupiscence," a passion defined as the appetite for pleasure[13] and found in the "concupiscent" part of the soul. Let me therefore clearly distinguish these three: intellectual desire (or will), which is one of two parts of the intellectual soul; sensory desire (or appetite), which is one of two parts of the sensitive soul; and concupiscent desire (or appetite), which is one of two subparts of sensory desire. (Reference to Figure V-A will help.)

Apprehensive is impossible as an English version of *pars apprehensiva*, the cognitive part of the soul, since "apprehensive" now means "worried." "Apprehending" is usable, since it is general enough to leave open the kind of cognition meant.

a. The intellect, the power of apprehending, of knowing, is, when locked into the composite that constitutes human being, entirely dependent on the deliverances of the senses, particularly on the inner sense called "imagination."[14] Nothing could be more interesting than Thomas's expanded version of Aristotle's theory of the non-sensory human intellect's cognitive connection to the sense-affecting world of nature, but here I must be curt: The inner sense, the imagination, receives through the outer senses and then stores in memory "phantasms," images, likenesses of particular material objects. From these the intellect abstracts an "intelligible species," a non-sensory form such as informs corporeal matter—but not in its individualized particularity. Hence "species," as we use the term, means a kind or class. This species is not an ideal object, something the intellect perceives, but rather a *means* of understanding. Just how the outer senses deliver images and how the intellect abstracts is not our business here. In any case, I don't quite understand it, though I see why these acts are necessary to Thomas's purpose: to keep the human being securely tethered to the whole Creation without losing the separable function of thought. Consequently it is hard to find an author who exceeds Thomas in cognitive down-to-earthness. There is *for us no knowledge not based on the senses.* For this purpose the apprehending intellect has subparts. Of these, the discursive reason, which makes arguments about this temporal world, is most relevant to the passions.[15]

Even the intellect's knowledge of itself is only possible through observation of itself in action. Is the intellect then an active or a passive power? This question is of consequence because it illuminates the meaning of the passivity of the passions. In fact some people think of the passions as belonging to a passive intellect, which they identify with sensory appetite.[16] Thomas, elaborating on a brief passage in Aristotle's *On the Soul*,[17] speaks not only of the active intellect but, for humans, also of a passive intellect, two aspects of one power. For the intellect is not only at work, it is also receptive; Aristotle says it is sense-like. Moreover, the human intellect, being finite, is really never fully active, but is ever passing from potential to actual, and that is one of Thomas's meanings of "passive."[18] So there is written into the *Summa* that basic human affectivity which will come to the fore in Spinoza and Heidegger. For whatever else "passive" may mean, it means being somehow affected, and when even the highest power is in some aspects passive, the human being must be quite thoroughly a receptive being.

b. The will is the power of "appetence," of desiring, wanting, wishing, longing, in short, of inclination, *reaching* toward something—as distinct from apprehending, which is more receptively activated.[19] In Thomas's Aristotelian physics all natural beings have inclinations, fire to rise, rocks to fall, each to go specifically where it belongs or to become specifically what it is meant to be. But human beings have knowledge and can go anywhere or be, in a way, anything. Therefore their desire is voluntary, and inclination is directed by choice, and choice is rational desire. The same object can be known and desired, but it is known by the intellect as knowable and desired by the will and chosen as suitable or good.

Choice is will in the aspect of election—of deciding on this or that, of judging the way to take. Thus cognition must be engaged: The intellect counsels, the will elects. Thomas refers to Aristotle, who speaks both of an appetitive intellect and an intellectual appetite. To the question of which power moves which, the answer is: Will moves intellect—to concentrate, to focus, to learn. But intellect is above will in its comprehensiveness—in its understanding of the will itself, in its commanding counsel, in its apprehension of being and good: "These powers include one another in their acts." Nonetheless, of the two parts of the intellectual soul, the desiring power is more immediately related to the sensory part. (It is not, to be sure, differentiated, as is its corresponding sensory desire, into "concupiscent" and "irascible," since its level of universality is above these temperamental details.) Thus it is a reconsideration of the will as mover and actor, and of its object, the good, which leads immediately up to the "Treatise on the Passions" in the *Summa*.[20] The closer we come to the passions, the more their particular objects matter. The will, however, has a general object, *the* good, and it takes the intellect to present determinate good objects to it. Thus the intellect ultimately moves the will—in this aspect it is called the "practical" intellect. So the passions, after all, are going to stand under the aegis of knowledge from above and, as we are going to see, also from below—since obviously we become passionate only about something we have somehow apprehended, that is, had in the senses.

Thomas now considers certain passions, fear and the lower appetites, with respect to the will.[21] Does fear cause voluntary or involuntary actions? His sensible answer is that it causes both, but with the voluntary prevailing. Throwing cargo overboard during a storm is an example: We will because we must. The acts of the lower desire, concupiscence, on the other hand, are not treated so forgivingly; they are voluntary, since they come from inclination and "the will can resist the passion."

On the bright side, the will is the power of enjoyment, delight, and love. Here we discover that rational desire is not only for ends or for the one last end insofar as they or it are not yet obtained, but also for the fruition, when the will is at rest: What is possessed only in intention is indeed enjoyed, but imperfectly; it is the end obtained that is perfect enjoyment.[22] This is the viable positive between two defaults—Socrates' early analysis of desire, and with it pleasure, as canceled when fulfilled, and the later Romantic recoil from satisfied desire in favor of unconsummated longing.

The questions about the will which are the prelude to the passions in the *Summa* are centered on good and evil in human acts, since rational desire is always for the good. So the question arises: To what extent is the higher power of desire susceptible to the lower, corrupting sensory desire? The answer is: greatly. For a human being in the grip of passion is a changed human being; to a being so affected, what seems good and fitting is different from what it would be in a calm state. The rational will rules, Thomas says, quoting Aristotle, not as a despot rules a slave, but as a governor rules free man who can disobey—and even sway the governing authority. So sense-desire may sometimes move rational desire.

Perhaps the notion of will as rational desire seems harmlessly reasonable at first, but I find it difficult to understand. The question it raises for me is skirted by Thomas in his analysis of the will, and Aristotle, whom Thomas means to follow in matters philosophical, is equivocal just here. How really are willing and wanting related? Willing is, it seems, aggressive and resistant; wanting is passive and succumbing. Will is active, desire is passive. That desire might be thoughtful, governed by a rationally apprehended good is plausible, but in what aspect is it willful? I suspect that the will as rational desire is a hybrid notion; perhaps it borrows its active-passive role from the dual aspect of the intellect as agent and as patient, when it goes actively about the work of receptive knowing. The consideration of the will would not, to be sure, particularly belong here, did its way of being—since the soul is unitary, and the lower powers flow from the higher ones—not tacitly affect Thomas's understanding of the passions.

Aristotle, I think it is fair to say, does not have a notion of will. His word *boulesis*, which passes into Latin as *voluntas*, "will," though close to *bouleusis*, "deliberation," means mere "wishing"[23]—as occasionally does *voluntas*. *Boulesis* is only doubtfully a part or power of the soul; it is rather an activity we sometimes engage in. It is similarly doubtful whether for Aristotle appetite is a separate part of the soul at all or belongs to all parts at once. Thus the two notions don't mesh. At one point, to be sure, *boulesis* is said to be appetite, but at others it seems to be distinguished from it.[24] So will as rational appetite is not really Aristotelian.

The pagans, it seems to me, did without a will in our sense; they managed to squeeze it out, speaking in hindsight, between practical thought and biddable desire (except perhaps for some Stoics).[25] But the Christians required the notion of a power of choice that was radically free and rebelliously pervertable; Augustine first enunciated the features of this novelly required capacity of the rational soul, its will-power;[26] Thomas's will, too, seems to bring together, perhaps somewhat incongruously as I said, the force of Christian free will with thoughtfully good-directed desire.

The human affect of the lower, sensory sort is, perhaps analogously, likewise set out altogether through appetite, that is, as a longing for an *object*. Hence there is little room either for those objectless feelings called moods that will come to the fore in modern times or for the non-desirous imaginative affects that come to be called "esthetic" feelings in the eighteenth century. Even pleasure, in some respects the high point for Thomas, will be quite anomalously conceived as a desire, although it is, in the Socratic understanding, more desire fulfilled and so quenched, and in the Aristotelian tradition more a concomitant of activity than its spur.

5. *The sensitive or sensory soul.* In one aspect this appetitive power is sensual, and thus the center of the soul is given over to desire, to the passions; on occasion Thomas does indeed speak of the sensitive soul as centrally sensual.[27] But desire cannot work without knowledge, so the complete middle part consists of a desiring (appetitive) and a cognitive (apprehending) part, as shown in Figure V-A.

a. Naturally the sensitive soul's cognitive part consists of the senses. Senses are by nature passive, that is, receptive powers. (Nothing will more effectively separate humans from the world than the modern discovery that the senses actively construe it.) There are first, the exterior senses, which are moved by an external sensible object through the sense organs provided for them. They are sight, hearing, smell, touch, and taste. Of these, the last two are the most material and the most basic. Thomas follows Aristotle in thinking that touch (to which taste is related) is necessary to all the other senses and so primary, the sense of senses.[28] Whether that be true or false, it shows once more how close to the tangible world Thomas is—and why Aristotle is his mentor. The pagan philosopher, though his world is eternal and not created, gives Thomas the means for appreciating God's Creation.

The inward or interior senses are the most interesting, since they function as the interface between organized matter (body) and activating form (soul). The "common sense" is the "root," the point of convergence for the exterior senses; in it all the deliverances from the separate outer senses are both distinguished and brought together in a sensed object. Moreover, in this sense is located the very awareness of sensing an object as object that completes the act of sensing. So here arises "sensitivity"—awareness of ourselves as sensory beings, a differential internality beyond Aristotle.[29]

Of the function assigned to imagination and its storehouse, memory, both of which are consequent on common sense, I have already given an indication. Finally, there is a sensory kind of rationality: the "estimative" power that judges the use or good of sense-deliverances. We share the whole apparatus of sensory cognition with animals, including judgment, whose human version is called the "cogitative" sense.

From the sensitive soul also issues locomotion, through which the passions become active in the world.

b. So now we have come to that spot in this huge psychosomatic organism in which the passionate powers or capacities are seated: the sense-related desires, passivity *par excellence.* Since sense-appetite mirrors intellectual desire on a lower level of universality, and intellectual desire is for the good in general, the passions are for the good in particular, this or that good thing. So from the very beginning passions are drawn most naturally by something good, though, of course, things go wrong.

Moreover, as rational desire, will, is moved by the intellect and its reason, so sense-desire, the passions, are moved by the "cogitative" power, sometimes called the "particular" reason, which addresses individual intention and is mirrored in sensory apprehension.[30] So, again, from the very beginning passions are responsive to the higher reason of the intellect, and so the governance implied in the top-down hierarchy of the rationally willing soul (which is the mirror image of the deliverances from the bottom-up, receptive cognitive soul) is maintained;[31] the soul's gradations are connected.

Of course, as I said, sensitive desire is apt to go wrong; hence virtue, vice, and sin come on the scene. These are not in the diagram, for they are not powers of the soul, but rather conditions of perfection or defect in the powers.[32] Sin and virtue are distinguished in this one sentence, "Sin is compared to virtue as an evil *act* to a good *habit*" (my italics).[33] Vice, as defect in general, comprehends sin, theological vice. The three will be briefly taken up in Section 7.

3. How Are the Passions Passive?

Thomas takes seriously the passivity expressed in the term *passion*, which will remain the main name for human affect for the next half millennium, when a more motoric word, *emotion*, will largely replace it. He begins his "Treatise on the Passions," Questions 22–48 of the Second Part of the First Part of the *Summa Theologiae*, with the question: Can there be passion in the soul? The question arises—as the objections to the intended positive answer articulate—because suffering, which is the literal meaning of Greek *pathos*, Latin *passio*, seems to imply materiality, that is, the capability for being affected (for that is what Aristotle means by matter), as well as the concomitant movement and, moreover, the kind of decay that may come with being intensely affected.

Thomas explains that "to suffer, to undergo, to be acted on" (Latin *pati*) has three senses. It might mean simply receiving a quality without attendant loss, as when air is illuminated; or losing a deleterious quality, as when one is healed from a disease; or—and this is the most proper sense—losing a quality, as a "patient" has lost his health.

Note that this emphasis on the primary verbal meaning has a philosophical origin. "Active and passive," doing and done to, are the ninth and tenth of Aristotle's basic categories, features that can be said of any being, and certainly of any human being, for whom mastering or being mastered, by one's self or an other, are life-determining conditions. In particular these categories matter because happiness (*felicitas*, whose more spiritual synonym is bliss, *beatitudo*), the end of all human desire, is understood by Thomas, as by Aristotle, not as a *passion*, affect, or feeling but, on the contrary, as an *activity* of the soul. Ultimately, though, it is not even an activity of the higher desire, the will, but of the highest cognition, the intellect—for it is the contemplation of God.[1] Earthly happiness is not passive either. It is an activity in which the agent acts not toward an outside object, as when we burn or cut something, but on itself, as when we fulfill ourselves by feeling, thinking, willing, contemplating. Attention to activity and passivity will turn out to make it possible to distinguish among happiness, pleasure, and delight—with, it seems to me, considerable consequences both for the insight into, and the living of, a human life.

So Thomas regards the passions as tending toward the "suffering" sense of the word, albeit all three senses apply to the soul. Though even pure thinking has a receptive aspect, the passions belong to the soul-matter composite, and the whole human being undergoes them, for they involve somatic change. This change may be positive, but the characteristic sense is that of loss: "But sorrow is more naturally called a passion than is joy";[2] passion is primarily suffering.

Thomas immediately goes on to place the passions in the desiring (appetitive) rather than the cognitive (apprehending) part of the sensitive soul.

Why that part rather than the other? After all, the objectors point out, not only is there no feeling until there is some cognition, but the desiring part of the soul seems more intensely active than the knowing part—which is, hence, relatively more passive, that is, receptive; thus it is the more likely locus of passions. Moreover, passion appears to depend on the power of the sense organs, and these belong to the apprehending part of the sensitive soul. (This issue, whether passions are cognitive, has come to dominate current emotion-discourse.[3])

Thomas answers that the passions or affections (*affectiones*) are "drawn toward" something in the agent, something in itself good (or bad). The cognitive faculty comes to know by the medium of representations (*intentiones*); it does not acquire the thing itself. But the good (or bad) that desire is drawn to is in the agent-thing itself. So passion, in its passivity, wants, needs, the thing directly, and that is how desire operates. Another way to see it is that a passion, by its very meaning, implies in effect a lack—for passion as a capability is potential and requires to be actualized by a very particular external object. Cognition, on the other hand, is in its nature more active, self-directed, closer to self-sufficient perfection. Desire only *seems* more intense because the body is involved. (Note, though, that in this context the ultimate receptivity of the human intellect is underplayed.)

Finally, the question is: Why do the passions belong to sense, rather than to intellectual desire, to the will? After all, there is an intellectual passion for God, and the universal good that is the object of the will ought to produce the most intense passion. Thomas replies that the passions he is talking about involve the body; the higher desire is indeed non-physical. (In fact, beings that have no body at all, like God and the angels, have no passions either; they perform acts analogous to those we do from passion, but dispassionately; obviously we cannot know what that "feels" like.) The intensity of a passion comes not just from the power of the passion-inducing agent, such as the universal or particular good, but from the—here Thomas uses a wonderful word—*passibilitas,* the ability of the "patient" to become impassioned.

So now the passions are seated in the soul according to their passivity, through which a part of us is drawn to and in need of actual bodily things: With that part we need physical possession of their *good,* while with another part we are fulfilled by their trace in our mind, their *truth.* So ends Question 22, the first in the Treatise on the Passions.

4. The Ordering and Enumeration of the Passions

The primary differentiation of the passions by which they can be ordered comes through the division of sense-desire, of sensuality, into two distinct powers, "concupiscent" and "irascible." Thomas had established these earlier in the consideration of Man,[1] and he now takes them up in Question 23. His terms are in fact all but unusable in English; "concupiscent" intimates lust, and "irascible" bad temper. In Latin they refer respectively to strong desire and indignant spirit. What he means by the first is the soul's desire for something sensory that is pleasurably fitting, in short, that sense-desire which is simply an inclination to seek something presented as pleasurable by the senses—or to avoid what is unpleasant. The second power comes into play in adversity, when sense-desire needs a spirited champion for fighting obstacles to its getting what it wants. Thus the passions of "irascibility," an angry fighting power, always arise out of the concupiscent ones and terminate in them; they are indirectly desirous.

I might note here that this division of the soul has its remote root in Plato's *Republic*, where the soul is divided into three parts, reasoning, spiritedness, and desire. There, however, though the spirited part includes such thought-connected passions as indignant anger and pride, it is not particularly concerned with obstacles to possession, and though the desirous part contains the appetites in the lower sense, it is not much engaged with love and joy in Thomas's sense. Furthermore, Thomas thinks— wrongly, I believe—that Plato treats these parts as separate souls, while in the *Summa* he insists over and over that not only is the soul one, but also that its powers are mutually implicated, the lower being in the higher "virtually" (as implied), the higher being dependent on the lower for their intake.

He defends the division by reference to the claim that passions are distinguished by objects. Some objects are simply delight- or sorrow-inducing; these define simple desire. Some are arduous and difficult to come by or to get away from; these define spirited or fighting desire.

Objects differentiate passions in yet another way: They are contraries in being good or bad, and so are the passions that are drawn to, or recoil from, them. Thomas discerns only one passion that has no contrary. (Contraries, in logic, oppose each other more colorfully than mere negation can effect; for example, love and hate are contraries, as distinct from love and non-love, that is, indifference; these latter are called contradictories.) The one such passion is anger (*ira*), after which the spirited desire is named. Anger has a contradictory, to be sure, namely calm or non-anger. But it has no contrary because its object is a bad thing already at hand, which makes spirited desire either give up and turn sad or resist and turn angry, it being too late for avoidance or recoiling. What is interestingly observed behind all this logic is the uniqueness of anger as a passion that goes nowhere: It cannot flee the bad that is already at hand, and it cannot turn into its "irascible" contrary, for that would by definition mean pursuing a good already present, and such a good would not present a difficulty of attainment.[2] Thus, if you're angry, first calm down so you can reset your feelings.

Thomas is now ready to list the discernible pairs of passions under the two powers. There are eleven in all:

Sense-desire: love and hatred, desire and aversion, joy and sadness.

Spirited desire: hope and despair, courage and fear, and the singleton, anger.

So ends Question 23.

The next question is a necessary interlude: Thomas treats of good and bad in the passions. I will postpone this topic to Section 6 on virtue, vice, and sin, except to say that Thomas wants the reader to keep in mind that, of the healthy passions, some are good when well directed, while others are good in their very nature and are thus virtues.

In Question 25, Thomas turns to the ordering of the passions just established. The spirited passions function, so to speak, in the midst of the simple sense-desires. The latter first initiate a movement toward a good object and then find repose in it, while the spirited desires take their cue from and clear the way for the straight desires to get their way. Thus the spirited desires are less complex *in conception,* for they are only an in-between movement. On the other hand, the spirited passions often *in effect* precede the others, as hope comes before joy. But, all in all, the simple desires have precedence, because they *are* simple, and the spirited ones exist to be in their aid: Joy is, in our vernacular, "what it's all about."

Then what is the first sense-desire? It is love—even before desire or pleasure. The order is: love-desire-pleasure. Why? When we look at the abstracted order of our intention, our goal, the listing is, to be sure, reversed. We must first feel anticipated pleasure, that is, the imagined enjoyment of a good; thence arises the longing for it, desire, and that finally issues in love, our firm attachment to an object. But in actual occurrence, the order that counts is as stated. We first experience a "tendency toward a goal," an attaching attraction, love; next comes a movement toward that goal, desire; finally we find the repose of enjoyment, pleasure. The contraries—hatred, aversion, sorrow—are in the same relation, except that sorrow and pain, being attainments of evil, are weaker than pleasure and joy,[3] and their repose is more like death. In other words, love intends to effect a "real union" as its end, but it is already a union through our inclination to and "aptitude" for the object. To me it seems wonderful that Thomas's logic of love catches a human fact: In the beginning there may be a moment of pure untroubled love that precedes the rise of longing desire.

The first of the spirited desires is hope because it is close to love. Since it is also a theological virtue, I will take it up in Section 6.

"Movement" is a pervasive term in the Treatise on the Passions that needs a brief comment.[4] Thomas uses this word for all the psychic commotions by which we are disturbed or moved, those which the Stoics called "perturbations of the mind" and the moderns will call "emotions." He means it analogically: Psychic motions have agents that exercise their active powers on the passions of the soul. These are to be understood "in terms of an analogy (*secundum similitudinem*) with natural agents."[5] A natural agent attracts (or repels) bodies, first inducing the pertinent movement by communicating to the passive object its own quality, which will then produce in the object-body a tendency to incline toward the agent. Second, if the passive object is not in the place where it naturally belongs, the agent will cause it to move there. And third, the agent can be said to be the cause of the passive body's coming to rest in its natural place. This is an account of motion in the terms of Aristotle's physics, in which the power of attraction is located in the attracting goal as a final cause; this agent-cause can be a natural place or some object-good. (Thus the agency is not, as it will be in Newtonian dynamics, in the bodies themselves, in their power to attract each other reciprocally.)

The analogue of this power of attraction in the passions (and, *mutatis mutandis,* of repulsion) is given in these terms, whose first exemplification is love: The desired object produces a sense of affinity (*aptitudo*) in the impassioned soul, next it induces the movement toward this congenial good, namely desire, and finally, the good obtained, the soul is in that repose which is called delight or joy.

There is some trouble with the analogy, plausible and, as common speech confirms, apparently unavoidable though it may seem, for the soul cannot itself literally move. Thomas had grappled—very insufficiently, it seems to me—with that objection raised in the very first question of the Treatise: "It is true that suffering and being moved don't belong to the soul in itself but belong to it accidentally, as Aristotle says." Aristotle is here much more subtle than Thomas. He says, recall, that, granted that the passions are movements (*kineseis*), we can't say that the soul gets angry as we might say that it builds a house; better say that the human being is moved by means of the soul. The movement is, then, not *in* the soul, but something reaches it and something comes from it: external movement results.[6] This is not the place to enter into the everlasting perplexity of how soul is moved in itself, or moves and is moved by the body. It will be yet one more reason for those inclined to find the soul an unperspicuous notion to drop it altogether: Neither its internal, nor its received, nor its causative movements are *observably* assignable to it. In any case, I think Thomas might agree to this version: The "feel" of passion, of affect, is *as* of a psychic motion that is effectively evinced in the region of the heart or on the skin or in the limbs.

I now turn to the ordering of the passions. The simple desires precede the spirited ones, and love is first in the first group, then desire, then delight. How are the remaining passions to be ranked under their respective powers, or even before that, with respect to each other?

Thomas tries several ordering principles, first, that of the successive coming into being of the passions. This order would perturb that just established by the two aforementioned powers, the spirited and simply desirous: Love and desire (and their contraries) are still first, but thence arise spirited hope and fear (and their contraries), thence anger, and finally joy. Thus joy and anger have variable precedence of succession in these passion-economies. As for precedence of worth, in all the pairs the positive emotion outranks the negative one. Yet with respect to poignancy, although joy is the culmination ultimately wished for, it is anger, *ira*, the last of the spirited passions, which is "most manifest";[7] it is distinguished by giving its name to a whole power, because when anger occurs all the other emotions feed into it.

If, however, the order is by intention, which means by the end or goal, joy (and sorrow) are still the chief passions because that is what we finally want (or are averse to). Again, if the order is by time, hope is principal because it conditions the "appetitive movement" that begins in love and desire[8] (and similarly with fear and the hate and aversion that lead to it). Each of these taxonomies has some justification. Thomas sticks with that already established for the simple sense-desires, and he adopts for the spirited desires an order in which fear and hope are not ultimate passions simply but only furnish the temporal ends of movement into the future; their opposites too, despair and courage, along with anger, are secondary because they are, so to speak, supine in the present. To be sure, the taxonomic approaches are even more complicated than my version shows and most people's interest will bear, yet somehow, sometime, one has to come to grips with what's what in one's psychic economy.

He is now ready to consider each of the eleven passions in turn.

5. The Particular Passions: Simple Desires

Here is the list of all the passions in two columns:[1]

Simple sense-desire (concupiscent)		Spirited desire (irascible)	
Passion	Number of Questions	Passion	Number of Questions
Love	3	Hope and Despair	1
Hatred	1		
Desire (*concupiscentia*)	1	Fear	4
		Courage	1
[Aversion]	0	Anger (*ira*)	3
Pleasure (Joy)	4		
Sorrow	5		

Four preliminary observations:

1. Sorrow—and its remedies—leads the way in consideration given; this signals that passion is suffering after all, whence a theory of passion almost always has a therapeutic aim. Pleasure, joy, delight, the positive passions, are nonetheless high-points, while the negative contraries of the other passions are downplayed.

2. In both columns there is one passion whence the power is named: desire (*concupiscentia*) and anger (*ira*).

3. In both there is an unexpected listing: pleasure, the concomitant-feeling, and courage, a virtue.

4. Desire's contrary, aversion, has no entry (nor does despair, but it is treated with hope). The very brief reference to aversion is under desire; Thomas claims that it has no name and downplays its force. In fact, he had already given it *two* names, and they are strong: "flight" and "abomination" or "disgust" (*fuga, abominatio*).[2] It is of interest here that Descartes will display a similar uncertainty. He says that desire *has* no opposite and then waffles about it; he says that insofar as desire does have "abhorrence" as its true opposite, neither member of the pair is concerned with a good or bad *object,* but they are only two different complementary *excitations* of the soul. I think that this indecision about the valence of negative desire is a sign of, though not an explanation for, a wonderful human (or divine) fact. Longing desire is an almost universal passion of the soul, when indifference or aversion might, conceivably, be our most common propensity. (I recall reading about an African tribe, the Ik, who under extreme life pressure were reduced to complete passional negativity.) And moreover, finding objects of desire in the world is our general experience, when the world might imaginably contain nothing we long for beyond our exigent needs. There might, so thinkably, be nothing but arid hell within and vacant hell without.

I have wondered as well whether, besides an implied affirmation, a significant suppression might not be lurking behind these difficulties. The proper contrary of desire which seeks a pleasure is, to be sure, the flight from or disgust with the unpleasant—an aversive psychic motion induced by repulsive object. But another opposition is thinkable: the attraction—for aversion come under the rubric of (negative) desire—to an object in itself repulsive. At least it is thinkable in well-advanced modernity when the wetly morbid, phosphorescently putrid, odorously disgusting, the sinner and the *belle-laide,* become well-described objects of inverted delight. For Thomas the perverse, the unnatural, is a human possibility located in rational volition.[3] That the sensitive soul might be *naturally* perverse, turned to the bad *as* bad, is perhaps not thinkable for him as a Christian Aristotelian or for Descartes as a rationalist. Could it be that certain experiences are excluded by certain frames of mind? Or, more likely, overlooked? Well, not really, because Thomas does not leave unconsidered the possibility of loving evil—more intimately known to Augustine, who as a youngster stole some inedible pears for the mere contrarian thrill of evil-doing.[4] Everything human has, after all, always been somehow known to all fully sentient humans.

I won't attempt to report on all eleven passions. Full of perspicuous observations and cogent distinctions as Thomas's treatments are, there are nearly two hundred pages of them, enough to cloy even an avid appetite for fine discriminations. Instead, I offer an abbreviated report on six that are both illuminating for themselves and particularly pertinent to past and future thinking about the passions.

A. Love

Love (amor)[5] here naturally belongs to sense-desire. It is, in Thomas's words, a *coaptatio appetitus sensitivi*, "a close fit [of the object] with the sense-desire," an attachment to some good, and a *complacentia boni*, a very pleased satisfaction with that good. (There is, of course, also an intellectual love seated in the will without the senses.) It is a passion, for there is an agent, the attractive good thing, which is the cause—not of the consequent motion toward it, which is desire, but of the "disinterested" love-attachment to begin with. So love is not, as noted, a motion toward, but just the *complacentia boni*, the satisfaction in, the sense-object deemed good. What seems to me so well observed is, as I said, that the first stage of love is not necessarily desirous; that is subsequent—the follow-up.

Thomas distinguishes mere *amor* from *dilectio*, a word similar to *electio*, "picking"; it is a love that includes an element of rational choice. Thus *amor* is more passive and *therefore* "more divine" than *dilectio*—for a human being can come to God more swiftly when drawn by love than by reason. Here passivity trumps activity: Ultimately we are passive beings—not reaching but drawn; this is the shade of Aristotle's attracting divinity in Thomas's God.

He also distinguishes desirous love from friendly love. In the first, we want an object not for itself but for us, as when we "love" some food. In the other, we want the good object for itself as good, and we want good for it: This is friendship, the real love.

What causes love? Only something good? Yes. For evil—and here Thomas considers and modifies the possibility of that occurring—if it is loved, is only loved when rationalized as good. As for the beautiful, which is often thought to be a cause for love, Thomas advances a remarkable understanding: The beautiful is the good plus cognition. "Good"—here is its operational definition—is that in which desire takes pleasure. "Beautiful" is what pleases as apprehended. That's why we favor sight and hearing; the senses that are maximally cognitive are most associated with beauty. So simple sense-awareness of, not the desire for, something good is the first cause of apprehended beauty, just as above love—and, in general, according to Aristotle, an image—precedes desire. Here is the very remote prototype of what will develop into estheticism, the love of beauty that is indifferent to morality—namely when the good no longer underlies the awareness.

Of course, knowledge must be a cause of love, for how can we love what we don't know? So, too, is similarity, understood in the two ways that match the two kinds of love: similarity in actuality, as when two friends are already as one in their realized qualities, and similarity in potentiality, in which the impassioned person hopes to assimilate another's actual good, which is the desirous sort of love.[6]

What are the effects of love? First, union—the accomplished real presence of the beloved, which love seeks insofar as the beloved is an efficiently moving cause; but also union in principle—the desiring of that perfect togetherness of which love itself is the formal, ideal cause. Next, a first mutual indwelling, through the apprehending power in which the beloved is ever present in thought and by which the lover is reciprocally in the beloved who wants to know all about him and go deep into his soul. Then a second stage of mutual indwelling through the appetitive power, in which lover and beloved are in one another's feeling and where desire is not for the other as a means to pleasure but as an end, a "deep-rooted delight," an "innermost love" lodged in the "bowels of affection."

There is also an "ecstasy" of love, literally a "standing outside" oneself, being carried away from oneself. In desiring love there is no real ecstasy because what we want, we want to bring within our grasp, but in the love of friendship we genuinely go outside toward our friend and his good. Friendship is more "ecstatic" than amorous love!

Jealousy, in the sense of zeal, is also an effect of the intensity of love, a resistance to whatever might diminish it or its object. Strictly speaking, then, jealousy should be an "irascible" passion; here it is counted not as envy, but as intense protectiveness.

Is hurt to the lover himself an effect of love? That depends on the object. If it is not suitable, or if its effect on the body is excessive, then love is harmful.

And finally, love's effects are universal, since love is the originating cause of every passion, including the spirited ones—even of its own contrary, hate, and even of the adverse emotion fear, since we fear to lose what we love.[7]

An *obiter dictum*: If accuracy is the sufficient condition for achieving poetry, Thomas's exposition of love has, for me, that severe loveliness which can be brutally described as "hitting the nail on the head."

B. Desire

Next is *desire* (*concupiscentia*).[8] Love, desire, delight (= joy = pleasure) are joined in a reciprocating movement: object to soul, soul to object, object to soul. The love object goes in to the subject, as it were, "making ... an impression" there (*faciens ... intentionem,* that's love), then the appetite moves out toward the object (that's desire), and finally the object is attained, is again within the soul (that's joy). So for Thomas desire is not a proto-passion, but a distinct passion enchained with other passions: a mediating, a passion of passage, a self-extending passion—*longing* for. . . .

The whole appetitively sensitive soul is named after it, since it represents figuratively the soul's "motion" toward the object that has impressed itself on the soul, and that is the way of appetite. The intellectual part of the soul also desires, and desires so intensely that in fact it "overflows" into the lower desire and makes the body serve spiritual things. But the higher power's longing is called *desiderium,* while the lower power's desire is called *con-cupiscentia,* signifying a composite origin, in soul and body. Recall here that the Roman godling of love is Cupid, as in cupidity, who covets erotic possession.

Desires can be non-natural (not to be equated with un-natural). The natural desires, when the object is agreeable and pleasurable to the subject in its very nature, are shared by man and beast; for example, both want to sleep. The non-natural ones belong to humans alone for they depend on *apprehending* the object in a certain way, namely as appealing, which it is not necessarily by nature; only humans sometimes long for sleep as a dream-venue. Thus this desire rests on cognition, but also on choice. No rubric is held open for *un*-natural passions.

The infinity of desire is a major Platonic topic, for it marks the unsatisfactoriness of the life of pleasure. Thomas approaches it through his natural / non-natural distinction plus the Aristotelian differentiation between actual and potential infinity. Actual infinity, which Aristotle rejects as unthinkable, is the totality of an infinite set, such as, for example, mathematicians call "aleph null," the actually infinite set of all natural numbers taken at once. Potential infinity is simply an indefinitely proceeding progress of increase by addition or of decrease by division; Aristotle admits only this latter infinity as physically possible in his finite world.[9] Objectors say that if desire were infinite, actual enjoyment would be impossible, and this is close to what Plato thinks. It is my reason for dwelling on the logic of desire—that and the fact that the constitution of desire, which for some writers is, as I said, the root affect, is ever interesting, both as an intellectual problem and as a real-life conundrum.

Thomas answers, then, that natural desire is not actually infinite since man, being finite, soon gets enough. Yet desire is potentially infinite because we always get thirsty again, in spurts. (This is not, however, Aristotle's meaning of "potentially infinite," as noted.) Yet non-natural, that is, specifically human, desire *is* infinite, that is, indefinitely continual, because it is excited by reason, and reason proceeds, by stops and starts, indefinitely onward; it can amplify desire indefinitely. This treatment of the infinity of desire is, it turns out, less sterile than it seems.

C. Pleasure

Right upon desire follows desire attained, that is, *pleasure* (*delectatio* = delight).[10] Pleasure and its failure, sorrow, are naturally of overwhelmingly great interest to Thomas—nine of the twenty-three questions considering the eleven passions are given over to them. Not only is pleasure the culmination of all the simply desirous passions while sorrow is the moving cause in the "contentious" or arduous passions, but the passion itself is far more differentiated than even love. Thomas raises twice as many questions about its nature and causes, and adds specific considerations of good and evil.

He first considers whether pleasure *is* in fact a passion.[11] The objections give all the Aristotelian reasons for it not being a passion. Indeed, it is emphatically not a passion for Aristotle, but rather an activity, perhaps even activity itself, and it isn't even a sensory process. Yet on this score Thomas follows Augustine, who ranks pleasure among the passions, and he parlays Aristotle into compliance: To say that pleasure is an activity is not giving its essence but its cause. He does have a point. Even for Aristotle pleasure *is* the activity only in a manner of speaking; it is rather its bloom or perfection—though that certainly does not make it a passion. Why this departure on Thomas's part? It may be that under the dominating notion of the will, whose downward influence turns all human affects into various states of desire, there is no room for a formal acknowledgment of a desire-superseding yet somatically expressed feeling such as Aristotelian pleasure. Yet Thomas keeps all its descriptive features: Pleasure is a perfection of our condition, which puts us into harmony with our nature. As a completion, it is all there at once. It is therefore atemporal in the sense that, though it occupies time, it doesn't grow into its own by lasting through time. Once the pleasure is there, it is all there, at its every instant; in modern parlance: "It doesn't get any better than this." Neither Aristotle nor Thomas seem to take account of the careful, moment-by-moment pleasure-calculation of competent hedonists. Nonetheless (and this is opaque to me) Thomas talks his way into calling it a movement, since passions are motions. As I have said, this peculiar skewing of Aristotle—and of the nature of pleasure—seems to be a consequence of the notion of a will that is a rational desire. When so powerful a notion is injected into a "system" (which is how Thomas treats Aristotle's works), all the terms tremble.

Thomas adds two terms under *delectatio,* "pleasure." They are *gaudium,* "joy," and *laetitia,* "a heart-swelling rejoicing," terms used by the Stoics. I mention the latter because together with *cupiditas,* "root-desire," *laetitia* will be Spinoza's fundamental affect.

Joy is a species of pleasure, the pleasure of the soul alone. The objects that give bodily pleasure can give rational pleasure, but not the converse. That is to say, physical pleasure can have rational resonance, but, the implication is, some rational pleasures don't move the body. I wonder. Isn't there some palpable excitement in all rational activity? But then Thomas turns out to be thinking mainly of that intellectual pleasure, seated in the intellectual appetite, which we have in common with angels. It is indeed completely non-physiological, and so, strictly speaking, not a passion. But, Thomas argues, the pleasures of intellect and spirit are greater than those of the body, both because their object is better and because the activity itself is finer: The union of its proper good with this power is "more intimate, more perfect, more firm."[12] I think this is a half-knowledge in us that survives its continual contravention by personal experience.

He asks, however, of sense-pleasure: Which sense gives the most pleasure? Touch is most useful and in that respect most pleasurable, and this preference for food (taste is a type of touch), sex, etc., we share with animals, but sight is most pleasurable to humans alone because it gives knowledge.

Are there non-natural pleasures? Here Thomas does briefly admit that besides the strange cravings of the physically sick, there is a sickness of soul that makes humans take pleasure in such practices as cannibalism and bestiality. Finally, he asks whether two pleasures can be contraries—for this cannot happen in virtues. But yes, since pleasure is related to the affections of the soul as natural repose is to the body, and bodies can come to rest in opposed places, so can there be pleasures that interfere with each other. Thus ends the question on pleasure in general.

Next comes a long question on the causes of pleasure, which I will summarize briefly.[13] As Aristotle says, pleasure arises in unhindered natural activity, that is, not as a process but as a concomitant of activity;[14] the pleasure can be in the activity itself, like learning, or in the end attained, like the possession of knowledge: "[E]very pleasure can be traced to some activity as its cause."

Movement too is a cause of pleasure. (Recall that activity—Greek *energeia*, Latin *operatio*, from *ergon* and *opus*, work—is as distinct from movement as its completion is from a process or full engagement from the approach. Activity is "realized potential" in the language of the schools.) "Three things are necessary for delight or pleasure: a delightful good, a delightful union, and third, the recognition of that union." Each of these requires episodic movement and plentiful variety for us changeable human beings. The good we enjoy now we will probably not enjoy later; the union becomes oppressive. Moreover, we prefer for our recognition of a union to come in stages that allow us really to grow into and oversee the whole. Of course, a being who does not need change, who grasps things instantaneously, would have and does have the most continuous pleasure.

Are memories and hopes sources of pleasure, being of things no longer or not yet present? Yes, but real, present union with a present sense-object is more pleasant, says Thomas the realist. Romantics would not agree: "Heard melodies are sweet, but those unheard / Are sweeter."[15] Can sorrow cause pleasure? Yes, because even a present loss brings to mind the good that is gone, and a remembered sorrow carries along the prospective pleasure of subsequent assuagement.

Other people's actions can surely cause pleasure. It gives pleasure to be well treated; others' appreciation of one's goods is pleasurable; conversely, a friend's good gives pleasure as does an enemy's ill. So do one's own good deeds give pleasure: in their present effect, since the friend's good is felt as one's own; in the final end, because there is the hope of reward from God or man; in the ready source, which is one's own power to help.

Is similarity a cause of pleasure? Yes, because similarity is a cause of love, and love is pleasure. But there are cautions—likes may be excessive in combination, or they may hinder each other in competition.

Finally, Thomas asks whether wonder (*admiratio*) causes pleasure. Since wonder, once a state of mind rather than a passion, will be made by Descartes into a full-blown, indeed a leading—though not fully approved—emotion, this question makes an interesting background to his revision. The objectors Thomas quotes already express all of Descartes' own doubts: that wondering expresses ignorance, that it impedes learning by emphasizing obstacles, that knowledge attained is better than the way to it (the very notion Romantics will reverse). Thomas in reply takes wonder to mean "wanting to know"; thus it is a desire. Hence the implied hope of attainment is an attendant pleasure. This is a sensible solution—though not quite what Socratic wonder meant. It seems that the ambivalence about *admiratio* (Greek *thauma*) is expressed in the term itself, as it is in English: Wonder means at once puzzlement and admiration, a sense of ignorance of, and of attraction to, its cause—which must thus be somehow unknown, yet somehow known.

Now Thomas turns to the effects of pleasure. The first effect is literally "dilation," "latitude," "expansion," all that is later expressed in *laetitia*. This is an enlargement that comes from the opening of one's heart to and receiving a congenial good and reposing in it. Here is the loveliest treatment of Thomas's—and anyone's—favorite condition![16]

But then arises the question whether pleasure in turn makes for desire, the desire for more; in other words, whether it contravenes itself as a fulfillment, a repose. No, not as pleasure itself, but sometimes through our not yet perfect possession of the object, as on hearing the first lines of a poem, we want more—or when, because of an imperfection in ourselves, though the object is complete we need time to take it in, as in our human knowledge of God. Physical pleasures weary us, and so we long for variety, but in nonphysical pleasures there is no unhealthy excess and no tedium. They perfect

nature and are free of fatigue. (Here Thomas interjects, just as I was demur-
ring: except insofar as contemplative activity involves certain bodily powers in humans.) But can just any pleasure obstruct reason? Unexpectedly,
Thomas says yes; it can undermine prudence, that is, practical judgment, by
focusing our attention too closely on just one enjoyable object, by its own
tendency to excess, and by filtering reason through the special vehemence of
bodily changes that pleasure effects. On the other hand, pleasure does make
an activity perfect in two ways: by being a sort of "supervenient," that is, a
gratuitous bonus, and by focusing the agent more eagerly on the work. Here
Thomas implies, not quite consciously, I think, that pleasure is an oddity as a
passion insofar as he takes it, following Aristotle, as a complement to *action.*

Then Thomas considers goodness and evilness (*malitia*) in pleasures.[17]
Why wouldn't what undermines prudence, what we share with the beasts,
what has no legitimate art devoted to it, be sometimes evil? Thomas is sensible. Some pleasures are good, some evil. We do naturally need some sensual pleasure; pleasures can be good when the higher or lower appetite is
reasonable. But certainly not all pleasures are good; as Scripture says: "Some
rejoice in wrongdoing and exult in very bad things." Thus Thomas faults
both Stoics and Epicureans. Since not all pleasures are rational, not all are
virtuous; some are only relatively good, apparently good, good for someone who is in an abnormal condition and is taking pleasure in something
only circumstantially good. Some pleasures, however, are absolutely good,
namely when the object of a passion is good in itself. So much for *de gusti-
bus non est disputandum,* for the relativity of taste.

Is there a pleasure that is the greatest good? Thomas here takes up the
ever-interesting relationship of pleasure to happiness (*beatitudo*), which is
the end of human life and cannot be without pleasure. This article of the
Treatise is presented as a review of Plato's *Philebus* and shows that the dialogue aims both too low and too high: Plato's description of pleasure as
an incomplete process applies only to physical pleasures; his understanding of the greatest pleasure applies only to the (metaphysical) Good, which
is beyond human participation. Thomas himself is thinking of a supreme
human pleasure that *is* attainable, the enjoyment of (a personal) God.

Finally, pleasure *is* a measure of good and evil, but only as it occurs in
the higher desire, the will, whose repose in a good *is* true pleasure; a human
being is judged good or bad chiefly by what his will takes delight in. But,
Thomas adds without break, this means deeds, actions, not mere good will.
One observation: So the will *is* in some sense passive, insofar as it is affected
with delight, yet at the same time it is the immediate principle of deeds. To
take pleasure in good is to do it—no mere intention here.

The Protestant view will turn this order around. Intentions will come to
outrank deeds (witness Kant), as faith outweighs works. In passional matters, Thomas's Catholic realism is one pole; the other might well be said to

be Kierkegaard's Protestant subjectivity. This polarity, I think, distinguishes individual temperaments as well.

D. Sorrow

Pain and sorrow (*dolor, tristitia*), pleasure's contraries (and the last of the desiring passions), occupy the most questions of any passion, because Thomas now includes a question on remedies (as he will later for anger, the last of the spirited ones).[18] Here is confirmed his humane wisdom; these prescriptions might actually help. They are certainly in line with contemporary self-help advice, though pitched a little higher.

Once again, he begins by delineating the nature of the notion. Pain has every characteristic of pleasure in the negative: Instead of attainment there is loss of a good thing or unity with something bad, where "bad" is a "privation" of good. (Thomas reminds us here that evil is for him nothing in itself but the absence, or removal, the de-privation, of good.) Physical pain appears as a kind of illness in the body, but it is really a passion of the soul. Sorrow is actually a species of pain. As joy is interior pleasure so is sorrow *interior pain,* the pain arising not from exterior perception (*apprehensio*), but from the interior senses, imagination and memory; hence sorrow concerns present, past, and future, while bodily pain is only from an ill now present. Since excessive pressure is what hurts, the sense of touch is the primary locus of pain.

Sorrow really is contrary to pleasure, though it can lead to pleasure indirectly, as when grief over sins merits consolation. Sorrow may even be a pleasure in the sense of making one an eager seeker for the absent good.

Are all the sorrows in their generality contrary to all the pleasures? Yes and no, for sorrows and pleasures are avoidances and pursuits respectively, and any pleasure may serve as remedy for any sorrow, though they might be specifically diverse.

One pleasure has no contrary. Contemplation—properly speaking, that is, if it is not of things harmful or saddening—is intrinsically pleasant and is a perfected activity, the beholding of truth. For extrinsic reasons, pain may incidentally occur if sense-cognition is involved, since the sense organ may be stressed out or the object disagreeable. But real contemplation is an activity neither of the sensory body nor of the sensitive soul; it is neither exterior nor interior but beyond, of the intellect, and if there is any distress it is only incidental. "Affliction of the flesh" may indeed be an indirect accompaniment of mental contemplation of truth, says Thomas, ever down-to-earth. But it cannot infect the pleasure itself.

Is sorrow more to be avoided than pleasure is to be desired? (This article raises, but only implicitly, the romantic possibility of desiring desire, pleasure being the fruition of desire.) Thomas says no, since he wants to emphasize the dominance of good over bad, giving as one reason that the cause of pleasure is all-agreeable, while nothing is all-bad. Thus sorrow is always partial, pleasure perfect, and desire for pleasure is naturally stronger than flight from evil. There are exceptions but they are circumstantial—for example, the more we love, the more overpowering our sorrow at a bereavement.

Is bodily pain greater than sorrow? It might seem to be, because exterior pain is real and life-threatening, while interior pain belongs to the imagination only and you can live with it. Nonetheless, it is not so. Apprehension by imagination and reason is more profound than that by the sense of touch. Here we see how deeply the apprehending side of the sensitive soul is involved in rousing the passions. For, Thomas says, the sorrow that comes from the interior senses is more directly repugnant to desire than pain from the exterior senses. A look at Figure V-A on p. 151 will show what he means. The internal senses are closer to sense-desire than the bodily senses, diagrammatically and psychologically. Experience confirms Thomas. People do put up with physical pain in the interest of interior pleasure; they may even rejoice in it.

Finally, Thomas distinguishes kinds of sorrow: by its *object,* namely "one's own misfortune"—hence pity, in which one feels another's pain as one's own evil, and envy, in which one regards the other's pleasure as one's own evil; by its *effect,* namely "fugitive desire"—hence anxiety, not unlike the modern mood, in which we are so weighed down that we see no "refuge," or torpor, not unlike our depression, in which things get so bad we can't even speak and express our feeling.

The next topic is, as it was for pleasure, the causes and effects of pain in general.[19] "If privations were in apprehension what they are in things themselves," one would not ask whether the cause of sorrow was loss of good or union with evil, for loss of good, simple lack of good, which is what evil is in reality, would cover the case. But in the soul even "privation has a certain status (*ratio*) of being," so that evil can be a contrary, a concrete opposite as distinct from a mere contradictory; its logical nothingness can make us nauseous in our interior soul. Thomas's reflection on positive privation is the more interesting for being psychologically plausible. Though we may understand evil as a privative notion, we don't *feel* the bad as mere absence of good. He can now say that sorrow is caused by evil that is present, which makes it much more vivid than it would be as mere privation of good. Is desire also a cause of sorrow? Yes, insofar as there is delay in the getting, or complete removal, of what we long for.

For in these considerations Thomas relies heavily on the analogy of Aristotelian physics, in which the center of the earth below acts as attracting end and the body's weight as instigator of the motion. In this figure, desire is analogous to weightiness, driving the soul to its center of attraction. What is dubious yet telling in Thomas's exposition is that it would be, I think, more in Aristotle's spirit to see the physics as the analogue of the soul's motive powers than to illustrate the soul's tendencies by those of the body.

I shall curtail the account of the next two emotions, pain and sorrow. The *cause* of pain, pain being the impeded longing for a good, is that the unity with the object is thwarted because the force of desire is overborne by a superior power; again the analogy is to a physically stronger agent that decomposes a heavy body so that it loses its natural tendency to move downward to its natural place.

So also for the *effects* of pain and sorrow. Great physical pain, such as a toothache, can interfere with learning, for it, most of all, skews the soul's directedness; it preoccupies the soul more acutely than can pleasure. External pain is even more intrusively disruptive than interior sorrow, for even wild sorrow can focus us on study as a distraction from itself. Sorrow also effects an "*aggravatio animae,*" a "weighing down of the soul." Thomas here says explicitly that the effects of passions are often metaphorically described in terms of physical analogy because there is indeed a similarity—presumably because the passions have bodily expressions: Love feels warm, pleasure expansive, sorrow "aggravating."

Sorrow and pain are, moreover, debilitating to external activity. Finally, sorrow hurts the body more than do the other passions, for it causes bodily changes, that in the physical matter should be in a certain right proportion to the psychic movement of desire, to be out of kilter. While the movements of love or joy are not naturally inimical to bodily vitality (though they may be so in excess), those in which the motion of desire is rebuffed and reversed, so that it becomes aversive and withdrawn, are simply harmful to human life.

So pain and sorrow appear to be more in need of remedies than the other emotions. Thomas supplies them.[20]

First, pleasure can mitigate pain and sorrow, for there is a certain repose of desire in a congenial good, while sorrow is repugnance. Just as any bodily rest relieves any bodily fatigue, so any pleasure will, so to speak, generically relieve pain; at least pleasure and pain diminish each other, as the thought of a friend's death is somewhat relieved by some present good.

Weeping assuages sorrow, for what hurts, hurts more when pent up within. When the soul's attention is turned outward by the release of tears or words, sorrow is lessened. This is the advice still given today by grief counselors.

A friend's fellow feeling (*compassio*) will help. On the physical analogy, grief is a weight that is lessened when two bear it; what is more, the sufferer feels loved and that gives pleasure; when a friend grieves with us the pleasure we get outweighs the increased sum of communicated grief. In modern terms, sharing sorrow is not a zero-sum, but a (desirably) negative-sum game.

These passions are also mitigated by the contemplation of truth, for that is the greatest of pleasures. To be sure, knowledge has its pain because it is difficult to attain and because we learn so many things contravening our wishes. Still, the contemplation of truth attained is a human good pleasurable in its very nature. Even though the speculative intellect does not move the soul by virtue of the thing it contemplates—for it reposes in its contemplative fulfillment—the very activity is good, and the higher powers of the soul do flow down into—inundate, as it were—the lower ones.

And now the wonderful last word on this passion of sorrow, following hard upon the advice to contemplate truth: Sleep and take baths. The bodily state, which is out of kilter in pain and sorrow, will be restored, and that will cause a mitigating pleasure. This really works, especially the baths.

Finally, Thomas asks: What is the relation of good and evil to pain and sorrow? Every sorrow is, unconditionally speaking, a bad thing. But circumstantially it is right that we should have such feelings in the presence of evil. So can sorrow be a decent, honorable good, even though it happens against our will—which then finds itself, to complicate matters, in opposition to God who sends the grief? Yes, because sorrow involves the recognition and rejection of bad, insofar as it is regulated "according to the rule of reason." Can it be a useful good as well? Yes, insofar as it is not a mere feeble contrary desire in the face of a bad thing already present, but arouses the movement to repel the sorrow-causing evil. Finally, is the pain of the body the highest bad? No, the objectors say, there is a pleasure that is the highest good, happiness (*felicitas*), and not getting it is the worst thing. But, Thomas replies, there is something yet worse: not judging true evil to be evil, and even worse, not rejecting it—and similarly, judging something to be evil that is really good and thus separating oneself from it. So certainly the body's pain is not the highest bad, nor sorrow the greatest evil, for sin (*culpa*) is a greater evil than its punishment—though it brings sorrow.

I have switched here from "bad" to "evil" and back to translate *malum*, which, according to its context, sometimes means bad in general and sometimes morally bad, that is, evil. Earlier on Thomas had used *malitia*, which is unequivocally a moral term.

With the question concerning the good, bad, and evil in pain and sorrow ends the consideration of the passions that are desires simply, unimpeded at least in respect to the impetus of the appetite, the passions of the "concupiscent" power of the soul, the sense-passions. Now come the fighting, strenuous, spirited passions.

6. The Particular Passions: Spirited Desires

"Angry," "spirited," "contentious," "arduous" are the adjectives for the passions that belong to the "irascible" part of the soul, the part that deals with adversity, with inhibited, checked desire.

Thomas works in a tradition that had absorbed the Platonic notion of spiritedness (*thymos*) as a part of the soul, but the question is whether the resulting distinction in the passions is true to life. The arduous and angry passions do seem to be what we post-Freudians would call "passive-aggressive." They are parasitic on the simple sense-desires but they add an element of attack: "All the contending passions presuppose the desiring passions," to the object of which they add "not only possibility but even arduousness."[1] So it is not in the object that the qualification of arduousness lies.

What really is the difference here? Take love, hatred, and anger. Love can certainly be disappointed in its object, but the result, as Thomas sees it, is sadness and languor, not aggression. Confusingly enough, hatred, which is, like all the passions, caused by love—indirectly, to be sure, since love of one thing causes hatred of its contrary—is also said to be without aggression. Thomas quotes Aristotle, who says that hatred is for people under a general aspect, for their character and class—this rather defangs its personal bite. Anger, on the other hand, is for the particular individual who has done us harm; it is thus more sharp-set.[2] We passively just hate thieves in general and want the police to get them, while we become aggressive with an individual who takes what is ours.

So is the concupiscent-irascible distinction mostly a matter of pushing the passions into the shape required by a misunderstood—or deliberately transformed—traditional distinction? No, it seems to me that in general there really is in experience a difference between those affects that are simply a longing or wanting, directed towards or away from something—these being the truly passive passions—and those others that have an additional element of resistance to danger and opposition, though the object is no different. Some passions feel supine and others get one's back up. It may not be the only or even the most obvious taxonomy (that latter must surely be primarily by contraries or by temporality, which will be Descartes' scheme), but it *is* recognizable. One way to characterize it is to say that spiritedness gets distributed over its various inciting situations.

A. Hope

Of the arduous passions,[3] hope is listed first and provides a kind of model to show how the object determines the spirited passions. In the case of hope, that object is a thing that is good, is in the future, is possible, but is arduous to attain: expectantly energetic wishing. However, I will take up the passion of hope later, together with the synonymous virtue.

B. Fear

Fear is listed second. It is the most vehement of emotions, and turns up high in every list into modernity. For Thomas, too, fear is a model passion because "most properly those movements are called passions which imply something hurtful."[4] Here Thomas helpfully reviews passivity: In a way, both intellect and sense are passive, since they are aroused by their object; the passions are the cases where a bodily organ is involved; the harmful "passions" are most properly so called. Fear certainly hurts and is therefore most truly a passion, though sorrow still comes first, inasmuch as it is for a present hurt, while fear is for the hurt to come. Yet it is not altogether of the future, because the bad thing is already present in the imagination. For Thomas fear is a very specific passion because it has a very specific object, the precise contrary of hope's. For the fear-object is disagreeable, difficult, and thought of as impossible to resist, while the hope-object is agreeable, expected, and still to be worked for. Fear is a natural inclination, though there is unnatural corrosive fear that opposes our natural "desire to exist."

There are various types of natural fear, among which Thomas lists first—interestingly—laziness, the fear of exertion (perhaps because it is close to the monk's affliction, *acedia*), then of embarrassment and of shame, the fear of loss of reputation, respectively, for an act now being committed or for one already committed. All kinds of formidable and intractable situations give rise to different fears.

The general object of fear is, as was said, a future bad thing. Naturally bad things, like death and disintegration, whether naturally or violently caused, are especially objects of fear; guilt is feared but often not powerfully enough.

Fear itself can be feared—a truth that will ring in American ears through Franklin Roosevelt's exhortation on facing the Great Depression, "[T]he only thing we have to fear is fear itself."[5] The unexpected is more fearful, especially the suddenly imminent. Evils without remedy are especially fearful, and if they are perpetual or long-enduring they are superlatively frightful.

Causes of fear: Love, as was said; for love disposes us to fear being deprived of something good; lovers fear loss especially. Deficiency, for fear has two causes in which the defect may be lodged: the disposition (the underlying material, as it were) of the one who is afraid, and the acting object (the form, as it were) that gives the fear its shape; fear comes about if a person's disposition is defective, too weak, or if the assailant is overpowering, too strong.

What are the effects of fear? First a kind of contraction, a withdrawal, as when the dying concentrate their remaining strength within, or when citizens abandon the outposts to hide inside the city. Next, a wish to take counsel, an anxiety to get advice and help. Then trembling, paling, tooth-chattering, for as the vital spirits flee inwards, the external members undergo all sorts of physiological changes. And finally there is the effect of fear on action, which moderate fear will make more deliberate, but overwhelming fear will impede.

The contrary of fear is daring (*audacia*).[6]

C. Anger

Anger (*ira*)[7] is the eponymous passion for the "irascible" part of the "appetitive" part of the "sensitive" part of the soul, and the last to be considered by Thomas. It is also the most anomalous, for one thing because it has no contrary, no positive opposite. (It has a contradictory, non-anger or calm.) If the essence of the passionate anger is righteous indignation, it is indeed hard to think of a true contrary, though such a contrary was implied in a saying popular in the 1960s: "If you're not part of the solution, you're part of the problem," meaning that a lack of reformist passion was a positive fault. And so anger has a certain relation, for Thomas as well, to justice.

Thomas asks first if anger is a narrowly focused or an inclusively general emotion, for pain, pleasure, and hope are involved in it. As so often in the Treatise, he begins by giving a lesson in philosophical distinctions, here of generality. Anger is not as truly general as is love. For love is a root cause of all emotions, while anger is rather a concourse of the emotions just named. Anger arises when one has suffered pain and, therefore, both desires and hopes to exact punishment. So too is the object of anger complexly apprehended: The object seems bad insofar as it is the agent who has done us an injury, but it feels good as the target upon which it is a satisfaction to visit punishment.

Anger, *ira*, has given its name to the irascible part of the soul because it is indeed preeminent among those passions that have an arduous element. Both the revenge itself and the object on which it is inflicted can be harrowing to deal with, especially when anger involves a matter of some magnitude.

Moreover, anger is a passion that involves reason, not in a direct way, as if anger were called up by reason, but, so Aristotle says, in an ancillary way, insofar as reason articulates the perceived nature of the injury for the passion to fix on. Anger is also very natural, more so even than desire, at least from the point of view of the subject, the angry person. Desire may be more natural in animals, but humans, being rational by nature, are more apt to be aroused by what they *understand* as opposing and threatening them. There is, in fact, a certain human temperament—the choleric—that is especially given to anger, while some temperaments are by nature calm. Is Thomas tacitly admitting that there is a possible contrary to anger after all, a kind of calmness beyond mere apathy, something like Aristotle's opposite to anger, gentleness?

Compared to hatred, anger is less deleterious and less grave. Though it desires something bad for its object, it does so not as hatred does, namely absolutely, but as tempered by reason and even as in pursuit of justice. The angry man's desire is to inflict a punishment for which the object can understand the reason; a hating man simply wills an injury. So anger and justice are indeed connected. In fact, though it is possible to be angry even with inanimate objects—as when we bang a tool that's gone dysfunctional, I imagine—usually anger is concerned with people in respect to justice and injustice.

Anger is typed by the ways it intensifies: easily roused—wrath; long-remembered—ill will; vengeance-desiring—rancor.

These are the effective causes of anger:[8] It is always caused by an injury done, and done to oneself in the inclusive sense, to one's near and dear. Hatred can be aroused simply because of what the object *is*; anger needs a particular reason. All causes can be reduced to one: slight—contempt, spite, insolence; thus it is the intention that matters. One's honor or personal quality (*excellentia*) is at stake. Thus excellence in a person is a main source of indignation, for its protection makes one vulnerable to slights. (Yet so do personal defects.) Slighting from insignificant persons is particularly galling, though the anger is softened if they repent and humble themselves. The dead, who have already met the final evil and who are in any case insensitive to hurt, are not objects of anger. (Here common experience might disagree; the dead can be objects of a whole lifetime of anger.)

Oddly, though Thomas has promised remedies for anger in the question heading, he gives none. This might be mere oversight, or it might also be to the point: How can anger be assuaged, except by getting timely satisfaction or by forgetting over time (which Thomas in fact mentions later)? No passion settles in more and is less amenable to generalized remedies.

Next, Thomas tells the effects, the first of which actually *is* a remedy, precisely the pleasure that comes from vindication.[9] There is among the effects also a physical "fervor" around the heart, but not like the sweetness of that produced by love. It is sharper, as loss of a good is more sharply felt than ever was its presence.

Anger, which is amenable to reason, also impedes it. The objectors point out that anger does respond to reason, that anger reasons well because reason demands openness, and anger is not insidious but expressive. This comes from Aristotle, who is plain wrong; people eat their hearts out in silence, as Thomas will soon say. But Thomas disagrees on the grounds that the upsetting physical effects of anger are so strong as to inhibit reason, which, although it does not directly use them, still requires well-functioning sense organs. To be sure, there is a certain expansive magnanimity and manliness in anger that distinguishes it from desire, which is soft and insidious and felt to be shameful—but that, Thomas says, doesn't mean that the angry person *really* knows what he's doing.

Finally, Thomas asks if anger is particularly apt to cause taciturnity. Yes, both as it uses reason and as it impedes it. It can go so far beyond the bounds that, as I just suggested, it ties one's limbs and one's tongue. "But if the turbulence is not that great, then out of the abundance of perturbation of the heart there follows the speech of the mouth."

So closes the last question of the "Treatise on the Passions." I have done small justice not only to its acuteness of observation and its incisiveness of understanding but especially to its language, which appeals to me for being at the same time tried-and-true and ever-fresh. The Treatise contains not only a very full phenomenology, that is to say, a descriptive inventory of the passions, but exhaustive philosophical analyses and, finally, moral evaluations. For the passions are close to virtues and vices, and I will now give a brief account of how Thomas treats that relation.

7. Virtuous Passions, Passionate Vices— and Sin

For Thomas, as for the ancient writers, the passions are tightly involved with virtues and vices—and for Christians with sin as well. When passions will later turn into emotions, certainly in name but naturally also in quality, this alliance is largely broken off. I have before me half a dozen contemporary books on the emotions, picked randomly off my emotion-shelf; not a one of them so much as has an index entry for virtue or vice. One reason—more will be brought up later—is that while passions are thought of as good, bad, or evil, emotions tend to be regarded as well or ill. It is an odd fact that the affects named after supine suffering, the passions, were thought in their time to be so much in need of suppression or at least control, while the affects named after expressive psychic movement are now regarded as requiring cherishing tendance and managing support. Could it be that passions suffered were more lusty than emotions expressed?

In the *Summa* the close relation of passion and morality shows up not only in the introductory question, which is devoted to the good and bad of passions in general and to pleasure and pain in particular, but even more in the fact that certain passions later turn up as theological virtues or sins. Hope is the most clear-cut case, since the name for the passion and the virtue is the same.

Among the vices there is despair, the passion contrary to hope; it has a dual relation to *acedia,* which is a sin, that is, a vice with respect to God's law. Whereas despair is due to an excess of hopeless desire, *acedia* is a failure of desire, but both lead to inaction, to withdrawal.[1] *Acedia* belongs to that sphere of unfocusedly debilitative mental states which will later be called "moods." These are the objectless feelings, predominantly of depression— though Thomas finds a sort of diffuse object for *acedia*: "disgust with divine good." Thus he ranks it among the mortal sins, those deadly to the spirit. An example of religious virtue is charity, the spiritual love of God, on which all the other virtues depend; it corresponds to sensory love among the passions on which, in turn, all the passions depend; faithful fortitude corresponds to passionate daring; joy appears as an effect of charity rather than a stand-alone virtue. In general, the passions have their counterparts most overtly among the theological virtues, but more implicitly among the social virtues, which are more externally directed.[2]

Let hope stand as the example of the difference between passions and virtues. Hope was the first of the spirited passions but it is the second of the three theological virtues, faith, hope, charity. As a passion it is the spirit-stirring desire for a future good that is hard but possible to get. As a virtue it has exactly these features, but what makes it a virtue rather than a passion is that it belongs to the faculty of rational desire, to the will rather than to sense-desire. Thus it is a choice. What makes it theological rather than "cardinal" (that is, one of the chief pagan virtues) is that its object is "blessedness," that is, the attainment of God rather than of human good.[3]

The best way to marshal these involvements is through a brief account of the relevant terms and their relations: passion, virtue, vice, and sin.

Passion (*passio*), to recapitulate, is, taken philosophically, a movement in the matter-and-form, that is, the body-and-soul composite which makes up a human being. The body, being organic matter, is potential, which means it is passively responsive to the informing soul and receptive to affections from the world of external nature. The soul is the active principle. It has, however, also a receptively potential, passively suffering aspect—as does, indeed, even the intellect itself. Thus the soul is capable of experiencing passionate affects. Such passion, though by unperverted nature directed to good, is nonetheless properly speaking, a suffering: Sorrow is thus more "passionate" than delight.

Virtue (*virtus*) is not an affect but a—good—habit. A good "habit" is something we "have," a quality, a disposition of the soul for doing things best from the point of view of its own nature, a condition that enables it to act at the peak of its power. A habit is more or less deliberately acquired— though God is its ultimate cause—and it is settled, long-lasting.[4]

Both desiring parts of the sensitive soul, that which desires simply and that which desires spiritedly, are subject to virtue, not as they are appetites *per se,* but insofar as it belongs to them to obey reason and to be capable of habituation. In contrast, the cognitive part of the sensitive soul, the senses, are not quite capable of virtue—not even the interior ones, imagination and memory. For though they have something like a habit, a facility, it cannot be a perfection of these powers themselves because truth, their object, is never completely in *them* but rather in the intellect. So virtue is properly only *related* to desire, without *being* itself a passion. Thomas summarizes the reasons: Passion is movement, virtue is habit; passion is good and bad, virtue is good; passion begins in appetite and ends in reason, virtue is just the reverse.[5] I should say here that the treatise on the particular virtues— personal, social, and theological—and their contraries is simply enormous: one hundred and seventy questions, set out in the Second Part of the Second Part of the *Summa,* and what I am reporting is an infinitesimal sampling.

Vice (*vitium*) is the habit of doing bad things in general. Passions turn vicious when, instead of being sense-movements toward good or from bad, they turn away from the "order of reason" and become disordered and irrational. Thus fear's contrary, daring (*audacia*), can become audacity in the English sense of reckless insolence.[6]

Sin (*peccatum*) is more restricted than vice, as vice is narrower than badness. Thus badness > vice > sin in class extension, but sin > vice > badness in active intensity. For though every privation of good is bad, vice is the particular badness (*malitia*) of passion gone wrong. Sin is even more specific, since it is not a habit but a real *act*. The immediate cause of sin is the will, for sin is voluntary, freely chosen evil.[7] The passions do affect the will, though indirectly, because a lower power cannot purposefully move a higher, as the body—mere matter—does not move the soul. Yet the passions can distract the will and diminish its attention to its proper good object. Moreover, imagination and sense-judgment, which are violently affected by the passions, may impede the will—as in people who are out of their minds.[8] Hence sins, evil deeds, committed in a passion are thereby alleviated (as we still have mitigating legal categories for crimes of passion). Passion is, in fact, related to the will before and after its exercise: Passion *may* distract the will but it *cannot help* being moved by an intense act of willing.

The above is just a rudimentary approach to Thomas's huge treatment of the virtues and vices, which is complex as well as consistent, systematic as well as humane.

Blessedness (*beatitudo*), finally—its slightly less theological-sounding synonym is happiness (*felicitas*)—is not to be found among the passions or virtues, and its consideration precedes them.[9] For it does not belong to the sensitive part of the soul but to the intellectual part, not to the will but to the intellect, not to the practical but to the theoretical intellect. (See Figure V-A on p. 151.) To be sure, pleasure, the repose of desire, is a *concomitant* of blessedness, but no passion is a *constituent* of it. It is the completed activity in the sense of fulfillment; it is man's best moment, the highest power engaged with the highest object, a creature's activity fulfilled in an uncreated object, God. Thomas follows Aristotle's understanding of happiness as an activity in accordance with perfect virtue and in taking that activity to be contemplation and its object, God. So his blessedness differs from Aristotle's happiness as the Christian God differs from the pagan *Nous*; whether that is much or little I need not consider here (but, very much, I think). What does bear pointing out again is that when happiness is not a passion—which is just what it *is* taken to be in the contemporary psychology of emotions—the distinction between it and passionate pleasure is much crisper, with obvious effects on moral discrimination. For not only is it easier to condemn certain pleasures when happiness is divorced from them, but felicity and blessedness become far finer ends when they are disjoined from such pleasure.

8. The Leap from Thomas to Descartes

Four centuries separate the "Treatise on the Passions" of Thomas Aquinas from *The Passions of the Soul* of my next author, Descartes (1260s to 1649). If it were my purpose to give a historical account of ideas, the incremental transformation from a medieval to an early modern work to be found in intermediate links would be indispensable. Who can doubt that people think onward, basing themselves on their immediate predecessors? Thus the development of notions, especially insofar as it is carried on in works of no particular distinction, appears in some degree continuous. But then again, as in the "punctuated equilibrium" of biological evolution, in which the life of species undergoes sudden "jerky" changes followed by stasis,[1] a new era breaks forth abruptly in certain seminal works. Perhaps it comes about as a release of the pent-up impulse of less adventurous writers, perhaps as a flare-up of originating genius. This is not the place to think that out. However it happens, this arrival of the new is most boldly in evidence when we look at authors widely separated in time. There is, moreover, another justifying factor for comparing authors, especially modern authors, to their more remote ancestors: The more original the thinking, the more reference it *tends* to have not to the immediately preceding but to the remotely antecedent tradition. On that level, *in*-novation tends to be conceived as *re*-novation, *new* birth as *re*-naissance. The comparison between Thomas and Descartes, of which I will give the sketch of an account below, seems to me, apart from the main point—which is to think about human passion—to be a lesson in what it means to live in a dialectical tradition, one that spirals up (or down, perhaps), coming full circle through diametrically opposed positions to modified coincidence on a new level. Maybe that's a digression; to me it seems a bonus.

In any case, the comparison is warranted because of Descartes' scholastic learning. I'm tempted to say also that Thomas's works contain many intimations of modernity, that in fact much of the non-technical basis of modernity was *apprehended and rejected* by Christian writers, as by the pagans before them.

Descartes' relation to the scholastic tradition, to medieval book-learning, is intimate and cagey—outrightly acknowledged on some occasions, surreptitiously abrogated on others, now deliberately circumvented and then again forthrightly flouted. The last is the mode he adopts in *The Passions of the Soul*, the focus of my next chapter, where he insists on the absolute novelty of his revisions of older treatments. For his Method of discovery this claim is surely just, in particular for its application in mathematics, which resulted in the invention of what we now call analytic geometry (based on the Cartesian coordinate system) and for the related conceptual revolution that transformed the concrete counting numbers of ancient mathematics into the abstract magnitudes *x, y, a, b,* appropriate to modern equations but used ubiquitously.[2] Cartesian geometry and equations in general are now high-school subjects, a routine tool of modern technique. In physics his specific discoveries, being too much governed by his metaphysics, had less staying power and were superseded by Newtonian dynamics. In metaphysics itself, which touches *The Passions of the Soul* most nearly, his innovations proved most persistent and most problematic.

So this seems to me the bridging moment, the time for a succinct comparison between Thomas, the tradition incarnate, and Descartes, the propagator of newness. Their works stand to each other as a comprehensive and differentiated synthesis to an initiating and deck-clearing simplification.

1. *The source of self-knowledge.* For Thomas all human knowledge comes initially through the senses, and the soul, a substance, knows itself through first apprehending external objects.[3]

For Descartes the self—the "subject" of later philosophy—emerges after a radical divorce from the senses, and the object of this new pure self is a newly construed nature. Thomas connects man to the Creation to emphasize God's dominion; Descartes distances the mind from nature to facilitate natural science. Thus the turn to modernity consists only in part of the Baconian call to the observational use of the senses; its other part is the Cartesian requirement of abstraction from them to make nature mathematical. The medium of apprehension is for both Thomas and Descartes the "light" of the intellect, a metaphor that goes back to Plato. But what for Thomas is a light from God, is for Descartes a "natural light."[4]

2. *The number of substances.* For Thomas substances, real beings, are multitudinous, as many as are the immaterial essences beyond nature (angels) and the immattered essences (sensible individuals) that comprise nature; together they make up the Creation. There is above them a unique being, beyond the category of substance, God.[5]

For Descartes there are only three substances, meaning self-subsistent beings having independent existence: the non-extended thinking reality; the extended reality, which is a matterless, weightless, non-sensory continuum; and beyond them, God. Thus a pure self, the human being, faces a pure non-self, extended nature—as well as a God who functions remotely though continuously as a creator and as a maintainer and immediately as a guarantor of human knowledge. The effect of this starkly oppositional relation of mind and body on the understanding of the passions is very great, as indicated in the next paragraph.

3. *The union of soul and body.* For Thomas, following Aristotle, the soul informs the organic body as its material, so that body and mind are

conceived as functionally complementary constituents of a totality.[6] Consequently the union of mind and body is not a problem *for* metaphysics—though it might be one *in* metaphysics in so far as the Aristotelian notion of form-and-matter, equivalent to potentiality-and-actuality, is problematic.

For Descartes the union of soul and body is inexplicable; that is the consequence of his two opposing, semi-self-subsistent, substances. For far from being in the mode of potentiality, for him the body has independent substantiality.[7]

Both Thomas and Descartes speak of the soul as diffused over the whole body. For Thomas that follows from the form-matter relation; for Descartes, who centers the soul's influence on a gland in the brain, it is a problematic assertion.

4. *The constitution of the soul.*   Thomas collects under the name "soul" a highly diversified set of powers or parts, of more than merely distinguishable, indeed unmixable functions. Yet the soul is one in number, and the upper parts contain the lower "virtually."[8]

As for substances, so for the mind Descartes accomplishes an enormous simplification. In effect he abolishes that soul which is traditionally understood as a hierarchy of powers turned toward the body in its lower rungs. The Cartesian "thinking thing" is a unit without parts; in particular, Descartes abolishes the middle and lower elements, the sensory and vegetative soul. He assigns the lowest, the merely animating function, to a literal fire in the heart (as did the Stoics), and the sensory function to the animal spirits, backed by a material physiology.[9] This reassignment of sensation plays a great role in his *Passions.*

Both Thomas and Descartes reject Plato's simile of the soul being in the body as a sailor in a ship,[10] but for opposite reasons—Thomas because he regards it as implying that, since a ship's complement includes different specialists, there must be several different souls in a human being, and Descartes because a sailor is not "intermingled" with the ship as the thinking thing is—somehow—with the body. I think these different interpretations signal what each has trouble with: Thomas with the unitariness of the tripartite soul, and Descartes with the union of mind and body. Thomas's problem reaches back to Aristotle; Descartes' is his own.

There is another issue concerning the thinking soul, one about which Thomas is explicit and Descartes is silent. Is all intellect or mind one, or is it individuated? Thomas argues for individual intellects; Descartes simply does not say (!) whether or how *res cogitans* is individuated; *res extensa* is indeed all one, with only movement to differentiate its bodies.

5. *The mutual embrace of will and intellect.*   For Descartes the upper third thus becomes a unified, pure, independent "thinking thing" which,

though strictly one, has—not quite perspicuously—numerous capabilities, of which will and perception are primary, as they are for Thomas.

For Thomas the relation of the rational appetite (will) to the apprehending understanding (intellect), especially in its practical aspect, is involved to the point of equivocation. Will and intellect embrace *each other*—in different respects, to be sure, though they remain distinct. Yet "absolutely" the will is nobler than the intellect—while the intellect gets hold of what is highest.[11]

For Descartes intellect and will are modes of a unitary mind—not a partite soul. Though reason is a universal tool, it is finite in power. We are not omniscient. The will, on the other hand, is "in a sense" infinite, for its scope is equal to God's.[12] We can will any object of volition; we are, so to speak, omnivolent. This view is of importance in the *Passions,* where Descartes wishes to account for, and give advice on, the control of the passions. Such advice would be vain were the freedom of the will not as comprehensive as the scope of its interest. Thus of the two sorts of thoughts, willing and intellecting, volition represents all the soul's action, and by mere willing it can, through that little gland, produce the required bodily effect. Everything else is passion in an enlarged sense that includes all the adventitious perceptions that happen to arrive through the body and those that arise of necessity in the mind itself. Thus will and intellect are here distinguished as action and passion, but both are equally thoughts (*pensées*); moreover the body, the active source of affects in the soul, can sometimes react passively, and the passively cognitive soul can sometimes be active. Not a plain situation!

As far as I can make out, for Descartes the freedom of the will is thus pretty nearly total, including the liberty to doubt anything; the will can assent to truth but also willfully fall into error. Hence virtue is primarily of the will; it is volitional control to be applied freely to the internal management of the passions.

For Thomas, will is not, as for Descartes, a power of mastery, but rather a desire, an "appetite," connected to reason. Thus it is bound by its object, the good, as intellect is necessitated by truth. But it is free to consent or not when the connection between a particular choice of good and the final good is not proven or provable. Thus the will in Thomas is object-directed, not control-directed. It makes all the difference to his view of the passions, insofar as they are normally sense-aroused and always appetitive. It is not so much tight self-control as soundly-directed desire that straightens the passions.

6. *The mediating imagination.*   But how do external objects affect the soul? For Thomas, as for Descartes, the imagination mediates between the immattered external substance and its matterless internal idea; hence it is through the imagination that the passions are aroused. For Thomas

the means of ingress from the outside world to the soul is the abstracted "species"; for Descartes it is a difficult, staged process of mathematicizing abstraction. This abstractive process has, however, no immediate bearing on *The Passions of the Soul,* in which the question of the imagination, though central, is folded into the mind-body problem—it is fudged.[13]

7. *Passions and actions.*   The effect of these differently constituted souls on the understandings of the passions is large. Thomas must make an argument for why the soul, the formal active principle as against the merely potential body, can indeed be passive, for he regards the passions as belonging to the soul alone. Descartes, on the other hand, must make an argument for why the body can be soul-lessly active. So he implicitly denies that the body is material in the old sense of being potential—that it is receptive to becoming *this* body by being informed by the soul. For all matter is itself substantial—it is, in fact, one substance—and is, recall, diversified only by differential motions;[14] these motions *are* its "actions." This last claim is a necessary preparatory step in what will be his major thesis: that in the passions it is mainly the body that acts.

Both authors attach the passions to a physiology involving heart, heat, blood. But of course Descartes is far more specific, and since he locates the point of mutual passionate impingement of body and soul in the brain, he denies its traditional location in the heart. (Thus begins the retreat from introspection to clinical observation in matters emotional, since we can note our heartbeat in passion, but we can't sense our brain cells firing.) As I mentioned, both authors think of the soul as in some sense united to the whole body. But for Thomas it is so as the form of the entire body; for Descartes it is so because the body, though divisible as extended, is indivisible as organic. This explanation is involved in an equivocation: Descartes says that the pineal gland is the "principal" seat of the soul where it acts merely "in a more particular way," but he also says it acts there most "immediately"; he must mean that the soul's effects are diffused over the body, not that it is "jointly united" with the whole.[15] The main point is this: For both authors the passions proper arise as the soul's response to the body and are particularly related to perceptions of well-being or harm. But for Thomas the soul is the animator of the body, so that, while the body is a conduit for whatever sensory objects affect the soul, it is in the soul alone that the passions are "moved." Descartes' version, which seats the soul in a gland, moves the body front and center in human passion.

8. *Objects.*   For Thomas the passions are diversified by their objects, because the powers of the soul are distinguished by their acts and these by their objects.[16] Since by the different powers Thomas here means the pleasure-desiring (concupiscent) and the adversity-resisting (irascible) parts of

the appetitive sensing soul, "object" is taken very broadly—"formally" is the scholastic term. It is that good and bad which fits the passions belonging to that power; for example future bad fits fear and future good fits hope, both passions of the irascible capacity.

For Descartes, "object" means the external object of the senses, which is in itself neither competent to differentiate parts of the soul by eliciting their activity nor qualified as good or bad. Thus the basic distinction of "concupiscent" and "irascible" parts falls away—though he does admit faculties of desiring and being vexed, among many others.[17] For him too the passions are valued as useful, namely toward inciting the soul to will that to which they have already alerted the body. The great difference is this: Thomas finds objective good or bad in the Creation, while Descartes rather attributes a relative usefulness to external things, a utility explicitly not proportionate to a difference in their own natures, but to their harm or profit relative to the human body.[18] Here is yet another of those indices of modernity I will be noticing as I go—the turn from intrinsic goodness to relative usefulness in the valuation of objects.

9. *Definition.*   For Thomas the passions are implicitly defined in terms of the meaning of passivity, together with their siting in the powers of the soul. Descartes too begins with a reflection on patient (soul) and agent (body) as separable, the one being the recipient, the other the perpetrator. The event, however, the excitation in the soul, is one, and he defines passions explicitly as such excitations—he says *émotions,* the first use of the modern word by any author here cited—suffered in the soul but caused by the body.[19] I think that his motive for reiterating the identity of passivity and activity is to disallow the Aristotelian analysis of substances as conditioned by two complementary principles, passive potentiality and actualizing activity.

Thomas engages in the circumscription rather than the definition of the passions. As I said, the system itself places them. Descartes defines them very definitively, and his definitions are expressive of his way, which is to let the issues be guided by traditional terms and the outcomes by reaction against them; the object is to insinuate gently an abruptly new approach, a new way of seeing the world.

10. *Enumeration.*   Both authors mean to classify the passions so as to get an exhaustive enumeration. Thomas achieves this by combining the two functions of parts of the appetitive sensory soul, the concupiscent and irascible, with the attractive force of good and the repulsive force of bad and with certain temporal considerations to get eleven passions in all. Descartes, who denies that the soul has parts, enumerates and classifies the passions—essentially but implicitly—by their relation to time and, on reviewing his

enumeration, gets six primitive passions from which an indefinite number of others originate. In other words, Thomas offers a systematic and complete enumeration; Descartes an empirical and open-ended one.

In both authors the paired opposition of passions is important, since they are almost always linked to good and bad, or harm and utility respectively. Thomas finds only one passion that has no contrary—anger—because calm, its opposite, is not a positive passion with respect to good or bad. Descartes finds two, wonder and desire—wonder because it occurs in us antecedent to judgments of utility, and desire because aversion, its scholastic opposite, is to Descartes simply a concomitant of every movement of desire; to seek anything is to avoid its privation. Thus he forestalls any pure unidirectional desire for an absolute good; by fiat every desire is also an aversion and every good a utility.

11. *Orderings.*   For Thomas love is, from the chief point of view, the root passion, the first of all positive passions, because love is that attraction and attachment to the desired good that precedes all other positive passions.

For Descartes wonder is first, because it is the astonishment at something newly experienced, the simple sense of something extraordinary, which can make us learn and remember. Here, between those two chief positive passions, we see exemplified the turn from an object of love desired for its objective goodness to an object of wonder whose quality of newness arises in relation to the subject and induces there an emotion valued for its usefulness.

For Thomas love is, accordingly, simply "satisfaction in what is attractive," and union with that object is a resulting feeling of oneness, an effect of love rather than love itself. On the contrary, for Descartes love is by definition the wish to join oneself to objects that appear *suitable,* so it is possessive as well as subjective at its inception.[20]

Thomas orders the unfolding of love as follows: First, love, which is an attachment to a good object; then, desire, which is a longing to have it; last, joy, which is the repose in its attainment. Descartes borrows and oddly perturbs the sequence. The reason is that for him love itself is the volitional union with an object not so much good as suitable; desire is really the *same* volition directed to the future; joy is the enjoyment of the union. Thus in fact, love, desire, joy can all be simultaneous. Since desire has for Descartes no contrary, the withdrawal or aversion that is accompanied by hatred and sadness is said to be always referrable at the same time to some suitable good sought as well as the opposite evil shunned. Descartes concludes that "we can see very plainly that it is only one passion that does both."[21] Both because I cannot match my experience with such a doubly directed passion and because Descartes takes this occasion explicitly to oppose the Scholastics, I imagine that in conflating desire and aversion he is here engaging in a significant innovation.

What could it be? I surmise that as actions of the body, the coronary agitations of desire and aversion, which are said to be very strong, are not physiologically distinguishable. Moreover, since the suitability is not, as for Thomas, in the object itself but in its mental representation, there is no *objective* exterior source in which attraction or aversion are distinguishable. That is indeed a new beginning: Desire is a totally relativistic passion whose two opposing psychic tendencies are quite subjective.

12. *Locomotion.* For Thomas human locomotion originates in the soul; for Descartes—mostly—in the body. The Cartesian animal body is an automaton, moved by internal physical causes or external sense objects.[22]

The consequences for our environing world are great. Animals, for Thomas, are passionate. For instance, judging the inside from outward behavior, he says they have hope, as when they are moved by the sight of prey. For Descartes animals are automata; perhaps even the higher animals lack thought and thus soul, for he has rejected the merely sensitive, animating soul-parts. Consequently humanity is—and this is another Stoic echo— in one aspect set apart and against its object of study and use, nature. Here Thomas, who accords to animals the power not only of estimating what to react to and how but also of remembering experiences, is much closer to contemporary animal ethology than Descartes.[23]

The feature exemplified by Descartes' view of animals is one that makes his treatment of the passions, albeit somewhat harsh, yet very interesting. In its disruption of the affinities of Creation, in its opposition of body to soul, and in its trust in science before the fact, it displays a sort of necessary first extremism in the pursuit of a new beginning: Phase Three of our Western tradition, Scientific Modernity that succeeds the Faithful Middle between us and Philosophical Antiquity. If the affects are first reduced in stature at this willful inception of modern times (Chapter VI, on Descartes), the opposition that is the animating principle of this tradition will soon restore them to a significance beyond all former bounds (Chapter VII, on Spinoza).

chapter VI

The Passions of the Soul as Actions of the Body

Descartes and the Obscurity of Clear and Distinct Ideas

1. Descartes' Title: Cunning Candor

René Descartes' work on human feeling is called *The Passions of the Soul* (*Les passions de l'âme*, 1649). It was the last of his books to be published in his lifetime (1596–1650). He thought of it as resolving two great issues. The first was the question of the union of mind and body, a perennial problem exacerbated in his own metaphysical system, which separates—evidently radically and irreconcilably—extended and thinking being, the substances underlying body and mind respectively. The second, not unrelated issue was the purpose of philosophy: how it can make life serene.

The title seems plain enough. The small book is about *passions*, what we now call emotions. Descartes uses the word *émotions* of any commotion of body or soul: Passions are thus a subclass of the emotions.[1] (Much later, in English "emotion" will supersede "passion.") He says *the* passions, indicating that he will be comprehensive, and these passions are *of the soul,* where they are traditionally located. But there is a novel implication, which will be the crux of the treatise: "Passions of the soul" here implies "actions of the body." In his metaphysical works it is the mind that acts, that finds in nature the matter amenable to its operations. Here, in his work on human nature, the body acts on the soul.

For Descartes uses the word passion with full awareness of its primary meaning: something which is done to the soul, which it suffers, is passive under. That the passions, though they have a physiological expression, are often just-bearable afflictions or curable errors of the *soul,* was part of ancient wisdom. That they arise in the *body* and have their effect in the *brain* is contemporary science. In *The Passions of the Soul* they arise in the body and affect the soul; this is a neat marker of beginning modernity. Thus Descartes' book is pivotal between the old and the new.

In one of the two anonymous letters prefacing the *Passions,* the author says that he writes "as a physicist," not as orator, nor even as a moral philosopher.[2] The oratorical reference is meant to put distance between his work and Aristotle's *Rhetoric;* the moral abjuration is a ruse—the *Passions* ends on a moral note. What he intends is to explain physiologically the commotions of the active body that the soul experiences as passions. I might say here, proactively, that Descartes, who is probably the writer of these letters (each of which is followed by a reply signed by himself), says, quoting from his own Preface to his *Principles of Philosophy,* that he had no "opportunity to carry out the experiments needed to support and justify [my] reasonings."[3] Hence these fluent explanations in terms of motions of the blood and the "spirits" are apparently just speculation on his part and no longer of the first interest to us—except insofar as they outline in a remarkably prescient way the elements of the contemporary physiology of the emotions: blood, nerves, brain.

Descartes' prefatory claim not to be writing as a moral philosopher is, as I said, belied by the work itself. Descartes was at this phase of his life less interested in the scientific enterprise than in the use of the knowledge gained to live well. So the aim of the book is the discovery of "a general remedy for the passions" that are to be feared, and its conclusion is that wisdom is what makes us masters of such passions as may be pleasurable when well managed. Descartes himself calls such regulation of Desire, one of the primitive passions, "moral philosophy."[4]

This little treatise is chock-full of such equivocations and contradictions; past a certain point they result, I believe, neither from Descartes' disingenuousness nor from carelessness (the former being, to my mind, the more venial sin), but from the crossing of his method, which requires hard-edged claims, with his metaphysics, which precludes straight answers.

The word *soul* of the title exemplifies the difficulty. Traditionally soul is a complex notion that collects under one term that which animates, that which feels, and that which thinks. Thus the soul is a sort of hierarchy of faculties; the lower the rank, the more closely involved it is with the body. Descartes knows all about this tradition, and he was certainly reminded of it by his critics. Nevertheless, he establishes a mental substance that is in principle incapable of composition with the body, so that the soul which the *Passions of the Soul* brings on the scene is an *ad hoc* adaptation, a jury-rigged notion devised to make a physiological treatment of the passions plausible. He was evidently well aware of this fact; his reply to his most acute objector, Gassendi, on the matter of the soul is blatantly evasive.[5]

I want to remark here that Descartes can be read in two ways. One is to take him to speak candidly but to waffle or contradict himself as he changes his focus or his mind. The other is to regard him as a cunningly disingenuous writer who guides the canny reader to his well-secreted offensive opinions by intimations and clues. He can seem by turns straight and sly, plain and complex, earnest and ironic, faithful and heretical, consistent and incongruous. He writes, in sum, sometimes with candid simplicity and sometimes with crafty complexity. For example, he is often proudly innovative and then claims, in his summary treatise, the *Principles of Philosophy,* that "this philosophy is nothing new but is extremely old and very common."[6] I'll call it as I see it, now as candid, now as cunning, for what else is to be done?

2. Method, Metaphysics, Man

In his earlier works, Descartes is concerned with the way of inquiry: *Rules for the Direction of the Mind* (1628; "Mind" translates *ingenium,* the inborn capacity for intellectual activity broadly conceived)[1] and *Discourse on Method* (1637). The lesser fact of these works is that he proposes a specific set of rules, a method (as in "scientific method") for making discoveries; the greater fact is that he sets any human inquiry on the track of a "methodology," that is, a predetermined way of achieving mastery over a subject, adopted on the general principle that the approach will discipline the subject. Perhaps one might call Descartes' method a Continental, a more intellectualized, and rigorous, reprise of Bacon's *New Organon* (the title means a "new intellectual tool," for exposing nature's secrets). It is indeed a new *organon,* as opposed to Aristotle's old one by that name, which was an instrument of thought, a logic. The Cartesian method will haunt *The Passions of the Soul,* as it haunts us.

The Passions of the Soul seems to mark the final stage of this methodological preoccupation; had he lived past 1650 and found the means, Descartes might—so he intimates—have turned back toward actual physiological experiments so as to throw light on the actions of the body that cause the passions of the soul. This somatic problem had already been inherent in the *Rules* and was explicitly proposed in the *Treatise on Man,* a part of a work called, with stupefying simplicity, *The World* (or *Treatise on Light,* 1633). It was published only posthumously because Descartes was frightened off by the condemnation of Galileo at the hands of the Inquisition. No wonder: In this work Descartes, godlike, offers to bring into being a "wholly new" world; it is in fact just our world viewed anew, scientifically. So too in his *Meditations* he will reverse the order of *Genesis,* in which God creates what we—not the books of the Bible—call Nature, before he sets Man within it; Descartes, on the other hand, insures human—or rather his own—existence before he constructs, in six episodes, a nature amenable to man's mastery by mathematical physics, particularly in Meditations II and VI. The *Treatise on Man* begins with the proposal to describe first man's body, then the soul, and then to show how the "two natures would have to be joined and united to constitute men who resemble us." Descartes writes in the *Passions* as if this work realized the proposal, as if the union of body and soul had here as satisfactory a treatment as is possible.

To me it seems that the great central works of his middle age, setting out his metaphysics, the *Meditations on First Philosophy* (1641) and the *Principles of Philosophy* (1644) which reviews the results in summary form, *precluded any solution*. A bald way to put this is that his method and his metaphysics together make an account of man impossible. So much the more important is it to sketch out here the Cartesian ontology, that is, his account of being, leaving aside for the moment the following intriguingly complex questions: Did Descartes change his mind or did he contradict himself? If the latter, did he do it purposely or inadvertently? Or did he have a solution up his sleeve which escapes me? I will attend only to those elements of his metaphysics which bear on the *Passions*; in particular, that means omitting Descartes' account of God, which most exercised his contemporary critics.

Here are the basic notions:

1. It is necessary first to find something certain, that is, something that certainly exists. This necessity was not, as far as I know, felt by the earlier writers here considered; the story of its genesis as one of the marks of early modernity could and does fill books. To put it very abbreviatedly: When the source of knowledge is relocated from the steadfast lucidity of a substantial object to the natural light of the conceiving intellect, trust in the object's being must needs turn into concern for the certainty felt by the subject, the knower. Descartes discovers that he as thinker turns out both to exist certainly and to know that fact with certitude, that is, without any doubt. Doubt is that mental state in which the mind unsettles itself because its ideas are *obscure* and *confused*.

Hence to drive out doubt is to gain the footing for certainty. Descartes' way is to use his intellectual imagination (the *ingenium* of the *Rules*) to throw everything methodically, deliberately into doubt. This doubt has little to do with a crisis of faith; it is a "hyperbolic," that is, an experimentally extremist mental position, assumed to regain one's sure foothold. He aims to free himself once in his lifetime from all preconceived opinions arising from sense perception and even from mathematical proofs; he means to assert his free will in assenting to or withholding assent from beliefs—without, however, applying this doubt to real life. For this life, Descartes says, must go on while he refounds the world.[2] The *Objections* to the First Meditation, contemporary critiques by competent opponents, are full of acute criticisms of Cartesian doubt. Again Descartes does a god's work: the unmaking of the world in preparation for its rational rebuilding. Descartes' six meditations are, as I intimated, truly a second Genesis, apparently taking place over the six days of Creation, as intimated in the beginning of the Second Meditation.

What is left when all has been doubted is—as one might guess—the doubter, the knower of doubt himself.

2. *Cogito ergo sum:* "I think, hence I am"—this most famous of Descartes' conclusions occurs in that form not in the *Meditations* but in the later *Principles.*[3] Thus I take it that Descartes meant there to be an inference from "I think" to "I am": *ergo* means "hence," "therefore," although in its first appearance in the *Meditations* he does not put the dictum so succinctly.

The inference from "I think," or, more accurately, "I am thinking" (the continuative present), to "I am, I exist," seems obvious on the face of it—for how could I engage in *doubt,* which is *my* thoughtful activity, unless *I* existed? Nonetheless it is full of problems. A first one is logical. Does not the thought "I am thinking" presuppose or contain the conclusion "I am" analytically, that is, in its mere meaning? Has anything been, in fact, *inferred?*

A second problem is in the supposed specific inference: Does it follow of necessity that because I am thinking, therefore "I" exist—that *an I* exists, especially in the way Descartes will conclude that it does, namely as a substance? For a substance is, traditionally, a being that steadily and self-subsistently *underlies* its activities, while for Descartes it seems to *be* an activity itself, the thinking, that *is* the substance—a rather strange notion, a reified Activity. Imagine that Aristotle had made his divinity, who is all *energeia,* into a *thing*! This substantial ego-thing is, however, said to be dependent on God—though only for its existence; it is otherwise free.

But could it be, one might surmise, that this thinking being is not so substantially thinglike; perhaps it is ephemeral, evanescent—fluid, at least? The transition from acting to being seems to be even more dubious when the proposition is stated as a condition with the personal pronoun italicized: "If *I* am thinking, then *I* must exist." For whence is it known that it is an "I" that thinks? Maybe it is a "we" or an "it"—"*It thinks,* one should say, as one says *it is lightening.*"[4] In any case, I myself have often had the experience that the thinking—which, to be sure, I am host to—isn't done by me alone but by itself or even an other. Neither its terms nor its necessities seem to be particularly *mine.* Thinking happens; am *I* necessary to it? It seems likely but not indubitable.

A third reservation about Descartes' great initial conclusion is in line with his self-assimilation to God. His proposition, insofar as it is an argument, is—remarkably—analogous to Anselm's famous ontological proof of God's existence, employed by Descartes himself.[5] It argues that God's existence follows from his essence, from his defining features: *What* God is includes *that* he is. Similarly, since for Descartes, a human being is essentially a "thinking thing" (*res cogitans*), it exists by reason of its essential nature:

Thinking *includes* existence! This way of considering the proof brings out something further about it that is both crucial and dubious. Any activity in general *might* be said to imply the existence of an actor (though neither his existence nor his substantiality seem, as I just suggested, to follow necessarily), but the thinking activity in particular, which Descartes defines as awareness of internality,[6] also *gives knowledge of his existence* to the thinker. For him "I think" entails "I *know* I think." Rational consciousness can discover itself, can become self-conscious. It seems to be true, but is it an inference or just a simultaneous apprehension?

3. So, returning to a notion already broached, "*the* I," any *ego*, is an entity, a substance that thinks. For him it follows that it is a thing, *res*, a reality. Before, he had made a leap from "thinking is happening" to "*I* think." Then he jumped the other way: from the ego-agent of thinking to a thinking *thing*. Descartes pronounces himself a thing. To put it accurately, he asks, "What am I?" He answers, "A thing that thinks. What is that? A thing that doubts, understands, affirms, denies, is willing, is unwilling, and also imagines and has sensory perceptions."[7] Later he will say, and we will see how important this is to the passions, that there are really only two modes of thinking, "the perception of the intellect and the operation of the will." Of these, the will turns out to be far more potent.[8] He is, in sum, a mind primarily, definitively; his mind is better known to him than his body; it is more *he*. But the mind is a substance, an existing thing that is self-sustaining, needs nothing to keep on being except "only the concurrence of God."[9] Descartes does not think we can become aware of this or of any underlying being as existent except through its principal, defining attribute. Mind's principal attribute is thinking, whose aspects have been enumerated above. So he knows himself as a thinking thing and infers himself to be a substance. He suppresses this problem: Being an "I" and being a "thing" might be incompatible. To acknowledge and resolve that perplexity would require more ontology than Descartes wants to provide.

How many such substances are there? The *Meditations* are indeed "meditations." Traditionally that means musing in all the modes of thinking, including imagination of the intellectual kind such as radical doubt requires and of the sensory kind such as the figures of geometry involve.[10] Descartes' musings in the *Meditations* are thus introspective and written down entirely in the first person singular "I." However, in the more objective *Principles* Descartes writes the plural "we." Now two other substances will soon come on the scene, God and Nature; God is certainly unique, and nature seems to be all one as well. But while it is usual to speak of Descartes' "three substances," it seems to me that minds, being one *type* of substance, must be plural in *number*, as the "we" of the *Principles* implies, and there must be as many as there are humans—though he does not say so, as far as I know.[11]

That plurality appears to be the more necessary in view of the central function assigned to willing, which is in its nature an insuperably ego-istic activity.[12] Perhaps that fact about the will is the source of Descartes' certainty that
thinking is a first person singular activity. It is the will that makes the human
mind god-like: It is maximal, indeed infinite, in scope. Through it, "I understand myself to bear in some way the image and likeness of God."[13] Since
the power to will comes from God who is perfect, unaffected by envy and
deception, will in itself is incapable of mistakes. These come about because
"the scope of the will is wider than that of the intellect," and it is from the
will's *exceeding* the understanding that error and sin arise. One might ask
why such excesses of the will are not *its* mistakes; its inerrancy seems to be
ascribed to its being partially beyond, and so without, intellect. In any case,
this primacy and perfection of the will resonates in the *Passions,* and so does
the plurality of minds.

4. I could be myself, could be a thinking thing, if there were no world
besides and no imagining and sensing of bodies. So I can and must methodically throw in doubt all "adventitious" ideas, all awareness such as comes to
me not innately because it belongs to my thinking mind by its very nature
or is invented by myself at will, but such as comes at me from the outside,
from the world, through the senses. For there might be nothing behind
these deliverances or nothing true in them. How, having thrown the world
in doubt, does Descartes regain it?

He needs a guarantor, not only of the ideas of an outer world that come
to him but first of his own innate ideas. Or better, he needs criteria by which
to judge the truth of his own thinking and also a warranty for the criteria
themselves.

The criteria are in accord with his mind as being naturally luminous, as
having a "natural light." Ideas that are thus illuminated are *clear* as being so
accessibly present to the mind that all obscurity is overcome, and they are
distinct as being not only clear but so "sharply separated" from others that
all confusion is deleted.[14]

That is as much as to say that warranted truth is Descartes' *sense* of crisp
patency, hard-edged illumination. Clearly it is a treacherous kind of certainty that depends on the mental light in which ideas appear. So an under-
writer is needed, and that is God. God guarantees the trustworthiness of
our natural light—which had first, by a perfect (or vicious) circle, delivered
God to us. I have no idea whether Descartes regards this God as an object of
real worship or as an intellectual stop-gap at most—and himself as a creature or as a colleague. He does say that God is not just another substance of
our sort. For if by substance is meant a thing that depends on nothing else
for its existence, we—being not only created by God but also maintained
in existence by him—cannot be said to be self-sufficient substances in the

same sense that he is. Yet, once again, apart from our depending on God for our being and staying in existence, we too depend on nothing else. Here is more light thrown on the human substance in its autonomy; it will have a bearing on the *Passions.*

Why does the thought of God guarantee not only innate knowledge, above all logic and mathematics, but also sensory affections? Because God, being perfect, cannot be thought to deceive us. Thus the natural world, the world of bodies, exists, and I have true knowledge of them.[15] But bodies are not minds.

5. They are in fact a third substance. There are mind and body, radically different from each other, and God who makes and maintains both *and* assures that the latter is knowable to the former.

The primary attribute, or rather essence, of body is space understood as extension. Body is *res extensa,* the extended thing. What is extension? First, it is that about body in general which *underlies* sensory qualities that come through the human, organic body's senses, such as warmth through touch, fragrance through smell, or even figure that appears to the imagination. The substrate extension, however, is perceived "by the mind alone."[16] And there it is a clear and distinct idea—and innate.

Second and more crucially, body is external to the "I"; it is perceived as *outside*: ". . . on the one hand I have a clear and distinct idea of myself, insofar as I am simply a thinking, non-extended thing; and on the other hand I have a distinct idea of body [evidently my body and, through it, bodies in nature] insofar as this is simply an extended non-thinking thing."[17]

Now the imagination has to come back in. The mind can *be* mind without imagination and sensation, but it cannot *know* bodies. The mind, which is turned inward when *thinking* extension, must turn outward toward *body,* and this it does by *imagining.*[18] We need not ask here what extension as purely *understood* might be, but extension *perceived* in the imagination is shape, position, number, motion. Extension is measured quantitatively.

The extended thing is always imagined as having measurable dimensions.[19] This is Descartes' vision of nature: All the sensory qualities of bodies being removed—including even heaviness and solidity—this is a ghostly mathematicized world, the world of our physics. Thus gravity too is not a feeling of heaviness but a measurable effect, and bodily solidity is not a sense of tangibility but a configuration of resisting forces. Descartes, in fact, goes beyond the classical physics that eventually prevailed—Newton's—in erasing the difference between space and body altogether, in not even admitting the physical dimension of mass. Material things "are capable of existing, in so far as they are the subject-matter of pure mathematics . . .";[20] the physical sciences are branches of mathematics. In the extended spatial continuum, individuated bodies (in the plural) are only temporary configurations of space continually moving out of position. I think, as I said, that body as the substance occupying extended space is *one* continuous geometric matter, a plenum coincident with space: "And this extended thing we call 'body' or 'matter' . . . The nature of body consists not in weight, hardness, color, or the like, but *simply in extension*" (my italics).[21] This strangely disembodied body, abstracted from all sensory, so-called secondary qualities, counterintuitive though it is, makes perfect sense if we regard the motive; motive tells the tale. This is a world capable of being known very clearly, distinctly and so certainly—nature prepared for apprehension by the science of sciences, mathematical physics.

Nonetheless, and this is most important for the role of the passions, sensory qualities do inform us, not of what really exists in bodies, but of "what is beneficial or harmful to man's composite nature."[22]

Imagination then, which plays a central though discreetly treated role in the *Passions,* "seems to be nothing else but an application of the cognitive faculty to a body which is intimately present to it."[23] *How* does a mind apply itself to body? Or the body to the mind? To be sure, as the mind has, as active, the imagination to turn toward the body, so it has "the passive faculty of sensory perception," which could be activated only by the reality of the opposing substance[24]—a proof, incidentally, that the latter, the external substance, exists. In other words, there is plenty of gear provided to turn the mind outward and also to absorb into the mind that which is external.

But: Body and mind, thinking and extension differ totally. "Body is by its very nature always divisible, while mind is utterly indivisible."[25] A thinking thing has no parts—aspects perhaps, but no divisions; it is "quite single and complete," a claim important in the *Passions.* The extended thing is exactly what its name says: It is extended, stretched away from itself, a composite each of whose homogeneous parts is outside the other; its very nature is to have parts; that makes it *both* part-by-part outside itself and as a whole on the "outside" of mind.

Descartes is very positive about the distinction between mind and body, but he also repeats that mind and body—his own body—are conjoined.[26] It is this union that causes us to be so unaware of their radical independence from each other, a lack of awareness that only attentive meditation can cure. Yet this imaginative intellectualism cannot, I think, cure the sense we have that a human being is formed by the living interdependence of body and soul. Indeed, Descartes will admit later that this union is itself different from both body and mind—a third something, perhaps even a fourth substance, but he cannot, by then, explain it. It is inexplicable—not in the enticing way that the experienced union of body and soul might be a stumbling block to reason and a mystery to faith, but in the peremptory way that the rational joining of two notions conceived to be each other's foil is a bare impossibility alleviated by no saving grace.

Descartes is very chary of explicit descriptions of substantial extension. He may have been satisfied, in the main, with his earlier characterization of geometric extension in the *Rules for the Direction of the Mind* (1628), where the purpose was to express extended objects in mathematical terms. From that point of view, extension has dimensions (a measurable aspect), unity (an assignable unit measure), and shape (a capacity for configuration).[27] Certainly mind has none of these, but that distinction does not tell us what extension *positively* is. The trouble is that extension itself is the defining essence of body, and it may seem excessive to ask what, in turn, the essence of extension is. Yet that is what we need to know if the union of mind and body, so crucial to the passions, is to be made intelligible. We will see how Descartes manages in his *Passions*.

I might add that his dual problem, that of the nature of space iself and of its meeting with mind, is neither new nor yet resolved in its own terms. It haunts philosophy, from the space-like receptacle of Plato's *Timaeus*, which can only be apprehended by a "bastard reason," through the spatial intuition of Kant's first *Critique*, which can be got together with the understanding only through that "blind though indispensable function of the soul," the imagination. And, be it in metaphysical or in physiological terms, it haunts all accounts of the passions ancient and modern: How does the body that has real parts "interface" with the soul that has only virtual ones? For nobody doubts that our passions involve both.

3. Why Study Descartes on the Passions?

Before saying why Descartes' treatment of the passions is, in spite of its unpropitious setting, important to thinking about human affect, let me recapitulate the chief difficulty that I see in it and in the curious solution Descartes propounds. Again, it is not a local problem special to this inquiry that he needs to solve, but one built deep into his metaphysical framework: The knowing mind and the object he intends it to know, body, have no conceivable interface.[1]

Descartes was far from unaware of the problem. He had a favorite pupil, Elizabeth, Princess of Bohemia, for whom alone he composed the *Passions* and to whose penetrating questions he responded. To her he wrote on May 21, 1643:

> [W]e have for body in particular, only the notion of extension, from which follow those of figure and movement; and for the soul by itself, we have only that of thought, in which are comprised the perceptions of the understanding and the inclinations of the will; finally, for soul and body together, we have only that of their union, on which depends that of the force that soul has to move the body, and body to act on soul, causing its sentiments and its passions.[2]

What then follows is as puzzling as it is interesting. Since it needs to be an admitted fact that body and soul interact—and crucial to his theory of the passions that the body in particular act on the soul—Descartes must explain this fact to the acute Princess. He first tries an analogy: As we falsely but easily and efficaciously attribute heaviness as a real, movement-causing quality to body—recall that the extended thing, as mathematical, has no attribute of dynamic mass—so we conceive the manner in which soul moves body. Elizabeth replies that she is too stupid to understand how a false idea could help to explain how an immaterial substance can move an extended one. We might feel the same, especially since he had once insisted that there is only one sort of material motion—locomotion.[3]

Descartes regards it not only as a brute fact but as a principle of his philosophy that the mind is such that all three effects, sensations like sight, feelings like pain, and emotions like joy, can be produced in it by movements of and in the body.[4] So a month later he answers Elizabeth that he should indeed have explained the three kinds of notion, soul, body, union, and their operation—but proceeds to do something else: to persuade her that, though "it is very necessary to have understood, once in a lifetime, the principles of metaphysics . . . it would be very harmful to occupy one's intellect frequently in meditating upon them. . . ."[5] Instead one should spend most of one's time in "the relaxation of the senses and the repose of the mind" (surely the most unexpected Cartesian advice—and gratefully received). A few hours a day should be invested in the exercise of the imagination—the faculty of the mind, recall, that represents body to the mind, and is thus the center of what it is fair to call their *unio mystica*. This letter is plainly a diversion from the problem.

Earlier Descartes had replied to another acute objector, Arnauld, that body and mind, being substances, must be complete taken in themselves, but in another sense they must be incomplete insofar as they form a union with, are "referred to," another substance to make a third "self-subsistent thing. . . . Mind and body are incomplete substances viewed in relation to man who is the unity which they form together."[6] Let he who can understand the metaphysics of this—it is, in any case, the motives that matter: the desire on the one hand to give the mind an opposing, soul-less, will-less object that it can completely master by the natural light of the intellect and on the other, the need to admit that this object must come to us through *our* bodies, which must therefore be connected to our minds. This body-connected mind is what is called traditionally a *soul*. This soul receives more than intellectually assimilable perceptions; it receives also causes of affects—feelings and passions.

Descartes has an ingenious, cunning way to face the problem "as physicist." He shrinks the interface of body and soul to a physical point of contact, a dot in the brain, the pineal gland.[7] The soul "is joined to the whole body"—I think that means "is affected by and affects the whole"—but it exercises its functions immediately on this gland, as does the body in its turn. The reason for the choice is that, whereas all the other parts of the brain are paired, the pineal gland alone is, as far as he knows, a single organ, and best fits our thoughts of any thing, which come as singles. (There are in fact other single structures in the brain, the hypothalamus and amygdala for example, which are indeed particularly associated with the emotions by brain scientists. The pineal body actually secretes the hormone melatonin and is thought to be involved in circadian, "day-round," rhythms.) Descartes has ingenious explanations for the way the animal spirits impact the gland locally with what we call information and carry causes of movement away from it to the extremities. His explanation of the soul's effect on the gland, however, is skimpy.[8] It is interesting that he admits an indeterminacy that seems to me still to operate in brain science: Whereas it is possible to trace the brain activity subserving a mental event, it is not possible systematically to interpret an excitation in the brain as a very specific human affect without some introspective report. Descartes says clearly that the same brain impression can have different passionate effects in different people; neuroscience corroborates this.[9] He does not appear to realize that if that is ultimately true he cannot really explain the passions "as physicist"; there can be no *certain* science of the emotions.

What is this soul that is *moved by* and moves the bodily brain in a material point? Here I will say in brief what it is not; in the *Passions* it will be described positively.

It is not, as the soul in Plato's dialogues, a whole of parts with different psychic jobs. It is not, as in Aristotle's works, the principle that makes a mere body into an actually living one, for which purpose it has specialized parts or aspects—Aristotle doesn't much care which. Descartes cares very much that the soul be one unitary whole, for several reasons, a tacit one probably being its pointlike contact with the body. In fact, however, it is under no actual description an undifferentiated unity. It needs to have, and is accorded, different powers—will and intellect, while intellect in turn has numerous different perceptual modes. This dissonance of claim and practice leads to Descartes' numerous tacit withdrawals, reversals, modifications, and inexplicit contradictions. I cannot keep from pointing out that Descartes' frequent appeals to simplicity, self-evidence, and easy apprehension must be taken as invitations to wariness. They signal that confusing problem is being swept under the rug—a rug transparent and opaque at will. This is not Socratic playfulness, willingness to live with perplexity, or Thomist faith, acceptance of principles surpassing human reason, but a purposeful reaching for the impregnable position.

What makes the *Passions of the Soul* so important nonetheless? There is a writer at the beginning of modernity, Descartes' great successor and traducer Spinoza, whose metaphysics is practically made to explain human affects (Chapter VII; his relation to Descartes is set out in Section 8 of this chapter). But first, and necessarily so, there is Descartes, whose metaphysics does just the opposite, and that fact—that he leaves so vexing a problem-legacy—is precisely one of the elements of the *Passions* that makes it interesting. Here is a list of benefits:

1. We see in general how different metaphysical frameworks illuminate (or skew) the conception of the passions and cause their enumeration, order, and value to differ, and in particular how a philosophy intended to make the mind master comes to grips with the fact that the passions are powerful.

2. We see how the passions look to a physicist and physiologist. Descartes is here quite consciously the initiator of modernity, in particular of an early version of the James-Lange theory, the notion that the passions are an excitation of the psyche caused in the body: The body is aroused—and we feel it. An adaptation of this theory to discoveries in neuroscience is current. To be sure, it, like practically everything, can be found in Aristotle's *On the Soul*,[10] where he says that there are several approaches to the passions and that the physicists will attribute them to physiological causes, such as surges of blood that heat the heart—which jibes with Descartes' own account. What is new is the single-mindedness of the explanatory mode and its detailed breadth. Moreover, although Descartes himself did not have the means to advance the physiological and neurological investigations of the passions very much, he was, as I said, remarkably prescient in pointing to the places to look for them—blood, nerves, single brain structures.

3. He is, thus, with Bacon, a most articulate leader in the revolts against the ancients, especially since he was so well trained in the tradition. He writes of the passions as "though I were treating a topic which no one before me had ever described."[11] What he writes is indeed new, but new in the peculiar way that marks the dialectical, that is, argumentative, tradition of Western philosophy. The new edifice is built from the re-hewn stones of the old; the terms are received but the use is remodeled.

4. A particular reversal of the ancients and the consequent tradition appears in the attribution of *action* to the body; among the ancients, the sensory body—and through it a part of the soul—is mostly thought of as passive. Poetically, it is the suffering victim of external agencies: "Eros whacked me with an ax"; philosophically, it is the passive material to be governed or informed by the soul. This new notion (though like so much else prefigured by the Stoics) of the body as the main actor in the passions will

play a foundational role in the *Passions,* and it gives much food for thought: What or who is in charge of us?

5. It turns out that it is not easy (if it is possible at all) to find a new principle for a complete and graded enumeration of the passions from which their analysis can follow. Descartes' method provides such a taxonomy to consider. In particular his claim to completeness, which is in line with the assertion in the *Principles* that "there is no phenomenon of nature which has been overlooked in this treatise,"[12] stimulates the question: How crucial is completeness as an explanatory value?

6. The *Passions* is, in spite of Descartes' disclaimer, a book fraught with moral implications. I know no avowedly rational contemporary writer of our day who is not in some respects a Cartesian, either in going at problems with Descartes' analytic method or in regarding the world in some aspects "as physicist," which means, in the case of the passions, physiologically and thus mathematically, as measurable. For example, who among us balks at quantitative evaluations of our emotional health, and what pre-Cartesian would have dreamed, even in a nightmare, of such a procedure?

For Descartes, however, the deliberate benefits to be derived from the same principles that ground our unconscious Cartesianism are the discovery of new truths, the forming of wiser judgments, the elimination of disputes by means of the clarity and certainty of the principles, and the general disposition to live serenely and harmoniously.[13] The *Passions* in particular is intended to promote wisdom; there might actually be something to help us practically in this book.

4. Actions of the Body: Passions of the Soul (First Part)

I will begin now with the text itself, namely with the First Part, which is titled "About the Passions in General," subtitled "and Incidentally about the Whole Nature of Man." I take this to mean that any consideration of human passion will necessarily involve reflections on the composite human being, body and soul.

A. Actions and Passions

In the first article of the First Part Descartes starts with the attack on the ancients and the claim of utter newness mentioned above. In the same article, however, he makes a first crucial assertion that seems to me to be in fact taken from the tradition: Action and passion are one and the same thing, though differently perceived on the part of the actor and the subject of action, respectively. This view of the relativity of doing and being done to—which seems to imply that there is one event, a passion to the subject and an action to the doer—is to be found in Aristotle's *Metaphysics*.[1] What is new is the apparently narrow but consequence-laden claim that the body acts—can, somehow, act—on its own. For, to repeat, in the main tradition, speaking in sum, the body is subject to affections, to passions, particularly afflictions—which are felt in the incarnate part of the soul. The mind too has a passive aspect insofar as it is receptive to being;[2] it is, primarily, however—or its ideas are—the source of motion and action in the worlds of appearance and being.

But that the body act on its own requires that it should be a substance (not a semi-being or a potentiality), and that is a belief held only by the ancient materialists, for whom it is in fact the *only* substance. So it is indeed the newly required junction of two fundamentally diverse substances, body and mind, that lies behind Descartes' project of explaining the passions physiologically. In other words, the body has to be real if a physiological explanation is to carry weight, and it has to carry weight if the sure and certain science of the world is to be brought about; the mind has to be real if the passions are to be mastered, and they have to be masterable if wisdom is to be philosophy's achievable aim. It follows that the mind will also be shown to act on the body, so that, by the time Descartes has made all his numerous modifications, *both* substances, body and mind, turn out to be *both* active and passive.

Nothing "acts more immediately on the soul than the body it is joined to."[3] Of course, bodies outside us in turn act on our sense organs and hence within our body. As a consequence our body is, it seems, both a conduit and a barrier—in any case, a modifying mediator between the world and the soul. Here is a new sort of subjectivity: The ancients tend to locate the cognitive distortion of the outside in the unreliably variable nature of the sense objects; these dubious aspects are now attributed to a possible disconnect between an object's properties and our physical sensory reception.[4] Whatever else it does, this view focuses attention on the inner structures and functions of the sensitive body. This body is highly differentiated.

The soul, on the other hand, is essentially single.[5] Why does it matter so much that it should be one? The claim is, in this book, Descartes' most drastic departure from the ancients. Their psychology tends to be partite, three parts for Plato, five for Aristotle, three with quite a few subparts for Thomas. These are specialized faculties, the lower ones devoted to animating the body and sensing its changes. I must point out here that the unity of the soul, which Descartes asserts most definitely, is by no means clearly understandable.[6] Not only does he speak of the soul as having "innermost depths" and an "interior," but it has diverse functions that, to be sure, he names "faculties" rather than "parts," and all of which he calls "thoughts." But they seem to do mutually exclusive work, such as representing and willing;[7] I will, however, go here not so much with what he actually achieved but what he intends. So why does Descartes intend it?

First, I think because he wants clarity and, in this case particularly, distinctness. The soul, however, that in its lower reaches is capable of being embodied is a metaphysically complicated, or if you like, a murky, notion. He wants sharp distinctions such as will keep extended body exclusively mathematicizable and unextended soul correspondingly indivisible. Moreover, it is a rule, a part of his method in this book, that we must be able to distinguish within ourselves what is entirely attributable to the inanimate body, that is, to the body apart from soul, and what is not.[8] Second, since the soul acts on the body as a whole and does it through a tiny area of contact, a picture of the soul that is, even if only figuratively, a topography, a divisible extended territory, is very inconvenient. The whole soul is both to be acted on and to act through the pineal gland and should therefore be unitary, expressible in a point. Of course, such a soul is not a source of heat or motion and so it is not the cause of death. (As so often, this assertion is later qualified). A living human being is like a wound-up automaton that stops when it runs down, not because the soul departs.[9] So, third, a unitary soul is sufficiently independent of the body to outstay it as a whole. Moreover, there are no parts to engage in a psychic struggle with each other, which is the principal purpose of the Platonic partite soul. The mental struggles we are aware of are entirely due to opposing movements imparted by body and soul to the glands.[10] Thus Descartes disapproves particularly of the traditional division of the whole soul into sensitive and rational, appetitive and volitional. Both the former and the latter pairs are for him identities, and these identifications will turn out to signal the most characteristic Cartesian notion—the domination of the will over the whole soul. It is as thinking wills that we are substantial.

And fourth, though really first and last, what has already been broached: The soul "is of a nature which has no relation to extension or to the dimensions"; it is indivisible since there is no such thing as one half or one third of the soul.[11] Descartes goes on to say—for he must here say something—that the organic body too is one and in a way indivisible, since it becomes defective if any organ is removed. Since divisibility is essential to extended body, this claim is either a sophism or the tacit admission of a new substance different from *res extensa*; *res organica*, one might call it. But then, what of the fact that the body is a mechanism, an inorganic assemblage?

B. Physiology

A large part of the *Passions* is devoted to a very confident exposition of the physiology underlying the passions,[12] although Descartes had not, as I mentioned, the means to carry out anatomical experiments. I shall briefly note the elements which, though then very prescient, are by now left far behind.

Descartes accepts Harvey's discovery of the circulation of the blood but not its cause in a pumping heart; he thinks it is due to heat in that organ. This heat is in fact responsible for all bodily movements—it is why Descartes rejects the pump theory—including that of the limbs, in which it ultimately causes the contraction of opposing muscles. For his purposes in the *Passions,* the main organs are the blood and the "animal spirits" produced in the brain by the heat of the heart, which is carried to the brain by the blood. Thence these spirits animate the body; they are the mobile successor of the old animal or sensitive soul and the forerunners of both electrical brain activity and the transmitting nervous system. They run through the body by means of little sheathed filaments, the nerves. These nerves, in a reverse motion, also carry to the brain excitations from both the external and internal senses, such as sense impressions and pains, whence originate our felt sensations. The soul is not involved in such bodily "feels." The evidence comes, for example, from reflex motions such as closing our eyes at the sudden thrust of a hand, even though we might know that it is a friendly gesture.

This is the body understood as a machine, which will now act on the soul. It is interesting that Descartes does not mention touch in his list of external senses, although it is the sense of senses in a bodily machine, since in physics direct interactions are by touch. Perhaps he is suppressing, in this organic context, the mechanical interaction that all external objects are supposed to have with the body, even those that seem to affect us by the distance senses, like vision.[13] In any case, the chief emphasis is on the internal animal spirits, or "spirits," as Descartes says for short. They can act entirely without the soul—though the will can influence them.

C. Perceptions and Volitions

The soul is so far totally pure, that is, unmingled with the body, and completely unitary, that is, partless. It will now be shown to be passive under the body's action and to be partly passive and partly active in itself.

The soul thinks, but thinking comprises many functions divisible into two genera that have been carried over from the *Meditations*: perception and volition. Cases of perception—or "knowledge"—are generally passions because it is "often not our soul that makes them such as they are, and because it always receives them from things that are represented by them."[14] The actions of the soul are its volitions; it is the loftier function. They terminate either in the mind "as when we will to love God," or in the body, as when we move our legs.

As volitions may issue either in soul or body, so perceptions are caused within both. Those in the soul come about by the will's attention; they might be invented imaginings or intelligible ideas. Those in the body come either by the sense organs and the mediation of the nerves, as do sense perceptions, or arise within our body, as do hunger and pain; all these are actions of the body but passions of the soul. There are also involuntary imaginings, like dreams that come about haphazardly because the spirits course at random in the brain; they too are among the passions. (See Figure VI-A.)

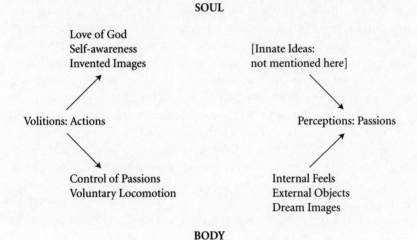

SOUL

Love of God
Self-awareness
Invented Images

[Innate Ideas:
not mentioned here]

Volitions: Actions

Perceptions: Passions

Control of Passions
Voluntary Locomotion

Internal Feels
External Objects
Dream Images

BODY

Figure VI-A

This chart maps the functions of the soul as 1. divided into willing and perceiving (left and right), and 2. as it executes them by itself and as joined to the body (top and bottom). The innate ideas and the intellect play no appreciable role in the *Passions of the Soul*, which is not about certain knowledge required for the mastery of nature, but the applicable wisdom useful for the mastery of self.[15]

For this is what the passions proper are: They are defined as perceptions that differ from all the soul's other thoughts.[16] They are "excitations (*émotions*) of the soul which are referred to it in particular and which are caused, maintained and strengthened by some movement of the spirits." Here is the word "emotion" (which will not displace "passion" in English until Hume employs it) used in its most suggestive sense: a commotion of the soul, "which the close bond between the soul and the body renders confused and obscure." There are no other thoughts "which agitate and shake" the soul so strongly. Descartes makes it part of their definition that they cannot be referred to a commonly "known proximate cause." He seems to mean that we never know where passions come from—whether from an external object moving our nerves or from some internally caused excitation. Descartes is perfectly traditional in this view. The passions of the soul are murky, however clear their physiological causes. There are, he adds, self-caused excitations of the soul—our volitions; these latter will be the soul's actions.

D. Representations

The soul wills, and those volitions are, once more, what Descartes calls actions. Thus it acts on the body, "and the whole action of the soul consists in this: merely by willing something, it makes the little gland to which it is closely joined move in the way required to produce the effect corresponding to this volition."[17] There is here no such thing as an ineffective volition—to will freely is to will effectively. This straightforward view will obviously have great moral import.

But the soul also acts within itself, and these actions originate *and* terminate within the soul. It attends, assents, imagines, and even loves willfully. If this book were about the soul's faculties rather than its passions, I would ask how any of these actions can be willful, that is, at our initiative, rather than caused by the object, be it a matter of interest, a proposition, an image, or an object of love. But here I just note the ultimate power of the will in the Cartesian soul with respect to two activities that seem to be, as it were, passivities: imagining and loving.

Descartes, as I said, considers that invented images are volitional. It is a trait of modernity—as lively now as ever—that the imagination is usually regarded by both artists and amateurs not as receptive to the inspiration of the Muses, who channel a tradition, but as creative in the manner of a God, who commands that there be a new world.

Not unsimilarly, he thinks that our love of God is active, willed, a sort of inverse passion. Love will be defined as "an excitation of the soul caused by the motions of the spirits which incite it to join itself in volition to the objects that appear to be suitable to it."[18] The love of God, on the other hand, is exceptional because it *starts* with our will, which then brings about a passion that is in fact an action.

Indeed in the soul, "active" and "passive" seem to get mixed up, because volitions and perceptions are so intimately related, for example, in the case of self-awareness. Descartes says that, for our soul, it is an action to will but a passion to perceive that it wills; these are nevertheless a single thing, to be named after the loftier thing, the will.[19]

The reason for this equivocation is so interesting—though not the subject of this book—because it involves us in the deepest question concerning human knowing: Is it primarily receptive, as the ancients thought, or constructive, as the moderns claim? Is our soul at its highest in the receptive activity of contemplation as Aristotle understood it, or in a forceful operation of the will as Descartes did?

There is one aspect of the question that does need to be mentioned here: representation. Perceptions "represent" objects to the soul, and passions are directed toward objects.[20] These external objects, which occur as the occasioning causes of the cognitive perception or of the passion which they excite, exist in the mind as symbols or pictures of themselves. The effort of the *Meditations* is, after all, largely that of removing doubts about the truthfulness of the representations, that is, of the objects as they are present idea-wise in our minds. Thus representationality in general is basic for Descartes.

Now consider representations more particularly. They appear as the images of the imaginative faculty, which seem to be picture-like, quasi-spatial, resemblance-representations. This faculty always plays a great role in those passions that are not mere blind feels such as simple sensations like pain, but are excited by representations of objects—the intentional passions. So it does in the *Passions*. The imagination and the imaginability of the intellect's ideas are a fascinatingly complex Cartesian topic in respect to the top and middle of the (purportedly unitary) Cartesian mind,[21] but for my purposes it is at the bottom, where mind meets matter, that the interest lies. How is the non-extended soul capable of giving room to a spatial picture? Such images are certainly rife in Descartes' account. For example, the pineal gland, in "acting immediately on the soul, makes it see the object causing the passion." "Make see," *fait voir,* does not seem to be used metaphorically here.[22] The perplexity is a more sharply focused version of the ever-mysterious body-mind union. Its non-resolution, inherent in the particular difficulty of explaining how a "thinking thing" can harbor a quasi-spatial representation, means that Descartes hasn't quite explained how passions can be object-directed. To this critique Descartes might—this is merest surmise—reply, "But consider that it isn't the *object itself* but our apprehension of its *utility* that rouses passion."

E. Morality

The First Part of the *Passions* ends—as will the other two—with Descartes writing after all "as moral philosopher," for he now considers the power of the soul to control the passions.

The principal effect of the passions is adaptive: They incite the soul to will what they simultaneously prepare the body to do, say to flee in fear or stand boldly.[23] (This is a partial prototype of Darwin's "serviceable" theory.) Moreover, the soul can will to remember by driving the spirits—through the agency of the gland—to memory traces in the brain. (This is a prototype of present memory storage and retrieval theories.)

Then the moral application of these capabilities is this: There are what are now called autonomic movements, those not at all or not easily subject to volition, like the dilation and contraction of the pupil; our passions too are not directly subject to the will. Yet we can, willfully, make representations, that is, generate to ourselves mental images that are *opposed* to those which incite the passions we mean to reject. Note how vitally important to morality the image-making imagination is after all! Thus fear can be conquered by representations of the greater security and glory to be won by standing strong, etc. This mental device does not always work, because of the autonomy of the blood and the spirits, but even there the will can have a restraining influence.[24]

Descartes takes the occasion to reiterate his opposition to a psychic struggle in the moral control of the passions such as the ancient theories of the partite soul involved. He says that the body alone opposes our reason. The soul is a unitary thinking thing, not capable of self-opposition.

However, once again, he temporizes: We imagine that the soul undergoes a struggle of different powers because we successively succeed and fail in quelling the somatic conditions. Thus the soul feels driven in opposite ways at once, and the effect can be conceived as a kind of struggle.

It is by the outcome of the struggle between body and soul that we tell a weak soul from a strong one. Strength of soul is the ability to make its judgments, true or false, prevail over the body. Hence those resolutions that rest on knowledge of truth are the ones that prevent repentance, the bitterest of all passions.[25]

Descartes ends the First Part by reiterating his chief therapeutic moral principle, the Aristotelian theory of habituation, now in physiological form—a somatic ethics. It consists of disassociating by training the movements of the brain from certain events, just as setters, who are naturally inclined to chase a partridge, are trained to stop dead until they hear the gun. Thus even the weakest souls can "acquire a quite absolute dominion over their passion." One might say that here Descartes is in effect managing to be a moral philosopher "*as* physicist."

5. The Order and Enumeration of the Passions (Second Part)

The Second Part consists of four subparts: 1. the *enumeration* of the passions and the ordering that makes it possible, which I will dwell on; 2. the definition of the six primary passions; note that the description of each passion, which might be called its phenomenology, namely the account of its psychic appearances and its physiological symptoms, precedes its definitive formulation; 3. the accompanying physiology, which I shall cut short; and 4. the role of those excitations of the soul that depend only on our will, that is, the role of *morality*.

In the First Part, Descartes applied his Method insofar as it prescribes analyzing the subject of inquiry into its parts, here body and soul. In the Second Part he follows its enumeration requirement.[1] As I said, enumerating the passions is no mean trick; Descartes wrote to Princess Elizabeth about it several times.[2] The difficulty lies in finding that principle of ordering which will give not only a rational but also a complete list; his book is after all about *the* passions of the soul. We already know—and here Descartes acknowledges it—that this principle cannot be physiological because the gland does not act determinately and because some passions are in fact actions initiated by the soul.

His actual principle of enumeration introduces a new factor, one alluded to above: ". . . [O]bjects which move the senses do not excite different passions in us" through their particular diversity but by their usefulness for disposing the soul to will the execution of things useful to us. So he will investigate "in how many different ways that are important to us our senses can be moved by their objects."[3] Note that Descartes equivocates: Are the passions excited by cognitive perceptions of usefulness or are the senses themselves judges of utility? The latter possibility might derive from Thomas's "estimative sense." It would confirm the body's initiative in arousing the passions. In any case, the first enumerating principle in theory is: by the *degree of usefulness.*

In practice a second ordering obtains: by *temporality,* as displayed in Figure VI-B-1. The rest of this Section (a–e) will be a commentary on that chart of the passions. I should observe here that its innovations are mostly piggybacked on traditional issues: physiological concomitants, suitability of object, passions with or without opposites.

A. Wonder

Perhaps the most remarkable feature of the ordering of passions is the placing of wonder as the first (Figure VI-B-1), where is marks the temporal mode of newness—Descartes' very own.[4] Wonder is the old incitement to learning, the beginning of the love of wisdom. But it was not itself listed

1. Protopassions: Before Good and Evil

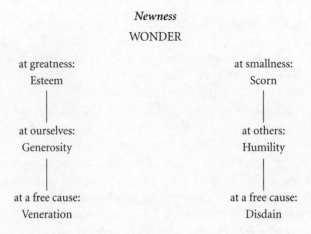

Newness
WONDER

| at greatness: | at smallness: |
| Esteem | Scorn |

| at ourselves: | at others: |
| Generosity | Humility |

| at a free cause: | at a free cause: |
| Veneration | Disdain |

Figure VI-B

2. Passions: Under Good and Evil

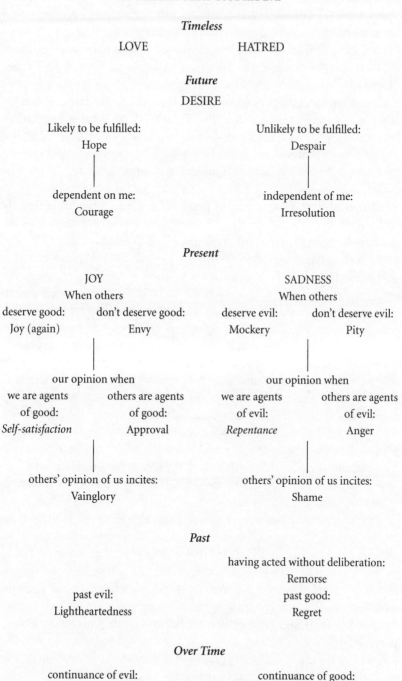

Timeless

LOVE   HATRED

Future

DESIRE

Likely to be fulfilled: Unlikely to be fulfilled:
Hope   Despair

dependent on me: independent of me:
Courage   Irresolution

Present

JOY   SADNESS
When others   When others
deserve good: don't deserve good: deserve evil: don't deserve evil:
Joy (again)   Envy   Mockery   Pity

our opinion when   our opinion when
we are agents   others are agents   we are agents   others are agents
of good: of good: of evil: of evil:
Self-satisfaction   Approval   *Repentance*   Anger

others' opinion of us incites: others' opinion of us incites:
Vainglory   Shame

Past

having acted without deliberation:
Remorse
past evil: past good:
Lightheartedness   Regret

Over Time

continuance of evil: continuance of good:
Sadness Diminished   Distaste

Figure VI-B *(continued)*

among the passions by the ancients—though it was by Thomas and will be by Spinoza. A suppressed reason for Descartes' attention to it may be that he wants cognitive wonder to supplant faith in miracles.[5]

It is indeed called a passion in the *Passions* because of its powerful brain effects, but it is a peculiar, a unique, passion in several ways. Since it arises from a first encounter with some object that surprises us, its occurrence is not preceded by any experience of that object's suitability. Hence it is actually not a proper passion in Descartes' sense at all, since passions have just been tied to adaptive helpfulness—a very modern notion, for it used to be thought that passions were destructive afflictions on the whole. I call it a *protopassion* because it lacks that judgment of suitability which is the first feature of passions.

It is, moreover, physiologically peculiar in affecting the brain directly without relation to heart or blood.[6] It has no opposite because it is a kind of "startle reaction" whose null condition is indifference.

Descartes has an ambivalent attitude towards his first passion, which causes him to return to it over and over. Defined as a sudden surprise of the soul, it serves to focus psychic attention on its inciting object and to keep the senses fixed on it. Thus we learn and retain in memory what we were previously ignorant of, and hence it disposes us to the acquisition of the sciences. Yet if we wonder too much or too long we become habituated to finding everything wonderful and addicted to seeking novelties.[7] Stupid people are too dull to wonder while astute people soon begin to see the regularities. (An aside: This passion for novelty, grown into a greed for the new, is called *curiosity*. Edmund Burke will regard *it* as the first of the passions[8]— for every major passion there is someone for whom it is first—because it is simple, characteristic of children, and blended into all our passions; I think he means that into every live affect, even the direst, there is mixed a drop of wondering curiosity: "What's happening?" Heidegger, just to get the whole gamut, will damn it as a prototypically inauthentic way of existing.)

It turns out that Descartes is anticipating a tendency of modernity to regard wonder as a temporary psychic condition due to ignorance to be superseded by warranted knowledge—while nonetheless recommending curiosity as part of the scientific temperament. It is this ambivalence toward novelty—to seek it in order to nullify it—which is prefigured in the *Passions*. And thus wonder, whose temporal mode is newness, rightly heads the list in a book that means to found what we call modernity. This modern wonder differs, *toto caelo*, by a whole world, from the old Socratic wonder: The former is a non-marvelling astonishment at something extraordinary; the latter was a marvelling perplexity aroused by something very ordinary.

Descartes returns to wonder in the Third Part, when passions meld into virtues. And there wonder develops an ego-istic aspect that is truly novel:

As marveling *wonder at ourselves* insofar as we have free will and can control our volitions, it gives rise to Descartes' master passion, generosity.

Enter now a third ordering principle besides utility and temporality, that of "primitive" and derived passions.[9] There are only six primitive, originating passions from which all the other passions are derivatives by composition or specification. These secondary passions fit easily into the time-scheme of the primary passions (Figure VI-B-2).

How does Descartes know there are six primitive passions? He claims that their enumeration is both totally new and complete. (The derived passions are not practically enumerable because their number is indefinite, but in principle they are reachable through the primaries.) In particular Descartes criticizes the old division of the sensitive part of the soul into *concupiscent* and *irascible*, that is, into desire- and anger-harboring parts.[10] How, he asks, can all the passions be derived from these? The answer, I should say, is to hand: "Irascible" refers not just, as he claims, to "being vexed," but to spiritedness, while "concupiscence" does, to be sure, refer to desire but in a larger sense than Descartes admits—for desire traditionally includes love, which Descartes separates out, as the diagram shows. Curiously, this separation is the result solely of his time principle of order, for love and desire are, in his understanding, identical except for the future-directedness of the latter. I think he criticizes the old concupiscent-irascible distinction just because he eschews any division of the soul.

How, then, does he know which and how many primitive passions there are? He reviews, as he says and the as Method dictates, those listed and finds "with ease" that only six are simple. The accuracy of this proceeding depends on the list being complete to begin with and the descriptions of the derivatives as originating from the primitives being correct—in other words, it is largely traditional and only somewhat empirical—and mostly improvised. For example, the notion that in love there is a lot of heat around the heart[11] is traditional. It may be that Descartes thought that the physiology of the emotions offered some empirical evidence for ordering them. It is, however, entirely unclear how he knows the considerable detail he gives of the organs involved in informing the brain, or the size and speed of the spirits coming from it to the members. The physiology seems, in fact, to be *ex post facto* with respect to the psychology. Moreover, it is hard to discern in it more than very rudimentary diagnostic indices useful for ordering the passions. Probably the ordering rationale, though inexplicit, yet lies on the surface: The one disinterested passion, wonder, is first because its formal object, the *new* (at all times), precedes engagement. Then, naturally, follows that most celebrated pair of passions, love and hate; then comes their moving principle, desire, and finally their consummation, joy or sorrow.

The primary passions, then, can be set out in a neat arrangement of single and paired:

WONDER (no opposite)

LOVE   HATRED

DESIRE (no opposite)

JOY   SADNESS

The derived passions will be more particularly taken up by Descartes in the Third Part.

B. Love and Hatred

Of the passions proper, love and hatred are first because they are the very embodiment of the suitability feature: Love is defined as "the excitation (*émotion*) of the soul, caused by the motion of the spirits, which incites it to join itself in volition to the objects that appear suitable to it"—here suitable means, I think, useful;[12] hatred is, analogously, a will to be separate. This may seem a pretty cramped rendition of humanity's premier passion. It is clearly the consequence of not allowing love to be a species of desire. Descartes explains what "joining (or separating) oneself in volition" in love (or hatred) means. It is a stable state of *present* fulfillment, a condition of union (or disunion) attained by our consent. For that reason, future-directed desire is not necessarily a part of love.

C. Willed Love

I pause here to say something about Descartes' understanding of the will, since it plays so primary a role in the *Passions,* and the phrase "in volition" (*de volonté*) is so often repeated here and elsewhere; in these places Descartes uses *volonté* for the faculty, will, and *de volonté* for the activity, willing or volition. It cannot, I think, be said that by reading the applicable passages, one knows what it means to have a will. Perhaps that is impossible. But the circumstances of its operation are laid out particularly in the *Principles* and the *Meditations.*[13] The modes of will listed are desire and aversion, assertion and denial, as well as doubt. The operation of the will—here, of course, meaning the free will—begins in indifference, volitional "imperfection," inconclusiveness. This indifference seems to mean the condition of being without sufficient reasons for deciding; Descartes thinks of it as an incomplete condition. Then the thinking thing, the mind, deliberates, and that involves the intellect, which judges by its natural light and delivers clear and distinct truth. The will immediately inclines in accordance with the intellect's knowledge, and this assenting or denying constitutes the spontaneity and freedom of the will—being moved off-center by true understanding.

Nonetheless it is not the intellect that rules, but the will and resolution is all. As was said, the human intellect labors under the limits imposed by God on a creature, while the will is completely unrestricted and infinite, for it is indivisible, so that no part of it can be taken away. I take this strange argument to mean that will—not intellect—is the innermost faculty of the human mind, the one most remote from extension and so least subject to even metaphorical partition. It is, one might say, the most opposite to indefinite extendedness—infinite intensity. That is its nature, mastery is its work: We are unextended beings who can dominate nature and must master ourselves. For people used to thinking that the will's indifference before it is determined by thought and fixed by choice *is* its freedom rather than its moment of imperfection, and that the will, being determined by the intellect, is less or at most *equal* to the latter in scope—for them, Descartes' notions will be hard to swallow. That is evident in the *Objection* to the *Meditations,* longer than the work itself.[14] Descartes' novel version of a will—whose freedom is to be determined by truth but whose power is in the infinite reach of its intensity—is perfectly fitted to dominate the soul and its passions.

To return to love. It is "in volition," then, by the will, which may act either on the body or within the soul, that we join ourselves to another and imagine ourselves as part of a whole.

Descartes reinforces the importance of the imagination in this union by referencing deadpan the most imaginative work on love I know, Plato's *Symposium,* where this coupling of lovers is presented in a hilariously physical image. The centrality of the imagination is reinforced in a letter to Chanut dated February 1, 1647, usually referred to as "the Letter on Love." It occurs there in respect to that love of God which is not a passion but a volition. How, Descartes asks, could it ever become a passion—as it sometimes does—when here the soul is "detached from the traffic of the senses" and so unable to communicate its love to the imaginative faculty? He has an answer: We imagine as an object not God, who is unimaginable, but our love itself which consists of our will to unite ourselves to God; that idea itself will produce the bodily heat around the heart that causes a violent psychic passion—another ego-istic, self-referential emotion.

This then is the passion-circuit for volitionally generated passions directed to internal objects: object → volition → body → soul. Recall the contrasting route for the response elicited by external objects: object → body → soul → body. That the former terminates in the soul and the latter in the body defines them respectively as interior and exterior passions; what is typically Cartesian is that the body is involved in both.

D. Desire

The Chanut letter helps in another respect. Descartes wants to keep desire out of the definition of love, because, I think, he wants to preserve his temporal ordering principle, the only comprehensive one he really has; it, recall, distinguishes love from desire merely as present from future union. Thus he says that benevolent love is not essentially different from concupiscent, that is, desirous, love; these phenomena are merely effects, not parts of the definition.[15] But as anyone who has had the experience knows, ingenious definitions notwithstanding, love without longing is but a supine satisfaction. In fact, desire gets mixed up with it continually in the *Passions,* for some loves, he says—those not so purely and unpossessively fixed on the object itself as is parental love—indeed desire possession.[16] Moreover delight, a specification of love, is also sometimes a species of desire. The delight of beauty incites us only to look, but the delight in the one whom we imagine as another self, which is the most powerful at a certain age and season—spring, I imagine—makes us *want* to unite with that other self, since our brain has received an impression of our own defectiveness without that other. Usually we desire to join ourselves to just one such other at a time, because Nature does not make us imagine that we need more than one other half (!). It is in this article that Descartes cites the *Symposium* (without acknowledgment) and admits that this passion is the one usually called love.[17] So we might say that the more he descends from the definition to the living experience, the more confusing the exposition gets, which is only fair; desirously delighted love is a confused representation, as he himself says.

In the Letter he says even more explicitly that the soul's love is confused thinking attributable to prenatal and early childhood experiences of the satisfaction of physical wants. These confused bodily passions and their physiology still shadow rational adult love and its judgments. That is why, he says, the nature of love is difficult for us to understand. Is he insinuating a deflation even of spiritual love? In any case, the definitive presentation in the *Passions* is to be taken with a grain of salt. For "confused thought," aroused in the soul through the nerves, has been termed in the Letter, as it was earlier in the *Principles,* the mark of *all* the passions; for Spinoza it will be their very nature.

Hatred, the opposite of love, is not so highly differentiated by object, because the evils from which we separate ourselves are not so distinctly noticed by us.[18] Were there, I ask myself, no devotedly precise antipathies in seventeenth-century Europe? Molière will know better.

Desire has no opposite; it is *one* desire that makes us either seek or avoid an object, tend toward it with love or turn away from it with that hatred which is traditionally called aversion. Thus desire is, as was said, speciated by delight and abhorrence. The latter is instituted by nature to represent to the soul "a sudden and unexpected death";[19] I imagine Descartes means an abrupt reversal of the physical processes. One might ask why, if he wants to be novel in avoiding aversion as desire's opposite, love might not similarly be said to be a passion without opposite but to have a positive mode, love proper, and a privative one, which would be called hatred? The reason is, I think, that love, being present and actual in time, is already committed, so to speak, to being then and there, in itself, positive.

E. Joy and Sadness

Joy and sadness are the last of the primitive passions. "Joy (*joie*) is a delightful excitation of the soul, wherein consists the enjoyment (*jouissance*) it has of the good which the impressions of the brain represent as its own."[20] It is the fruit of the goods that the soul possesses, for they are as if not possessed when they are not enjoyed. It cannot be said that this definition tells us wherein the *émotion* of the soul consists: Of course joy must involve enjoyment. Joy is probably close to what elsewhere is called pleasure. Its condition is attainment or possession of the object, its fulfillment is a fruit, or as Aristotle says, a bloom. "Good" is commonly said to be something we judge to be agreeable to our nature, so joy comes from having what fits us, what is good for us.

There is also a joy in which what we possess is our own to begin with, intellectual joy.[21] Once again, while we are embodied, the imagination intervenes even when this good is "in no way whatever imaginable," and by forming some impression in the brain turns the action of the soul into a passion. Thus even our purest thinking "can hardly fail" to take the physical detour into the brain. (This seems entirely plausible. It is, I think, common experience that even the least sensory intellection is accompanied by some figurative representation and if so, the brain is probably involved.) Sometimes, Descartes says, this *émotion*, joy, and its opposite, sadness—which he calls not an *émotion*, an excitation, but an unpleasant languor—are thoughtless. There are times when we feel joyful or sad without distinct notice of good and evil; Descartes says that this means these passions form impressions in the brain without the soul's mediation: When the weather is fine we feel irrationally cheerful. Here experience seems to have trumped the theory which does not permit such direct effects.[22] Physical pain and pleasure do not necessarily occur in tandem with joy or sadness, but being testimonials of the body's good or evil, they do usually induce those passions in the soul.[23]

There follow the articles on the physiology of the passions, on accompanying phenomena such as laughter and tears, and on the external indices of the passions.[24] A sample of the physiological etiology is from the article on love.[25] Descartes tells how, after the understanding has represented to itself some object of love, the animal spirits, nerves, and muscles go into action; the heart is unusually heated; the spirits are larger and more agitated than usual and strengthen the first impression of the lovable object in the soul so that it dwells on that thought. "And this is what the passion of love consists in." It is, in short, a physiologically reinforced impression that a suitable complement has now been adjoined.[26] Elizabeth cannot have found this satisfactory.

F. Usefulness

The Second Part closes with a reiteration of the usefulness of the six passions. They are by nature given to the soul insofar as it is joined to the body, and their natural use is to preserve and perfect the body. Descartes goes so far as to say, in his methodically reductive mode, that fear, which is often cited as the model passion and is near the top of most lists, is not a particular passion at all, but only an excess of cowardice. His rationale—a very rationalistic rationale—is that it is never useful. Recall that usefulness is, together with the physiological feature of being caused by the spirits, the chief identifying mark of a passion. The principal ingredient of fear is—paralyzing—surprise, that is, stupid wonder, which we can forestall by forethought.[27] To me, the fact that fear gets short shrift in the *Passions* is indicative of the bold volitional morality that governs the book.

One of the negative emotions, sadness, might be even more necessary than joy, since to repel harm is a requirement of survival. Here again the Darwinian view of the emotions is in prospect.[28] Nonetheless, Descartes warns, the usefulness of the negative emotions is imperfect. They are not always immediately correct indicators of good and harm, and they tend to exaggerate conditions. We should correct them by experience and reason.

The useful passions are, moreover, so not only to the body but also to the soul. Love—for this reason incomparably better than hatred—joins a good to us that makes us more perfect; what is more, that union is followed by joy. Even an ill-founded joy is preferable to sadness, except when the latter leads to action. Likewise, an ill-founded joy is more harmful than false sadness, because the former leads to rashness while the latter makes for prudence.[29] Here is yet another passion-order by utility.

All these four passions incline us to action only through the mediation of the desire they excite. Therefore the regulation of desire is "the principal utility of Moral Philosophy."[30] The most common error concerning desires is to fail to distinguish "the things that depend entirely on us from those that do not depend on us"—pure Epictetus, unattributed. So it seems that the passions are useful to the body through exciting desire, which is, recall, willing the future things suitable to us. Moral philosophy is useful for controlling that desire. The control is necessary only for other-dependent desire. For there is no excessive ardor for things that depend on our free will, which are always good. There are two specific remedies for vain desires. One is the virtue of generosity.

The other is reflection on Divine Providence, which will teach us not to depend on Fortune, a chimaera arising from an error in our understanding. Instead we will accept that, except for those things that depend on us, our fate has been determined from all eternity,[31] for we can desire only what is possible. Therefore what does not depend on us we can consider to be possible only insofar as we think it depends on Fortune, which is simply a term for our ignorance of all the causes necessary to produce an outcome. So when it does not occur, that shows that the necessary cause was lacking. However, if we had known that, we would have considered the event impossible and so would not have desired it. Here is the clever Stoic argument for desiring only what we can completely control. It is watertight but somewhat unpersuasive, because it is, as far as I know, part of real, indefeasible human desire to long for the impossible—and then, against all rhyme and reason, sometimes to obtain it.

Indeed there seems to me to be a rift in Descartes' world. His old stoicism requires self-mastery and self-limitation, but his new science expects unlimited dominion over nature. Moreover, though self-mastery was a long-standing moral maxim for him, it was another maxim to act firmly and decisively—and masterfully—in the world even on doubtful opinions once adopted.[32]

Descartes indeed borrows extensively from ancient Stoicism, as he had even in his first writings.[33] His orderly enumeration, his establishment of the few generic emotions, his temporal classification—these are all Stoic ways, as reported by Cicero. But there are also great differences (besides the basic fact that he is not a pantheistic materialist). The Stoics regard the passions as errors of judgment and as pathologies of the irrational part of the soul. Descartes thinks of them as utilities and locates them in a unitary soul. The Stoics think that the best life is without emotion; Descartes does not think so at all. Indeed he chides Chanut for thinking that, because he, Descartes, has studied the passions, he has lost them. On the contrary, he finds them so good and useful that "our soul would have no reason to want to be joined to the body . . . if it could not feel them."[34] What he has in common with the Stoics is the insistence on moral self-sufficiency, on self-dependence.

Toward realizing, in this work on the soul, the self-dependence of the thinking self, Descartes introduces the—more than a little discomposing—notion of an *inner* excitation, one caused in the soul by itself unaided by the animal spirits. It is, in effect, the idea of a self-activating passion. These inner excitations, being most intimately ours, prevent exterior disturbances from having the power to harm us. Thus they are very useful, but don't they vitiate the system which is based on the bodily origin of the emotions? At any rate, the soul, in seeing itself thus invulnerable, comes to know its perfection and a contentment with itself that is the concomitant of virtue. Virtue is introduced in the last paragraph of the Second Part and becomes prominent in the Third Part.

What then are these internal excitations, these self-activating emotions on which "our good and our ill depend principally"?[35] Though they are our refuge from the passions, Descartes says next to nothing about them, only that they are often accompanied by their exterior passion-doubles or even opposites. One example he gives is—perhaps inadvertently, who can tell?—hilarious: A man weeps with genuine body-activated, soul-passive sadness at the funeral of the wife he was used to. But in his innermost depths—wherever they are in the unextended non-partite soul—there is excited an unbidden secret joy.[36] I observe without comment that earlier on a live mistress was cited as a typical object of love.[37]

The supreme remedy for the passions, however, is still virtue.[38]

6. Particular Passions: The Turn to Virtue (Third Part)

In this part Descartes reconsiders, in a more moral vein, the particular passions that are species of the six primitive passion-genera, shown in Figure VI-B together with their differentia. Here the passions are closely related to vices and virtues, though more to the former. "Virtue does not seem to partake of the nature of passion as much as vice does."[1]

How to distinguish a virtue—or vice—from a passion? For one thing, passionate excitations are more evident externally. More definitively, the virtues are dispositions (that is, not primarily excitations) of the soul, "which dispose it to certain thoughts, so that they are different from these thoughts but can produce them and conversely be produced by them."[2] True virtue is included under wisdom, Descartes says in a letter to Elizabeth,[3] and proceeds from knowledge of what is right; vice usually springs from ignorance. So Descartes is appealing to the famous Socratic dictum that virtue is knowledge, but with a modification: He interposes a "disposition" between knowledge and virtue, which are directly joined by Socrates. A disposition is probably more that firm resolve (mentioned in the letter) to reason correctly and do right than it is an inborn propensity. It is a combination of Aristotelian habituation with Cartesian volition. Since the pure virtues so defined and taken together are "wisdom," wisdom is what the *Passions* ends with.

A. Picked Passions

I will choose some particular passions from the forty or so listed and described in the Third Part, those that stand out in some way. I begin with esteem and especially self-esteem, which I mention first because it is such a current preoccupation—not, however, in a form Descartes would approve. Today, it is a therapeutic expedient not necessarily related to desert. But Descartes says the only good reason to esteem ourselves "is our free will and the dominion we have over our volitions." And then, "It renders us in a way like God"![4]

The whole list ends with "lightheartedness" (*allégresse*, Figure VI-B-2) which, he says, is not particularly noteworthy but is put here to follow the order of enumeration—of which a moderately attentive reader will surely have lost track but which he regards as a sort of completeness-warranty.[5]

Not too far from the middle come two opposed passions that Descartes singles out as the *sweetest* and *most bitter* respectively: self-satisfaction and repentance.[6] The former is a species of self-dependent present joy. It is not so much the quiescent tranquility and repose of conscience that comes from constantly following virtue—a taste for which pertains to the Stoic temperament—as the joy derived from a freshly done action one thinks good. It is an *ex post facto* passion, the excitement after virtuous deeds, the sweetest because it depends on ourselves. It can also be dangerous, however, when it turns to pride and bigotry. Here he issues a wonderful blast against the bigots who revel in false self-satisfaction, "exterminating whole peoples just because they do not accept their opinions"[7]—Descartes in the benign mode of modern tolerance. Repentance is, then, the opposing passion, a species of joy, useful in inciting us to do better, but harmful when people feel guilty without knowing for sure that what they did was bad.

B. Generosity

Having spoken of the first, last, and middle species-passions, I come to the one most interesting to Descartes, who devotes the largest number of articles to it, for it is "as it were, the key to all other virtues."[8] It is *generosity*, a species of the genus wonder and thus in part what I have called a protopassion, one which may be excited without reference to the goodness or badness, the utility, of its causal object. Generosity is defined as self-esteem for our free control of our volition—another self-referential passion. It is hard to see how this passion, which is the first to turn out to be a virtue as well, is *not* actually about the goodness of its object, the self, though of course it is a peculiar object. Truth to tell, the subordination of both self-esteem and generosity to wonder is unperspicuous—for surprise at the novel extraordinariness of its object is its defining feature, and why should that be the essence either of self-esteem or generosity? Descartes doesn't quite believe it himself and struggles to make things fit: What is ever newly marvelous to us in our esteem for ourselves and in the virtues that cause it is not so much the set of well-known reasons for our ordinary self-respect, as the fact that there should be such an infinite power as our free will in so infirm a subject as ourselves. Those considerations "always give off new Wonder." Cartesian generosity is, it seems to me, the very protopassion of the newly discovered ego: the "I," the "subject," of the great Continental systems that establish modernity.

Generosity, which makes a man esteem himself as much as he legitimately can, consists then only in this: He understands, first, that nothing truly belongs to him but his free will and that he should be praised or blamed only for his good or bad use of it. And he feels, second, a "firm and constant resolution" to use it well and never to lack the will to undertake and execute everything he judges to be best. This is what it is "to follow virtue perfectly." Thus generosity is the virtue of *resolving to be virtuous.* In sum, the master passion is a form of amazement at our power of control, albeit self-control—a strangely cramped first twist on a word denoting, even before the later "liberality," high-bred noble-mindedness. Whatever the name, this Stoic resonance carries into later modernity. Thus Kant will begin his introductory work on morality with the claim that nothing in or beyond the world is unqualifiedly good "except a good will."[9]

Humility, "low-to-the-ground-ness," is only an apparent opposite to generosity insofar as the traditional name for *generosité* is indeed "magnanimity," "large-souledness." Descartes has chosen for the latter, his key virtue, the French term because (he now explains) he thinks this passion-virtue is misunderstood in the Schools.[10] They adhere, I imagine, to the Aristotelian meaning of magnanimity as "greatness of soul," a virtue primarily concerned with due honor and noble liberality and including no reference to that post-pagan notion, the free will; it would certainly be a virtue opposed to humility were that too not a post-classical notion. But Descartes' generosity, although he appreciates its reference to gentle birth, that is, to natural superiority, is not at all opposed to humility; rather the most generous are most humble, humble with a "virtuous humility," since the essence of their virtue is self-control, free will used well. (No writer included in this book comes across as haughty as this commender of humility.)

What makes this generosity so central is that it is the virtue whose exercise is the supreme remedy for the disorders of the passions.[11] It is possible that the self-excitation referred to at the end of the Second Part, which is there abruptly associated with "following virtue diligently," is actually exemplified by generosity and humility. For these latter are actions of virtue "and at the same time passions of the soul," namely insofar as the animal spirits strengthen them.[12] (How dispositions and excitations may be identified, how virtues are also passions, is not further explained.) Generosity is in fact that movement of the spirits which first belongs to wonder, combined with both love and joy; that is to say, generosity is defined as wonder specified by composition with these two. Furthermore, generosity makes one not only esteem *oneself* but esteem oneself for doing good to *others.* The generous are "courteous, affable, and of service to everyone." This is a meaning of generosity closer to ours, and it makes this passion-virtue the *only* virtue that issues in a general benevolence, benevolence not attached to personal love. Because generous people esteem good works more highly than their own interests, they "are entirely masters of their passions," be it desire, envy, jealousy, fear, or "hatred of men, because they esteem them all." Generosity is indeed the cure for all passions, because it is—the essence of Stoicism—wishing for nothing not in one's own control and not even caring much for what isn't.[13] Note, however, that with the aid of Cartesian science the sphere of that control is expansively huge.

In fact, each part ends with a call for the control of the passions, the First with a recommendation of physiologically based training and the Second with the suggestion of a remedy in psychic self-excitation. The Third, which early on names the passion-virtue of legitimate self-esteem, that is, generosity, as a remedy for disordered passions, ends with a general remedy for all the excesses of the passions. It is a remedy said to be both most general and most easy to practice: Mind your physiological indices, let the blood cool, be wary of the imagination (as the Stoic emperor enjoined), delay judgment when under its influence, postpone action, distract yourself and divert your thoughts; when long deliberation is impossible at least quickly rehearse the counterarguments. In short, dampen the unprofitable passions.

And now the very last paragraph. Here, once again, Descartes uninhibitedly retracts what was so definitively asserted earlier, namely that "our good and our ill depend principally on inner excitations, which are excited by the soul itself."[14] Now he says:

> Finally, the soul may have pleasure by itself. But as for those that are common to it and the body, they depend entirely on the passions, so that the men they can move the most are capable of tasting the most sweetness in this life.[15]

This sweetness appears to be far richer than that of self-satisfaction, formerly the sweetest of passions. It is true that this life has also the most bitterness for those who misuse the passions or who are opposed by fortune. (Recall that there is supposed to be no fortune.) Wisdom, he ends, teaches us to become such masters of the passions and to manage them with such ingenuity that their evils too "can be easily borne, and we even derive joy from them."

So ends a seminal treatise that combines confident assertion with ready retraction, brisk definitiveness with unabashed equivocation, proud innovation with tacit recourse to the tradition, hopeful emphasis on experimental science with a speculative physiology, and a determined reliance on the metaphysics of distinct substances with an insistence on a human union that the theory itself forestalls. But if the theoretical exposition is surely obscure just by reason of its attempted lucidity, the practical advice might be sage just because it is wisely ambivalent.

7. Transition: Descartes to Spinoza

No philosopher of stature was, I think, ever more indebted to a predecessor for the mere terms and less for the meaning of his thinking than was Spinoza to Descartes. The *Passions* and the *Ethics* are only a quarter century apart, but let no one conclude that closeness in time or terms entails similarity in thought; a vocabulary may be in the air, but there it oxidizes and is transmuted to new uses.

Both authors focus on the passions, Descartes as his final effort, Spinoza as his fundamental project. Both authors seat them in a metaphysics, their scheme of the way things ultimately are. But Descartes' account of human and natural substance makes, as I have been at pains to point out, the union of body and mind that the passions seem to require problematic to the point of impossibility (while, to be sure, opening the way to a first neurophysiological account). Spinoza's theologically conceived nature, on the other hand, is practically tailor-made to account for affective humanity (not that other perplexities don't appear), for the divinity that is, makes, and moves nature is in its essence an affective substance, as I will explain in the next chapter.

Here are the main items, as I discern them, that Spinoza borrows from Descartes and wholly transmutes:

1. Both limit the enumerable substances. Descartes establishes three (mind or thinking thing, body or extended thing, God) and maybe a fourth (the human union of soul and body). Spinoza derives everything that is from one substance, called God-or-Nature. They both choose their beginnings carefully—Descartes by the order of knowing, beginning with the ego, Spinoza by the order of being, beginning with God. Both use the language of attributes and modes, though for Descartes modes do not belong to God since God has no variations, no modifications;[1] for Spinoza modes belong eminently to an infinitely modified God.

Thus, when Descartes does say at a point that by "nature, considered in general" he understands nothing but "God himself or the order and disposition God has established in created things,"[2] that seems to be an equivocation. For how can God be at once the separable creator and inherent in his creation? Spinoza would say it is impossible; his God is not a creator but the creation itself.

Let me add that Descartes thinks that it is not within our grasp to reconcile human free will, which is self-evident, with divine preordination, which latter our knowledge of God's power and our piety nonetheless require us to accept;[3] Spinoza evades this problem.

2. For Descartes, clarity and distinctness are the criteria of truth in thought. The passions are confused and obscure insofar as they come from

the body's action.[4] For Spinoza too, action, passion, clarity, and confusion are basic terms. But since the body and mind do not interact—a drastic solution to the chief Cartesian problem—the body does not causally influence the mind, whose passivity is all from within and whose confusions will turn out to be identical with its passions.

3. As for substances, so for primary passions. "Passion" is Descartes' translation of Latin *affectus,* which is the term Spinoza will use.[5] Descartes derives all emotions from the six primitive passions; Spinoza too looks for an order of enumeration and finds instead one master passion from which all the others flow; it is desire, the very essence of man. For Descartes desire, a primitive passion, is precisely not volition, not the soul's active principle; for Spinoza desire and will are the same. For both, morality requires favoring the actions of the soul over its passions, but for the former, action is willing, and for the latter, contemplation.

4. Descartes is ambivalent about the role of the object in shaping the passions. He says that the individual objects of love are too many to help distinguish species of love. But then he does wish so to distinguish desires, which he accomplishes by making them, illogically, follow the species of love.[6] Spinoza does think that the affects are differentiated not only by their object but also by the way individuals are affected. Spinoza's closer conjunction between the passion and its object is made possible by his rejection of an—indeterminately—intervening physical effect of the body on the soul.

5. Consequently the definitions of particular passions differ significantly, whether they are nominally similar or not. Just two examples: Wonder (*l'admiration, admiratio*) is defined by Descartes merely as a passing surprise at an object newly encountered; for Spinoza it is the entrenched imagination of something that has no connection with the rest; this definition derives its meaning from the fact that for him disconnectedness *is* confusion. Love (*l'amour, amor*) is defined by Descartes as a motion of the spirits that incites a volition to join oneself to a suitable-appearing object; Spinoza says it is pleasure accompanied by the idea of an external cause. In Spinoza's definition there is no mention of spirits because the body does not act on the mind; none of suitability because the affects are all together *defined* as enhancements; none of volition because will and desire are the same and all particular affects are derivative from desire; and finally there is no mention of joining, because, Spinoza says, alluding critically to Descartes in the relevant article, that union with our object is not of the essence of love but only a property, for love is quite conceivable without the will to union. In sum, for Descartes love is an imaginatively willed condition of union incited by the body; for Spinoza it is a life-enhancing aspect of the mind.

6. Descartes' conception of an intellectual love of God is analogous to his definition of passionate love: "Uniting oneself entirely to God in volition," one desires nothing but that God's will should be done and knows that nothing can befall one that is not God's decree. This love is delineated in the letter to Chanut referenced earlier: The love of God raises difficulties because it must be intellectual. First, God's commonly considered attributes seem to be too high to be "suitable" to us, and second, since we cannot visually imagine anything about God, we cannot love him sensuously with the passion that is an action of the body. This fact, he says, has convinced some philosophers that only through the mystery of an incarnate God of the Christian religion do we become capable of loving him. Yet there is another way: to consider that God is a thinking substance which, in that respect, we resemble. Moreover, though his knowledge *is* infinite, ours *strives* to be. We must not be so absurd as to wish to be ourselves gods, but we must meditate on his infinity with gratitude for the knowledge he has given us. And this fills us with extreme joy. Thus, speaking philosophically, it *is* possible to love God.

I do not know if Spinoza knew the letter, but his intellectual love of God, the famous *amor dei intellectualis,* the culmination of his chief publication, the *Ethics,* is almost point for point its reversed reflection. To Spinoza, God is not a substance separate from us in essence but similar just in the fact of being a substance. God is rather the very substance of which human beings are modes. Hence the love of God is no union with an other but self-love of a sort. This affect is no more a passionate love than Descartes', yet it differs wholly in being a *self*-realization, and in being not volitional but contemplative. Above all, whereas Descartes, writing about the love of God in private, employs an elevated tone in the service of a rather pinched affirmation, Spinoza, before the public, uses the severe geometric mode to mask his nonetheless palpable ardor.

chapter VII

Human Affect as Our Body's Vitality

Spinoza and the Price We Pay for Resolving All Oppositions

1. The Stock Antitheses of Thinking about Feelings

Here is a Table of Opposites, of antithetical notions, into which fall, apparently very naturally, my own—and other people's—reflections about human feelings:

Body	Soul
Body	Mind
Nature	Humanity
Impulse	Freedom
Desire	Virtue
Inclination	Morality
Partiality	Impartiality
Passion	Action
Passion	Virtue
Affect	Imagination
Emotion	Reason
Heart	Head
Feeling	Thinking

The vertical terms of the pairings are pretty interchangeable, because the left column expresses the sense that there is something that belongs to us without our doing, that comes on or over us, that we are given or possessed by. The right column refers to something that we are at least in part responsible for exercising. That isn't to say that we don't exercise our bodies or cultivate our hearts, but that the powers on the right initiate that work. Around the middle of the table morality, a judgment of good and bad, shows up, but not everyone agrees that the right and respectable side is more sound—much less, preferable. The pairings can, of course, be shuffled.

What the double column expresses as a whole is that thinking about the feelings begins unavoidably as a *contrasting,* because reflection is done on the right side, by a human power. This power, by that very fact of thinking *about* the feelings, shows itself as distinct from—no, opposed to—them; these feelings on their sinister (*sinister* is Latin for "left") side seem in their turn to oppose our thinking as an enigmatic opponent which confronts and rebuffs and bedevils it, even as it captivates and imbues us.

There are also many stock distinctions that are not exactly antithetical. For example, desire, pleasure, and pain are sometimes distinguished as basic feelings from the more structured "intentional" passions; or the objective side of a passion, the particular thing or event that arouses the passion and that it "intends," is distinguished from its subjective aspect, the feel of the affect; or those feelings that are aroused by a discernible object are distinguished from those that arise for no evident reason; these latter, which are about nothing concrete, will later be called "moods" as distinct from emotions.

Thus, speaking very generally, thinking about affects tends to begin by distinguishing feeling from thinking itself and the passion-object from the impassioned subject. In sum, when thinking turns "inward" in meditative soul-searching (as distinct from "on itself" in intellectual self-consciousness), it comes upon its alien and fascinating other, its complement and sibling, born of a common parent who is that very subject or self. This self then often reveals itself as preoccupied by interests other than the truths of its thinking. It is captivated by an object, whose objective nature it must, as a thinking self, labor to discriminate from its subjective feeling.

2. Why It Is Very Fruitful to Come to Grips with Spinoza

Now imagine a thinker who finds a way to overcome these oppositions, to resolve or obviate or mitigate them. One would want to understand him, if only to see what price in assent to counterintuitive originality would be demanded of us for a release from this forked stick.

That thinker, Benedict Spinoza, needs this justificatory preface because his work, the *Ethics* (completed in 1675 but published posthumously), repels the beginning reader by its bewildering novelty, its quirky use of scholastic terminology, its exasperating mathematical presentation. Once it opens up even a little, though, it breathes a sort of sweet jocundity.

Here are five more reasons why the *Ethics* is worth attending to.

1. Of its five books, the last three are most specifically concerned with what Spinoza calls "affect"—human feeling. He has more to say about this

topic than even Descartes and Hume, and what he says is more—I am tempted to say—stupefyingly new than any other treatment I know of.

2. The *Ethics* is balanced on a range of cusps, not in time but in thought —between Biblical tradition and rationalism, Parmenidean monism and multifarious Nature, sober Stoicism and God-intoxication, ontological Scholasticism and anti-metaphysical existentialism. I hope I will be forgiven all these "isms"; they are shorthand for recognizable but transfigured elements of Spinoza's book.

Precisely because he absorbs and transcends such a variety of traditions, he stands not astride the mainstream but aside from it. There is something of what the Germans call *Winkelphilosophie,* "hole-in-corner philosophy," about the *Ethics,* as if it were written—as it no doubt was—in a close Dutch chamber out of incessant soul-searching (a colleague of mine calls its style "rebarbative," that is, "crabbed, repellent"), but which promises an uncanonically fresh perspective. In his *History of Philosophy,* Hegel, giving an appreciative critique of Spinoza, his most kindred predecessor, says, "When one begins philosophizing, one must first of all be a Spinozan. The soul must bathe in this ether of a substance, in which everything which one supposed to be true has perished."[1] I will have to speak more clearly of Spinoza's substance before long. My point here is that by absorbing, combining, and reinterpreting traditional notions Spinoza manages to make a new, as it were, pristine, field in which the old oppositions no longer figure and we can begin anew. Probably the best instance is Spinoza's assimilation of Descartes' philosophy. Much of the agenda of the *Ethics* is set by Spinoza's opposition to Descartes, most explicitly to his treatment of the passions. Hence the most crucial terms are Cartesian, but they now serve to subvert the very Cartesian dualism that gave rise to them. These announcements will, I hope, gain concreteness as we go.

3. Spinoza is the most likely patron for the fairly new preoccupation of neuroscience with the emotions. The working postulate for neuroscience is usually represented as being the identity of mind and brain. Spinoza's system offers a deep-laid ground for this hypothesis.

4. I also have a very personal reason for being glad to have come, albeit late, to the *Ethics.* Spinoza—though surely not any actual text—was a household word in my youth (as it was for many other liberal-thinking Germans). For my father, an assimilated German Jew practicing medicine between the two World Wars, Spinozism was the *religio medici,* the physician's faith, because, I imagine, it allowed a practitioner of science to sideline the question of a personal God while endorsing his professional reverence toward nature. Thus Einstein said, "I believe in Spinoza's God, who reveals himself

in the harmony of all being, not in a God who concerns himself with the fate and actions of men."[2] I should mention that very different types—the Romantics, Nietzsche—had earlier discovered (or construed) something to admire in Spinoza: his nature- or vitality-worship.

5. Finally, the *Ethics* invites study because, granting all its thorniness, it is a beguiling text; it is one long rejoicing in the way things are, "God-intoxi-cated," as that arch-Romantic Novalis said, yet entirely without piety, and as I began by saying, a resolution of the antitheses that, almost inescapably, bedevil thinking about the passions. But before one comes to that realiza-tion, its very difficulty is an incitement. It is rare that one gets to laugh *at* Hegel, but it can't be helped when he says in the same place that Spinoza's system "is very simple, and as a whole easy to grasp." It is in fact simple and *therefore* hard to grasp and also, I have come to think, because it doesn't work at crucial junctures. Yet the double effort of trying at once to compre-hend momentous meanings that are at first recalcitrant to common sense and to question the ultimate unintelligibility of notions that seemed com-prehensible does really push thinking about the passions pretty close to its limits.

I might mention here that, since it is through learning Spinoza's use of terms that one begins to understand both his system and his spirit, I will often cite Spinoza's Latin, which will frequently be quite recognizable and will add resonance to the English version.

3. Hopes and Helps

Let me remind my reader (and myself) what I'm hoping to get at, and where I'm looking for help. I am hoping to come near an answer to the question: What does it mean to feel? Perhaps I can exclude some impossibilities, clar-ify some intimations, or even just ask the right questions, first among which might be whether the question is even well asked. What would it mean to know what it means to feel? Can we ask what it is *like* to feel?[1] For example, are we content with a metaphorical answer such as the word "emotion" itself suggests, that the soul is analogous to a body and can be "moved out" of its place by some thing, and that is the feeling of a feeling?

Meanwhile I must try not to lose just that feel of feelings—mine or pos-sibly another's—even while doing exactly what will have that effect: opening the protective cocoon of mute internality and probing its sensitive matter with penetrating thought.

The help that comes from personal experience needs a lot of supple-menting, since what we know most immediately is fugitive as well as opaque. If the conversation of friends offers the bloom of responsive spontaneity, it is the study of books that offers extended, coherent, and deep treatments, from which I get ideas I could not come by on my own and against which I test the truths I finally accept as my own.

And that is exactly what the *Ethics* is good for. My own formulations just above show me that I am thinking in the oppositions that I listed in the beginning of the chapter, and the study of this book will show me entirely new possibilities—but also the limits of my acceptance.

There is, however, a dilemma in allowing oneself to be helped with a particular problem by a systematic writer. The parts are tightly bound into the whole and take their meaning from it. In this case, the lowest elements of the system are actually deduced from its pinnacle: What the passions are follows logically, through a few intermediate steps, from what God is. Therefore we cannot get the wished-for insights without engaging the *whole* philosophy, and that is why this chapter is the longest devoted to one philosopher. For as far as each of the ancients to whom I have appealed is concerned, while his thought is not incoherent, neither is it systematic; it is neither a logically derived hierarchy nor a totally rational synthesis—though I should say right now that even if the latter phrase truly describes, for example, Kant's critical system, the former does not quite rightly characterize Spinoza's thought. His presentation is, to be sure, deductive, top-down, but his meaning circles back on itself. The beginning is also the whole, and this whole is closer to a vital organism than to a logical structure. My point is, however, that if we may call on Plato's figures or Aristotle's terms or even on the Stoic's wisdom concerning the passions without regarding every last term of their philosophizing—not so with Spinoza.

On the other hand, the bulk of contemporary writing about the emotions is only loosely and inexplicitly grounded in the nature of things. Therefore whoever has a philosophical interest—meaning an interest not satisfied by mere description and analysis—had better go to the great foundationalists, out of favor though they may be at present, and of these Spinoza is chief with respect to the affects.

4. An Interlude to Throw the Way of the *Ethics* into Relief: Adam Smith's *Theory of Moral Sentiments*

This digression may strike the reader as antic, yet to me it seemed needful—to throw the *Ethics* into relief with the most elegantly enlightened, sweetly reasonable work on the "sentiments" I know of and which, for all that, has certain specific affinities with its thought-burdened forerunner. So here is writing to make Spinoza on the passions look crabbedly idiosyncratic. The *Theory of Moral Sentiments* (1759) was composed by Adam Smith almost a century after the *Ethics*.[1] It was based on lectures to young students; it is likely that Jane Austen read in it in her youth; it was available as a popular work and either shaped or jibed with her mirthfully undeluded clarity.

Spinoza, in contrast, was first proscribed, hated, mistaken for an atheist, for example, by Hume; later on revived, romanticized, and again mistaken for a pantheist; but whatever currency Spinozism gained, the *Ethics* was never, it seems, a popular book, always out of the mainstream, always more alluded to than read. I doubt that Jane Austen would have found him congenial and must make shift to live with that judgment.

Adam Smith, known to Americans now mostly as the patron saint of our presumed economic mode, is a wickedly elegant writer whose amiable skepticism, velvet wit, and workable wisdom testify to his keen eye for humanity's ways.

Despite its title, I for one have discovered no grounded "theory" of the passions, nor even a definition of his key word, "sentiment," that is, human feeling. Smith writes as someone who thinks that facts not in doubt have no need of foundations, and that a cunning circularity is a sufficient account for the irreduceable reciprocity of individual and social morality. Others may think that just such facts call for an inquiry into the roots—that that's philosophy; what his book addresses instead with a wonderfully wise worldliness is the amendment of the passions: moral instruction. So is Spinoza's *Ethics* an incitement to morality; its last two fifths are about the management of the passions. But this teaching is so completely bound into the preceding metaphysics as to make it, as I've now said more than once, if philosophically moving, also personally daunting, while Smith's work is simply delight.

Moral Sentiments operates with three moral-psychological terms, "sympathy," "propriety," and "the impartial spectator." *Sym*pathy is an innate countervailing force to natural human selfishness. (The latter is a propensity acknowledged in a very different, more approving key by Spinoza.) Sympathy is *not* our ability to *feel* ourselves into another's feeling—that is what we would call *em*pathy. It is rather our ability to *imagine* ourselves into others' situation and *hence* to *re*-feel their sentiment in that setting: Smith's morality requires a vivid imagination *and* cool distance—a novelist's temperament. A particularly charming example of the difference is Smith's account of our *inability* to sympathize with the state of being in love, which tends to seem ridiculous to us, for, "The passion appears to every body but the man who feels it, entirely disproportionate to the value of the object; and love, though pardoned in a certain age because we know it is natural, is always laughed at, because we know we cannot enter into it."[2] Jane Austen must have been delighted with this sentence, though she might have balked at "always." The subtlety of this observation seems to me to lie in this: that while we are bidden to imagine generic human situations vividly enough to summon a shadow of the passion a fellow human would feel, yet the circumstance of being-in-love is so acutely and particularly tinctured by the object that we cannot reproduce it. We cannot see "what he sees in her or she in him." (The particularity of passion is also Spinoza's theme.) So we judge the sentiment disproportionate, improper, and insofar as it is harmless, we snicker.

Let me emphasize: What Smith intends by sympathy is *not* what we mean when we say "I feel your pain," that is, "I *enter into your sentiments*." Instead he intends this: "I *imagine* your situation, and I put *myself into your place*." Then I watch to see what feelings arise, and it is these, my feelings, by which I judge propriety." Thus Smith is surely the novelist's philosopher—certainly Jane Austen's, whether she had ever read him or not. (It is not known.) I think that she envisions a situation, watches her people's reaction to it, puts herself in their place, feels her feelings, and by these she judges the propriety of theirs.

We—I mean us, living now—have a locution handy for the many cases when we are too craven to express moral condemnation. We say, "That's inappropriate." It's a degenerate version of Smith's term of moral judgment, "propriety." Propriety is the criterion by which we assign praise or blame to a passion. It is the suitableness or unsuitableness, the proportion or disproportion, that the affection seems to us to bear to the object which excites it and the decency and gracefulness of the consequent conduct. The spectator's judgment of propriety is intimately connected, is in fact simultaneous with, the "sympathetic emotion of the spectator."[3] When we sympathize, "feel with" others, we approve their feeling and its effects as being proper. "Proper" here has no overtone of "prim," but rather of "just" in the sense of well-adjusted, of being a good fit of self and world. It is sensibleness qualified as moral elegance.

What keeps our judgment, which connects sentiment to virtue (or vice), from being entirely partial, that is, in our terms, subjective? Who judges impartially? We have within us an "impartial spectator," an objective observer, a moral doppelgänger, as it were—less guilt-ridden than a Christian conscience, fairer than mere personal preference. This figurative "ideal man within the breast," a "demigod," of divine extraction, judges himself not in accordance with a desire for praise, but for the attainment of "praiseworthiness"—and others similarly.[4]

But by what "peculiar faculty" does the impartial observer judge propriety? By his own sympathy! This imagined "man within" has been appointed by God the "immediate judge of mankind."[5] It follows that, both for himself and others, "the precise or distinct measure by which this fitness or propriety of affection can be ascertained or judged of . . . can be found nowhere but in the sympathetic feelings of the impartial and well-informed spectator."[6] And what is the criterion of judgment? It is a set of "general rules" formed by the experience of the approbation or disapprobation expressed by "every body around us," by society. Its members have, of course, come by their judgment just as we have. Consequently propriety rests on a *per-*

fect circle, or better, a continual reciprocity of individual and societal judgment—which may be dubious as a rational theory but is perspicuous as a
human fact, our socially conditioned, individually breakaway nature.

If one master feeling is to constitute our moral humanity, our admira-
bleness, sympathy seems to me more humanly plausible than the apparently
cognate "pity," conceived by Rousseau only four years earlier in his Essay
on the *Origin of Inequality,* which was known to Smith. That sentiment,
an "inactive passion," belongs to a creature of theory, the natural man, an
uncorrupted pre-social being who satisfies his healthy self-love while doing
"without reflection" the least possible harm to others.[7] Sympathy, on the
other hand, requires civilization, above all a well-cultivated imagination,
which seems to me indeed to be the more plausible source of social pity.

Moreover, this sympathetic "theory" has, as I said, what can be a very
appealing double quality: It is humanly well observed, and it is philosophically quite unfounded—sceptical. These features are two sides of one coin.
We recognize ourselves and feel that our amendment will indeed not derive
from too high a principle. Moreover, the great moral antitheses are col-
lapsed—nature and morality, passion and self-control; we are good or we
are bad by nature. And although Smith has no exalted opinion of human
nature, he allows nature itself to even the score. Though we are creatures of
emotion, yet it is a feeling that controls our feelings. Moreover, the light of
this reasoning succeeds wonderfully in bleaching the bulk of moral systems
down to a common color: Plato, Aristotle and the Stoics are all said to make
virtue coincide with propriety. This interpretation is perfectly plausible if
each description is ripped untimely from its philosophical womb. In Smith's
account, virtue for Plato is each mental faculty's confining itself to its proper
sphere, a reductive version of the *Republic.*[8] For Aristotle virtue is the mean
between moral excesses, which is, again in Smith's account, the propriety of
the degree by which one is affected by the object of one's passion, a stripped-
down appropriation from the *Nicomachean Ethics.* The Stoics he assimilates
by explaining that their virtue requires that one should look only to propriety understood as acting in accordance with principle while endeavoring
not to be affected by the success or failure of the outcome, surely an airy
reading of Stoic "consistency."

Smith's propriety, at bottom, is a kind of affective counterpart to truth,
which is commonly defined as the fitting of our thought to the thing; it is,
namely, the fitness of our feeling toward an object. It is the very essence of
sweet reasonableness, eminently practicable even in our day, though here it
comes down to us dressed in elegant period costume.

But this "theory" happens to leave unexplained both what it *means to
feel* and what the imagination is, such that we can figure within ourselves
another's world and judge of its appropriate sentiment. What is our nature,
such that we harbor within ourselves a second self whose scope is larger and

less "selfish" than that of our host self? I am dwelling on Smith's philosophical foreshortening (which continues into current emotion studies) because I was, as I said, looking for a mode that, because it is a world's width—a polar distance—away in style, intention, and thesis from Spinoza's system, will throw it into relief and will yet evince similarities. Smith is surely that world apart from Spinoza, who writes learnedly and goes to ultimates and gives neither fellow-feeling nor passion properly proportioned to its object any place in his abstruse ethics. Yet there is, remarkably, one main element of Smith's theory that resonates strongly with Spinoza's philosophy and makes the two akin: what constitutes Smith's inner spectator, the moderator of passions, is just his *im*partiality, his not taking a *partial* view but regarding the *whole* situation without bias. Impartiality in the deepest, literal sense—non-particular regard to the whole—turns out to be Spinoza's way of overcoming the passions as well. Here is more than a coincidental wisp of a similarity, for it reveals something weighty: that thinking, however done, is apt to find feeling insularly private, passively particular. So I return from Smith's observant sweet reasonableness to Spinoza's comprehending joyful radicality, this much the wiser by this interlude: that whatever the fashion, thought will come on passion as *partiality.* It will be of the passionate essence in the *Ethics.*

5. Spinoza's *Ethics*: The Alpha That Is the Omega

What marks the *Ethics,* what makes it so different from other founding philosophies and repellent to the ordinary reader is its axiomatic-deductive presentation. It has the organization of a mathematical textbook that begins with some definitions and axioms and then proceeds to prove propositions. The definitions are, to be sure, more like those of Euclid than of modern mathematics. They delineate, implicitly, what it is that exists, or will be shown to exist by its very definition. The axioms have only *ex post facto* perspicuousness, which is to say that before you see them in use you don't see their bearing. The propositions, as Spinoza's admirer Hegel observes—it seems to me rightfully—are "laborious, useless torture."[1]

It is a curious form for a book that means to engage in ethical persuasion, that hopes to turn our passive affects into active virtues by showing us what passions really are. Who wants to prove propositions as a prelude to practicing virtue? And it is even more curious for a system in which God is truly the Alpha and Omega, the first and last thing. For in a deductive system the particular conclusions, as they are more remote from the general first principles—the axioms and postulates—are also more concretely visible and complexly full of content. Thus Euclid derives all the rich consequences of parallelism and figural similarity from a bare "postulate," the somewhat opaque demand that we should accept without proof, possibly even as *unprovable,* that if a straight line crosses two others such that the inside angles on one side of the crossing line together equal less than two right angles, the lines on that side will eventually meet.[2] So in a deductive system the interesting truths exist only potentially in the alpha and are successively developed as it approaches the omega.

We must wonder what, beside the then current mania for the "geometric way," should have caused Spinoza to employ this manner of presentation, for he was the most recalcitrant of contemporaries. One reason may have been his theory of how the mind holds ideas, namely as proposition-like assertions, affirmations of content in the tone of a mathematician: "I say that . . ."

I think, however, that in the main it was just that very axiom-derived character of the geometric way, viewed under a philosophical aspect, that made it seem to fit the presentation of his thought. For, unlike an axiomatic geometry, an axiomatic ontology begins with what is not only first but also highest, which has the riches of the consequents patently within it not simply potentially but *actually,* and these beginnings are merely made explicit and expressed in the particular consequents. Thus the particulars will have been involved in the first things as elements of a whole, and conversely, every least circumstance is strictly, necessarily, a consequence of the beginning, which is always concretely *there,* preserved and displayed in each effect. In sum, the demonstrations show forth what is already fully actual in itself, though only potential for us. This pattern pre-figures perfectly Spinoza's philosophy. But I think—heresy or not—that readers, content to know that it is possible, can ignore its execution, or they are likely never to get the good of the whole system. In any case, the illumination is usually in the "scholia," the notes to the propositions.

The system, then, begins with God. Even the greatest of the previous theological summations do not claim that God is first in our apprehension. Thomas asks whether God is the first object known to the human mind. His answer is, not so: "God is not the first object of our knowledge. Rather do we know God through his creatures," through his works.[3]

But what if God is not a creator but an all-encompassing being, the one and sole substance? Then we, being of him or in him, must begin and end our knowledge with him. Thus Spinoza's *Ethics* is the sum of theology as written not by a dependent creature but by an intrinsic part of God. That is not to say that this particular Benedict's peculiar existence *necessarily* follows from God's, but that any particular human mode, by exemplifying *that* there are human beings and *what* they are, follows from, expresses, the way God is. Just so a particularly shaped triangle appears in a proposition, but it is not *that* triangle whose properties were deduced as necessary. We must now see what substance, mode, and expression mean.

Hegel says that "Spinoza is the chief point of modern philosophy: either Spinozism or no philosophy." (Spinoza's modernity consists, I imagine, in making physics the divine science, as we will see.) The analogous point in antiquity is Parmenides, the discoverer of Being—that all there is, *is*, that there is truly nothing outside Being, that All is One in Being. A caveat: Here we are not to be misled by reading no-thing as Nothing, as if it were a thinkable external complement to Being. When we come to consider mood, which is objectless affect, feeling about nothing, interpretable as the feel of Nothing, this proscribed way of thinking will become humanly crucial. But the Spinozism that Hegel equates with philosophy discovers God as *all*-inclusive Being, with no Nothing within or beyond.

Our modern Parmenides, then, thinks that there is but one Being, the divine Substance. There lurks in the background his avatar's great unstated postulate: "Something exists and Nothing is not an element in or about it." As an axiom it is perhaps not so self-evident if you are in the mood to cavil—recall that for Descartes the existence of anything at all was so little self-evident that he went about proving a particular case: that he, at least, existed—but it is surely unavoidable if you want to live entirely in the positive.

In short order, Spinoza elicits from his mere understanding of substance that there can be but one, that it is its own cause, that it is infinitely rich in attributes, and that its being *what* it is—its essence—necessarily involves *that* it is—its existence. Since this chapter is intended to be about the passions, neither the larger plausibility nor the narrower logic can be the issue here, and it must suffice to say that the initial implausibility of Spinoza's theology wanes, at least for me, as I allow myself to be carried along in his way of thinking. That is not, however, the same as being convinced; it is just reading with willingness.

The consequences most important to my subject are 1. that this Substance becomes in due course recognizable as endowed with the usual divine characteristics—it is called God nearly from the beginning—such as omniscience or all-knowingness and omnipotence or all-potency, and an additional, most important, radically heretical feature, which might be called "omni-essence" or all-beingness. God is all there, is unique, and all there is, is God, is one. Thus everything is, in its way, of God's essence—essence being defined as that without which a thing can neither exist nor be conceived. Spinoza's notorious phrase is "God *or* Nature."[4] In traditional theology, nature, the world, is created by God. Hence it is, though dependent on him, separate from its creator and affected with non-being precisely *as* creature. Spinoza's *Deus sive Natura*, "God or, if you like, Nature," signifies that both terms, creator *and* creature, apply to the one Substance; any distinction is only aspectual.

Out of the many problems one might address, I will pick one that becomes of particular interest for the human passions. God is a perfect plenum—all that can be is *in* him. There is no defect in his being and in the world that is identical with him. There is nothing negative comprised in him, as there was no Nothing beyond him. That condition is supported by Spinoza's famous sentence: *Omnis determinatio est negatio*, "All determination is a nay-saying." He is expressing, I think, two thoughts at once: "Anything that departs or delimits itself from the whole and becomes particular thereby consigns itself to the status of a lesser being, one afflicted with negativity," and "Nothing that is a part gains a positive nature of its own just from its own determinate particularity." Spinoza gives an example: A triangle's nature is "contained in the Divine nature solely by the necessity of the Divine nature and not by the nature of an essence of a triangle."[5] Thus nothing is what it is on its own, but everything is *comprehensively implicated* in the universe. The last part of this sentence carries a tremendous burden of consequence. Consider that some philosophers of the Western mainstream accord to the particulars of the world a certain stubborn liveliness and recalcitrant individuality; these are, for better or worse, responsible for the motion and variety on display in nature.

Aristotle goes so far as to call the individual "*This*" substance *par excellence*. To deny that particulars are separately *something* means, from the point of view of things, that the Whole has gathered to itself all worth and interest. Here is the mother of all "contextuality" (the contemporary notion that it is its environment which defines the thing). From the point of view of the thinker it means that nonbeing, substantial nothingness, cannot be in his thought for, as Spinoza says, an idea about nothing is a non-idea; that means in turn that there can be no true falsity (so to speak) in our thinking. Instead such ideas, defective ideas, have another, ingeniously conceived, characteristic which will become of the greatest importance in explaining the passions: *inadequacy*, understood as *partiality*.

In abjuring substantial nonbeing, the kind that enters positively into separate beings to give them their unstably various character—Plato, recall, terms it Otherness, a bonding kind of counterbeing, a principle of pervasive differentiation—Spinoza has to face a problem: God-or-Nature is full of motion and variety, of apparently determinable, definable, differences. If we must not speak of them by negation, by saying "this is *not-that*," how can we think of the parts? What does it mean to think only positively of particulars? And what is error (or deception) if it is not saying what-is-not? How can God be one and all alone, all and altogether Being and yet infinitely full of differences? We can see what a metaphysical feat it will be to solve this problem if we consider that Spinoza's ancient counterpart, Parmenides, drew the obvious conclusion that the one Being has no motion, no variety, no parts:

"You will not cut off Being from holding onto Being." Most astonishing is the immediate consequence: "For it is the same: to think and to be." For Being, in its inclusivity, makes all that is its own, the same.[6] This turns out to be precisely what Spinoza thinks, but he must account for this sameness insofar as it is also *apprehended* as different.

Because I am concentrating on the human passions, I will truncate Spinoza's account of what God is in himself (Part I) and what he is to us and for himself (Part V), thus in effect curtailing the Beginning which is its own end and which in its circle encompasses the particular human realm. But I must say that one reason Spinoza knows so much about our passions is that he is intoxicated—an accurate word for his so prosaically presented thought—by a love of God, an intellectual love (*amor dei intellectualis*), a blissfulness (*beatitudo*) that partakes of, joins in, the love that God has for himself.[7] Through it Spinoza knows, for example, the ultimate power of affect, but also that not all our affects are passions, states we *undergo*; some are actions, activities we *engage in,* such as activating our intellect. It is in the light of this ultimate active love that human passions are conceived. That they are, as appears to me, well conceived gives cause for thought not in the scope of this book—theological thought.

Let me give the titles of the parts of the *Ethics,* for the reader's orientation:

  I. *On God*
  II. *On the Nature and Origin of the Mind*
  III. *On the Origin and Nature of the Affects*
  IV. *On Human Servitude or the Force of the Affects*
  V. *On the Power of the Intellect or Human Freedom*

I have no doubt that in placing the explanation of the affects in the middle part Spinoza was signaling their central importance to human life (as did Thomas). I should repeat here that the Latin term is *affectus,* usually translated "emotion." But emotion is such an expressive word in a different context, and so designed to make Spinoza's originality sound *outré,* that I've stuck with "affect"—literally something done *to* us (*ad-facere,* "to do to"). Thus Parts III and IV together trace the laborious road by which something done *to* us is transformed into something done *by* us, the road from servitude to freedom as Spinoza understands them.

We are, however, prepared for this ascent in Part II, in which the terms of the mind are set out: "The modes of thinking (*cogitandi*), such as love, desire or whatever affects of the mind are signified by a name. . . ." So, strangely, begins Axiom III of that part, telling us that thinking and feeling are not separable. No, more: that they will be regarded as one and the same. Here we have identity number three: God and Nature was the first, Thinking and Being the second, and now Thinking and Feeling. Is this Hegel's "night in which . . . all cows are black"?[8]

6. Attributes: The Discernible Aspects of God

Of course not. The term "attribute" is the key both to God's identity with nature and to our being *at once* both thinking and natural beings, or speaking more ordinarily: having minds and bodies which—though there is no way to make *this* thought ordinary—are identical. I am here taking "natural beings" to mean "physical" nature or moving body, something that is not mind but the object of mind, which object Spinoza will in fact show to be body.

The divine Substance, one and all alone, has in its plenitude every humanly conceivable *and* inconceivable *attribute.* In fact only two of them are accessible to us—thought and extension; Spinoza submits no reason why just these two. In their names they answer to Descartes' two substantial "things," in common belief they correspond to body and mind. "Soul," the mediator between them, the usual locus of passion, is conspicuously not on the scene. The spectacular news will be that they are all one in God, hence identical in us. We are, to introduce a second crucial term of the system, but *modes* of God.

But first, what is an attribute? The word itself signifies a feature we "attribute" to any substance: *ad-tribuere* "to ascribe to." It is an aspect (as perceived by the intellect) that constitutes the essence of the Substance—*what* it *is.* But Spinoza will show that the essence of the Substance does not differ from its existence—*that* it is. This claim, an old scholastic technicality, will have the widest consequences for human affective life.[1] The identity of "what" and "that" signals that attributes are not mere ascribable properties. If you consider as a counterexample, say, a golden globe, you find that it cannot be unless it is round, since that is of its essence, but it might not be golden, for that is a property which is accidentally ascribable but not needed for its existence as a globe.

It does indeed seem to Spinoza that these two attributes, thought and extension, are our perspective on God, his aspects *for us.* And yet they are also "expressions" *of God,* or we could not make the attribution to his essence.

Here are questions, mooted before, that I cannot resolve definitely, nor do I see that anyone can: How does a god-substance that is totally unitary express itself to itself or show itself to us under different attributes at all, how can it be rich in distinctions at all? More pressingly, how can it express two attributes that are, as are bodily extension and ideational thought, describable as antithetical? One is thinkable only as having measurable dimensions, weight, color, etc., while the other is conceivable only as non-dimensional, weightless and without color. We might well say that whatever the extension that underlies the body is, that thought is not. For extension is stretched out, extending away, so that each element is *outside* the other, which is, however, the same as itself, while thought is just the opposite: Its very nature is to comprehend and enclose, each idea being curled *about* an intended content distinguishable from thinking itself. Recall that Descartes was driven by these oppositions to posit a thinking thing and an extended thing as the two basic substances.

I don't want to suppress here the fact that the "coincidence of opposites" in God is a topic of the mystics, or that Thomas, though incidentally, defends the possibility that opposites might exist in God.[2] But Spinoza is no mystic, and Thomas is thinking of a God who is a Creator and thus *above* his creatures, so that his argument does not apply to a God who *is* nature. Thus paradoxes are no way out. That cavil lodged for future reference, I'll proceed.

(We might ask, on the way, whether there are "modes" of God besides the human one, beings fit to know the infinitely many other expressions Spinoza attributes to God—though that inquiry soon becomes fantastical, and is in fact a favorite topic of science fiction).

Now comes a crucial consequence of the two-attribute notion: If they are just aspects of one substance they cannot be causally related, for primary attributes are not each other's ground or cause. They cannot connect except through their one expressive substance. They must run strictly in parallel. I say "run" because motion belongs to bodies as essentially as time does to the human mind. And bodies and minds are indeed "modes" of the divine attributes called extension and thought.

This is the moment to say what "mode" means and how it is related to attribute. Attributes are, recall, not properties of God. They are rather analogous to powers of production, expressions of his omnipotence, belonging to, or better, constituting his essence. Spinoza's phrase, repeated several times, the one that has defined him and caused scandal, is, once again, *Deus sive Natura*, "God-or-Nature." God *as* nature has two aspects. Under the first he is *Natura naturans*, which might be translated as "Nature-at-it," nature being nature, which is God in his power as he is in and for himself. Under the second he is *Natura naturata*, which means "nature performed," "nature the result of nature," "nature enacted," which is God as he is expressed in his productions.[3] It helps to think of the Latin meaning of the verb that yields nature: *nasci*, "to be born"; nature is becoming and having become. Of course, in his producing-nature God is *identical* with his product-nature; he is, after all, *causa sui*, "cause of himself."

The modes are what descend from God as his effects, his products under his attributes.[4] As I said, the attributes, thought and extension among them, are infinite, which is here, in Spinoza's scholastic language, not a quantitative but a logical term. It means "necessary," not limited by being contingent or dependent on circumstance. Some of the modes are similarly infinite. There are the modes or effects under extension: the motion and rest of the con- figurations of nature in the narrower physical sense—differential motions as they distinguish body from body. There are the effects under thought, expressed in the mode of the ideational: ideas.[5] From these two infinite modes descend two finite, contingent modes known to us: the human body and mind. Here is a table of descent:

0. God or *Natura naturans*
1. God or *Natura Naturata* expressed in two infinite attributes perceived by us:
    Extension and Thought
2. Two infinite modes of these attributes:
    Physical nature and Ideas
3. Two derivative finite modes:
    Body and Mind

Note these three strange consequences: Thought → ideas → mind; conse- quently the mind *is*, by descent, a—finite—idea. The parallelism of attri- butes descends all the way down to us, for we are modes of God. But these nowhere tangent parallelisms are also identities, for God is one. We, as finite minds and bodies, are thus the inseparable products of God as Thought and as Extension.

7. Human Beings as Two Ways of God: A Mystery

Modus means "way." We are ways of God, expressing finitely two of his infi- nite attributes. Thus we are a duality of body and mind, in tandem but not in touch. How can we make this unconnected yet identical duality, this appar- ent paradox whence our passions become intelligible, itself understandable? One might try to describe the modes as "isomorphic," as having some sort of identical structure; it turns out, they don't. People have also tried to get hold of the duality by the example of known physical dualisms such as the two valid descriptions that can be given of a moving electron, namely in terms of a particle that travels linearly or a wave that spreads in space.[1] The trou- ble is, it seems to me, that these descriptions together obey the "Principle of Complementarity": Though both work, when one is applied it *excludes* the simultaneous use of the other. Thus complementarity *seems* analogous to Spinozan parallelism in that both the extensional and the thinking descrip- tion are true and that they mustn't be crossed. It is disanalogous, however, in that the two physical descriptions it governs are *mutually exclusive in their terms*, whereas the Spinozan attributes are said not merely to belong to *one identical substance* but also to be, so to speak, *identically parallel in all their descriptive features*. I think there are no analogies to Spinoza's conception. It is *sui generis*, marvelously and disturbingly one of a kind.

8. Dual Humanity: Body and Mind

We are getting closer to us human beings. We are modes of God, ways in which he expresses himself. (I will, from theological habit, use the masculine gender when I say "God," the neuter when I mention its philosophical name, Substance.) Thus we exist, in all our aspects, from and in him, that is, from and in Nature, which is yet another term for God. Man in nature is, however, not "a kingdom within a kingdom";[1] properly speaking he is not "in" but *is* Nature.

So we must first consider what the human *mind* is. The mind *is* an idea, in fact, a composite idea.[2] We usually think of the mind as "having," not being, an idea. Evidently Spinoza takes "idea" to be not a static object like a picture, but an activity, capable of different approaches to its object, for this mental activity—we might say "ideation"—is about, or *of something*. Spinoza calls this something the *ideatum* or idea-content.[3] It seems an obvious notion and leads to lots of trouble.

The human mind has one unique *ideatum*: It *is* the idea *of* a particular object "actually existing," namely its own *body*, a mode of extension.[4] It is, observe, an *idea* body we have in mind.

Why "actually existing"? Because we cannot think of what is not; for Spinoza, recall, to think is to affirm, to say yes to what we think about. Whatever it is we have above all in mind is not half but wholly there. (Recall, in contrast, Plato's understanding of the visible as being "mere" appearance, enmeshed in nonbeing, so that to think of an item of nature is to have hold of a half-being.) Moreover, how could we have an idea of our mind's body as not actually existing? It is, after all, the actually thinking mind's parallel mode!

Why our body? Here we come to Spinoza's most spectacularly novel version of the mind-body union that bedeviled Descartes and still does any thoughtful embodied being. Our body is our mind's object because body is what we know, and it is *all* that we know—except for our own mind. To know our own mind, to have self-knowledge, is then to reflect on an idea whose content is our own body. This second-order thinking will become very important for managing the passions.

In the second part of the *Ethics*, which deals with the mind, a set of axioms and propositions is interjected that could well be regarded as the foundation of physics, the science of mere bodies in motion.[5] It is followed immediately by a similar consideration of the human body, that is, of physiology, the science of sentient bodies. Through our own body's mod-ifications—Spinoza says "affections" (*affectiones,* as distinct from *affectus*)—comes our knowledge of other bodies of either type. So we are, as it were, at two removes from external bodies: We know them *only* through our own body's modifications,[6] and we know them *only* in our mind—as we repre-sent our body to ourselves as the mind's ideatum.

Therefore to say that the content of our master-idea, that is, our mind as a whole, is our body, is to say that the near-exclusive object of our thought is nature in the narrow sense: God as expressed as the attribute extension. And since this nature is in our mind, it is identical with the science of nature, that is, with the laws connecting all bodies; that is why physics is founded in the part of the *Ethics* dealing with the mind, and why as minds we compre-hend nature.

The reason why Spinoza can really mean this is precisely that he posits extension and thought as perfectly parallel. Bodily nature perfectly expresses thoughtful nature and the reverse.[7] As our bodies are more apt for being passive or active in the nature-world, so our minds, in perfect parallelism, are more apt for being impinged on or being active in the idea-world.[8] But they do *not* interact, they merely mirror each other, though even that opti-cal figure is false, since it implies that one mode is *causing* the mirror effect in the other.

This mutual non-intervention between thought and extension can be grasped logically. Spinoza considers conception and causation as co-exten-sive: Whatever is explained as conceived through something else must be thought of as caused by it. Thus, since thought and extension are conceived as independent, it follows that they are also causatively unconnected.[9] But I think the ultimate reason for the non-interaction between the attributes and modes known to us—and any others—is theological. If there were inter-causation, if the modes affected *each other,* there would be little local turbu-lences, initiating sources in the Nature that *is* the divinity. Not only would the attributes, which are supposed to be different expressions of one and the same essence, God's being, be pried apart into a causing and an effected element, but Nature, a necessary complex, a whole that proceeds from the whole which is itself, from God who is *both* all of nature *and* its first cause—this Nature would be subjected to internal initiatives. God's expressions would breach their conceptual independence to become causally originative in each other.

So how do we know that our body or other bodies in fact exist, since we have no direct testimony from them? What if the physical parallel were simply our fantasy? Spinoza does provide for our imaginations, our fanta-sies, not indeed being positively false—that cannot be—but for going wrong from "*lacking* the idea that shuts off their existence."[10] Bodies, however, are *not* fantasies, for the difficulty of nature's reality, at least, is soluble for us humans in that we may, so to speak, kick it upstairs: All that belongs to God's essence exists, and bodies, as one of the modes in which his extensional attribute is expressed, therefore exist—not that any individual body necessarily exists, but there *are* bodies. And these are what we have in mind.

9. Thought vs. Extension: The Parallelism of Dissimilars

I think a good way to wrap one's mind about Spinoza's curative strangeness, his astonishing solutions, is to see what about them is—I think, terminally—unintelligible. I want to say that no philosopher I have ever read has solved without stubborn remainder the problem posed by an uncircumventable fact: that we think about things and in doing so seem—somehow—to get hold of some of a world. The problem is, in fact, "aboutness." That what we know is mostly bodies and that we know them through our own, that we are somehow in sync with the world and that our mental life is somehow synchronized with our bodily life, that our two ways of being run concurrently—all that is somehow grantable. But Spinoza's parallelism is not merely temporal; our mind is not only synchronized (though non-tangent) with physical bodies. It is also structurally identical, the way two parallel straight lines are both lines of the same shape. The trouble is that the mind is *not conceivable* as structured like its *ideatum*, its idea content, which is its body.[1]

Let me set out my problem by using that figure of parallel lines, two straight lines everywhere equally distant, standing for mind and body respectively. A better model would, however, be two lines, one straight (extension), the other looped (thought):

They might, like parallel lines, never touch, but they won't be conceivable as identical in structure either.

Put it to yourself this way: I perceive (Spinoza's term) my body and its affections. What does the body in its realm do reciprocally? Here is a true sentence: "I *think about* bodies and ideas." Now fill in its extensional counterpart: "Bodies ___?___ ideas and bodies." It can't be done, for bodies are modes of extension, and extension is constitutional outsideness; bodies can't be "about" anything—perhaps "around" something, but here the container and contained are identical the way an idea-action and its idea-content are usually not. (Aristotle says, to be sure, that the passive intellect "becomes all things,"[2] but he does not say that it is nothing but what it becomes.) Thoughts have what philosophers call "intentionality"; they intend something, are directed to something that they comprehend, wrap themselves about, but do not entirely assimilate. Bodies have extension;

their parts constitutionally tend away from each other in space though as matter they are the same in kind. Moreover they have on some level impenetrability, while minds are as permeable as anything can be.

One way to conceive the parallelism as really an identity—the structural identity required—is to appeal to "Leibniz's Law," which says something fairly obvious: that items are identical if they have every property in common. There are, however, two logical types of property, called "extensional" and "intensional" in logic (not to be confused with the extensionality of space and the intentionality of thought). In our case, extensional properties would be those that owe nothing in particular to their turning up under either the attribute of thought or extension (in the spatial sense), that is to say, they are not determined through their class. Rather, such properties would be neutral as between mind and body. Examples would be properties of order and connection: Within each attribute and mode, be it as the body that is the mind's idea or as the body in corporeal nature, the body would undergo and cause the same number of effects in the same spatial and temporal order and would display the same complexities of connection.[3]

So conceived, that is, extensionally, the items under both modes would indeed be identical by Leibniz's Law, which is generally understood to apply to extensional properties, the neutral ones. But there are also intensional— note well: s not t—properties, those that come from the class, or better, those that tell the nature of an item insofar as it is described as being of a certain kind: of thought or of extension, of mind or of body. In respect to their intensional properties, the two kinds differ, I would argue, radically. The great difference is in the intentionality—note well, here t not s—of thinking, its aboutness. Of course, if you concentrate on the "neutral" properties, since body-in-the-mind is an ideationally representational parallel of body-in-physical-nature, their identity is logically unexceptionable. But what about the fact that thought has the reflexive character of both being an idea and harboring an *ideatum*? Can the identity of the attributes' elements be saved by a logical restriction?

Supposing even that a way were found to construe the physical world so as to give it mental-like structure. It would not solve the problem for Spinoza, because such bodies could then not come essentially, intensionally, under the attribute of spatial extension. The same might hold for the converse: A mind with truly physical structure—a current preoccupation— might not be Spinoza's kind of mind, for that is representational in his way: It consists of ideas which *are* mind but are also *about* non-mind.

Mind indeed appears to be a hyper-mode, so to speak: It is "about" or "over" objects; not so the converse. The book, the *Ethics,* is written by a mind about the body; *we* are minds thinking of bodies. But bodies don't reciprocate, and there is no name for such a somatic function. There is a built-in deep asymmetry between the two attributes and their modes. Indeed, Spinoza will exploit it in his theory of the passions: Without it, without the active comprehension of thought, we could not control our passions. Put thus, it is not news; almost all writers—though not Hume— consider that the mind has a function in mastering feelings. But once again we will see how strange and fresh even this hackneyed notion will be within Spinoza's system.

10. Interlude: Once More the Question in Question

Asking about feelings is a most questionable enterprise. For while feeling can suffuse, envelop, challenge, derail thinking, it can't pose questions to it—except figuratively. This observation is a specific version of the body-mind asymmetry just noted before. So Spinoza, who goes far in identifying affect and thinking—he speaks, recall, of the "modes of thinking (*cogitandi*), such as love, desire, or whatever affects of the seat of thought (*animi*) are signified by name"—yet nonetheless speaks *about* the affects primarily— what else indeed can a thinker do?—from the point of view of thinking, as if they belonged to the body, the mind's idea: "Man thinks" is an axiom of the part of the *Ethics* on mind, not "Man feels."[1]

It matters here that affects be signifiable by name, for in order to think about them we have to focus the mind so as to bring ideas to bear on some reminiscence, some revival of our feeling, and we are incited and directed to do that by its name. But then the passion soon becomes a dangling specimen, shriveled and discolored. That is the dilemma on which analytic writing about the emotions, particularly modern academic writing, is hung up. In civilian life students of the affects are, we may suppose, passionate beings like all humanity. The trouble is that, when officiating as reflective analysts, the question they must ask themselves—as must even, at some point, the most behavior-oriented researchers—the question "What does it feel *like* to feel that X-emotion?" is an invitation to a self-examination that is also a self-distancing. The fact of that distance may be first expressed in half-dead, hackneyed simile: "It feels *like* a vise around my heart" or "It feels *as if* my heart was on fire." The next step is, if truth be told, "I've lost it"; "like" couldn't hold it.

The point of these observations is that Spinoza has found a way—without either yielding up the primacy of thought or discounting the affects—to reduce considerably the mutually exclusive otherness of feeling and thinking that perforce obtrudes itself when the latter tries to comprehend the former. The particulars will take a little setting out, but it's worth it. First, the body's role in our affective life must be delineated, for so far it may have seemed as if the mind had feelings on its own.

11. Affections and Affects: Motions and Emotions

So it is time to turn to feelings. Bodies can be affected by other bodies and by themselves. Spinoza calls the internalized motions by which bodies are other- or self-modified *affectiones* and the idea of these motions *affectus* (that's both a singular and a plural). *Affectus* is therefore translatable as "emotion," but "feeling" is better, because modern English writers often do use that term exchangeably with "affect." They mean by it something less specified by its cause or object and more basic than an emotion: sometimes a state of the body of which we are conscious in an emotion (or which according to the James-Lange theory *is* the emotion), sometimes, if emotion is understood as primarily a judgment, as its accompanying feel, sometimes just the experiential aspect of the psychic motion—the fact that it moves the soul metaphorically out of its place.[1] Spinoza might be said to have a theory of the emotions based on a theory of feeling; I think that any philosophical inquiry into the passions must reach the mystery of affectivity, that is, of feeling simply. Spinoza, in his top-down mode, starts with this affectivity and the question of how we are, such that we feel. Well, then, how, what, are we as feeling beings?

> By an affect (*affectus*) I understand (*intellego*) the affections (*affectiones*) of the body by which the power of action of the body is increased or diminished, aided or restrained, and at the same time the ideas of these affections.[2]

Of course, he can bring his intellect to bear on the bodies themselves only by his parallel-attributes postulate. All we know directly are "the ideas of these affections," and they are what this part, on the affects, explicates. Ideas, recall, are always affirmative. They do, indeed, have a content, but the idea-activity itself is to affirm, to say yes to the content. *So the idea which is an affect is the idea of an affection*; Spinoza repeats in the general definition that this idea is one "by which the mind affirms of its body or any of its parts a greater or less force (*vim*) existing than before."[3] The accusative of *vis, vim,* is actually in the American vocabulary; it means vigor, vitality.

We have now been told what feeling is. It's that simple: *To feel is to be mindful*—recall the mind *is* the idea—*of the liveliness of our body*. We know its vitality from its changing conditions, its affections. The body doesn't have feelings—it has accesses of power.

But, once more, we must not be fooled into imagining that we know this *from* the body. We have no contact with it; all we know is ideas, which run parallel to our body. The vitality or infirmity affect us mentally, as an idea. Spinoza uses the phrase "the idea which constitutes the form of the affect"; I understand this to mean that the idea gives the affect its thought-mode, for "form" refers to the intrinsic nature of the thing, here the idea.

Has anything been done here, or is this just an eccentric case of the tendency that has afflicted emotion study from the Stoics to contemporary "cognitivists," the tendency to reduce—or upgrade—feeling to knowing? I don't think so, for as affects are ideas, so also are ideas affects. Perhaps, however, not absolutely all ideas are affects, for there are apparently ideas neutral with respect to the increase or diminution of the body's power. These are the aforementioned ideas of ideas, which are not caught up in particulars.[4] That most ideas are affects is the remarkable solution I was talking of in the Interlude on questions above, and it is rich in implications.

Recall first that an affect is that aspect of an affection or modification of a body by which the body gains or loses vitality, and that we perceive it as the object of an idea; we have an idea of our bodily power—but not as a mere sense of existence. Rousseau, a hundred years later, speaks of a *sentiment de soi*, a "feeling of self," the atemporal moment of enjoyment of one's own just being there.[5] Spinoza's sense of existence is dynamic, "differential," so to speak. Spinoza says, however, that this increase or decrease is not comparative, as in "Today I feel more energetic than yesterday," but "involves truly more or less of reality than before" (*plus minusve realitatis involvit, quam antea*). I understand Spinoza to mean that the sense of dynamism is absolute, that it is not a relative quantity involved in continuous passage but inherent in each moment—what in modern physics would be represented as an instantaneous acceleration: dv/dt. This sense of non-relative onwards-feeling (which seems nonetheless to be comparable in memory) will be the name of the first and fundamental affect: *conatus* "striving," "trying," in the sense of self-impulsion. In the physics of the time, *conatus* was appropriated as the term for a body's apparently internal tendency to make a first movement and to maintain its motion;[6] one might think of it as the dynamic body's analogue to the soul's vibrant stasis that Aristotle called *energeia*, the fulfillment, complete in every now, of a body's capability or power (*dynamis*), but with an added element of push. Thus there is no restful completion, but to be is to strive. Goethe (who encouraged the first publication of Spinoza's complete works) famously has the angels say, "Who ever strives and labors trying— him we have means to save."[7] And indeed, *Faust*, a definitively modern work, is a paean to striving (*Streben*); the lines quoted were said by Goethe to be the key to the work. But the impetus of the *Ethics* is a far more deeply grounded affect than the expansive restlessness of Goethe's runaway medieval scholar.

12. Thinking Thing: The Human Being as a Mind That Is an Idea

But if so much must be made of the fact that Spinoza identifies affects with modes of thinking, that is to say, with particularized ideas, then before showing how the whole theory of affect is developed from "impulse" (the translation I will settle on for *conatus,* because it covers physical and psychical strivings), I should try to say what an idea, what thinking, is. For what is the good of saying that it is a consequence-laden notion to call feelings ideas, if ideas are not illuminatingly characterized? There are, as I said, plenty of theories that reduce the emotions to appraising rationality, but Spinoza's view is not thus reductive.

The *Ethics,* however, gives very spare guidance. "Man thinks," presented as an axiom, must mean: Take it as given; it's the first thing to know and not to doubt. That the mind *is* an idea must mean, as I said, that ideas are activities, that we "ideate." (There is a parallel in Hegel's use of "Concept," which is self-moving, not a mental object moved by mind.) The summary definition of an *ideatum* is "a conception of the mind which the mind forms by reason of its being a thinking thing."[1] That "a true idea must agree with that of which it is the idea (*ideatum*)" means that ideas have the character of aboutness.

"Thinking thing" comes from Descartes, and this suggests that some help might come from Spinoza's earlier presentation of Cartesian thought. There we learn that thinking (*cogitatio*) is consciousness simply.[2] From Spinoza's fragment *On the Improvement of Human Understanding* we get a useful analogy: As men used simple material tools to make in time more and more complex ones, so the intellect makes intellectual instruments of greater and greater complexity. I interpret this to mean that ideas are self-activating tools working to master their contents. There follows the thought—corroborated in the *Ethics* and crucial to the theory of affects—that ideas can be regarded *in themselves,* as they are intrinsically, quite apart from their contents. In particular we can ask whether an idea considered in itself without relation to its object "has all the properties or *intrinsic* [my italics] predicates of a true idea."[3] A true idea is an *adequate* idea, as a false one is inadequate. Since inadequacy is *the* hallmark of passion I will explain it as soon as I have tried to say—sketchily—what it means to be the human being presupposed by the *Ethics.* It means to be conscious (though what consciousness is, is beyond telling non-circularly), and it means that consciousness is structured as mind, as a thinking entity. Thinking, in turn, is the particular—Spinoza's word is "determinate"—delimited case of having, or better, of being an idea. For the mind *is* an idea and we *are* minds (and, of course, simultaneously but non-tangently bodies). Ideas are activities, tool-like in being busy on or about, in intending, their idea-content—which has, once more, *no* direct connection, no causative connection to its physical counterpart that exists in the bodily mode under the parallel attribute of extension. Ideas *in themselves,* quite apart from their content, can be inadequate, which will mean confused and *partial*; that, in turn, will mean *passionate.*

So this is what it means to be a human being: We exist in one mode as a mind that works on, conceives, contains, its contents. These may be either bodies-in-thought, which are for our mind idea-contents, or they may be ideas-of-ideas, thoughts of thoughts, by which we reflect on our own thinking. In our other mode we exist as bodies.

To me this understanding of my human nature is not so much convincing as illuminating, for it touches base with every ultimate human mystery: how consciousness is related to ideas, what ideas are and do, what it means to have a body and a mind, and more to my point, how the passions are *thinkable*. I will let the good of Spinoza's metaphysics be in its bold address of alluring enigmas.

13. Interlude: Emotions as Bodily Feels

It might be good to say here what Spinoza's theory of affects cannot be. Just as it is not a reduction of emotions to a kind of (good or bad) reasoning, so it is not a reduction of emotion to bodily feels. As I said, there is such a theory, set out by William James in his famous essay "What is an Emotion?," and simultaneously by C. G. Lange.

The James-Lange theory says that directly upon perception of an exciting fact there follow bodily changes, and "*our feeling of the same changes . . . IS the emotion.*"[1] According to James, common sense says that we meet a bear, get frightened, and tremble, then run. But his hypothesis says we meet a bear, tremble, and as we run, we feel frightened, in that order. James, to be sure, restricts his hypothesis to those emotions that have an obvious bodily expression, emotions like fear, anger, lust; there are also mental excitements that are not distinctly felt in the body. But for the "standard" emotions, bodily arousal, mediated by the brain as feeling, *is,* without remainder, the emotion; if we abstract in our consciousness the bodily feel, no "mind-stuff" is left behind.

Experiments, for example testing the emotional responses of people without bodily feelings due to spinal injuries, have been inconclusive.[2] Moreover, the James-Lange theory requires that emotions be differentiated by physiological effects, but evidently very different stimuli, say, hearing beautiful music and watching an autopsy, presumably emotionally differently fraught, can have identical physical effects, such as scalp-tingling.[3]

Yet, together with Spinoza's, the James-Lange theory plays the role of patron saint to contemporary neuroscientific investigations into the emotions. They differ, however, quite completely insofar as James's theory depends on the body's inducing mental states causally. Spinoza happens to regard our body's external affections, such as trembling and growing pale, as having no relation to the mind at all, causally or in parallel.[4] This brief account of the body-first theory is useful also for pointing out a remarkable feature of Spinoza's theory: It obviates the distinction that bedevils many accounts, that between feels or feelings (close to the body) and emotions or sentiments (close to the mind). Spinoza's distinctions among affects never differentiate types of that kind. Affects are affects, first and last, only some are differently apprehended from others, as we will now see.

14. Inadequacy : Adequacy—Passions : Actions

We are ready for one of the *Ethics'* most startling notions: that "passions," affects, can be either passive or active. *There are active affects.*

This novel claim—for its time—is the direct consequence of the understanding of affects as ideas, and I now want to say again that, conversely, all ideas are ultimately affects. For although there are ideas of ideas, reflective ideas, still our primary ideas are of the body's vitality. Indeed it seems to be that even the secondary reflections are, perhaps more remotely, imbued with the body's more or less existentially auspicious affections. But, recall that that is what an affect is: the idea of my actually present body's affections, meaning either modifications by other bodies or our own ideas as we imagine things that help or hinder our power of action.[1] Spinoza does postulate that not all such affections affect our vitality, but that possibility depends on a fact of physics: that the relative motions of bodies or their parts can be so proportioned that a body's internal or external situation does not change in moving.[2] We have to keep in mind that physics, the science of the motion of bodies, will be deeply and wonderfully involved in human self-knowledge. It was to be expected, if our mind *is* the idea of our body.

Ideas can be true or false, but not in the traditional way that is still current in ordinary life: We think we have a good idea if it matches up with the thing it is of. The scholastics speak of *adaequatio intellectus et rei,* "the making-equal (adequation) of intellect and thing."[3] But for Spinoza we are, as beings who have an intellect, on a different track from these things, that is, from bodies. So we can't match up our thinking with them,[4] and once again, Spinoza innovates on the back of scholastic terms. For nonetheless our ideas have adequacy or, what is far more interesting (and usual), inadequacy. Ideas are intrinsically true (now interpreted as adequate) or false (inadequate) not either as they match the *things,* the bodies, themselves, but as they "come together" with their ideated content.[5] That content, as an *ideatum,* is never at fault: In fact, a bad—deficient—thing as a content will only be so because we know it inadequately.[6] There is no content that lacks being—for as I reported before, there is no lack of being, no substantial privation or nonbeing in God's plenum. All the inadequacy is in the mind, in the "ideating" itself.

So what causes falsity—and therewith passion—is rather to be called inadequacy than falseness or badness. What makes the idea-instrument inadequate? It is a "mutilated" and confused idea, an imperfect idea.[7] I will set out below what our grades of thinking are, such that inadequacy can come about. But what it itself is, can be stated now. In sum, inadequacy is incompleteness, lack of comprehensiveness, *partialness*. In particular, it is conceiving a cause that is "inadequate or partial," that is, a cause that does not completely account for its effect. By using my intellect I should be able, by inspecting the cause alone, to see how a given effect necessarily comes from it; I should see it "clearly and distinctly"—a phrase borrowed from Descartes meaning brightly lit as a whole and unconfused in its parts.

When our conceptions are obscure and confounded, we are passive with respect to our bodies' affections. (Again Descartes: Spinoza offers a remarkable elaboration of his claim that the passions of the soul are the actions of the body.) And this is what human *passion* is—*having inadequate ideas of our world and ourselves,* seeing the physical causes themselves inadequately, not being in mental command of the complete context of all that affects us, or alternatively—transferring our idea's inadequacy to its contents— supinely allowing opaque causes to work their effects on us. We are, so to speak, less there, less existent, when our affects are passive rather than active; an active being *is* more fully than a passive one.

This is how Spinoza himself explains it:

> Thus if we can be the adequate cause of these [bodily] affections, then by affect I understand (*intellego*) an ACTION (*actio*), if otherwise, a PASSION (*passio*).[8]

How can we be adequate causes—causes at all—of our physical conditions, into which we cannot intrude? It will turn out, as it must, that there is no free causation at all, no interference of the will with the order of nature. Moreover, neither can we think as we will; the order of ideas is also necessary. So if I say that being a cause, adequate or inadequate, of my affects just means coming to have clear and distinct ideas of my physical vitality, I haven't said how I can, given the determinism of ideas, work myself into that clarity. This ultimately insoluble perplexity will become acute as the analysis of the passions turns into their ethical management in Part IV of the *Ethics*.

Meanwhile, having left things for us to last, we do come to some humanly recognizable results, the results meant for us all. Most people—at least most people who are all there—do, I think, regard themselves now and then as passive under their passions, that is to say, as affected, "upset" by them— done to rather than doing. Furthermore it is our general experience, I also think, that when we focus on the cause, expose it to light and delineate its elements, we feel less afflicted by the outside and more in charge of ourselves and—this is the peculiarly Spinozan insight—that greater clarity about our bodies and their interactions with the rest of nature gives us more active control of our lives. Recall that for Spinoza all ideas are asserted beliefs, affirmations, yea-sayings.[9] Since thoughts are willing affirmations, to employ the will and to use the intellect are one and the same, so there is no quite idly held idea; all ideas are expressible as "propositions," as logicians call posited thoughts. Therefore, as I understand it, the more comprehensive and complete the hyper-idea that is our mind becomes, the more its contents (some of them about itself), become clarified and differentiated, the stronger, the more forceful it will be, enriched with the sort of "propositions" two hundred and fifty-nine of which do indeed constitute the bulk of the *Ethics*. And the body will flourish in parallel.

Spinoza has answered Hume here before the fact. Hume is the rare writer who says unabashedly that the reason does and should serve passion, though, of course, he has a very meager notion of thinking. Spinoza answers: Reason can and should master passion. For reason (*ratio*) will be the grade of thinking (*cognitio*) that turns inadequate into adequate ideas.[10]

Again there is a novelty that seems to me to be in accord with experience. When we have successfully irradiated suffering out of our passions by the light of reason, when we have thoroughly put fear, anger, hate, any monomania, perhaps even lust, in their place, when we have seen them within the whole of things, we are not left with an empty neutrality, with bare rationality. Instead we feel ourselves as active. A passion thoroughly thought through does not cease to be an affect, but it is now an active one, an enhanced sense of our body's strength and mastery. For this enlargement is not merely a control of the body's internal feels, such as the thumping of the heart and the coursing of the blood when we face, say, an object of the attractive—or repulsive—passions. It is a widening of our entire scope to what Spinoza calls elsewhere "the face of the whole universe,"[11] and the attendant expansive pleasure in our situation, no matter how parochially painful it may be.

15. Physics and Physiology: The Prerequisites for Blessedness

Recall always that there is an unbreakable wall of separation between body and mind and that they are nonetheless each other's exact "mirror," the modes of one substance, God. Spinoza does not scruple to say that as our body is more fit for doing and receiving more actions, so is our mind more able, and as our body is more independent of other bodies, so is our mind more adequate in its understanding.[1] But he must mean two things: that under God, those endowed with a sounder body will have a sounder mind, and that for us, the better we understand and discount the way other bodies affect our body, the less we suffer from its affections and the more active our intellect is.

Suppress for a while what is unintelligible in this doctrine for the sake of seeing what it accomplishes. This mode of allowing things to proceed is called the Principle of Charity in hermeneutics (the theory of interpretation). Get all the good you can from a work, well knowing that our intellect is finite and somewhere, way in, something is going to be terminally enigmatic.

I understand Spinoza to say that the study we engage in to make our ideas adequate and our affects active is the study of nature in the narrow sense: motions and the bodies they differentiate and impel. It is of these that he sets out the principles.[2] Spinoza has a tremendous respect for our body, the one which is going to be understood through the coming science of physiology: We don't—yet—know what our body can do, he says. For everything can be deduced by the mere contemplation of nature, and all that we imagined would need the direction of mind can happen by the laws of nature alone, above all, the construction of the human body, which surpasses all human artifacts.[3] Here is an invitation to study natural science in the interest of ethics, because in the "face of the whole universe," in the "natured," that is to say, realized, nature that is both God himself *and* his product, we can read ourselves—a body among bodies obeying natural laws present to us in mind.[4]

Once the notion has come into the world that we know ourselves by looking nature as a whole in the face, that physics is humanity's mirror, it settles in, in various forms. Thus Kant will say in his *Critique of Pure Reason* that, in order to have that sense of our inner self which arises within us in the form of time, we first have to have experience of bodies in space, for these alone give time determinateness; we need some permanent material object against which to perceive regular change, as a fixed sundial registers the moving sun.[5] And, for Kant this world of extended nature is itself one of the two aspects of what we are in ourselves, insofar as we shape all our sensations spatially—just as Spinoza's extension is one of two attributes whose modes we are in God. These are not the only respects in which Spinoza anticipates Kant.

16. Interlude: Spinoza and Neuroscience

This is a moment to mention the way Spinoza's *Ethics* anticipates an ontological grounding for neuroscience. The study of emotions as they activate or are activated by the brain is fairly recent, though long called for by the James-Lange theory. It is fair to say that neuroscientists tend not to care much about the philosophical grounding of their science, partly because they have other things to do, partly because the science itself is by its very postulate antimetaphysical. It says that the *brain* is the mind or, more carefully, that its neural patterns determine consciousness. While Spinoza says that "the mind *is* the idea of the body," the neuroscientists can be taken to say that "the body *is* the underpinning of the mind," meaning that somatic and brain activities together prepare a complex dynamic neural structure which either *is* the mind or allows it to *emerge,* immediately and without recourse to anything extra-physical. One might think of this view (if it worked) not as the converse, but as the complement of Spinoza's body-as-mind—*as the mind seen from the body's point of view.* That would be the solution to the very asymmetry I noted before: that God's two attributes don't seem parallel. For the mind thinks *about* the body, but what does the body do reciprocally? In neuroscience it at least *underpins,* subserves the mind—allows it to emerge.

Let us, once again, leave aside these much agitated questions—whether scientists themselves, looking at brains, can possibly be just brains or whether "emergence" is a theory of consciousness-eventuation or just a kind of hand-waving—to attend to one of the several pioneers in the fairly recent neuroscientific study of the emotions who is of somewhat philosophical temperament and regards Spinoza's philosophy as giving guidance to his science. He is Antonio Damasio, in *Looking for Spinoza: Joy, Sorrow, and the Feeling Brain.*[1]

Damasio's own theory is, to begin with, of the James-Lange type insofar as he regards emotions as the observable movements of the body, either external, such as expressive gestures, or internal, such as somatic chemical alterations or encephalic electrophysical wave patterns. But while emotions play out in the theater of the body, feelings, he says, play out in the theater of the mind. His terminology reverses the common understanding, as does James's. Feelings are for him the higher level, being the conscious notice we take of our emotions; emotions are physical and evolutionarily first. "In brief, the essential content of feelings is the mapping of a particular body state; the substrate of feelings is the set of neural patterns [i.e., emotions] from which a mental image of the body state can emerge."[2] I will presently point out that Damasio's theory comes close to but does not perfectly jibe with Spinoza's, in which bodily affections are also, as the lowest level of thinking, represented in the imagination—though, of course, here they are not "caused" by the body. Damasio is rare in his frank admission that the emergence of a mental image from a neurophysiological emotion—or indeed any brain event—is so far largely a puzzle.[3] Consider, for example, a fascinating discovery that the brain patterns are sometimes isomorphic with the stimulus: Macaque monkeys, shown various patterns, form neural patterns that are graphic images, copies of the stimulus in the visual cortex.[4] Yet it helps very little with the ultimate puzzle of consciousness, that is, with the "mentality" of the mental image: the fact that the monkey sees, and that *we* see both what *he* sees (the external stimulus) and its image patterned in the brain (which *isn't* what *he* sees), and that we, in reflecting on the situation, form a mental image of both (which *we alone* see).

Now if the patterns were such as, for instance, to frighten the monkey, what would be the feeling component? It is old wisdom that all but the most immediately physical "feels" require a mental image and that most images are emotionally charged [Ch. X, Sec.5], but just how is that charge to be located in the image? The physical neural pattern is said to *be* the emotion; the mental image is said to *be* the feeling. But the mental image appears, for Damasio, to be a representation, that is to say, to be in some sort of—not necessarily visual—correspondence with the neural pattern it images. Yet it seems unlikely that a feeling, what is usually called an emotion, is representational, that it is some sort of spatial version of something that is itself spatial, like a neural pattern, albeit one that changes in time. The open question here, piggy-backed on the problem of consciousness, is: Can a mental image be *the* feeling or does it merely convey it?—in which latter case, far from being a solution to the problem of felt feelings, the image complicates it by adding the issue of representationality. Spinoza escapes this problem, so central to the neuroscientific consideration of consciousness, because affects are not the bodily affections themselves as apprehended in the imagination, but rather their idea insofar as it evinces an increase or decrease of the body's "power of action."

What Damasio considers to be Spinoza's real breakthrough is, first, the very notion of our mind as the idea of our body and, then, the thought of a correlation, the parallel process that represents the one by the other. Although Spinoza knows little of biochemical processes or neural pathways, he assumes, Damasio thinks, a "mechanism" by which bodily events are represented in the mind—and it involves the brain, the *cerebrum*.[5] There seems to be a fallacy here, because the mechanism for both Spinoza and Damasio may work from body to brain, but not from brain to mind. It works neither for Spinoza, because the correlation is emphatically not a causal connection, nor for Damasio, because neuroscience has not yet—if it's in principle possible—made evident a brain-mind causation (as distinct from a correlation). Nonetheless, the main attraction the metaphysician exercises on the neuroscientist is the very fact that both body and mind are based in one substance in such a way that the mystery of their causal interaction simultaneously appears to be obviated along with Cartesian "substance-dualism," which is a scandal to present-day brain science.[6]

It is, however, hard to see how the one-substance theory would be helpful, unless accepting it signaled that Damasio is actually resigned to and relieved by the ultimate impossibility of finding a causal connection—and is grateful to the metaphysician for finding the formulation which allows him to hold onto non-substantial mind while finding through experiment ever more specific brain patterns that appear to be closely correlated with the conscious mental experience known by introspection—without having to worry about their causal connection. This course appears wise when you ask yourself how one would class such a nexus—as physical (manifest directly to the senses) or mental (expressible only indirectly through words).

Finally, there is a specific aspect of Spinoza's theory of affect that is particularly in accord with Damasio's and all neuroscientists' evolutionism: Emotion, joy above all, is an evolutionary outcome, and its associated maps signify optimal physiological coordination, a greater capacity to act, as sorrow signifies the opposite. As emotions, joy and sorrow are witnesses of the body maneuvering itself into survival; as feelings, they are sensors of the waxing and waning life within. Damasio's understanding of emotion, arrived at experimentally, is close to that expressed by Spinoza: the affection of the body by which its power of acting is increased or diminished.[7] The residual problem is: Who or what *feels* the feeling?

This interlude on a scientist's co-option of a metaphysician not only shows how future-fraught the *Ethics* turns out to be, but also introduces problems, to be considered later, that bedevil the current science of emotions.

17. Impulse: The Proto-Affect

We have at last worked our way down Spinoza's deductive system to the passions—and actions—proper, that is, to the affects (Part III). There is one that comes before all others: *conatus*—endeavor, trying, urge, exertion, push, impetus. I have, as I said, chosen to use mostly "impulse," partly to preserve its physical meaning. (In physics impulse = force acting over time, $f \cdot t$.) Impulse, being the basic affect, has absolutely determinative significance in Spinoza's theory, connecting the passions to the theological ground and to the ethical end.

Here is what "impulse" is not: It is not quite the drive to self-preservation, whence springs that basic right to life that is a fundamental for the political writers of Spinoza's time. And while it is not the scramble to stay alive, neither is it quite the fulfillment of human being, the often mentioned vibrant stasis that is not a motion, which Aristotle called *energeia*. Yet it is some of both. It is dynamic.

For Aristotle *energeia* and *dynamis* (I cite the Greek words to recall the survival of his terms in our physics) are related as the actual to the potential. *Energeia* is the fulfillment of *dynamis*, which latter is potency or the capability for coming into full being.

Spinoza enunciates:

> Impulse, by which any thing whatsoever is impelled to persist in its existence, is nothing besides the actual essence of the thing.[1]

In the proof of this proposition, he keeps using the phrase *conatus sive potentia*, "impulse or power."

Thus first, impulse is no longer for Spinoza what *dynamis* was for Aristotle: a mere capability, a mere potentiality, a transition that cancels itself as it passes into fulfillment. Instead it is now power, potency, a permanent dynamic state that *is*—IS—the actual essence of the thing: *energeia is dynamis*; essence (what it means to be a thing) *is* impulse (that it wants to go on existing). With this notion Spinoza, incidentally, makes an end run around the scholastic mainstream, since Thomas says explicitly, "No creature's doing is its being, for that is God's prerogative, and no creature's power to act is its essence, for that too is God's prerogative."[2] Spinoza could, of course, answer: Human beings are not just God's creatures but one of his own modes of being.

That is to say: It is the very nature of everything that is an entity, in particular it is *our* very "whatness," our essence, to be impulsive, dynamic. Spinoza uses scholastic terms. It is our essence to be impelled to persist in existence. In English: *What* we are is *nothing but* our trying to ensure *that* we are and are ever more—not forever, but in ever greater degree. For our potency or power waxes (and wanes) by its (or our) very striving. So this impulsion to exist *is* not just preservative, it is *expansive*.[3]

It sounds pretty bare (and *toil*some), but it is the source of all joy for Spinoza. For to exist in this dynamic way is to be actual, as is God—of whom we are, after all, a mode, that is, one way of his being. God *is* as productive in his omnipotence, which is his "naturing" (*naturans*), and he *is* equally as his production, which is his "having natured" (*naturata*). So we too express what we are by being it actively. This existential trying to exist can be called self-preservation only at a minimum. It is in fact self-amplification.

Conatus is nature-wide, but it also has human-specific names. When referred to our minds alone, it is called will (*voluntas*); when it refers to mind and body together, it is called appetite (*appetitus*); when it refers to conscious appetite, it is called desire (*cupiditas*). "Desire is the very essence of a human being, conceived as set (*determinata*) to do something out of some given affection of itself."[4] This whole definition should be in capitals. It shows why the impulse to exist is aggrandizing: It is in us desire, and desire is acquisitive.

Lest anyone suppose that this is innocuous term-mongering, Spinoza ends the passage by setting its meaning out as follows:

> It may be gathered from this, then, that we are impelled by, will, seek or desire nothing because we deem it good, but on the contrary, we deem it good because we are impelled by, will, seek or desire it.[5]

Readers might well clutch their heads: Here is a work called *Ethics* in which will equals impulse and what is good is defined by our desire! Spinoza is setting the stage for his own affective morality, which as ever with him, will double-invert the standard tradition: turn it upside down to recover it for something beyond the normal. I will come to it toward the end.

18. A Return to Negativity and the Partial Spectator

Meanwhile, recall that some affects are inadequate ideas. Inadequacy is the only kind of falsity an idea can have, for there is nothing in God's nature, there are none of his ways, be they extended or thinking things, that are, to coin a phrase, positively negative. Spinoza's Nature is not, after all, God's creation. Creatures, Augustine says, are and are not; they are because from God they *derive* existence; they *are not* because they only *have* being derivatively and *are* not being.[1] But Nature is God, and its modes have only affirmative being, absolute positivity, undetermined by negation. For merely to think of them, to define their essence, is to affirm it, for essence implies existence. All that can be thought of exists, and no existence is in and through itself destructible—though it is vulnerable to assault by another existence.[2] Things can indeed destroy things and so we, and all the conceivable modes, are finite, contingent, destructible.

Clearly our impulsive urge, in its two aspects, our body's vitality and our mind's activity, are of the utmost consequence in this universe, and confused *conatus* is our vulnerability to its incursions.

But recall that the activity of the mind is in the adequacy of the ideas that constitute it and its passivity—its vulnerability to destruction—in their inadequacy. Recall too that inadequacy is primarily *partiality*, in the related senses both of incompleteness or non-comprehensiveness and of the disorientation that comes from "being partial" (as the phrase goes), of being thoughtlessly, lopsidedly, engaged. I can't help observing here again how oddly close Spinoza's contemplative monitoring, the adequate ideation of the mind that is made of God, comes to Adam Smith's Impartial Spectator, the ideal man in the breast, who is also divine.

19. The Specificity of Passion: Its Object

We have finally finished what seemed to me the necessary preliminaries, to come to what we now call the emotions. Of these the deficient kind, the passions, are more humanly illuminating for this book and the actions more philosophically remarkable for thought in general.

To begin with, passions, as ideas, have an object which they are "about." And now Spinoza makes an observation that is very nearly the most helpful to be found in any writing about affect and, I think, nowhere else so positively put. Technically stated: The passions are qualitatively determined by—or express—their object.[1] Humanly interpreted: My feelings take their "feel" entirely from what they are about. Anyone can say that (though few do, Thomas, for instance, though only generically, Sartre more particularly),[2] but only Spinoza gives its metaphysical ground, his understanding of idea and *ideatum,* of active mind and positive object.

For that impassioned man or woman who has ever been oppressed—even while overjoyed—by the sheer confusion attending the assault of feeling, or grieved—even while exulting—by the powerlessness it revealed, Spinoza's observation will come as comfort. It means that the almost unbearable specificity of the affect comes from its object, and that the patient's attention should go to *it*—should go to making its idea as clear and distinct as possible. Thus, to become personal, we can either rejoice in it in full awareness or cure ourselves of it. It means that the poet's question should not, primarily, be "How do I love thee? Let me count the ways," but "What is your substance, whereof are you made?"[3] For the first reflects on oneself as passionate and leads to generalities about affect, while the second goes out to an other as object and articulates cognitive specifics—and specification relieves passion, for the burden of passion is largely in its unspeakable uniqueness, in its inexpressible particularity. The insight seems to me to work not only on erotic and temperamental affects but also on esthetic effects, whose elusive and confounding uniqueness is generally agreed to derive immediately from the particular qualities of a work of art. The labor of clarifying and distinguishing the object of a passion brings a wonderful relief that includes a positive profit: insight.

Here is another way to think of Spinoza's assertion that "the nature of any one passion must therefore of necessity be so explained that the object by which we are affected is expressed." This injunction reaches across the species: A horse's desire is equine, a man's human.[4] I take that to mean that horses and humans focus their desires on species-specific objects. The formulation is a little ambiguous, as it needs to be, for of course the passion as mere passion—aside from its object—also has its own formal characteristics. That is why different affects can, after all, be discerned and defined, as I will report shortly.

This view of passion as receiving its character largely from its object underlines Spinoza's powerful individualism. Metaphysically, there are for him no general essences, whatness-bestowing forms. For when essence *is* existence—as it is for God-or-Nature—then each individually existent being must have its individual essence. For nothing can be conceived that is more individual than existing. And so for Spinoza existence, even though it applies to every being, is most emphatically not a universal term, since as essence it is particular to—and here I anticipate Spinoza's ethics proper—what every human being makes of itself. Hence the only generality comes from a collection *we* happen to make and denominate, such as is expressed in the name "mankind." Thus, precisely as modes of God, our existence is our very own; we are not constrained by a common essence.

Here, to engage once more in "isms," Spinoza shows himself as the heir of medieval nominalism, the claim that only individuals exist and universals are mere names, and also as an ancestor of modern existentialism, the claim that individual existence is prior to and determines essence. Nominalism tends to be a consequence of thinking of God's power as total, unconstrained by prior requirements of essential being. Its implied individualism will, however, as we can imagine, make the social passions and actions problematic. For our root affect is, accordingly, concerned with our own, our individual existence—which has its pathos for a man so personally benevolent as Spinoza.

20. The Passionate Affects: Preliminaries

That root affect is the impulse of every being to be, and it is now specified as *desire*, the human being's conscious appetite, which is called impulse when it is referred at once to body and mind. This is, exactly, what we do ordinarily call desire. The tradition wavers about whether to term desire an emotion. One might say either that Spinoza has obviated that question by simply calling all feelings affects, or that he has solved it by showing how all emotions must spring from desire, the urge to be and to absorb being. As the underlying affect, it is single; most of the derived affects that follow will be opposing pairs. Of these, the negative is, in Spinoza's positive vein, less powerful, and moreover, we avoid it as much as we can.[1] I think Spinoza makes these affect-pairs opposites rather than considering one as just a deficiency in, or an excess of, the other for two reasons. The first is, as he says of sadness specifically, that such defects or privations would be nothings, while all the passions can in fact enter into the positive actions of a soul, as we will soon see.[2] The second reason is that the affects can mingle and induce "fluctuations" of the mind, waverings that are to affect what doubt is to imagination.[3] This condition would make less sense if the opposites were just oppositely signed positions on an affect-spectrum.

One more observation on the emotions in general: Joy and sadness, the parent affects, evince preeminently—as they must—the fundamental duality of action and passion; the active mind is ultimately affected only by the joyful member of the pair.

21. The Passions

The first offspring, born out of human *conatus* or desire, are joy and sadness, *laetitia* and *tristitia*. Some people translate these as "pleasure" and "pain," mostly, I think, because they are, after all, states of the body. But they are the *mind's idea* of the body; joy is the mind's *glorying* in the body's increasing power: The body flourishes and we think the better. It is typical of Spinoza to use spiritual language of God's Nature. For *laetari*, the verb, occurs in all sorts of sacred texts, in particular in the Latin translations of the Hebrew Bible, for example, *Laetamini cum Ierusalem et exultate in ea*, "Rejoice with

Jerusalem, and exult in her."[1] "Pleasure" or its verbal forms would be flabby in these contexts—and in that of the *Ethics*. "Joy is a human being's transition from less to greater perfection." Perfection = existence = essence = actuality = power,[2] but "less to greater perfection" goes with the understanding of joy as a *transition*, an increase in the plenitude of our body's power or actual existence, or rather, our idea of it. Joy is not a state of equilibrium but one of felt increase. This expansiveness must not be comparative, that is, a confused sense of "better now than before," of a transition from negative to positive, but there must be really, affirmatively, more existence felt as an absolute increase at each moment.

How, one might ask, could any thing undergo an access of existence? We tend to think that a thing either exists or doesn't. Existence seems to be an undefined term of the *Ethics*, but whatever else it might be when defined, the human being's existence is dynamic—to be is to be active, like God who "natures," and of that dynamism there can indeed be more or less. Thus joy is quite naturally the second affect; one might say that it is the feel of the body's now trying and now succeeding, and thus in every now.

Here is joy's descent: Impulse (all of Nature's propensity to exert existence) → appetite (the human impulse of body and mind at once) → desire (conscious appetite) → joy (successful desire). Since desire is impulse, it is our essence; since it is of body and mind together, it is affected by the affections or modifications, interior or external, that our body undergoes; since affect is, in our minds, the idea of increased or diminished power of action, desire is defined as our being set (*determinata*) to act; since joy is successful desire, it is activity toward perfection.

Perhaps "expression" or "derivation" would be a better word than "descent" for the relation of joy to human impulse, that is, to desire. There are as many desires as there are particular objects of joy, an infinity of them. So joy and all the other derived affects can be considered as articulations of impulses by objects.

Now this is strange. Who thinks of desire primarily as being determined (in both senses, impelled and resolved) to act? We think of it as longing, perhaps incidentally active, but more likely and more characteristically passive. So actually does Spinoza, for desire arises from the body's affections, and our ideas of these may be quite confused, inadequate, passive. Desire is a *passion* if we are inadequately the cause of our body's affections—those that empower or victimize us—and of our ideas of them.[3] What "cause" could mean here is first and last a puzzle, for recall that while we *are* bodies, we *know* of them only as ideas. But of that more will be said when we come to the active affects, the virtues.

Since joy is successful desire, it shares in the possible passivity of desire. It can be more or less causal as it is more or less clear and distinct. There are also purely bodily passions; these appear to be cases where we are mindlessly or unconsciously driven by the affections of our body—the difference between the philosopher's joy and the drunkard's pleasure.[4] Since the body is an idea, this would take some explaining—perhaps it is an inadequacy that doesn't quite reach even the level of what Leibniz calls the soul's stupor, in which nothing is distinct at all.[5]

When our ideas are insufficiently active, that is, causative, we are affected with sadness (*tristitia*), joy's opposite—perhaps "depression" is not the wrong term. In sadness our vitality droops.

All the other aspects are composed or derived from these three.[6] Spinoza numbers forty-eight of them. The definitions that make up such lists can't help but be somewhat concocted and, with the exception of some crucial spots, correspondingly boring (except perhaps for Hobbes's in the *Leviathan,* because he is so witty; for example: "*Sudden glory* is the passion which makes those *grimaces* called LAUGHTER," or, more to the point since it must have been noticed by Spinoza: "*Joy,* arising from imagination of a man's own power and ability is the exultation of the mind which is called GLORYING," and "*pleasure* . . . a corroboration of vital emotion, and a help thereunto"). Hobbes's "glory" seems to be joy in the acerbic mode.[7]

So I'll pick four of the remaining forty-five which seem to me revealing, either as dead right or as startlingly new.

The first passion after the three basic ones is wonder (no. IV), Descartes' first. Recall that wonder is for Socrates in antiquity the readiness to marvel at the obvious, thus the beginning of philosophy and so not really a passion; to Descartes it is indeed a passion and the first enumerated one. It is our astonishment at an object insofar as it is novel; it is, so to speak, the "startle" passion, before any judgment we make of usefulness, and it is to be gotten over. In Spinoza's list it occurs as first of the derived passions, in order, I think, to go Descartes one better: Wonder is the mind's "imagination" of something in which it stays transfixed (*defixa*) because the object is disjoined from everything.[8] It is not really a dynamic affect at all, but a "distraction" of the mind. So its cause is not novelty and its effect is not being startled, but just the opposite: It is the pseudo-affect of being stuck for want of a cause why the mind should go on. If wonder was primitive for Descartes, it is—worse—stale for Spinoza. Why this resistance to what in ancient philosophy was *the* humanly admirable disposition? Both authors are devoted to natural science, which, rather than dwell in questioned beginnings, tends to progress to demonstrable answers. That is one reason. But for Spinoza, having defined it as he does, wonder becomes the very model passion for inadequacy, which is, recall, in one aspect, disconnectedness, incompleteness of understanding. We are a mode of God, and as such we, as partial gods, ways of his, are meant to strive for comprehensiveness, to drive toward omniscience, not to be stuck in a fixation.

Thus, strange though it seems, it makes good sense that Spinoza immediately transits to contempt (no. V), for contempt is overlooking: The mind is so little touched by its imagination of something that it imagines things not contained while overlooking those contained in its object. In other words, contempt is wonder gone inventive from sheer inattention. This adverse definition encapsulates Spinoza's humanity: Nothing, *properly regarded*, is, in fact, contemptible.

The word "imagination" has now come up several times. It is closely related to inadequacy and hence to passion; it will be explained soon.

Love is next (no. VI). What writers know of love is, I think, the test of their usefulness. Spinoza says, dryly, "Love is joy accompanied by the idea of an external cause," and he thinks this "explains the essence of love with sufficient clarity." As it happens, it does that, it seems to me—when unpacked. As so often, Spinoza's formulation is first a negation of, and an alternative to, one previously on offer, that love is the lover's will to unite himself to the object of love. That's only a property, he says, and signifies merely that will is the mind's impulse, which underlies the joy. What his definition positively does is once again to put the object, its idea, in the center, so that the strength and quality of our passion is determined as much by *what* we love as by *how* we love. Spinoza, to be sure, knows a lot about the subjective aspect of the passion. He sets it out in numerous propositions that are kept severely metaphysical by using the Cartesian language of things, yet keep slipping into the language of persons and are so keenly to the point that they sound naïve. For example: "When we love a thing similar to ourselves, we are impelled to bring it about that it should also love us." Or: "The greater the affect with which we imagine a thing loved to be affected towards us, the greater will be our feeling of glory."[9] There are many more; he is particularly acute about the fluctuations of love and about the simultaneities of love and hate in a lover when the object of love moves closer to someone else. Hate (no. VII) is love's opposite, a depressed state induced by an external cause, together with an impulse to "cut off its existence." Who has not found ugly relief in a dream in which he—or she—"cuts off the existence" (*secludit existentiam*) of an unresponsive object of love?

The understanding of love as determined by its object will be very helpful to Spinoza in delineating the love of his own life—the "intellectual love of God." For it is the manner in which God exists—as the *whole* of divinized nature—that makes such a love possible; in the knowledge of God, a passion is turned completely into an action, for it is *ipso facto* comprehensive. This active love will put all the passionate love in the shadow. I think Spinoza regards all existences, rightly known, as worthy of love, but insofar as concentration on individuals is the very definition of partiality in both senses—predilection and incompleteness—that love is an inadequate idea.

The last listed passion is lust (*libido,* no. XLVIII), desire and love "of the commingling of bodies." It is one of five affects that have no contraries because, as I understand Spinoza, if lust indulged is lust enjoyed, lust thwarted is not lust replaced by a contrary affect; the lust remains. Moreover its apparent contrary, chastity, is "potency (*potentia*) of mind," not a passion but a virtue—virility, one might say, under the attribute of thought. But since Spinoza thinks that the mind's alertness depends on the body's vigor, the monk's vow is not privileged as a virtue.[10] Indeed whoever thinks that Spinoza is just against physical pleasure hasn't got the idea:

> Since, therefore, those things are good which aid the parts of the body to fulfill their function, and, since joy consists in the fact that the power of a human being, insofar as it consists of mind and body, is helped or increased—all those things then which bring pleasure are good.

There are many more such passages, even to approving the enjoyment of perfumes.[11]

What is wrong with lust is not only its tendency to excess but something much more revealingly consonant with Spinoza's drive for "impartiality," for comprehensiveness. Spinoza names an affect that cannot be excessive because it is not partial: "Of joyous pleasure (*hilaritas*) there cannot be too much, but it is always good, while melancholy is always bad."[12] It is a pleasure of both mind and body, but here it is not a physical member that is a locus of the pleasure, since "all the parts of the body are equally affected." This is wonderful: Spinoza's preference for a humanly diffused over a physically localized passion evinces, I think, a feminine sensibility—in the service of comprehension!

One last passion: pity (no. XVIII), to show how Spinoza can seem most odd when he is most sensible. "Pity (*commiseratio*) is pain accompanied by the idea of harm which happened to another whom we imagine similar to ourselves." *Commiseratio,* shared misery, "I feel your pain," is not approved by Spinoza: "Pity in a human being who lives under the guidance of reason is in itself bad and useless."[13] It is pain and so it is bad, depressing; it is, in short, a passion in the worst way—inaction. "Act and rejoice" is the right watchword, that is, be active rather than passive; do something and do it not from immediate feeling, but upon reflection. I might add here that some other Christian virtues, humility and repentance, are singled out for disapproval; the one is bad because it is pain resulting from loss of power; the other makes you "twice as unhappy or weak as before." There go insecurity and guilt feelings, good riddance: "Pangs of conscience, remorse (*conscientiae morsus*) is depression accompanied by the idea of a past thing whose outcome was contrary to our hope."[14]

Let this sampling represent the whole ingenious list, and let me repeat its all-important principle: Since all affects are derived from impulse, which is in itself a push to the better, the passions that are positive with respect to impulse all have the names of those affects we ordinarily tend to be for. Moreover, these have greater potency than their contraries; in particular "the desire which arises from joy" (Spinoza must mean "is specified by joy") is stronger than that drawn in by pain.[15] From the positive passions will be drawn the virtues. But these depend on clear thinking, so it is time to explain cognition, the kinds of knowledge of which our minds are capable.

22. Of the Degrees of Knowledge: Imagination, Reason, Intuition

In the *Ethics* Spinoza makes short work of his theory of knowledge, however crucial it might be to his theory of affects. I will do likewise. It seems to me that the degrees, the "three kinds" of knowledge he sets out, closely track Plato's *Republic,* as is likely for a cognitive theory that represents an ascent, a ladder of knowledge—to the Good in the *Republic,* to God in the *Ethics.* For there is in such hierarchies always cognition of what is perceived confusedly, experienced vaguely, and remembered from words heard and formed into images; these both Plato and Spinoza call "opinion" and "imagination." Next comes cognition from common notions and adequate ideas of the properties of things; this Plato calls "thinking" and Spinoza "reason." And the third stage is cognition of formal essences, which we see directly with the intellect; this Plato calls "thought" and Spinoza "intuitive science."[1]

Let me here state the obvious: A theory of staged cognition is made to order for converting passions into actions. That transformation, however, is accomplished by increased adequacy, which means a more global comprehension. But that is precisely what the stages will provide in their ascending order.

For Spinoza, then, the third kind of knowing "proceeds" by the intellect, "from the adequate idea of the formal essence of certain attributes of God to the adequate idea of the essence of things." (Plato says "form" or "idea" and means a separable being; Spinoza says "formal essence" and means the individual essence as it is in itself and coincides with its *ideatum* when the idea is adequate.) "Things" I take to mean the above-mentioned "face of the whole universe," which intuitive science reaches with the help of analogical insight.[2] In other words, this highest knowledge is a theology of Nature as a whole, and its affect is that intellectual love of God already mentioned. I will turn to this love at the end.

The middle genus of knowledge is what we ordinarily call reasoning or thinking, for example, mathematics and logic with their axioms. It is the genus in which the *Ethics* is written, though its perspective is that of intuitive science.

As always, the lowest kind is the most interesting because there mind meets body or, in Spinoza's terms, has body most directly in mind. Spinoza's theory of the imagination reflects everything he thinks about the human mind.

First of all it is a representational theory, meaning that cognitions begin as affections of our body; this body, remember, *is* itself our hyper-idea, our constituting idea. This idea re-presents to us—that is, in our mind— "images" of external bodies as if they were present.[3] These images are never in themselves false—ideas never are—but only insofar as the mind lacks the idea that "cuts off" (*secludat*) the existence of the thing which does not in fact exist. (This cutting off or excluding is Spinoza's way of avoiding negation; he is the aboriginal philosopher of the positive attitude.) So fantasies can be accounted for: They arise when we fail to cut off the idea of existence from the multiple images that have become confused in our finite mind. Thus too general ideas are formed. Recall that Spinoza rejects real universals as being the imagined generalizations of the vulgar. They arise when the mind imagines like bodies together confusedly, comprehending them in various ways under one or another property. (It is, recall as well, left to reason to clarify and distinguish properties.) So associative memory arises, which for Spinoza is the imaginal re-presentation of the chain of affections the body undergoes. And thus it happens that we regard things as contingent when true reason knows them to be necessary in themselves; the imagination comes to expect certain chains of events, and if it is disappointed it "wavers" and loses faith in a fixed future.[4] Here appears the wholesale determinism that will figure strongly in the ethical part of the *Ethics*.

Above all, the imagination is responsible for affect. No, more: "Affect *is* imagination" (my italics), since it "indicates the present constitution of the body."[5] In other words, imagination is closest to affect, because it images the disposition of the mind's constituting idea, the body, as it is affected by other, external bodies. Thus affect is more intense when we imagine nothing that cuts these off; our affects are most vivid when their causes are now present. And that happens in the imagination: Our bodies channel other bodies that affect them through our senses, and so we simultaneously perceive the object whose perception *is* a confused affect and thus a passion. Here, in one stroke, is resolved the ever-present problem of the relation of "apprehending" image to "appetitive" passion. The image that represents the object is itself its affect; to perceive is to be affected, impassioned.

But since the imagination is the cognition most prone to confusion, it is the sole seat of inadequacy and so of all the falsity Spinoza admits. Thus it is what passionate humans begin with and what clear-thinking philosophers leave behind. I take the object of cognition to be the same in all three stages, though modified by becoming increasingly adequate, that is to say, more and more tied into the whole of nature.

I think the imagination is the source of inadequacy in three ways. First, as a capacity it is "vagrant"; it is cognition from "wandering experience" (*cognitio ab experientia vaga*), a cognition to which everything seems contingent, accidental; by the same token it is multitudinous; the number of its affections is confusing and is mastered only by deceptive generalizations.[6] Second, as consisting of representational images, it is particular; Spinoza does not say this explicitly, but an image as a singular presentation has every mark of partiality, non-comprehensiveness.

The third incompleteness is temporal. The imagination is much focused on the present; it is by the bodies present that we are most affected, and it is present existence that matters: "The mind . . . tries to imagine those things that increase or help its power of acting,"[7] where "imagine" does not mean "fantasize," but "make present, real." For the imagination belongs to a mind that *is* the idea of the body existing—now. (There's a mystery here, to be considered below.) This temporal present is not, I hasten to add, where or when we see "the face of nature"; that face we rather behold "under the aspect of eternity."[8]

So the affects are passions insofar as they are, to begin with, imaginal, meaning feels attached to pictures; that is how Spinoza comes to say that affects *are* imagination. With this theory Spinoza comes down on the hither side of an old dispute: No one thinks that the imagination does not figure strongly in the emotions; the question is whether images in themselves are affect-fraught or are the intrinsically neutral instigators of emotion. [See Ch. X, Sec. 5] The point is that he decides for the affective character of images not extraneously but on the basis of a theory of cognition that *includes* the affects. There is no setting aside such a philosopher.

23. From Passions to Virtues

The next question, and the penultimate project of the *Ethics,* is: How do we manage the affects? Thus Part IV, "On Human Servitude, or the Force of the Affects," is devoted to that problem.

The answer is, of course, to turn the passions into actions. Writers on the passions have always noticed that some passions of the soul shade into excellences of the mind and some names for emotions are also the names for virtues, and that was never so much a difficulty for those who regarded thought itself as a passionate activity as for those who sharply distinguished the warm heart from the cool head, passion from reason. For Spinoza it is no problem at all, since passions and action are both affects. Recall that bodies being affected *means* that their power of action is increased or diminished, that our mind *is* basically or constitutively the idea of our body so affected, and, that being the very definition of affect, our mind is in effect *constitutionally affective.* But, Spinoza explains, as we are able to be the adequate or inadequate cause of the affections of our body, so our affects are active or passive.

Everything falls out from that explanation,[1] which will become clearer below. This is the place to point out an interesting consequence. Spinoza does not have a theory of the *soul*—what parts it might have and how it relates to the body—for traditionally the soul is that aspect of a human being in which the body touches the spirit or reaches the mind. For Spinoza the physical neither touches the non-physical nor does it get to the mind, but rather its idea constitutes the mind to begin with.

Yet as so often in the *Ethics,* because everything is involved in everything (and who can doubt that it is so in truth) the development of this solution to the problem of managing affectivity—to turn passions into actions—is also somewhat involved.

24. Passion Pitted against Passion: Practical Advice

"We are said to be passive when something takes place in us of which we are only the partial cause." Our passivity, however, pertains to a part of nature that cannot be clearly and distinctly understood through itself alone, a part which the laws of our own human nature do not completely elucidate.[1] This consideration implies an astonishing piece of theology, because it means that we, as ways of God, are, in being bid to be active, instructed not only to make ourselves like him who is *causa sui* and so to be our own cause, self-sufficiency incarnate, so to speak, but also to become omniscient, all-comprehending physicists. It would not be a totally new ambition, though one which leaps back over Christian to Aristotelian theology.

Nonetheless it relieves our wonder at Spinoza's extremism to read that this desirable self-causation is in fact impossible to achieve completely for human beings. We are too much enmeshed in nature to be our own adequate and adequately known cause. Our vitality is too limited and so far surpassed by external causes that we must suffer changes and in time lose our physical existence.[2]

Spinoza's advice for practically "coercing" a passion is in fact totally sensible: fight passion with passion, with a contrary and stronger one that will "cut off" the previous one. This affect will of course be an affection of the body. When he says, famously, that an affect can only be coerced by a contrary and stronger affect,[3] this is not primarily a piece of psychological wisdom brought on to correct the traditional view that thinking and habit can control passion. It is, rather, the immediate fallout from Spinoza's system, for what but affect is there available in it to fight affect?

We seem to have surrendered action here to some sort of passive power, that of the stronger passion. It is an expedient and interesting loop in the development toward full human activity, which is, however, justified by Spinoza's notion of passionate power.

25. Good and Bad: Joy and Sadness

Recall that the positive passions, being expressions of our body's vitality, are always more powerful than their opposites. Now Spinoza takes a foreseeable next step: He identifies joy with good and sadness with bad. Good, in turn, is identified with what is useful and bad with what is harmful. And again, the useful is what helps and the contrary is what hinders our power of acting. So this is the chain: joy → good → useful → increased power of action. Ripped from this chain the identification of good and useful sounds utilitarian, an ignobly sensible sort of human ethic. But if the extreme terms, joy and action, are considered, it was a foreseeable development in this theology of ethics. For full activity will be the joyful love of God, of which more at the end.

Here is another way Spinoza has already put it (since joy is derivative from desire): "We desire nothing because we deem it good; but on the contrary we deem a thing good because we . . . desire it."[1] If this appears to be perfect relativism—the good is what anyone happens light-mindedly to want—that is a false appearance. For although this desire is our deepest being, we may be confused about it: Our deeming may be deleterious to our being.

A reference to the Platonic dialogue *Euthyphro* is illuminating.[2] There Socrates raises—but does not resolve—the question of whether the gods are to be lovingly reverenced because they are holy or are holy because we reverence them. Spinoza answers this question in a way, I imagine, contrary to Socrates' thinking but that would have earned his admiration: God is good because he is our joyful desire. But that desire is the very spring of life and indeed the way of God himself.

So yet another way to think of our condition is that neither God nor we have a final cause; we have no good beyond our own desire to direct and determine it. For God has nothing outside him to cause him to act, and we, analogously, as ways of God, have no goal beyond being ourselves. Spinoza does, to be sure, allow us to form some general exemplary ideas of perfection, though these are not in themselves good goals, but only "notions" of ours which we resort to when we are ignorant of our appetite.[3]

26. Desire of the Mind: Will

The dots in the quotation two paragraphs above signal the omission of a term: the will. To fill in: "[we] have an impulse, we will, seek or desire it." These are all one.

But if will is the same as impulse, from dull instinct to half-aware incli-nation to full-blown affect, then there is no free will. For impulse arises from the "laws of our nature," from our existence, and free will would intrude itself into these necessities and make a new, a "spontaneous," beginning ("spontaneous" being from Latin *spons*, "free will," that is, "originating impulse").

That is exactly what Spinoza means. We and nature are totally deter-mined. For God as Nature is *necessarily* what he is. He does not, so to speak, interfere with himself or second-guess his own omniscience. And we, his modes, are not "a kingdom within a kingdom," who can set ourselves apart, disturb rather than follow the order of nature, who have ultimate power over our actions, and who are free from determination by things external to ourselves. Just the contrary is the case.

27. Insoluble Problems

Nevertheless, we have control of our bodies, although we are constituted under two of God's attributes that are forever non-tangent, parallel. We can turn passivity into activity and become causes, even though the turn from passions to actions is entirely in making our *ideas* adequate, that is, in changing our mind. We are free, though all our ideas are necessary in them-selves and obedient to the connections of thought, just as the body is obe-dient to the parallel laws of nature. As we will see, we do have connections to other human beings as minds, and we do act on them, yet we know them only through the affections of our bodies.

I think Spinoza cannot solve these quandaries. They dog every philoso-phy that requires ethical freedom in the face of natural and logical necessity and that allows some manner of independent existence to the physical and the non-physical realms. I leave out of account here the even harder per-plexities that arise for the two extreme antithetical approaches intended to obviate these problems, the one that reduces all mind to matter, nowadays the brain—and the other that makes all reality ideal. Kant's system, devised more than a century later, seems to me to be, despite his specific demur-rer,[1] most closely related to Spinoza at least in respect to the duality and its perplexity. Kant established a realm of necessity, namely nature and its laws, and a realm of freedom, namely morality and its commands. The two are absolutely without causal connection. For natural things always func-tion under the deterministic temporal sequences of natural causation, while moral beings occasionally extricate themselves from the necessitations of their natural inclinations to act under the free, timeless commands of a rational will. Certainly their actions affect the chain of natural events but Kant, otherwise a model of philosophical probity, is shameless, one might say, in putting the problem as if it were the solution: It transcends the power of our reason to say why this moral decision has that originating effect in the world of experienced nature, why an originating act in the realm of freedom is a necessary effect in the world of nature; we only need to know that the realms are, though not interactive, yet not incompatible.[2] We *can* redirect the course of nature without disturbing its entirely determined natural causality.

For Spinoza, of course, the two realms are perfectly parallel, but the problem is analogous: How does our mind, by clarifying its ideas, become a cause of the body's affections? Perhaps it is by modifying what goes on in our nethermost, imaginative kind of knowledge—for most of the propositions about the passions are, of course, about what we imagine—so as to effect an increase in our power. That is what Spinoza in fact says.[3] But how does this act of cognition modify our bodies? This is the problem Kant too will fail to face squarely. Could it be through God's knowledge, which is, after all, the common ground of both of our modes, body and mind? Spinoza does not say. But there is still a prior, insuperable difficulty, the universal necessity of Nature insofar as it is both body extended and mind thinking. How can we, parts, mere modes of God's two attributes, intervene even in our own minds? How can we have spontaneous ideas? In other words, how can we be the responsible originators of what goes on in our imagination, reason, or intellect? So both perplexities—"How can I as a thinking thing affect my body and others through it?" and "How can I even modify my own ideas?"—appear to be intractable.

And recall that if we could explain how we originate thoughts, it would still be a question, a wider version of the problem just broached, whether sheer *adequacy* of ideas—supposing we were able to make them clear and comprehensive by our original effort—was rightly called *action*. "Naturing" God, to be sure, produces by merely being what he is, but how do our ideas turn into causes by becoming self-sufficiently complete? How, by just being acutely attentive to the world and observing it to its widest extent, do I *do* something? Can the mind's cognition indeed be more than a kind of shadow play of the world of externalities? It is a beguiling notion experienced by every lover of learning, a notion analogous in the realm of philosophy to the thought that faith moves the world in religion. But is it metaphysical sympathetic magic?

The perplexity very immediately concerned with those virtues most easily recognized in ordinary life, the social virtues, derives from the difficulties already set out. Spinoza, himself a model of these virtues, certainly thinks that human beings are to have human relations, but there are two difficulties, which will be borne out by the characterization of those active social affects. First, how do we even know of other minds? We know of what is external through our body's affections. But we are not told whether there are—or how there even could be—marks of bodily affections that effectively convey one human being's mind—a partial, individual mind, not the mirror of the face of all nature. Yet we do apprehend other minds somehow, though Spinoza himself says: "[W]e clearly understand what is the difference between . . . the idea of Peter which constitutes the essence of the mind of Peter and the idea of Peter as it exists in the mind of another, say, Paul. The first directly explains the essence of the body of Peter, . . . but the second idea indicates rather the constitution of Paul's body than the nature of Peter. . . ."[4] He doesn't seem to explain how *we come by* this idea of *Peter's idea* of his body, which is his essence, that is, himself as a mind.

Once again this genus of difficulty turns up in Kant's system: There is within it no way other minds can come to us, for we perceive only the outer appearances; the minds themselves are inaccessible.

That is one metaphysical difficulty on top of which there is a second, ethical one—that Spinoza's understanding of human being is so highly individualistic that it might be called, though not quite rightly, egoism[5]—not quite rightly, because just as his theory of the good as the useful did not encourage any utilitarian calculus of greatest happiness, so his theory of impulse toward increased vitality as being of the human essence does not preach self-regard; it rather characterizes what human existence, understood as a particular way of God, means. Nevertheless, it will take peculiar-sounding arguments to parlay the self-assertion of individual existences into the basis of social virtues.

What is the good of attending to a text so beset with perplexities? Well, to begin with, I cannot think of a work that is not so beset when pressed. At any rate, don't we study philosophical writings largely to learn what price is to be paid for certain valuable acquisitions, and don't we think out things on our own largely to find out what problems follow from what solutions and what questionable antecedents we can tolerate for the sake of their livable consequences? I cannot think of a book of which this is truer than of the *Ethics*—that the conclusions are beguiling enough to make one wish eventually to find the premises at least intelligible.

28. The Social Virtues of an Impulsive Being

I'll begin with those virtues that relate us to other human beings, just to get them over with, as it were. For in spite of what I've just said, in spite of the bracing astringency of his formulations, there is something—to me—insuperably offputting about Spinoza's prescriptive description for dealing with others. He was, by every account, an impeccably just, benevolent, and courteous man and a sort of democrat in politics.[1] So, I imagine, plied in his spirit these ways of virtue would show much humanity. (Incidentally, *humanitas* is for Spinoza, significantly, not a way of being—for we are expressions of God—but the desire of doing what would please other human beings.)[2] Here, in brief, are the virtues that concern our community with our fellows.

Human beings can oppose each other under the assault of passionate affects, but if they live under the guidance of reason they always necessarily agree.[3] The greatest good that comes from virtue is common to all. That is not accidental but arises from the very nature of reason, for it belongs to the essence of the thinking human mind to have an adequate knowledge of the eternal and infinite essence of God.[4] Yet to try impetuously to make others love what I love makes me hateful to those who are pleased by other things; to try, however, to lead them by reason is humane and benign. The desire of doing good engendered by a life lived according to reason is called piety; what we desire and do, that is, what we are the cause of insofar as we have the idea of God and know him, is called religion.[5]

All this, perhaps innocuous-sounding, preaching concerning the social aspects of belief is insidiously revolutionary: It takes the mediation of Christ out of the way to God, divorces churchgoing from piety, and proscribes forcible conversion. Then comes the political teaching of the *Ethics*: Since each human being exists by the supreme right of nature, does by this right what follows necessarily from his nature, judges for himself what is good or bad, and consults his own advantage, there will be contrariety and conflict because of the partiality of the passions. So human beings must give up their natural rights; they will do this in accordance with the proposition that a passion can be checked only by a greater passion: Everyone refrains from the desire of inflicting injury through the greater fear of incurring injury. By this law of fear, society is held together.[6]

Finally, private social life is under the aegis of the following chain of propositions: What is useful to human beings is what most agrees with their nature and thus is common to them. Since it is reason which most agrees with common human nature—for the passions are particular and there-fore divisive—the human being who lives by reason is most consonant with other humans, and such a human being is most active and powerful in his own behalf. Therefore he who seeks to do himself most good, to be most useful to himself, will also be most useful for others.[7] There is, after all, a cool truth in this: Those who flourish will be most helpful; they are most capable of Spinoza's version of friendship, the friendship of the free.[8] It is time to see what these self-cherishing virtues are, and how they work.

29. The Individual Virtues

The first thing to notice is that there isn't a list of virtues as there was of pas-sions, for virtues, such as justice, equity, piety, and religion, are only passions illuminated by reason, passions adequately sited in the whole of things. It is reason that turns passions into actions.

> By Virtue (*virtus*) and Power (*potentia*) I understand the same, that is, virtue, insofar as it has reference to man, is his essence or nature in so far as he has the power of effecting something which can be understood by the laws of that nature alone.[1]

And:

> The more one tries and is able to get what is useful to him, that is, to preserve his being, the more he is endowed with virtue. . . .[2]

In Part IV of the *Ethics,* Spinoza speaks of acting under the guidance of reason: To act absolutely according to virtue is nothing else but to act according to the precepts of reason. And that, in turn, is nothing else but to understand; what is conducive to that is alone useful. The precepts of reason—act and live according to virtue, preserve your being, seek what is useful—all mean the same thing.[3] This is no longer fighting passion with passion, but transforming it into action by adequately understanding what is affecting us. This is "virtue = power": becoming active from the inside, from our own nature and its necessities, its "laws" alone, not allowing the idea of other bodies to impinge on our minds.

It therefore comes as no surprise that the virtue of virtues is fortitude (*fortitudo*), which term we are, I think, to hear literally: "strengthfulness," forcefulness, from Latin *fortis.* Its two complementary sub-virtues are *animositas,* literally "animatedness," spiritedness, courage, the desire to hold on to what is rationally ours, and *generositas,* literally "attachment to our genus," the impulse to friendship (in contrast to Descartes' self-esteem).[4] Note how Spinoza likes to hear Latin literally, which leads to some startling renamings of virtues. (Could it be because he in fact received his Latin tuition outside his Jewish childhood community?)

Is this doctrine of virtue Stoic? Well, at most it's a very revisionist Stoicism. The Stoics thought of the passions as false judgments whose correction by an application of the will would, for the most part, *damp* the emotion, while Spinoza thinks of the passions as confused ideas whose clarification *strengthens* the affect; moreover, recall that the will itself is the root affect: impulse. Spinoza indeed regards the real difference between himself and the Stoics as being in that very will, above all because they believe it to have command over our passions, while he denies its freedom.[5]

It bears repeating that the virtues are affects, joyful affects and, to begin with, as closely related to the body as are the passions. Right in a section of Part IV on the political and social virtues, Spinoza inserts two more propositions on the body, reminding us that what is useful to a human being is that which makes the body sensitive to being affected by, and more active in affecting, other bodies, and which keeps the parts of the body in the right equilibrium of motion and rest.[6]

Strangely enough, it seems to be easy to misread the *Ethics* on the above account. There is a poignant story by Isaac Bashevis Singer called "The Spinoza of Market Street." It—at least as I read it—makes this point: Dr. Fischelson is as miserable a specimen of a sidelined, physically and materially down-and-out ghetto scholar as one may conceive, who, though more dead than alive, and always wretchedly aware of his body, does nothing day and night but study the *Ethics*, disdaining the pleasures of food, fellowship, exercise, and certainly sex. On his floor in the dank house on Market Street where he has a room lives the ugliest and most asocial spinster imaginable, Black Dobbe. This bizarre pair wonderfully find each other. There is a wedding night that "could be called a miracle." At dawn Dr. Fischelson arises, and standing at the open window looking out into the extended divine substance, into the face of the universe, he murmurs, "Divine Spinoza, forgive me. I have become a fool." It's rather the case that he's *been* a fool. What book, we are—I think—invited to ask ourselves, had he been reading? How could he think that "according to Spinoza emotion was never good"? How could he miss that the body's increasing vitality is joy and belongs to each individual human essence? Was it because you can't become a Spinozan through a scholarly fixation on the *Ethics*? Or did—and this I doubt—Singer himself miss the book's message? I doubt it, because he lets Dr. Fischelson, on a bad evening, read and fail to make sense of just those propositions that deal with that knowledge which is inadequate because it is partial, because it doesn't get beyond its own body's perceptions to the face of the whole universe.[7] The ghetto scholar has missed both the book's loci of joy: the vitality of the body and the comprehension of the intellect. But he's found it as an unlikely lover.

30. Freedom as Necessity

Part IV of the *Ethics* was "on human servitude or the forces of the affects," that is, about the passions to which we are subject and the reason that puts us in control. Part V will be "on the power of the intellect or human freedom," that is, about the highest knowledge: intuition, a yet further degree above reason. This part no longer offers a mere set of precepts, but a way of life.

The free man was, to be sure, delineated in Part IV, insofar as he is enmeshed in the ordinary vicissitudes of life. We are told how, under the guide of reason, he is freer under political law than in a solitary state,[1] how he chooses among goods and faces dangers, and all sorts of salutary and sensible things. One observation is of particular interest because it states bluntly the contrary of the thesis held by another philosopher who will appear in this book, Heidegger: that human beings must live "towards death." Spinoza says: "A free man thinks of nothing less than death, and his wisdom is a meditation not of death but life."[2] In the *Ethics,* human existential finitude is to be contemplated, but life is not to be dominated by death; the book is all positivity.

What then is freedom (*libertas*) in the absence of free will? It is not, as think the ignorant, who are "conscious of their actions but ignorant of the causes that determine them," the power of the mind to move the body.[3] It is instead existing by the mere necessity of one's own nature and being determined to action by oneself, meaning by one's own essence, alone. When the cause of action comes from the outside, that is compulsion.[4] Spinoza makes a crucial distinction between necessity and compulsion. By the latter the thing is passively compelled, by the former it is freely being what it is, through the necessary laws of its own essence. "You see, I do not place freedom in free decision but in free necessity," he says in an explanatory letter.[5] This apparent paradox can be made more plausible by being phrased like this: Any thing—it could, strangely, but consistently, be a body or a mind— is free when, as it acts, nothing interferes in the unconstrained working out of its nature. The final part of the *Ethics* will show how the intellect effects human freedom by letting us be ourselves through ourselves.

31. Freeing the Imagination

So human freedom is active self-realization in accordance with the idea (which *is* our mind) of a body as vital as possible. Therefore Part V returns to the imagination, which, being closest to the body, is most involved in its strengthening. Recall that it is not understandable how we ourselves influence ourselves according to precepts, though there is no question that a book called *Ethics* is giving advice on how to live. Furthermore, it is not intelligible how our mental activities can influence our body when they can only "mirror" them. Spinoza actually begins this part by chiding Descartes for setting up the mind and the body as radically different, as separate substances, and then trying, absurdly, to find a way for the mind to have dominion—through the will—both over the mental and the physical part of the passions, all by a little gland in the brain.[1] But does Spinoza's parallel-attribute setup solve the problem?

At any rate, he now repeats this central doctrine, that mind and body are not in a causal connection, that a passion becomes an action through our clear and distinct idea, and that we can form such ideas of every affection of the body.[2]

There follows a series of propositions—really observations—about the passions that are at once in accordance with the system and, as it seems to me, with our experience:[3] that affects arising simply from "free," that is, logically unconditioned, imagination are stronger than those "modally" bound, that is, induced by things known to be necessary, possible, or contingent;

that those affects arising from presence are stronger than those induced by absence; that those with multiple cause are greater; that as long as we are not assaulted by affects contrary to our nature, by bad affects, we have the power of disposing the affections of our body according to the order of our intellect. Furthermore, the more inclusive the imagination is, the more it flourishes; the more connections an image has, the more often it is excited.[4] Here Spinoza inserts a long, wise note on what to imagine and think about so as to control the vicissitudes of passion: Envision the situation as adequately as possible (a foretaste of Adam Smith) and rejoice in increasing knowledge.[5]

32. The Intellect's Body

And then suddenly:

> The mind can bring it about that all the affections of the body or images of things bear on the idea of God.

For "there is no affection of the body of which the mind cannot form a clear and distinct concept." So starts the delineation of the affect that is the purest, most preoccupying, and most potently active: the intellectual love of God.[1] I cannot pretend to know it as an affect, but I will try to describe it as a concept.

Perhaps a way in is through a very summary history of its object, Spinoza's God. For although it is *sui generis*, alone in its kind, there are many forerunners, of which three are: the Goddess of Parmenides' poem who dwells at the center of being—which is also its circumference—and receives one who is ready to learn that Being alone *is*; the divinity of Aristotle's *Metaphysics*, *Nous*, who moves us without being moved and is contemplated as Mind by minds; the God of Cusanus's *Learned Ignorance* who is the unfolding and enfolding of all things. Each is different but in all the divinity is not the creator of nature but *is* respectively Being or Activity or the All, and we *are* in or toward or through the divinity. To attain such a divinity is—and this is the point—a possible human achievement: "He who understands himself and his affects clearly and distinctly loves God," the more so, the better he understands himself through them. Such clear and distinct conceptions are indeed in our mind's power, as stated above. Hence Spinoza's expositions function also as exhortations.[2] The injunction to strive for our proper divinity does not, however, preclude retaining our proper humanity.

Spinoza has just said that we can attain God through the imagination. The imagination is, however, the way in which the mind regards present things and evidently forms images derived from past and future objects. In other words imaginative cognition is temporal.[3]

So the love of God appears to diversify: There is a love by the imagination, carried on by us as ways of God in time and through his particulars: "The more we understand particular things, the more we understand God."[4] The particulars are studied and seen in their connection through physics (in which our body is the conduit for knowledge of *other* bodies) and physiology (in which it is the counterpart of affects in *our own* minds). This is the study of God as he is expressed in the infinite ways that specify his incident attributes. For us, these are bodies in nature as they affect our own body, that body as the idea which constitutes our mind, and our mind as it knows itself. In a letter writen in the year the *Ethics* was completed (1675), Spinoza calls this vision to be attained—the phrase was quoted earlier—the "form" or "face" or "configuration" or "the countenance of the whole [extended] universe" (*facies totius universi*).[5] He had spoken of "the knowledge of the union of the mind with the whole universe" in the fragment mentioned earlier, *On the Improvement of the Understanding,* which was composed more than a decade before the *Ethics.* Then, however, he regarded such knowledge as a merely human perfection. Slowly it must have turned for him into that highest and most ardently active affect, the intellectual love of God, the reunion of a divine Mode with its supporting Substance.

But the same love of God is also to be felt "under the aspect of eternity" (*sub specie aeternitatis*). Now we learn what we might not have expected, that there is something eternal about our mind which remains when the body is destroyed, namely insofar as that mind is conceived through God's essence. However *that* post-somatic eternity is to be taken, there is eternity also in our knowledge while our mind is still the idea of a body now existing. For besides the temporal imagination, we have the higher forms of cognition: reason, which is the necessary preliminary clarifying knowledge, and finally the direct intuitive knowledge of the intellect.[6]

This eternity while the body is yet with us is an atemporal knowledge of essence alone. For while the infinite, the unending, ways of God have essences that imply their existence, some contingent or particular ways are always going in and out of existence, though the essence remains in the surviving others. All human beings die, but there are always human beings perpetuating the human essence by their individual existence.

This intuitive knowing of essences—not, to be sure, as separable forms, but as adequate ideas of the mind—is our greatest impulse. "Is or ought to be?" we might ask. Is this a necessity of our nature or an attainment to be devoutly worked for? Experience—and the tone of the *Ethics*—says the latter: The final proposition of the work speaks of restraining our lusts so as to reach the bliss of the highest love. Physical lust, *libido,* the kind here to be restrained, must be that passion insofar as it tends to excess, since we have heard nothing of an inherent badness of *libido* before; for Spinoza the body, which is, after all, *the* object of the mind, is not bad, only less good.

Moreover the love of God is itself that restraint; recall that only affect can fight affect and that the power over a bad, that is, an opaque, affect is itself an affect. Evidently this circle is the consequence on the grandest scale of freedom understood as necessity.

33. The Ultimate Affect: The Love of God

What does this ultimate affect feel like? It is the bliss of blessedness (*beatitudo*). The more capable the mind becomes of intuitive knowledge, the more it desires the same.[1] It is closeness to God: Knowing oneself and one's body under the aspect of eternity is knowing oneself in God and as conceivable through God, even as God simply. God loves himself with infinite intellectual love.[2] Love for human beings is, recall, the joy that comes from an external cause, but God is his own cause. Thus God enjoys *himself,* and that very joy is his power of being, of being Nature—and of knowing it, for God *is* Nature and is also its *intrinsic physicist*—both. The human mind's love of God is a part of that very same love, a part of the knowing self-love of Nature, its very vitality. In humans this expresses itself as "acquiescence, resting content," which is the greatest pleasure.[3] Earlier on, Spinoza had called it *acquiescentia in seipso*; I would translate: "Saying Yes to oneself."[4] We may figure to ourselves a pale reflection of this blessed affect: the knowledgeable affirmation—rarely felt—of the face of things seen as a whole and of ourselves as necessarily enmeshed in that whole. Here striving has reached a steady state.

34. The Stock Antitheses Resolved

Eccentricity is, I think, an honest kind of originality. By and large, philosophy is not supposed to be original, meaning ingenious, but rather adequate to the way things are. The mainstream thinkers are, to be sure, original in the sense that, incited by the problems left by their immediate predecessors, they return to the origins to shape the responses that constitute the tradition. There are also—often very avidly received—oracles who devise brilliantly original schemes that happen to hit a contemporary nerve but are not totally trustworthy. And then there are—a very few—philosophers who are off on their own whilst absorbing the most disparate parts of the tradition; they fashion wonderfully strange and utterly serious answers to their very own questions. So Spinoza asks and answers the question about the emotions that is simply below the notice of the mainstream writers: What does it mean in the nature of things to be a being open to affect? We get from him not only an acute phenomenology of the human affects (meaning a description of the ways they appear), but also a philosophico-theological account (meaning a God-dominated metaphysics) of ourselves as basically affective or emotive beings, of the relation of our minds to our feelings, of the hierarchy of affects, of the control of our passions, of the bearing of natural science on our affective life, and of an ultimate love that is implied in our very existence itself. All of these ideas have been—albeit sketchily—set out above, and together, in answering the question of human affectivity, they contain resolutions to all the oppositions that seemed to have been unavoidable in thinking about our feelings. They are still unavoidable, for as I have been at pains to point out, their resolution depends on a metaphysical theology that is as problematic as it is deep. But at least we now have the wherewithal for getting beyond these oppositions, if only in one particular speculative venture.

Let me now end this chapter by listing once more the stock antitheses with which I began—I cannot think of many others—together with Spinoza's resolutions:

In speaking of the passions, Body and Soul are, then as now, quite normally distinguished in ordinary speech (though "psyche" might now be more comfortable). In the *Ethics* the soul, as the traditional place where the body meets the spirit, has disappeared, since there the body is in itself a mode parallel to the mind, but for us as thinkers an idea, *the* idea of the mind. Therefore so also has the body-soul opposition been obviated.

The opposition of Body and Mind has disappeared as well, for the reason just given: Mind *is* the idea of the body. Moreover body and mind are parallel specifications of Extension and Thought, and (unlike the Cartesian extended and thinking thing) these are ultimately identical as attributes of God.

Nature and Humanity are not opposed as what is determined by laws and what has spontaneous free will, since as a part of extended nature the human being lives under the same necessity as do bodies.

Impulse and Freedom are not opposed, because all existence is governed by impulse, and freedom is not its opposite but its fullest realization.

Desire and Virtue are not in opposition, since the greatest virtue is in fact an adequately-conceived strong desire.

Inclination and morality, in the Kantian antithesis, are but different terms for the same opposition of desire, which is here superseded.

Partiality, the particularity of passion, is not antithetical to objective Impartiality, but is convertible into the latter by a comprehensive clarification, by attaining an adequate idea of the affect.

Passion and Action, our suffering under affects or our being in control of ourselves, are not opposite states, but only less or more adequate conceptions of our affects; we go from one state to the other by the clarification of our ideas, since action is reconceived as passion clarified.

Nor, more generally, are Passion and Virtue any longer antithetical, since virtue is passion adequately conceived.

Affect and Imagination, whose mysterious melding—mysterious because they spring from, or are, different faculties—was before and is after largely a problem too delicate for robust study, are here simply brought into unity by identification.

Spinoza's resolution did not take hold. The reason is pretty plain. His onto-theology is too strange. Instead the words change: Emotion and Reason, Heart and Head, Feeling and Thinking—these are the new expressions for the old basic antitheses in the century after Spinoza wrote. To one of their chief exponents, David Hume, we will now go, a distance of only a little more than half a century in time but of a whole universe in thought.

chapter VIII

The Passions as Reflective Impressions

Hume and the Price We Pay for Scepticism

1. Spinoza as Hume's Predecessor

Were readers to infer that the passions were not a subject of lively comment in the two-thirds of a century that separated Spinoza's *Ethics* (1675) from Hume's *Treatise of Human Nature* (1740), they would be the victims of my particular intention: to attend to those texts on the passions that are in themselves substantial and are embedded in full-fledged philosophical systems. Of course there were numerous treatises written in the eighteenth century both before and after Hume, especially on the moral management of the passions—elegant self-help books.[1]

There is, however, a really immediate connection between the two works, and it is primarily negative. Spinoza is the named author to whom Hume devotes more pages than to any other in the *Treatise*[2]—pages of excoriation: Spinoza is "uniformly infamous" for his "hideous hypothesis." Hume refers to those "gloomy and obscure regions" whence derives Spinoza's "famous" atheism, "the immateriality, simplicity, and indivisibility of a thinking substance . . . [which] is a true atheism." The objectionable features of this doctrine, so opposite to Hume's—who, however, gets himself into gloomy regions on his own account—are simply consequences of the unity of the universal substance, the substratum, as Hume calls it, of all modifications. Hume concludes that as a result we can never conceive "a specific difference betwixt an object and impression," since in this doctrine ideas are derived from preceding ideas and these can never represent to us, that is, reach, objects of "external existence." Oddly enough, Hume's own theory of perception is exactly in the same case; nonetheless he concludes, although "this may at first sight, appear a mere sophism," that the unintelligible doctrine of one—or many—simple immaterial substances, especially of the immaterial soul, prepares "the way to a dangerous and irrecoverable atheism." For

Spinoza's system is incoherent on all counts, just as are those of all theologians—who must, consequently, it would seem, all be atheists as well! Hume does not explicitly make the connection between some of the well-taken difficulties of the *Ethics* (which I have pointed out) and atheism, nor can I make out what game other than *tu quoque,* or you-too-ism, this denier of all human knowledge concerning divine efficacy is playing.[3] In any case Spinoza's system was for Hume the antithesis of his own. And though he does not refer to Spinoza's theory of the passions as inadequate ideas, he must have seen the antithetical character of passions so understood and of his own theory—which is, in summary, that the passions are reflective impressions, and as such are just what they are and are never to be clarified or completed by thinking, for reason is quite inert with respect to them.

Yet Spinoza and Hume also seem remarkably alike, in certain respects and on the surface. I think this similarity derives from what in Hume's case is called empiricism, or reliance on observed experience, and in Spinoza's case, naturalism, or faith in the science of extended bodies. (For some reason, Spinoza is tagged in the text books by the polar term rationalism, when it should be, if there has to be an "ism," "theological affectivism.") Both, above all, reject human spontaneity or free will in favor of a somewhat obscure necessitarianism, and both think that pleasure and pain define good and evil. Also, both think of human nature as initially or originally affective, and both consider passion to be controllable only by passion. Both suppose that the passions are specified by the multiplicity of their objects—Hume in every case and Spinoza at least on the lower affective level. But these experientially induced surface coincidences are very differently grounded in the systems, and this fact itself is fascinating, if one cares about the variety of roads that all lead to Rome.

2. Why Study Hume's *Treatise*?

The *Treatise of Human Nature* is a young book—Hume was twenty-nine upon the publication of its six hundred-some pages. It evinces at once the dark, lost melancholy that must depress and the brilliant, assured reductionism that can elate a young sceptic, and it is brusque in its certitudes and prolix in its arguments. It is an infuriatingly difficult book whose main intentions are crystal clear, and it is a coolly rational treatise composed with youthful intensity. These are attractive qualities, and in addition the book is composed in what seems to me an engagingly elegant style (though it has been snobbishly said that this Scotsman trying to write idiomatically English English never quite succeeds;[1] this fact is, however, beneath my threshold of discrimination, since I'm not myself a native speaker.

So here is a book written with forcefulness about the passions—as Spinoza wrote with joy—and since this quality becomes rarer as the literature on the emotions accumulates, it is in itself a reason for studying Hume's extensive treatment.

There is another reason, compelling by its very equivocality. Skepticism of Hume's continually qualified sort induces endless complexity, express-ible in multiple diagram-like expositions. Indeed, all "x is nothing but . . ." reductionism—Hume's work is full of it—tends to trail complications. Partly it is the result of his ardent attempt to cover up the essential base-lessness of any faithfully skeptical view of human nature; he really cannot say in a final—which has to mean in a metaphysical—way what a passion is, whence it comes, or what causes it[2] (albeit "cause" figures largely in his explanation). But even if these diagrams function to cover up baselessness, they also operate to uncover very subtly observed and cleverly analyzed features of the passions and especially of the model passion, *pride*. The privileged position of this usually derided passion is itself of great interest; we learn how pride comes forward when the self falls apart. Thus Hume's multifarious divisions, distinctions, and derivations do, in a way, constitute definitions both of the passions in general and of pride and love, his chief examples, in particular—and that in spite of the fact that he himself repeat-edly terms the passions indefinable because they are too original, too close to simple facts, to permit reference to underlying terms.

There is a fourth reason for reading Hume's *Treatise*, besides its exuber-ance, elegance, and analytical complexity, one which is terminological. Pas-sion, emotion, affection, and sentiment are all terms applied to the subject of my book. To trace their time of appearance and shifts of meaning would be a huge task in the history of concept-formation.[3] Hume's usage marks a moment in this history when the main term, "passion," is about to be replaced by "emotion." Hume often uses both equivalently, but at one point he seems to distinguish the passions from the emotions as more violent (by which he means not injury-inflicting, but forceful, very vivid); here the emotions appear to be a gentler enclave within the passions, those pertain-ing to beauty and deformity, that is, the esthetic passions.[4] He is, however, consistent neither with this nor any other relation of the terms. "Sentiment" might be construed as still more diffuse, in particular the moral sentiment, which is "intermixed" with the esthetic emotion[5] and is "often so soft and gentle that we are apt to confound it with an idea."[6] "Affection" seems to be used for a feeling whose object is another person, as we still use it (unlike Spinoza's *affectio*, which applies to bodily sensations).

What appears to be established is that Hume was the first to use the term "emotion" liberally and in a sense familiar to us: first, as differentiated from bodily "feels" of pleasure and pain; these Hume terms "sensations" (see Fig-ure VIII-A, p. 297); second, as quite distinct from, and unamenable to, reason and, in a major reversal of the tradition, now even its master. Here Hume's theory is a pivot point between the terms and connotations of the old philosophical and theological mainstream tradition, which taught that the intellect or the principled will is the natural master over the passions, and the newer moral theories, which pit rationality against emotion, favoring either the head as in the Enlightenment or the heart as in the Romantic reaction.

To be sure, this crude schema makes little sense without a discussion of the deep difference between intellect (intuitive thought) and rationality (logical thinking) and the consequently different relation they have to passion and emotion respectively. My purpose here, however, is only to place Hume at a turning point, at the initial moment of a shift in the treatment of the passions that has momentous consequences. Henceforth the focus of social attention will have shifted (not always and not irreversibly) from a fearful respect for the passions as causing the too-passive soul to suffer and wreak havoc, being seduced by a possibly unworthy object, to an anxious defense of emotion as stimulating the enervated soul into a movement that causes the subject itself to feel more intensely existent. As emotions, the affects henceforth fade somewhat from both the philosophical and theological consideration of human nature and become a secular "psychological category," which is "morally disengaged, bodily, non-cognitive and involuntary"[7] (though the bodily cause of emotions is a Cartesian, not a Humean notion). This emotion-category, which has been shaped and expanded by understandings from psychoanalysis to linguistic analysis, from evolutionary science to neurocience, is fairly current, and its features are the focus of debate. The great systematic philosophers, Kant and Hegel particularly, of whom one might expect treatments in the grand style of Descartes, Spinoza, and Hume, in fact write of the emotions rather unthematically in their major systematic works. Partly, I want to say, this is because the former are seeking the springs of human psychic motion at a level deeper than the emotions as a "psychological category" occupy. That is also one reason the emotions are displaced in certain major works of theology and philosophy by another sort of affect, to be dealt with in the next chapter: *mood.*

A fifth reason for reading Hume's work should really be shown by extensive quotations rather than by mere telling: his complexly differentiated accounts of the varieties of human passionate life (and in fact of animal passions as well), which are usually ingenious, often caustic, sometimes kind, on occasion youthfully clueless, and always thought-provoking. Some of the complexities, however, might be more absorbing to work out than interesting to read about, but I'll do my best to be, at least, more clear than the original and less prolix.

A final reason is that Hume's kind of philosophizing, "if just, can present us only with mild and moderate sentiments."[8] And so it is the exemplar of a philosophy which, as it evades heights, also avoids harm.

3. Preview: The System of the Passions

Taken grossly, Hume's theory of the passions is simple to state, at least with respect to his model passion, *pride* (or its opposite, humility).

    1. Every case of pride has an *object* and a *cause*. The object (as in "the object in view") is *self*—such as a self is for Hume, namely nothing but a concatenation of perceptions. The cause is a *subject* (as in "the subject of interest"), that is, something that is ours and interesting to us, either our internal sensation or, most particularly, an external thing, a possession that by its qualities, such as beauty or strength, gives pleasure; this pleasure is the *essence* of pride—but it is only its crux, not the whole complex. (Readers must train themselves in Hume's usage of "object" as a person and "subject" as a thing, which is half-askew of ours.)

    2. All the contents of the human mind, called "perceptions," comprise *impressions* and *ideas,* the former usually entering with the greater force or vivacity of sense impressions and feelings, the latter being their usually fainter images as in thinking and reasoning. This theory of knowledge is put in the service of the terms just set out. The subject-causes with their qualities and the object-self with its perceptions give rise to impressions and play host to ideas respectively; these in turn produce new impressions and ideas by *association*—impressions arousing resembling impressions, ideas causing or producing ideas; impressions and ideas, apparently, also cross-associate.

    The full title of Hume's work is *A Treatise of Human Nature: Being An Attempt to introduce the experimental Method of Reasoning into Moral Subjects.* As he works out the subtleties and modifications required by this method, the terms diversify and their relations ramify, often not quite consistently, until only a series of diagrams can track them somewhat clearly. So I have to say that alternative versions of the figures I offer in Section 6 are quite defensible (though I doubt many people will want to redo them). However, in order not to make the presentation too complex I have chosen the versions most plausible to me, and what follows can be read as an explication of, or as the subtext to, the diagrams provided. I cannot resist the observation that, in matters philosophical, when you deliberately deny depth you seem to have to embrace compensatory complexity. Hume speaks often and with proto-enlightenment crispness of the commonsense immediacy and patent self-evidence of his observations, but his explanatory text is baroquely elaborate.

4. Problems and Griefs: Perceptions of the Mind

Since my purpose is to clarify Hume's theory of the passions, it seems neither altogether avoidable nor yet quite suitable to start with a discussion of his theory of knowledge—which the diagrams do seem to require. For on the one hand, we look for a serious theory of the passions to be closely integrated with the philosopher's fundamental understanding of the mind or soul, as Hume's most surely and admirably is. Yet on the other hand, that understanding is itself so problematic that the very coherence of it with the consequent system of the passions casts a shadow on that system.

So I will try to say—briefly and thus inadequately—what the problems seem to me to be. Hume's term "perceptions" of the mind signifies all that enters awareness, but it probably also hints that the mind is by itself bare of ideal, that is, immaterial contents. It is in itself nothing but a small set of relating operations, the associations set out in Figure VIII-D (p. 298). The terms to be related are, first, the *primary* impressions, which are "perceived," meaning that they come adventitiously through the senses from the outside as sensations, or from the soul itself ("or body, whichever you please to call it"[1]) as pains and pleasure, whence come many emotions and passions. Thence, second, are *derived* the ideas, which differ from impressions by no mark except their diminished vivacity. Hume thinks that he need not "employ many words in explaining this distinction. Everyone of himself will readily perceive the difference betwixt feeling and thinking."[2] And so I do, though the difference does not seem like a mere degree of force, since I have in mind numerous other marks that distinguish feelings, that is, sensations and emotions, from thinking; they will be set aside here. I shall, however, say a word about the difficulties with the relations between perceptions in the account of association.

The distinction between impression and idea is problematic—or rather the blurring of that distinction which results from making them qualitatively identical (for they only differ quantitatively, in their intensity). But so is, even prior to that, the term "impression" itself, especially in the case of "sense impression," which cannot help but imply that *something* is pressing on us, *is making* an impression. But Hume is expressly—and terminally— sceptical about the relation of impressions to their originating causes, for "'twill always be impossible to decide with certainty, whether they arise immediately from the object, or are produced by the creative power of the mind [that would be stark solipsism!] or are derived from the author of our being."[3] The impressions themselves are just what they are, and in that sense real enough, but as for conveying an idea of the actual existence of an object answering to the impression, that is quite possibly an illusion; existence is a mere inference of the mind, based on experience gathered from a series of perceptions.[4] The problem is that while well-articulated scepticism is argumentatively unassailable—for who can contend with a reasoned plea of ignorance?—the consequences are humanly insupportable—for who can live without somewhere touching *terra firma* in some more solid way than the therapeutic amusement of "a game of back-gammon" that Hume is driven to seek?[5] To be sure, in his system ordinary people are still allowed a peculiar feeling of or belief in reality and existence such as makes life viable;[6] it is only the philosopher's certainty that is said to be impossible to achieve: The doubts and denials of the *Treatise on Human Nature* are more positive, so to speak, than the affirmations.

These consequences are palpable in the Conclusion to Book I, "Of the Understanding," which forms, as it were, the prelude to Book II, "Of the Passions." This concluding section is a very black passage in this huge work whose general tone is so bright, not to say perky. It is a cry of philosophical melancholy, of rationally induced grief. Hume feels himself "invironed with the deepest darkness." The chief reason is "not, indeed, perceiv'd in common life"; it is our ultimate ignorance, when all our sense of reality has to rely on is the vivacity of our perceptions (which is but a property of our imagination), when all our reasoning supplies no solidity or satisfaction, and our choice is between false reason or none at all. "Here in the house I find myself absolutely and necessarily determin'd to live, and talk, and act like other people in the common affairs of life"; notwithstanding the fact that, or better, just because, this "philosophy has nothing to oppose" the philosopher's splenetic passion, his melancholy.[7] It is a curiously candid comment on the human effects of a philosophy that bases itself solely on experience, that is, on impressions and their derivatives, and eschews all elements not so arising, that is, all immaterial substances.

"Where am I, or what?" is the first of the questions that has wrought upon him, and I imagine—it is a pure speculation—that the proximate cause of the black mood is the immediately preceding section on the notorious problem of "personal identity." This is the perplexity concerning selfhood that arises when there is no psychic substance to hold together the bundles and chains of perception that then constitute the self. Such an underlying principle cannot emerge from any impression, because our self is not any *one* impression but a disparate sequence of them:

> [W]hen I enter most intimately into what I call *myself*, I always stumble on some particular perception or other, of heat or cold, light or shade, love or hatred, pain or pleasure. I can never catch *myself* at any time without a perception, and never can observe any thing but the perception. . . . They are the successive perceptions only, that constitute the mind. . . .[8]

"These variable and interrupted objects"—the objects intended in the impressions—cannot betoken an identity of self. Such an identity is a fictitious ascription, a false connection of disparate, atomic perceptions. Identity is solely the product of the relations of ideas, that is, of association. Well might one ask what it is that induces and supervises these associations. Within the *Treatise* this agency seems to be the imagination, but of course it too participates in the insubstantiality of the episodic mind. Meanwhile Hume prefers to rest in the ultimate undecidability of the problem of personal identity.[9] I think, however, that he will try to alleviate what I am tempted to call the serious sceptic's unbidden guest, existential unease, by establishing as a model passion, of all affects, *pride.*

5. Pride in the Tradition: The Morally Ambiguous Passion

Not only is the whole first of the three parts of Hume's book on the passions devoted to pride, but to it are attached all the theoretically significant observations. I think Hume had a double motive here. First, as I said, in the absence of an assured personal identity, pride takes up a primary self-asserting role, and second, in his display of the "experimental method," it is the principal example of the most complexly complete human affective scheme.

Pride is notoriously double-faced. There is a proper pride, the ancient great-souledness, and there are several bad prides: among them the Satanic willfulness of Christian theology and the ill-judged pleasure arising from a man's over-estimation of himself of Spinoza's *Ethics,* that peculiarly human folly so insistently said to be absent in Swift's rational horses and so slyly shown to be over-weeningly present in them, a diatribe against which "absurd vice" concludes *Gulliver's Travels.* Hume too, whose very system calls for pride to be allied to virtue as the "agreeable impression" of our satisfaction in our virtue[1] (contrary to custom, as he observes), does not scruple—as is his insouciant habit—to term pride vicious when it is "overweening conceit."[2] Perhaps it is most accurate to say that Hume gives pride a new place in human nature: It is the passion that holds us together, that supplies, as we will see, an occasional objectivity to our selves in place of our lost permanent identity.

I might point out that in its function and importance it is close to Descartes' generosity. Self-esteem is a human crux from modernity's beginning to its current end. It is surely concomitant with the discovery of *subjectivity,* self-consciously personal self-hood, fascinatingly contrary to its predecessor, *soul,* which was a more generic, natural being, to be viewed by its possessor with objective amazement, but rarely with anxiety. The bridge is Christianity. But enough of broad strokes.

6. The True System of the Passions: The Double Relation

In seven diagrams, I will try to marshal and explain the terms and relations that go into Hume's theory, experiential and analytic, of pride and similarly constituted passions. (The lower-case Roman numerals in the headings refer to the Sections of the Second Book of Hume's *Treatise.*) This diagram-set is, if anything, somewhat less daunting than his "True System."

A. *The Perceptions of the Mind*
(i–ii, Figure VIII-A)

Hume reviews the first division to be made in the perceptions, that of impressions and ideas, in order to make further distinctions that are necessary to the theory. The *impressions* can themselves be divided into *original* and *secondary*. This (left-hand) division consists of sensations, which "without any antecedent perception arise in the soul" from outside bodies affecting our senses or from our own body: sense impressions and feelings of pleasure and pain. They and their causes are not to Hume's point. (In fact, it may be that further philosophical inquiry in this direction would quickly be balked by the radical undecidability of the origins of primary impressions.) To be sure, "bodily pains and pleasures are the source of many passions, both when felt and consider'd by the mind; but arise originally in the soul, or in the body, whichever you please to call it"—this is the undecidability—"without any preceding thought or perception."[1] Thus Hume has not—and ought not to have—anything to say about bodily feels simply: They are primary adventitious facts, while the passions come from within the mind.

So he confines himself to the secondary (right-hand) impressions, those that have arisen in the mind from ideas or are derived from primary impressions.[2] These "reflective impressions"—the apparent oxymoron is deliberate, for there *are* impressions that arise, in turn, from ideas, and these derivative or secondary impressions are essential to the theory—are distinguished as calm or *violent*. The calm (left-hand) side of the division is once again set aside; they are the esthetic emotions. It is by this division that Hume seems to distinguish the softer, more evanescent feelings as *emotions* from the more forceful and sturdy passions.[3]

These violent feelings are the *passions proper*, and they are immediately distinguished into what turns out to be the most interesting division (though subtle to the point of evanescence), that between direct and *indirect* passions. The direct (left-hand) ones, which are again to be set aside, arise immediately from pleasure and pain.

The indirect passions are somewhat more capable of analysis. For though "'tis impossible we can ever, by a multitude of words, give a just definition of them," we can describe them by an enumeration of their circumstances, having captured them, as it were, by their names, which we get from general use.[4]

The indirect passions too mostly come in positive and negative couples. In fact, the nearly universal antithetical pairing of passions derives from their common origin in pleasure and pain. The indirect passions are, how-

A.

The Perceptions of the Mind (i–ii)

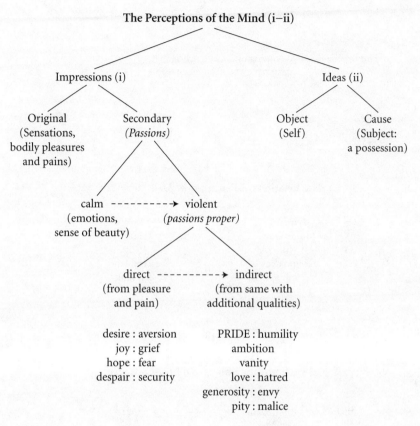

B.

The Qualities of the Mind (iii)

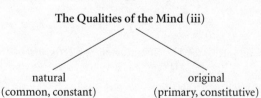

Figure VIII

(continued on following pages)

C.

The Economy of Principles (iii–iv)

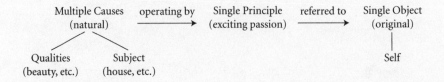

D.

The Relations of Perceptions: Association (iv)

of
Primary
Impressions
(by
resemblance
only)

of
Derived
Ideas
(by
resemblance,
contiguity,
production)

E.

The Double Impulse
of Passion-Impressions and Idea-Causes (iv)

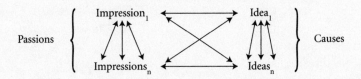

F.

Suppositions: The Operation of Subject-Causes (v)
(Pride and Humility)

Figure VIII *(continued)*

G.

The True System of Double Relations (v)

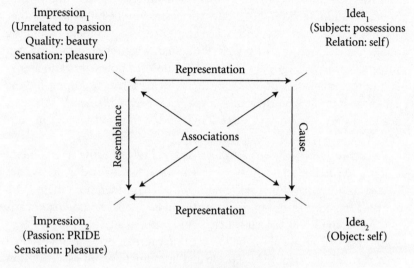

Impression₁
(Unrelated to passion
Quality: beauty
Sensation: pleasure)

Idea₁
(Subject: possessions
Relation: self)

Representation

Resemblance

Associations

Cause

Representation

Impression₂
(Passion: PRIDE
Sensation: pleasure)

Idea₂
(Object: self)

Figure VIII *(continued)*

ever, conjoined with other qualities (specified below for selected passions) and therein consists their distinction from the direct passions. Chief among these passions are PRIDE and its—less considerable—negative, humility. But love and hatred, which occupy the second part of the book on the passions, are also in the indirect column. It will be of great significance that these passions, unlike pride, are in fact, cross-referenced with the direct passions since desire plays a part in them;[5] its absence in pride makes it a "pure" and self-sufficient passion, a sustainer of self-sufficient selfhood.

Hume candidly says that he cannot justify or explain this distinction between direct and indirect passions "at present." Here is a half-acknowledgment of the fact that seems to me to reveal the real difference between his and Spinoza's system: For Hume, what I want to call the "passionacy," the essence of passionhood, must be an ultimate given; passions are original facts, representing nothing, referring to nothing, and not susceptible to truth insofar as that is adequacy of some sort[6]—either to an external reality or to an internal, ideal sufficiency. (That is to say that their relation to their inciting event is purely *de facto* and ultimately inexplicable.) Hence they are incapable of further explanation. For Spinoza, as we have seen, particular passions and passionateness are grounded in human affectivity, which is in turn part of a philosophical theology. It makes every sense that Hume should single him out for attack.

The second major part of the mind's perceptions are the *ideas,* the usu-ally—nothing in the *Treatise* remains unqualified—fainter images of the impressions. For the purpose of analyzing the passion of pride, ideas are given two functions or offices, so that the distinction here is not of kind but of operation: the idea that excites the passion in the mind and another idea to which the mind is turned when so excited.[7] These functions and the double relation built on them yield the system which is Hume's very own contribution, and a large part of the book is devoted not so much to apply-ing it to the established passions for their elucidation as to submitting the passions to it for its confirmation—just as an experimental scientist begins, once his observations have yielded a hypothesis, to invest himself in con-firming it.

These two idea-functions are *object-self* and *subject-cause.* The "object" of all proud passion, that which we have in view, that toward which we are directed, is our self. "When self enters not into consideration, there is no room either for pride or humility"; pride and its opposite, humility, invari-ably involve an idea of ourself which is "more or less advantageous."[8]

But this self cannot alone be the exciting cause of pride. Hume gives a pretty formalistic reason: Since pride and humility have self as a common object, if the self were also the sole cause of these passions, it, being homo-geneous, would always excite both passions equally at once, and they would cancel each other. Indifference would be the permanent state.

So there must be a cause or productive principle besides, which can be "placed on" a vast variety of subjects—"subject" in the sense of something on which we focus. These subjects have to belong to the self, be they inter-nal, such as qualities of mind ranging from good judgment to integrity, or bodily excellences from beauty to dexterity in making things, or real pos-sessions from country to clothes.[9] One might ask what it means for a man to have a quality of mind in the absence of an underlying mind, but that is too disruptive a question here. "Here there is a passion plac'd betwixt two ideas, of which the one produces it, and the other is produc'd by it. The first idea, therefore, represents the *cause,* the second the *object* of the passion."[10] "Produc'd" here is clearly meant to apply to the idea of self, not to the self itself; but then, since Hume admits no substantial self, he might be con-strued as saying that the passions, especially pride, do indeed produce such self as we have—a pretty spectacular notion. These terms may be abstruse, but the case is well observed. Thus Homer says of purple-dyed ivory cheek-pieces in a king's treasure that "they are for two things: to be the beauty of a horse [and] the pride of the horseman."[11]

Now one more distinction is necessary, that between the subject and the quality "on which it is plac'd." This "placed-on" locution appears to be Hume's way of trying to avoid thought and to talk of underlying substance and inherent accident—though Hume does fall into it himself,[12] for the subject has to have attractive characteristics to become a cause of pride, such as the strength of one's body or the beauty of one's house. The latter quality shows that the calm, esthetic passions are, after all, involved in producing the violent ones.

B. The Qualities of the Mind
(iii, Figure VIII-B)

However the properties or qualities of the mind are to be explained, two of them, each other's opposites, are distinguished as belonging to the "constitution of the mind," and these are the characteristics amenable to the influences of the causes of pride. We have a primary or natural impulse toward certain causes of pride: Power, riches, personal merit, are operative constantly at all times and for all people; it is human nature. This same holds negatively for their opposites, the causes of humility.

But these causes, natural though they be, are *not* original. Hume means that they are not each adapted to the passions of pride or humility by some distinct "new principle" or original quality. On the contrary, since the causes of pride are pretty commonly operative, each subject produces pride by some general quality and works by way of common circumstance. Thus owning a handsome writing desk makes us proud by the same principle as does owning its chair. Recall that for Spinoza, on the contrary, each cause of an affect colors its feel; Hume's accent is not on the high specificity of the "violent" passions—though it might be more so for the milder emotions.

What is original (as well as natural) is the attachment of the passions of pride and humility to self as object; there is in us a primary impulse, an original quality of the mind, that is its distinguishing characteristic. "Original" here describes (its meaning varies) a quality that is "most inseparable from the soul, and can be resolv'd into no other. And such is the quality, which determines the object of pride and humility."[13] Pride and humility pertain to the soul—and that's ultimate.

C. The Economy of Principles
(iii, Figure VIII-C)

Hume compares his moral philosophy to the Copernican Revolution: The ancient Ptolemaic astronomical system was so intricate and complex that it had to give way to something more simple and natural. "To overload our hypotheses" with "a monstrous heap of principles" is proof, Hume says, that none of them is just right. ("Hypothesis" is a term borrowed from ancient astronomy, which aimed to "save the [heavenly] appearances" by rational hypotheses, the axioms of geometric astronomy.) This observation is unavoidable: His principles are few by fiat of generalization, but while this parsimony leaves the particularity of appearances unexplained, it does not in fact make the system simpler.

So: A great number of causes, that is, subject items with their qualities, naturally operate by one common (but unspecified) principle to arouse the paired passions of pride and humility in one object (or self) that is originally (or inherently) prone to them.

D. The Relations of Perceptions: Association
(iv, Figure VIII-D)

At this moment Hume recalls the part of his theory of the understanding that explains how impressions and ideas are related among themselves and to each other. Its general term is *association*. The mind is a heap of atomic perceptions constantly changing but not entirely chaotically, not without "rule and method."[14] The mind passes from one idea to the other in three specific ways: by *resemblance* (similarity), by *contiguity* (next-to-ness), and by *production* (causation). Impressions are also associated, though "with this remarkable difference": Their association is by resemblance only.[15] For example, we associate father and son as they come before our senses not because they stand next to each other, or because one engendered the other, but because they look alike.

Again only the briefest sketch of the difficulties that might arise in thinking through the relations of perceptions is in place here, and again a reminder is necessary that there is scarcely any positive statement in the *Treatise* that Hume himself does not modify with exceptions, restrictions, and reversals. Above all, this "uniting principle among ideas [that is, association] is not to be considered as an inseparable connection . . . nor yet are we to conclude, that without it the mind cannot join two ideas . . . but we are only to regard it as a gentle force, which commonly prevails."[16]

First then, we might ask what agency exerts this "gentle force," since the mind, no unitary, persistent being, is "nothing but a heap or collection of different perceptions united together by certain relations [the very relations to be explained] . . . though falsely endowed with . . . identity."[17] At one point Hume calls in, reluctantly, the material brain—here he is very modern—to explain how the "animal spirits" (those Cartesian forerunners of electrical currents) excite ideas. However, the brain here is but an intermediary; it is the mind that "is endow'd with a power of exciting any idea it pleases" by dispatching "the spirits into regions or cells of the brain, in which the idea is plac'd."[18]

So the mind is after all the exciting agency, and moreover, the material brain falls under the sceptical doubt concerning bodily existence and thus cannot be definitively explanatory. Perhaps then it is each impression or idea that has the inciting cause of the pertinent relation inherent within it, as each body in Newtonian dynamics is sometimes said to be the cause, by reason of its measurable mass, of the attractive force by which all the others accelerate toward it. Analogous inherent relations might well explain the causal association that produces idea from idea, or the contiguous association in which an idea moves and so excites the one next to it. For an idea of the impression of an extended thing must be extended, Hume argues, so that continuity is a literal feature of certain ideas by which they might assert themselves.[19] Moreover, Hume seems to allow such relations as continuity and succession to be *in* the objects and thus "antecedent to the operations of the understanding," though we cannot, after all, "ascribe to these objects an inherent power or necessary connection." For we do not observe this power directly but infer, or better, ascribe it from contemplating our internal feeling or experience.[20] Let who can unscramble this welter of suggestions.

Resemblance, however, the widest of associating relations, does *not* seem to be at all intelligible as an inherent relation. For let two configurations be as similar as two eggs, the one cannot thereby have *excited the other* or even just *likened itself* to it (that is, evinced a similarity) all by itself without some inciting or comparing agent. And that must be our mind—which is also the "We" of the book—understood as the self-consciousness of this mind's objects and actions, the "idea of an idea," that "certain *je-ne-sais-quoi,* of which 'tis impossible to give any definition or descriptive, but which everyone sufficiently understands."[21] But that is the difficulty not to be entered into here much further: how to understand sufficiently what is neither to be defined nor described, and to accept claims of consensus as demonstrative finalities.

What accounts for that "remarkable difference" between impressions, above all the passions and their ideas, for the fact that the former are related only by resemblance[22]—and what really is resemblance? It seems to be in the first instance pictorial likeness, for it appears immediately to the eye. Could it also be some other type of similarity, such as can be intuited by the mind? It does not seem to be the one that we might first think of, namely that proportionality of corresponding lengths which together with the quality of angles defines the similarity of geometric figures—for that is listed as a separate relation.[23] Whatever the case, I think—though Hume does not say—that impressions are related by resemblance alone because they are radically atomic; each impression is a separate perception, in itself unconnected to an other, and resemblance is, as I have surmised, the essentially *un*inherent, purely comparative, and therefore purely external, relation. Moreover since impressions are largely of sensory origin, and sight is the predominant sense, they tend to be visual, that is, pictorial. Thus their primary relation might well be with visually like impressions, or with impressions similar at least in the mere fact of visuality. Yet it must be said that in Hume's system of passions, the *production* of impression by impression through resemblance is obscure. The productive relation seems to be more causal than fits the fact of resemblance. For how can two pre-existing items be caused—*ex post facto*—to resemble each other?

There is, furthermore, a resembling relation that is absolutely crucial but different from the resemblance that associates impressions with each other—and also ideas in parallel fashion. Hume does not distinguish the nature of this third resemblance—that of impressions with their derived ideas (which are really weak impressions)—from the resemblance that associates impressions with impressions and ideas with ideas. Perhaps there is not in fact a qualitative difference, yet this third resemblance relation does seem to exercise a productive or causal agency, that of re-presentation, for impressions are said to cause by a constant conjunction ideas that resemble the impressions. Unlike the unmixed resemblances, this relation is not reciprocal, for ideas do not cause primary impressions, though they do cause secondary ones. The relation is, however, representational, that is, ideas are "copies and representations" of impressions, which, if they are simple, the ideas "exactly represent."[24]

Since all these relations and cross-relations will be needed for the True System of the passions, it matters for its intelligibility how they work and where the obscurities arise.

E. *The Double Association of Impressions and Ideas (iv, Figure VIII-E)*

Hume now goes on to make this cross-production explicit for the special case of the passions. The mind cannot hold an idea constant for a long time; it proceeds, in the imagination, to pass to another by the (nonbinding) rules set out before. Thus one idea, an idea of a subject such as causes pride, associates with itself a number of others. A like association holds for impressions; thus one passion, such as joy, "naturally throws itself into love, generosity, pity, courage, pride and other resembling affections." (Here "resembling" means: so connected that where one arises the others immediately follow.)[25] Note that the direct passions, such as joy, here enter into the generation of indirect passions such as pride. One cause-idea, then, brings on several others, as one passion-impression gives rise to multiple others. But there is a third relation involved in the generation of an indirect passion, the kind that requires qualities beyond mere pleasure and pain. This third relation (which apparently goes both ways, since ideas give rise to reflective impressions) is the one between the first impression, which is the initial passion, and the "hundred subjects of discontent" (or content) that comprise the secondary ideas; these are the multiple imagined subjects related to the initial cause. This cross-relation "bestows on the mind a double impulse" that makes for a passion of "so much greater violence."[26] The explanation of the fierceness of passion has here begun in terms of the reciprocation of perceptions; a physical analogy might be the sympathetic vibration or resonance by which an oscillating system can build up an enormous, sometimes catastrophic, response from small inputs of force. Hume is offering a complex account of the self-ratcheting-up of passion. Being puffed up by pride or apoplectic with anger are familiar examples of the multipler effect from mutually inciting mental representations.

F. Suppositions: The Operation of Subject-Causes
(v, Figure VIII-F)

Hume now articulates explicitly the basic hypotheses or suppositions concerning the workings of the subjects that are the external causes of pride and humility, namely the things possessed. He supposes it to be generally true that many causes give pleasure and pain by the mere quality of the sensation, such as beauty or deformity, quite independently of generating any pride or humility. He further supposes that each subject is "determin'd by an original and natural instinct" to be related to self and that its object is always the self. Thus he pins down the *essence* of pride and humility which is caught in the diagrammatic center, as it were, of these suppositions: By its qualities, such as beauty or deformity, the subject causes pleasure and pain independently of pride or humility. By its second peculiar quality of pertaining to the self, it excites a second pair of painful or pleasurable emotions that are the *sine qua non* of pride. By its relation to self, which is, I think, actually identical with this second quality, the subject is related to self as the object that feels the pleasure or pain and so the pride and humility. These passions are therefore encompassed 1. by the causing subject's particular characteristics, 2. by its pleasure- or pain-giving qualities, and 3. by its relation to the self as object.

G. The True System of the Double Relation
(v, Figure VIII-G)

Now "the true system breaks in upon me with an irresistible evidence."[27] The *established* "properties" of the passion-impressions, namely their object-self and their sensations, pleasant or painful, are now put together with the *supposed* properties of the subject-causes, namely their relation to self and their independent tendency to produce pleasure or pain. (This, Hume's own summary, does not quite match the exposition of his analysis as set out above, but then no earlier exposition in the *Treatise* ever does quite jibe with a later one; here's a writer who would have benefited from a word processor.) He says the following:

> That cause, which excites the passion, is related to the object, which nature has attributed to the passion; the sensation, which the cause separately produces, is related to the sensation of the passion: From this double relation of ideas and impressions, the passion is derived.[28]

The cause with which Hume begins is the possession, be it of a personal characteristic or a thing—for this cause stands, as Figure VIII-F shows, behind the whole event. Perhaps I should have put the idea side of the system, subject-cause and object-self, on the left side of Figure VIII-G as coming first, for the impressions involved, here on the left, are not primary but secondary, that is to say, mediated by ideas. Hence Hume's emphasis on the subject-cause; the right top corner of the diagram is the pivot point of the system, for it becomes a cause of passion precisely as an idea—derived from sensations, to be sure, as Figure VIII-E shows—rather than as an immediate sensory experience.

The double relation, then, involves two impressions (left): The first is calm and has an appealing esthetic or similar quality; the second, derived from the first, excites, or better, *is* the excitation of the pleasurable passion of pride. Similarly two ideas are involved (right): The first is that of a subject, a thing or personal characteristic, related by possession to the self; the second, derived idea is that of the object at issue, again the self, the possessor.

These four terms are associated: impression$_1$ to impression$_2$ by the relation of resemblance, the only option (though not a very plausible one), and idea$_1$ to idea$_2$ by the relation of production or cause, Hume's relation of choice for this association of ideas. The impressions and the ideas are, of course, also related, the first to the first and the second to the second (and, it turns out, crosswise as well) *not* by the representational association through which primary impressions turn into ideas, but by some causal version of this copy-relation by which ideas produce secondary or reflective impressions:

> Nature has bestow'd a kind of attraction on certain impressions or ideas, by which one of them, upon its appearance naturally introduces its correlative.... When an idea produces an impression, related to an impression, which is connected with an idea, related to the first idea, these two impressions must be in a manner inseparable.... 'Tis after this manner, that the particular causes of pride ... are determined. The quality, which operates on the passion, produces separately an impression resembling it; the subject, to which the quality adheres, is related to self, the object of the passion: No wonder the whole cause, consisting of a quality and its subject, does so unavoidably give rise to the passion.[29]

It is this cycle of incitements that results in the violent, indirect passion of pride, which I have tried to schematize in Figure VIII-G, though I doubt that I have pulled together all the different starts definitively; it may be impossible. But perhaps enough is enough.

7. The Afterlife of the System: Reconsiderations and Retentions

I might say here that for his own part, and for all the self-saving force of pride, Hume recommends the calm, esthetic branch of the passions. To these belong both a "delicacy of passion," which is an exaggerated emotionality, and a "delicacy of taste," which is a heightened sensitivity; the latter is more conducive to happiness and awareness. I take it to be a description of the calm passions of Figure VIII-A.[1]

Hume was clearly proud of his system—which is certainly the most elaborately ingenious one known to me—and it survives into a later piece, "Of the Passions" (1757),[2] which is largely taken from the *Treatise* but so rearranged that the direct passions get pride of place. The double relation for the indirect passions is, however, retained, though presented in more succinct form:

  0. Idea → impression: The idea of beauty produces the sensation of pleasure.
  1. Impression → impression: The sensation of pleasure is related to the passion of pride.
  2. Idea → idea: The cause of pleasure is related to self.

Hume also introduces in this essay what might be called a chemical theory of the mutual influence of different types of passions,[3] by which they calm or excite each other. Again a tabulation will make the parts clearer:

The Chemical Theory

Passions	Opposites	Results
1. Contrary	unconnected	non-influencing, like diverse liquors in different bottles; the mind is divided
2. Mutually destructive	connected	miscible, like alkali and acid in a solution; the mind is neutralized
3. Simultaneously present	same but viewed contradictorily	immiscible, like oil and vinegar in an emulsion; a fused third, a self-disparate, passion is produced

In sentences: 1. When opposite passions, like joy and grief, arise from quite different sources, the passions will alternate, as when a man now rejoices at the birth of his son and then grieves at the loss of his lawsuit; the mind "can scarcely temper the one affection with the other." 2. When one and the same event has a mixed nature, the passions become "mutually destructive" and leave the mind calm and tranquil. 3. If passions, like hope and fear, concern the same object which seems now good, now bad, and the event seems now probable, now improbable, they will subsist simultaneously as a union or *fusion* of unassimilables. (This last item is my interpretation of what seems to me an incoherent text.)

Hume then adds a conversion theory to account for the mutual influence of passions that are already established: "The predominant passion swallows up the inferior, and converts it into itself."[4] For example, in love, a lovers' quarrel gives additional force to the prevailing passion, and occasional anger also enhances it.

With the intra-passional theory and the double relation, Hume considers that he has shown the passions to obey a "regular mechanism, which is susceptible of as accurate a disposition, as the laws of motion, optics, hydrostatics. . . ."[5]

The chemical theory had in fact been prefigured in the *Treatise*, where Hume says that, while ideas are largely impenetrable to each other, passions "are susceptible of entire union; and like colors may be blended so perfectly together, that each of them may lose itself" and contribute to a new whole.[6] It seems to me that Hume is here close to our experience; in fact, mixed emotions, whether they leave patients apathetic or conflicted, are a current scientific subject. Yet *how* this fusion and conversion can occur within Hume's system (or out of it, for that matter) I cannot tell, the less so since for him passions are, after all, impressions, though secondary ones, and therefore supposed to be associable only by resemblance. Or is it perhaps that certain emergent effects in the mind are neutralized rather than the standard passions themselves?

I mention the chemical theory especially because a version of it is applied by Hume to the explanation of the perplexity of tragic pleasure. The perplexity that can and ought to be very keenly felt is how we can take strong pleasure in the viewing of terrible catastrophes. In his essay "Of Tragedy" (1757),[7] Hume says that it is not sufficient to refer to a notion we might have lurking behind our participation in the tragedy that the spectacle is only a fiction. He therefore adds that the force of imagination, the charms of imitation, the delights of eloquence all seem to join in converting the painful passions into pleasant ones. The agreeable effects of the finer arts mollify the harsh affections that the real object in a tragic situation would cause, and *fuse* with them to produce the tragic pleasure, a simultaneity of contradictions. Hume adds that in real life the principle even acts inversely: When the subordinate, that is, the negative passion becomes predominant it swallows up the positive one: "Too much jealousy extinguishes love."[8] By his "immiscible" theory he must mean "overwhelms" rather than "puts out."

8. What Is Engaging about the True System?

I suppose I should say why this system does—for all the mildly infuriating looseness of its arguments, the complexity of its differentiations, and even its occasional callowness—seem to me to be engaging.

First, Hume is proud of it just because it *is* a system and such an intellectual artifact is always in some aspect illuminating.

Second, it fits neatly into the design of the *Treatise*, putting to use the terms of the understanding set out in the first book, while allaying the sceptical and self-despairing melancholy with which that book ends. For this system of passions, based on the double association of impressions and ideas, is really designed for, or better, derived from, the model passion of pride (humility being the recessive member of the pair).

Pride is, however (as I mentioned), the one passion capable of restoring to some self-satisfaction and self-sufficiency the exploded self that unsettles Hume. Pride cannot, to be sure, return identity to the Humean mind, but it brings it about that the self becomes an object, an object that must have at least as much persistence as has the subject, the possession, be it material or personal, that excites the natural propensity to pride in the self. (Recall that Hume seemed to say as much in Section 6 A: The passions, pride in particular, "produce" the idea of self.) It is pertinent here to recall that for Hume there is no self apart from perceptions;[1] now the ideas that cause pride tend to be pretty long-lasting—houses and such—and so the proud self is also pretty stable.

But more: Pride is, Hume says, a pure emotion in the soul, unattended by any desire, and not immediately exciting us to action."[2] He must mean that in pride—as he understands it—we rest content and complete for a while, for we already possess what we want, and it causes "our idea of ourselves [to be] more advantageous" and us to be elated—*us*, "the identical person, of whose thoughts, actions, and sensations we are intimately conscious." To me it seems significant that here for once an "identical person" appears, though personal identity of the mind has earlier been dubbed a fiction.[3]

Third, some features of the passions in general that Hume observes really ring true. Certain passions do seem to arise directly as qualifications of pleasure and pain, while others involve aesthetic qualities. Some passions are directed primarily to other "objects," some essentially to self. Feelings and thoughts, once a passion is developing, do ratchet themselves and each other up.

Fourth, the analysis of pride in particular seems, complications aside, true to life. There *is* a kind of very common pride that springs essentially from the pleasure in fine possessions: "House-proud" is the pertinent adjective, and Hume has captured it. As a consequence he can also distinguish the passions that are not thus self-involving, and in the second part of Book II, "Of Love and Hatred," he does just that.

9. Limitations and Expansions of the System

Hume's various theories of the passions are thus sketched out. To return to the *Treatise,* Part I of Book II ends with sections on "limitations," specifications of rules obtaining in the "general system" as applied to pride. There follow sections detailing the causes, such as one's own virtue, beauty or health, property and riches, reputation and fame.[1] These are acutely observed and complexly specified: Hume's young man's reflections on the pride-ridden world makes one nod and smile. Hume's serious agenda, however, is to fulfill the promise of his book's subtitle, "An Attempt to Introduce the Experimental Method into Reasoning." He intends to test his system against the facts of observed experience. That he succeeds is no surprise: It is, after all, his system, applied to his experience. Yet even to my mind, sceptical of scepticism, there are some strikingly good fits, which corroborate the System (or hypothesis) if not as a philosophical illumination, then at least as an analytical-descriptive method.

He goes on to apply his system to animals, in analogy to the ways of anatomists who "join their observations and experiments on human bodies to those on beasts" to corroborate their hypotheses. Since pride and humility "are really nothing but the power of producing agreeable or uneasy sensations," this passion ought correspondingly to occur in animals, for they have, on observation, "the same relation of ideas, and deriv'd from the same causes" in their minds as do men.[2] Thus swans, turkeys, peacocks, nightingales are visibly vain. Hume concludes:

> My hypothesis is so simple, and supposes so little reflection and judgment, that 'tis applicable to every sensible creature; which must not only be allowed to be a convincing proof of its veracity, but, I am confident, will be found an objection to every other system.[3]

That may be an illusion; students of animal ethology are doubtful about anthropomorphic interpretations of animal emotionality, except, perhaps, for the primates nearest us.

I have quoted Hume's conclusion, characteristic as it is, mainly because it draws, finally, attention to a significantly missing element of the system: The passions are essentially unrelated to reason, that is, they make no implicit judgments and involve no comparison of ideas. (Even the so-called "reflective" impressions are not products of reason.) Later Hume will say that, since "our passions . . . are original facts and realities compleat in themselves, they cannot be either true or false, contrary or conformable to reason." For reason is concerned with the real relations among ideas, such as are not involved in passions, since these latter are each self-complete and without necessary reference to others.[4] Thus passions are neither true nor false—they just are. Hence they are unamenable to reason, neither judged nor guided by it—on the contrary, the reverse holds: One of Hume's best-known dicta is "that the reason is, and ought only to be the slave of the passions."[5] I suppose this means technically that passion could and should force reason to subvert its own associative functions.

10. Love and Hatred: The System without the Self

Hume then turns to love and hatred, *perhaps* because, if you consider both sexes and all ages, they are the central passions, but *certainly* because they are to bear out the system, as the fifteen pages of Section ii, "Experiments to confirm this system," make clear.

I will attend to the positive side of the pair. The oppositional pairing of most passions is a given for Hume, but it is of interest to him mostly because he uses it once more to show that the object and the cause of love and hatred are not, "properly speaking," the same: Once again, if it were so, if the common object (the focus of interest) of either passion were at the same time their cause (their inciting reason) it would excite these contrary passions simultaneously and equally, and they would simply cancel each other; we would be passionless. Here the "object" of love is, naturally, not one's own self, as it was for pride, but "evidently some thinking person," though an other.[1] (Recall that the object is that on which the passion "directs its view," is focused.) This turns out to be not much of a restriction: Part II, as did Part I, will also end with an application of the system to animals; in fact "to the whole sensitive creation," for though the thoughts of beasts are not so active in tracing out the relations that cause love in humans, yet they do have judgment.[2] Indeed Hume had earlier made a very modern-sounding *behavioral* argument for animal thinking: Animals' actions *resemble* those of ours that are "guided by reason and design." Notice that animals are held to be less passionate, thus, perhaps, more rational than humans![3] I again make a point of Hume's inclusion of animals to remind the reader here how important it is to him that the human mind should be stripped of all "subtility and refinement" and its work brought as close to *instinct* as possible.[4]

The object at which love is directed is, then, some thinking person, meaning a being capable of "virtue, wit, good sense and good humour." But now follows a puzzle: Hume insists that the subject (recall that for pride this was the house that bore attractive qualities) is to be distinguished not only from the lovable personal qualities of which it is the bearer, be they of a virtuous or beauteous sort, but also from the object. Yet it is hard, when thinking of plain love, to see how subject and object don't coincide here.

The person who is the object of love seems also to be the subject of lovable qualities.

But Hume means it, quite coolly. His first example distinguishes between the esteem of which a prince is the object and the stately palace that he possesses, which is the cause of the esteem, and he repeats such examples, in which the object of esteem and love *is* not but *possesses* the subject whose qualities cause the love. Here is the outcome: Love and pride are produced by the same, endlessly various qualities *viewed as possessions* and are closely related. Hume is writing here in a politically consequence-laden tradition, which views one's goods, one's qualities, and one's self all equally as possessions; thus Locke speaks of "the property which men have in their persons. . . ."[5] (Lest, however, this convertibility of personhood and possessions be blamed on—or credited to—the invention of English commercialism, let us recall our Homer. Where else do beautiful wealth and human stature more directly reflect on each other?)

Now Hume himself sketches a diagram in words: "'Tis evident here are four affections, plac'd, as it were, in a square or regular connection with, and distance from each other."[6] Here is my construction of the square:

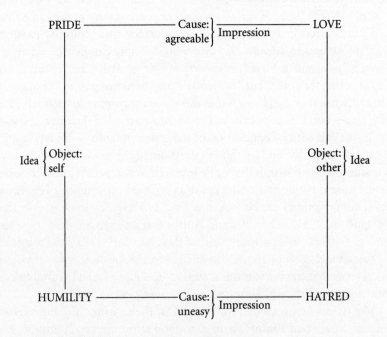

And thus, the "line of communication" between pride and humility is the self; between love and hatred it is the other; between pride and love it is agreeableness; between humility and hatred it is uneasiness; the objects *are* ideas, namely our idea of the other; the causes *excite* the impressions, namely passions.

This dry exercise has the express purpose of testing whether the system can, besides analyzing single passions, display their connections of love and pride, hatred and humility. The imagination (not much in evidence so far) here comes forward as the chief agency of the mind in the "transfusion," "passage," "transition" of these passions into each other by variations of objects and causes. Hume develops a multitude of subtle exemplifications of these interrelations, some amusingly observed from life, some drily fabricated from a systematic motive; none deal with love as I—probably it would be fair to say, as we—feel it. This theoretical subjection of passion to analytical reason is a pretty mechanical affair, but it will prove useful below for explicating the origin of erotic love.

The rest of this part is mostly devoted to the causes of love, which draw in their train other passions: first, the desire for a close relation, which operates on us by resemblance and, since it is involved with the self, is immediately related to pride. Then, benevolence, in some systems falsely conjoined with love, which is consequently regarded as nothing but the desire for the happiness of the object. Hume observes wisely that the passion in fact often occurs without such benevolence. I think he might have gone farther, since, folly though it be, most of us would rather have our love unhappy close to us than happy far away—well, up to a point.

Next come compassion and pity, which give Hume the occasion for an analysis of sympathy. This is a passion that will eventually be of great interest to Hume—and thence to Adam Smith—because this powerful principle produces "our sentiment of morals in all the artificial virtues." These are the virtues invented for the good of mankind. Sympathy arises from the resemblance relation: "All human creatures are related to us by resemblance,"[7] and so their passions, their pains and pleasures, strike us in a lively manner and produce similar emotions in us. This production must be subsequent to the resemblance-effects; passions, being reflective, go through ideas, and a lively idea is easily converted into an impression. We can see that sympathy is, like pride, a reflective impression, but it differs in being initially based on our resemblance to others rather than on our regard for self. Sympathy also differs from pride in that affliction and sorrow, negative passions, are the stronger instigators in sympathy, while in pride pleasure plays the greater role. Here are elements of Smith's theory of moral sentiments in preformation.

Next comes malice, which "imitates the effects of hatred, as pity does those of love."[8] Then Hume considers the mixtures of benevolence with pity and of malice with anger; finally he treats respect and contempt and shows their affinity to pride, since a comparison with ourself is involved. And thus, with a chapter on amorous passion, ends the consideration of all passions that have an admixture of love or hatred. If the complex involvements of love in life are confounding, on paper they are positively laborious!

For the explanation of erotic love, Hume introduces the notion of a "parallel desire." The term seems poorly chosen: "Parallel" desires, strictly speaking, can't establish connections (being, by definition, non-intersecting), but what Hume means is that the soul's most refined passion, a feeling of esteem, and its grossest one, the "appetite for generation," are mediated by the love of beauty to produce sensual love.[9] Hume says that this account holds for any system, but also that it confirms his double relation: It is only because impressions and ideas reinforce each other that this trio of emotions coalesces in the amorous passion. In it, to be sure, appetite for the flesh and appreciation for beauty do play a part, beauty even being the initial mover. Yet the whole catalogue of love-related passions, although having an other as object, is primarily related to pride, to the sense of self that is derived from what we "own," either as our own internal qualities or as external subjects of qualities. Pride not only holds us together but connects us to others. It is the root of love. For Hume, it is *the* master passion.

Here is a neat construction offered in a gentlemanly voice, but it does not, I think, sit well. For the pagan, pride was the warrior's passion, for the Christian, Satan's sin—both more likely to lead to lust than love. For Hume, it is the proprietor's boast, and that also seems to me a poor beginning for the passion that is supposed to focus on an other. Proper pride may be a *condition* for sound love, but I am not convinced that it is its "*origin.*"

11. Pleasure/Good, Pain/Evil, Virtue/Vice, Loose Necessity

The passions so far considered have been the indirect ones, to be found in Figure VIII-A, and defined as requiring qualities beyond pain and pleasure. Now Hume turns to the other, the simpler branch of "violent" passions, the direct ones, "which arise immediately from good, or evil, from pain or pleasure." Thus begins the third and last part of Book II, the *Treatise*'s book on the passions, and we learn right away that pleasure/pain = good/evil.[1] I think it is pretty plain that Hume does not regard pleasure and pain as passions proper but as sensations, original feelings "that immediately produce passions. . . . They are the chief actuating principle of the human mind"; without these sensations "we are, in great measure, incapable of passion or action, of desire or volition."[2]

So the direct passions, being immediately generated by pleasure/good and pain/evil, are somewhat more directly related to virtue and vice. They are therefore placed close to the third book, called "Of Morals," that concludes the *Treatise*—which is, after all, said in its title to be about "Moral Subjects." For a similar reason, Hume now introduces a long disquisition on the will, the gist of which is that he obviates the usual opposition of free choice and necessary connection, by denying both. The facilitating term lies midway between them and is taken over from his theory of natural causation: "constant conjunction."[3] This term denotes the *de facto* connection of events from which the mind infers a *presumptive* causal connection for which there is no real evidence. Constant conjunction is to be understood neither as spontaneous, that is, as free, nor as deterministic, that is, as jigged. I would call it "loose necessity," loose because there is no inherent causal nexus, necessity because it does, after all, constantly occur. Applied to morals, this type of loose connection means that we are entitled to infer from like actions to like motives—this action tends to be produced by that passion. But since reason only *discovers* these causes and effects of pain, pleasure, and their consequent passions, it can never *produce* moral action, nor can it combat immoral action; at most it can conjecture outcomes as a bystander. Hence the notorious dictum already cited, that "Reason is, and ought only to be a slave of the passions...."[4] Moreover, since a passion is "an original existence ... and contains not any representative quality, which renders it a copy of any other existence," it cannot be either true or untrue. For truth, Hume takes for granted, consists of the agreement of a copy or representation with the original it represents, and reason has the function of ascertaining this agreement. An interesting implication of these reflections is that passions are constitutionally *non-representative*; this seems to be a fundamental feature of feeling.

All writers who embed their study of the passions in a philosophical system eventually slide into the virtues and vices. It happens partly because some passions bear the names of virtues and vices, partly because the control of the passions by virtue is a chief object of morality, while morality itself is to be rooted in the way human beings are: passion-ridden. For Hume, however, the transition is particularly easy, because morality is itself a sentiment that is in closest relation to two other sentiments, pleasure and pain. A sentiment is, after all, an affection much as is a passion, and differs from one only in cognitive complexity: Pleasure, pain, and moral sentiment are original impressions, while passions are reflective impressions.

But it must be said that it isn't clear, at least not to me, why the will and the direct passions are stowed away just here. The will plays a very small role in the remainder of Book II, and the virtues and vices that are said to pertain most intimately to the indirect passions had already been very explicitly treated in an earlier section on the indirect virtues.[5] There "the moral hypothesis" is unequivocally stated:

> For if all morality is founded on pain or pleasure ... all the effects of morality must be deriv'd from the same pain or pleasure, and among the rest the passions of pride and humility. The very essence of virtue, according to this hypothesis, is to produce pleasure and that of vice to give pain. The virtue and vice must be part of our character in order to excite pride or humility.[6]

According to this exposition, virtue and vice (which might, after all, be said to constitute morality) are even anterior to the sensations of pleasure and pain, since they produce it, though Hume wobbles on this order even within one page (which is why the moral sentiments are not located in Figure VIII-A). I think, however, that ultimately virtue and vice do come first, insofar as they are the occasion of a "soft and gentle" sentiment, which Hume will call the "moral sense," and will make the basis of his morality.[7]

At any rate, pride, traditionally proscribed as the root of sin, is now redeemed:

> [T]hese . . . are to be consider'd as equivalent with regard to our mental qualities, *virtue* and the power of producing love or pride, *vice* and the power of producing humility or hatred.[8]

After some ingenious but questionable observations on the opposite effects of space and time on the vivacity of passions—a spatially remote "now," he claims, is far more vividly present to the imagination then a temporally distant "here"—Hume takes care of desire. He disposes of the most direct of all passions, which is Spinoza's prime affect, in a sentence: Desire "arises from good consider'd simply"; the will exerts itself when an action of body or mind may attain that good.[9]

12. Philosophy as Hunting

Hume finishes his book on the passions with a section called "Of curiosity, or the love of truth," a passion he regards as too peculiar to fit under any previous heading. Here is an irresistible contrast: The very passion Socrates ridicules as distracting to truth-seeking, curiosity,[1] the very antithesis to wonder, is the one Hume identifies with the love of truth; I might call it inquisitive rather than inquiring wonder. And in this spirit the section continues: "[T]here cannot be two passions more nearly resembling each other, than those of hunting and philosophy. . . ."[2] For both, the pleasure lies in "the motion, the attention, the difficulty, and the uncertainty," and for both, the passion is not derived from the end. This end must, to be sure, have some utility. However, we become passionate about it only in the course of the pursuit; indeed its value is disproportionately small compared to the effort. Hume mentions a partridge as the purposed end on the hunting side and leaves us to supply the analogous term on the philosophizing side. Then he offers a second analogy to philosophy: gaming. And indeed, after him some English-speaking philosophy does turn into an analytical chase and a linguistic game, and its motive does seem to be that peculiar love of truth Hume calls "curiosity." Curiosity will turn up elsewhere in these pages, now praised, now scorned, depending on the writer's view of the knowable world.

And here too, at the end, the pure love of knowledge, which "displays itself in the sciences," for a moment rears itself up and is disjoined from common curiosity, after all. The latter has, nonetheless, the last word. "Let us," Hume says, "search for the reason of this phenomenon," namely that of nosiness.[3] It is, he says, that the vivacity of the idea of our neighbor's affairs engages the fancy and gives the sort of pleasure we get from a moderate passion while simultaneously the information we obtain allays uncertainty and prevents uneasiness.

With this indulgent view he simply ends, and I am tempted similarly simply to stop. It is a curious web of tightly woven complexity and wandering loose ends, this second book of the *Treatise,* whose scores of phrases of assurance—"'Tis obvious," "'Tis evident"—seem, oddly, to call for nearly two hundred expatiating pages. Perhaps, however, I should refer the willing reader to my Section 2, where I did detail the profit in studying Hume's so simplistically intended and so analytically complex theory of the passions, so often referenced and so rarely set out. But what is finally captivating is this disclaimer from the end of Book I, which affords the reader the pleasure of watching a brilliant young man elegantly eat his cake and have it too:

> On such an occasion [the exact and full survey of his book] we are apt not only to forget our scepticism, but even our modesty too; and make use of such terms as *'tis evident, 'tis certain, 'tis undeniable* . . . I may have fallen into this fault after the example of others; but I here enter a *caveat* against any objections . . . ; and declare that such expressions . . . imply no dogmatical spirit, nor conceited idea of my own judgment . . . which are sentiments that can become . . . a sceptic still less than any other.[4]

chapter IX

Mood as News from Nothing

Kierkegaard, Heidegger, and the Age of Anxiety

1. Mood Situated and Delineated

Who can doubt that human beings have always been moody—affected with unfocused feelings, feelings the harder to deal with for being "vapourish," as they said in the eighteenth century—without certainly assignable cause or distinctly discernible object, not quickly exhausted like a squall of passion nor relievingly expressive like an access of emotion.

Yet mood is an explicitly defined theme neither among the ancients, nor those people-between-the-ages, the medievals, nor for the early moderns, with whose distinctive writers the first eight chapters of this book were concerned. Yes, there are passions and states that are unmistakably moodlike, such as the racking *aegritudo,* the soul-contracting distress that Cicero could not shake off, and the debilitating *acedia* ("non-caring") and *anxietas* ("narrowing"), that spiritual disgust and constriction of the soul to which monks are prey. Yet Cicero's suffering had a clear object, his much-loved daughter, and a definite cause, her untimely death. So also the religious' sadness—for *acedia* and *anxietas* are both species of *tristitia,* sadness, wonderfully defined as "flight of appetite" (*fuga appetitis*)—is regarded not as a helpless mood, but as a willed vice, or rather as a mortal sin, the monk's dis-ease: *morbus melancholicus,* which is defined as "disgust with the holy life."[1]

Corresponding to this inattention to the objectlessness or—as we have learned to say—non-intentionality of moods is the ancient lack of concern with their cure, especially notable in the Stoics, for whom the self comes to the fore and passion therapy is so central.[2] Perhaps one might say that the pagan ancients have a propensity for overlooking what is not crisply objective, for evading subjectivity or attributing its symptoms to the body. I am thinking of the old Hippocratic theory of "humours," the four body fluids, which are held responsible for four corresponding "temperaments." These are the conditioning propensities for mental states, among which *melancholia,* the "black-bile" affect, is the one still most spoken of. There is a part of an Aristotelian work specifically devoted to melancholy that points to the groundlessness of that mood (which can, of course, rise to madness): "So it is with daily spiritlessness (*athymia*): Often we feel as if in pain, but for what we cannot say." There is here a recognition of two kinds of depressive affects distinguished by psychiatrists: "endogenous" moods that have some internal psychological cause which is hard to pin-point, and "exogenous" ones that are occasioned by identifiable external events. The former are harder to treat. Responsibility lies, however, not with the sick soul but with the humoral temperament: "All melancholics are abnormal not because of disease but because of nature."[3] That was precisely the general judgment about the most complexly grand American melancholiac. His law partner, Herndon, said—and dozens agreed: "No element of Mr. Lincoln's character was so marked, obvious and ingrained as his mysterious and profound melancholy. . . . It was part of his nature and could no more be shaken off than he could part of his brains." Yet it sometimes approached madness, a natural condition in the sanest of men.[4]

I won't say much more of melancholia, because what was—even for that anatomist of melancholy Robert Burton—still something of a poetic mode, an inspired madness, is now recognized—and perhaps diminished—as a "mood disorder," a disruptive, pharmacologically treatable mental dysfunction: manic-depressive (now bipolar) illness, which includes the melancholias. (Something of that revelatory dignity, however, does survive into modern psychiatry. Thus Freud says of the melancholiac that "it may be that he has come very near to self-knowledge; we can only wonder why a man must become ill before he can discover a truth of this kind.")[5] Of interest here is that Burton subscribes to the ancient sense of the inward-directed circularity of melancholy: "Sorrow is both cause and symptom of this disease." And for its agony he quotes John Chrysostom (the Greek church father of the fourth century C.E.), who calls it "a most inexplicable grief . . . a perpetual executioner, continual night. . . ."[6] If you want a picture of it, look at Dürer's *Melancolia I* (1514) as she sits, "super-awake," surrounded by the gear of knowledge and practice, focusing fixedly, staring intently—at *nothing.*[7]

On the other hand, I will have a lot more to say of anxiety, a more current term than melancholy, and an affect which, although it has also been medicalized, retains its sense of a humanly expectable affliction. My choice of mood (which is usually regarded as an endogenous affect, literally a feeling "*generated within*") as the tone-setting feeling and of anxiety (literally, a strangling constriction) as the exemplary mood of modernity is, I will claim, defensible or at least half-defensible. Not a soul really knows whether human affectivity has changed in the literate millennia, but everybody knows that context, the circumstances of time and place, changes, and so may the dominant affects.

"Contextuality" is the shibboleth of post-modernity, but I am appealing to folk wisdom: As the setting changes new notions become thinkable and are indeed thought and then feed on themselves, or conversely, someone has a new idea and forthwith the world has changed and has become the world for that idea. Happily it is not my project to think out this "chicken or egg?" problem. Happily, I say, because we haven't even got so far as to know whether it is to be solved philosophically or historically, rationally or empirically (though the present inclination—whether intellectually or circumstantially driven, who knows?—is all toward the latter approach in each pair). I will simply content myself with observing that the affect of mood, moodiness, came to the fore in concert with a roiling conglomeration of ideas and events that seem, in all their diversity, to make a coherent complex. It is describable to a first approximation as the confluence of subjectivity and science, ego-istic inwardness and human mastery of nature, individualism and public pressure, and dozens of antitheses more with all their pre-conditions and consequences.[8] The most eventually burdensome of these—the more so for first being taken too lightly by the Enlightenment—is a new obligation to think through the human place in the world, that is, human existence, just when distractions and displacements most obscure the human situation. Yet it is in these very circumstances that there occur what appear to me the most ingenious understandings of mood and the most original appropriations of "anxiety" (sometimes rendered "dread")—those of Kierkegaard and of Heidegger (Sections 2 and 3).

I am far from claiming that objectless mood or "existential" anxiety are exclusively historically conditioned, recent phenomena or that they have displaced the old passions, which under the newer name of emotions are surely as alive and well—or ill—as ever. In his dramatic poem "The Age of Anxiety," written at the end of the Second World War, W. H. Auden has the most reflective of his characters singing of "the *ages* of anguish" (my italics). Under this long view anxiety, though intensified by war, when "everybody is reduced to the anxious status of a shady character or a displaced person," is just the perennial crisis of faith now and then come front and center. Perhaps mindful of Kierkegaard's "deliberations" on anxiety, the same character "suggests":

> All that exists
> Matters to man; he minds what happens
> And feels he is at fault, a fallen soul
> With power to place, to explain every
> What in his world but why he is neither
> God nor good, this guilt the insoluble
> Final fact, infusing his private

Nexus of needs, his noted aims with
Incomprehensible comprehensive dread
At not being what he knows that before
This world was he was willed to become.[9]

What one might safely say is that mood becomes thematic in modernity, and anxiety is its emblematic exemplar in more recent modernity—in philosophy, psychology, poetry, and ordinary consciousness. In the first section of this chapter I will list, in a cursory way that convicts me of notion-dropping, some of the circumstances that are conducive to mood-affects.

But first let me locate mood very generally in the economy of affects. What makes mood interesting in this context is that it does seem to be a distinct kind of affect, particularly as opposed to the object-directed passions-or-emotions, distinct in being objectless, non-intentional, endogenous.

Here is a little table ranking various kinds of affects by their intentionality.

2:		Passions	
1:	Feelings		Emotions
0:	Feels			Moods

"Feels," in Anglo-Saxon parlance, are the intentionless bodily sensations, including sheer somatic pleasure and pain. The "higher" psychic pleasures and pains, and atmospherics, sometimes called "feelings," are somehow "at" or "from" or "for" something; we get diffusely enjoyable feelings from or have them for the wilderness we camp in, but we directly fear a black bear—acutely and objectively. Passions like fear, then, are at the top of the pyramid in being vehemently object-directed and object-imbued. Their very name implies a suffering impingement by an acting object: wanting, fearing, hating *something*; grammatically they act accusatively on their direct object, but semantically they are its victims, aroused by its power. Emotions are certainly intentional, tending toward their objects but with a greater emphasis on our expressive reactions to, and subjective reconfigurations of, that object. Moods, finally, return to the null state in being object-divorced, like feels, but of the soul.

Of course, none of this works perfectly. For example, a mood could surely be triggered by an external event, though if the thought of it became stuck as the object of the feeling one would probably call it an emotional fixation rather than a mood. And conversely sometimes emotions bleed into moods. So can passions appear as feelings: Who has not felt accesses of love or tenderness summoned, objectless, by music?—though surely those diffuse affects only show that love always lies in readiness, waiting to precipitate its object.

Nonetheless, even giving complexities their due, objectless or very remotely occasioned anxiety is a powerfully distinctive feeling, so apprehended both by the complexly melancholy Dane, Kierkegaard, who thought it "the most terrible spiritual trial," and by the simple English curate Wentworth, who, as a true Protestant priest, understands that it is

> our highest sensation—higher than any positive enjoyment in the world. It used to sweep over me like a wave, sometimes when I opened the door, sometimes in a letter—in all simple ways.[10]

2. Between Hume and Kierkegaard

This section must be either scandalously short or unconscionably long. I'll opt for the first. That resolve, however, drives me into an approach in which I have, ordinarily, no faith (except perhaps as a laboriously achieved *ex post facto* summation): the naming of eras as if they were pre-given containers into which authors come packaged. Nonetheless, to get from Hume to Kierkegaard (their relevant works are just a century apart: 1740, *Treatise of Human Nature*; 1844, *The Concept of Anxiety*), I will name the English Neoclassicism of the novelists that followed in Hume's wake; then the French Enlightenment of the philosophers to whom Rousseau, Hume's exact contemporary, half-belongs; next the German Romanticism of Schlegel and Novalis, among whose spiritual progenitors Rousseau was; to come finally to the Dane Kierkegaard, who gave the deepest formulation to that characteristic aspect of Western modernity, the mood of anxiety (whose sometimes conscious complement—and sometimes mask—in the West's West, America, is—no, used to be—obligatory optimism).

A. Hume, Defoe

Hume's writing is a very formulary for an "age of feeling" that was what one might call the soft underbelly of a brightly reserved Neoclassisism. From the first, the new, *the* modern genre of the novel had been lyric poetry's more expansive complement in the cause of what in the early nineteenth century begins to be called subjectivity—concentration on the inward self. Not that the Greek lyric poets with whom this book begins did not know what it was to be in the grip of passion. But that's just the difference: For them not the "I" is to the fore, but the divine tyrant Eros who is eros "personified," or rather, that is how it looks from our inside-out vantage point—the emotion is *extruded*. From theirs it was divine Eros who had entered and captured the soul—the passion is *suffered*. It is interesting that the Neoclassical writers reveled in the personification of the passions; what to the lyric poets of the sixth century B.C.E. was the accurate report of a *human event* is in the writers of the eighteenth century C.E. a popular and potent *literary figure*.

The personification seems to stand for the "substance" of the object. Allowing the passion itself to be impassioned, the form of the personification positions emotion as standing warily between being a subjective and an objective
experience. . . . As in Hume, passion creates a person.[1]

Recall, however, that this impassioning the passion is just what Socrates
censured previous speakers in the *Symposium* for doing to Eros; in psychic
matters, there's nothing new under the sun.

Daniel Defoe is said to be the father of the novel. *Robinson Crusoe* (1719)
is the true avatar of novelistic subjectivity. Twenty of its twenty-six chapter
titles began with the word "I." It turns to "we" when Friday, the friendly savage, joins him. In its expurgated, perky children's version—the first book
I, like many European children, ever read *to myself*—it is a most objective
account of practical ingenuity, a handbook of survival skills; it is Robinson,
"Everyman," at his jack-of-all-trades best. The unexpurgated version, however, is a novel of isolation, despair, loneliness, and of what we would call
"existential anxiety," that is, forsakenness.[2] Hence "Crusoe" the "man of
the cross." It is a moody book, this early novel.

The genre will continue in this vein. Friedrich Schlegel, one of the
founders of Romanticism, will say that the Novel, *Roman* in German, "is a
romantic book," designed to be read privately, *to oneself,* giving an imaginative or even fantastic form to a sentimental, self-revealing content.[3] As ever,
there is a forerunner in antiquity, albeit late antiquity: Augustine records
in the *Confessions* that his mentor, Bishop Ambrose, most amazingly read
books silently to himself, not even moving his lips—surely an index of a
new, Christian subjectivity.[4]

Hume, however, had, in the *Treatise,* drawn attention to the complement
of private subjectivity—its easy accessibility to social influence:

> [H]atred, resentment, esteem, love, courage, mirth and melancholy; all these
> passions I feel more from communication then from my own natural temper
> and disposition. . . . The passions are so contagious, that they pass with the
> greatest facility from one person to another, and produce correspondent move-
> ments in the human breast.[5]

Hume formulates the condition for any particular affect to arise and for the
literary expression that ensues. First, it is indeed feelings that, in the absence
of a continuous personal identity, make the person, and second, these feelings, though eminently subjective, don't always originate in an "I." They are
got by contagion, and the person (or better non-person) that evinces them
is thus "socially constructed" (as we say). Indeed, in the absence of a steady
self, the passions, particularly the self-regarding ones like pride, come, as
was shown, particularly to the fore. Traditionally the human soul is unified by the dominion of reason, but, of course, for Hume reason is to be the

acknowledged slave to the passions. However, he pays a price for the candor of his skeptical empiricism, to wit, the dark melancholia, this skeptic's notorious confession with which the *Treatise* begins, not entirely unlike Crusoe's depression and like his, also to be dispersed by fixing one's attention on the practical world of fact.

Ideas, assents, moral judgments are each a feeling for Hume: "nothing but . . . feeling or sentiment." "Nothing but" is the ever-present marker of Hume's reductionism from the complex to the ungrounded; it is the expression of the anti-metaphysics that drove him to despair and then energized him. The age he presides over is thus "the age of feeling," of sentiment, sensibility, sentimentality, social and subjective at once. It is a social flowering of something mostly new under the sun as such: "Among the ancients we find no trace of sentimentalism," rightly says an American onlooker.[6]

The many writers on emotions of the time are neither mainly concerned (as Hume was not) with the relation of the passion to its object—for it is no longer the chief determinant of the affect, the feeling[7]—nor (and again Hume is the model) with a metaphysically-sited psychology.

B. English Novels of Sentiment

Novels of the period expressed what had become the passion of fashion. The most famous literary example is Lawrence Sterne's *A Sentimental Journey* (1768), which tells of a trip to France he had dashed off on, forgetting, in his "light attachment to reality," as Virginia Woolf puts it, that England was at war with France.[8] In these slim and charming two volumes, Sterne expressed his sensibility in his small-grained observations, his sensitivity in his widely inclusive humanity comprising disreputable characters of either sex, and his sentiments of every sort and for everything in his ever-ready responsiveness. The extant volumes end thus, wonderfully *in medias res*: "So that when I stretch'd out my hand, I caught hold of the fille de chambre's."

The equally popular counterexample in point of *joie de vivre* is Henry McKenzie's *The Man of Feeling* (1771), whose "hero," Harley, weeps his way through this slight but very popular novelette, living and dying by his sensibility: When Miss Walton responds in suitably chaste circumlocutions to the sick-bed confession of his love, he expires forthwith. Or take Jane Austen's much later *Sense and Sensibility* (1811; Miss Austen read Sterne). Its antiheroine Marianne, who has an overplus of sensibility, nearly kills herself traipsing about brokenheartedly in the wet grass of spring. "It is not every body," Elinor, who has all the sense, had said before about her sister's earlier fall rambles, "who has your passion for dead leaves." It is Marianne too who gives the conversation in the drawing room "the powerful protection of a very magnificent concerto"—the forerunner of restaurant mood-music, which, I am told, is intended to protect diners' privacy while imposing on them—Hume-like—an enveloping common feeling, with a probably equal access of comfort.

Books belonging to the period keep finding a philosophy behind these expressions of sentiment, but they seem, in truth, to intend nothing beyond a general "world-view" (or better, "self-view") and its particular sense of moral opprobrium. Thus they run from Lord Kames's inveighings against inflated, unrestrained, "emotional extravagance," or false feelings and their expressions,[9] through warnings from motherly types against novel-reading in general, particularly of the Gothic kind, to the elegant spoofing and vivid depiction of the consequences of unreserved emotionality by Jane Austen.

C. Rousseau

For the most seriously reflective treatment of sentiment, one must, like Sterne, cross to France, where Rousseau, contemporaneously with Hume, is recovering—or constructing—the modern self as it is by nature, both by self-inspection and through a philosophical or "hypothetical" history of mankind's staged development from savage to civilized man.[10]

As the writings of the English "age of sensibility" were social in the drawing-room sense, so Rousseau's sentiments are social in the civic sense. Natural man, Rousseau says in his *Second Discourse*,[11] is animated by two "first and simplest operations of the soul," principles that are sentiments preceding reason: love-of-self (*amour de soi*), which is the ardent interest in one's own self-preservation and well-being, and pity, which is our natural repugnance to seeing any sensitive being suffer; pity moderates love-of-self. *Sentiments* abound in Rousseau, and they morph into each other as mankind becomes civilized: healthy self-love (*amour de soi*) into vain self-regard (*amour propre*), pity into the reasoning philosopher's self-isolation from suffering, the solitary savage's primitive sentiment of existence into the solitary thinker's pure "sentiment of existence unmixed with any emotion," that is, the momentary happiness of idle reverie.[12] Rousseau thinks of this state as the only one of which one might say, "Would that this moment could last for ever." Goethe's Faust answers, saying to his devil:

> Were I to say to any moment
> You are so beautiful, oh stay!
> Then may you cast me into fetters
> Then shall I perish with a will.[13]

The two quotations seem to me to show the difference between proto- and full-blown Romanticism: from reverie to restlessness.

What then is a *sentiment*? I make it out to be neither a propensity for any particular passion, nor an object-focused emotion, nor quite emotionality in general, but an evolving ready-affect-state, so to speak—an under-lying feeling of a certain protean quality, coming in various hues. In its constructed indeterminacy, it fits Rousseau's way of philosophizing, which is a daring exposé of the degenerated human condition supported by a secu-larized historicizing myth of the Fall, the very antithesis of Thomas's siting of the human soul in an atemporal metaphysical economy.

D. German Romanticism

I now jump over to the German Romantics (named from the revived medi-eval romances, the chivalric, exotic, and overtly emotional tales, that had come into vogue). Romanticism, a multifarious movement united by a dis-tinctive type of emotionality, is the common denomination of this clan. Rousseau had exercised great influence on the *Sturm und Drang* ("Storm and Stress"), the early literary phase of German Romanticism, particularly through his *Confessions*.[14] But that sentiment of self—which was for Rous-seau so oddly characteristic at once of the natural savage and the renatural-ized sage, a sentiment which he thinks would, as things are at present, not be good for men other than himself to experience[15]—now becomes an ele-ment in a movement, and a way of life. Romantics have a characteristic "life-course." It is a life of daydreams and reveries together with an unbalancing entanglement of the conscious and unconscious, resulting in "a hovering and wavering" about life's choices and in a gravitation toward misfortune, whose ground is an overwrought sensibility and a heavy-weighing sensu-ality. In this dark soil, however, bloom "the charming flowers of phantasy," and along with them a poignant striving for light and freedom.[16]

The chief of such flowers is "the blue flower" of Novalis's *Heinrich von Ofterdingen,* Romanticism's emblematic novel, begun in 1799—and char-acteristically unfinished. The blue flower stands for the bluish vapor of the Infinite, that beckoning non-goal that Romantics, like the hero Heinrich, are in search of. It was, evidently, not just the poet's young death that prevented the novel's completion. *The Blue Flower* (1995) is a perceptive fictional account by Penelope Fitzgerald of the period in Novalis's short and charac-teristic "life-course" when he was writing his novel. It paints the Romantic picture: unaccountable in love, attracted to illness and death, longing for the indefinable, and devoted to an incompletable search.

It is impossible not to mention the philosophically serious Schiller here. Although he was on bad terms with the more self-indulgent German Romantic circle, in his defining essay delineating two poetic modes, "On Naive and Sentimental Poetry" (1795), he declares himself a sentimental poet. This "sentimental" category captures the non-objective, world-inflect-ing inwardness of disciplined Romanticism, as opposed to the simple, straight, childlike, grand relation to nature of vital Classicism. The poets of this latter mode (whose incarnation is Goethe) *are* nature and are the *guardians* of nature; the former *seek* nature and are the *avengers* of nature lost. This is pretty strong language, which, however, does delineate the deep essence of romanticism anywhere, anytime: feeling-charged, reactive subjectivity. The rest is antic by-play.

Thus an acute analyst of romanticism as it resonates in politics says in 1919, "The philosophical problem of the age [is] the opposition of thought and being and the irrationality of the real." The consequence of the romantic's living his life in a "subjectivist reserve" is that he cannot find real reality. The political result is not indifferent: The supposed revolutionary romantic's waffling before reality entails leaving things as they are—the inadvertent conservatism of radical dreamers.[17]

I should say here that there is one Romantic poet, Hölderlin, the most difficult and philosophically interpretable of them all, who feels particularly close to Rousseau. He wrote an ode to him and, in the hymn called "The Rhine," actually alludes to the very Rousseauian reverie cited above. One interpretation has it that Hölderlin understands Rousseau as announcing in that reverie a turn from sense perception to the sentiment of existence, thus going beyond the old primacy of the sensuous object to a new "ontological priority of *consciousness* over the object." This would indeed be the "crucial moment in the development of Western thought."[18]

A question relevant to my project—to understand theories of passion (by now emotion) in their philosophical framework—is whether there is in fact Romantic philosophy—or can be; its harsh critic, Heinrich Heine, doubts it.[19] Thus German Romantics indeed associated themselves with German Idealists, with Kant, Fichte, Schelling, and Hegel, who generally failed to reciprocate. I trust the assessment of the logician, Rudolf Carnap, who speaks of Romanticism as a "life-feeling" (*Lebensgefühl*) and *ipso facto* not quite compatible with an all-too-systematic philosophical idealism.[20] For what came *to* the Romantics in feeling-fraught meditations—Novalis called philosophy "properly nostalgia, a striving to be at home everywhere"[21]— came *from* the philosophers as laboriously rational "ground-works." In some fundamental respects, the two camps were indeed on common ground: subjectivity as self-conscious selfhood, radical individuality up to solipsism, imagination as the world-making faculty, and a fascination with infinity. But the so-called idealistic systems were not *the* grounding for Romanticism; in fact these philosophers were, as I said, leery of Romantic extravagances.

Most to my point, however, the great Idealists offer no extended thematic treatments of the emotions. One might, of course, say that Hegel, the ultimate Idealist but also the modern Aristotle, writes, as did Aristotle, about nothing but desire, and desire is surely a feeling. It is, however, the desire (*Begierde*) not for an opposing object, but *for itself.* Abstractly put: The self, the desiring subject, strives to develop *itself* as the desired substance. Humanly put: We strive to bring out what is in us and to appropriate what is other so that the world we conceive is both ours and real. The logic of this progress is a dialectic of desire.[22] But this is, after all, not so much a philosophy of affect, as affect serving as the motor of philosophy.

E. Kant's Anthropology

However, one of the four, the least Romantic, indeed usually reckoned to belong to the late Enlightenment, wrote quite a bit on the affects—Kant. He is the very philosopher whose morality Coleridge, the most philosophically inclined of the English Romantics, rejects as "false, unnatural, and even immoral . . . [because] he treats the affections as indifferent . . . in ethics." Thus, in his *Critique of Practical Reason,* Coleridge observes, Kant holds to the stoic principle that a man acts more virtuously when he does so from mere duty than when "his *affections* were aidant to, and congruous with, his Conscience."[23]

Coleridge's charge is not false. Kant in his critical works, even in his work on esthetics, the *Critique of Judgment* (1790), finds the affects and passions cognitively inconvenient; indeed, he sounds like a Stoic:

> But in fact any affect is blind, either in the selection of its purpose, or, if that were to have been given by reason, in achieving it. For an affect is an agitation of the mind that makes it unable to engage in free deliberation about principles with the aim of determining itself according to them.

In a footnote to this passage Kant distinguishes affects from passions as occasional bad from settled worse:

> Affects relate merely to feeling, whereas passions belong to our power of desire and our inclinations that make it difficult or impossible for us to determine our power of choice through principle. Affects are impetuous and unpremeditated, passions persistent and deliberate.[24]

The feeling of pleasure (and unpleasure) fares somewhat better, since it is functional. It is not merely a state, but one of the three representational faculties of the soul and, moreover, in a mediating position: cognition, pleasure, and desire.[25]

Kant's economy of psychic powers as sited in his system is brought together in his *Anthropology from a Pragmatic Point of View* (1798). "Pragmatic" here describes an inquiry into what humans as freely acting beings do, can, and should do. Such a "philosophical anthropology" relies on a system of mental presentations as well as on experience of the world. (Kant charmingly observes in a footnote that a cosmopolitan city like Königsberg on the River Pregel is a place sufficient for gaining knowledge of both humanity and the world.)[26]

The *Anthropology* is, *mirabile dictu*, pleasant reading and full of wonderful detail. It proves that it is indeed not for any want of practical experience or acute observation on his part that Kant's ethics is so uncompromisingly rational—meaning that to be moral is basically to be rationally self-consistent, that is, uncompromisingly principled.

What is of most relevance here is his naming and systematizing of the capabilities of the soul (*Gemüt*) engaged in the affective life, which occurs in Part I of the book. Of course, cognition comes first. The *Anthropology* being a post-Critical work, the account is an empirical, introspective, psychological version of the soul, consistent with his three *Critiques* (*of Pure Reason, of Practical Reason, of Judgment*, 1781–90). Accordingly, the first book of Part I is about the cognitive aspect of the soul, which has an acting faculty (*facultas*) and a passive receptivity (*receptivitas*)—understanding and sensing. Here, however, cognition is not considered in the mode of the *Critiques*, as "transcendental," that is, as the ground of "pure" experience, but as embodied experience based on the physical senses and the sense-derived imagination.

The second book deals with pleasure and unpleasure (*Lust, Unlust*), sensual and intellectual. They comprise "feeling" (*Gefühl*), the middle of the three root-aspects of the human soul: ". . . [Feelings] cannot at all be explicated on their own; . . . we cannot have insight into them but only feel them . . . and consequently we can explicate them only in a meager way . . ."[27] It is of course a—rare—explicit statement of the very problem anyone writing on the feelings meets with first, that of trying to know oneself as a non-cognitive consciousness.

Sensual pleasure is called "delight" (*Vergnügen*) and is understood in Spinoza's way as our feeling that life is being advanced, "unpleasure" as the feeling that it is hindered. Kant follows an old notion that every delight must be preceded by a pain, that animal life is a "continual interplay of the antagonism of pleasure and pain." Not only is pain "the goad of activity," but a continual increase of delight-pleasure would in fact lead to "a quick death by joy." What a way to die!

Kant asks the question broached in the Platonic *Philebus*: whether delight is just a negative, the relief from pain, or is actually positive, the prospective sense of an amenity. We can guess beforehand that only the first can happen, for time drags us irreversibly from what is present to what is to come, and the only cause of the feeling of delight can be that we must necessarily go out of this present, though it is undetermined into which other present we will enter, as long as it is in fact an other.

Kant seems to be saying that time, in the *Critiques* our "inner sense," has a forward structure such that pleasure is for us essentially in change—not an atemporal bloom on our activity as for Aristotle, but a release from pain with an uncertain prospect. Thus Kant's first example of delight is the attraction of gambling, because it is a continual alternation of fear and hope.

Intellectual pleasure is the feeling for beauty or "taste" (*Geschmack*). It is the ability—a higher version of the primary sense of its name, a capacity of the tongue to be specifically affected by the "smack" of sensory matter—to judge beauty and to appreciate the outward signs of morality. Its particular agency is the imagination.

So far Kant has presented the root-faculties of cognition and feeling. The third, desire, is to follow below.

F. Schopenhauer, Nietzsche

Here I am drawn to digress into the future, to follow a ways the fate of "feeling," that is, pleasure and pain. Whereas for Kant pain is merely temporally prior to pleasure, Schopenhauer sees it as absolutely first. It is a view consonant with his understanding in *The World as Will and Representation* (1844) of human being as essentially an incessant striving to live—the *Philebus* problem fraught with *Weltschmerz*:

> Every human life without exception courses on between willing and attaining. Wish is in its very nature pain: Attainment quickly gives birth to satiety: The goal was only apparent: Possession takes away the charm.
>
> There follows either a new want or a consequent desolation, emptiness, or boredom; the battle against these latter is as much torture as is the fight against acute want: Whatever nature or luck may have done, . . . the pain essential to life cannot be avoided. . . . The unceasing efforts to dispel suffering achieve nothing more than to change its shape.[28]

Nietzsche in turn will criticize Schopenhauer as fundamentally misunderstanding and devaluing the will by taking desire, instinct, drive, to be its essence. Schopenhauer's view is, to be sure, not quite that of the major tradition, for there the will is *rational* desire. But his perspective is abetted by the fact that in German the verbal noun "willing" is *Wollen,* which also means "wanting, desiring" simply. Nietzsche takes this "driven" view as a misconstruction which leads to a feeble hatred of the will and to an attempt— which Schopenhauer is indeed guilty of—to relieve us of its lashings, to subvert it in favor of a will-less, pure, disinterested contemplation that seeks to see the world of appearance as a purely esthetic representation. Nietzsche thinks of the will rather as the master of the desires; it is what shows them "their way and measure," in a world whose appearances are not a show but our reality.[29]

It follows immediately that Nietzsche revalues the feeling of pleasure. It had been an accompanying bloom of activity; it had been a mediating judge of desire. For him it is a sense of the increase, as unpleasure is a sense of the decrease, of power: "Where pleasure appears there power was felt," he says.[30] This is sheer Neospinozism, the universal impulse to maintain existence by exerting power, and pleasure as the sense of the transition from less to more existence—albeit now set not in a pantheistic but a panatheistic world. It bears on this point that Nietzsche in his descent to Hades was admitted to converse with Spinoza along with other heroes of his; they seemed to him— and to me—more alive than the living.[31]

Thus pleasure is for Nietzsche a differential feeling, the conscious sense of an increase of power, as a decrease is noticed through a weaker pleasure down to unpleasure, and this is decadence. Unpleasure is now no longer the pessimist's inescapable cross, but the motive ingredient of, the necessary goad to, all action, since force can release itself only where there is resistance. So here unpleasure works as the stimulus and charm of life (*Reiz* means both) and strengthens the will to power. Pleasure, then, registers the differential in power. But more. Nietzsche ratchets up the sum of pleasure: Pain and unpleasure are not really opposites, for if pleasure is described as a "plus-feeling" of power, unpleasure is not thereby defined as a pleasure's negative. On the contrary, pleasure might also be said to be "a rhythm of small unpleasure-stimuli"; the great example is sexual intercourse. But this definition is not convertible (as it would be if the terms were truly coincident): Many little accesses of pleasure do not (as Kant thought) in their turn result in pain (Nietzsche here seems to use unpleasure, *Unlust*, and pain, *Schmerz*, more or less interchangeably). Moreover, since pleasure and unpleasure are not, after all, causes but concomitants and thus value judgments of second rank, it is not these feelings that human beings really seek but "a plus of power." So much the less is it true that "man strives for happiness."[32]

So pleasure was for Kant a feeling at the center of the soul, a flight from pain and thus a spur to action in time; it was for Schopenhauer submerged in the want at the base of human nature, reduced to its negative, the inescapably burdensome pole of pain that invites escape into esthetic contemplation; and it is now for Nietzsche the measure of the living being's consciousness of its power, paradoxically merged with its negative, pain, to increase its potency. This sketch history of Central European pleasure has turned into a story of pain!

Now that Nietzsche is on the scene a reader might wonder why his works do not play a larger role in this book. I know no writer who is a more formidably acute—and dangerously subversive—psychologist of passion. But his insights are delivered over a number of books in aphorisms that flow together in a powerful drift but don't seem to be meant to cohere in an ordered theory. Nietzsche represents himself as reacting both against Rousseau's self-pampering submission to sentiment with its unbridled *ressentiment,* a mood-like feeling of social inferiority, and against Romanticism, in which Christian and Rousseauian ideals join with its false cult of emotional extremism to form a complex born not of strength but of neediness.[33] He is thus reacting against the reaction to the coolly rational Enlightenment but without at all returning to it.

Spinoza—who, recall, is Nietzsche's predecessor in regarding human existence as fundamentally expansive—did, just for that reason, denigrate the passions for their passivity; Nietzsche, however, accepts them for their reality: Let it be, he says,

> posited that nothing is "given" as real but our world of desires and passions and that we can't get up or down to any other "reality" but just to the reality of our instincts (*Triebe*).[34]

And, as we have just heard, he exalts them in their vehemence. We lust even for a deep pain. Passion when it has passed leaves behind a "dark longing." The moderate sensations seem insipid in comparison. "One prefers, it seems, any vehement pain over flabby pleasure."[35] It is his recurrent theme that it is one of "the great crimes of psychology" to have branded all strong feelings of pleasure, among them high spirits, lustiness, pride, and daring, as sinful temptations. So too are the moralists guilty who demand the extirpation rather than the control of passion, who want to dry up rather than impose an economy of affect on the grand desires, the passions of power, of love, of vengeance. In sum, mastery over the passions, not their weakening or extermination! The greater the master-force of the will, the more freedom the passions may be allowed. For the fear of the passions is already a symptom of weakness, of a collapsing forcefulness in the vigorous inhibiting of the impulse. There are three types of passion, each making its own demand on a soundly potent discipline. There are dominating passions, which are actually the supreme form of health, almost its definition; there are opposing and conflicting passions, very unhealthy for causing inner ruin; there is a contiguity of various passions without contradiction or connection, healthy but changeable without going anywhere.[36]

Thus Nietzsche demands control of the passions for the sake of their concentration. (Note, incidentally, that Nietzsche has reinvented Hume's passion-chemistry.) And so, in the defense of that anti-metaphysical metaphysical root of human being, the Will to Power—it seems, oddly, to need a lot of protection—Nietzsche wants "to transmute all the *Leidenschaften* of humanity into *Freudenschaften*"—"suffering-passions" into "joying-passions."[37] Consequently he is rich in *aperçus* about the management of the passions, beginning with their cultivation. The "salient point" in allowing the replete soul-vessel to overflow into overt anger or love is an extra drop of "good will toward passion (which is commonly called the evil one)." He warns against the courtly attempt to suppress the vulgarity of passionate expression without repressing the passions themselves; the ultimate outcome would change the passions into a graceful game. He points out the danger to the free, restless, living spirit of letting passions become opinions and letting these in turn, from the inertia of spirit, rigidify into inflexible convictions.[38]

Next, he mounts a fierce, obsessive attack on what one might call the mingy passions, in particular the aforementioned *ressentiment*, the territory of the "physiologically unlucky and worm-eaten, a whole quivering worldly realm of underground vengeance, inexhaustible, insatiable in outbreaks against the lucky, happy ones," the reaction of herd-man, characteristic of the morality of slaves.[39] It is interesting that the passion for freedom that Kant, the republican, recognizes as humanly first is for Nietzsche, the exceptionalist, part of a slave-morality: The aristocrats revel in reverence and devotion.[40] Which aristocrats were these? one wonders.

But the focus of Nietzsche's antipathy, so pervasive as to bring down on him what this master of psychological exposé must least have wished for, a suspicion about his own human-all-too-human humanity, is pity—*Mitleid* in German, which might be translated as "suffering-along"; "sympathy" is the exact Greek-derived term. The Stoic tradition and Spinoza in its train had disapproved of pity as a vain duplication of suffering, but Nietzsche truly despises it. Christianity is a religion of pity, of sympathy with God— "the excess of 'pity for God' belongs in a democratic age"; so does pity for social distress, for society with all its unfortunate, vice-ridden, and broken ones, with the rebellious oppressed who "long for mastery and call it freedom." Nietzsche offers a higher, more long-range pity, the pity for the diminution of humanity that follows from the attempt to do away with grand suffering. His pity, whose object is no particular individual "with" whom he suffers, is for the general waste of precious potencies.[41]

As it is socially diminishing, so pity is personally demeaning. He describes it, an all too recognizable picture of aspects of our therapy culture, as

> the shabby characteristic of sympathizing that has as companion the effrontery to insist absolutely on being helpful, and intrudes its quackery without the slightest hesitation over the cause and kind of the sickness.[42]

As it happens, pity is not the only psychic motion that puts paid to passion. There is also a healthy obituary for sentiment: The Nietzsche I savor, mordantly pointed, not globally overwrought, says, "A witticism is an epigram on the death of a feeling."[43]

I think Nietzsche uses "affect" more broadly than "passion": It is psychic arousal with the element of pro and con. "To live with an enormous and proud composure (*Gelassenheit*), always apart—. At will to have and not to have one's affects, one's for and against, to condescend to them, for hours on end . . ."—this is the opposite of the vehement emotion, the sudden discharge of a wild affect, used by the sickly to find someone to blame and to dull their pain.[44] Thus for Nietzsche the quality of any affect lives in its discipline, in a lightly-handled subjection to the pressure of a will that is not repressive but concentrating.

Asked for the origin of affects, Nietzsche goes bluntly—and very modernly—physiological: "Affects are a construction of the intellect, a *fiction of causes* which don't exist." A reason is sought in something injuriously, dangerously alien, so as to make our bad mood intelligible. Thus generalized somatic sensations are interpreted in affective terms. For example, a flow of blood into the brain with a sensation of choking becomes so regularly associated with certain sights that we call the event anger and say that "the affect was aroused" by these sights, that is, by an opinion of their relation to us. But it is a belief in miracles to suppose that affects, physiologically based, are excited by opinions. It is really the case that each such excitation already includes a judgment on itself, an answer to the question: Does it further our feeling of power or not?[45] This is Nietzsche's version of the appraisal theory of emotion.

Physiology is not, however, ultimate after all, since it is but an expression of a prior cause:

> The question is finally whether we acknowledge the will as actually *acting,* whether we have faith in the causality of the will: If we do—and at bottom our faith in that is just our faith in causality itself—then we must make the attempt to posit the will's causality hypothetically as the only one.[46]

I said earlier that Nietzsche's treatment of the passionate affects is more a drift than a system. By now it may have become clear that it has to be that way, since his philosophizing inextricably combines two features: It is personal and historical. It is personal in that his insights are, drop by aphoristic drop, more the distillation of an intellectual agony than the products of constructive thought. Their occasion is the present decadence, the diminution and demeaning of present humanity, and—who knows?—perhaps anxiety about the potency of his own passions. It is historical in that his perspective is genuinely temporal (rather than timeless), envisioning the Western past under the aspect of a glory-seamed decline, the present as a pivotal prelude to a new age, and the future as the restoration of degenerated mankind. Nietzsche is the depth-historian of the past, the clear-headedly agonized watcher of the present and of the future—if not the divinely inspired prophet, yet both the illuminated announcer of a hoped-for salvation and the cool prognosticator of a historical necessity. And that's the difficulty, at least for me. For to regard him as a mere contemplative would be an insult. Then to whom, for what, are these books written? Is he agitating for a historical necessity? Is he an activist empowering power? These questions arise, but happily needn't be resolved, in these pages.

Nietzsche does, after all, finally introduce two "metaphysical" principles. One, the "Eternal Return," is intended to give some sense of stability to the uncertainties of temporal unwinding in the long—very long—run and some ground for prognosticating and accommodating the immediate future. This circle-like principle is related to the second one, the Will to Power, *conceptually* as movement to mover but *actually* as an identity: Will and Return as one *are* this very self-moved, ever-recurrent becoming. Analyzed out, it is the principle of motion, the *Will*, that bears directly on human passion—in philosophy as their ultimate explanation and in reality as their cause. And yet it actually *is* the world itself, self-created, self-destroyed. So it might be called *causa sui*, its own cause:

> It lives off itself: Its excrements are its nutrients. . . . This world is the Will to Power—and nothing beyond. And you yourself are this Will to Power—and nothing beyond.[47]

What a strange coincidence, once more, with Spinoza's God, and what a divide in affect!

I hope I will be forgiven for this long disruptive leap ahead. It is meant to show how differently such elementary affects as pleasure and pain—"feelings" *par excellence*—appear under different philosophical frameworks. I am acutely aware that such synopses in their disparate perspectives cannot succeed in delivering the full wisdom of the texts—though perhaps a foretaste. I want to remind the reader here that an earlier account of pleasure and desire in texts by Plato, Aristotle, Freud, and in recent research was similarly chronologically out of order though thematically in place [Ch. II, Secs. 6–9]. These temporal displacements are, in part, expressions of my small faith in the power of time over human nature. There is, to be sure, novelty, which is by definition time-positioned, but is it thereby time-conditioned? But back to Kant's desire.

G. Back to Kant

The third book of the *Anthropology* then treats of the third root-faculty (cognition and feeling having preceded), that of desire or appetition (*Begierde, appetitio*). The definition of desire is typically Kantian. It appears abstractly remote and springs back suddenly into common experience:

> Desire is the self-determining of the power of the subject through the representation of something futural as an effect of that representation.

In simpler words: To desire is to represent to ourselves in the imagination something yet to come and by that image to rouse our ability to act. A mere wish is, then, such an imagined object without any investment of power in the actual "production" of the object or situation. There is also a "moody" (*launische*) wish, a desire without definite object (*appetitio vaga*), which is only the empty longing to leave behind one's present condition.

Habitual sensual desire is called inclination. An inclination which the subject, that is, an "I," cannot or can hardly control is a passion; here self-determining is more like self-affecting. The German word is revealing: *Leidenschaft*, "the condition of suffering." Kant distinguishes, as I said, passion from affect, which is more immediate; it is a feeling of pleasure or unpleasure in a present situation which does not even allow the consideration whether or not to surrender to the feeling to arise in the subject. Affect takes the soul by surprise through a sentiment that disrupts the psychic lay-out. "Affect acts like water that breaks through the dyke; passion like a stream that digs itself ever more deeply into its channel." Affect and passion are each other's reciprocal—the more of the one, the less of the other.

Kant, who likes quantitative descriptions of feeling, has a second definition of passion: Passion occurs when the reason is prevented from comparing one inclination with the sum of all, when its calculation of comprehensively sound desirability fails. If affect is intoxication, passion is—in the Stoic vein—sickness. For desire is satisfied and stilled by the attainment of its object, but passion is always connected with a rationally based persistence—which is why animals are not passionate. Here is Kant's acknowledgement that human passion is shot through with abetting rationality. Consequently passion can be palliated but not cured, nor does it want to be, reason having lost its universality and become a rationalizing partisan.

As Thomas divided passions into desirous and harsh, so Kant divides them into "ardent" and "frigid." The ardent passions are combined with affect and come in two kinds, the inclinations for freedom and for sex. The cold ones are the passion for honor, domination, acquisition (*Ehrsucht, Herrschsucht, Habsucht*; Kant points out that these words end in *sucht*, "sickness," as in *Fallsucht*, falling sickness or epilepsy).

What seems remarkable here is the very notion of a passion for freedom as individually congenital—the newborn already cries because it does not have the freedom of its members—and as historically primitive. The former is a Kantian idea, but the latter is Rousseauian, for Rousseau thinks that the natural savage will be socialized out of his primitive natural love of freedom.[48] It is the more remarkable since mature freedom, one of Kant's central preoccupations, turns out to be the very opposite of a passion: It consists in the use of our will, a higher, transcendental, non-sensuous faculty of desire, to thwart our personal inclination in the interests of a universal morality. What intervenes is educational discipline; the road to freedom is through necessity—obedience.[49]

The work ends with the highest physical good, the greatest sensual enjoyment—rest after work—and the highest moral-physical good—human socializing. There follows a disquisition on dinner parties, for: "To eat alone (*solipsismus convictorii*) is unhealthy for a philosophizing scholar." Sometimes Kant is in his writing—as he was in life—positively charming, here in a grayish, hypochondriac way: rest after work as the greatest sensual enjoyment! Well, perhaps in the long run.

In the (still-current) debate over the nature and relation of desire, feelings of pleasure, and cognition, Kant takes a clear position. These are three separate powers of the soul, and they are not derivable from a common basis. I can think of no ancient who thought, as Kant does, of the feeling of pleasure as a *faculty* or a part of the soul.[50] For the ancients it is always a concomitant or reaction, whereas for Kant it is a sort of non-rational judgment, as the "estimative" sense was for Thomas and emotion will later be for some cognitivists.

Cognition is in turn tripartite; one might go so far as to say that the tripartite soul as a whole is in fact a kind of magnification of this cognitive trio. In order not to burden the reader with what would be an exposition of the *Critique of Pure Reason*, I will simply say that the power of interest here is a middle and mediating faculty between Reason and Understanding. It is called Judgment, and its function is to decide whether an instance falls under a given rule; in this operation the imagination is crucial. To Judgment as a part of cognition, corresponds Feeling (pleasure and unpleasure) in the soul as a whole, to Practical Reason (rational desire or Will) corresponds Desire in the whole—the highest faculty to the nethermost.

The Epicureans accorded the two feelings they recognized, pleasure and pain, the function of judging choices and avoidances.[51] So also for Kant, this feeling-faculty of the soul judges, by finding objects agreeable or disagreeable (presumably with the help of *understanding*), whether a desire is to be engendered and pursued, whether its object agrees "with the subjective conditions of life."[52] Here lower, sensory desire has *pleasure*-feeling as its *antecedent*. For the higher rational desire, the will, it is, however, the other way around: The good will is attended by a *moral* feeling as its *consequence*. It is a special sense of self-contentment, the satisfaction in having done one's duty.[53] Thus, while the highest and lowest faculty share the name Desire, they are each other's inverses in their relation to feeling.

Kant in fact distinguishes the upper and lower desires just referred to as *Begehren* and *Begierde*, wanting and lusting. There are all sorts of fascinating implications, for one thing, the soul, cognitively top-heavy, is a disparate collection. The faculties are, to be sure, very systematically interrelated and, moreover, inhere in the subject, the self. But they have no common ground—understanding, pleasure, desire are ultimately distinct. Whereas for Aristotle and Plato there was something that bespoke a common root, something sensuous or sense-like in the highest desire and something amenable to rational control in the lowest, while pleasure was not judge but participant, for Kant there is only hard suppression of sensuous inclination by rational will, a battle of non-kindred faculties.

Another novelty is the interposition of pleasure and unpleasure as a *feeling* coming *between* two powers or faculties. In Plato's *Republic* this was the place of "fuming" spiritedness, one of whose affects Kant has relegated to the "cold passions" of desire as *Ehrsucht*. This is clearly a post-classical human being, in whom pleasure rather than spiritedness mediates between knowing and desiring.

A third observation is that feeling is positioned as non-cognitive; it merely expresses the condition of the subject itself, and this complete subjectivity is demonstrated by the fact that feeling does not refer to an object. We do, to be sure, take pleasure *in* an object (or pleasure could not "judge," that is, react to the object), but pleasure does not "intend," is not directed *to* an object, it rather flows from the object. Therefore feeling, that is, pleasure, does not give us objective knowledge of an object[54] but only of ourselves in relation to it. Pleasure had been thought of variously as a proto-passion, a passion, an accompaniment of fulfilled desire, and of fulfilling activity. Now it is the central ultimate constituent of the soul as subject, feeling in a restricted sense: Feeling *par excellence,* self-feeling, feeling one's feelings.

Here, then, is the fourth implication: Looked at analytically, Kant's notion of feeling as objectless subjectivity, as representationless self-feeling, is not so different from what I have called mood. It is as if he were giving official recognition to a hitherto unformulated capacity of the soul: As the cognitive subject can turn on itself reflectively in (Critical) thinking, so the affective self can stay subjectively within itself in what Kant calls feeling. Perhaps, then, Kant, the champion of Enlightenment, has a central affinity with Romanticism, after all.

H. Back to Romanticism

The Romanticism I have presented is selective; I have dwelt on its objectless subjectivity and its essayistic philosophy. But the Romantics were also great collectors of folktales, recorders of tradition, researchers into language, passionate botanizers and cosmologists, deeply interested in the organic wholeness and significance of the phenomenal world. Novalis himself, as well as being a deep student of the cognitive subject as it appears in Kant and his successors Fichte and Schelling, was a devotee of mathematics. Yet mathematics was for him "the element of the magician," in the sense that he was preoccupied with Kant's problem of "synthetic a priori judgments." These are judgments in which the human subject brings forth *out of itself,* on the basis of a deep hidden productive power called the *transcendental imagination,* terms and propositions which have a content that goes beyond a mere analysis of a sentence's subject term. Among those synthetic, non-empirical, propositions are the concepts and axioms of mathematics. Novalis appropriates Kant's cognitive theory to ask, "Is there an . . . absolute art of discovery? Is a genius possible . . . ? Is magic possible?" And he says, "Everything real created out of the *Nothing,* as for instance the numbers, . . . has a wonderful affinity with things of another world. . . ." Mathematics is for him "a product of mental self-activity"—the antithesis of Hume's empirical mathematics, mathematics derived from experience.[55]

Here, finally, is an example of the subject-centered mathematicizing that seems to preoccupy Romantic writers:[56] In ancient astronomy the circle, with its single center about which is circumscribed a self-congruent periphery on which a star is borne in uniform motion, was the symbol of perfection. Now the ellipse comes to the fore as "not only a human- but a world-hieroglyphic." Its double foci, light from each one of which is reflected from the curve into the other, symbolize reflective human self-consciousness, while as an orbit its variable curvature expresses the non-uniform, anomalous motion of the planets—and of human souls.[57] Thus the very cosmos becomes an expression of our inwardness.

The sentimentalism and Romanticism I have so scantily delineated were not only a new individual but also a new *social* phenomenon. By "social" I mean that people who were similarly circumstanced infected each other, as Hume discovered of himself. I have no doubt at all that people throughout our Western history, even those redoubtably "naïve" Greeks, have always been moody, that is, in fancy terms, endogenously affective—most certainly so in Hellenistic, Roman, and Medieval times—and that these affects were partly social dis-eases. Augustine's *Confessions* is the acutely observed and candidly memorialized account of the moody unease suffered together by a band of friends, until the author himself, their leader, was, by conclusive conversion, released from the sensual and intellectual entanglements that had been at once the precondition for and the obstacle to faith.

Once more: How does any affective mode, how does this moody emotionality in particular, become a social movement? What brings it about that people open themselves to and find in themselves, ways of feeling that then become acknowledged and even respectable? What caused mood to become one of the signature feelings for our time? I don't have an answer.

For while I find all the explanations advanced by the human disciplines suggestive, they also seem to be inherently inconclusive. Those in terms of historical antecedents are non-necessary; those in terms of social conditions are circular; those in terms of psychic constitutions are hypothetical. I suspect that large explanatory terms are at bottom summary, often merely metaphorical names for the phenomena whose causes they are meant to state. Even so directly acting a cause as weather—the diaphanous ether of the Hellenic heavens as opposed to the low, lowering sky of northern Europe—are more similitudes of moods than explanations. To be sure, the Romantic phase called "Storm and Stress" expresses in its name its consonant atmospherics; the Gothic-Romantic novel *Wuthering Heights* by Emily Brontë is a prime example of the actual influence of stormy weather on mood. Yet was it not the Mediterranean Stoics who started us on the road to inwardness and the African Augustine who wrote its greatest account?

A new music divorced from liturgy and turned expressive, a new religion turned from dogma and works to self-searching and faith, a new bourgeoisie and its pampered women deprived of purpose,[58] a new devotion to human individuality paradoxically exacerbated by social constraints—all these "causes" (and dozens more that we could all produce within the hour) seem to me, then, to be descriptions more than explanations. But happily I have not included it within my brief to solve the problem of the possibility of intelligible history or of explanatory social science: whether the historians' eras and the social scientists' structures present to us real originary forces or just *ex post facto* summations.

All the preceding part of my penultimate chapter was intended to lay a predicate for Kierkegaard's discussion of the mood of anxiety, the most meaning-fraught of all modern affects, whether we know why or not. To get there I have largely bypassed the English Romantics—Kierkegaard's philosophical roots were German—who differ from the continental ones (with whom they were indeed acquainted) more in style than in this essence:[59] a preference for a diffuse sort of emotionality and a willingness (or perhaps a necessity) to turn over their grounding to philosophers in whose hands it is then no longer Romanticism but Rationalism. Even Coleridge, philosophically inclined as he was, cried out about himself, "O Lord! What thousands of Threads in how large a Web may not a Metaphysical Spider spin out of the Dirt of his own Guts / but alas! It is a net for his own super-ingenious Spidership alone!"[60]

Kierkegaard was an irate anti-Hegelian, but he is at one with Hegel about a characteristic feature of German Romanticism: "Romantic irony." Friedrich Schlegel, *the* Romantic spokesman, says that irony has its proper home in philosophy and that it is "on the inner side the mood that overlooks everything and raises itself instantly above everything conditioned. . . ." Hegel protests against irony as willful "infinite absolute negativity," as the "feeling of the empty, vain subject" and its "self-conscious frustration of what is objective."[61] Kierkegaard borrows Hegel's terms of criticism for his dissertation *The Concept of Irony* (1841). In his own words:

> [I]n irony the subject continually wants out of the object, which it achieves by being at every moment conscious of the unreality of the object.[62]

I cite Kierkegaard's negative relation to Romanticism here to engage in a speculation: Like irony, mood in its objectless negating subjectivity might be said to be inherently Romantic, or better romantic, that is, not bound to a period but rather to a set of characteristics. Could Kierkegaard's novel, positive, interpretation of that non-object be regarded as a way to save anxiety and its moody mode from Romantic-style philosophizing, so as to accord it depth with hyper-epochal precision?

3. Anxious about Nothing: Kierkegaard and the Mood of Freedom

Whether we are lapped in pleasure, constrained by misery, or dully suspended between these, mood is generally recognized as being about nothing in particular. That is how it is distinguished from emotion. It is the difference between feeling blue and feeling grief. Later the question will come forward why the moods of interest to philosophers tend to be downbeat: disgust, nausea, resentment, boredom, anxiety. It is not so surprising about psychiatrists: Who consults a soul-physician about exhibiting even irrational exuberance—unless it is a bipolar phenomenon?

Moods, from black depression, blue devils, brown studies to gray unnamed dis-eases are hard to get at. Emotional imbroglios can be faced down, not so misty moods. Yet they can sometimes be dispelled by diversion.

A. Pascal

That is just what Kierkegaard's true predecessor, Pascal, observed: Men seek diversion; they "are fond of hustle and bustle"; they cannot be alone. "The sole cause of man's unhappiness is that he does not know how to stay quietly in his room." For this is "*Man's condition*: Inconstancy, boredom, anxiety."

> The only good thing for men therefore is to be diverted from thinking of what they are, either by some occupation which takes their mind off it, or by some novel and agreeable passion which keeps them busy, like gambling, hunting, some absorbing show, in short by what is called diversion. [Recall that these two diversions are Hume's philosophy-analogues.]

Why is that? We are cast into finite dimensions in number and time but "the finite is annihilated in the presence of the infinite and becomes pure nothingness. So it is with our mind before God. . . ." Thus our unavoidable condition is:

> *Wretchedness*: The only thing that consoles us for our miseries is diversion. And yet it is the greatest of our miseries. For it is that above all which prevents us

from thinking about ourselves and leads us imperceptibly to destruction. But for that we should be bored, and boredom would drive us to seek more solid means of escape, but diversion passes our time and brings us imperceptibly to death.

The "more solid means of escape," to which boredom is a goad, is faith, which is "God perceived by the heart, not by reason."[1] Pascal seems to me to be speaking of what might be called existential depression, the persistent wretchedness that is inherent in human existence, an existence strung as a tiny finitude between two infinities, the immense and the infinitesimal, while impelled by instinct and passion to mask its situation by diversion. Heidegger will make use of Pascal's notion that boredom might recall us from our dispersion.

An uncircumventable sense of nothingness borne by a persistent mood about nothing in particular it surely more humanly significant than a passing flare-up of emotion. And so mood is now recognized, in the sense of being admitted as a revealing human fact—revealing both of human subjectivity and of man's situation in the world. Recall that the religious tended to suffer from the monk's mood, but that it was not then understood as it is now to be analyzed: as a universal human condition (Pascal) or as an original prelapsarian state (Kierkegaard) or as an existential-metaphysical disclosure (Heidegger). It was rather a sin, a sin of disgust with the monk's vocation, to be cured by concentration on the divine object, not on the human subject.

B. Kierkegaard

Kierkegaard combines the two approaches by discovering anxiety as the answer to a theological problem, which he treats psychologically.

Let me say up front in two sentences what he discovers and sets out in *The Concept of Anxiety* (1844)[2] that is relevant to this book: Anxiety is a mood which is about nothing, as common speech shows. That "nothing" is not mere absence of an object but is the intimation of the possibility of being free—to sin.

Thus Kierkegaard's problem is, to begin with, theological: original sin and its heritability. That is the framework for his understanding of anxiety and his incidental but consequence-laden analysis of mood.

Kierkegaard had thought about anxiety before, in *Either/Or* (1843). There he understood anxiety as a sort of *predisposition* to a sad emotion, "the organ by which the subject appropriates sorrow and assimilates it"; it is reflective rather than objective, as linguistic usage shows: When I say "my sorrow" I can mean the *object* I sorrow over; he thinks "anxiety" is never used that way. Moreover, for us moderns anxiety is temporally extended and not about the momentary present; "Greek sorrow, on the other hand, like the whole of Greek life, is in the present time"[3]—which seems to say that

Greeks didn't have anxiety, surely a half-truth. I think it is safer to say that they didn't make much of it.

Now, in *The Concept of Anxiety,* he goes much deeper. His problem is very precisely set out in the subtitle, to the explication of which Kierkegaard's Introduction is devoted: After "The Concept of Anxiety" comes "A Simple, Psychologically Orienting Deliberation on the Dogmatic Issue of Hereditary Sin." I'll take it back-to-front and briefly. But I must warn that this exposition loses the Kierkegaardian flavor: the colorful complexity at once reconditely learned and eccentrically playful, the recurrent categorizations both obscurely abstract and personal, the dogged anti-Hegelian Hegelianism, the incessant mordant polemicism—and the bold clear strokes of absolute originality breaking through all the baroque indirection.

"Anxiety" is the subject, but its occasion is hereditary sin.[4] "Hereditary sin" (*peccatum haereditarium*) is for Kierkegaard's purpose the more revealing name for original sin (*peccatum originale*), defined by Augustine as both originating and originated sin, that is, as sin which is *both* causal for us and caused by us (*peccatum originans* and *originatum*).

The problem, then, is what sin was and is, such that Adam, created and not born, first became sinful and we, born and not created, became sinful through him. For in both major Christian traditions "Adam enjoys the well-meant honor of being more than the whole race, or the ambiguous honor of standing outside the race." And this, "fantastical" though it be, is indeed Adam's case—but it is also ours. For as first man, or any man, he was "at once himself and the race." That is what it means to be an individual belonging to a genus, a race—to be both himself and the race. So neither was Adam (though first) different from us nor are we as individuals different from him: "Through the first sin, sin came into the world. Precisely in the same way is it true of every subsequent man's first sin that through it sin comes into the world."[5] If sin is thus individual, then the problem of hereditary sin is: How did Adam *first* become sinful and in such a way that we, his heirs, both become sinful *through him* as humans and are also responsible as individuals? This contradiction is the task. Otherwise put: In the tradition, Adam's actual sin precedes the condition of *sinfulness,* that is, the propensity for, or possibility of, sinning, but for subsequent humanity sinfulness—the established possibility of sinning—conditions sin. This means that Adam was at once outside the human race and yet our forefather in sin.

I want to say here that this problem need not be alien to a non-Christian reader: Does the sense of sinfulness, which at least some self-aware people cannot escape, that sense of being likely to be bad and to do everything wrong from way back and aboriginally—does that sense come from our generic humanity or from our individual character? That anxiety, whose theological meaning Kierkegaard will discover, surely has a secular translation.

This problem, sticking with the subtitle, is declared to be a "dogmatic issue," which means that hereditary sin is to be simply accepted as a teaching. Sin must be treated in a certain "mood"—"an error in modulation is just as disturbing as an error in the development of thought." That mood is "earnestness." Sin is not to be treated esthetically, tragically, metaphysically, or even ethically, which modes all dispel that earnest mood. It is most properly the subject of a didactic sermon,[6] delivered dogma.

Instead, Kierkegaard offers a "deliberation," an inquiry more tentative than didactic, which is not so much empirically, positively psychological—for psychology as a science is no more than any other (except dogmatics) suitably modulated for sin—as it is psychologically "orienting": We are directed not toward the observation of actual sins, which are nothing to the point, but toward possibilities. Such psychologizing deliberates on the "real possibility" of subjective sin. Like an Archimedes it sits undisturbed and "traces the contours and calculates the angles of possibility" of possible sin. Dogmatics, on the other hand, deals with its ideal possibility, which means, I think, that it does not involve itself in Adam's subjectivity, his personal proclivities, but in his human capabilities.[7] Finally, the deliberation is called "simple," a word fraught with anti-Hegelian import: Sin is *not* a logical moment to be overcome, annulled, in a dialectical movement; it is and remains insuperably what it is.

Thus Kierkegaard now meditates on the condition of Adam's soul. Was it different from that of subsequent men, who are, because of Adam's sin, born in the condition of "sinfulness"—by which, once again, I understand Kierkegaard to mean the precondition, the propensity for sin? Was he outside of mankind in the primal condition of his soul?

Adam is himself the race; what explains him explains humanity and vice versa. But he committed sin number one, which is different from just any one sin because it *first* brought sin into the world and sinfulness into Adam. This sin was a qualitative leap, a discrete change in man's quality, not a quantitative, continuous accrual of a growing species-propensity. Sin, once in the world, does have such a quantitative history, but it cannot explain how sin is individual yet inherited.[8]

Again: Adam was innocent and lost innocence by guilt, being in that like all succeeding men. So, once more, the question is: What distinguishes the Fall, the first sin? Kierkegaard, once again, resists attempts to build up a continuous "quantitative" explanation—one of which claims that the very prohibition of eating from the tree, in conditioning an escalating concupiscence, led up to the commission of the sin. The psychological explanation he gives "must remain in its elastic ambiguity" from which guilt breaks forth in a qualitative leap. Here is that explanatory ambiguity:[9]

Innocence is ignorance. Kierkegaard takes the story of *Genesis* to say just that. An innocent human being is psychically at one with his natural condition. "The spirit in man is dreaming." Here, spirit is what unites physical and psychical man; it is human self-consciousness, the self-awareness of the soul within a body.

Anxiety is thus, first, "a qualification of dreamy spirit," meaning a change in its essential nature: The pre-self-conscious Adam, when awake, is simply, straightforwardly soul and *also* body, experienced together, simply "posited," a fact. In dreaming, this posited, simply given, unity is suspended and turns into nothing.[10]

Second, anxiety arises in sleep, which is a state

> of repose, but there is simultaneously something else which is [to be sure] not contention and strife, for there is indeed nothing against which to strive. What, then, is it? Nothing. But what effect does nothing have? It begets anxiety.[11]

The concept of anxiety, Kierkegaard points out, is almost never treated in the psychology of his day. It is altogether different from fear, which refers to something definite, whereas anxiety is "freedom's actuality as the possibility of possibility."[12]

This sentence, which editors have emended as an iterating slip of the pen, is, I think, nothing less than Kierkegaard's adaptation of Aristotle's definition of change and of qualitative change in particular; in fact Kierkegaard refers to it. Aristotle's definition might be put this way: Change, the process itself, be it of place or quality, means that something which has the possibility (or potential) to change is in effect fulfilling (or actualizing) that potential *as* potential: It has not yet come to its completion, its finally fulfilled being, but it *is actually in the process* of "realizing its potential," as we say.[13]

Now Kierkegaard regards actual freedom as possibility, so becoming free, or being in the process of gaining freedom—which is what anxiety signifies—is indeed the possibility of a possibility. Freedom, which is potentiality or possibility, is actualizing itself as an ability. Freedom's possibility is not the choosing of good or evil but rather the possibility of *being able,* the mere intimation of our *capability for being bad* (or not).

This is how Kierkegaard feels compelled to speak. The reader might like a simpler, less fey formulation: Adam's pre-subjective dream (where by "a subject" is meant a self-conscious being) is of the possibility of being able to act on his own. It seems to me to correspond exactly to a familiar feeling: the uneasy intimation that one *could* do all sorts of things, including very bad ones—that, as we say, "I have it in myself" to do anything, and so, to do my worst.

Anxiety, considered dialectically as a movement of the intellect, has just the psychological ambiguity Kierkegaard is looking for. It is "*a sympathetic antipathy and an antipathetic sympathy.*" We still speak, he says—evidently the Danes do—"of a pleasing anxiousness." Children in "profound" cultures evince this as yet guiltless, not yet burdensome anxiety when they are captivated by the adventurous, the monstrous, the enigmatic. "Temptation" is, I imagine, another word for the mutual embrace of sympathy and antipathy.

"That anxiety makes its appearance is the pivot upon which everything turns." In it, spirit intimates itself to itself before it becomes overt. There is a catalyst, as it were—a word from God, a prohibition and a judgment: "You shall surely die."[14] Adam in his ignorance understands neither the meaning of eating the fruit nor of incurring death. But they make anxiety both more ambiguous and more focused:

> The infinite possibility of being able that was awakened by the prohibition now draws closer because this possibility points to a possibility in its sequence.[15]

This is the uttermost point of innocence. Its anxiety is related to the forbidden. It is the end of the psychological explanation. That Adam actually commits the sin, does the prohibited deed, and surely dies, is then a matter of dogma, a fact that proves the possibility.

Anxiety is thus the "presupposition" of hereditary sin, which explains it "retrogressively" in terms of its origin. Its actual origin is told in a "myth of the understanding," which "allows something that is inward to take place outwardly." In this myth the woman is first to be seduced. Adam was created; Eve is derived. She too is innocent, but she has, by reason of being derivative, a presentiment, a disposition, a kind of sinfulness in her from her beginning. For she is more sensuous than the man because her life was made to culminate in procreation. Therefore she is also more anxious—more free to sin, as it were—than Adam.[16]

That the Fall occurred, that sin in fact came into the world, is not explicable by psychology, by science. It is a "qualitative leap" in the nature of human beings. But Eve's making—something between creation and birth, it appears—prepares the condition. First of all was anxiety, "the final psychological state from which sin breaks forth." Second came Eve and with her generation. Thus the generation of mankind is now feasible, a mankind "quantitatively," escalatingly, sinful from birth.

Third, though sensuousness is by no means sinful, because there is no human history without sex, so without sin there is no sexuality. For sin brings reflection and self-consciousness. Thus naïvely sensuous sexuality turns into sinful sexuality.[17]

Kierkegaard inserts a digression on a subject already taken up in this book: Post-naïve sexuality is preceded by a state of anxiety that is expressed as "shame" in the sense of modesty (*Scham*). Here spirit finds itself as yet without sexual urge, that is, without relation to the other body, and so it is ignorantly innocent, yet extremely aware of being embodied, in a body with a gender difference. (Such shame is, I've noticed, evinced especially by pre-puberty boys in the period Freud called "latency.") Shame without sensuous lust is "of nothing." "And yet an individual may die of shame." It is the deepest pain because it is inexplicable.[18] It is not made explicit where in the story of the Fall *Scham* occurs; in traditional accounts it is immediately after, when the pair covers its nakedness. But Kierkegaard, regarding it as a half-knowing innocence, must be thinking of himself as correcting that sequence; shame-modesty precedes, indeed prepares, the Fall.

By sin, sensuousness became sinful, and each generation becomes quantitatively more so as it becomes more reflective. "This may be expressed by saying that the nothing that is the object of anxiety becomes, as it were, more and more a something." It becomes a "complex of presentiments" from which an individual leaps into actual sin and guilt, and this is hereditary sin, strictly speaking. Anxiety about sin produces sin: Evil desire, concupiscence, is not innate, but in "the impotence of anxiety the individual succumbs and is ambiguously guilty and innocent."[19]

Adam's anxiety is unique because by him sinfulness came "*into the world*": Henceforth Creation appears in a different light; it is sunk in corruption; it is objectively anxious. Kierkegaard expresses doubt both over a notion found in Schelling, that creation is anxious because God created it in a mood of anxiety, and over Hegel's introduction of the negative as a dialectical force in the world. Hence it is not clear what the world's objective anxiety might be. Is it a sort of "melancholy spread over nature"?[20] Granted that Adam is, in some sense, responsible for the "subjective anxiety" that has been so deeply delineated—is he also to be blamed for its infecting the world? I cannot tell whether Kierkegaard has really, without equivocation, resolved his problem of heritable sin: Was Adam in or out of the human race, and how is humankind his heir?

Nor can I pretend to care much about that question. What draws me to his treatment of anxiety is much less that it is taken up—with minimal acknowledgment—by Heidegger into his even deeper and more fundamental analysis of human existence, than that it describes a very familiar feeling, a widely shared mood of modernity.

But is it so modern? My report of the *Concept of Anxiety* relies on its first two chapters. The rest of the deliberations consider varieties of personal post-Fall anxiety and the way "the individual through anxiety is educated into faith." There is, however, also a section on anxiety under paganism.[21] The pagan version of anxiety is *fate*, an external relation to spirit; the—notoriously—ambiguous Greek oracle is voice of this personal yet outside force. The pagan's relation to fate is anxious because fate appears, equally ambiguously, at once as necessary and as accidental.

This understanding seems to me exactly right, and it is exemplified in Oedipus, *the* tragic hero. The ancient, at least the Greek, counterpart to modern anxiety is indeed fate and "its object is nothing." That nothing is expressible in just this ambiguity: Fate is neither an unavoidable providence nor a manageable contingency. Oedipus's tragedy is exactly consonant with this analysis: Who can tell wherein his failure, his flaw, really consisted? The word for this flaw-or-failure is *hamartia,* which Aristotle regards as the tragic hero's distinguishing attribute, the "tragic flaw,"[22] and which in the Greek New Testament has become the word for sin. Was this flaw a fault in Oedipus or a fate upon him—a proto-sin, or a fixed necessity? Under such questions the object of Oedipus's fear, the deed to which, as he early on learns, his fate consigns him (killing his father and marrying his mother) does, from his point of view, evaporate. He will have "done nothing." Sophocles in *Oedipus at Colonus* wonderfully dramatizes this by the mode of Oedipus's death: He dies like no ordinary mortal who leaves a corpse when he goes. Instead he is *annihilated*—a man pursued by nothing, absorbed into nothingness. His guiltlessly polluted body disappears without a trace—a resolution for himself and a blessing to the place, to Athens, where his anxiety is permitted to be finally nullified.

So the ancients knew anxiety, for surely Oedipus, like Adam, is not only unique but generic as well. And yet there is a difference between our anxiety and theirs: It doesn't even make much sense to ask what it felt like—subjectively—to be a heroically tragic Oedipus or a grandly driven Antigone. They were not twenty-four/seven subjective selves but beings living in that concentrated moment produced by the device of dramatic unity, the one action/one day temporality of tragic drama observed by Aristotle.[23] I imagine that the viewers took their cue from these great spectacles and seldom made much of their own anxiety or acknowledged in others a more mundane kind of anxiousness. That they did not as ordinary human beings now and then feel, just as we do, the invasion of nothingness, I cannot believe, but I imagine that their subjective anxieties were purged by the fearful fate, this ancient dread, borne by their tragic heroes. When, however, the gods and their fate-proclaiming oracles cease to be in the picture, pagan anxiety is no longer an elevating fate, is no longer the privilege of kings, to be exhibited to the city on the tragic stage with a terrific resolution. Instead it becomes the common condition, lived out somewhat miserably in private (or at the doctor's office), with pharmaceutical alleviations.

From this perspective, what Kierkegaard has done, and Heidegger will do, might seem like an attempt to return to humanity in general some of the grand significance of a mood that was once engrossed by kings and heroes. Yet, as it turns out, both insist that not all people have "learned to be anxious in the right way."[24] Sometimes then, probably predominantly, anxiety is just ordinary anxiety, and so this question must remain open: Whether these royal, tragic, theologico-psychological, existential explanations may not be *too* deep for so unstrung an affect.

And not only individually unstrung—socially conditioned as well. Thus J. S. Mill, in his *Political Economy* (1847), criticizes the claim of socialism to achieve that "freedom from anxiety" which would be a great gain for "human happiness."[25] This mood, possibly socially curable, is a far more mundane experience—not high-flown anxiety about human existence but ordinary, generalized worry about material livelihood. But back to the extraordinary mood—for with respect to human affectivity, what is ordinary must arouse our sympathy, but what is exceptional will attract our interest.

4. Anxiety as the Openness to Nothing: Heidegger's Metaphysical Mood

The most significance-fraught interpretation of the mood of anxiety I know is to be found in Martin Heidegger's "What is Metaphysics?" (1929).[1] Much later Heidegger wrote a Postscript to this essay (1943) and then an Introduction (1949). In these he first implicitly—that is, enveloped by the blue smoke of sacral language—and then explicitly retracts the thesis of the essay—that anxiety gives access to metaphysics—because now, at this turn in his thinking, metaphysics is to be overcome;[2] he does not, however, withdraw the essay: "For the genuine question is not canceled by the found answer."[3] There is also a quite different, equally interesting, earlier analysis of anxiety in *Being and Time* (1927).[4]

The study of Heideggerian texts is an uneasy task. All the other works in this book, no matter how high they fly, were written by men who, as far as I know, had probity, decency, and humanity—sane, ordinary virtues. Is it to the point? It is a tricky question. For though I believe that what Plato expresses in his Socratic dialogues is the truth—that it is of the essence to the future credit of philosophy as a way of life which is *at once* humanly involved *and* contemplatively withdrawn that Socrates should *be* what he preached—it does not follow that the question of whether a bad man could be a genuine "lover of wisdom" is ever after absurd. Philosophy might be conceived as having evolved in such a way as to induce so agonized a sense of a crisis in human existence and so high-flown a view of the inexpressible extraordinariness of Being that ordinary virtues fall below sight. One might then judge *for oneself* the personal humanity of such a philosopher both from the teachings of his work and the reports of his life. That private judgment would not, however, relieve one from the obligation to deal with his as with all texts: to penetrate, expose, second-guess the *work* as far as one's ability went; there would be no warrant for questioning the *author* as part of the interpretation.

But with Heidegger—of whom I am speaking—that purity of focus is nearly impossible to maintain. Heidegger was deeply involved with Nazism; he distanced himself from the Nazi party only eventually, from the National

Socialist worldview, never. That was his public face; his private conduct was endlessly deceptive, particularly toward fellow philosophers.[5]

How does this uncomfortable digression bear on this section? It is an expression of my queasiness with the text in a general and in a particular point. In general, there is the question of Heidegger's philosophical probity. First, all philosophers naturally distinguish themselves from their predecessors, but Heidegger's meager, qualified acknowledgment of Kierkegaard and Pascal, who surely gave him the central notion of anxiety as well as a number of resonant phrases, is something else.[6] Second, all philosophers I have ever read massage a little; usually it is the venial sin of molding some subordinate matter to fit their trusted systems. With Heidegger's texts one has to be continually suspicious: Has what seems like depth been surreptitiously won through linguistic sleight-of-hand? Is an obscure passage the expression of an unacknowledged perplexity, of a depth just beyond saying, or perhaps rather of a wrong but convenient turn willfully taken? That last raises the most curious philosophical quandary: Can a philosopher be wrong and yet deep, are there falsely deep disclosures? Can such willful falsity be deeply interesting? To explain that possibility would be to have explained the possibly positive truth value of the false. It is an old problem with many approaches. In its resolution lies the possibility both of philosophical inclusiveness and of human tolerance, but also of false entanglements. But here I have to let this perplexity go, and opt to make the most of these prime texts on anxiety.

Yet a particular point of uneasiness that is not circumventable concerns Heidegger's analysis of anxiety itself. Anxiety can be seen from the perspective of creaturely finitude (Pascal), of psychological sinfulness (Kierkegaard), of psychoanalytical pathology (Freud), of a historical condition (Auden); in each of these approaches the mood of anxiety is a revealing, troubling, affective outcome but not the ultimate source of all disclosure of human existence.

Not so for Heidegger. His "analysis of existence," intended as a replacement for the old, quasi-empirical "philosophical anthropology" such as Kant practiced, reaches for an absolutely radical grounding of the structure of human "being-there" (*Dasein*, usually translated as "[human] existence"). As we will see, the mood of anxiety will play a uniquely privileged role in this structure. But this position will be achieved by a very strict exclusiveness: Not everyone is actually thus fundamentally affected, and not all empirical phenomena of anxiety are here taken into consideration. Is the analysis then perhaps a highly selective psychology of an all too particular experience surreptitiously levered into an ontology of human existence? Has the urge to go deep displaced the desire to tell truth? Has the wish to distinguish the elect overcome the care for human commonality? With these misgivings voiced, I will begin by telling as clearly as I can how in the essay

"What is Metaphysics?" (1929), anxiety discloses what "is" (the scare-quotes are essential) "behind the physical" world (which is English for the "metaphysical" realm).

A. "What Is Metaphysics?"

The essay itself is a gem. It is written, bizarre as that may sound, in a Heideggerian version of the Hemingwayesque style: short, hard-hitting sentences. There is no argumentation, to be sure, but after several readings, the text is rationally expandable. Although the logician Carnap termed its "pseudosentences" meaningless upon logical analysis, that is itself illogical, for it begs the question: Heidegger's essay is an attack on positivist logic.[7]

There is also a Postscript (1943), which in an uncandid way means, as I said, to save the essay while nullifying its answer to the question "What is Metaphysics?" The recourse is to speak of a questioning that goes beyond metaphysics, "a thinking that has already been absorbed in a surmounting of metaphysics." Since a part of the Postscript deals with misunderstandings of the essay, I shall refer to it briefly. The still later Introduction (1946), while enveloping "What is Metaphysics?" in later Heideggerian language (that is, a mode of speech in which language-play bears the burden of thought), is actually more an introduction to *Being and Time* (1927) than to the essay in question; it ends, however, with another effort at salvage by insinuating that the main question of the work is one that is, in fact, clearly only a next question tacked on at its end: "Why is it the case at all that there are beings and not rather nothing?" I want to inject here that this is a truly radical, a truly modern, a novel question (not, to be sure, novel to Heidegger, who now feels obliged to explain why he once took it without attribution from Leibniz[8]). Before the modern thinkers, serious questioning stopped before it asked, "Why Being and beings?", "Why God's Creation and creatures?", not to speak of "Why God?" For those who mythologize or believe that the world and its denizens were made or created—from Plato on—attribute its being simply to God's generosity, including Thomas who means thus to derail the question of why God made the world.[9] Those, on the other hand, who think that the cosmos and its contents were unoriginated and infinite in time—I'm referring to Aristotle—also hold that it is absurd to ask "whether" it is, for that is self-evident;[10] so much the more would it be absurd to ask the question "why" about that which has no beginning, and so no intended finality of direction. (There is, however, the fact that absurdity can't be attributed to an unasked question.) The Leibniz-Heidegger question is deeply modern, it seems to me, in that human thinking deliberately breaks through any sense of ultimates and declines to feel rebuffed by any *ne plus ultra,* by any injunction that says "go no farther!" One might call this uninhibitedness ontological daring—or shamelessness.

Now to the essay, of which I will try to explicate mainly the part concerned with the anxiety of human existence, existential anxiety.[11]

The essay begins with an attack on positivistic science, that is, on knowledge that admits in its relation to the world, in its actions, in its research, only "beings themselves (*das Seiende selbst*)—and beyond that, nothing (*nichts*)"; that is to say, science deals with worldly facts and nothing else. Positivistic science regards the nothing as "nothing-worth" (*das Nichtige*), null and void, invalid, even as a horror-phantasy. Yet it itself does rely on negation, or at least acknowledges it. For science appeals to the law which decrees that contradiction is to be avoided, that "either A or *not*-A but *not* both at once." To ask, however, about "nothing" is to engage in contradiction, for if by definition thinking posits an object, that is, a something, then to think of nothing is to think a contradiction: nothing as something. That—and here is the crux of Heidegger's attack on standard logic—must be the end of any inquiry into nothing, if indeed that logic and the rational understanding it supports are to be the highest authority.

Now Heidegger works out the question: Are the ordinary logical negations that positivistic science uses without further thought (that is, in routinely denying what contradicts the facts or its own laws) prior to or, perhaps, dependent on the Nothing? If Nothing is nothing but—and here follows a slew of negation terms such as only German is capable of—negation (*Verneinung*) of beings as a whole, if it is simply not-beings (*das Nicht-Seiende*), then it must be ranked under the more inclusive class of "the nothing-sort" (*das Nichthafte*), and thus, as it seems, it will be subordinated to "the negated" (*das Verneinte*). Does "negatedness" (*die Verneintheit*), and thus negation, then, represent the higher class under which the Nothing falls as a special kind of "the negated"? Or is the reverse the case: Is negation possible only because the Nothing is more original than negation? The latter is what Heidegger asserts: The Nothing, a metaphysical mystery object, is prior to negation, a rational human activity. "The" Nothing—I have gone from the grammatically multifarious nothing (noun, pronoun, adjective, adverb) to the unambiguously nominal Nothing—is not attainable by logic. Then how?

Before coming to the crux of the matter for my purpose, that is, the nature and function of anxiety, here are two reflections on Heidegger's procedure so far: First, he himself never once speaks of "positivism," but it seems clear to me that his interpretation of science and its logic plays out against this suppressed background term by taking it at its word as intimating a rejection of the negative. Second, the source of the logicians' irritation with this essay is in the skewing of the sensible reading of the claim "that science is concerned with beings and with nothing beyond." Heidegger, not otherwise a great giver of credit, attributes the claim itself to the Positivist French historian Taine, who means that science deals in facts and nothing besides.[12] Now Heidegger deliberately mishears that description to say literally that scientists are indeed, though *unwittingly*, concerned with the Nothing, because besides the facts they also, implicitly, involve the no of negation. It is this cunning reading which permits him to establish the rank order of negation and Nothing.

How then do we find the Nothing if logic is not up to it? We cannot, in principle, get a grasp on—and so *go beyond*—beings as a whole. But we do find ourselves *in the midst* of beings as a whole. There is a kind of cosmic background noise by which beings as a whole shadow and unify our mundane day, no matter how splintered into this or that diversion is our existence. It is a "condition in which we find ourselves" (*Befindlichkeit*; the Germans say: "How do you *find* yourself?" for "How *are* you?"). A basic form of this condition is "being in a mood" (*Gestimmtsein*). "Mood" in English is related to musical "mode," a fixed structure of tones, like the major and minor scales, conveying a definite coloration of feeling. Similarly, the German word for mood, *Stimmung*, is related to the verb *stimmen*, in which two separate words have been blended, that for using the voice and that for harmonizing or tuning.[13] Consequently in Heidegger's works *Stimmung* is often translated "attunement," though this loses precisely the common meaning: mood.

Heidegger gives two first examples of moods that attune humans to beings as a whole: One is boredom, in German *Langeweile*, "the long while." "Deep boredom, wafting hither and thither in the abyss of existence, like a silent fog, pushes all things together, human beings, and oneself along with them, into a strange indifference. This boredom reveals beings (*das Seiende*) as a whole."[14] (Pascal had assigned a similarly dubious saving grace to boredom.)

Heidegger adds a brief afterthought: Joy in the presence, not of just any person but of that human existence which is loved, can also be such a revelation. It is the only time that I know of when an unalloyed positive effect plays a revelatory role for him, albeit only a secondary one. On the other hand, boredom gets a further hundred-page treatment, reported below.

Such attunements are not mere occurrences but disclose, each in its way, the basic events of our existence. Thus what we are in the habit of calling feelings are neither mere concomitants and phenomena of our thinking and willing attitude, nor its causal impulses, nor conditions that we happen to be in and that we somehow come to terms with, but *indices of our existential condition*. Yet just when such moods make us face beings as a whole, they also hide the Nothing from us—presumably precisely because they turn us *towards* beings. Is there, then, an event, an attunement that reveals the Nothing in its very own revelatory sense? Does there eventuate in the existence of a human being an attunement that brings it before the Nothing?

This event is possible and also actual—albeit rare enough—only during the moments of the basic mood of anxiety.[15]

Anxiety is not fear of this or that determinate being. In fear, which is about something definite, the fearful human being is fixed in its condition, petrified as it were, and in its urgency to save itself from the object of fear, it "loses its head" and becomes insecure with respect to everything at once.

Anxiety does not permit this confusion, for anxiety is rather saturated with a peculiar serenity. To be sure, anxiety is always "anxiety about . . ." but not about this or that. This indeterminacy is not, however, a mere lack of determinacy, but is the essential impossibility of determinability.

It is familiarly said that in anxiety "something uncanny gets to one." Who is the "one" and what is "uncanny"? We cannot say. As a whole, it gets to us. As in boredom, everything sinks into one indifference, but with this distinction: Instead of drawing us into this indifference, anxiety distances beings from us—though, as we will see, from that distance they turn toward us. This distancing of beings as a whole is oppressive. All beings slip away, "no hold at all remains," and we are overcome by this "not-any" (*kein*). Thus "anxiety reveals the Nothing."[16]

Anxiety holds us in suspension because it makes the beings as a whole slip away—and that is "uncanny." In German the word is *unheimlich,* which means literally "un-homey," exposed, "unaccommodated."[17] And it is not you and I who feel uncanny as individuals but as a "one," as a human existence which feels through and through the trembling of a being suspended.

The proof that anxiety reveals the Nothing comes when anxiety has receded. In the clarity of the fresh memory we must say: What we were anxious about was actually—nothing. "Indeed: The Nothing itself—as such—was there."

The rest of the essay answers the question, What is metaphysics? In anxiety, beings as a whole are neither annihilated (*vernichtet*) by our doing nor negated (*verneint*) by our reasoning. Rather the Nothing itself reveals an essential activity for which Heidegger invents the word *Nichtung,* "act of not-ing"; it is of the essence of the Nothing itself to evince a "repelling referral" (*abweisende Verweisung*) to beings as a whole. The phrase is mystificatory wordplay, signifying that from the perspective of the Nothing the Being of the world comes to light in anxiety: "In the bright night of the Nothing of anxiety first arises the original openness of beings as such: that they are beings and not nothing."[18] From the viewpoint of the Nothing human existence has access to the whole of things.

This Nothing is not an object nor a being nor an opposing not-being, but belongs at its very origin to the essence of Being. Being (*Sein*) is distinguished from beings (*Seiendes*) as its transcendent ground is distinguished from the world.[19] The Being of beings is *not* itself a being. We are thus brought up against Heidegger's pretty well-concealed nihilism: "In the Being of beings eventuates the act of not-ing of the Nothing," he says in passing. As Heidegger explains in the Postscript, the attribution to him of nihilism is an "errant opinion" if interpreted as an invalidation of living and dying in the world, but he can hardly deny that he does assert a kind of transcendent nihilism.

Thus the two questions raised are now, Heidegger thinks, answered: First, it is the Nothing which first makes negation possible; negation is the "displaced evidence" of the Nothing in our existence, which we could never recognize did we not have the aboriginal Nothing in view. Second, metaphysics means questioning beyond—"transcending," that is, "climbing beyond," the beings of the world. Therefore the question concerning the Nothing both infects and embraces metaphysics. Only because Nothing is revealed at the bottom of human existence can the alienating strangeness (*Befremdlichkeit*) of beings come upon us so that we experience estranged astonishment (*Verwunderung*); this is not, I think, the ancient wonder which would be *Wunder* and signifies more a marveling than an estrangement.

Heidegger takes up a long repressed misgiving: The human being can truly exist and have a relation to the world of beings only in the effort of "holding-itself-into" (*Sichhineinhalten*) the Nothing, meaning that it takes and holds a place beyond beings. But that happens only in anxiety. Then shouldn't we be constantly suspended in anxiety, he asks, and didn't we ourselves admit that this original anxiety is rare? Indeed, he answers, anxiety is always there but it is asleep, suppressed, largely by our diversionary busyness. "It is always there because the being-suspended-into (*Hineingehaltenheit*) the Nothing of human existence on the basis of a hidden anxiety makes the human being the placeholder of the Nothing." But in our finitude it is precisely not up to our decision to be thus anxious, to transcend the whole of beings at will. I think this is a way of saying that anxiety is an affect and thus not in our control. But that would imply that the entry into metaphysics is not our choice to make, and the achievement of genuine existence not in our power. I think it *is* what Heidegger means: The breath of anxiety, he says, "trembles continuously through human existence, . . . most securely through an existence that is daring at bottom." But that does not mean that that daring human being *does* anything in particular toward achieving this mood, for "original anxiety can awake at any moment in human existence. . . . The depth of its sway corresponds to the nugatoriness of its possible occasion."[20] Authentic anxiety is, so to speak, existential grace.

Is this anxiety a recognizable mood? Is it descriptively, phenomenologically, plausible? Are there actual human beings thus attuned to Nothing? Can one abstain from feeling an incongruous sentimentality in the description of this original anxiety as being "in a secret alliance with the cheerfulness and mildness of creative yearning"?[21] I think *no* to all of the above, but then I am not an altogether charitable reader—except in one, the main, point: I know of no other writer who can be credited with having assigned so ultimate a function to a mood. And though "original anxiety" may be more an invented than a described feeling, its actively inciting Nothing more a metaphysical mystery than a revelatory experience, and its glorification more an idiosyncratic exaltation than a communicable devotion—still, it seems to me that, particulars aside, Heidegger has told an unforgettable truth in "What is Metaphysics?": Moods are human affects that tell not only how *we* are but what *our world* is.

B. Being and Time

Mood in general, in its revelatory capacity, here called "disclosure" (*Erschliessen*), is treated in Heidegger's best-known work, *Being and Time* (1927).[22] In the framework of this book, anxiety functions quite differently from the way it does in the slightly later "What is Metaphysics?" (1929), where, however, that change is not noted. I infer from this tacit disparity that there is, for all its suggestive originality, something forced in both analyses. Both have undoubted depth and yet are somehow—this is a puzzle—not quite seated in the way of things, as a plug might not quite click into its socket. Yet I do think that to have missed these analyses is to be the poorer in thought-perspectives.

   Being and Time is written on two levels: the "ontological" and the "ontic" (from Greek *on*, being, and *logos,* account). The latter is the level of our familiar, daily existence. The ordinary answer to the question "How are you?" is given "ontically": "Fine." Yet in the respect I'm concentrating on, the candid answer might be in terms of a mood (*Stimmung*), say, "I feel anxiety," or of "being in a mood" (*Gestimmtheit*), such as "I'm in a bad mood" and "I'm in a sad mood, feeling blue," or even in terms of that gray moodlessness (*Ungestimmtheit*) which we call "having the blahs."

   This ontic inquiry is levered—actually lowered—onto the more fundamental ontological level where human beings question and try to give an account of their own existence. In *Being and Time,* the human being is called *Dasein.* Literally it means "There-being," that is, the being that exists, is there, in its world. Nonetheless, Heidegger insists that *Dasein* should rather be read as "the being that *is* openness."[23] It is curious but precise language for us receptively moody beings, whose very existence is confirmed in our self-questioning and our attentiveness to our moods. In such ontological inquiry we reach down to the *a priori*, that is, to the very first, the prior, foundations of the way we are.

   What underlies our daily moods on the ontological level is called by Heidegger *Befindlichkeit.* Translators struggle with this meaning-fraught abstraction: "State-of-mind" is a very bare translation, "self-findliness" a bizarre one. More expansively, we might say "the-condition-in-which-one-finds-oneself-existing." I say "existing" because Heidegger must have had in mind the phrase *ist befindlich,* which means "is to be found, exists, is situated" somewhere. (This is not the occasion to inquire whether *Befindlichkeit* is prior to *Stimmung* by terminological fiat or by an insight into human existence.) The condition in which we find ourselves in fact conditions our way of being, namely as *Dasein*: The relevant paragraph is headed "*Das Da-sein* as *Befindlichkeit.*"[24] This is what the latter word signifies:

> *Existentially inherent in the condition of finding oneself existing is a disclosing directedness toward [Angewiesenheit auf: also "dependence on"] the world out of which something of concern can be encountered.*[25]

This ontological term thus articulates one of the meanings of existence: to be open to a world that commands our concern.

"Finding-oneself-in-a-condition" is meant to express that each human existence has, so to speak, already found itself, though not in some sort of self-perception, nor in a condition of the soul or in a certain apprehension of experience; but this finding of oneself as "always already" in a mood is rather an *attunement* to the world. Or, more generally: We cannot leap beyond our own being-there in the world. It is our precondition, this finding ourselves as "always already" somehow situated in the world. Heidegger calls it "thrownness" (*Geworfenheit*), our having been cast beforehand into the condition in which we find ourselves.

Thus *Befindlichkeit* is analyzed into three features: First, the disclosing to us of our "thrownness"; second, the disclosing of the world as a care, a concern of ours; and, third, the disclosing of an aspect of the world familiar from the forgoing account of "What is Metaphysics?": that we exist within it as a whole.[26]

Now to the "ontic" counterpart of attunement: mood, *Stimmung.* The human being is "always already" attuned, in a mood, be it of imperturbable equanimity or of inhibiting despondency. Heidegger singles out the sallow "untuning" (*Ungestimmtheit,* which is not to be confused with a bad mood, a "mistuning," *Verstimmtheit*). In this untuned state, being (*Sein*) is revealed as a burden to being-there (*Dasein*), while "being-attuned" (*Gestimmtsein*) brings being (*Sein*) to its "there" (*Da*). In plainer words: Our moods are intimations of the meaning of our existence; they might help us answer the question: What does it mean to exist, that is, to *be* both *there,* in the world, and *open to* it?

But in its daily life, that is, ontically, the human being is not up to its moods. Instead of giving in to them and pursuing their disclosure of being, it evades them. Yet precisely in that evasion is revealed its surrender to its "there," its world. It doesn't care about the burdensome character of being that mood could reveal, least of all when relieved by an elevated mood. Even rational enlightenment cannot overcome the "phenomenal matter of fact" that moods bring—or could bring—human existence face-to-face with the condition of its thereness, "which answers with a stare of inexorable enigmaticality." Yet human beings flee from this confrontation *with* the world by taking refuge *in* the world.

It is, however, equally a falsification of the phenomenon to relegate moods to the preserve of the irrational, for irrationalism is just the counterpart of rationalism: The former talks squintingly whereof the latter talks blindly.[27]

Here is a difficulty I cannot quite solve. Heidegger begins his analysis of what are ontically termed the affects[28] by calling "the condition-in-which-one-finds-oneself" the ontological foundation of the ontic "moods." Now it is the ontological condition that has "modes," fundamental ways of differentiating itself, among which are fear and anxiety. Thus anxiety is not among the ontic, lived moods at all in *Being and Time,* for it is on a different, higher level from them—the ontological level. (Fear too is problematical, since it is usually called an emotion, as having an object.) This much only seems clear to me, that Heidegger thinks that the ontic affects *all* fall under the general class of mood, that every emotion too is dependent on an attunement as precondition. He does not, to be sure, say so explicitly on this ontic level, but he is very clear about it on the higher level.

Heidegger wants to demonstrate the "phenomenon" of *Befindlichkeit*—it is most expressly not a faculty—through one of the fundamental modes, fear, in anticipation of the prospective parallel interpretation of anxiety. This ontological fear is not the individual propensity to fearfulness but a deep possibility of essential *Befindlichkeit.* The analysis of fear finds the following fourfold structure: 1. Fear is *of* something, the threatening object that is approaching from some as yet uncontrollable but determinable quarter, whence it may arrive or not. 2. Fearing *itself* discovers fearsomeness not by first positing an evil and then proceeding to fear it, but because fearing is an ever-ready possibility of *Befindlichkeit,* which has already disclosed a world in which something fearsome may approach. 3. Fear is *for* something, namely for the fearing being itself; fearing discloses the being's threatened abandonment to itself in the face of a threatening world. 4. Fear can be in *behalf* of another, an indirect fearing that does not really fear the frightening object but fears through the other for itself, that is, for the possible loss of togetherness with another.

The anxiety of "What is Metaphysics?" thus seems to be, as it were, downgraded in the terms of *Being and Time,* reduced from a mode of the ontological condition-in-which-one-finds-oneself to an ontic mood, though within the essay that very mood or attunement seemed to be fundamental. As I said, the analytic level of mood is somewhat unclear between the two

works. At any rate, in the book (which, recall, preceded the essay), anxiety had already been established ontologically as a fundamental condition
(*Grundbefindlichkeit*), akin to fear though a grade deeper.[29]

The analysis of anxiety begins with that phenomenon of the *flight*
into, the absorption of human existence in, "the world of care-taking" (*die
besorgte Welt*).[30] "Care" (*Sorge*) has a triple sense, expressed in three locu-
tions: "caring for," "being full of care," "taking care of," that is, cherishing,
worrying, managing. It is the basic unifying ontological context established
for all human existence. Its discovery does not, however, precede anxiety
but follows from it. The analysis of anxiety will first reveal this caring as
a fundamental characteristic of human existence, of *Dasein*. Caring gives
its ultimate meaning to the Germanic phrase "always already" I have used
several times. Ontological care is the basic existential condition of a human
being as "always already" there, ahead of itself, as it were, in being ever and
always already engaged with and involved in the world: care-full or careless, both being modes of care.[31] Care brings together the whole meaning
of existence.

The reason anxiety is the key to ontological care (the basic condition of
Dasein) is that proneness of the human being, already observed in its deal-
ings with its moods, to take fright at, yet to flee into, the world. (I keep calling the human being an "it" because an unindividuated, ungendered being
is what Heidegger seems to have in mind.) Fear was *for Dasein* itself, but it
was *of* something definite *within* the world. Such fear, Heidegger says, could
not arise were there not anxiety behind it. For anxiety is also a flight, a more
primordial one, of human existence from its world, again a "rebounding
recoil," in which *Dasein* flees *into* what it flees *from*. Heidegger speaks of the
human being's "declining," "lapsing into," "falling to" (as in "coming under
the dominion of") the world. The verbs are *verfallen* and *verfallen an*; the
allusion is of course to the first *lapsus*, the original sin, the Fall, though "falling" is now a concept of ontological motion, not an ontic state of sin.[32]

Here it might help to insert two descents of concepts. Neatly perspicuous though the parallelism seems, the two columns—problematically—
don't actually match up in the analyses of *Being and Time,* since there care,
anxiety, and fear are, as I said, all modes of *Befindlichkeit,* that is, they are all
ratcheted up into ontology.

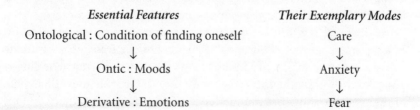

Essential Features	*Their Exemplary Modes*
Ontological : Condition of finding oneself	Care
↓	↓
Ontic : Moods	Anxiety
↓	↓
Derivative : Emotions	Fear

Human existence takes flight into the busy preoccupied managing of its world to save itself from a caring involvement with the world, and since care is its most fundamental characteristic, it turns out to be in flight from itself. It is necessary to say here that by caring Heidegger does not mean something warm, cuddly, and close up. On the contrary, existential care is a cold, demanding burden that requires a lonely heroism of *Dasein*. Care is not now to my point, except insofar as it certainly entails distance from the mundane, the worldly everyday world. That distance is what anxiety has provided to *Dasein*.

Anxiety in *Being and Time* is not entirely without an object, an "of" such as fear is of; in that respect one might call it a semi-mood. Yet this object is not something definite inside the world, certainly not that ever-cited fear-object, the black bear. It is totally indeterminate. Nothing to hand within the world functions as that before which anxiety is anxious. To anxiety nothing in the world is relevant; the world is characterized by total insignificance. What threatens is "nowhere" (*nirgends*). But "nowhere" in particular is not nothing, for it implies a region, the "country" in general. *Gegend*, like "country," is derived from what lies *entgegen, contra*, facing the observer—ex-tension. It signifies the openness of the world for *Dasein*'s being spatially within it. What is revealed in anxiety is a refractory inner-worldly territory of nothing and nowhere. Anxiety is of the *world as such*. What oppresses and constricts in anxiety—Heidegger plays on the etymology of "anxiety," *Angst*: Latin *angustia*, German *Enge*, meaning "narrowness"—is not simply the sum of all that is present, but its very *possibility*. *That* is what Heidegger means by the "world itself," "as such."[33] Thus the Nothing in particular, which anxiety is anxious about, turns out to be a "something," namely everything that might possibly come at us, "come to hand" in the world. Anxiety is anxious about being-in-the-world itself. Thus being anxious first discloses "the *world as world*." (Recall that Kierkegaard had connected beckoning and repelling *possibility* with anxiety.)

Just as fear, besides being afraid *of* something, also feared *for* something, namely the existence of the fearing self, so anxious *Dasein* is anxious *for* something, namely its own ability to be in the world. In anxiety the world has nothing to offer, not even the fellow existence of others. Anxiety isolates and individualizes human being. And it turns out that what, in that condition, *Dasein* is anxious about and what it is anxious for is the same: its being-in-the-world, its being among beings. Ordinary German speech says, "I feel (literally, "it is for me": *es ist mir*) un-homey (the literal interpretation of *unheimlich*, normally "uncanny")." Anxiety brings *Dasein* back from its lapsed absorption in the world. *Dasein* loses the matter-of-course "feeling at home" of daily life with others who have equally lapsed into the ordinary life of the general public. Trust implodes and *Dasein* becomes solitary. But on the ontic level *Dasein* averts its eyes, so to speak, from the condition in which it ontologically finds itself and lapses into the existentially undemanding and humanly comfortable managing care for its world. But it would not so lapse were it not ontologically threatened. Our ordinary anxiousness is the innerworldly appearance of a hidden "proper" (*eigentlich*, often "authentic") anxiety, which is an ontologically defined prelapsarian condition; the ordinary feeling of an occasional uncanniness is its masked derivative. Even "the physiological triggering of anxiety," says Heidegger, "is only possible because *Dasein* is anxious for itself in the very foundations of its being."[34]

Later in the book Heidegger goes further. Anxiety is not only a phenomenon of alienation from a world in general, that is, a world which is nothing in particular. Rather for that rare, resolute human being who experiences it properly, anxiety is the possibility of "*the* one mood that does not inhibit or confuse him. (Here Heidegger actually uses the masculine pronoun for *Dasein*.) For it lets one be free *from* the "possibilities that are 'nullities'" ('*nichtigen' Möglichkeiten*) and lets freedom arise *for* the authentic ones."[35] *Nichtig* is seriously derogatory: These innerworldly possibilities, those not approached from beyond, are now—not quite surreptitiously—condemned.

Instead, an authentic possibility of human existence, absolute and "unoutstrippable," (*unüberholbar*), certain but indeterminate, is brought forward: the possibility that *Dasein* can *not* exist, that it can and must die. This possibility demands the full acceptance of the truth of the death that is "coming at us." (The word for "future" is *Zukunft*, "coming-towards.") That death, which is only and always one's own, is not a matter of the empirical observation that all men die. It is rather the condition in which one finds oneself, the condition of anxiety, that keeps open the threat which arises from *Dasein*'s very own singular being. Through mood in general, human existence is brought before the fact that it has been thrown into the world; in anxiety in particular it finds itself "before the Nothing of the possible impossibility of its existence."[36] (Note again the—skewed—echo of Kierkegaard.) This human being lives with the full awareness that as it exists, so it can and will, at a date uncertain, not exist. It becomes authentically anxious; in German the verb for "being anxious" is reflexive: *sich ängstigen*, which I render as "self-anxious" below. This is for Heidegger the human high point: when the single human existence has revealed to itself its lostness in the world's thoughtless, self-less "generality" (*das Man*, which is the impersonally indefinite pronoun *man*, "one, somebody, people" turned into a neuter noun). It is then brought

> *before the possibility to be itself, unsupported by a care-taking social care* (besorgende Fürsorge: "managing social welfare"), *but to be a self that, released from*

the illusions of self-less generality, faces facts [to attain] *a passionate, self-assured and self-anxious* freedom for death.[37]

There never was a more radically isolating individualism; against it the often-deplored Tocquevillean-American individualism is child's play. Thus anxiety, as Heidegger describes it in a course of lectures given while *Being and Time* was in the writing, far from being a fear of death, is rather the very feeling Descartes denied that we have: the affect of being itself—pure, naked being-in-the-world;[38] it *is*, however, a harsh version of Rousseau's dreamy "sentiment of self." So much the more is it clear that between 1927 and 1929 (the book and the essay) anxiety had undergone a reversal from facing a Nothing that *is* the world to facing a Nothing that is *beyond* the world, from an existential to a metaphysical Nothing. The anxiety in the face of the latter Nothing seemed to me not so obviously a real human affect; the uncanny sense of not being at home in the world when confronted with the former is surely a familiar, if not frequent, experience for many people. But here the bald question is: Does it have the import assigned to it? Is the eerie sense of alienation many of us have—surely more than Heidegger grants—sometimes felt really so deeply based, so revelatory?

Since Aeschylus first said in so many words that "learning is by suffering" (*pathei mathos*) into our time when we have learned to lever every misery into a learning experience, and books extracting the blessing of wisdom from the pain of misfortune abound, people have learned to make the best of bad affects. But that very fact gives me pause in two ways. One is a reluctance to believe that because an affect comes unbidden over me, I am justified in regarding it as bringing news from Nothing. This doubt is recognizable as a form of *the* question behind my project: Are we fundamentally affective, and if so, does it follow that affects come from and perhaps tell of the very ground of our being? Or could it be that, while we are at *bottom* affective, we are at our *height* thought-ful and find our way to what truth we attain through thinking?

It is clear that Heidegger thinks the former. In his explanation of the "condition-in-which-one-finds-oneself," which is really *root-affectivity*, he gives as good a delineation of such affectivity as I have read. For this condition is the ontological background of all aspects, moods, and emotions. He says that

> *It lies in the condition-in-which-we-find-ourselves* (Befindlichkeit) *to be a disclosing dependency-that-refers-us* (Angewiesenheit) *to the world out of which what-comes-to-concern-us* (Angehendes) *can meet us.* We must indeed turn over, on *ontological* grounds, the primary discovery of the world to 'mere mood.'[39]

Pure intuition, Heidegger says, could not discover the human world; even understanding is "always already" attuned, in a mood. This seems to me the most unqualifiedly thought-inducing aspect of *Being and Time*. I should say here that as the title of *Being and Time* announces, this root-affectivity of human being is itself further interpreted as temporality. But the exposition of this ultimate framing of human existence would take me too far away from feeling.

My second misgiving concerns the relentless fixation on the grim moods, which Heidegger masks in the heroic language of the self-discovery by which a *Dasein* finds itself not as a being busy among beings in the world, but as an existence alone, mortal, and aware of itself as a self. That fixation is in want of refutation, for it bears the mark of something idiosyncratically forcible. But before considering the possibility of interpreting the world through a better mood, I want to set out a diametrically opposite role that anxiety can be made to play—anxiety not as disclosure of human existence, but as a repression of human instincts.

5. Anxiety as the Repression of Instinctual Impulses: Freud's Mythological Mood

The effluvium of un-pleasure seems, so far, to hang indispersably about modern moodiness. Not only is anxiety the main and most metaphysical mood—when it is not a pathology—but depressive diversion, unassuageable longing, the "vapours," *ressentiment,* disgust are the moods that get most space in literature, fictional and reflective. Even as the popular swarm of coping books attest to an assumption of common dis-ease, these moody moods are also deemed to be deeper than the felicitous ones, which are regarded as superficial. A root metaphor for thought seems to have been reversed—discarding a buoyant ascent to heights for a brooding descent to depths.

Practically speaking, it is not so hard to say why moods, once they have been articulated as a recognized way of "finding oneself to be," are so insidiously dominating. By reason of being unspecific in scope they seem to be universal, and by reason of being diffuse in us they pervade our world. But what makes the bad moods more moody than the good ones? Boredom, nausea, disgust will reappear in the final chapter, but let me here say just a word about the psychological pathology that anxiety was even before it became a metaphysical revelation. I am thinking of Freud's many writings about anxiety, which, though beginning earlier than Heidegger's, simply don't figure in *Being and Time*. For that book eschews, along with psychic naturalism, the "ontic" varieties of experience that ordinary men and women have—to its detriment I think.

Freud's psychoanalytic theory of anxiety has a thirty-year history of qualifications and finally a great retraction; unlike Heidegger, who pretends to seamlessness, Freud readily admits to his revisions.[1] The earlier theory explained anxiety as caused by libidinal repression, in which aggregated and unexpended excitations turned directly into anxiety. An additional claim was that "*the act of birth is the first anxiety-experience and thus the source and model of the anxiety-affect.*"[2]

Like Heidegger, Freud eventually thinks of anxiety as an affect that is 1. future-directed since it is a reaction to danger, 2. connected with indeterminacy and objectlessness, and 3. turns into fear when it has found its object.[3] In the later development of the anxiety theory, Freud does not give up repression (that is, the banishment of painfully unacceptable instinctual impulses or ideas from consciousness, where they may, however, turn up again in a transmogrified form) or the origin in birth trauma, but he modifies their order of importance. "And that it is the libido [the sum of psychic energy that is, or is associated with, an instinct] which is thus transformed into anxiety we no longer claim."[4]

The later theory is attached to a tripartite "dissection of the personality"; thus the psyche with which psychoanalysis is concerned—the soul of old—is once again a triple composite. Freud conceives it topographically, like a geographic territory with distinctly functioning populations that also mix (Figure IX-A, p. 366).[5] I mention this representation because, as I intimated, it shows this Freudian soul as a version, in a new setting, of the tripartite Platonic soul in the *Republic* and the *Phaedrus*. Recall that the three parts of that soul were all mutually influential, and interaction is exactly what Freud has in mind. Indeed one might regard psychoanalysis as an inquiry into the actual dynamics among the parts, which is a missing element in Platonic soul-analysis. I might observe here too that Freud argues vigorously that in a real science the subject-ego can and must become an object to itself, that it can "treat itself like other objects."[6] And that is exactly what pits Freudian psychoanalysis against its near-contemporary opposite, Heideggerian existential analytic: Heidegger regards *Dasein* as that kind of being which *exists,* by which he means precisely that it is *not* a subject in a sense of an underlying self, but a being that "has always already *stepped out beyond itself* (*ex-sistere*)" into the world. "Consequently it is never anything like a subjective inner sphere."[7] Even less is it an object like any other entity that positive natural science might study.

Thus Freud is, in contrast, rightly to be considered a naturalist of the soul as, in a sense, Plato was: The soul has parts and is observable, differing from the rest of the natural world in being self-observed.

Recall that Plato's three parts were: Desire, Spirit, Reason. Desire, seat of the consuming passions, withdraws itself from reason altogether in some people, and even spirit, the place of self-regarding ebullience, though more amenable in most of us, is not fully thoughtful. Yet neither of them is "unconscious" in Freud's sense:

> We call a psychical process unconscious whose existence we are obliged to
> assume—for some such reason as that we infer it from its effects—but of which
> we know nothing

—at least at the moment when it is activated. The psychoanalyst then infers
an intention "which did not put itself through" and proposes it to the patient,
who may recall it from its latency or consign it to permanent unconscious-
ness.[8] Socrates, who certainly thinks he can and should study and know of
himself whether he happens "to be some sort of beast even more complex
in form and more tumultuous than a hundred-headed Typhon" or something simpler and gentler,[9] never supposes that any expert can do this for
him, and do it better than he himself could, by applying a technical soul-
theory. Nor does he think that there is an underground reservoir of passion
that is in principle unreachable by his own reason, yet obeys laws of psychic
dynamics that are analogous to a rational physics with its dynamic forces.
That there are such psychic forces, the instincts, is for Freud "*our mythology.
Instincts are mythical entities,* magnificent in their indefiniteness."[10] So, as
he admits with startling candor, Freud is as much a maker of paradigmatic
soul-myths as is Plato.

For his late theory of anxiety, Freud very aptly borrows a Nietzschean
usage: The Unconscious is named by the Latin impersonal pronoun: the *id,*
the "It" that is ours but is not an "I." It is atemporal, alogical, amoral. It is not
identical, for the reasons just given, with Platonic desire, but it is analogous
to it as being the place of the Libido (Latin for "desire").

"Above" it, in Freud's diagram, is the province of the Ego, where anxiety
breaks out. Recall that its Platonic counterpart, spiritedness, the agent of
self-regard, was both a mediator between desire and reason and a patient,
suffering under the harsher desires. Analogously to the sentry-like spirit,
the ego perceives threats, for it is Janus-faced. It is directly involved with the
perception of external reality, "the "perceptual-conscious," and also with the
control of internal instincts: "We might say that the ego stands for reason
and good sense while the id stands for untamed passion."[11] Here, to be sure,
the ancient analogy slips some: Platonic spirit is reasonable but it is not reason. Accordingly Freud paints a picture somewhat divergent from the soul-
chariot of the *Phaedrus*: The ego is not, like the spirited white horse of the
soul-chariot, *yoked* with the horse of desire, but rather it *rides* the id-horse;
it is, however, a strained rider, for the libidinous horse, being the source of
"locomotive energy," often runs off on its own.

The Freudian ego in fact has *three* tyrannical masters whose demands
it must mediate: external reality, the passionate id-underworld, and, a new
third, the super-ego. This third power, a supervisory bystander, sets the standards to be obeyed; if the ego fails, it is punished with "tense feelings of infe-

riority and guilt." Platonic governing reason has here turned into Freudian punishing morality. I call it a *"by-*stander" because it not only oppresses the ego from the top but also reaches by it, so to speak, to merge with the id. This merger is typified in the Oedipus complex, in which a libidinous infantile attachment to the parent of the opposite sex is eventually "precipitated" as a strong identification with the parental authority, to emerge as a severe command structure that has been internalized. Both Platonic *logos* and Freudian super-ego are made for rule, but the former *should* rule and rule by persuasive wisdom, while the latter *does* rule and rules by the most irresistible of forces—internal compulsion.

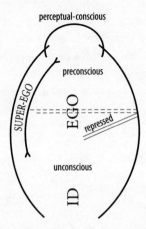

perceptual-conscious

preconscious

SUPER-EGO

EGO

repressed

unconscious

ID

Freud points out that the space occupied by the id
should be "incomparably greater."[12]

Figure IX-A

This transformation of lucid, being-directed, receptive reason into a harsh, rule-directed commanding authority amounts to a formulaic perspective on the relation to rationality of the two originating philosophic phases of the West: Greek antiquity and European modernity. But with respect to the narrower topic at hand, anxiety, the super-ego completes the array of forces that drive the ego, when it is obliged to admit its weakness, to break out in anxiety—realistic anxiety regarding the external world, moral anxiety regarding the super-ego, and neurotic anxiety regarding the strength of the passions in the id.[13]

Freud is now ready to give an account of the actual dynamics, the psychic mechanisms by which anxiety comes about. Having shown that the ego, as the place both of harmonizing struggle and of forcible rationalizations, is the place of anxiety, he can simplify and stabilize his theory.[14] Anxiety is now, more straightforwardly, a signal announcing a situation of danger. Whereas before anxiety was complicatedly created by repression, the new theory reverses that: Anxiety makes repression. The exemplary case is, again, the Oedipus complex. To begin with, a boy's anxiety is *at once* neurotic and realistic, internal and external: He feels internally threatened by his love for his mother, the demand of his libido, and precisely because he feels it as an internal danger, he must avoid it by renouncing his love. But it became an internal danger only because it conjured up an external danger, that of castration. Freud regards the boy's anxiety about castration as quite realistic, since people evidently regularly used to threaten male children with cutting off their penises; indeed, circumcision is, he says, a relic of the castration actually practiced in primitive puberty rites. So the boy represses his love for his mother—as a *result* of his internal and external anxiety.

This anxiety is, of course, somewhat more like fear, for it has a real object. But Freud mentions other more diffuse anxieties leading to repression, among them the primal trauma of birth already mentioned, the "model of all later situations of danger." In fact every stage of development has its appropriate anxiety which is left behind in the process of maturing.

At the last stage there appears the generalized fear experienced by the super-ego, which "should normally never cease, since in the form of moral anxiety, it is indispensable in social relations."[15]

The ego's kind of reasoning, rationalization—meaning the forcible finding of reasons, even spurious ones—comes into play in the dynamics of the repression that issues from anxiety. When the ego feels weak against the id's instinctual impulses, it goes into an energy-minimizing thinking mode. Like a general in a war room, who hopefully shifts model figures to win his battles in the small before moving real, large forces, the ego engages in an anticipatory, small-scale, spurious, satisfaction of the instinctual impulse and thereby incidentally reproduces its initial unpleasurable anxiety. That anxiety signal brings into operation the pleasure-unpleasure principle, which, in accordance with its nature, namely to lower tension, carries out the repression by thrusting the anxiety into the unconscious, the id.

What happens there? The answer is—suspiciously—complex. In the id the pleasure-unpleasure principle has unrestricted dominance, and it transforms the offending instinctual impulse, sometimes causing its extinction, sometimes its regression to an earlier stage. The id is very powerful compared to the ego, but the latter *can* influence it, especially by calling into action, upon anxiety's signal, the aforementioned pleasure-unpleasure principle. Yet in renouncing its influence on the repressed impulse by acquiescing to the consequent act of repression it once again shows its relative weakness. All this activity is, of course, totally submerged.

Finally Freud asks, "What is actually feared in anxiety?" I think he takes this "step backward" as a chance to formulate the objectlessness that, after all, should characterize anxiety. The answer is that from the birth trauma on, every situation of danger calls up the "state of highly tense excitation, which is felt as unpleasure" and which cannot be mastered by being discharged.[16] Such breakdowns of the pleasure principle are "traumatic moments." Consequently what is feared in every sort of anxiety, what is the true object of anxiety, is the reemergence of such a moment. For the pleasure principle does not guard us against objective but only against psychic injury. The solution to the question "What causes anxiety?" is then prosaic, for it is quantitative. What originally turned a real event, such as being born, into a traumatic moment, what paralyzes the pleasure principle and threatens the ego with danger, is simply the great magnitude of the sum of excitations, an "excessively great libidinal demand." Later on a sort of secondary anxiety may arise as a signal threatening a repetition of such a moment.[17] Present anxiety is about old anxiety.

This, then, is the other great theory of anxiety in the twentieth century. This one deals with the psyche in developmental, mechanistic, quantitative, that is, in basically naturalistic, terms; the other deals with an existence in ontic, structural, existential, that is, in ultimately ontological terms. For the former, anxiety can have internal or external causes; for the latter, a mood "comes neither from the 'outside' nor the 'inside' but arises as a way of being-in-the-world from that very way of being."[18] The physician regards serious anxiety as a common case to be effectively treated; the philosopher regards genuine anxiety as a condition of authenticity, a rare condition to be soberly celebrated. Both regard it as a centrally important aspect of human being. For a doctor who sees cases, that fact needs little explanation; the physician's problem is rather why anxiety was by then so socially entrenched a condition. This question arises instead for the philosopher: Is anxiety really the most revealing of affects?

6. In a Better Mood: Bollnow's Rehabilitation of Happiness

In his perceptive phenomenological account of the nature of moods, *Das Wesen der Stimmungen* (1941),[1] Otto Bollnow takes issue with Heidegger's ontologically based philosophical anthropology. To begin with, he sees a problem with the method. Heidegger uses the case of anxiety as exemplary for all moods, on the hypothesis that they all have the same fundamental structure and that their role in human being is similar. This assumption obviates all particular empirical inquiry and dismisses all the variety of human experience.[2]

I must say here that even for Heidegger anxiety is not the only fundamental mood or attunement. Just at the time of "What is Metaphysics?" (1929), during the two years after *Being and Time*, Heidegger delivered the above-mentioned very long lecture series on Boredom, in German *Langeweile*, literally "the long while" (1929–30).[3] Heidegger distinguishes the boredom that comes from determinate and from indeterminate boredom-sources. That is to say, boredom can have a precise or vague intentionality.[4] There is also a third, more profound boredom, that holds us in a limbo to be explained below.

The essence of all boredom is that time becomes long—the time, namely, that *Dasein* whiles away in the midst of beings. This while, though *Dasein*'s own time, is concealed from *Dasein,* which unreflectively uses it up. In boredom this while, which becomes long, is not mechanically counted clock time but *Dasein*'s proper lived time. The limits of *Dasein*'s "whiling," instead of being the *now,* the today, expand to manifest the indeterminate while of human existence. This indefiniteness is an expansion that is not liberating but oppressive; this long while "holds [Dasein] in its spell" (*Bann*).

In this condition of boredom *Dasein* is left empty, delivered over to all the beings as a whole, which deny themselves (*sich versagen*), thus announcing (*ansagen*) the *possibilities left unexploited*. This is the limbo *Dasein* is in when it exists inauthentically in a phaseless *expanse* of the "long while" rather than in the *moment* of possibilities. Such an authentic moment has its prospect and its retrospect—its true temporality that includes within itself intimations of all the phases of time, namely future, present, past.[5]

Thus boredom, the "long while," is a second fundamental mood or attunement. In "What is Metaphysics?" the Nothing that transcends all beings revealed itself in anxiety; in these lectures, beings as a whole deny themselves to bored *Dasein,* which is under the spell, the ban, of unpunctuated, pointless time. Yet in that very state that sharp crack in time, the "glancing moment" (*Augenblick*) still presses upon us as that which has been lost together with "the vanished shortness of the while": the moment of *active existence.*[6]

Thus Heidegger does consider another mood; nonetheless anxiety, which is first presented merely as an exemplary mood, is, as Bollnow points out, actually treated as the mood of moods. But since no sufficient grounds are given for regarding anxiety either as a representative mood-structure or as the finally fundamental mood, the question arises: Is all human existence that is not focused on existential anxiety really to be regarded as an inauthentic, spoiled condition?[7] Bollnow is here implicitly calling Heidegger's bluff, for the latter always draws back from the plain admission that the inauthentic modes, albeit they all bear morally derogatory names like "falling" and "falling-apart," have in fact been devalued by him.

Bollnow now embarks on the project of showing that the elevated moods have at least as much to say about the way things are as the depressed ones. Thus happiness (*Glück*) as mood can claim at least as much power to disclose reality as the negative moods. (Recall here that, though the word we render as "happiness" meant neither an emotion nor a mood for Aristotle, but a fulfillment of the soul at work, for us it does tend to be a feeling, and not necessarily an object-directed one—thus a quasi-mood.) For anxiety and other low moods isolate human beings—Heidegger, to be sure, regards that as a revelatory plus—while the joyful and happy moods tend toward communion. What is more, such elevated moods show us reality as supportive rather than oppressive. Heidegger denies exactly that possibility by speaking of the "burden of being" that must be taken up and by asserting that the "elevated" (*gehobene*) moods "alleviate" (*entheben*) and thus mask this heaviness.[8] But Bollnow points out that in such elevated states, from joyous moods through high inebriation to blissful ecstasy, the world is, to be sure, transformed, but reality is not thereby annulled. What is nullified is rather the opposition between the self and an alien world.[9] Against Heidegger, Bollnow appeals to experience of such revelatory moods gathered from notable literary records. He does not, however, provide a countervailing ontology. Perhaps—I am speculating—an ontology of elevated *moods* is not possible because genuinely philosophical positive affectivity is not moodlike but passionate. I mean that exhilarating affects are not about nothing, are not objectlessly indeterminate, but are about something, are more or less crisply object-directed, even when they, yet vaguely, anticipate the object they long for. Bollnow does point out that the boundaries between moods and feelings (*Gefühle*)—he means emotions—are somewhat fluid. Nonetheless, for him too the distinction is fundamental, and, moreover, the moods again have priority over emotions. The former are as a thoroughbass to the melody of the latter; moods are as the psychic frame around emotional events: "The intentional acts in their directedness and modulation flow forth from this subsoil of mood."[10]

This notion that mood is deeper than passion seems to dominate the Existential-Phenomenological school of thought: "Mood . . . constitutes the elementary foundation of experience."[11] Much deep analysis and acute observation regarding the affects comes from this school, but, finally, they may be mistaken about the priority of mood over emotion. Mood may not go as deep as they think. It may be a kind of soul-coloration, an affective tinting that easily shades into what is called *Laune* in German, "whim" or "caprice."[12] The preference may be a kind of Romantic hangover, a socially induced or at least encouraged form of terminal subjectivity, moodiness levered into position as the human ground. The very fact that moods when good are, although so mistily musical, yet shot through with gleams of visual reminiscences, and when bad are, although so paralyzingly pall-like, yet active with stabs of pain, might be evidence of their epiphenomenality. To me it seems possible that moods, our attunement to the world, do not arise from our deepest affectivity at all but are indeed epiphenomena, that is, piggyback effects, of our quasi-perceptual representational imagination, a power that can have no place in Heidegger's *Being and Time*. For as I have repeated several times, *Dasein*, human existence, is not a soul that has an inside and outside; its very being is a direct openness to its world and *not* a capacity for representing the world's beings within; *Dasein* has no *room* for the depictive imagination.[13] But imagination, whose relation to affectivity and interiority will be taken up in the next and last chapter, is that very capability for re-presenting the outside world to the inside soul in affect-laden images. It must be a significant circumstance that in this chapter the moody mode that arose in the froth of Romantic imaginative subjectivity ends up as the fundamental feature of a severely imagination-devoid existence. Perhaps that betokens a latter-day tendency toward simplifying sophistication, toward imageless abstruseness. Perhaps it even presages—strange to say— the contemporary flight from the patent but cumbrous analog mode into opaque but efficient digitalization.

chapter X

Our Times

Theorizing

W ith respect to emotion studies, the last century can be divided into decades of freeze and decades of torrent—though these telescopic overviews of artificial time-territories are intellectually dubious from two aspects. First, we (at least I) never know enough to tell the exact story, and second, people are not conveniently conformist epoch-sheep who amble as a flock one way in a given quarter-century. Let this account then stand as a shaky bridge by which I get myself and the willing reader from one significant text to the next.

It does seem, however, that spatial territory plays a real role in the study of emotion in the first part of the last century. On the European continent wrote the founders of what would be the schools of Psychoanalysis, Phenomenology, and Existentialism. But they were little regarded in Anglo-Saxon lands, where they seemed at once abstruse and woolly: They were not empirical but introspective, not linguistically analytical but verbally ingenious. This went against the English-speaking grain and led to a freeze on emotion studies, as various hard-edged, reductive schools captured adherents: Logical Positivism, Behaviorism, Language Analysis—positivist approaches in the sense of demanding patent, verifiable evidence and precise, stripped-down language.[1] "Emotivism" was, albeit by indirection, one way to denigrate emotions. The notion was introduced by Ayer,[2] who traced his indebtedness back to Hume's logical empiricism, via Russell, and Wittgenstein. The idea was that ethical pronouncements, that is, assertions of value, are neither true nor false, that they are without truth value but are "emotive," partly expressions of feeling, partly injunctions. Ayer is not overtly against feeling, but he does eject its study from philosophy redefined as a department of logic, namely as the inquiry into the formal consequences of definition. Emotion is thought to be too much the antithesis of such logic, too private, to engage inquiry concerned with truth.

I shall select for presentation one writer from each approach: Sartre will represent a first-fruit of Phenomenal-Existential philosophy; I will there subjoin a brief consideration of certain emotions expressive of Continental *mal de siècle* and its sequel. Ryle will then be asked to stand for the Language-analytic and Behaviorist point of view. Both texts to be considered fall within the first half of the twentieth century.

Around mid-century a thaw set in and with it a torrent of science-style emotion studies. I do not exactly know why this happened—probably the release of post-World War II energy and the discovery of a large untilled field had something to do with it, along with a rebellion against reductive rationalism, accompanied by an outbreak of avidity for practical empiricism, followed by a spate of scientific theorizing. Partly, though, the sense that a new era has begun is, it seems, an artifact attendant on the notion of cutting-edge research, which augurs into the future as the past silts up behind it—bibliographically, I mean: Approaches that buck the trend simply get buried as dead on arrival.

An example of the earlier work done in this empirical-theoretical mode will be that of Tomkins. Eventually the most concrete advances in the neurophysiological underpinnings of the affects come to center in brain science, while conceptualizations and theories of emotion burgeon, especially of the cognitivist sort that emphasize the belief element in emotions. I will try to find my way through the chief presentations.[3]

1. Experienced Emotion: The Continent

A. The Magicking of the World: Sartre

The magicking of the world is the crux of Sartre's theory of emotion.[1] The attempt to describe human experience by acutely concentrated introspection that is the initial effort of Phenomenology,[2] combined with reflections on the way human beings are in the world that is the burden of Existentialism, produced this most appealingly eccentric theory of the emotions that I am aware of. It is sketched out in Sartre's *The Emotions* (1939). In sum, Sartre thinks that emotions are a magic we work subjectively on the world, a transformation by which we annihilate an objective threat as in fear, or possess an objective pleasure as in joy. It sounds a little counterintuitive but gains some plausibility through its Phenomenological frame and its Existential focus.

Sartre starts from the observation of consciousness: Emotions are not, to begin with, experienced the way psychologists tend to present them: as "posited," that is to say, as consciously acknowledged; they are not at first self-conscious perceptions of a conscious state. They are rather just *immediate* apprehensions *of* the world. Here Sartre is adverting to the notion of intentionality: Every emotion is primarily intentional, *about* an object. Thus it is essentially objective—though the object might be imaginary—rather than self-absorbed. Fear, for example, is determined by that which makes us afraid and which we want to flee, be it bear or bogeyman. Hence we pass very immediately and unreflectively from the ordinary "world-to-be-acted-on" to the charged "world-to-be-fearful-of." The world impinges on us at once as object and as fearful; it catches us, so to speak, self-unawares.

Hence this is *not* what happens:

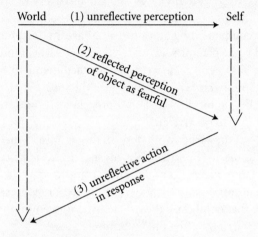

And this is what *does* happen:

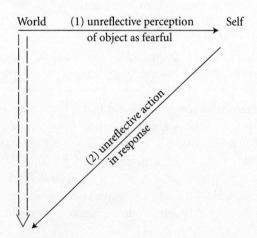

The second, immediate course is not unconscious but it is, in Husserlian vocabulary, "non-thetic," that is to say, not accompanied by a conscious "positing," an acceptance of the situation: I am, rather, impelled to act at a certain spontaneous existential level in the world. The world exigently demands my action, and I have "a pragmatistic intuition of the determinism of the world."³ Simply put, the world makes me respond with immediacy and along certain necessary routes—not unconsciously, yet directly. If nothing is in the way, I react calmly.

Emotion, then, is that direct response when the paths prescribed are too difficult, when the world becomes too "urgent," and all ways are barred. Emotion is the magical transformation of this world from the one that is "exigently" given, intransigently deterministic, to another that is more manageable. We cannot get hold of the world as it is, so, under unsustainable tension, we seize it as otherwise. It is the same kind of reconception that occurs when, by a sudden shift of perception, we see in a picture figures not visible before. That is the phenomenon of "aspect seeing," which was, contemporaneously, so central to Wittgenstein's thinking. It occurs when, say, a wedge-shaped outline may look like—is re-visioned—now as a triangular hole, now as a mountain, now as several imaginable other things.⁴

Such emotive behavior is not like most other behaviors; "it is not effective." Yet "if emotion is a joke, it is a joke we believe in."⁵

Sartre's illustrative examples range from trivial to serious: from Aesop's proverbial unreachable grapes, re-envisioned as too green to be desirable, to the wild animal at the sight of which one faints, thus annihilating—not, to be sure, its real presence—but one's consciousness of it. This is eliminating danger by bowing out of its—and all—presence. Similarly in sadness for a loss, one withdraws from the bereaved world and makes it as one wishes it: affectively neutral. This is the aspect of Sartre's *Outline* that will later range it under "conative," that is, desire-driven, theory.

The positive emotions might seem more difficult to place within this theory, but Sartre explains joy in the same terms: We are psychologically inertial. Thus the realization of the full delight in being, say, reunited with an object of love or friendship takes time; the object of pleasure "only yields itself little by little. . . . Joy is a magical behavior which tends by incantation to realize the possession of the desired object as instantaneous totality." Joy works the magic of anticipatory possession, possession that outruns psychic readiness. It seems to me this observation does much to redeem the whole somewhat *outré* theory. Here is its summary:

> Thus the origin of emotion is a spontaneous and lived degradation of consciousness in the face of the world. What it cannot endure in one way it tries to grasp in another. . . . ⁶

Hence emotion is a mode of existence in the world, of world-consciousness—a way of "being-in-the-world" in Heidegger's sense. That means that the body has a merely expressive, submissive role in the emotions: Consciousness changes the body, which is a thing among things used by consciousness as its means of incantation. "Physiological manifestations are, at bottom, very trivial disturbances."[7] This is a position diametrically opposite to that of the most successful current theory, in which physiology is primary. Sartre says, however, that small physical fluctuations do account for the "delicate" or intimating—as distinct from "weak" or damped—emotions. A slight discomfort warns us, by a "modified wonder . . . of a disaster dimly seen"; thus is profound disaster subtly anticipated.

Sartre tackles, quite by the way, two old problems. First, the "list" question: He denies that there are just four major types, fear, anger, sadness, joy. To begin with, there is an infinite variety of emotional consciousnesses, because each object qualifies the affect. But also, since each emotion is temporally sited and thus modified by its forerunner, each successor emotion receives its tincture from the previous one: Thus fear passing into anger yields a new type of anger, that of anger incorporating surpassed fear.[8] That the emotions are multifariously colored by their particular objects and finely qualified by their temporal setting seems to me close to a last truth about them.

A pertinent aside here to show Sartre's taxonomic insights bear on the most current problems: The age-old question concerning the taxonomy and naming of the passions turns out to be closely related to the recently acute problem concerning the identification of emotions with biological conditions. For the connection of brain events and physical responses with particular emotional arousals requires established protocols listing and naming the latter, since such identifications depend on laboratory subjects' self-reports. But those names come, perforce, from the subjects' ordinary language: "fear," "sadness," "happiness." The emotions so named are, however, far too coarse, perhaps one might say, too pure, to designate much actual human feeling; most emotions are composites, blends, or meldings (as Hume and now Sartre had observed). They are also, indeed primarily colored by their object, origin, and setting. They are, moreover, too equivocally, too incongruously related to the biological processes being observed to yield an exact science of emotion; there seems to be, at least so far, no exact homology, no fixed structural analogy, nor any precise symbolic relation between the realms of observable biology and of felt affect.[9]

The second old problem is that of "false" emotions. Falseness in emotion, says Sartre, is not a logical propositional characteristic but an existential quality. False emotion is a behavioral comedy, a mimicking of, say, joy or sadness. But it is not an actor's mimicry, which is an emotionally disengaged behavior, addressed to and functional in a fictional universe. The behavior of false emotion is not sustained by a special dramatic world; it occurs in a real situation and is a voluntary, if not fully conscious, attempt to invest through magic real objects with qualities that are as false as the faked emotion, a semi-self-foolery.[10]

Sartrean emotion-magic is a near-*unconscious* fabrication, and so it raises the question: Can emotions be roused at will? The Stoics thought that they could be extinguished at will, and most people agree that they can at least be controlled. But what about emotional self-excitation; is it enough like physical self-stimulation to be feasible? Most of us have indeed had the experience of working ourselves into a temper (children do it willfully quite often) or some other emotional state, such as making deliberate shows of affection in order to summon some—sorry—simulacrum of it within. There are, in fact, current techniques for fostering emotions, useful both in daily living and as a method for particular action.[11] It might be, however, that the modern, subjective emotions are more amenable to such manipulations than the old, subjugating passions.

Is Sartre positively or negatively disposed toward the emotions? Once the magical world is delineated, consciousness tends to perpetuate it; this world "is compressed against the emotion and clasps it"; the attempt to get away from the magical object only emphasizes its grip and gives it stronger "magical reality." (Here is an existential anticipation of the South American literary mode of mundane magic called "magical realism.") Now the world's objects are captivating; consciousness is unrealizingly caught in the magical world it has made and come to believe in. For, so Phenomenology teaches, it can *know* itself only through its intentional objects; it always must transcend itself, meaning that it must go beyond itself in tending toward objects, being *empty* in itself. Unconfronted consciousness is limpidly transparent, inactive. Hence Sartre's insistence on the specification of an emotion by its object.

And therefore, "Freedom has to come from a purifying reflection on or a total disappearance of the affecting situation."[12] There is, it turns out, a rational-reductionist and an anti-imaginative denigration of the passions. The positivists practiced the former; Sartre has adopted the latter. For we achieve our fully free being in the world by de-magicking it through a cathartic cognition of our emotional construals.

The theory of the *Outline* is carried into *Being and Nothingness* (1943), where it is lodged in the Phenomenological—and Existential—ontology of which I give the most minimal sketch here.[13]

It is the earmark of Sartre's existentialism that the world's being has no natural essence, no positive "whatness," but is—the terminology is Hegelian—as a "Being-*in*-itself," a brute being that "transcends" or lies beyond the phenomena, massively, opaquely undifferentiated. Yet "nothingness haunts being,"[14] and it is thus negatively that the latter gets its characterizing distinctions. Spinoza's maxim was that all determination, that is, every fixation of features, is negation; Sartre converts it (as had Hegel before him) to say that all negation is determination.[15] Hence it is negation, which it is in fact lodged in massive Being, that distinguishes it into a plurality of beings.

There is, however, a second kind of being, Being-*for*-itself, a being that is present to itself, namely human consciousness. Consciousness questions Being-in-itself and so wrenches the "in-itself" continuity of this inertial being away from it. Brute being thus actually receives the negations within it from the "concrete nothingness" of consciousness. What does it mean to say something so contrary to ordinary thinking, that the distinctions within the non-conscious "external" world ultimately come from consciousness? It is somewhat obscure to me, but Sartre seems to mean that a conscious being is never quite one with the object its questioning intends or with itself as it is present to itself. It is *not* its object, not at one with what it perceives, and it is *not* itself, not self-identical. This constant, world-affecting slide into "elsewhereness," that characterizes consciousness in the absence of a stable essence, is indeed the source of human freedom, of the ability to become what we choose to be. More to the present point, the nothingness of consciousness is concrete in not being the abstract opposite of in-itself being; it is rather sited *in* reality, and thus it *pervades the world* and introduces its negations into it: The external world is—somehow—inhabited by consciousness. The nothingness of Sartre's *Being and Nothingness* is both a borrowing from Heidegger and a departure, since in his *Being and Time*, *Dasein's* nothing is an experience of transcending the world of ordinary living so as to face it, while for Sartre nothingness is immanent, built both into the world *and* into consciousness.

A similar but possibly clearer way to talk of Sartre's world-discerning nothingness is to consider that to ask questions about any one being, any object, I must negate its close causal interconnection with other beings *and* I must interpose a clear distance, a nothingness within myself that distances me from the object so as to allow it to emerge *for* myself, reveal itself *to* me. Thus it can be said that "Consciousness is a being the nature of which is to be conscious of the nothingness of its being" and thereby of the negating distinctions of the world. That is not merely a way of describing a human being as a being capable of negating, of re-moving, being; it is a way of possible conduct, a distancing, nothingness-interposing way. Derivative from it are all sorts of annihilating behaviors. They are our common human way. Sartre calls them "bad faith." This is the setting for magicking the world in emotion in *Being and Nothingness.*[16]

Lying is an example, but it is only one sort of "bad faith." In emotional self-deception the non-self-identicality and self-chosenness of consciousness both come into play. Sartre picks sadness to illustrate the theory: It is an attitude I have adopted—as is proved by the fact that I can be distracted from it—adopted "as a magical recourse against a situation that is too urgent." And since there is "no inertia of consciousness [as there is of things], for consciousness is of itself empty," I must continually *make* myself sad: The being-in-itself of sadness keeps escaping me while haunting me. "I am not what I am" and I am not quite conscious of what my consciousness effects. Clearly, magicking is not deliberate lying, though it all but obliterates any distinction between genuine and false emotion.[17]

I should note here that other affects, love, desire, hate, are treated in *Being and Nothingness* but not under the aegis of the magical theory. Rather the heading is "Concrete Relations with Others," and the description is in terms of the impingement on one's own or the other's freedom and the appropriation of the other as an object.[18] This perspective puts each passionate consciousness into the incessant conflict with itself and the other. It is an account at least as dispiriting as it is veracious. Existentialist existence and its accounts are not given to jocundity.

B. Existence and Its Discontents

This existence, cast atomically into the world, has its peculiar discontents, among them nausea, disgust, ennui. In old antiquity the passions that illumine the human essence are vehement and strongly object-directed: spirited anger, erotic love, and tragic terror. In recent modernity the emotions that shed light on human existence are delicate and self-referring, practically non-intentional: anxiety, boredom, and the vertiginous nausea that is the feel of being an unnecessary being involved in a gross, absurd world, a fascinated disgust that comes from contact with its hypertrophic life, and the dull ennui that follows on the demise even of mere curiosity.

Of course, this sketch is a half-truth; ordinary modern humans have, as those before us, a superfluity of brutely vehement feelings. I am reporting here, first, on a subclass of tone-setters who actually cultivated the exquisite sensitivities whose very symptom is a lack of lively affect, particularly of sound desire. They colluded in the "social construction" of these affects, for which a legitimizing delineation of subjective experience in literary works is often trendsetting.

There followed, particularly starting in the earlier part of the last century, a monographic, secondary literature in which the aberrant and morbid affects get objective recognition: Previously still-proscribed perversion is thus given public status by permissible pedantry; the real moral dilemmas of such philosophical and scholarly acknowledgment and appropriation are set out by Roger Shattuck in *Forbidden Knowledge*.[19]

All the moody affects mentioned above—anxiety, boredom, ennui, nausea, disgust—are interrelated. Of this depressive complex, anxiety, treated at length in the previous chapter, has received the existentially deepest interpretations—where "existential" refers to the way human beings find themselves cast, "thrown," into the world without the anchor of a divinity or fixed human essence. But boredom has now unquestionably become the most extended, endemic and epidemic feel of modern times. And, although the word itself is first cited in 1864, its meaning also has the longest history, for the monk's acedia is the recognizable forerunner of the secular "psychic anorexia" or "atrophy of desire" that marks boredom: "Our former Age of Anxiety has given way to an Age of Boredom." All these facts and quotation come from Patricia Spacks's study, *Boredom,* which recounts the state of mind as it is mirrored in literature.[20] To some extent the diagnosis, written at the end of the last century, may be superseded by a return to the age of anxiety in a time of "asymmetrical warfare," that is, war against a stateless, armyless, covert enemy. But for the well-entrenched residue of the epidemic, dozens of reasons for modern and postmodern boredom can be given: leisured affluence, routinized work, over-stimulating entertainment, etc., etc.

I think, however, that the ultimate cause is to be found in the very condition that is rightly named "modern": "Modern," *modernus,* is the Latin word for "just now"; modernity is the temporal mode of quickly—more and more quickly—changing nowness, of the demand for and subjection to novelty, for innovation, be it in the sphere of experience, invention, or interpretation. Heidegger's analysis of curiosity and its expectable turn to tedium highlights a characteristic aspect of modernity and its post-modern appendix.

i. Nausea   Nausea was brought to the fore by Sartre, first in his novel *Nausea* (1938);[21] it later appears in his philosophical work *Being and Nothingness.* There Sartre says that his term *nausea* must not be taken as a metaphor from physiological disgust, but rather as "the foundation . . . for all concrete and empirical nauseas" such as those caused by spoiled meat and excrement. This nausea in itself is, however, an "insipid taste," a non-positional, that is, not consciously affirmed, apprehension of myself as a brutely factual existence; this taste is a dull and inescapable sense of myself as a contingently existing bodily being, a sense only temporarily mastered by pain or pleasure.[22] Sartrean nausea is the counterpart in importance to Heideggerian anxiety; they differ in accordance with their philosophies: As Heidegger distances human existence from the world, Sartre involves it with the world. Accordingly in *Nausea* the narrator, Roquentin, experiences, oddly enough, quite vividly—such is the art of the novel—this elusive half-mood in all its tonalities, from its "relief" in profound boredom to its immediate return in a willed nightmare of civilization-disgust.

The nausea of *Nausea* is centrally a novel way of coming to grips with the Cartesian doubt about the fact of human existence and its need for certification by human consciousness. Nausea is a kind of "visceral cogito."[23] It certifies existence but this certainty is no steady platform for a cognitive project. For it implies something awful about existence: that it is *de trop,* superfluous—an unnecessary contingency, just an "extra" in a pointless play:

We were a heap of living creatures, irritated, embarrassed at ourselves, we hadn't the slightest reason to be there ... and I—soft, weak, obscene, digesting, juggling with dismal thoughts—I, too, was *de trop* ... even my death would be *de trop*.[24]

This unnecessary life, this unaccountable, radically absurd life in a body, displays a kind of meaningless teeming, a hypersensitivity both of the inward-turned imagination and of its body in sensory contact with things: a "horrible ecstasy" before the gross, absurd world.[25] That is what makes a novelistic account of nausea so sensorily—coloristically and tonally—vivid. The nauseated man is always *in extremis* under sensual impressions and subject to sexual impulses tending to criminality—and then again to quietism. Thus Roquentin's entry:

Tuesday
Nothing : Existed[26]

Radical contingency is a discovery of the medieval Nominalist theologians (Ockham in particular), who, regarding all universal essences as mere names and therefore not able to trammel the omnipotence of the Creator, made of the non-necessity of each and every uniquely novel individual an occasion for faith. The dismalness of these typical modern existential affects is, so it seems to me, even more deeply a consequence of nominalism secularly reconceived than of the gloomy historical setting, from the premonitory dis-ease of the turn of the nineteenth century to its dreadful realization in the two World Wars of the twentieth. As I write this, there sounds in my ear the text of a Bach setting of Matthew 8:26, "O ye of little faith why are ye so *fearful*";[27] the Greek word of the New Testament text, *deiloi,* is closer to "vilely wretched" than to "afraid," but anxiety is germane. It seems that existential nausea is a sort of obverse of faith. They have this, at least, in common: It is next to impossible to decide whether they are willfully discretionary or receptively passive states.

When the meaning of existence is precisely its brute "mereness," an encompassing indifference ensues,[28] that "*insipid* taste" of the nothingness of existence which can become the experiential basis of existential freedom—the one acknowledged human necessity, that of doing nature over, of self-creation.

ii. Disgust   Disgust is obviously close to nausea; for Sartre it is actually a peculiar—evidently too personal—mode of nausea, that in which I am conscious of myself as being an "object-for-others, a body with deformities, so that I feel an anticipatory disgust for my too-white flesh. . . ."[29]

Disgust has a curiously opalescent character, like putrescence itself: There is fascination and repulsion in it at once. Huysmans depicts this double effect in his *mal-du-siècle* classic of the sick sensibility, *Against Nature* (1884).[30] The hero feels "a perverse craving" for the "nauseating snack," a "disgusting white mess" that a squalid, snot-nosed urchin is eating (a lump of skim-milk cheese sprinkled with garlic on a grimy hunk of bread). The passage points up a feature of disgust delineated by Aurel Kolnai in his essay *On Disgust* (1927),[31] a feature that makes it the complement of Sartrean nausea. Whereas nausea is mainly the repelled sense of existential nothingness, disgust is the repulsion from hypertrophic nature—both are too-much-impinging apprehensions of existence:

> [T]here is undoubtedly associated with the extinction of life in putrefaction a certain—quite remarkable—augmentation of life: a heightened announcement of the fact that life *is there.*[32]

It is not, however, every pathological activity that becomes disgusting, but only what pertains to the body when it obtrudes itself *as* bodily, by too close crowding or loveless proximity or the exposing of its interior or the magnification of its imperfection. The last is an experience Swift's Gulliver has among the monstrously large Brobdingnagians; it is even the prototype experience of what is later called "the eroticism of disgust," for Gulliver has hilarious relations of the flesh with one of these female giants.[33]

Thus there seems to be a *haut-goût* attached to putrescent odors and tastes such as smelly cheeses and gamy geese; they evidence the life of organic off-ness and of dead flesh. Another kind of somatic obtrusiveness is profuseness: "All fecundity is simply disgusting."[34] One could go on and on.

All these gustatory disgusts are, however, mostly acquired, hyper-sophisticated feelings, which derive their edgy attraction from savoring some substance just short of the positively putrid. Surely most disgust is simply inborn protective physical repulsion from things bad to ingest or touch; it is a feel rather than a feeling. "Disgust" refers, after all, to taste (Latin *gustus*); it means dis-taste.

What is more to my point is metaphorical disgust—existential and moral. Recall that Sartre speaks of "the insipid taste of existence," an existence that nonetheless teems with the glow of decay—the taste of these high-toned nothings causes existential disgust.

Moral disgust too is interpreted in the light of the "coquetry" exuded by "the surplus of life in disgusting formations . . . the swollen overloadedness of vitality or of what is organic,[35] that is, viscous and slimy, as opposed to what is inorganically dry and structured. Kolnai gives as a strangely persuasive example our reaction to mendacity: It is not possible to lay hold of a liar or betrayer; he is hidden by "a layer of slippery, dirty vitality," a "putrescence and semi-flourishing." He is a slimy character, as we say, who has the feel of moral corruption. "And then surges up the image of a formless, homogeneously pappy, pulpy, carious mass." In a liar it is not that the hard-edged values of honesty disappear, but rather that they live on in diminished, deformed, and dissolving moods.[36] Kolnai is a master of the vocabulary of the shuddering retraction of the senses.

"The image surges up." Is moral disgust then merely figurative, though the simile is imposed on the prime and most pervasive figure of the West— the soul seen as body? There is indeed a very pertinent novelistic realization of esthetic moral disgust: In Oscar Wilde's *Portrait of Dorian Grey* (1891), the progressively dissolute morality of the sitter is tracked by the actual dis- solution of his likeness on canvas; his image becomes disgusting. I think, however, that in the case of moral disgust, which is not, as is existential nausea, a half non-intentional mood, but is a vehemently focused emotion with a vivid intentional object, the somatic image of the soul is more than a conceit. Nature—maybe evolution—has done the clever thing here. In making us imagine spiritual corruption as physical putrescence, it has made our body recoil from evil as from foulness, in accordance with the fact that it is, after all, through the body that we give effect to our morality. And yet, a sophisticatedly spoiled taste might find a fascination precisely in embod- ied evil. But these are mysteries of the perverse will and its seduction of the senses that are beyond *this* book.

iii. Ennui   Ennui, a potent part of the modern affect-complex, is a French term, from *esse alicui in odio,* "to be in a state of hatred or disgust toward something"; in Late Latin *inodiare* becomes "to render loathsome" and thence *ennuir*; it comes weakly into English in the verb "to annoy." "Ennui" itself predates "boredom" by a century in England. From the first, it includes a sense of weariness and carries to this day a more metaphysical sense than boredom—especially in its Anglo-Saxon use, which the Conti- nental ontological interpretation of boredom has not reached.[37] Ordinary boredom is companionable. Its confession calls forth the colluding smirk of an open secret and the recollecting snicker at the all-too-true, unhelpful old motherly fudge:

> Life, friends, is boring. We must not say so.
> After all the sky flashes, the great sea yearns,
> we ourselves flash and yearn,
> and moreover my mother told me as a boy
> (repeatedly) "Even to confess you're bored means you have no
>
> Inner Resources."[38]

These are not the tones of existential despair.

But those tones *are* exactly the notes sounded by confessions of ennui. The most characteristic passages here cited—from French writers of the nineteenth century, who wrote most revealingly on this state of mind—are taken from the chief monograph on accounts of ennui in literature, Reinhard Kuhn's *The Demon of Noontide* (1976).[39] Ennui seems to pick out a special sort of emotion, namely that which, if it has an intentional object at all, has a negative one. Thus it is at once a state of the soul, a persistent affect, an existential mood.

Kuhn distinguishes four marks of ennui: It begins in the soul but affects the body; it is independent of external circumstances; it is also independent of the will; it involves a sense of estrangement from the world and its meaning. The first mark of ennui is emphasized by the fact that Baudelaire, one of its experts, often calls it by the lymphoid organ that is supposed to be its seat, borrowing the English word "spleen," (as the English borrowed "ennui"). The fourth mark is its very definition:

> The state of emptiness that the soul feels when it is deprived of interest in action, life and the world (be it in this world or another), a condition that is the immediate consequence of the encounter with nothingness and has as an immediate effect a disaffection with reality.[40]

The manifestations are in one direction morose joylessness, up to despair, in the other an arrogant sense of superiority up to a sense of godlikeness. "Schizophrenics, supermen, artists, and saints"—these are types affected by ennui—a choice affliction.

Ennui offers a curious kind of immortality. Thus Baudelaire writes:

> Ennui, fruit of bleak incuriosity,
> Takes on the proportions of eternity.[41]

For ennui withdraws the sufferer even from curiosity, the frantic version of real interest, and turns the mortal span, whose perhaps unconscious spice is that it is measured, into this-worldly time-without-end. One self-observer draws this conclusion: Ennui cannot engender suicide because it is itself already post-mortal, a death-in-life: witness those who die of ennui Sunday afternoon

> because they see Monday coming
> and Tuesday, and Wednesday . . .[42]

Indeed the Lord's day in a secular world is often devoted to ennui. I remember the heartfelt French children's song: "Les enfants s'ennuient le dimanche."

About Kuhn's middle two marks, however, I have doubts. Though ennui may be more "endogenous" than the real emotions, external circumstances do seem to figure. Some self-descriptions of those affected show that cramp-ing social conditions, personal isolation, physical debility, and unhealthy regimens are very much the background causes of ennui.

To be sure, there may be a pure ennui that is perceived by the sufferer as purely endogenous:

> I mean . . . not passing ennui; not ennui through fatigue. . . . Instead I mean this perfect ennui, this pure ennui, this ennui that has neither misfortune nor infir-mity as its origin, which is consonant with the most blissful of all imaginable conditions—in brief, this ennui that has no other substance than life itself, and no other secondary cause than the clear-mindedness of the living being. This absolute ennui is in itself nothing but life laid bare when it contemplates itself with lucidity.[43]

This apotheosis of a revelatory ennui is coincidental with Socratic sobriety, and Valéry has indeed put its description in Socrates' mouth. There is a cer-tain arresting naughtiness in making a Greek virtue of a French vice, espe-cially when this philosophic transfixing of the world has so little in common with the characteristic morose alienation from it felt in "normal" ennui.

So also is the will not invariably powerless against ennui. The accounts of monastics' struggles with *acedia* as a sin—*acedia* being unmistakably the theological forerunner of secular ennui—show that victory over "the noon-tide demon" was a moral possibility.[44]

Why, really, are anxiety, nausea, disgust, and ennui thematized and thus legitimized by tone-setting moderns? That is, thank goodness, a question beyond this book, one with too many speculative and too few compelling answers. Has the natural, human, social world revealed a new aspect of itself? Have too many souls lost their normal spring, or have the gods that troubled us receded so that we must now plague ourselves?

I pass on now to an astringent view of the affects that would, it seems to me, treat the existential pretensions of these self-observed internal states somewhat dismissively—did they come to its notice.

2. Externalized Emotion: Ryle

The reductionists are, at least, not wordy.[1] It ought to be simpler to report on Ryle's *The Concept of Mind* (1949),[2] which is in its style of expression as in the tempo of its thought the antithesis of its Continental Phenomeno-logical and Existential contemporaries—but it is not so. As so often in brisk, no-nonsense writing, it's clearer on the page than on reflection.

Ryle did not wish to be regarded as the founder or follower of a school.[3] His chief book, however, as the title implies, is a theory of the mind and so belongs to, or rather initiates, a philosophical direction called "Philosophy of Mind." But the work is also meant "to rectify the logical geography of the knowledge we already possess."[4] Such negative inquiries belong, incidentally, to a great philosophical tradition: Some of Plato's dialogues seemed only to show up error and were hence called in antiquity "anatreptic," that is, "overturning" or refutational.[5] Once again, however, since one can refute anything only from a position, very powerful positive opinions in fact drive the book; the two most to the present point are "Ordinary Language Philosophy" and "Behaviorism."

"Ordinary language philosophy" is the notion that concepts are fixed by common linguistic use and that by attending to the way that terms function in ordinary speech one discovers what words in fact signify and what uses are aberrant or illogical uses. I will say up front that most of my difficulties with Ryle's own theory of the emotions stem from this philosophy, which is reasonable in theory but requires a truer ear in application than its practitioners seem to me to evince. At least what ordinary people (who are presumably the speakers of ordinary language) are said to mean by ordinary-language philosophers is in crucial cases not what I would agree they mean or what I myself mean. I will give an example taken from John Dewey's "The Theory of Emotion" (1894),[6] which is on various points an—unacknowledged—forerunner of Ryle's work. Dewey says: "When we say that John Smith is very resentful at the treatment he received . . . we do not simply, or even chiefly, mean that he has a certain 'feel' occupying his consciousness. We mean he is in a certain practical attitude, has assumed a readiness to act in certain ways."[7] But that isn't at all what I mean. I mean just exactly that he is in a certain inner "state," since I know very well the seething condition of eating one's heart out, suffering in silence, holding it in, and keeping a stiff upper lip—and I wonder that, if not the American Dewey, then the Englishman Ryle wouldn't know this kind of thing too. To me it seems that ordinarily when I speak of someone's feelings I mean that they feel them; what they are ready to do—here's part of our trouble with each other—who knows?

"Behaviorism" comes in roughly two sorts. The first is the radical-reductionist "scientific" type propounded by the psychologist J. B. Watson, who introduced the term in 1913. In this theory, internal states of consciousness are simply bypassed—and effectually repudiated—in favor of observable behavior, in particular the responses to controlled stimuli. It was B. F. Skinner who later disowned the inner contribution to human behavior explicitly, throwing its whole burden on environmental conditioning.

Ryle's behaviorism belongs to the second, "philosophic," type, which works in tandem with the linguistic analysis. For him emotions, along with other mental occurrences, are "dispositions" to behave in certain ways. Here too he is anticipated by Dewey, who described the emotional experience as "a disposition, a mode of conduct, a way of behaving."[8] Neither writer is reductionist in the sense of devaluing or denying internality. In Dewey's case, however, the emphasis is all on the practical effect of affects, while Ryle concentrates on the way in which language is—here a literal meaning, not Ryle's own, comes in handy—utterance, an "outering" that yields up whatever is available to us in respect to internally felt emotions of others. His analysis is, as I said, by turns simple and subtle—and terminally puzzling.

Let me get Ryle's rectification of the putatively prevalent Cartesian myth out of the way: This prevalent "official doctrine" says that every human being has a body and a mind. The body is a spatially extended mechanism and is externally observable. The mind is not spatial and not publicly witnessable; only I am privileged to take direct cognizance of my mind's states and processes; its career is private. There is thus a polar opposition between mind and matter, and their admittedly necessary interactions are mysterious. Moreover, our language about other people's minds, including their emotions, expressed in our use of "mental-conduct verbs," is thus about their "secret histories," which cannot but be inaccessible to us directly.

This doctrine is, Ryle thinks, absurd. He calls it "the dogma of the Ghost in the Machine," meaning that some elusive thing seems to be working our bodies from a metaphorical inside. He means to prove that it is in principle, that is, logically, false. It is, in fact, a "category-mistake." Such a mistake occurs as an error in the level of the class meant in a proposition. Here is Ryle's example: A visitor is shown the classroom buildings, the library, the gymnasium, and the dining hall of a college. Then he wants to know: "But where is *the college*?" The visitor is mistaking the category of "a college" for that of its various buildings.

The Cartesians' category-mistake came about thus. At the root is the fact that Descartes regards mind and body equally as things. Since mental processes are not mechanical they must be non-mechanical, but both events are in the category of "thing" and thus describable in terms of stuff, attribute, state, process, cause, effect. As the visitor thought of "the college" as yet another edifice, so Cartesians thought of minds as yet another machine, "a spectral machine." So the absurdity lies not in saying that bodies exist and minds exist. Rather it is absurd not to understand what this saying signifies: not that there are two different species of existence, but that there are two "logical tones of voice" in which the word "exist" can be used. Mind and matter belong to different logical types, and it is a category-mistake either to pit one against the other on an equal basis or to reduce one to the other.[9]

I inject here in passing the observation that these claims impose a heavy burden of proof that Ryle does not, in fact, supply: From what ontology comes the knowledge of the difference in the logical category of mind and body? And even if it is granted, is it clear that, if they cannot be logically confronted with each other, they might not, nevertheless, still be analogously compared? An example would be the pervasive somatic simile for the soul, which displays differences on the grounds of similarity.

Here is the application of Ryle's critique to the emotions: First he sets it down in general that when we describe people as exercising qualities of mind, we are not really referring to occult episodes of which their overt acts and utterances are the effect—because this has been shown to be absurd—but instead we are talking about the overt behavior itself.[10]

Now comes the expected question: How do you construe a statement such as "He boasted from vanity," for Ryle has eliminated vanity as an occult, internal cause of such an assertion? The meaning he opts for is that "the boasting satisfies the law-like proposition that whenever he sees a chance of being admired and envied by others he does what he thinks will bring that about." Ryle thus substitutes for impossible empathy into a private place, to which only one agent possesses "privileged access," a permissable inference from a public rule. For about insight into the other's mind, he says that "no one could ever know or even, usually, reasonably conjecture that the cause of someone else's overt action was the occurrence in him of a feeling."[11] This would appear to be the direct denial of the "sympathy" that animates Adam Smith's moral sentiments. And even if someone said—which they never do—that his own boasting was *caused* by a preceding, private vanity-itch, this would be weak evidence. Moreover, then no one could directly test any motive.

It is interesting and disconcerting that Ryle appeals at this point to that old "impartial and discerning spectator" as generally a better judge of a person's motive than the person himself. For recall that Smith's "impartial spectator" of a man's motive was *not* primarily a public other, but the man himself within himself. His own view, Ryle says, is directly contrary to the notion "that an agent possesses a Privileged Access to the so-called springs of his own actions. . . ." It is equally interesting how oddly close this behavioristic denigration of unaided introspective self-knowledge is to psychoanalytic practice, though the latter offers a way: through the trained analyst.

So a feeling or emotion is no longer the cause of behavior—apparently not because it actually isn't—Ryle appears to be agnostic on that point—but because it isn't available to comment in an acceptably overt way.

If feelings aren't causes, still deeds do have motives, and those motives are corrigibly discoverable—discoverable by an inductive process which leads precisely to a law-like proposition similar to the one mentioned. Imputed motives, despite their name, are hence not conceived as motive impulses from behind but general rules from above—not as motive *causes* but as inductively derived and generalized *explanations*.

Internality, a.k.a. the soul, accessible to just one person in the Cartesian world, seems to be open to none in the Rylean realm, since it is not only inaccessible to the public, but even the possessor himself has never reported experiencing the "itch" of an emotion. Here is a case where I doubt the logically preoccupied behaviorist's ear or feel for what people may say: "I was itching to boast" is something I have in fact often observed in myself (and in my students) and have even sometimes reported.

Motives, the living out of law-like propositions, can be called traits of character. A motive then is not an internal causal energy but just the *inclination* to do certain acts and feel certain feelings. "Inclination" is the most important term in Ryle's emotion vocabulary. He distinguishes inclinations from agitations, somewhat along the old lines of "propensities" versus "flare-ups." An agitation requires an inclination and a factual impediment, as eddies require a current and a rock. Thus, if an inclination is somewhat analogous to habit, then Dewey's definition of emotion nearly fits Ryle's "agitation": "Habit is energy organized in certain channels. . . . Emotion is a perturbation from clash or failure of habit."[12] The significance of this similarity is that, while Ryle includes agitation as an emotion-type, his chief interest is in the higher-level behavior which in the emotion-context is attributed to inclinations, and whose general term is "disposition."

Ryle does find four emotion-types: inclinations, agitations (or commotions), moods, and feelings. The first three are propensities, not occurrences, "and therefore do not take place either publicly or privately." Feelings, on the other hand, are indeed occurrences; we experience them. But they are not causes of actions; on the contrary they are consequences: "We wince and shudder, because we are inhibited from acting purposively." Moods are temporary conditions, tendencies to have certain feelings: In a lazy mood we tend toward feelings of lassitude.[13] These detailed typologies are all gathered from our socially learned way of speaking about the terms; I will concentrate here on the inclinations, the "dispositional properties" as evinced in emotions.

What are these dispositions to which are reduced—and here the word is in order—the highest-level feelings, the settled calm passions, as Hume called them? No terms in Ryle's book are, it seems to me, more subtle and more slippery than these, which bear the burden of the emotion theory: inclination, propensity, disposition, tendency; in fact he devotes a central chapter to them.[14] The subtlety and slipperiness coincide in the function they fulfill: to eschew the need for an opposition of mind to body by staying out of all inwardness, to attribute no causality to the proscribed ghost that is commonly thought to be the emotion itself, and to analyze one person's emotion through analyzing the speech of others about it.

There seems at first to be a straight answer to the question: What is a disposition? It is simply such behavior as makes us expect fairly regular episodes bearing the earmarks that we have learned to call by a certain emotive or cognitive term. The mental conduct is then nothing but, is reduced to, a disposition, meaning an observer's expectation that a certain behavior will probably occur. Inclination seems to be disposition in respect to the emotions. The inclination to anger is then nothing but the observer's expectation that angry episodes will occur; there is no Anger beside or beyond these anger-agitations. When the inclination is analyzed, it is explained in terms of a law-like proposition motivating the actor.

The slippery subtlety of the dispositional view of the emotions has two aspects. One is that it seems to be too hard to get a firm grasp of the nature and location of a disposition. Is it anything at all besides my prediction about you? On what in the actor—not an allowed, yet an unsuppressible question—does the likelihood of certain behavior depend? If it is something like potentiality,[15] how can I understand it in the absence of an ontology providing for actualization? So the first difficulty is that I am now—because of logical commitments—unable to ask "Whose inclination is it anyway?"— since it isn't mine as an interior possession.

The second aspect, already broached, is that I am no longer the first expert on my own affective life. Nor can I any longer follow the old Socratic injunction to know myself, in the sense of looking within to see whether "I am some sort of beast . . . complex in form . . . or something simpler and gentler."[16] Nor is the theory particularly interested in distinguishing passions from virtues; indeed most of Ryle's examples of emotions—vanity, laziness—would in fact be called character flaws in ordinary language. In that sense the analysis of what we quite normally and competently say turns out to be pretty prescriptive of what we ought to think.

Ryle had the grace to say at the end of his book that for all he knew, the Cartesian two-world myth might have been better for concrete psychological research than behaviorism.[17] Indeed the early, bold version of the latter had, in its ultra-objectivity, inhibited emotion research for a half century. Such research took off, however, a decade after Ryle's last classic of sophisticated behaviorism was published. As in other fields, so in emotion studies, the scientists turned out to be less inhibited about the useful availability of subjective emotion experiences than some philosophers.

3. Empirically-Based Conceptualization: Tomkins

The explosion of emotion studies—the successful countermovement against the positivist freeze—is not strictly in my purview. Emotion research is designedly interdisciplinary: "physiology, neurology, ethology, physiological psychology, personality and social psychology, clinical psychology and psychiatry, medicine, nursing, social work, and the clergy . . ." are involved, but notice: no philosophy.[1] The often massive studies are empirically based and backed by particular "conceptualizations" belonging to the system of choice. Some of these will later be exploited philosophically, where I call "philosophical" those expositions that aim determinedly to take no terms and distinctions for granted, and try to lay bare their roots—a fair enough attempt, since the terms in fact precede the observations. They set the experimental agenda.

Wherever the intention is to fit the emotions into a system, the first effort has to be to discern and marshal them, to produce a list and then a taxonomy such as primary, secondary, and mixed; positive, negative and neutral; human only and all-primate; vehement and gentle; intentional and less or non-intentional; propensity-like and flaring—to name some recurrent organizing categories.

Lists are, perforce, first; they precede orderings.[2] Their multiplicity shows that they are non-binding, and of their making there is no end. When devised in the absence of a basic theory of human nature, there is something adventitious about them. Generally, it seems to me, the product is less interesting than the possible ways of coming by it, from simple inheritance to linguistic observation, from self-observation to clinical protocols.

One such way is derivative from Darwin's claim that emotional expression is humanly universal and visually identifiable. My personal difficulty with this theory in books is that without captions I can practically never recognize the emotion illustrated more closely than as distressed or pleased; it's a little better in life, though all the subtle mixes are often not readable on a real face, even a familiar, one.[3] Nonetheless, the listing of emotions that includes the most interestingly novel item I have come across, Silvan Tomkins's, is based on facial expression.[4]

His guiding concept is that of an interactive "affect system," affects being brain-controlled biological mechanisms, triggered by definable stimuli and playing out according to a time-sequenced program. "Affect" is thus fundamentally biological; Tomkins does not use the term "emotion," which is, however, introduced into the context by Nathanson, who understands "feeling" as the awareness of affect, and "emotion" as an (expressive) affect compounded with accretions of experiential memory;[5] most contemporary writers use some such distinctions, tweaking them to suit their conceptions.

First on the list of the affects of Tomkins's system is "interest or excitement, the primary positive affect which has been most seriously neglected." Its facial indices are "eyebrows down, track, look, listen, . . . the far-away look . . . tracking an early memory or idea."[6]

It is indeed true that I have come across no previous listing of "interest" among the affects and, moreover, had not thought of it as the "emotion"— into which it develops, namelessness notwithstanding, in Tompkins's own long description.

Yet what good affect (in the general sense) is more familiar, more a way of life, to the unwithered human being whose species nature it is, as Aristotle says, to "stretch out to know"? Intellectual arousal may not be the most vehement, but it is surely the most reliably persistent and exhilarating of passions. It may be that only the name is novel for the very familiar passion intended—though possibly this term is the best of them all, for "interest" is derived from the Latin verb *inter-esse,* "being right among, in between" things and people, participating, involved.[7] Perhaps what the ancients called "wonder" is its initial step; the next is "philosophy." Wonder, reflective thought, and what is for one modern, Spinoza, "the intellectual love of God" are high-end examples of the interest-affect.

The reason why "interest" has not appeared in the emotion lists seems to lie in its meaning-history. The noun's time of origin is obscure but post-Roman. Once established, it began to assume, in the sixteenth century, a very modern economic meaning. It is sober, prudent, rational, worldly, Machiavellian, self-interest—at most a counter-passion, at war with and counteracting the impulsive passions.[8] In the late eighteenth century the objective notion of "having interest," "being interesting," as attributed to something exercising fascination or attracting curiosity came into vogue.[9] In the last century Heidegger wrote:

> *Inter-esse* means: to be among and between matters, to stand in the midst of a matter and to persist in it. But for today's interest only the interesting counts. It is that which permits having already become indifferent in the next moment and being relieved by something else, which touches one as little as what preceded. . . . In truth, this judgment has degraded the Interesting to the Indifferent and has soon consigned it to boredom.[10]

It is easy to see why these overtones of "interest" should inhibit its recognition as a better-than-mundane, a—so to speak—disinterested interest, a *cognitive passion.*

Tomkins brings the interest-affect on the scene as one which, though biologically based, plays a special humanizing role. For, like the good affects in general, it is critical in powering "the Image, . . . the centrally emitted blueprint which organizes the totality of subsystems in the human being in the interests of goal achievement." But interest is, as distinct from fear, shame, or joy, a "general impersonal asset." I understand that "impersonal" feature to characterize an essentially species-characterizing, *human* excitement. As such it has two aspects: First there is our interest in, our excitement over, what is *necessary* to sustain existence (an affect perhaps attributable to animals also). This interest is of primary utility insofar as "one's sexual drive and one's hunger can be no stronger than one's excitement about sexuality or about eating." Thus it is interest that arouses basic life-supporting "drives," not the other way around, as is usually supposed in psychoanalysis and behaviorism. When interest is extinguished the drives fail, as in severe depression.[11]

The second aspect of interest is concerned with the *possible*. This interest is aroused not by what preserves life but by what enhances it: Interest in the possible makes the difference between mere life and the good life. Tomkins names "science" as a consequence of interest in the possible, for science, though it may support the basic viability of the species, can also go beyond to improve or even destroy it. "The realm of the possible is equally the realm of the wonderful, the trivial, the distressing and the terrifying." Interest under this aspect arouses cognition, along with other "sub-systems," just as the other interest aroused the drives. In fact "radical intellectual creativity," given sufficient ability, is ascribable to the sustained intensity of "a passion for ideas and the pursuit of truth."[12] Here a research psychologist has rediscovered *the* humanizing affect of old, philosophical *eros,* and has set, perhaps quite intentionally, a certain limit to the evolutionary-adaptive theory of affects.

This might be the place for a brief note distinguishing interest from curiosity, in German *Neugier,* "news-greed," a linguistic windfall exploited by Heidegger, for whom it is among the "fallen" modes; it is the diversionary, unsteady, behindhand, runaway, squinting counterpart of the authentically present moment, called in German the *Augenblick,* the "glance of the eye."[13] It is the tradition to think ill of curiosity, from pagan Plato denigrating the indiscriminate "lover of sights" who "facilely wants to taste all learning and comes to it with gusto,"[14] through all the philosophers seeking wisdom in otherworldly truth, as well as the religious embracing spiritual concentration. Thus in the Christian context Augustine writes:

> There is also present in the soul, by means of the bodily senses, a kind of empty longing and curiosity, which aims not at taking pleasure in the flesh but at acquiring experience through the flesh, and this empty curiosity is dignified by the names of learning and science. . . . It is called in the divine language "the lust of the eyes."[15]

And that proto-modern, Hobbes, says in his acute way:

> Desire to know how and why, CURIOSITY, is a lust of the mind, that by a perseverance of delight in the continual and indefatigable generation of knowledge, exceedeth the short vehemence of carnal pleasure.[16]

Thus curiosity, for all its levity, has often been the the dark yin to philosophy's bright yang—precisely fitting its contours and exactly betokening its contrary. Hume, to be sure, equates it with the love of truth, since he wants to make philosophy "experimental." But the longer tradition may be summarized thus: While philosophy leisurely generates knowledge in a love more satisfying than physical desire, curiosity indefatigably procreates in unassuageable lust—and produces obsolescent information rather than deepening wisdom.

Curiosity of a small format used to be especially attributed to women in whom, it was thought, a greater personal penetration together with a restricted sphere of action combined to induce it.[17] Instead, in our day, children as yet undamped by social pressures are credited with curiosity. In them alone is it a generally acknowledged virtue—in them and perhaps in old ladies given consolatory credit for keeping young. Thus interest in the sense delineated by Tomkins is not mere curiosity but is, so to speak, curiosity plus the *gravitas* of steady, far-seeing, biologically grounded but not necessarily adaptive engagement—a scientist's tribute to a survival-indifferent affect.

4. Emotion and Knowledge: Cognitivism

A. *Things Fall Apart*

Things fall apart: Theories, approaches, schools—these are the rubrics, like currents and vortices in the torrent (in which this book is a drop) of emotion studies in the last half-century. Let me give a *short* list of them; the classification into theory, approach, and school is fluid:

> *Feeling theory:* a theory of emotion as pure affect.
>
> *Behaviorism:* a school focusing on overt evidence.
>
> *Linguistic analysis:* an approach to emotion through the investigation of concepts and common language.
>
> *Cognitivism:* a theory of emotions as evaluative judgments.
>
> *Conative theory:* emotion as desire-based choice.
>
> *Evolution:* the theory of emotions as heritable adaptive behavior.
>
> *Contextualism:* an approach that considers historical and social circumstances as determining the nature of emotions.
>
> *Social construction:* an extreme case of contextualism, regarding emotions as social products.
>
> *Rhetoric:* an interpretative approach particularly to the political implications of emotion-language.
>
> *Neuroscience:* the neural networks of the brain as the seat of emotions.

There are also some outliers, refreshingly eccentric treatments.[1]

Two of the treatments listed have been predominant, and they have been in a strained but close relation to each other. One is Cognitivism, to be treated below. The other is the brain-scientific approach, which began in the 1970s. It has actual progress to show, at least in its own terms.[2] This neuroscientific approach has been slighted in this book for two reasons. First, the highly technical findings are available to me only in the popularized versions written by the researchers, who, though precise in their scientific terminology, are not always equally perspicuous in their reflective language. Second, the progress made by scientists intent on research programs for the discovery of physiological and brain events "subtending"—or, some also claim, constituting—the emotions does not seem to get any closer to the questions asked by laypeople of a reflective turn of mind. The most fundamental queries remain—perhaps fatally, that is in principle—unresolved.

There seems to be, for instance, an unnegotiable fissure between *observing* a physiological or brain event and *having* a feeling or emotion. Indeed, the science itself seems to define itself in terms of the difference between these events, for it proceeds on the hypothesis that emotional states, discerned introspectively, must first be reported for the science to go to work. These protocols in fact direct the research, at least for normal affectivity, for who, in the absence of overtly abnormal behavior, can look for a significant, subserving brain event unless it is identifiable by a concurrent emotion event that is verbally reported? The neurological activity would be only very speculatively interpretable. Moreover, the very relation of these two supposedly coordinate event-realms seems to be a—very basic—postulate, unobservable in principle. The trouble here appears to be that objects of science, on the one hand, are supposed to be patent to the eye or to a recording device. Such objects are exposed in space and evolving in time; they are external almost without a remainder. Thus, when a body in motion is to be scientifically described, we do not attribute to it relevant inner states unamenable to similar spatio-temporal descriptions. On the other hand, the feel of our feelings does not have similar patency, similarly determinate spatio-temporal structure; it is not, strictly speaking, a "phenomenon," an appearance. Hence no one could, I surmise, write a compellingly subtle romance from the unidentified log alone of the hormone or brain activity of a human being in love.

More specifically put: No account of body and brain functions even matches—far from being identical with—an introspective account of how a human being feels a feeling. The scientific accounts are pitched too concretely as physical observables and too abstractly as schematic interpretations; the holism of a felt affect seems to be of a different sort. Our *speaking* to each other of our passions seems to be precisely a way of circumventing the hugely complex activities of our somatic selves; conversely, "we" who feel our feelings are out of the observer-brain loop. One might say that the brain seems to be a peculiarly selective one-way window between us and ourselves. It projects evidence that we are having emotions to outsider observers, but it doesn't display what matters about them to us as insiders. Or, once more: We speak without having our brain in mind; the brain, in turn, lends itself to observation without, as it were, speaking its mind.

What a layperson would then like to know is whether observable brain events *can*, in fact, sometimes show a precise one-to-one correspondence with the emotional propensities or flare-ups—whether, granted the undeniable, that psychic experiences are subtended by brain events, they match exactly; it is a recurrent question of this book. The answer seems to depend, in the first instance, on the possibility of analyzing a feeling or an emotion verbally into its components, of producing an exhaustive phenomenal inventory of an affect. I wonder whether the multitudinous aspects of impassioned internality aren't self-involved in a way that defies being laid out as analytically articulable complexes—meaning in itemizable elements and levels or by any analysis involving multiple variables or even variables themselves derived from variables. For surely even emotions that seem simple often turn out under introspection to be many-faceted, reason-entangled imbroglios at any one moment and, moreover, to have some sort of interactive development in time. That master of interiority, Augustine, says: "... [T]he hairs on a [human being's] head are more easily numbered than the affects and motions of his heart."[3]

Again, one would like to know whether some nameable type of causal relation can be established between body and soul. Are conscious efforts consequent upon or concomitant with or prior to brain events? Though it seemed to be the case that such events have been observed as preceding action-choices, is this globally so?[4] Is it possible to show that *no* psychic disposition or motion ever *precedes* a physical effect—contrary to the common belief of "folk psychology": We can, for example, or so people think, work ourselves into a fit or will ourselves to calm down—*we*, as psychic first agents. Is that an illusion?

So, hampered both by incompetence and misgivings, I have mostly stayed away from neuroscience. I must take its findings of emotions as evidenced in observable brain events on faith, but I simply cannot tell whether its reductive attitudes toward emotions as conscious experiences are even falsifiable.

One more observation, however: There *is* an often-mooted notion brought in to bridge the gap between body and soul, matter and consciousness, brain and mind, and to settle them into a continuous hierarchy: emergence. With a sufficient gathering of complexity the first item in these pairs will eventuate as the second one. Brain will emerge as mind. So, say, two parts of hydrogen and one of oxygen will form a molecule, which will evince the experienced properties, the "qualia" of water. But try as one will to understand it, the term "emergence" is more a hopeful description than an explanation.[5]

Cognitivism, on the other hand, the other predominant school, must be dealt with, above all because it is so inclusive a theory, comprehending at once attacks on, and assimilations of, other theories. Of these I note especially what is called the "feeling theory," which is somewhat differently understood in different places. In Anglo-Saxon parlance feelings (or "feels") are direct experiences, which include such events as sensations and itches; here the feeling theory is a "folk-theory," the common-sense notion that emotions are a subset of feelings, those that have objects, while pure feelings are mere "qualia" ("suchnesses" is the closest I can think of in English) and have no intentional objects.[6] On the Continent, on the other hand, "feeling theory" is the affective *complement* of the rationalism represented by Descartes and Hume. Here feeling renders the German word *Gefühl*, a seventeenth-century coinage from the verb *fühlen*, close to French *sentiment* (but distinct from *Empfindung*, which has a meaning more like the English "feeling" above).[7] This version of feeling theory regards emotions specifically as passivities, affects undergone as opposed to activities of thinking. Descartes is one chief proponent.

My point is that cognitivism both opposes and absorbs the notion of a pure and passive affectivity, of feels and feelings in either theory. It has two very diverse, not to say opposite, aims.

But first let me give the stripped-down definition of essential cognitivism: Emotions *are* judgments.[8] And that sentence can be taken to mean that emotions have the logical structure of certain propositions and that therefore a logicizing approach to emotions is inherently appropriate. This was the way of the English founders of the cognitive theory, Errol Bedford in "Emotions" (1956), Anthony Kenny, in *Action, Emotion, Will* (1963).[9] A second understanding of the sentence construes it as having the opposite aim—to rescue the passions from the hegemony of reason, their (supposed) Western patrimony of subjection, by showing that they have cognitive independence *as* passions and are not "sporadic and 'irrational' intrusions" but "provide our lives with meaning." And more: "Our passions constitute our lives." This is the way taken by the American founder of the cognitive theory, Robert Solomon, in *The Passions* (1976).[10] It is immediately evident that this version of the theory is destined to undergo much tinkering, perhaps even to be modified out of recognition, since it seems, on the face of it, to save the passions from the "myth of passivity" imposed by rationalists—by rationalizing them after all. I will give brief reviews of Bedford's, Kenny's, and Solomon's theories.

Before I go on to these, some words about the sense I must be conveying in citing Yeats: "Things fall apart: the center cannot hold."[11] It certainly isn't my meaning that "mere anarchy is loosed upon the world"; the trouble lies rather in a plethora of unreconciled and partial rational results. And since it has been the presupposition of this book that the passions are more vividly illuminated when sited within philosophical wholes, be they built on basic foundations or ordered to final ends, the situation does look a little chaotic.

My approach is, I think, not very hard to defend as a working method for marshalling views but not so easy to justify as a way to establish truth. For these grand wholes of philosophy are obviously even less easy to *reconcile* than the narrower partialities of scholarship, while to *cannibalize* such frameworks for handy parts to cobble together would break up the very integrity that gives their passion theories stature. Therefore the justification for my—somewhat unfashionable—interest in grounds can hardly be, it seems to me, in culling a theory from this tradition, but rather in showing how and why the inquiry into human affect might be thought to involve all the world there is. But why then are there no compelling large groundworks or frameworks on the contemporary scene?

The tradition, our "Western" tradition, begins with that pair of complementary antagonists, Parmenides and Heraclitus. It has ever since been dialectical, that is to say self-refuting and self-reviving. Notions, like their mortal thinkers, followed each other in time: The prime objects of inquiry were, roughly speaking, Ultimate Being, the Creator-God, Human Existence, always accompanied by reflections on the World as nature and as human artifact. The modes of those reflections were, again grossly, representationalism, empiricism, critique, to cite examples from this book. These thought-complexes were, as I said, in time because the people who entertained them lived in time, but they were, once conceived, also simultaneously present—apart from any claim about the timelessness of truth—because the people who in all seriousness took issue with them, modified, deconstructed or refuted them and so kept them alive. This progression—not necessarily a progress—of notions was evidently felt as an incitement to, rather than as a discouragement from, large positive philosophizing. Why not now?

It may simply be the fortuitous failure of large philosophical gifts, a possibility about which there isn't anything to be done and little to be said, except that the rarity of the ability to make knowledge cohere just isn't proportionate to the universality of the desire to know—and to publish. Perhaps the dialectical notion that quality, whether regarded logically or temporally, eventually falls into quantity, that any unique character eventually turns into multitudes of indifferent items—quanta[12]—actually describes the drift of intellectual history. More seriously, a cause for the decline of comprehensive philosophizing may have been inherent in the very forcibleness characteristic of incipient modernity: the exigent drive to find an absolute, a presuppositionless beginning or a certainly existent being or a set of absolutely first axioms or a mind cleared of illusions. Each such short-shrift rebellion against the inherited givens of the tradition raised a counter-rebellion, which exposed the hidden presumptions of the most recent shape of modernity and recast it in a new system.[13]

Eventually, in the last century, a weary disgust with the search for systems based on absolute beginnings expressed itself as a countermovement in "anti-foundationalism," a rebellion against all the rebellions.[14] "Rebellion" literally means, as Locke points out, a return to war.[15] Once established, however, the uprising achieves legitimacy as a "revolution," a term that in early modernity meant primarily the orbital paths of the planets—including *the* new planet, Earth[16]—but later became the mode-word for a modern pattern of progress. Without really entering into its complexities and consequences, I want to observe only that the practitioners of foundationalism—among whom were the founders of modernity—*as well as* the adherents of its recent nemesis, anti-foundationalism, seem to have a new relation to tradition: They want to cancel and supersede previous illusions and mistakes; they want to go back to war, more than they want to save and be served by preceding views. The principal ancients too were radical in their search for roots and beginnings (*archai*), but they inquired *in medias res*, seated in the midst of affairs, and often found a place for opposing views, if only as aspects of human opinion that it is profitable to take into account. My point is that the moderns *par excellence* not only founded a new phase in the dialectical tradition of the West but founded it, willfully yet self-underminingly, as a phase of continually superseded new starts, each meant to be the ultimate beginning—and yet each contumacious rebellion damped down into a canonized revolution.[17] (I say "*a* phase," in the faith that there will be a fourth coming, despite the unmodern stuckness expressed in naming our present "post-modernism.")

I enter these very general but not very original reflections because they do have some bearing on the dispersed aspect of current emotion studies. Philosophy, which in the medieval university curricula had played the role both of complement to theology and of the culmination of the liberal arts, eventually lost its hard-fought contest for dominion over the other faculties. As in the course of the later nineteenth century and largely under German influence, universities acquired the features of specialization, departmentalization, electives, graduate studies, and professionalization, philosophy became one field and one profession among others.[18] In particular the ideals of academic scholarship now apply, among which are the production of "original" work contributing to the advancement of knowledge, however small the increment, as well as proper referencing of recently preceding work, be it for critique or credit, while allowing "dated" contributions to lapse. Moreover, neology (novel technical jargon) is valued both as a mark of originality and as a sign of the professional initiate. Neither the required originality nor the expected contribution nor the citational tether nor the amnesiac cutting-edge nor the rewarded neology seem to me to have much to do with furthering philosophical reflection, but they have indeed produced that general "zeal for theory construction" operative also in emotion studies.

Thus the state of the intellectual tradition and of its present chief establishment combine to generate some unanchored profusion. A certain impatience for all the incomposable theorizing has been felt among professional philosophers themselves and has been expressed by Amélie Rorty.[19] Her particular explanation of the proliferation is that since emotions do not form a "natural kind" they will therefore never be clearly and cleanly distinguishable from motives, moods, and attitudes such as beliefs, fantasies, perceptions, decisions, reasons, etc.[20] Thus, in the absence of a clear determination of the nature of the emotions, theories are produced idiosyncratically. For the "working condition of theory construction" is what on the Continent is called the "hermeneutic circle" and in Anglo-Saxon countries, "bootstrapping"—the back and forth between specific case analyses and more comprehensive theories. Yet the generalizations of constructed theories can't, she judges, accommodate the often very acute special studies produced by the "pieceworkers" if they are not framed as a "relatively complete philosophy of mind/philosophical psychology."

That last sentence is, of course, a version of my working principle, but it may be asking for the impossible in the setting assumed. For the Philosophy of Mind, within which most contemporary studies are indeed framed, cannot, it seems to me, by its very character, produce the required "one plan with shared assumptions and purposes (say a Thomistic factory . . .)" in which the findings of the "pieceworkers . . . can . . . merge smoothly into the entire program." The reason is that Philosophy of Mind is a collective term covering not only several disciplines, such as linguistic analysis and philosophical psychology, but also many problems that arise *among* the disciplines. Furthermore, having Wittgenstein and Ryle among its progenitors, it is, with its reductionist ancestry, as far from a Thomistic factory as possible. I wonder whether a theory conceived within the Philosophy of Mind, that is, one capacious enough to site and so to define the passions, would not end up by being parricidal—I mean, by taking down its own parameters.[21]

Perhaps the question "Why have things fallen apart in our time?" has a purely quantitative answer, one that can be put simply in terms of proliferating production, but I doubt it. I think there is a qualitative explanation in terms of the features of academic scholarship cited above, and that they all conspire to replace the perennial polemical *preservation* of philosophies through dialectical confrontation with the mutually assured *destruction* by academic debate. A particular characteristic of philosophical scholarship in line with its modern paternity appears to be a reluctance to read earlier works as if they *might* contain truth. It seems to go against the academic grain to entertain the diverse philosophies of the tradition not as simultaneously or serially nullifying refutations now largely of "academic" interest, but as presently alive, powerful, possibilities. But such a reading might be useful at the least for gaining some sense of the way particular human experiences are entailed by larger frameworks and, perhaps, for finding a coherent set of livable opinions for ourselves—even for justifying those we already have. Having said that, I turn to some founding works in cognitivist theory that must be grappled with since in some aspects it does represent a serious attempt at coherence.

B. Justification, Judging, Judgments

Justification, judging, and judgments are three modes of regarding the cognitive content of emotion. They are represented respectively in three founding texts of cognitivism.

i. Bedford   In 1957 Errol Bedford published an article subsequently much cited, in which he introduced the notion of emotion words as *justifications*.[22] Bedford continued Ryle's attack on "feelings" (the bugbear of modern emotion theories), although he criticized Ryle's "dispositional" account as incomplete. He attacked the then prevailing "feeling theory" as involving a fundamental logical mistake, that of treating the subtly differentiated emotion terms as the names corresponding to feelings, thus attributing a richness and clarity to the inner life of feelings that it doesn't possess. I must ask where, then, all the fine-grained emotion talk comes from, and comment that this claim about the lack of differentiation of basic affectivity seems to me far too reductive. For example, the many emotions felt around the heart—high-heartedness, heart-soreness, whole-heartedness, "the heart high-sorrowful and cloy'd"[23]—all these feel subtly different, and those discriminations are in fact underlain by a multitude of differences in the physiology.[24]

Against Ryle, Bedford particularly urges that emotions are not just explicable as individual propensities or behavior trends but also as arising in a *social context*—in personal relations and institutions. I want to observe here that the ensuing social construction- and context-mongering can sometimes be irritating from two opposite perspectives. One is that its proponents seem to present as novel discoveries knowledge surely as old as the hills. For example, on those monumental Athenian pots of the eighth century B.C.E., the Dipylon grave markers, there are represented mourning men surrounding the bier of a dead person, with their arms akimbo above their heads, perhaps meant to be tearing their hair. There were also female mourners, known in the trade as *Klagefrauen*.[25] (When archaeologists wax typological they speak German). These mourners were probably commandeered or hired to express and surely also to incite grief; they knew how to make grief, just as modern Greeks know how to "make *kephi*," that is, festive fun. Yet surely there were real people at those funerals who tore their hair in the spontaneous self-mutilation that goes with terrible grief. Surely it is an absurdity to call Achilles' paroxysm of hair-tearing grief at the moment when he hears of his one intimate friend's death[26] a social construction! Surely everyone knew, even absent terminology, what feelings were socially constructed or at least contextually appropriate in, say, love. Yet they surely also knew a more natural and more poignant feature of passion, the one that every adolescent at heart, whether young or old in years, has experienced: the lonely, asocial sense of having been singled out, set apart, isolated, made at once proudly and abjectly unique by passion.

Thus the proponents of the social construction of the emotions—that case of contextualism where the context is society—are irritating from a second perspective: For the truly passionate affects their outside-in approach is so insufficient. La Rochefoucauld's epigram that "There are people who would never have been in love if they had never heard talk about love," has been cited as an anticipation of the contextualist or social-constructionist approach.[27] I just cannot believe that his witticism can be generalized; there may be such people in Society, but in ordinary Life, it is just those—mostly teenagers—who have no idea what hit them who are hardest hit; in any case it is practically impossible for the young to take in—actually to *hear*—conventional talk of love before the event, or at least in advance of the readiness.

Bedford's influence extends beyond his name-recognition into the recent "rhetorical approach," as set out by Daniel Gross in *The Secret History of Emotion*.[28] This approach "puts the question of politics front and center." For "rhetoric is at once an embedded cultural practice and an inventive attitude which allows us to reflect critically upon those same cultural practices."

What then is rhetoric when it is viewed as other than the learnable skill of persuasive speech?

> As opposed to univocal speech that would mean the same thing everywhere, rhetoric is always in brackets ... [for it] presents the possibility that things might be otherwise. ... [A]s opposed to the philosophy that posits language as a mirror of nature, rhetoric is an inventive attitude toward language and the world where "emotion" names one important way in which language and the world connect.[29]

What is the consequence of seeing rhetoric as the art of constructive equivocation? It must mean that people's public speech is to be interpreted not as univocally truth-telling (or simply deceiving), but as sub-textually status-defining, and so as society-constructing. If, however, the social environment is—largely—constructed through rhetoric, then it is also construable through rhetorical analysis. Consequently Gross's emphasis in respect to emotion is on certain second-order phenomena, on the interpretation of social, even economic rubrics found in speech—what he calls its "economy of scarcity" and its "shadow economy." These terms convey "Emotion's uneven expression over different sorts of people, its apparent dysfunction in the humiliated or depressed or even its utter absence in the politically disaffected."[30]

An example comes from the rhetorical interpretation of the Late Stoic Seneca's book *On Anger,* in which, Gross claims, anger and apathy are treated as "scarce resources." For since, "socially speaking, the slave deserves little compared to the monarch, his capacity for anger also differs dramatically." Here I must remind the reader that the Stoics were in fact as universalist in their apprehension and attribution of human emotion as one can well be. So the rhetorical reading is here indeed highly inventive; in any case it is somewhat woolly. Is it the capacity for the affect or the opportunity for expression that is dysfunctional? And how, in general, would we know how the dispossessed and consequently *silenced* classes really felt? Though, to be sure, we meet them in Greek and Roman comedy, where their emotions, anger included, seem, however, quite ebullient. Such evidential difficulties as there are notwithstanding, the rhetorical thesis is put forth very positively as a version of social constructivism:

> Emotions . . . must be read as markers of social distinction rather than just expressions of human nature essentially shared by all. Instead of wondering perennially why it has taken so long to extend the range of human compassion to women, to slaves, to non-Europeans, to the poor, the disabled, and so on, we would do better to track the history of terms such as *pride, humility, pity,* and *compassion,* and see how they have been mobilized for strategic purposes; how, for instance, particular communities are composed by the notion that they have a monopoly on that compassion that would be extended to others.[31]

I see the following basic problems with this project: How do you weigh, apart from the political inclinations of the rhetorical analyst, the influences of shared human nature against the impositions of social distinctions? And how do you track the inherently untrackable: what millions of inexpressive human beings living over millennia of bygone times felt in the inner sanctums of their heart of hearts?

The main legacy of Bedford's article, logically prior to social construction, is, however, the introduction of the notion of "appraisal."[32] Mere-feeling theory fails to elucidate both the fact that we regard attributions of emotion as explanatory of behavior and the fact that we regard emotions themselves as justified or unjustified; indeed, it speaks for the appraisal thesis that emotion terms and moral vocabulary often overlap. Bedford argues not only that statements referring to emotions—keep in mind that this is a theory of *statements interpreting behavior,* affectivity having been put out of commission—are explanations that go beyond the individual's behavior to a social context, a set of relations among people, within which the behavior makes sense. The second part of his claim, which enables the first one, is that they are *appraisals* and *justifications* that can in turn be judged. To say, for example, "I loathe his filthy ways," is to express an aversive appraisal, to embed it in a social context that values cleanliness, and to justify the aversion. One might put it this way: Emotion words are almost always implicitly qualified by a "pro" or "con." This is the essence of the incipient cognitivist theory.

ii. Kenny   Anthony Kenny, who is generally regarded as the initiator of cognitivist theory, does not in fact cite Bedford's article in his book (1963), which fact is of interest only because it signifies that the thing was in the air. Only Kenny goes deeper, beyond the observed justificatory feature of emotion words to the formal character of emotion speech as a kind of *judging*. He does that by means of an analysis of the "concepts employed in the description, explanation and appraisal of human conduct" in general and of emotions in particular.[33]

This is my moment to enter misgivings about "conceptual analysis." The approach is, to my mind, a most needful first stage on the philosophical way when carried on in the mode of exploratory futzing-around, but a most off-putting conversation-stopper when presented as productive of definitive conclusions. I entered a similar reservation for ordinary language analysis above, which has, in fact, also been subjected to sharp technical critique,[34] but my general trouble with it—a layperson's trouble—is that my sense of what the speaker might mean and the language might say is so often askew of the analyst's. So too with the analysis of concepts; I will give particular cases below.

"Conceptual analysis," breaking up a concept (usually gotten hold of by a term) into its constituents, is used by Kenny to discern and establish "propositional attitudes." These are the types of mental states expressed in such language as "I judge/believe/desire that. . . ." One can see right away that cognitive theories of emotion—those claiming that they are justifications or judgments—would depend heavily on reviewing such attitudes. The cognitivists therefore regard those very physiological events that constitute emotions for William James as irrelevant to the explanation of emotions.

They find support for the disjunction from experiments in which the autonomic nervous systems (ANS) of human subjects were differentially stimulated, but these differences turned out not to correspond systematically to the labels by which subjects reported their consequent emotions. These findings are no longer fully accepted, though it does seem that in severe spinal lesions "visceral" feelings like fear and sexual arousal are diminished—yet again, on the other hand, "sentimental feelings are significantly increased."[35] Thus, in the absence of conclusive correlations, mental states appear to give better access to the emotions than physical arousals.

Two other kinds of science, however, cognitive science (which deals experimentally with the mind as a problem-solving mechanism) and brain science (which traces neurological responses in the brain associated with controlled stimuli), do help the cognitive cause because their theories locate "appraisal" early enough in the flow charts of the affective process to make the latter appear plausibly "cognitive."[36]

What Kenny had done to start off these diversely framed and differently supported theories—they might well be called a movement—was to analogize emotion-having, or rather its linguistic expression, to judging in general and desiring in particular. Here is the crux: Both judging and desiring have objects, both are intentional.[37]

This is the same intentionality that played so large a part in distinguishing emotions from moods. Kenny fixes its precise formal features:

Objectum specificat actum: "The object specifies the act." This medieval adage is found in Thomas and comes from Aristotle, who says that, in thinking about the soul, the consideration of its activities should precede that of the powers which engage in them, and that the objects which are responsible for the activities should precede both.[38]

I have surmised before that this way of looking at passions, that the objects both move and shape them, is among the most important insights we can entertain about them: Our affects are—not without remainder, but significantly—qualified by the object they wrap themselves about, take in, intend. So the two great questions are perforce: What belongs to affect in itself, and what to object on its part?

Kenny points out that traditionally the object specifies in two ways: First, different real objects specify the same action very differently, as killing mice is very different from killing people. But, second and more broadly, different "formal" objects specify what *species* of actions they can activate to begin with; for example, only "the difficult" can be striven for (hence Thomas's strenuous passions) and only "the lovable" can, formally speaking, be loved. Kenny adds that a formal object should not be confused with an internal accusative such as "dreaming a dream" and "dancing a dance," since the dream or dance, the so-called "cognate objects," are not, as are formal objects, beyond and separable from the action. Here is the promised example of a conceptual analysis, that of the cognate object, that seems to fall short of real-life meaning: The poet asks, "How can we know the dancer from the dance?"[39] and we go on to think of the ways; more so even for a dream than a dance; after all, people used to think that dreams were sent:

So [Zeus] spoke and the dream went when the word was given—
Went right away and came to the swift ships of the Greeks.[40]

In my experience, dreaming a dream is, much like imagining an image, an image being a pseudo-product (at least for me), since imagining is much like doing something about *something,* like attentively viewing a sight.[41] A cognate object *can* be conceived as really objective: feeling our feelings.

Warned by that mismatch between linguistic analysis and life, I also have misgivings about the "formal object," for all its respectable scholastic ancestry. A cautionary case is that of Spinoza's practice. Though it may be that when he spoke of the passion being determined by its object he sometimes meant the formal object, yet I think he had in mind a more concrete stimulus, one more capable of particularizing the passion. Sartre certainly did. Be that as it may, I can think of examples where human understanding is evinced by allowing that striving might not always be for the difficult rather than stipulating beforehand—thus putting logic before meaning—that if, say, the felicitous is striven for it must in fact be hard: We sometimes labor over what is inherently easy. Nor is the eaten always the edible, for Job asks, "Can that which is unsavory be eaten without salt?" and answers forthwith, "The things that my soul refused to touch are as my sorrowful meat."[42] And above all, I know that love is not only for the lovable but sometimes for the deplorable:

> O, from what pow'r hast thou this pow'rful might
> With insufficiency my heart to sway?[43]

Without our being overstrict about the actual determination of mental activity by its formal object, it seems, however, to be the case that unless we admit some generic relation between the particular actions here called emotional attitudes and their objects, the relation of an emotion to an arousing object might become a mere contingent matter of fact. The consequence would be that every person's realm of emotion-arousers would be completely personal, and people would rarely agree on something being lovable or hateful or comforting or scary. But, yet again, it seems to me that it needn't be so if emotion and object *mutually* informed each other. For then our inborn passion-propensities would play a part in finding and forming responsive object-targets. In conceptual analysis, it seems to me, logic and human understanding are often at odds.

Kenny, however, thinks that the proper analysis of Descartes' and Hume's mistake, which he takes to be the incoherent relation between the passion and the object, especially its goodness or badness, is this: They ignore the formal, logical restriction placed on the object with respect to the particular propositional attitude: "What is [logically] not possible is to be ... proud of something one regards as an evil unmixed with good," he says. But once again, this seems to me to try to solve a great moral and, finally, theological question—that of the perverse will—with a logical analysis. When Satan says proudly, through the chilling fire of his hell within, "Evil, be thou my good,"[44] does he mean, as the logic of the formal object demands, that he desires a good, though he *calls* it evil (a nasty but merely terminological rebellion against God)? Or does he rather mean that for him the formal object is askew with respect to the emotional attitude, since in him evil has in reality taken the place of good, and that its darkly void essence is what he is in fact making his own? Would a logician have the power of decision over the reality or unreality of evil? The real-life relation of formal object to feeling aroused does not seem to me so unexceptionably tight. Enough said about the first feature of formalized intentionality, that the object activates a formally specific feeling.

So far the distinction between intentional and non-intentional actions has not been set out. The difference is easy to illustrate—though it may seem at first counterintuitive: Killing a mouse is non-intentional and fearing a mouse is intentional. Kenny now calls to aid Franz Brentano, who reintroduced the medieval notion of intentionality into modern philosophical psychology.[45] What distinguishes just any subject → action → object relation (like a mouse-killing) from any intentional relation is, Brentano says, "a property only of psychological phenomena; no physical phenomena display anything similar." Intentionality, "aboutness," thus serves as the specific characteristic of consciousness.

Actio manens in agente: "Action remaining in the agent" is the feature by which it is recognized. Action dispatches the mouse; fearing keeps it in mind. The killed mouse is dead, but the feared mouse is unharmed by the fear (though perhaps not by its consequences); the object remains contemplatedly serene in the agitated soul. So also for imagined, judged, loved objects: Propositional attitude by itself, as Auden said of poetry, "makes nothing happen," at least not to its intentional object. Thus the object of love, which love is "about," feels thereby no arms around it. Of course, Auden didn't believe in the inconsequentiality of poetry anymore than we believe in the impotence of our mental acts. What is meant is that, logically analyzed, a mental or psychic act keeps its object within and does not change it, though the intended object might change the subject. This is illuminating, since it gives criteria for the difference between psychic and physical action.

However, the criterion of non-change, once again, does not seem quite right in living fact. For since an intentional object, at least in the case of emotions, will surely modify the intending subject, it is hard to see why the subject could not in turn work on the affect, the internal object, as in actively imagining we modify a mental image. But if we modify the object within, then, thinking further, is it really the case that this internally transformative intending changes no external object? Suppose a person entered, as it were, another's mind as the intentional object, say, of the emotional attitude called love. Might not this internalized—and thus "idealized"—object, now seated in and possessed by the lover's mind, effect a very large change in the real external counterpart, the beloved—if he as much as got a whiff of its existence, though the action that in fact "passed over into exterior matter"[46] might be vanishingly small, the merest look? A niggling, squishy consideration perhaps, but what a potent situation!

There is an important question incidentally broached by this occasion, namely how to explain propositionally the passage from the interior action that is proper to intentionality out into external deeds, small or large. It is treated by Kenny through Wittgenstein's distinction between "the meaning of an utterance" and "meaning an utterance."[47] A famous illustration from Greek tragedy occurs to me: "My tongue swore but my heart remained unsworn," says Euripides' Hippolytus.[48] Not only does this motivational differentiation in ways of uttering—saying something meaningful and meaning what you say—clarify the relation of articulate expression to determined action, but it helps Kenny's argument on the way. For next he needs to establish the formal parallelism between judgments and desire-statements.

First Kenny, without much ado but with good warrant, *ranges the treatment of emotions under desire*: "For the connection between emotion and behavior is made by desire."[49] Now if the parallelism of judging and desiring is to be at all persuasive, a certain strong distinction between them must be preserved; only then is the formal similarity acceptable.

That distinction is precisely that a judgment is *true or false* depending on the objective facts, so that it is tested by a standard of *verity*, while a desire-expression is *meant or not meant* depending on the speaker's subjective intention (in the sense of what's in his heart), and obeys a standard of *sincerity*. Truth accrues to judgments from the outside, meant intention adheres to desire-statements from the inside. That said, judgments and desire-statements look for the rest similar: There is a speaker who utters a judgment- or an affect-verb like "I think" or "I feel"; these express the respective "propositional attitudes." Then there is a "that" clause; reports of intentional states, be they truth- or desire-stating, although they can have a number of grammatical forms, can usually be expressed more accurately in a "that" form: "I think him wrong" means "I think that he is wrong"; "He wants the stars" means "He desires that he might own the world." Finally, after the "that" comes a clause expressing the subject's judged or desired relation to the intentional object: regarding him as mistaken or as wanting the world.

Emotions have, however, just been ranged under desires. Therefore if desire-statements are like judgments, then *so are emotion-statements judgment-like*. So begins Cognitivism—as linguistic analysis, which is convincing only if you believe that linguistic form is the unfailing clue to the meaning of speech.

iii. Solomon   The full-blown thesis that "An emotion is a *judgment*" appears in Robert Solomon's influential book, *The Passions* (1976), which was preceded by an article and succeeded by years of modification and reiteration[50] of the argument that emotions were neither feelings (though they typically, but not always, involve feelings) nor sensations or physiological occurrences—for they are not occurrences at all. "'Struck by jealousy,' 'driven by anger,' 'paralyzed by fear' . . . are symptomatic metaphors betraying a faulty philosophical analysis." Emotions are not the irrational disruptive occurrences that Western tradition and linguistic habit represent them as being. They do happen in disruptive situations, but they themselves are more like purposive actions that we choose than occurrent happenings. To be sure, they never can be deliberate; they are in fact "essentially non-deliberative." Such emotion-judgments do not follow *upon* a neutrally cognized object or event, but they view these events immediately *through* the emotion. Thus Solomon is committed to the notion of pre-reflective, non-propositional, even bodily, judgments. He reiterates that emotions are not only *like,* but *are* judgments, namely judgments that are option-choices.

Yet it appears finally that what will really make us responsible for our emotions as choices is a *pre*-emotional, purely rational reflection. And that guiding reflection is—surprise!—the theory of cognitive emotion itself. Thus cognitivist theory carries moral suasion: If we deliberately adopt the theory of emotions as volitional judgments it will become true as it works itself into our unconscious, non-deliberative emotional choices.[51] That is not so far from Aristotle's view that sound-mindedness is the rational issue of rationally administered habituation. Only he never says, and I don't think he implies, that his *Ethics* is the direct means.

Because cognition was so ill-defined, Solomon himself long resisted the label "cognitive theory," though it "has become the touchstone of all philosophical theorizing about emotions." The same uncertainty holds true, of course, for "judgments," which range from pre-linguistic bodily responses (Solomon is inclined to identify all "affectivity" as somatic, but then equivocates by calling it "the judgments of the body"), through unconscious psychical discriminations and construals, to conceptually analyzable propositional attitudes. However, Solomon is not fixated on "logic alone" but is looking for "a way of understanding the peculiarities of emotion." How then might the umbrella theory of judgment be characterized in all its latitude? Solomon offers this: The cognition that is both symptom and constituent of emotion is "*having* thoughts . . . without necessarily thinking."[52] I take this

Sibylline saying to mean: Emotions are thought-ful but they are not modes of reasoning, thought-imbued but not modes of rationalizing. It seems true to me in proportion to its lax suggestiveness—"somehow" true.

C. *The* Eigenlogic *of Emotions: Everyone Joins In*

I've fabricated, for fun, the term *eigenlogic*, in analogy to a mathematical usage (*eigenvalue*). *Eigen* is a German adjective meaning at once "peculiar, inherent, characteristic, *own*" and also "odd, strange" as in *eigenartig*, "one of a kind, eccentric." For the obvious next stage in the quest for an emotion theory is to ask, "If the assimilation of emotion to standard rationality proves to be drily reductive, what does the converse condition, the formulation of a logic to fit emotion, look like? What is an emotion-specific logic?" I am moved to say here that the preoccupation with cognition, with finding some analogy of emotion to cogitation in respect to usefulness, is generally a— quite deliberate—diversion of the quest from what I think of as the aboriginal grail, *affectivity,* and from the first question: What does it mean to have feelings? The diversion is motivated by the sensible deflation of philosophy from interminable inquiries into realms beyond us (both those without and those within) to well-defined research on problems selected for solubility— whose solutions in effect lay the problem to rest and consign it to history: Identifying the useful and reason-like features of the emotions seems to be a feasible program, though it might mean shelving the inquiry into the emotionality of the emotions. On the other hand, the attempt to discover an intrinsic emotion-logic seems to me not at all diversionary, but of the essence—in the sense that the basic nature of emotions is indeed at issue.

So, then: Do the passions have a rationality in a sense of a logic of their own, one that will save them from arationality and, perhaps, from irrationality—and thus from a necessary subordination to reason? Oddly enough, it bears repeating, this approach to rescuing the emotions from such subservience evinces a conviction that nothing but rationality *is* in fact respectable. Whereas, in the long preceding tradition, the passions inspired fear and awe as *the other* of human reason, now they are to be appreciated for being only *another,* perhaps sounder, way of rationality. Pascal is punctually quoted by way of being the sponsor of affectivity as another way of reasoning: "The heart has its reasons, which reason does not know." But Pascal—if you actually open the *Pensées*—turns out to mean both more and less than that the heart has an alternative rationality, that of the passions. He means, first, that faith, the love of God, comes from the heart; here reason is bid to submit. But, second, he means that there are two ways of knowledge, by one of which—he calls it "intuition"—"we know truth . . . by the heart." The ways are not at odds but successive: Antecedent to demonstrative reason comes intuition into first principles, such as the tri-dimensionality of space, the nature of time and motion, and the infinity of number. "Principles are intuitive, propositions inferred." There is, to be sure, very little intuitive knowledge. But what there is of this knowledge of the heart, is not to be impugned by reason nor to be called on to justify itself by proof.[53]

i. Titles of books representing the various theories rationalizing the emotions testify to this preoccupation: *Emotions and Reasons, The Logic of Affect, The Rationality of Emotion*.[54]

However, what Solomon meant by the "rationality" of the emotions is that they all "have a common goal," which he recognizes as helpful. It is "the maximizing of self-esteem" that evidences "their intelligent purposiveness." Thus the devastatingly humbling and destructively corroding incidents of passion are downplayed. It is this feature of academic writing on the emotions that makes one—makes me—wonder whether the passionate life itself does not undergo some damping alteration in these settings.

The "logic" of the emotions turns out to be the collection of concepts that can be applied to elucidate emotion, such as the determining of its scope or compass, the fact of its intentionality or "aboutness," its intentional object type (for example, human, inhuman, or superhuman), its criteria or standards of judgment as an act of appraisal, and more. Thus the "logic" outlined here is not that *inherent in* the emotion, which would be some inner structure of first principles and necessary consequences, but the marshaling of concepts *brought to bear on* emotions by the analytic scholar. It might be the case that, insofar as these concepts help to make an emotion intelligible, the affect should indeed correspond to them in having some sort of intelligible structure. But it might also be the case that the passion which is thus structured is the passion analyzed, not the passion felt, the emotion co-opted for understanding, not the emotion harbored in the soul. It is a little as if the language of physical theory explaining two bodies' acceleration toward each other by mutual attraction were understood as exhibiting the internalities of their mutual love.

I am trying once more to express the initial quandary I felt in writing this book: How, if affect is truly other than thought, can thinking get near it, without impinging on it? The question is more delicate than the old, robust quandary of the comprehension of the world without by thought from within, since feeling and thinking lie so confoundingly close together, both *within* the soul. A kind of psychic "uncertainty principle" seems to govern the interaction of affect and thought.[55] I am supposing that this quandary might, in part, fall away if passion were to prove to have an intrinsic logic that would, to some degree, assimilate it to thought.

Solomon indeed offers no system of principles and necessary connections that amount to an *inherent* "logic of the emotions." For him that phrase means rather a loose group of notions, "a matrix of permutations and combinations of essential mythological and ideological structures."[56]

"Judgment" and "logic" are here, somewhat contrary to their nature, very soft-edged terms.

A less relaxed argument, which agrees that emotions are evaluative judgments, but gives that notion a precisely stated yet wider setting, is made by Patricia Greenspan in *Emotions and Reasons.* She points out that emotions sometimes play the role of justifications, "rationally required *motivational* supplements to belief," but sometimes the reciprocal situation occurs, as the emotions are themselves in turn justified through having played a valuable role in rational motivation (presumably to action). Thus passion "may be seen as working in the service of reason." —Here's a reply to Hume's notorious claim that "reason is and ought to be the slave of the passions."

I choose among her cases deep, unassuageable grief at an irrevocable loss, because it is "an extreme case of emotional passivity." For this passion is a dead end, she says, insofar as it seems that nothing short of repairing the loss can be done about it. So it is a good test case for her second notion, that emotions are sometimes justifiable as encouragements of rational motivation to action. The problem is how an emotion that is both supine and intense, so that the victim is at once prostrated by it and wallows in it, can be aiding rationality. Such grief lacks a possible ameliorative aim; how then can it function as a reason for action? The prime explanation, that the discomfort of a negative emotion motivates the sufferer to—presumably alleviatingly constructive and non-diversionary—action is absent here; there is none such—*except* that the victim may feel that containment of the grief would make it worse. In that case the grief would, I imagine, motivate its own expression, and that is presumably itself a healthy action. Thus in "grief behavior," self-interested and altruistic reasons coincide; the former occur insofar as the pressure of the discomfort is alleviated, the latter insofar as non-deliberate expressions of grief, "*torn from* the agent," as it were, fulfill an obligation toward the object of loss.[57] Such considerations show *that* emotion and reason may be mutually justifying, but not *how* it can be that they are so—by what *in them* and in us emotion is capable of giving reasons to reason, and of receiving in turn its due from rationality.

What I would like to understand could be put in this way: First say to yourself, "I think, and insofar as my thinking is intended to be demonstrative it follows certain inherent necessities articulable as a logic, and these are its axioms and rules of inference." Then form the parallel sentence: "I am impassioned, and insofar as my passion is to be recognizably rational it must follow certain inherent necessities, . . ." My question then is, can I complete the passion-sentence so that it is plausibly parallel to the thought-sentence? Does it follow that I can, to begin with, intend to direct a passion the way I can intend to focus my thinking on a stretch of demonstrative reasoning? Next, what is the passion-parallel for demonstrating something? Then, what is the necessity-analogue to a thought-logic? In sum, is there a peculiar passion-logic, *an eigenlogic for affects*?

In psychoanalysis, to be sure, a claim is made—it is in fact a better specified version of an older notion[58]—that the unconscious, the infernal reservoir of the passions, has its own logic, expressed for example in dreaming, that theater of appearance for the unconscious. But Freud does not really claim that dream-logic is different from normal logic, only that it is differently, namely visually and narratively, expressed—to bizarre effect. For example, logical consequences are represented as simultaneities in time, the disjunction "either-or" by the conjunction "and," and oppositions, like the contradictory "not," are disregarded or represented by a contrary.[59] Thus his dream-logic is not a new alternative logic but an accommodation of standard logic to the spatio-temporal exigencies of dreaming. It is in fact not passion-logic but picture-logic, or thought working in images; the categories remain the same but the cognitive mode has changed.

Logicians are concerned with the domains to be occupied by true alternative logics. I am far from following the highly formal exposition, but the problem, taken informally, clearly concerns the possible ways the circulating phrase "the rationality of the emotions" might be logically realized:[60] Suppose that a special content, a different area of discourse, requires an adjustment of the standard, textbook logic (the kind familiar to all of us at least in use if not formally). Will this be something like an extension of, a supplement to, the usual way—just some special-purpose addition to standard logic? Here Freud's dream-logic might serve as an example. Or will it be an alternative, a so-called "deviant" logic, one whose theorems and valid inferences will constitute a genuinely diverse system? If so, there is a next question: Is such a deviant logic a local aberration from or a global rival to ordinary ways of reasoning? Would such a passion-logic simply apply within the emotion-reservation of our lives or could it make a bid for rivaling or even superseding standard logic? The latter might be the stuff of a very illuminating science fantasy—*if* there is in fact a passion-logic, if one can make sense of the claim that as we reason as rational beings so we do something analogous as emotional beings—which implies that our passions are in fact actions directed by their own logic.

To be sure, if we take logic in its extended sense, as treating not only of the rules of valid inference but also of concepts and judgments, then the emotions had already been brought into logic by Kenny's analogizing of the propositional attitudes of judging and desiring—both have the form of a judgment in which the speaker (or thinker) expresses in a proposition an attitude of judging *or* wanting toward an intentional object. But though that analysis appears to show that emotions are judgments, it does not yet show that they are rational in the sense of having a logic. I say the analysis "appears to show" that emotions are judgments because of the above-mentioned pervasive trouble, one to which I can see only fuzzily evasive solutions: The analysis really only shows that linguistically articulated emotions, *propositional* attitudes, have the form of judgments—why wouldn't they?—but that needn't mean that the affects in themselves, in their inarticulate native state, are judgment-like. Moreover, these judgments—and this is general cognitivist doctrine—convey appraisals. But it isn't obvious to me that the inclination (or aversion) of the soul, which does indeed seem to be an aspect of every affect that moves it, its "valence," is best described as an "appraisal," which means, after all, "fixing a price" (Latin *ad* + *pretium*, price). The tendings-toward or shrinkings-from undergone by the soul, the expansions or contractions felt in the heart, seem more primal than the "appraisals" that might express the feelings *in words*: When I incline toward someone or something, say in love, it seems to me to be a next step, a reflective step, possibly immediate yet distinct, that makes me say to myself, "This is my good" or, in consternation and usually after a time, to the contrary, "This is bad for me."

Are there then ways of finding the emotions rational that do better than either just to declare them judgments of appraisal or, in a more traditional vein, to distinguish the logic of passion simply by its skewed premises rather than as a respectably diverse mode of reasoning?[61]

This is the moment to interpose a topic so far neglected: to report at least one, somewhat formal, criterion for distinguishing action from passion. It seems to be part of cognitivist theory to accept a derivative of the ancient distinction between reason as active and passions as passive. A contemporary version is the distinction between intended action done for a reason and emotional states. Here is an analysis by Robert Gordon:[62] I note first that in this argument the soul's felt passions are not pitted against the *mind's active reason,* since reasoning is simply out of the picture for Gordon; instead felt passions are distinguished from *behavioral action.* Second, Gordon terms fallacious some very common, related, ways of describing and, it seems to me, of feeling our feelings: that we are passive under our passions, that they happen to us rather than being brought about by us, and that they are not at the first instance under our control. These assumptions are mistaken, he says, because, closely considered, they turn the *passions* into actions, insofar as the passions seem to be *doing* things to us. From this aspect, "a" passion is a creator of commotion, a mover of emotion, and so a principle of action along with the activating object.

In fact, however, Gordon says, it is not the passion but a *state of affairs,* a situation, that acts on us. For like reasons, passions can't be said to be out of our control or to overcome us, because they are themselves resultant states brought about by situations, some of which might indeed have been in our control. The passivity of the emotions, then, is just in their being states in which some situation acts on us. But, it turns out, those situations themselves are attributable to our action.

This correction requires some pretty drastic language rectification, since people do ordinarily speak—have from the beginning of this book: "Eros whacked me with his ax"—of being overcome by feeling, losing emotional control, and feeling passive by reason of their passion. This language makes sense to them because, it seems to me, they think they are pitting their reason against their passion—that is the missing factor here—and they think of the passions as offering powerful passive resistance to efforts at rationality.

However that may be, the point of Gordon's approach is to frame this problem: How, if it is assumed that we are *not* passive in a state of passion, are in fact to some degree responsible, does the impassioned state differ from reason-informed action? The answer is in terms of disposition—attitudes and belief-contents, such as are appropriate to the cognitivist approach. This is how it works: When one acts for a reason, one's action is caused by an attitude, that is, a disposition to act and also a belief-content that argues for, says *something in favor of,* so acting; in fact the action is justified and even dictated by these two factors. Verbally expressed, such attitudes are value judgments.

The dispositional attitudes and beliefs that underlie the emotion are, however, not so related, since given the attitude, that is, the disposition to grow emotional, the belief *does not argue* for growing emotional. For example, if I am growing embarrassed, my belief does not favor growing embarrassed; rather it is concerned with the state of affairs that is causing my embarrassment. In other words, in actions what I believe, the *reason* for the action, argues for acting. In emotion what I believe doesn't argue for the emotion but concerns the causal situation or object: "The reason for an *action* entails a positive evaluation of *the action itself.* . . . [A] reason for an emotion . . . does not entail a positive (or negative) evaluation of the emotion itself," *but rather of its object.*[63] Therefore, in virtue of their causal structure, intended actions are subject to reasons concerned with good and bad, while emotions are not.

This conceptual-linguistic analysis locates the passivity of the emotions in the fact that verbalizations of reasons given for any motion bypass it and go to the causal object or state of affairs. One consequence of this approach is that by the same token by which emotions are, by their very structure, impervious to moral suasion, they are, as has been intimated, amenable to control through their causal objects. For these can, for example, be avoided.

It seems to me that the notion that the passions are passive through their peculiar intentionality, their receptivity to an object, rings true and is useful in the analytic context. But I don't think it can replace that passivity which goes with their being not just states but "affects," "done-to's." The object will raise the passion, to be sure, but pasionateness is also something in itself. For passions are, as it were, receptivities waiting to be impinged on, and through these receptivities we really are passive and suffer impingements whether we will or not. I am saying that these passion-propensities are prior to the eventual object of our passion and are ready to be *activated,* indeed often seek to be incited—by it, the object (or, in Gordon's terms, by "states of affairs"). And whether or not we've got *ourselves* into the situational mess, we suffer.

Now I return to the question of a possible rationality of the emotions that is more logic-like than is a mute evaluative judgment, a pro-or-con attitude. But there are really two questions here. One is, indeed: Do emotions always include an aspect of inclination or disinclination, of "for or against," in the light of which they could be called reasonable or unreasonable? The other is: Do emotions have a structure analogous to—if distinct from—discursive thought in view of which they could be called logical or illogical?

ii. Both of these meanings of "the rationality of emotion" are carefully and comprehensively analyzed by Ronald de Sousa in his book of that title.[64] To anticipate de Sousa's answer: Emotions are indeed evaluative, and they do have certain intrinsic and distinctive logical features, a true *eigenlogic.*

I begin with the latter feature, the logic, as de Sousa does. A first requirement is a "typology" of the objects of emotion. It turns out that the general object-directedness of emotions can be interestingly detailed. De Sousa establishes seven types of emotional object:[65]

Target: the "real object" of the emotion, what I have called the intentional object—for example, the object of love, a person.

Focal property and motivating aspect: the feature of the object that is the focus of attention and whose apprehension seems to incite the emotion— the personal attractions of that person.

Cause: the real cause of the emotion when the motivating aspect may not be the genuine incitement; what really caused the love may be a suppressed or background feature—perhaps that he looks like one's father.

Aim: the direction given, so to speak, by the emotion itself, what it makes us do or endows us with—for instance, it drives one to express love or allows one to gain in self-esteem from its success. (This intrinsic aim is not to be confused with some ulterior purpose to which the emotion might be put.)

Formal object: the object in its general fitness for the emotion—the person who is intrinsically unlovable (if there are such) is generally an unfit object of love; it is through the fitness of the formal object that an emotion is intelligible, makes sense, seems correct or incorrect to the public.

Propositional object: the relation to a belief expressible in a proposition that conditions some emotions—if she loves him and then learns that he cheats, she loses faith and the love is gone (well, in people with backbone in passion).

These object-types together structure an emotion. Are they well observed and plausible? It is corroborative that Hume had seen pretty much the same facets under different terms, which are here shown in a comparative chart:

Pride (in a beautiful house)

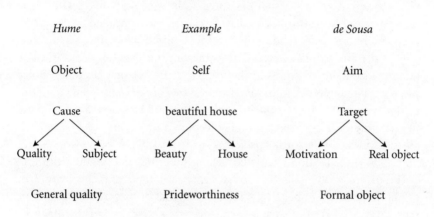

Hume	*Example*	*de Sousa*
Object	Self	Aim
Cause	beautiful house	Target
Quality Subject	Beauty House	Motivation Real object
General quality	Prideworthiness	Formal object

The types of objects having been established, the structure of an emotion can be shown in a "relational schema," in which an emotion type, say love, once distinguished by an observer through its formal object, the lovable, can be seen as a generalizable relation that operates over all the object types, somewhat as a function does over variables. Not all emotions have all variables; for example, love, de Sousa says, "typically has no propositional object,"[66] which is to say, we don't love or cease to love for conscious, articulable reasons. (It *does* happen; we can lever ourselves out of a painful passion by reasons.)

In Solomon's theory emotions were subjective: They didn't mirror the world, but they did shape it. De Sousa now looks for objectivity in the emotions (not to be confused with their "object"); he wants to find something that might make them more like perceptions. For perception is to a large extent "covariant" with the quality of the external object, though our own physiology and beliefs do contribute subjective elements. Perception is, however, distinguished from emotion first of all by the fact that it has sensory channels which, so to speak, deliver the object, while "there is no organ of emotion."[67]

I want to stop here for a comment on this latter significant observation, which, it seems to me, is what makes cognitivism possible. In the sphere of cognitivist concepts, emotions are "attitudes." "Attitude" (from Latin *aptitudo*) means a mental state, a sort of position or stance that the mind assumes. It sometimes helps to translate a term into Greek: Attitude would be *hexis,* the active condition of the soul (underlying virtue) that is contrasted with *pathos,* which latter is not a position of the soul but a possession—the soul is taken over, possessed, as it were: These older descriptions are possible because there *is* a sort of organ for the passions, namely the soul, or at least a part of it, say the sensitive soul. It is in fact conceived as a kind of receptor organ for objects of passion, as the sense organs are for objects of perception. The "mental attitudes" description favored by cognitivists places the emotions, since they have no definite soul-seats, in the same figurative space with all attitudes, so that they are not "encapsulated" (de Sousa's term) from rationality. Thus is dissipated—in a *very* general way—the mystery of the amenability of passion to reason; the passion-world is made safe for rationality. It seems to me to be a matter of very ultimate choice whether one prefers one's questions *unanswered* or *obviated.*—The cognitivist understanding obviates the discords of the soul by assimilating its parts to each other: All its parts or powers except perception are "mental" and all are "attitudes." So de Sousa's project is made possible by being worked out on an aboriginally homogenizing field—the mind of "mental attitudes."

Emotions in mental space do have more elements of subjectivity than perceptions; for example, in the former personal history and belief matter more. But what is of greater consequence, they have, even as mental attitudes, some of the receptivity to the object that characterizes perception. In other respects too emotion attitudes are closer to perceptions than to another attitude, that of belief. For beliefs can be hypothetical; not so emotions or perceptions: Emotions are ineluctable; seeing is believing. A belief, however, can be "entertained" without being actually believed, that is, without being "endorsed," posited. What seems impossible for a perception is hard, though to me it seems not totally impossible, for emotion: to experience an emotion without being "emotionalized" (my term) by it, that is, to experience it hypothetically.

A hypothetical emotion seems to be not totally impossible because I can imagine entertaining the ghost of a feeling, trying it on for size, "just for instance" so to speak, savoring its flavor without the feeling—Sartre's false feeling. Later on in his book de Sousa too will talk of "bootstrapping," of the self-deceptions of emotion, but isn't there a non-deceptive pretense of feeling (distinct from empathetic imagination), such perhaps as the inner attitude-taking by which actors prepare their roles?

The point here, however, is that emotions have, these contrary features notwithstanding, some sort of objectivity, some correspondence to reality. Objectivity, however, might possibly be regarded as more than suggestive of, as intrinsic to, rationality; this would bring emotions, insofar as they have marks of objectivity, somehow within the rational compass. In any case, de Sousa now goes on to analyze the criteria by which any state can be assessed as rational, including emotion:

First, *intentionality*, which means that the state is mental, being intentional in the sense discussed above, that it has an object which it is about, as love is love of someone.

Second, *success*, which means that the intentional state "attains" its formal object. For instance, in the rational propositional attitude of belief, the formal object is truth, truth being what any belief is in general "about." Unless a belief aims at truth—or desire desires good, or any emotion is about a fitting intentional object—the mental state will not be rational. Thus to hate the lovable is irrational (albeit all-too-human).

Third, *constraints*, meaning that rationality "which never [positively] prescribes,"[68] does, negatively, proscribe. For example, it forbids inconsistency. States of mind cannot be self-contradictory, incompatible with themselves, if they are to be rational; thus love and hate of the same object at the same time in the same respect is irrational (but, of course, a human fact).

Fourth, *origins-and-consequences*, a criterion which means that if there is an inconsistency or confusion it helps to inspect the beginnings and the outcome—how one came to love someone and where it's going.

Fifth, *minimal rationality* means that a state of mind is rational enough within its narrowly defined context to be assignable to the general category of "rational." Even a very eccentric love, given its peculiar story, has its reasons.

These diagnostic features seem to characterize pretty well a rational structure, a general logic of a state of mind that includes emotions. Furthermore, rationality "is always a teleological concept,"[69] meaning that it has a goal: success in its own terms. This success is a desideratum rather than a criterion; unlike the success listed above, which requires that the mental attitude fit its proper formal object, goal-success is the desired achievement of a material—meaning a particular—object.

There are, however, two types of success-seeking rationality: *cognitive* and *strategic*. The first seeks to fit the mind to the world, the second the world to the mind. It is a version of the old distinction between theoretical and practical thinking, more briefly, between cognitive belief and purposeful desire.

De Sousa turns to the question of whether emotion in general belongs to either or both of these. Emotion surely isn't just cognitive, though it has been shown above to have objective aspects, for to cognize lovability is not always to love. But it isn't all practical purpose either, for it has many formal objects, not all of which are "the desirable," nor is emotion always roused to pursue it. And it isn't a merging of both of these rationalities; one argument against such a close conjunction is that there is often a real, incomposable difference between the cognitive and the strategic aim in passion. For on the one hand you can, on occasion, eradicate an emotion or convert it completely by a mere change in belief. Thus (my example) when Queen Dido learns that the object of her passion, Aeneas, has his mind on history rather than on her, she implores her Carthaginians as she dies: "Hate, hate for ever / The Trojan stock."[70] Had she let herself live, her emotion for the faithless object of her love, having turned to hate, might well have died, done in by a belief of his unsuitableness as a lover. Yet on the other hand, you might not quench the purpose to love by hating the object; Dido's longing for love, a more general, "strategic" desire, might, she being an inflammable woman, have survived the loss of this cognitively devalued lover to welcome the next royal refugee from Troy. So: This particular love can quite die under sudden lessons that adjust the heart *to* the world, but the general longing persists, a residue of desire that has expectations *from* the world.

I might add here that John Searle also gives this argument as one of several explaining why an intentional affective state, that is, an emotion, is not a mere *conjunction* of desire and belief. Rather it is, he says, a strong form of desire *presupposing* a belief; if the belief is lost, so generally is the affect.[71] But desire does not *necessarily* come and go with belief; the two are separable.

Since emotion in general is neither purely cognitive, nor strategic, nor a melding of these, a third kind of rationality must be formulated. It will have parallels with the two at hand, but it will also accommodate *emotional desire* specifically, for in it the two rationalities of emotion, cognitive belief and strategic desire, *are* in fact brought together. De Sousa is saying that, while desire in general is not identical with emotion, there is a subclass of emotional desire. That emotion-desire can be a paradigm for understanding emotion. It won't, of course, be grasped as mere cognitive rationality and not even as just the functional desire of strategic rationality, of action-thinking, but as a third mode, now formulated as a kind of *prizing and valuing.*[72]

Before telling about this emotional desire, the account of which de Sousa calls "axiology" (from Greek *axios,* "worthy, valued," and *logos,* "account"), I want to remind the reader that these are old problems: Is desire different from passion or is it a protopassion, is it the root of all passion or is it one emotion among others? Is the good desired because of its own independent qualities or is the good simply what is in fact desired? If the formal object of desire is by definition the desirable and that is said to be the good, is the good here a mere name—we desire the desirable and name it the good[73]—or does it impose some obligation, some logico-moral prohibition on desiring the bad? These may seem like dry questions, but their answers determine not only our understanding of human affect but also finally of human action. One way to vivify the issue is to recall that it is indeed Satan's satanic determination to aim at the bad.

Back to de Sousa. As an introduction to "emotional desire," he distinguishes three types of desire. The first two types are 1. the objective desires, which, like cognitions, correspond to objective, real-world values and 2. the subjective ones, which, are for things valuable relative to us; these desires are respectively for things desirable because they are objectively good and stable and for things desirable simply because they happen to be desired by us, and therefore tend to be in their nature unstable, of the moment. This pair is generally regarded as belonging to "strategic" rationality, to reason driving toward success.

But there is the third kind of desire, "self-related" desire, which is neither objectively fixed on an external object, nor unstably, antically relativistic, but quite constant. This is the kind of desire that is above all vital to one's self-concept, one's personality. The capacity for passion itself is an example. That desire—the desire to *feel*—is not "strategic," not really fulfillable in purposive action, and yet our sense of being man or woman depends on it. De Sousa is surely right: Nothing hollows out our humanity like the flight of feeling, the inability to feel our feelings.

So that third, different rationality—the "axiological" logic already named —is needed to inform this self-related desire. Here de Sousa introduces his central notion, the source of the axiology, the *paradigm scenario.*

To begin with, this device is to replace the somewhat haphazard and essentially puzzling traditional list-making that proceeds from primary emotions, using them as building blocks or color blends. De Sousa's substitute notion works as follows: "We are made familiar with the vocabulary of emotion by association with *paradigm scenarios.* These are drawn first from our daily life as small children and later reinforced by the stories, art, and culture to which we are exposed."[74]

These originating childhood scenarios—the broadly Freudian background is pretty clear—not only provide the characteristic objects of specific emotion-types set out above, but they model the "normal response." The paradigm scenario acts much like the "ostensive" definition of a common noun: You point to an example of the thing whose name you want to give meaning to.

Indeed the paradigm scenarios both set up our "emotional repertoire" and "quite literally provide the meaning of our emotions."[75] The repertoire is preeminently that of formal objects. The "origin" of emotion-desire is in the paradigm scenario and this origin "constitutes the formal object's very definition." In other words, what will be in our emotional repertoire, in our capacity to find things lovable, contemptible, desirable, disgusting, will be there by reference to childhood scenarios. In these early memory-pageants, de Sousa is saying, we find the instance that is generalized into a paradigm.

This theory has the attraction of ringing utterly true to that part of one-self—of myself—that is even now just an expanded version of a child. More-over, it immediately struck me as familiar from a different realm and scope of discourse: Thomas Mann's works quite deliberately embody paradigm scenarios, especially so *Death in Venice* and *Joseph and His Brothers.* Mann's very own formula, his "element," as he says, is "myth plus psychology."[76] He means that his people live out in their uniquely individual psyche, often unconsciously, sometimes with full awareness, a mythical scenario, primordial and timeless, which informs their sense of self, guides their deeds, and gives meaning to their story. "Meaning" here is construed just as it is by de Sousa, as *reference to an antecedent event,* though the priority might be atemporal. Meaning *is* recollection.

De Sousa, however, naturally wants scientific backing. Therefore he draws on research in childhood development, especially on the way that "emotions are constructed out of dispositions."[77]

He then shows that the principles of rationality already worked out apply to these paradigm-modeling emotions. Since the formal object of the emotion, be the emotion objective, subjective, or self-related, is responded to under a dramatic aspect, because it is a "scenario" that sets the axiological appraisal, the object has a sensed value-quality, *apart* from either cognitive belief or action-directed strategy. Under the paradigm hypothesis *all* types of desire turn out to belong to de Sousa's third, the prizing-and-valuing kind of rationality.

Recall that the rational criterion of *success* was the attainment by the mental, intentional state of its formal object or "mode of appropriateness," which, in the case of an emotion, is that emotion's desire (meaning not that we get what we want but that the desire makes sense). This is the very fulfillment an aboriginal scenario provides. Note that, although the axiological aspect, the valuation and its inherent desire, are generic for each emotion-type (in fact, the only way an emotion-type can form a natural class is through a common formal object), each scenario, being an instance, has its own peculiar "feel." However, biological commonalities keep the scenarios from being too subjective. Thus reference to the scenario satisfies the criterion of success.

The scenarios and thus the emotions cannot arise until the child is capable of *intentionality,* of object-directed thought, as the rationality-assessment demands. Logical *constraints* apply to the way the paradigm scenario is interpreted, for instance: Is it permissible or rather wrongheaded to recall it under contradictory aspects? May it be coherently felt, say, as comic and tragic at once? *Minimum rationality* too is applicable; emotions are not to be criticized as inappropriate if the situation is relevantly similar to the paradigm. Thus emotions can be assessed for their "intrinsic rationality—a kind of correctness or incorrectness—in terms of the resemblance between a presenting situation and a paradigm scenario." So axio-logic *is* recognizably a logic, though a special one. Emotions *do* have their own logic whose enabling field is a memory-image.

After all that, the question might be: Why do we *need* (on the hypothesis, however formulated, that emotions are useful) emotions to be rational in their own mode when we already have a cognitive and strategic rationality—the old rationality? De Sousa says that axiological emotion supplies the insufficiencies of reason by "controlling salience."[78] He means—to compress a long argument—that emotion makes aspects of the world jump out as mattering to human beings, individually and generically.

I suppose de Sousa thinks that reason is too leveling to discern differential importance. It seems true that the type of understanding brought to bear on the world by a rationality conceived as a method of rule-directed mind operating on denuded objects, the type adopted by cognitivism, cannot achieve this human salience, and that emotion must be called in. Yet, I would submit, *that* only holds of modern rationality. The intellect of earlier times, conceived as receptive insight open to beings and their gradations, did better in highlighting human saliences than ever could the passions. *That, to me, explains the contemporary effort to make the emotions rational. They are to make up for, to supply, the deficits of modern homogenizing rationality.*

The paradigm scenarios have been severely criticized. For one thing, they seem too conservative: The passions are now understood as deriving from social constructions internalized in childhood; thus people are conceived as somewhat too constrained by childhood experiences, although they often in fact want to and do emancipate themselves from just these.[79] To my mind the chief obstacle to crediting childhood scenarios as the ultimate references of our affects lies in the common emotional experience of adolescence as a new birth and as a second childhood, one characterized by a sense of personal uniqueness and isolation never quite relieved by tribal loyalties or special confidantes: "No such thing has ever happen to anyone before, only to me." Surely the teens are a time of re- and self-construal of paradigms. Yet the notion of passion-paradigms by itself, aside from biological and developmental curlicues, seems very true to experience: Affective significance arises when (and only when?) the present moment connects with its memory-image.

I end this section with yet another approach to one preoccupation of emotional rationality, a tabulation of the *differences* between the emotionally and the intellectually rational mode by Aaron Ben-Ze'ev.[80] He conceives the logical elements listed below as "principles of information processing determining the meaning of events around us"; in other words, emotions are meaning-bestowing cognitions. The emotional approach is to be seen as doing better in each of these respects:

1. *Reality:* In the emotional world, that is, in our environment as actually perceived or imagined, changes are more significant than stabil-

ities and personal events than non-personal events. The intellectual world is oppositely structured; it is more static and more abstract.

2. *Events:* In the emotional mode the perceived strength, the reality, and the proximity of events determine their significance. In the intellectual mode, objectivity is dominant.

3. *Circumstances:* Emotionally, the more responsible I am for an event and the less prepared for it, the more significant it is; my perceived duties and actual unreadiness figure largely in my evaluation of it. Intellectually, the opposite is mostly the case; impersonal events tend to count most.

Here emotion is simply—and not always subtly—presented as the antithesis of intellect. One might point out that that is just what used to define them as non-rational. Ben-Ze'ev's explanation of the rationality of emotions starts from the endemic cognitivist critique of the supposedly traditional (actually, modern) understanding of rationality. He avers that its intellectual calculations, its logical operations, are too easily accepted as being optimal, that is, as "normative," in generating appropriate responses. Once this mistake is recognized, other mental mechanisms and modes will be acceptable as rational, such as emotions. For since they are frequently spontaneous—intense, fast, automatic, and not very aware—they, rather than the processes of intellectual rationality, will often produce the optimal response. All I can say is expressed in a Russian phrase I learned in my youth from a wisely sceptical elder: "Your word in God's ear."

5. The Role of the Imagination in the Passions: Few Take It Up

Why is this closest of conjunctions so rarely a specific theme? One reason is probably that the word "imagination" has a wide and a narrow use. The wide use, which I believe begins in the Renaissance, refers to the human power of making something new, even new worlds: creation. Its most extreme, hightoned expression occurs, to my knowledge, in a poem by Wallace Stevens in which (so I read it) the human mind's cognitions, the imaginative power, and the divinity are identified with each other:

We feel the obscurity of an order, a whole,
A knowledge, that which arranged the rendezvous,

Within its vital boundary, in the mind.
We say God and imagination are one.[1]

The mundane, hackneyed version of this divinization of a human capacity now pervades our speech. Anything that shows the least sign of being neither ordinary nor rule-driven is called "creative" and "imaginative," and amateurishness not withstanding, it is termed Art. This wide and almost boundless use of the "creative imagination" has so diffuse a relation to the emotions that it is nearly impossible to focus on. I shall try to provide a narrower sense below.

The professional arts, above all music, do indeed, I want to say parenthetically, attract a lot of inquiry into their relation to emotion. Music, however, is the quintessentially non-representational art, in the sense that ideas, mental imagery, and onomatopoetic imitation are often regarded as extraneous to it. (Schopenhauer was, I believe, the first to see music as that art which goes directly to the depths of the world and arouses passion while circumventing all representation, all visualizable ideas.[2]) Consequently the most common view among both musicians and their audiences is that music, instead of representing, *expresses* the emotion of the composer and sympathetically arouses a similar feeling in the listener. But the very lively critical literature asks whether it is the dynamic aspect of musical sound that arouses feeling directly or whether the effect is mediated by its significant symbolic forms—which would, after all, speak for some sort of representationality.[3] This and similar questions concerning the expression of emotion in all artifacts—whether the emotion expressed is the maker's, whether the emotion aroused is the perceiver's, whether the emotion conveyed is the artifact's—all these questions converge on this, the deepest inquiry: How does an affect, the most essentially un-exterior of human conditions, come to achieve sensory, not to speak of esthetic, external appearance? How is subjectivity "objectified"? I have, I think wisely, avoided this beckoning realm of tangles and pitfalls.[4]

I might say here succinctly what *representation* usually—and literally— means: It is some sort of image (not necessarily visual) of an original that is recognizable through it—and to which it is thus in some aspect similar. According to this way of speaking (there are others), a *symbol* also presents something other than itself but *not* in the mode of similarity.

In the fictional literary arts, too, questions of emotionality itself arise. (The art of rhetoric, the literary nonfictional mode most closely linked to passion, was discussed earlier.) Here the main problem is the non-being, or better, non-existence, of fictions: How can what has no "reality," no material thinghood, rouse emotions, and of what sort are they: pretended, purifying, sympathetic, empathetic? I would complicate the problem by directing attention back from the non-existence of *fictions in the images of art* to the complementary but cognitively prior non-reality of the *mental images in the mind*. In fiction, don't figures that have no reality arouse images that have no sense matter, which in turn incite feelings that—what? Are pallid, are pretenses, are "esthetic"? These quandaries of the arts, eschewed here as broaching too huge a field, have had ample, though inconclusive, treatment.[5]

A. Receptive Imagination

What, then, is the imagination such that it is receptive to passion? I want here to regress to that prior cognitive problem very little thematized in specialized emotion studies but very germane to this book: the imagination itself. Imagination, Greek *phantasia,* is originally understood as a power of sensing though without sensation, above all of seeing though with the "mind's eye," and also of hearing though with the "inner ear": "Heard melodies are sweet, but those unheard / Are sweeter."[6] It seems that those other senses that are associated by us with the receptor-organs of taste, touch, and smell do not produce images in their own mode; only the senses whose objects are distant and have some gestalt—that are configurations against a field—can, apparently, do that.

The immediate, interior products of the imagination are mental images, common phenomena of consciousness. That is the sense of "imagination" whose more precise functioning in emotion it would, within my context, be interesting to determine. The great battle of the late twentieth century concerning the "existence" of mental images I will circumvent here, supposing that all people reading this book can determine the fact sufficiently for my purposes by introspection, philosophers' denials notwithstanding; the experimental evidence seems to be, on balance, in favor of mental imagery.[7]

The question, then, is this: It may well be that nothing, but what is of the highest formality, can be thought about except with the aid of an image. To put it simply: The imagination is capable first of abstracting the visible form from the sensible matter and then of storing it in memory so that it is available to the intellect, and available to it in a way closer to its own ideal mode. That was Aristotle's teaching—"It is impossible to think without a [mental] image"[8]—and in updated terms it is still entertained.[9] Is what holds for intellectual perception perhaps also true for passion? Does human affect perhaps require inciting imagery, as cognition needs the filtering imagination? Does even a face-to-face encounter with an inciting object—even the very first one—lack its memory-image? Do we ever see the object of our passions for the first time? Is all feeling reminiscent and image-backed?

Probably not *all* feeling. There are quick and vehement visceral responses, gut feelings like frights and sexual arousal, that don't seem to leave much time for the formation of a focused mental image. Thus in erotic intimacy close-up is out-of-view; and then what Thomas calls *fomes,* "the law of the members," is apt to take over.[10] Yet even very sudden attacks of passion, like the proverbial erotic *coup de foudre,* are, as far as I know, often attended by swathes of coruscating imagery. It is probably safe to say that the farther away the feeling gets from the visceral, the more mental imagery is involved, and not only to arouse the initial affect but to shape and construe it once it is going. An example, only apparently to the contrary, in fact makes the point. Thomas Mann says in *Death in Venice*, "The felicity of the writer is the thought that can become wholly feeling, is the feeling that can become wholly thought . . . pulsing thought, precise feeling. . . ." It seems at first that feeling and verbal expression are here mutually assimilated without any image-reference at all, but not so. Both the sensory sight and mythic vision are in attendance. There is ever-present, in the flesh or in the writer's imagination, a certain living beautiful boy, and he is always imagined against the background of his antique paradigms: Eros and Hermes in one figure. He is the mediating image.

Probably no one would disagree that mental images do arouse feeling and can even be used deliberately to this effect, the most blatant case being the self-induced erotic imagery of daydreams. Nor need imagery be absent in the real presence of the original, though it has been claimed that an object's presence precludes its being imagined in the sense of "imaged." That's surely true only in the most literal sense, for in the closest somatic intimacy the other's image plays a most moving role—witness the sad significance of the case where the image called up is that of an absent third. Or the eerie case in Goethe's *Elective Affinities* where a husband and wife, each imagining other partners, engender a child that bears the features of those two others, a child born, as it were, of the congress of mental images.[11] I might even go so far as to claim that no one can be truly present to another's perception whose image is not in the imagination simultaneously.

And surely any object of passionate interest will be wreathed about with imagery, pictures, ornaments, settings, atmosphere—the more intense the focus, the more multitudinous the shades:

> What is your substance, whereof are you made,
> That millions of strange shadows on you tend?
> Since every one hath, every one, one shade,
> And you, but one, can every shadow lend.[12]

But except in those obvious cases of (not only erotic) self-stimulation which involve willful imagery, which way round does it work? Do imagining and its imagery bring forth feeling, or do feeling and its passions generate images? Is affect imagery in the bud, or are images prospectuses of desire? And once on the scene, how does an image carry its "cargo of feeling"?[13]

How, for that matter, does any mental moment carry that cargo? For William James makes the wonderful claim—astounding when you first read it, but when you try it on, close to experience—that simply everything carries a feeling, *even* what one learns in graduate school to call "syncategorematic" terms, those little words that seem to mean nothing on their own but function as connectives: "We ought to say a feeling of *and,* a feeling of *if,* a feeling of *but* and a feeling of *by,* quite as readily as we say a feeling of *blue* or a feeling of *cold.*" For the stream of our consciousness "matches each of them by an inward coloring of its own."[14]

If—my examples—you look into yourself attentively while you recall saying "if"—"*If* you loved me . . ."—you can *feel* the check, the inner hitch. For "if" implies "maybe not," and that impediment taints the content of the condition "You love me." So also for "and"; there it is a feel of a modifying linkage. "First you say you love me, *and* then you leave me." For, James thinks, our consciousness is a kind of stream of self-feeling in which the objects of our thinking are bathed, and which they in turn tint or roil with their own character. His "stream of consciousness" metaphor (which he himself did not regard as a prescription for emitting artily unpunctuated prose) intimates that all our apprehensions are floated on a sort of primal affectivity which *is* our "subjective life." One might say that he is Spinoza's phenomenologist, the observer of the basically affective consciousness. Of course, the mental images arising in that consciousness are *ipso facto* fraught with feeling, and they in turn imbue the streaming self with their more formal and stable sensory features.

Is there then no flat feelinglessness, no dispassionate objectivity? These two are actually different conditions. With the first, I am thinking of the condition the Germans call *Stimmungslosigkeit*—dull moodlessness, close to boredom or worse. Heidegger in a more significant vein calls it *Ungestimmtheit,* "untunedness." But this privative or failed affect, in which my subjective life is indeed lost to me, when there is an inner-world collapse, a high-pitched silence over a tuneless space, a presage of the World's end, when

> The Trumpet shall be heard on high
> . . . .
> And Music shall untune the sky[15]

does, it seems, have a feeling-tone of its own, gray-on-gray shot through with peals of black: It is not the flatly blank contradictory of our iridescent affectivity but only its characteristic contrary on a feeling spectrum. For even attenuated affect is still affect; a life of quiet desperation is still an affective life.

Is there then perhaps dispassionate objectivity; in particular, are there images that carry no cargo of feeling at all? Geometric diagrams, graphs, schematic drawings, all the pictures of reason, might be candidates.[16] But in my experience all the images of reasoning and thinking, up to the most focused nearly non-pictorial intellectuality, are in fact borne, if not on the stream then perhaps on the winds of consciousness: In activating the good ones, I have a feeling, the feel of being all there, swept along in the satisfying slipstream of concentration. For the rational images that most works of reason call on seem to sop up and give shape to the often subliminal pleasure of thinking. The pains are plain enough. So we are perhaps, for better or worse, never quite feeling-less even when untuned, nor dispassionate even—or even especially—when absorbed in intellectual objects.

The group of investigators who are most acutely aware of the necessity of images for thought on the one hand and the close relation of images to emotion on the other are, as far as I can tell, the cognitive and brain scientists.[17] While cognitive scientists devise arguments and experiments that reveal the underlying, usually unconscious, elements and processes operative in cognition, brain scientists look for their subtending brain structures and events. For both the felt phenomena are, albeit "epiphenomenal," necessary guides for pointing the research to its matter, perhaps partly explicable in its terms, but not really comprehensible from the science alone. Cognitive psychologists (dealing with the human part of cognitive science as distinct from artificial intelligence) cannot really say how the images whose underlying processes they trace come to be *images to the mind's eye.* They explain the generating *how,* not the phenomenal *what,* of mental images. Brain scientists can tell more and more what organs and neural systems subserve the emotions—cognitive scientists tend more toward the study of thinking and its images, while brain scientists have eventually become more interested in emotion and *its* images—but the latter tend to be modestly candid about being unable to say in their terms *what* an emotion is or what it means to feel it.[18] There are those, though, who simply reduce mental events to their functional or brain structure; they do in fact believe that conscious experience will have been explained in just these terms (where by "functional" are meant formal schemata of operation, abstracted from any particular material realization).

The point of bringing in these sciences is to get assurance that nothing physically observable speaks against the very existence of emotions, images, and their mental continuity. In fact no one doubts that we have emotions; moreover, it is, as I said, now an acceptable notion that we have cognitively serviceable mental analogue-images (images somehow space-like that have quasi-spatial picture features) and that the brain systems for emotions and memory are closely connected.[19] "Memories" may stand here for "images," since all images are memorial, both those whose aspect was originally conveyed in from the outside, through the senses fronting on the world (properly called memory images) and those that are originated inside as transfigured compositions of past sensations (called imaginary images). These latter, it used to be thought, were "breathed into" the soul, inspired by the Muses coming in, as it were, through the soul's back door.

This kind of image-memory is called "explicit"; there is also implicit memory, for instance, of motor and other skills. Of course, explicit memory is the receptacle for other modalities besides vision, coming from other receptors besides the eyes. But I focus here on the latter, because calling up or entertaining memory-visions plays so dominant a rule for most—though not all—people in personal life and because the enjoyment of narrative literature depends so much on the reader's ability to generate visual imagery, and also because even the hearing of music is often attended with visual imagery which, when shared by two, reveals them as soul-mates.

Even neuropsychologists tend, however, to speak much less definitively about imagery specifically than about memory in general. For example, it is not yet settled, since reports are conflicting, whether imagining is closer to sensation or to thinking, that is, whether seeing something in the mind's eye activates primarily the sensory cortex or the higher brain centers. It does seem to be agreed, however, that although the centers for emotion and images are in continual interaction (of varying intensities),[20] yet the conscious events they subtend are distinct: People sometimes experience nearly affectless memory-images (memories that are emotionally fairly flat) and also memoryless affects (affects whose current feeling-tone has lost its connection to their explanatory memory). Since, moreover, each of these mental phenomena does exhibit different brain activations, the folk-sense that images and affects are different kinds of consciousness is corroborated. On the other hand, often the brain activities subtending these diverse mental events are practically simultaneous and the experienced phenomena are all but melded.

It is a wonderful and confidence-inspiring fact that Augustine had anticipated some of the just-mentioned phenomena in his book on memory in the *Confessions* (c. 400 C.E.):

> For without being actually joyful, I remember myself to have been joyful . . . [W]hen I say there are four passions . . . I bring forth from memory desire, joy, sadness and fear. From memory I bring forth whatever I say in disputation concerning them. . . . Yet I am disturbed by none of these passions when I call them back to mind by remembrance of them. . . . Which of us would willingly speak of such matters if, whenever we named sadness or fear, we would be constrained to be sad or fearful? The mind itself, perceiving them by the experience of its own passions, committed them to memory, or memory itself retained them by itself, even though they had not been committed to it.[21]

I can't forbear observing that in emotion studies a little more affective recall might be of profit.

I turn now from the nature of the relation between emotions and images to its use. It is clearly to our advantage that images which represent the world as it is or as we wish it to be should jibe with emotions which arouse us to action. Such conveniences are usually, by interpolative reasoning, attributed to evolution, though one might ask whether it wouldn't have served us even better in this respect to evolve a more determined will—our non-emotive motive power.

That said, the question arises how exactly, besides being generally motivational or shaping the "paradigm scenarios" that fix our inclinations, the imagination, in the stricter sense of mental imagery, is helpful? One suggestion is that it makes empathy possible. Adam Smith's moral philosophy depended on "sympathy," fellow-feeling; empathy is even more "altruistic" because it is not "feeling *with*" but "feeling *as.*" It is getting into the other as an *alter ego,* another self. As Peter Goldie puts it, "a person *centrally imagines the narrative* (the thoughts feelings and emotions) of another person." Such imagining involves a sequence of efforts: first, to become aware of the other as a *center* of consciousness, then to characterize both the other person and his situation in some detail, and, finally, to put oneself in the center of *his* experience—not on the periphery looking in but at his exact vantage point.

Goldie distinguishes empathy from the mode of "in-his-shoes imagining," in which I retain something of my own self; I just imagine *myself* in the other's general situation. This is Smith's "sympathy" exactly. Hence in that kind of imagining I might even see a scenario in which I *encounter* the other person, since I *am* not he.[22] There are times when such imagining fails us. We cannot get into every character or imagine every situation and remain ourselves; what we know of the other's deeds outstrips our capacity for imaginative assimilation to him.[23] If I think, for example, of being bidden, as we now sometimes are, to put myself in the shoes of a terrorist, a moral perplexity promptly arises: How empathetically should we work our way into the soul of an evildoer? But where we are able to exercise such imaginative modes directly and without harm, they are clearly useful—in predicting others' actions, in making and moderating moral judgments, in being personally touched by fictions, and generally in enlarging our emotional scope, our ability to figure the world and imagine a beyond. (It seems to me, incidentally, that in mature intimacies of all sorts, there is more satisfaction in *regarding* than in *impersonating* the other, since otherness is just what we prize. It is different for the hero-seeking young.)

Another set of uses brings the imagination back home to ourselves. Ben Ze'ev points out that since the intentional object of imagining is non-existent, we can, being unconstrained by fact, imagine counterfactually—modify the present and envision the future to suit us, even undo the burdensome past. In other words, when the imagination is assumed to be emotional, it can allow us to live with positively charged illusions. Ben Ze'ev opposes the going professional wisdom, that mental health depends strictly on checking in with reality: Imagination in fact helps us live around that reality by discharging a harsh present, redeeming a tainted past, preparing a desirable future.[24]

It is obvious that there are dangers in lettihg the imagination re-construe reality and infuse the mind with positive feeling—a version of Sartre's magicking of the world. The danger serves to remind us of a crucial fact about the imagination, that it is at once spontaneous and discretionary, that in its genesis it is sometimes and in its persistence almost always amenable to discipline by thought. Thus thinking, imagining, feeling are lived as an inextricable trio.

B. Responsive Passion

And so I come to the basic question here to be faced: *What is passion such that it both generates and responds to the images of the imagination?* I am moved to remind myself at this moment that there is an even higher question which I am setting aside as being too deep for this book: What is thought such that it both needs and transcends imagination and both absorbs and masters feeling?

Such a meditation on image-involved passion will perforce be "phenomenological," that is, an attempt to call up and set out the phenomena of inner experience. I've tried to say why the pertinent sciences can't help, and other disciplines haven't developed much interest.

I'll begin with a brief review of three approaches to the question. Hillman gives one answer:

> [T]he image and the emotion are aspects of the same complex, so their confrontation with the fantasy image or symbol is the very stuff and ground of emotion. *It is the emotion in its formal aspect* [my italics]. The development of such symbolic forces is thus the development of emotion.[25]

The notion that emotion and image are to each other as material to form is wonderfully suggestive; the question is whether it can be given some detail. I'll try later.

Next, Opdahl starts with the notion of "codes" used in cognitive science. Codes are modes of symbolic representation of objects and events (and thus commit the user to a representational theory of mind). The two basic codes of that science are defined as verbal, propositional, digital on the one hand and imagist, spatial, analogic on the other. Often people choose between the "mind's eye" and the wordlike processing mode, beginning by retrieving both and then selecting the speedier one. For example, when you're first asked how many windows are in the front of your house, you're likely to visualize, to conjure up a mental image, of the house and then count. But if you are asked the same question soon after, though the image may be in the background, you'll more quickly retrieve the verbal memory.[26]

Now Opdahl does for codes what de Sousa did for logic: He introduces a third, an "affective code." He thinks of it as particularly applicable to literature:

> [I]t is a fact that some readers at some time imagine in the medium of emotion. To read the word "ball" is to think it as a word, visualize it as an image, or feel it as a mild emotion. . . . Just as the parts of an image combine to form a whole, and just as minor ideas combine to form a major thesis, so several emotions felt by the reader of a text combine to form the larger emotion that represents it. The result is not just what we feel *about* the ball but our feeling *of* the ball. . . .[27]

The ball here is not thought of as the intentional object of an emotion, what the emotion is about, but rather as the source of what is sometimes called its "feeling" (a word of many uses), or the "feel of it." That feeling *of* the object is somewhat more like an emanation apprehended from it than an emotion directed at it. He asks: "[D]oes the feeling *of* an object really serve to represent that object?" The answer is that it is indeed that feeling rather than emotion in its intentional sense that makes this mode of consciousness *meaningful*. That the affective code conveys meaning is the crux of Opdahl's argument, where "meaning" is an irreducible notion. It signifies simply an aspect that the fictional text *needs*, that completes it, brings it home to us in detail and as a whole.

How then is the affective code related to the imagistic code? Opdahl says that affect and image *blend*—that is, of course, the issue—and he has facilitated that blending by assimilating image and affect: The image that we apprehend while reading is usually not only private but sketchy, imprecise, indeterminate and hazy. For the mind simply does not have the capacity to develop each of many scenes in detail:

> We have a visual capability of sorts, but it is essentially non-optical and concerned with not images but meaning. . . . We imagine not specifics but something else, something that provides an illusion of the concrete and yet articulates the significance of the passage.[28]

So here is the phenomenological analogue of what is in neurophysiology called the "binding" problem, the problem of the union, of the integration of mental activities based on spatially different brain areas; it is solved by assimilating imagery to affectivity through meaning as the common factor. That's a beginning insofar as it raises the question, but also a foreshortening because it fudges the distinction.

Finally, Christiane Voss offers a "narrative" theory of the emotions, though only of the complex ones, like envy, shame, resentment (those that

are not intuitive but learned and require linguistic and imagistic competence). A narrative is a "synthesis of heterogeneous components." The components of emotion are: 1. intentionality, the object-representing aspect, be
it cognitive, evaluative, or imaginative; 2. overt behaviors; 3. physical-per-
ceptual aspects, that is, physiological changes and feels or feelings (*Empfind-
ungen*) in the primitive sense; and 4. hedonistic concomitants, feelings of
pleasure and unpleasure, sometimes called "valences."[29] "Narrativity" is the
very idea of the just-mentioned "binding" (*Verknüpfung*) of the elements;
it is the characteristic of a structure whose components have been brought
together by *associative* and *temporal* connections in a chronologically developed, meaningful whole. The temporal feature ensures that the unrolling of
an emotional state becomes part of its interpretation. The narrative character
of emotions entails that we *live* our emotions as a developing story and can
therefore *tell it* as a story, and in so doing digest and come to terms with it.
The synthetic result within each person lies in the integration of the episode
into a meaningful experience whose vivid emotion-charged external representation in turn carries emotional persuasiveness for others. It is through
our manifold experience with such scenarios that we are then able to—and
often do—abstract for reflection a more general type-like narrative for each
of these complex emotions. The point of this account for me is that the very
notion of emotional storytelling intends to bind together affect and image:
Emotions don't have a tale until they have a shape, an imaginative form.

So the question is now couched approachably: How do emotions attain
imaginative shape and images absorb passionate force?

It really is the case that the most-read emotion studies don't take up
imagination as a theme. The reason is, as I intimated, the apparently illim-
itable scope of the word. People are said to be using their imagination who
put two and two together to get, instead of prosaically four, felicitously five;
who think themselves "outside the box" or into another dimension; who
conjecture, guess, suppose anything whatever; who spin mundane facts into
marvelous fiction; who re-vision, "create"[30] or re-create things and scenarios. In its most antic meaning, imagination is fantasy, phantasms, phantoms,
phantasmagoria; in its most philosophical use it names our "transcendental" faculty for synthesizing thought and sense and even for solipsistic self-
and-world creation.

So arises the task of the limiting the meaning of "imagination"—pref-
erably to a defensibly primary use. I shall take that, as I said, to be the one
that ascribes to the imagination the capacity for making images, first of all
mental images, quasi-spatial re-presentations, likeness-like imitations. (The
Latin verb "to imitate" is based on the noun "image.")

There are, to begin with, affects—feels and feelings—that are fairly visceral and only slightly image-arousing, like a throbbingly felt and dully

imageless physical pain and a luxuriatingly sensed and rosy-cloud-lapped physical pleasure. It is from these feels, "inner sensations," as they are sometimes called, that we derive, I think, our notion of mere, objectless feelings. These do, to be sure, often have their cause in the somatic world, in the sensory source of hurt or blandishment, be it from outside or inside the body. But they are not about these causes. The headache is not "about" the noise that's assaulting us in the way a "headache" is about the grief we're been given, nor are chest pains "about" the heart that's failing the way a "heartache" is about the love that's left us.

Somewhat less somatic but also not yet imaginatively shaped is the current of affectivity, James's emotion-tinted stream of consciousness, or Heidegger's basic state of being mood-conditioned.

At the other end of the hierarchy of human capabilities is thinking—and it is *ipso facto* on top, because to make hierarchies and to write about them means to exercise this very ability *upon* the others. At its very height it is, once again, an imageless activity: the pure intellect intuitively at work by direct insight into its own beings of thought—at least so say the writers I venerate. Most of us, I would guess, can only get hold of that possibility very occasionally and by a forcible abstraction from the spatialized ways in which we are actually thinking—but that is, as I said, not the subject of this book.

Nor is the activity just below the intellect, the employment of the reason on its own constitutive structures and connections—logic—and its own object-constructs and proofs—mathematics. There is, I think, general agreement that both logic and mathematics as done by human beings call on a higher imagination, the spare images mentioned above, whose crisp, colorless diagrammatic figures are serviceable to reason. The ancients thought that spatial mathematics, geometry, was in fact reflected by reason into the imagination as upon a pure matterless canvas called "imagination-matter" (*hyle phantastike*), and so still thought Kant; it is what he calls "the pure intuition of space," a presciptive field into which the understanding inscribes axiom-bound figures.[31] This hard-edged imagery, at the opposite extreme of the woolly, visceral sort, is not particularly to my purpose either.

There is, then, a cognitive middle territory between the sensation-spare top and the sensory base. On it the more complex affects, sometimes called "secondary," those ranged above the primary sensations and feelings in having intentional objects and peculiarly human import, meet the lower imagination, in which such objects are imaged and our moods are sensualized, be it in vivid or mat colors, in defined or hazy figures, set in crystalline or opaque, crisp or vague scenes. This quasi-spatial field in fact *is* the quasi-sensory imagination. (I might reiterate here that I know of no way to speak of the soul's phenomena that is not figurative. It is a situation as confounding as it is wonderful: We are compelled to speak figuratively of the soul's capacity for figuration, hence the "quasi"-language.)

The objects upon which the passions are directed are at once their mental "intentions" and their sensory stimuli, the latter in so far as things and people address us first through our senses as sense-objects, and then, having passed into our memory, remain with us in recallable quasi-sensory images. I say, neutrally, "objects" because passions are—as everyone knows—directed both at material things and living beings. For example, greed for gold is a major passion. Why else would it be that "The King was in his counting-house, counting out his money"—not banknotes, I assume, but material pieces of glittering gold both sensuous and fungible, of which he surely dreamed at night beside his Queen when she was sated with bread and honey?[32] But more ethereal appeals to the senses can also become objects of love. Who has not spent the day longing to come back to the hearing of a music that has captivated the auditory imagination? (It does however seem to be the case that auditory memory, which sets the vocal cords silently but palpably vibrating and the feet tapping, is in that respect often more directly physical than is visual memory, which is not as physiologically overt.) Yet the keenest human passion is commonly agreed to be that preternaturally intense focus on another ensouled being called passionate love, which gets much of its wonder from seeming at once terminally inexplicable and fatedly fitting (though there *is* another candidate: self-regardant pride).

Passions of this sort—that is my point—may be aroused by and be about the real-world object, but they continue in its absence and are then most immediately about its image. Could we not substitute a mental image for the real object, our emotional life would have to be violently discontinuous. The imagination insures the continuity of the "intentional object" of passion. Could image-memory not serve where real presence fails, we would be forever inchoately impassioned, newly just in love at every meeting—and Dante could not have, "child as he still was, received [Beatrice's] visage into his heart with such affection that from that day forth never, so long as he lived, was he severed therefrom."[33] Let Dante's famous love for a Beatrice, existent mainly in "the book of [his] memory," be a reminder that many a passion has very little occasion in the world and is often directed even at an almost entirely imagined object, for fictions too can be the objects of life-long loves. And conversely, the realest living love can, in its very presence, be envisioned in the imagination, a phenomenon of double-vision denied by logicians and nonetheless experienced by lovers.[34]

So much only to establish that passions of the heart are related to images of the imagination by arousal, accompaniment, and aboutness. Hence the imagination seems closer to the affective than to the thoughtful self, as these delicious, just post-Elizabethan paragraphs assert, in which, *nota bene*, understanding is a "he," well-fooled by the imagination, presumably a "she":

> [T]he understanding looking into the imagination, findeth nothing almost but the mother & nurse of his passion for consideration, where you may well see how the imagination putteth greene spectacles before the eyes of our wit, to make it see nothing but greene, that is, serving for the consideration of the Passion.
>
> Furthermore, the imagination representeth to the understanding, not onely reasons that may favour the passion, but also it showeth them very intensively, with more shew and apparance than they are indeed; for as the Moone, when she riseth or setteth; seemeth greater unto us, than indeed she is, (because the vapours or clowdes are interposed betwixt our eyes and her) even so, the beauty and goodnesse of the object represented to our understanding, appeareth fayrer and goodlier than it is, because a clowdy imagination interposeth a mist. And here it falleth forth, as he which is most studious, is best learned; and commonly, he that is best learned, is most studious: so, hee that once apprehendeth the pleasure of the passion, ordinarily followeth it, and the passion increaseth the imagination thereof, and the stronger imagination rendreth the passion more vehement, so that oftentimes they enter but with an inch, and encrease an ell. . . .[35]

Yet for all his vivacity, Thomas Wright is not exactly clear about that mist which a cloudy imagination interposes between object and understanding and those green spectacles put before the eyes of our wit that tint the world fresh, hopeful and desirable. Is the imagination here, in coloring the object and beclouding the understanding, not itself impassioning passion, playing passion's role?

I want to plead that clarity requires—though theory may question—letting the imagination imagine and the passions feel, in particular, allowing mental images to be in the first instance affectively neutral; Aristotle observes that in relation to our imagination we can be as mere spectators,[36] not necessarily affected by our pictures, as we would be if they were sights we saw or opinions we held.

Moreover, there is the oft-cited phenomenon of arousing feeling by means of an image, especially in daydreaming: Sweet or sad, we summon the image and the feeling *follows*; the action of image-raising precedes the passion of weeping:

> When to the sessions of sweet silent thought
> I summon up remembrance of things past,
>
> . . . .
>
> Then can I drown an eye, unused to flow,
>
> . . . .
>
> And weep afresh love's long since canceled woe,
> . . . .[37]

Let me then put all the above thoughts together in a simple schema, not meant to rise to the level of a theory—a diagram of two routes connecting object, passion, image.

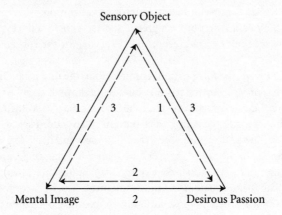

Outside arrows (counterclockwise):

1. The sensory object is taken into image-memory;
2. The image arouses desirous passion;
3. The passion goes out to the object.

Inside arrows (clockwise):

1. The object goes to desire directly; passion unmediated by the imagination is a definition of lust;
2. Passion coagulates into an image; a diffuse desire generates its own image-object;
3. Images "haunt" the object; the object accrues its own imagery about it.

The assumption here, a very common one, is that every passion has its affective base peculiarly located in desire. Passionate love, here the model, is that passion in which desire is for the intentional object itself and is positive. Fear is a passion in which there is indeed positive desire, though not for the intentional object of the passion, say a black bear, but for safety, while hatred is a passion in which the desire is in fact for the intentional object, say a loathed person, though it is not positive but negative desire, aversion, and a wish for their harm even to extinction.

Another assumption is that all the arrows may, on some occasion or other, face in the other direction, but that the solid outer arrows schematize what happens for the most part: That the sensory object deposits its image in the memory is generally if not universally accepted theory, expressed in the term "memory storage";[38] that desire as distinguished from mere appetite or lust requires a mental image comes from introspection and, happily, also from Aristotle—"imagination prepares desire"; and that passion once aroused first desires and then pursues its object is common knowledge.

So, finally, what is left is the question: Why are imagination and passion so mutually receptive? What exactly is it about mental images that allows them to give shape to, and be in turn invested by, passion?

1. Any image properly speaking, real or mental, is "iconic," meaning that it is a likeness.[39] A mental image, taken not as a neurological event but as a phenomenologically observable experience, is thus also a likeness: We see and identify things and scenes in our "mind's eye." Strenuous rear-action analyses meant to dispel the notion of these internal pictures are, it seems to me, very ineffectively fighting gossamer ghosts with steely swords—these images being just such stuff as dreams are made on.

I think that the iconic image serves passion in preserving, as I've said, its object, recollectably and recognizably, so that the feeling can continue and thrive upon itself. Moreover, the mental image offers a probably murky, amorphous passion a form—"Gives to airy nothing / A local habitation and a name"[40]—a name by which it can identify itself and a site, the object's image, to which it can shape itself. Moreover, just because the imagination is a gestalt-producing propensity, it includes also a ground, a field. And that ground often has an atmospheric coloration such as is readily inhabited by objectless mood; mood is vaporously imaginative.

2. Any image, and a mental image above all, presents an object in its absence. An image renders a thing as lacking those properties most characteristic of existence in the strict sense, namely "being here and now," in the world and its time: materiality, physicality, gravity, tangibility, predictable mobility. Ordinary images are tangibly material, to be sure, as is paint on canvas, but paint on canvas is not the material of which the object depicted is actually made. Mental images, however, don't even have that tangible substrate except in a manner-of-speaking mode, they are weightless, antically mobile, or quiescently atemporal "airy nothings." Intangibility is their element, and indeed imagined touch is curiously roundabout, since you must put yourself in the image—see yourself to feel yourself touching: quasi-touch by quasi-sight.

I think that the absent-object-image is, *ipso facto*, a particularly absorbent medium, a ready receptacle, of passion. For feeling, in going out to the object, is continually rebuffed—rebuffed even as it is compelled by the sheer, solid otherness, especially the ultimate psychic impenetrability of the object of love. But at home in its own psychic world, it can disport itself within and around the object's image with every proscribed expressive excess, just because the object of love is both there to behold and not there to resist—there, that is, in a phantasm, fully and familiarly accessible to contemplation and to possession by passion.

3. The mental image and the mind's eye are, then, untrammeled by the laws of physics, by the solidity and gravity of bodies. The mental image is scaleless; figures are the size that befits them. The mental eye is omni-perspectival; we can zoom in and out from particular detail to panoramic overview and go before, behind, between, above, below at will. The imaginative ground is tintedly vaporous or sharply defined; we can watch the atmosphere of a mood spread over it or work at the laborious recollection of a precise figure to be painted into its field. In part it yields playfully to our antics, in part it is firmly recalcitrant to our demands; it often lets us do what we will, but it also sends up unbidden images and bars longed-for appearances. It is indefeasibly spontaneous and freely manipulable.

Thus it is a fit canvas for passion in its volatility and its fixations, a space in which we learn the extent and limits of our feeling. It is passion's made-to-order playing field.

4. And finally, the imagination is anciently and ever the meeting ground of passion and thought and therefore the place where we can become adept at figuring realities and consequences. Some think that only passion has the force to fight passion and others that thought can prevail on passion by reason of its reasonableness. But whoever the combatants are in the fight for soul or self, the battlefield is still the imagination. For it is the ground on which the dimensionless intensity of passion extends itself into visible pictures, and also a space to which thinking—not always but often—controls access, summoning and forfending figures, just as Odysseus at the entrance of Hades admits or holds at bay the thronging souls with his sharp sword.

By Way of a Conclusion

On the Questions

Human passion is the all-pervasive, ever-elusive subject of this book—passion as seen through the writings of those who seem to me to have thought most deeply and largely about it. We think about anything by fixing it in our sights through questions; the more Protean the topic, the more crucial the way of asking. Here is a brief disquisition on question-asking in this book. First, then:

(1) Questions < problems.

Questions are fewer than problems. By a problem I mean a jigged question, a question constrained by the terms of a predetermined framework. The word comes to us through Greek mathematics, where a problem calls for a construction as its solution; it is distinct from a theorem, which demonstrates a truth. That the angles of an equilateral triangle are equal is easily shown, but first such a triangle must be produced.[1] For us moderns a problem requires that a difficulty arising in a setting be construed in such a way that a deconstruction of the problem is found, and it is resolved—goes away. But the question doesn't, since the problem was only one tightly tailored version of it. A solved problem is, thereafter, "of merely historical interest"; we are past it. There are usually several solutions to a problem:

(2) Problems < solutions.

Thus there are fewer problems than solutions. But if no solution really works, the framework itself becomes questionable; we become doubtful and begin to wonder.

Professional philosophers—in this respect usually post-Cartesians and post-Kantians in spirit—see it as their duty to formulate questions as problems within strict limits and to give certifiably correct solutions. Kant himself famously speaks of the strictly limited "island of truth" secured by the "solutions" of his transcendental analytic, surrounded by the stormy ocean of illusion on which we must venture only to become certain that nothing much is to be hoped for from this sea of metaphysics.[2] Meanwhile, however, the actors in the world bid us "live with uncertainty," and the "folk"—thus designated by the scientists of the mind—turn to religion for secure truths.

It seems to me that there is a fourth mode besides the certainty of limited problem-solving, the frissons of worldly riskiness, and the security of faith. It is *likelihood,* plausibility all things considered. Plato offers a model of the cosmos that is said to be an *eikos mythos,*[3] a "likely story" that has a fair chance of being a likeness—that has verisimilitude by the criteria of knowing and verifiability by the test of life. Likelihood is, in any case, what I aim for in this book.

Questions, as I think of them, are as little constrained as is humanly possible by a theoretical or technical jig—a jig being a mechanical device for guiding a tool. (I have adapted this notion of a jigged as opposed to freehand design, "the workmanship of certainty" as opposed to "the workmanship of risk," as a welcome metaphor for thinking. It comes from a book by David Pye.[4]) Although a prevailing opinion holds that such philosophical freehand thinking is unachievable, I think thoughtfulness consists, not in trying to be a-perspectival, but in being aware enough of one's perspective to include it in the account. Hence reflective candor requires the first person, often in thinking and, with restraint, in writing.

A question, then, is distinguished from a problem by being an open receptivity to the way things are. Such receptive concavities, intimations of answers that anticipate but do not jig the responses of thought, are as sturdy as they are delicate—easily lost but ever-recurring. All solutions are consequent on problems, being constructed to solve them. Answers, on the other hand, precede questions, draw them out, as it were, without completely configuring them, as would prejudgments. They guide the proverbial "thinking outside the box." Answers are attractively beckoning finalities. There must be, I imagine, fewer answers than questions, since questions are approaches. Perhaps all roads lead to the same limit, just as many hyperbolas approach one asymptote. It is, at least, a hope. Thus

(3) Answers < questions.

But if answers are *quaesita,* ever-receding and ever-sought, there are many fixed and formulated responses. And these are the very philosophical frameworks in the context of which I have sought the most well-grounded understandings of our affective life. Therefore

(4) Questions < responses.

For there are various ways to frame responses to essentially similar questions. And these are the very frameworks that set or elicit the terms within each of which multiple problems are produced. Thus,

$$(5) \text{ Responses} < \text{problems.}$$

Hence, collecting the terms:

$$(6) \text{ Answers} < \text{questions} < \text{responses} < \text{problems} < \text{solutions.}$$

Regard the above, if you like, as a *jeu d'esprit,* but I needed some terms to marshal the welter of thought-motions aroused by the subject. Within these terms, this book has dealt mostly with the responsive frameworks, the problems they raised and the solutions proposed. Now is the moment to articulate the inviting questions behind them and to attempt some answers.

One test of having wormed one's way into a "philosophy" is the ability to make explicit the question to which it is a response in a way slightly askew of the author's own formulation. I shall first try my hand at prizing out the questions behind the responding frameworks in the past ten chapters. Then, I shall attempt to recover my own questions, the questions going into this book, and finally to formulate the most likely answers coming out of it.

Chapter I.   The first question of the book is, "What hit me?" and the second, "Whence relief?" The responses are "Eros whacked me" and "Make poetry." Love, the prime and paradigm passion, is perceived as a passivity, perpetrated by a tyrant-god, a divinity who is passion-as-action, a passion imposed on a victim proudly distinguished by his gift, the abject suffering of desire.

That poetry relieves the sufferings of passion and even damps it is old and new wisdom. Jane Austen's Elizabeth Bennet asks, "I wonder who first discovered the efficacy of poetry in driving away love?" Hegel says, "[I]t is the writing of poetry especially that has the power to liberate one from emotional distress," and Heine sings, "Out of my great sufferings I make my little songs."[5] The poetry cure appears to gain its power not only from the decompression that comes from expression but also from the mastery the lover-poet gains over the beloved.

> So long as men can breathe or eyes can see,
> So long lives this, and this gives life to thee.[6]

But perhaps, above all, it comes from the diverting concentration of mind on the production of a perfect artifact.

One might argue that it is not love but proud anger that is the prime passion, the earliest in the Western tradition to get extensive treatment, in the *Iliad*, which begins: "*Wrath*—sing it, Goddess, that wrath of Peleus's son Achilles." Thus anger is the first word in our literature. It is not only the earliest, however, but as indignation at being wronged it is also perhaps the basic human passion, the proud shame-preventive. Perhaps the two together—the dual propensities for being battle-ready and love-prone— mark the full passion-gamut of human arousal: Ares and Aphrodite.

Chapter II.   The next question, asked by Plato, is, "Who is this god, Eros? Can he draw us up as well as bring us down?" Now Eros is seen as a needy half-god who, by the force of his own longing—a desire analogous to question-asking—draws human beings into the divine realm of pure intelligibility.

(A note to acknowledge a missing element in this book: The longing for what is highest is perceived as an *erotic* affect in both roots of the West, the Hebrew and the Greek. The *Song of Songs* of the Hebrew Bible is graphically erotic poetry traditionally, at least, interpreted as the soul's ardent longing for an elusive and temperamental God:

> By night on my bed I sought him whom my soul loveth. I sought him but I found him not.[7]

It was left to the pagans, however, to theorize about the relation, and by introducing a psychology that separates flesh from spirit or, in their terms, body from soul, they substitute for the expectant ardor of Hebrew poetry the active ascent of Greek philosophy.)

Then, what about that proudly angry, spirited element of our nature? It too plays a mediating role, between chaotic desire and ordering thought. Spiritedness—for Socrates the propensity closest to irruptive wrath—is the ethically most sensitive affect, tensed between wanting and obeying.

As for desire, when it is focused on its own satisfaction more than on a determinate object, it is pleasure-seeking, and then its very conception is doubly problematic. Satisfaction attained quenches desire and thus the very pleasure sought. But also pleasure-seeking is felt to have no natural bounds; pleasure is experienced as infinitely augmentable. Thus pleasure is at once self-extinguishing as satisfied desire and unassuageable as only fleetingly sustainable. Socrates' solution to these problems is both sensibly deflationary—the self-limitation of desire by the practice of rational moderation—and inspiredly elevating—the stabilizing of pleasure in the pursuit of intelligible beauty.

Aristotle will ask anew "What is pleasure?" and the response will involve his fundamental philosophical term: *energeia*, "being fully at work," actuality. For human beings that means acting in accordance with human nature at its best. This full involvement in a good cause has a *bloom* on it, its concomitant pleasure. Freud will reverse this active notion of pleasure as a perfection: Our deepest desire is *not* to be. Contemporary theories raise dozens of more or less technical problems about desire and give a diversity of solutions.

Chapter III.   Aristotle's great question asks, "What, in a world of motion ultimately induced by the attraction of the divine intellect, must be the fundamental feature of the human soul that activates the body?" His response is that first and last the soul is appetitive, *attractable,* hungry for physical and cognitive fulfillment. The problem "What is passion?" is then resolved in the light of our psychic organization: The passions are our nonrational appetites. They come in polarities, in pairs of extremes, and their moderation is *the* human goodness, understood as the mean between the extreme propensities. Though nonrational, passions are amenable to rhetoric, that persuasive speech specifically designed to reach them rather than reason. Thus rhetoric is an art that requires the listing and description of the passions; it demands solutions to the problems of marshaling the main passions so as to bring them under rhetorical management. Of the passions discerned, shame—the spirited aspect of impugned self-regard—proves to be most consequential, for like its unsocial twin, anger, it touches our *very own* being.

Chapter IV.   The Stoics have one overriding question: "How do human beings achieve control of themselves and their world?" They have a revolutionary theory of knowledge—that the world is known to us not directly but through representations in our minds, representations that are of various degrees of verisimilitude. This theory is, if not deliberately aimed at such control, at least conducive to it, for the world *is* as it is *to us.* Moreover, governing soul and apprehended world are homogeneous, both being matter in differential states of normal tension. Human passion is thus perceived as a problem of disruption, the problem of an upset in the order of our nature, a perturbation curable by the discipline of—material—reason. Thus Stoicism becomes a primarily therapeutic philosophy whose main problem is the confinement of desire within the scope of human power. In both its cognitive and moral orientation toward control rather than toward receptivity to Being, Stoicism is the ancient precursor of modernity.

Chapter V.   One question to which Thomas's *Sum of Theology* responds is, "How is the human soul sited in a divine economy?" A next question is, "How are the passions sited in the soul?" His theological response to both is, "Centrally." The passions are centrally located insofar as they belong to the "sensitive" part of the soul, which is placed above the merely life-giving and below the intellectual parts. The soul is receptive both to nature externally by its outer senses and to itself internally by its inner senses, and it is desirous or appetitive by the passions. These, being arational, want particular contingent goods, while the faculty of rational desire, the intellectual will above, desires good in general. Thus the organization of the soul offers one—mainstream—solution to the problem "How are passions related to desire?": Every passion is appetitive; passion is desire defined by its particular object.

The "Treatise on the Passions" of the *Summa* is the most extensive and acute phenomenology of the passions known to me. It is also a prolonged, comprehensive response to the question "What is a human being insofar as it is both a receptively embodied soul and an actively rational being?" To begin with, at least, it is the being who is sited centrally in the divine economy, and accordingly it has a hierarchy of hunger—for the world through the passions and for its creator through the will.

Chapter VI.   Descartes' ironically named *Passions of the Soul* is intended to be the solution to a problem posed by his own six days' creation of a new world in his *Meditations*. It is a dual universe of two antithetical substances, thinking mind and extended space. They are themselves responses to the question, "What must mind and nature be like for the former to have certain knowledge and sure control of the latter by means of the new sciences of mathematical physics and physiology?" For Descartes as rationalist, passions are indeed suffered in the soul, but for him as physiologist, they originate as *actions of the natural body*. The Cartesian problem is then, "How can there be a body-related soul when *res cogitans* and *res extensa* are in principle disjunct?" Descartes contrives a solution through the pineal gland, for him the only single structure of the brain, a dot-like conduit between body and soul. The treatment of the passions then requires a dual track: a material-scientific description of physical actions in terms of the new physiology of blood and nerves, and a morally fraught analysis of psychic passions with reference to a controlling will in the Stoic mode.

Chapter VII.   Read from the beginning, Spinoza's *Ethics* is an ontology: "What is substantial?" Regarded from its end the *Ethics* is an ethics: "What should a human being do?" The axiomatic response to the question of substantiality is: There is one self-caused substance, and its essence is power, the drive to *be*, in infinite ways. This is God, also called Nature. Human beings, along with all we call nature, are one of God's ways of being and participate in the impulse to persist and to exist maximally. Thus human beings are fundamentally affective, desirous of existing expansively. Then this specific, central problem arises for Spinoza: "How do human beings, in this setting of assertive potency, come to be passively affected?" The solution is that human beings are passive insofar as their self-conception is partial and inadequate. Our passions become active as our mind's ideas become more comprehensive, as we understand the objects of our affects in a larger context, for that is what the human mind is: the idea of our body and Nature's bodies as they affect us. What human beings should do, not by free will but by the all-governing inner necessity of God-or-Nature, is to strive to make the idea of nature that *is* their mind adequate to the reality. This increasing adequacy is a joyful science, the study of nature understood as the intellectual love of God. The ordered listing and definition of the human affects is a part of this study, necessary to its completeness.

This sole, great grounding of human passion in terms of an answer to the question "What is substantial?" seems to me to founder on an insoluble internal problem: God, the sole and unitary substance, is to be conceived under infinitely many attributes. These, being expressions of one substance, should be logically identical orders. The only two attributes accessible to human beings are their own mind, that is, an idea, and nature's extension, that is, body (Descartes' two substances modified). But these are just not as logically parallel as required. Such problems notwithstanding, Spinoza alone shows the way to ground our existence in our affectivity.

Chapter VIII.   Hume refrains deliberately from asking questions about the way things are. On the contrary, he can be said to pose this problem to himself: to construct a system that is minimally metaphysical. He finds the solution in an extreme version of Stoic representationalism, in which all knowledge appears in the mind as impressions of different degrees of vivacity and as mental operations relating these. An internal problem follows: How to construct the passions from such mental perceptions? Hume devises a system of extraordinary complexity construed from the mental operations functioning over the representational divisions. Perceptions are divided into impressions and ideas, impressions into sensations and reflexions. To these latter belong the passions, which are thus quite closely specified representations.

Pride is for Hume the paradigm passion, delineated in his terms. It alleviates, if it does not solve, a problem that arises from the project of banishing metaphysical substances, and thus the soul. In the absence of an ideal substrate, the mind has no continuous identity. The passion of pride constructs as much of a self as Hume's scepticism will admit. The Humean system of the passions is a fascinatingly infuriating exercise in the hypertrophy of miscarried ontological minimalism. But he *has* skewered pride by means of his acute distinctions.

Chapter IX.   "What is passion in and of itself, that is to say, what is its logical structure?" This direct question was always implicit in earlier treatments, but does not come to the fore until after a self-conscious social phenomenon has arisen—Romanticism. Romantics luxuriate in an affect that willingly lacks what passion has been generally understood to have: an object, more technically, the feature of intentionality, of mental "aboutness."

As a result (I surmise), even non- or un-Romantic philosophers—my examples are Kant, Schopenhauer, and Nietzsche—have a fairly new interest in "feeling," pure accesses of not necessarily object-directed desire along with pleasure and pain, each writer in his own philosophical context.

Affect in this non-intentional aspect is called "mood." The question is, "What is mood about?" The common response would be, "Nothing, really," meaning perhaps merely: nothing in particular, nothing sharp-edged. But this Nothing will now be substantively construed.

Kierkegaard has set himself the problem, "How did original sin originate?" He finds the solution in this Nothing of mood, of a particular mood, anxiety. Anxiety about nothing is the feeling of pure possibility, of a capability to do anything, to be good *or bad,* to sin. This innocence of ignorance that senses possibilities is Adam's original sinfulness, in which his actual first sin originates. Heidegger will transform Kierkegaard's spiritual construal of the Nothing of anxiety into a metaphysical mood.

Here is Heidegger's question, in my terms, "Suppose you feel yourself compelled to take down a metaphysical tradition that has lost its way. It has brought things to a halt by assigning to humans a common nature, an atemporal ideal essence. Suppose you mean instead to make a second beginning by analyzing human beings as *existences,* each as a *Dasein* and a possible 'opening to being.' *Dasein* is here and now, then and there, stretched into a temporal dimension and thrown into a worldly location; it has a choice of fleeing from or opening up to its world. The problem then is, 'What phenomena, primary and derivative, will reveal themselves?'" In its most genuine mode, its pre-rational receptivity, *Dasein* will be affective, attuned to the world. From that primal affectivity the particular passions will derive. Among these fundamental modes, or objectless moods, is one that is, once again, particularly revelatory: anxiety. Its Nothing is assigned diverse functions in different works. In one understanding it answers the question of questions, namely, "What is metaphysics and how do we come to it?" For it distances us from intra-worldly beings and makes us confront the Nothing beyond nature—a meta-physical Nothing that, so to speak, contains the world. In the other understanding anxiety alienates us from the ordinary nullities of the world and allows *Dasein* to exist not in the false fixities of ordinary life but frees it for its genuine possibilities. Here the mood that faces inner-worldly nothingness, again anxiety, answers the existential question, "What does it mean to be thrown *into the world* as a self unsustained by a human essence and thrown *on itself* as a being whose one certainty is that its existence will end, that it is mortal?" Never has an affect borne a graver—and tacitly grimmer—charge.

Chapter X.   The gauzy sentiments of Romanticism are superseded by the edgy, existential moodiness of existence on the Continent and by an astringent, anti-introspective behaviorism in Anglo-Saxon lands. The latter advances a problem that is a provocation: "What's the public evidence?" At this point emotion studies fall apart even as they flourish. The questions that shape themselves to ever-open answers go out of fashion, as do the large-framed responses. But carefully formulated problems and tightly constructed conceptual solutions abound, often concerned with the aforementioned analysis of emotional structure.

Among all of these theorizings, one approach, the "cognitivist," predominates. Its problem is to interpret emotions in such a way as to endow them with the dignity and especially the utility of rational judgments while preserving and exploiting their primitive priority. The solution, which has many executions, is to attend to the pro- and con- attitudes emotions exhibit and to construe these as pre-rational appraisals or reason-like judgments. The general problem with these solutions is that they might well be the analysts' projections of their own studious rationality upon the felt emotion rather than the extraction of a logic proper to it, though there does seem to be among them a genuine emotion-logic.

However the utility of appraisal-emotions might be conceived—as self-esteem-enhancing, as choice-facilitating, as salience-defining—it involves the imagination, whose myths, figures, and scenarios inform the feeling-matter and give it a local habitation and a shape. The final question of the book is, "What features of the imagination fit it to instigate, contain, configure, and maintain passion?" The response to this somewhat offbeat question acquires a certain precision from an analysis of mental images: their iconic, immaterial, and memorial quasi-reality. It turns out that the images in and of the imagination are, as it were, designed to accommodate affect.

I shall conclude with the questions that I myself brought as unformed urgencies to this study and for which the texts here treated supplied— besides useful formulations—likely responses, resolutions, and sometimes even theoretically satisfying and practically livable answers.

Question One.   Philosophers think about what people know, sometimes to confirm, sometimes to subvert common knowledge. *Is feeling even a legitimate object of such thinking?* To use a scholastic term that plays a role in this book, mustn't the "formal" object, the generically fitting object of thinking, be "the thinkable"? And if that is so, isn't thinking about feeling a confusion that contaminates the project at the root? Isn't it the logical transgression called a *metabasis eis allo genos,* a "passing-over into another genus"?

Nature, to be sure, is subjected to reason with humanly attenuating results in the most progressive of human endeavors, mathematical science.

Here warmth becomes a raised temperature, red a long wave in the color spectrum, heaviness a gravitational pull, insight a brain event. But the lucid beauties of scientific theory make up for the experiential loss, namely the bypassing of the sensory feeling, the *qualia* of consciousness, the activity of self. Truth to tell, thinking about the affects offers no similar compensations; the resultant theorizing isn't particularly handsome and is far from lucid. Just what is the—ever-attractive—perplexity?

Limit cases can be exemplary. An angel is a limit case, at the upper limit of the human world and the lower limit of the spiritual realm. Here is a poignant angelic experience:

A "kind of angel" sits on the rim of a well and, as he looks down to meet his face in the mirror of the water's surface, finds that he is a man. What happens next is a familiar human experience: The face that confronts us is one largely effaced from our daily life, for we never see it directly, and it is an ever-new surprise to us. "Why is *this* the mask I was given, this alien, contingent inadequacy?" But we humans can live with it since we own it to some degree. Even if we can't control its underlying structure (except, nowadays, by risky cosmetic intervention), its grooming and, what is more, its mobile expressiveness is somewhat up to us. Not so for the angel; for him the first mirrored sight of himself is devastating:

> The infidelity of his features confounded his perfect intelligence; they had assumed an air of the particular and accidental, and this expression had become so unequal to the universality of his limpid knowing that he was mysteriously wounded in his unity . . .
> And from eternity he never ceased to know and fail to understand.[8]

Here is an intellectual being facing the scars of passion, that "commotion strange,"[9] yet unable not only to grasp its peculiar particularity, but even just to admit into his pure intellectual consciousness its fact, marked in his visibly embodied face. Something analogous happens to humans from the opposite end: By the very endeavor of thinking about the passions, they may put to flight the feeling that is their element. For strangely, it seems easier—hard though it is—to temper passion by reason than to *grasp* it. Furthermore, whereas memory is easier to summon than to suppress at will (recall the man who was promised a fortune if he would but abstain for a day from thinking of a white elephant), the memory of a feeling is particularly barred from recall during ratiocination, much as dreams are prevented by longing.

That's not yet, however, the deepest version of our quandary, the inescapable human complement of the angel's trouble. We must wonder, "Is thought in principle incapable of wrapping itself about feeling without dispersing or deforming it?" Can we be naturalists of our emotions, having and observing them at once, as researchers focus on their objects? Or is it an impossible intellectual longing in us to comprehend our affectivity? Will a delicate surreptitiousness do it? Can we creep up on our feeling selves and take them unawares? Perhaps sometimes. Sometimes, between *our* noting and *its* muting, the nature of feeling finds utterance—in musing speech, sapient poetry, subtle prose. But rarely in studies.

Question Two.   Here is the currently much-maligned question that thus tends to get unsatisfyingly short or shallow shrift in emotion studies: "*What is human affect?*" There is much against even asking, but ever since Eve ate of the fruit of the Tree of Knowledge it is impossible not to wonder—eventually about its good and evil—but first about the whatness, the essence, of *human* affect.

(I omit animal emotion because there is no reliable access to it either from sympathetic analogies or empathetic introspection—thus the "feel" of the feeling is unavailable. Animal ecologists are generally committed to the occurrence of emotion especially in primates, though they can infer it only by intuitions about behavior.[10] "Animal emotions" opens a can of vermicular problems, for if animals turn out to have human-type feelings, they are, specific differences notwithstanding, our soul mates and entitled not to be used. But sufficient for this book are the problems thereof.)

The difficulty lies in the fact that to ask what something *is*, not what it is in a classifying scheme or how it operates or what it is for, but what it is *in itself*, to ask about its whatness or beingness or essence, it is necessary to have in thought a dim but steady intimation of one satisfactory and approachable answer; the "What is . . . ?" question is the prime example of a "final" question. But as researchers try to apply precise logical analysis to multifarious empirical findings, foundational notions become more and more fugitive. Thus in evolutionary biology the idea of species, in social biology the idea of human nature, and in emotion studies the idea of emotion itself is progressively dissolved.[11]

This last dispersion, most relevant here, is performed by Paul Griffiths, who argues that the general concept of emotion is to be eliminated from psychology because he can find no general psychological process, no common mechanism, in his review of a number of chief theories, theories mentioned also in this book: propositional attitudes, feeling theory, affect programs, psychoevolution (a science about which it is unclear whether it is just beginning or has come to its end),[12] social construction, natural kinds, and folk psychology. Griffiths' own hypothesis, which does meet his criterion of providing a common psychological mechanism for all emotions, says that emotions are really "a putative psychological category of motivational states that exhibit passivity." This formulation is not so far from "Eros whacked me," but Griffiths ends this way:

The research surveyed in this book suggests that the general concept of emotion has no role in future psychology.... This does not necessarily imply that the emotion concept will disappear from everyday thought. Vernacular concepts are involved in a whole range of non-epistemic projects. Concepts like "spirituality" have no role in psychology but play an important role in other human activities. But as far as understanding ourselves is concerned the concept of emotion, like that of spirituality, can only be a hindrance.[13]

I will, then, think and speak in the vernacular, since that seems to be the language of human significance. Yet perhaps even these stern requirements of science are less forbidding than the thing itself. There is plenty in the grand philosophical tradition to suggest the daunting difficulty of getting inside affect. Kant says of "the various feelings of the human soul, the feeling of the *sublime*, the *beautiful*, the *disgusting*, etc., without the exact knowledge and analysis of which we are insufficiently familiar with the main spring of our nature," that "as a careful observer will nonetheless notice, their dissection is far from accessible."[14]

More penetratingly, Hegel, a deep reader of the soul, says of sensibility, that is, primitive affectivity, that it is the spirit in its

> unconscious and unintelligent individuality.... What we merely have in the head is in consciousness in a general way, ... so that, as it is put in me (my abstract ego), it can also be kept away and apart from me (from my concrete subjectivity). But if put in the feeling, the fact is a mode of my individuality, however crude that individuality be in such a form: it is thus treated as my *very own*. My own is something inseparate from the actual concrete self: and this immediate unity of the soul with its underlying self in all its definite content is just this inseparability; which, however, yet falls short of the ego of developed consciousness, and still more of the freedom of rational-mind-life.[15]

Hegel is formulating the sense of the *particular* "ownness" that pertains to feeling in its hidden subjectivity far more than to shareable thinking in its patent objectivity—though the latter be a free act of *my* ego, even though I think "for myself."

Here I feel compelled to insert a reflection on word use. Should the word for affective subjectivity be "particular" or "individual"? I have used "particular" because in ordinary and traditional language it carries the sense of apartness by reason of detailed uniqueness. Thus in monastic communities "particular friendships" are proscribed for their individually focused separateness.[16]

The logical term for the ultimate element, however, is not "particular," which means *some* members of a class, but "individual," which means a *single* member in its ultimate non-generality. It is in virtue of individuality "that each one is a unique member of a class . . . [U]niversality and particularity are thinkable . . . only in conjunction with individuality."[17] But *omne individuum ineffabile,* "every individual is inarticulable," goes the dictum of logic. What makes the logical individual ineffable, un-speakable, is that all speech is general. What makes affectivity ultimately inexpressible is its terminal subjectivity.

Are these two mutenesses related? Certainly not every animate individual has an affective subjectivity; every slug is physically distinct, but *pace* Schiller, who says in the "Ode to Joy" that *Wollust ward dem Wurm gegeben* ("[Even] the worm was given voluptuousness"), I doubt that a worm has sentience, subjectivity, affective awareness, a sense of inwardness qualifiable by arousal. On the other hand, any being endowed with that ultimate subjectivity is, *ipso facto,* an individual. This individuality is not that qualitatively empty difference in external space that can distinguish items otherwise indiscernibly identical. It is rather an inwardness that, even if it were—a practically unthinkable but logically possible thought—identically the same in another soul, would nevertheless not be held in common and is, as the terminal "ownness" of a being, incommunicable—not only mine, but me, as in "it's me." That all but unthinkable thought induces a significant counter-reflection: Ultimately, human individuality is not as safely characterized by *uniqueness* as by self-enveloped "ownness," ego-less *inwardness*; it is ego-less because though mine, it is not the effect of a cognitively active I, as is thinking. At bottom, down there, it's not a self-consciously reflective ego but an awarely affected self, not a discerning agent but an arousable arena, not a construing function but a receptive field—in sum, not an *I* but a *me.*[18] It follows, incidentally, that "I feel your pain" is in principle false, and so (an example taken from Adam Smith) other people's love-sickness tends to vibrate our funny-bone rather than our heartstrings—actually a saving grace, socially speaking.

Yet perhaps it is not so much empathy into the *quality* of our affective states that is impossible as into their *factuality*: What we really cannot share is the indefeasibly stubborn fact of the passion we are suffering through "each world-without-end hour." For another's empathy is as a brief sally into a soul under siege. Thus the impossibility of effectively real empathy is only a consequence, not an explanation, of the residual privacy of our affective condition. Hence our condition may, as I intimated, not be unique— how would we know?—but it feels that way. Our veritable individuality seems to be purest subjectivity understood as self-aware inwardness, qualified as affectivity by different modes of arousal. So affectivity is inwardness variously aroused.

I must stop here, once more, over the crucial words "inward" and "inner," which I am using as if they were quite well understood. And so they are by people in general, though the professionals of thinking quite fairly require skewering of, rather than handwaving over, central terms. So I must try. It seems to me that to make one's way into this meaning one must borrow the *via negativa* of theology, the way of capturing what a thing is by saying what it is not.

Human inwardness, then, as I mean it, is not *essence,* for the human essence is just what is articulable. It is the conceptual expansion of the term "sapient hominid," the ideating animal; it says what we are meant to be. But what we are inwardly is precisely not "utterable," not to be outed, not capable of being turned out into public space without skewing and without remainder. Nor is it an *inside* defined by its enveloping outside, as a cavern is enclosed in the rock. For when we figuratively put the soul in the body we don't mean that like is contained by like, as a kernel by its shell, both extended beings. Nor is it, as was said, an *I* or *ego,* such as supports our conscious cognition—the "subject" of the great Continental systems. For my inwardness is my unique, unsharable own, while the cognitive *I* signifies personhood in general; all cognitive egos are, in principle, the same.

Nor, by its very name, is inwardness *evident,* externally very visible, though human beings manage to make plenty of inferences about its affective state, sometimes fatally false—but sometimes wonderfully accurate (and thus friendship comes about). So we speculate about others, but about ourselves we can, by trying, *know,* if not everything at least more than can others. Our way in is by introspection, for not only does our sentient body vibrate for us with its arousals, but, as I have tried to work out, this inwardness, this ineffable, unextended, non-cognitive, invisible, affective internality is given shape, place, and quasi-visibility for us in the imagination. Of course, it is an unabashed circularity to say that we find out about our inwardness—*what* it is and *whether* it exists—by looking within. That circle is, however, almost a model of true question-asking: Our inquiry is drawn on by an answer we can name long before we comprehend it.

In dwelling on the ultimate subjectivity of feeling, I am not, of course, saying that relief is not to be found in interpretative self-expression and that comfort does not come from sensitive sympathy. But though the roiled soul can be soothed—still *omne individuum ineffabile est* partly because it is *impenetrabile.* Its impassioned behavior can be observed, its emotional speech analyzed, its affects listed and outlined. But though the affected soul itself has indeed been touched, it probably cannot be *told*—either told to, or told by, an other.

Perhaps such sayable whatness as affectivity can lay claim to includes this essential concealment, a concealment purposeful and imposed, both. I have spoken of affectivity as a "qualification" of inwardness; I meant, here using unavoidably figurative language, the tensed tuning and quickening coloration up to the tempestuous roiling, "commotion strange," of the inner life. Perhaps—probably—just because our inwardness is so deep within and yet so exposed to external touch, it is by a forfending choice private, as it is by a contrary pressure expressive and, again by a logical necessity, ineffable.

Back to Hegel, who will articulate some of this sense. But first he observes of the somewhat higher intentional feelings, like grief, anger, and shame, that they "corporealize," embody, themselves. Shame, closely akin to anger, is a pertinent example, because its expression is in defense of my inner, my own self:

> In shame one begins to be a little angry with oneself; for shame contains a reaction to the contradiction between what I appear to be and what I ought to and want to be, and is therefore a defense of my inner self against my incongruous appearance. This outward expression of the spirit is embodied in the blood that is sent to the face.[19]

In explaining the blush of shame as the soul's taking possession of the body to express the incongruity of the person's public appearance and the soul's sense of itself, Hegel broaches a large topic neglected in this book: the *expression* of emotion. It seems to me that the most common incongruity between outer seeming and inner being stems from emotive expression itself. The sufficient articulation of thoughts is much more tractable than the adequate expression of feeling, for it requires two plain, learnable efforts—clarifying one's mind and acquiring the requisite vocabulary. But the expression of feeling is beset with opposing difficulties. If your expression is too uncontrolled, too incoherently spontaneous, like that of children, the observer can't figure out what's actually the matter. If it is too jigged, follows the typed gestures of your tribe too closely, the observer will infer that the feeling expressed is derivative, schematically ungenuine. Adequate self-expression, a balance between relaxing the reserve that protects the exclusivity of the inner sanctum and maintaining the control that effects the communication of nuanced feeling, requires a well-honed sensibility and a trained physicality. It is, no doubt, one of those byproducts of natural adequacy and sufficient schooling that may not be teachable but is, nonetheless, learned. The same holds for the listening that should complement such utterance. It, too, requires an art of translation, such as Adam Smith calls "sympathy." It means letting the confiding speaker's words become images and envisioning the situation until at least a shade of the feeling itself drifts up—much as in reading a novel.

Most interesting here is the very fact of affective expressiveness. Thoughts are communicated; feelings are expressed. Why are the latter capable—and in need—of being "ex-pressed," that is, squeezed out? Clearly, as I intimated, because they are so inward to begin with. Whereas thoughts are directly told in words that naturally intend and utter common and universal notions, feelings are indirectly shown by physical expressions and largely metaphorical language that tries to display what is private and ultimately unutterable. Conversely, people who fancy, or in fact discern, expression in animals also think they have a soul, some inwardness.[20]

Hegel next describes the great contributing source for the "feeling soul," deep memory. Even the consciously affected soul draws on an unconscious store. Hegel anticipates Freud here. His account of our hidden memory is vivid:

> Every individual is an infinite treasury of sensations, ideas, acquired lore, thoughts, etc.; and yet the ego is one and uncompounded, a deep, featureless, characterless mine, in which all this is stored up, without existing.[21]

That is, memory, until called up, is purely potential. Thus feeling is, once more, *ipso facto*, by reason of its terminal subjectivity and its unconscious material, though physically expressible, not easily reachable in itself. Its form is sheer inwardness, its matter is largely below overt existence, its mode seclusion, privacy.

I think from these classical grapplings a few elements come clear and can now be summed up. First, there isn't much to be said about the essence of passion without calling on the notion of a soul, meaning an entity both unconscious (note well: not non-conscious) and conscious, unaware and aware. It stores up experiences whose matter comes to it through the bodily senses and some of which, decocted as feeling, in turn instigate reactions in the body. *At bottom* (to redeploy a dead metaphor) we, as individuals, *are* this mine whose treasures lie largely in the dark and whose workings are very imperfectly directed from the top.

Next, the difficulty of speaking about feeling as feeling lies in this very arcane "ownness," this peculiar, deep subjectivity. Thus passion can "speak" *to* passion, others' or one's own, arouse or dampen it, more directly than reason, others' or one's own, can speak *about* it—for all its essentially greater communicativeness. Our passion-words systematically miss what passion *is*, which is indeed ineffable by reason of ultimate particularity.

Third, the object-related passions, and to some degree even the subject-related moods, indeed have objects. These give passions "objectivity" in two ways: The object determines diffuse affectivity not only in a formal, that is, generic way but also very specifically; each passion is detailed by its peculiar object. But the object also serves in a second way. It opens the passion to the understanding and judgment of bystanders; others can gauge the event—through its object. Thus objects rescue feeling from being quite obscurely "unintelligently individual." Hence, too, there can be *shared* passion. The object may be the same, as when fellow-citizens love the same country (it might even be a territory of the imagination), or the object may be different though the passion is similar, as when adverse patriots each love their own land. And then there is the miraculous case of *mutual* passion, when the object of two impassioned beings is each other—miraculous because the antic spontaneity of erotic love makes reciprocity, the confining of passion within the circle of two, so numerically improbable. Thus the rebuff to the loser in unreciprocated love is not just from the stark failure to attain the object, the other, but from the sense of that other's willful self-withholding; this other, the non-lover, in turn, feels simply unable—which in love is ever interpreted as "unwilling"—to rise to the occasion. "Eros . . . a bittersweet, intractable creeping thing," says the loser, preferring to displace the blame.

This is the moment to consider an evident difference between antique and modern affectivity. It is the latter, closer to my own, that I have been delineating. Yet I cannot bring myself to think that sapient humans have felt their feelings differently throughout their time in this world. They may, however, have attended more to different aspects of passion. Thus, it seems the ancients focused more on the object than the inwardness—until the Stoics changed everything.

Finally, affects, be they brute feels, diffuse feelings, objectless moods, or intentional passions, are arousals of soul and body, each by the other. As such, be they brief volcanic eruptions or long-breathed, banked excitations, we want them. Much may be said against them as deflecting us from our rational purposes or as disturbing the calm, serene tenor of a well-regulated life (the state of undistubedness praised by both Stoics and Epicureans). Yet most of us, for most of our lives, long more for the arousal of soul and body then we long for peace. We want to feel our feelings, and the *why* of that is ultimate, as Spinoza devised a theology to show. As for the *what* of it, I think I've talked a lot around the point—but that, after all, *is* my point.

Question Three.   Our thinking courses through our feelings, as our feeling floods our thought. *How* are *thought and feeling related?*

That they are distinct elements of our nature seems beyond doubt. The first deeply introspective character of the West, Odysseus, talks to himself, as head to heart: "Bear up then, my heart, you have been dogged by worse." And the latest science of the emotions, neuroscience, had its inception with the case of a brain lesion that left its victim intact rationally but impaired emotionally.[22] On the hypothesis of their discernible difference, I'll try my hand at a collection of their comparative commonalities and distinctions; I think of these items as phenomena of experience, both introspective and observational. Such a comparison of thought and feeling makes sense because, though feeling seems to have no proper procedural logic, it does have some fixed structures comparable to that of thought.

1. Feeling is—as if it were a malleable material—focused and qualified into passion or emotion by its form-bestowing intentional object, by which (this is one way to say it) the inner "ownness" of our subjective affectivity

becomes object-directed without becoming positively objective. Put more simply, we select the object of our feeling as particularly and peculiarly *for us*, as being uniquely compatible with our affectivity, but we also elect it because it is *other* than we and impinges on us, imposes its own character on us. Or again, in passion our most peculiarly private affectivity asserts itself by being captivated by otherness.

"Objective" thinking is similarly intentional—captured by an object, though not by its peculiar responsiveness to our own partiality. Rather the object occupies us in its public common nature, and the processes by which we get hold of the object are meant to be patent and articulable—logical.

And yet—affective intentionality and ratiocinative intentionality, already alike in their aboutness, can also borrow each other's mode. People think about objects that *affect* them as rationally attractive and develop feelings for objects they *think* well of.

2. Though there is a dull urgency of imageless feels and a high formalism of imageless thought, most feeling and thinking is accompanied by imagery, for feeling is expressed in imaginative figures and thinking becomes patent in spatial representations. Which precedes and which follows depends on the particular circumstance.

3. Both affects and reason have a kind of tropism, but there the similarity ends. The former *inclines toward or is averse from* its object or even its own condition, the latter is inherently *affirmative or negative*: "Reason . . . may be justly considered as the principle of approbation or disapprobation."[23] But the two modes of turning to or from are quite different. One's feeling is usually about an object and tends to be immediately and directly favorable or unfavorable, and consequently also variable. Though the poet says stalwartly, "Love is not love / Which alters when it alteration finds,"[24] that is not a general truth; passions often alter upon altered circumstances just because they *are* passions.

One's reasoning, on the other hand, is about a proposition and tends to be, or could be, worked out as a reproducible stepwise chain, ending in the logically derived affirmative or negative stable conclusion. I should qualify this differentiation for that highest of capabilities, intellectual intuition, direct insight into intelligible objects (as distinct from thinking in propositions). This intuitive intellect must be thought of as a passive receptivity and so—wonder of wonders—as closer to passionate affectivity than to discursive reason.[25]

4. Feeling, in its very irruptive contingency, is often experienced as having irresistible force; yet reason, in its linear necessity, carries a more inescapable compulsion: We do right to subdue our most whole-hearted feelings

on occasion, but when is it right to subvert our clear-headed logic? Passion as bitter bondage justifies rebellion, but sweet reason, no matter how unwelcome, requires our submission.

5. Feeling, we all know, may precede its object and go, fatally, in search of it. "As often happens with passionate people, he was mastered by anger but was still seeking an object on which to vent it."[26]

Something similar can happen in thinking, but more soundly. It is the very case of question-asking where the object sought is yet indeterminate, but the reason is receptively ready for it and only it. (There is, to be sure, a degenerate case of thinking: rationalization, when the belief or decision precedes the reasoned judgment. "No, no!" said the Queen. "Sentence first—verdict afterwards.")[27]

6. And once again the object: Mood has been delineated as objectless emotion. As such it has, as it were, two inordinate aspects—diffuse, sickly, vaporing, and indeterminate romantic longing, on the one hand, and the attunement of human existence to Nothing—an odd kind of Something—on the other. But while feeling that is not about something may be vapid, it is still feeling, perhaps even nauseatingly overwhelming affect.

Thinking too has a dual possibility. There is one down-to-earth argument that thinking about nothing is not even thinking, but also another, less literal acknowledgment that thinking about Nothing or Nonbeing is thinking of the highest sort.[28] Clearly human beings face nothingness in *both* of their aspects, their affectivity and their rationality; perhaps it is a mark of our basic solidarity with ourselves.

7. Finally the will. People know very well that, at least for the most part, feeling can't be willed, that is, chosen, but comes and fails spontaneously. Thinking, on the other hand, *can* be willed; it is called paying attention, and it is up to us. Attentive focusing on a desired object, wanted as knowable, is the will's great contribution—though it is also the only business the will can have with reason, whose necessities cannot be commandeered; moreover, once we are fully at work, choice is *de trop*, interest takes over; it obviates willing.

Yet the two capacities, affectivity and volition, have analogies, especially in their highest employment. Here is the message of a church bulletin I saw in Washington State: "Love is a choice not a feeling." That is good theology; the commandment of commandments says, "Thou *shalt* love the Lord thy God with all thy heart . . . ,"[29] and obedience to imperatives is a choice of the free will. As there is a love that can be moved by will, so there is thought that can be drawn by love; in these two ways are fairly summed up the theology and philosophy respectively of the pre-modern West.

How do feeling and thought come mutually to inform each other? The answer in terms of the subserving brain structures is that those involved in emotions and those involved in reasoning "project" to each other—emotion-circuits more to reason than the reverse.[30]

A suggestion framed in terms of introspective experience is that the venue of their interaction is the imagination, that intra-psychic arena in which desire rendezvouses with its object and thinking meets its matter. The ever-interesting question, "Which arouses which—desire imagination or the reverse?" seems to be undecidable. It depends, like the succession of feeling and thinking, on circumstance. "[I]mages are the brood of desire," but also "No animal is capable of appetite without imagination."[31]

Question Four. This next question I would not have asked on my own; it is obligatory because its implied thesis sums up a very old and a very new emotion-theory: *Are emotions judgments?*

I am not persuaded that emotions are such appraisals, understood as immediately trustworthy judgments of worth. I go with Shakespeare:

That I love her, I *feel.* That she is worthy, I *know.*[32]

The motives for assimilating our two root capacities are to restore to its healthy primacy the affective life, supposedly suppressed in the Greek tradition. Oddly enough the inventors of the notion that passions are judgments, the Stoics, had the opposite motive, since they considered them *erroneous* appraisals.

First, I see a small problem, arising right within the theory that emotions are appraising judgments, that nonetheless all but scuttles it: In cognitivist emotion accounts, there is *always* an opening, if only a hairline crack, between the apprehension of the situation and the responsive judgment, corresponding to the Stoic "pre-passion." A momentary first surge of emotion is, after all, acknowledged, and it is the reason why the cognitivist vocabulary uses emotion words. They are needed for this brief (or prolonged) moment; the theory doesn't seem to cover the complete process.

Second, it seems to me that the inclinations of feeling and the affirmations of reason, though they may indeed belong to the same genus (for they are both pro- and con- attitudes) are nonetheless very different in species (as set out in 3. under the previous question).

In sum: The feeling heart has no reasons, or only *ex post facto* rationalizations; the thinking head is supposed to put the reasons before the affirmation or denial. More: Passions are multifarious, reason is unitary; passions dither, reason considers; passions balance intensities, reason weighs possibilities; passions arouse, reason posits; passions possess us, reason is our tool, etc., etc.

Finally, our emotivity and our judgment are fairly often at odds, too often for even limited identification. Pascal speaks vividly of the ever-lasting ever-losing internal war within those who want to renounce the passions and become as gods, and similarly within those who want to renounce reason and become brute beasts.[33] To me it is clear that the effortful ability to bring our two psychic capacities into harmony is a major grace bestowed by Nature for keeping us on edge and all there—and if we deny the difference, we can't help her.

Question Five.   Socrates says that *his* question is "whether he happens to be some sort of beast even more complex in form and more tumultuous than the hundred-headed Typhon, or something simpler and gentler."[34] Who would have thought that Socrates' search for his true nature could become a research project: Is our inwardness ultimately "a completely unstructured mess" or a theorizable "information processing architecture" with discernible modules and chartable functions? This old question is the as yet inchoate problem, so far variously and inconclusively solved.[35]

No Socratic inquiry resonates for me as does this invitation to "know myself," to engage in that (not particularly personal) introspection which is the proper response to his question; it maintains its interest longer than a more subjective self-knowledge: Quirks fascinate, but they don't interest. My version of his question, which avoids the implied commitment to reason that is the mark of all the great ancients, is, *Are we fundamentally affective or rational beings?* The two most forthrightly opposing answers come from Aristotle and Spinoza. The former says, "The thoughtful part of oneself is what each of us seems to be."[36] The latter says: "Desire is the very essence of man. . . ."[37] Each says it in his framework, to be sure, and what I learn from the isolated statements is not, of course, which view is true, but that this is indeed a question by which to be preoccupied.

That we are embodied beings, that is, animals, is the first, the specifying, human fact; we are *homo sapiens,* the "sage" and speaking animal and—perhaps—by reason of that, the only surviving species of the genus *homo.* The second, taxonomic, fact is that evolutionary biologists regard those brain structures of *homo sapiens* that mediate emotions as more primitive, that is, as belonging to an older phase of hominid development. Very roughly speaking, they lie below those structures devoted to cognition—as if to underwrite the sense that affects come from deep within. A third, developmental, fact is that emotion seems to appear in us earlier than speech; infants are capable of distinguishing a limited range of emotions before they recognize speech.[38] These three biological facts underwrite my sense that it is precisely in what is traditionally called the soul that we are basically affective—for recall that the soul is traditionally that aspect of human consciousness that is experienced as body-involved. I think Spinoza is right:

As human animals, we want, at least when we are sound, to exist, the more expansively and comprehensively, the more joyfully. So far we are first of all affective. But why should we be finally, at our highest, what we are basically, at bottom? Why shouldn't Aristotle be right as well? Why shouldn't our hominid end be to live out our specific human difference, sapience?—especially since Spinoza's desire turns out to be for knowledge, and Aristotle's thought is, finally, a desire. Our joy is in living out to the fullest *particular* just the *kind* of animal we are.

Question Six.   But perhaps the passions in fact help to realize this human high point. *Are the passions revelatory?* Do we learn truths from them? Well, of course, they reveal us to ourselves. They give us experience of what it "is like" to be an affective soul. They tell us to what extent we are prone to passions and passive before them, and to what extent they are, as the Stoics say, "up to us." They reveal to us our individual differences, our own congenital passion-inventory, and our habitual affect-gamut; they really do reveal us to ourselves as we gape in awe and disgust, resignation and pride, at the antics on this internal stage. And they tell us about others, what likely or unlikely objects can rouse our fellow humans' emotions and in what ways. I saw a car sticker in my neighboring Navy Yard: "A man and his truck/It's a beautiful thing"—so that too can happen; live and learn.

But probably even more immediately they open us to the world by giving us a powerful interest in it. Perhaps the most precise learning experience is to be had from those passions that are most focusedly and acutely object-directed—principally love, which is essentially "magical awareness,"[39] the fanatical keeping in sight of, the inexhaustible interest in, the most acute being-for an object, human or non-human. An affair of love, whatever else it is, is a learning episode: one other being, type and token in one, as closely approached, as well explored, as is possible to us.

I began this book with the first poets of passion, who faced it with candidly abject panache. But there is a genre I might have put first, did I understand it better. Its very watchword is *pathei mathos,* "learning by suffering"[40]—tragedy. Greek tragedy is one long study of passion—contumacious passion pitted against an unaccountable cosmos—which leaves the appalled onlooker with a very dark knowledge, with tragic wisdom about deluded men and inscrutable divinity.

So the passions supply all sorts of deep though iffy sapience, of old as now. But in modern times it is rather the moods to which world-revealing functions have been assigned. These attributions of metaphysical disclosures to anxiety in particular seem to me hyperbolic. Yet our moods do show something about the world: what tints it can absorb, so to speak, from our affective perspectives—from untuned gray-on-gray to the high-toned glow of gold. Thus, mood poses a problem to reflection: What is it in the world as a whole that responds to human affectivity when the protective cocoon of daily business breaks open and leaves us vulnerably diffused? At the most, some trust in the disclosive powers of moods gives us the courage of our depressions and the confidence of our elations.

There is a currently popular belief that runs across all these meditations—that our emotional responses are culturally jigged, that they are prescriptive scenarios rather than natural responses. Of course our expression of feeling is shaped by our "culture"[41] (or its lack)—our language, our upbringing, our social relations, our literary education, you name it. That is so obvious that it is almost embarrassing to say it once again. Yet who can show for any time or place, back to those Neolithic master-painters in the Dordogne, that there is not in it at least one human being capable of feeling what you or I feel now? One such soul mate would suffice, for human capability is not defined by nose-counting; moreover, who is to say that the outliers aren't our proper paradigms? To give the earliest out-of-his-time example of the pagan West: Alongside the scores of heroic aristocrats encamped before Troy, Homer introduces one—one single—man, Thersites, who is everything they aren't: shamelessly unbeautiful, aggressively egalitarian, unabashedly whiny, a man of Nietzschean *democratic ressentiment*, not very lovable but recognizably ours.[42] No, I not only think that the passions, if they are revelatory of our species-fellows at all, must be so across times and places, but also that they are in their very essence our *own*, that, style aside, they are *ex*pressed from the inside, not *im*pressed from the outside.

So we learn from the passions about ourselves and the rest of the human world, precisely because they are at once species-wide types and individual-centered singularities. Strangely enough, they also help us to understand the physical world. For some of the early, the so-called Presocratic, physicists human passions served to recognize physical principles. Thus Empedocles says of the physical whole:

> And these things never stopped changing through and through,
> Sometimes by love (*philoteti*) coming together, all of it,
> Sometimes again borne each apart by the hate or strife.[43]

Later the Aristotelian unmoved mover will, himself dispassionate, set the cosmos in motion through attracting its love,[44] and it is imaginable that some terms of early modern physics—endeavor, impetus, attraction—had a passional resonance.

As moderns, however, our metaphoric way is the reverse. We describe our somatic affections in literal bodily language and our psychic affects in figurative physical phrases: "on fire, left cold, uplifted, cast down, transfixed, blown away." Such somatic metaphors, the ones that mirror "the body in the mind,"[45] teach us to discern through figures the postures and motions of the soul, the psychic stases and changes of emotion.

Nonetheless, I speculate that the other, the more venerable, way is worth an imaginative recovery; it is, after all, still the way of "primitive" people and other imaginative folk. Thus what the Presocratic philosopher thought as an adept is possibly no more than what the lay person had always known: that before the body served the mind as its figure the soul had pervaded nature as its explanatory principle. Hence what is now our normal metaphorical direction was then indeed the reverse. The emotions of the soul were perhaps originally not the "tenor," the literal subject of the metaphor, but rather the "vehicle," the term with the figurative force. Thus not, "The anger I feel is [like] a black fume in my soul," but rather, "That black fume rising to the sky is my wrath itself." But then, who knows whether such primal ways of seeing are, as they would be for us, just figurative? To be sure, among us this vision of the world is sometimes exploited sentimentally; then it becomes the "Pathetic Fallacy," the false ascription of feeling to nature, bad-faith poetizing. That's not what I'm looking for, but an occasional reprise of that fresh "empathy, an awareness of the feelings that something not sentient might be supposed to have"[46]—the un-Romantic sudden sense that the outer world might have its own inwardness, that things might have souls.

Question Seven. I'm about to end, but I can't do it without raising a question scarcely touched in this book, yet close to my heart: What distinguishes aesthetic feeling, the affectivity that is generally assigned to sensibility, that is, to a sensory receptivity bestowed by nature and refined by training? The term "aesthetics," that is, the science of sense-perception, was appropriated in the eighteenth century by Baumgarten for a branch of philosophy—the only one concerned with feeling specifically—dealing "with sensory experience coupled with feeling as distinct from the abstractions of logic."[47] I have omitted its consideration because it opens a large, specialized, and contentious area of inquiry involving the Arts. For the modern recognition of a specifically aesthetic response was an effect of the conversion of artifacts to be admired, made by artisans to be respected for their craftsmanship, into works of Art to be worshiped, created by Artists to be reverenced for their genius—and that is a forbidding arena.

Add to that "specialness" of the Arts another, quite incongruous, effect of more recent modernity: their accessibility. Two centuries after Baumgarten's book, Walter Benjamin published an essay entitled "The Work of Art in the Age of its Technical Reproducibility,"[48] in which he showed that, under conditions of easy reproduction, works of art (he was speaking of the visual arts) not only lose their original uniqueness but are ripped from their usually religious context to become "exhibitable" (*ausstellbar*), accessible to mere gaping mass-enjoyment.

Literary works had, of course, become technically reproducible with the introduction of printing in the mid-fifteenth century, and that great modern literary genre devoted particularly to the leisurely exploration of emotion, the "novel," that factual fiction presented as "news," was specifically geared to the opportunity of rapid propagation by print.[49] But even Benjamin could not have imagined what has now happened to music, that all the works ever recorded would become immediately available to be heard by anyone, anytime, anywhere. So what used to be, even within my lifetime, a rare experience, difficult to bring about and expensive to obtain, has become simply—and sometimes unavoidably—the circumambient air. And while even in our image-inspissated environment one must at least cast an eye on one of them actually to see it, and while even for the most rapidly read, gulped-down fiction one must at least keep one's eye on the page to get it, music can come to us in perfectly effortless passivity. For that is our sensory constitution; hearing is the naturally omnidirectional, naturally unoccludable sense.

No doubt this degrades our aesthetic sensibility, subjects us to unwanted, inescapable intrusions, and allows us to be diffusely and ignorantly inattentive, while the object, the music itself, is used as a mere mood-conditioner, becoming a need more than a recreation, a habituated relief from the taedium vitae normal to the alternation of working routine and scheduled leisure of our 24/7 existence. It happens to be a relief much more easily available and less demanding than human sociability. In fact, it appears that some people in our time spend much more of their life hearing music than conversing; digital music players can act as "conversation avoidance devices."[50] Such is the purists' severe if just indictment.

And yet—what more innocent, harmless way is there of moving the soul out of its ordinary slough of despond or even just its diurnal dullness? For that music moves the soul out of its crouch, erects and mobilizes it—in short, that it is "e-motional," is what even (or better, especially) the most aesthetically uncultivated listener senses. Who can doubt that "music be the food of love,"[51] and of all affective life?

I think I—we—should try to be less annoyed by the ubiquity of mediocre music and more knowledgeably aroused by the mystery of great composition. Very inadequately articulated, it seems to be the fact that there could be a temporal, sensory, and thus qualitative mathematics that develops by strict rules and inspired breaches, and that addresses the soul in so precise a rhetoric that it is only very approximately communicable in words—much like feeling.[52] A mystery of visual art or visualizable fiction, addressed above, was how the non-existent beings and places figured in the quasi-space of the imagination could touch us so strongly. Music, on the other hand, though it "annuls . . . spatiality in general," in the sense of eventuating in that one of the four dimensions in which we live which most arguably originates internally, that of time, nonetheless has its own—figurative—spatiality: Just as a work of architecture is a "frozen music," so a musical composition is a fluid dwelling.[53] So here a question is not only how speechless sound can signify so precisely, but also how so fugitive a structure can contain us so tightly. But above all the question concerning this remarkable—I might almost call it—isomorphism presents itself: They both, music and emotion, engender a sense of very precise and quite inarticulable meaning, so that music seems able to achieve that accurate exposition of our so intricately modified affectivity denied to words—almost as if it were the passion itself, appearing to the outer senses. Then how are we to grasp such a contradiction in terms: unarticulable specificity?

It must be plain why I didn't even try to pose such doubtfully askable, such obstinately dilettantish questions, which nonetheless cannot be approached without a professional's expertise. Still, they never cease to raise themselves, perhaps even most provokingly for the untrained amateur, the hopelessly inadequate lover of music.

Question Eight.   The hidden or not-so-hidden agenda of much writing on the emotions is either their control as demeaning passivities and unwanted commotions or their defense as vital parts of human nature victimized by hypertrophic rationalizing. The more recent polemics against a Western enlightenment supposedly unbalanced by reason are shadow-boxing: The tradition is, as ever, dialectical and goes both ways. My problem is how to frame the question for myself. I want to know, *Are the emotions good?* But should I mean "good for something" or could I mean "good in themselves"?

The current defense is usually mounted from the utilitarian aspect. The emotions are "good *for,*" good for asserting self-hood and raising self-esteem, appraising situations and marking salience.

The main active context of the question is, however, evolutionary: The emotions are good for the species. The generally accepted theory is that the emotions can be inferred to have evolved, as the "primitive" character of the brain structures mediating them attests. Their evolutionary origin implies that they were adaptive species-traits, universal to humans as biological mammals with complex social relations.[54] Of course, both among humans and their primate relatives the passions occasionally turn extremely maladaptive, threatening survival itself.[55] Since it is unclear that traits evolved by natural selection in the past are still adaptive in the present of our species—Darwin seems to have thought the emotions obsolete—and since the very concept of "for-ness" in evolutionary biology is vexed,[56] the question "What are the emotions good for?" is not really mine to ask. As an evolutionary question, it is too technically involved; as a psychological one, too much is to be said on both sides of the goodness question. For besides supporting—or devastating—group life, the emotions can also further the self-esteem, focus, and decisiveness—or the self-degradation, decentering, and confusion—of the individual.

Why not, however, simply ask, "*Are passions and moods a human good in themselves—thus not for mere life but for a good life?*" I believe that, whatever philosophers may think, people know the answer: Certain moments of passion and periods of mood are the high points of life. So the question is gratuitous, and that is what marks it as reflective; it does not require a solution, but desires insight.

I'll begin this way: What does it "feel like" to have no passions? People with certain brain lesions experience damped or depressed emotions, but the involvement of structures mediating thinking with those subserving emotion is such that the precise or complete excision of the latter seems to be in principle impossible; if there is responsive intelligence left, there is evidently also affectivity, albeit impaired.[57] The case of the true monopsychic human, the totally rational man—a *man,* not a machine, who does not feel his feelings, if somewhere he has them—seems not only to be precluded by our brain structure but also to be beyond our empathetic experience. For how can we feel our way to non-feeling? So it is left to the imagination, in this case especially active in science fiction, to represent such a being. All the world, but every Trekkie especially, knows Mr. Spock for being embodied Reason. In fact the three chief officers of the Starship Enterprise are so intensely complementary as to make up "at times, one personality."[58] The other two are Captain Kirk: virtuous spiritedness, and Dr. McCoy: emotional desire. Each of the trio therefore clearly represents one element of Plato's tripartite soul as set out in the *Republic,* though as individuals that leaves them incomplete and subject to irruptive transgressions into their banished part. Thus the Vulcan Spock has in him a volcanic reservoir of passion kept imperfectly under by an inheritance of severely repressive discipline. Nonetheless, his normal mode is the unflappable calm of logic. Yet his calculations don't have the repellently cerebral, ultimately monstrous neutrality which is one pole of the Romantic head:heart distinction. Rather his is a sweet reason that allows for humane moral judgment, and that makes Spock a fair figure for imagining a simply passionless existence unexacerbated by a coldly perverse will. What would it be like to be Mr. Spock? All Trekkies know that he is a lovable man who has, moreover, a certain pathos about him, a melancholy which is not *his* for himself but *ours* for him. And that's just it; our feeling of him cannot be his feeling of himself. He can certainly know himself, analyze his thinking functions, hypothesize an underlying, synthesizing "I" that does the thinking, see himself as a body, and observe others emoting. The affect-driven others do indeed baffle him, though that is no matter—they baffle us too. What then is lacking? What was missing for that angel on the rim of the well?

Here is the best I can do. He will see and think every object in every situation—prescinding from the contributing functions of his thinking—in *its* own nature. His condition will indeed be that of Valéry's angel, who says of his angelic intelligence that it "effortlessly consumes all creation, without anything affecting or altering it in return."[59]

What then is missing in any passionless being, Vulcan or angel, a being who is also endowed with a soundly receptive intellect? We ask, of course, from our perspective, that of human beings. For himself, such a hyper-human might well be capable of the dispassionate satisfaction of contemplative fulfillment. But from our point of view, it is pretty clear that what is missing is *subjective responsiveness*: The world would indeed be there *in itself*—but not *for him*; he would recognize its objects clearly and distinctly but he could acknowledge none as being something *to* him. Nothing would matter to him, have qualitative salience.

We humans, on the other hand, are beings of desire, a dual desire. We want to be ready to *receive* what the world offers in *its* own nature and to be taken over by its being. But we also want to be aware, to be present at the event, to *respond* to objects in *our* own mode.[60] We want to receive the thing as it is in itself *and* to be aroused by it as it is for us. Said yet another way, we want both being and meaning:

> [E]motions involve a double reference, both to the object and the self experiencing the object.[61]

The passions are a human good on the hypothesis that a second desire underlies all feeling. Besides the desire for the object, there is the desire to be fully sentient, to feel.

Moreover, human beings tend not only to welcome passion, because it is a *pleasure* to feel one's feelings, but to take *pride* in their passionateness, for it is testimony to their thereness. And they are proud not only of their positive but even of their negative affectivity, not only of being great in love but of being terrific in hate, not only of being victors in the pursuit but of being grandly afflicted victims of desire.

We take the poets' cry "once again" for mock despair and real exhilaration in being once again aroused in their depth and all there. (I take the need for strong stuff, for violence, for doing hurt or seeing it done, for "false paradises" and exogenous highs, to betoken a shaming deficiency in the capacity for psychic arousal—the flight into excitation in the face of failing excitement.) From little boys to old ladies, from being swung high on a swing to being ardently indignant at a wrong or warmly alight with a work—and of course, from being once again in the throes of love, be it for another human being or for any of the various lovable entities in the world or out of it—we all (no, most of us) want to be aroused in soul and to be fully aware of our condition, to rise, as the word arousal implies, to the occasion—*to feel our feelings.*

Thus our passions are indeed not only passively, supinely receptive but also actively, assertively responsive appropriations of their objects. Similarly our moods betoken not only our vulnerability to the vicissitudes of life and our capability for construing the world from our subjective perspective, but also the world's capacity for taking on the coloration of our feeling.

These proud possessions are spontaneous. Neither, it seems, can professional permission cause our failing feelings to flourish—quite the opposite—nor can our hypertrophic passions be effectively contained by merely rational prohibitions. Passion, its wisest students say, can only be controlled by counter-passion—which may indeed on occasion be the passion of thoughtful reason.[62] Possibly the most potent of these counter-passions is, in fact, pride. Our conscious affectivity is, it seems to me, normally shadowed by pride. When it fails we are not the willing, proudly self-confessed servants of passion sung by the poets—"Being your slave, what should I do . . ."[63]—but terminally passive, overcome, out of our control, not honorably conquered but beaten.

This passion-pride, this desire-exaltation, has three aspects. Of course, love will serve me one last time as the prime instance; the analysis, however, seems to me to hold as well for other intentional passions. First, there is our proud sense of having been chosen, some secular version of having, for better or worse, come to the possessive attention of a divinity, of being luckily blessed or honorably cursed by a receptive sensibility that invited possession. Second, there is our pride in the singular expertise, the excruciatingly specific and avidly private knowing that comes from the exclusive study of one object in its uniqueness, a partly ineffable cognition that subverts the standard marks of knowledge, universality, and commonality. And finally, there is our pride, as mordant as it is suave, at having seized, once again, the chance to know ourselves in our deepest—if not highest—soul.

Notes

By Way of a Preface: *On the Title*

[pages xv–xx]

1. W. B. Yeats, "Among School Children" (1928).
2. Aristotle's term for the dancer's way of being is *entelecheia he prote*, translated in many ways, but for my purposes as "primary persistent completeness," a perfected ability that comes before and stays through and beyond the action (*On the Soul* 412 a 22 ff.).
3. This question comes from Ann Martin, the first reader of this manuscript.
4. Thucydides, *Peloponnesian War* 3.82, on the effect of revolution on language.

chapter I
Passion Itself: *Poetry*

[pages 4–8]

Many of the early lyric poets' fragments are quoted from: *Lyra Graeca*, vols. 1 and 2, ed. J. M. Edmonds, Loeb Classical Library (1952).

1. Nietzsche, *Birth of Tragedy*, para. 9.
2. Ibid., para. 12.
3. Ulrich von Willamowitz-Möllendorff, "Zukunftsphilologie!" (1872), in *Der Streit um Nietzsches "Geburt der Tragödie,"* ed. Karlfried Gründer (Hildesheim: Georg Olms,1969).
4. *Birth of Tragedy*, para. 15.
5. *Republic* 607 b.
6. A millennium later Plotinus is still trying to explain their relation: Every soul or psyche, he confabulates, is an Aphrodite, and that her genesis is connate with Eros signifies that Eros is innate to the soul, *Enneads* 6.9, 9.
7. *Phaedrus* 235 b–c.
8. *Republic* 577 d.
9. *Rhetoric* 1367 a 14; *Lyra Graeca* 1, frag. 119; (see Frontispiece, herein).
10. Hephaistion, second century C.E.
11. *Lyra Graeca* 2, frag. 48; Dietmar Korzeniewski, *Griechische Metrik* (Darmstadt: Wissenschaftliche Buchgesellschaft, 1968), 119.
12. *Lyra Graeca* 1, frag. 81.
13. Anne Carson, *Eros the Bittersweet* (Normal, Ill.: Dalkey Archive, 2003), 8; *Iambi et Elegi Graeci*, ed. M. L. West, vol. 1 (Oxford: Oxford Univ. Press, 1972), 196.
14. *Lyra Graeca* 1, frag. 13, with Plutarch's context.
15. Ibid., 1, frag. 2.
16. Ibid., 1, frag. 1.
17. *Iliad* III 442, XIV 295.
18. *Odyssey* XVIII 212.
19. Hesiod, *Theogeny* 116 ff.
20. Ibid., 188 ff.

21. Parmenides, *On Nature,* frags. 12, 13.
22. Plato, *Parmenides* 127 b.

chapter II
Eros, Spirit, Pleasure: *Plato's Beginning*
[pages 9–67]

[Introduction: page 9]

1. For example, for poetry, Harold Bloom, *The Anxiety of Influence: A Theory of Poetry* (Oxford: Oxford Univ. Press, 1973).

1. Eros as Go-Between and Passion as Soul-Horse [pages 9–23]

1. *Phaedrus* 235 c.
2. *Symposium* 177 e, 198 d.
3. *Apology* 21 d.
4. *Symposium* 212 e.
5. Ibid., 178 d.
6. In the *Clouds,* on the other hand, there is a lot of bodily coarseness in action and praise for ancestral decencies in speech. Here lustiness is complemented not by respect for human nature, but for social tradition.
7. *Symposium* 192 e, 193 d.
8. Ibid., 191 a.
9. Ibid., 177 e.
10. Ibid., 203 e.
11. Aristophanes, *Birds* 1.695; produced in 41 B.C.E., two years after the dramatic date of the *Symposium.*
12. *Symposium* 203 d.
13. *Parmenides* 127 c.
14. *Symposium* 215 c.
15. *Charmides* 156 b.
16. *Symposium* 208 c, *Sophist* 230–31.
17. *Symposium* 204 a.
18. Hegel, *Phenomenology of Spirit,* "Preface," para. 5.
19. *Symposium* 204 c.
20. Ibid., 180 b.
21. Ibid., 205 d.
22. Robert Lloyd Mitchell, *The Hymn to Eros: A Reading of Plato's "Symposium"* (Lanham, Md.: Univ. Press of America, 1993), 44.
23. *Symposium* 206 a.
24. Ibid., 206 b, e.
25. Ibid., 206 c.
26. Ibid., 209 b.
27. Ibid., 208 b.
28. *Phaedo* 64 a.
29. *Symposium* 208 c.
30. *Republic* 510.
31. *Symposium* 216 b.
32. Ibid., 217 d.
33. Stephen Scully, ed. and trans., *Plato's "Phaedrus"* (Newburyport, Mass.: Focus, 2003), 86. In this section I will largely rely on this excellent edition, made by a teacher for and with his students.
34. On the fact that the dialogues are themselves written works see Charles Griswold, *Self-Knowledge in Plato's "Phaedrus"* (New Haven: Yale Univ. Press, 1986), 219–26.
35. *Phaedrus* 230 d.
36. Ibid., 257 b.

37. Ibid., 252 e.
38. *Republic* 473 c.
39. *Phaedrus* 247 c.
40. Dante, *Paradiso* 33.136 ff.
41. Scully, 106.
42. R. Hackforth, trans., *Phaedrus* (New York: Liberal Arts Press, 1952), 6.
43. *Phaedrus* 245 e.
44. Ibid., 246 c.
45. Ibid., 246 a.
46. Ibid., 246 d, 248 c.
47. Ibid., 249 d.
48. Havelock Ellis, *Studies in the Psychology of Sex* (1905) (New York: Random House, 1942), 193.
49. *Phaedrus* 252 c.
50. Ibid., 253 c.
51. Ibid., 253 e.
52. Ibid., 253 d.
53. Ibid., 237 d, 238, 245 c, 251 e.
54. Ibid., 253 d.

2. Spirit as Soul-Center and Desire as Soul-Base: The *Republic*
[pages 23–27]

1. Aristotle, *Politics* 1327 b 41.
2. *Republic* 368 e.
3. Readers notice that love plays a diminished role in the *Republic*. One possible reason is that in that dialogue the ascent to Being is by rational discourse and mathematical analogics, whereas in the *Symposium* and the *Phaedo* it is by impassioned rhetoric and imaginative metaphors.
4. *Republic* 435 e.
5. Ibid., 368 a.
6. Ibid., 435 e.
7. Ibid., 433 b.
8. Ibid., 437 a.
9. Aristotle, *Metaphysics* 1005 b.
10. *Republic* 439 e.
11. Ibid., 439 d.
12. Ibid., 439 e.
13. Ibid., 441 a.
14. Ibid., 440 e.
15. *Odyssey* XX 17.
16. *Republic* 441 b.
17. A careful analysis of *thymos* in the *Republic*, and an acknowledgment that the question of how reason can influence it is unresolved, is given in a lecture by Michael Dink, "The Structure and Guises of *thymos*," delivered at St. John's College, Annapolis, March 1996.
18. For example, Federalist No. 6.
19. *Cratylus* 419 e.
20. *Republic* 375 e.
21. The beginning of this line of thinking was in Carol Gilligan's *In a Different Voice: Psychological Theory and Women's Development* (Cambridge: Harvard Univ. Press, 1982).

3. Desire and Questions as Analogues [pages 27–28]

1. In the *Symposium* there is repeated play on the similarity of the sound of "love" (*eros*; genitive, *erotos*) and "lover" (*eron*) to the sound of "to question" (erotan), "question" (*erotesis*), and "I will say" (*ero*). The puns are especially audible in Diotima's speech making Eros into a philosopher; for one example: "The answer longs for (*pothei*) a further such question (*erotesin*, 204 d)"; here, to be sure, the answer desires the question, as when a half-satisfaction arouses

more longing. For another example, "Come, Socrates, I shall say: 'What is the love—or quest— of the lover of good things?'" (*phere, O Socrates, ero: ho eron ton agathon ti erai,* 204 e).

2. Ibid., 234 c; Scully, 11 n. 27.
3. Gabriel Marcel, "Desire and Hope," in *Readings in Existential Phenomenology,* ed. Nathaniel Lawrence and Daniel O'Connor (Englewood Cliffs, N.J.: Prentice-Hall, 1967), 281.
4. Aristotle, *On the Soul* 433 b 8.

4. The Word "Passion" [pages 28–29]

1. A. Walde and J. B. Hoffman, *Lateinisches Etymologisches Wörterbuch* (Heidelberg: Carl Winter, 1954), "*patior*"; H. Frisk, *Griechisches Etymologisches Wörterbuch* (Heidelberg: Carl Winter, 1960), "*pascho.*"
2. *Odyssey* VIII 490.
3. Aeschylus, *Agamemnon* 1.177.
4. *Philebus* 17 d.
5. Aristotle, *Metaphysics* 986 a 5.
6. Frag. 31, in Hermann Diels, *Fragmente der Vorsokratiker,* vol. 2, 7th ed. by Walter Kranz (Berlin: Weidmann, 1954), 152.
7. *Phaedrus* 256 b.
8. *Philebus* 36 a.
9. E. M. Cope, *An Introduction to Aristotle's "Rhetoric"* (London: Macmillan, 1867), 113–16.
10. Aristotle, *Categories* 1 b 27.
11. Something of the old sense of being the suffering subject is readmitted in a distinction between "internal and external passion," the former being a passion we identify with and accept as our own, the latter being one "that we regard as being in some manner incoherent with our preferred conception of ourselves." (Harry G. Frankfurt, *The Importance of What We Care About* [Cambridge: Cambridge Univ. Press, 2005], 63.) However, even this cold appreciation of passionate passivity is then rationally qualified into "inefficacy" (66).
12. Hegel, *Aesthetik* (1820–26), pt. 1, chap. 3, B II 3b.

5. The Perplexities of Pleasure [pages 30–32]

1. Floyd E. Bloom et al., *Brain, Mind, and Behavior* (New York: W. H. Freeman, 1985), 152–53.
2. Aeschylus, *Prometheus Bound.*
3. *Philebus* 11 b.

6. Socrates on Pleasure: Before the *Philebus* [pages 34–35]

1. *Gorgias* 491 e–501 d.
2. *Republic,* bk. IX, 581 c–588 a.
3. Ibid., 362 c.
4. Ibid., 566 d; 576 c, e; 580 b.

7. Plato on Pleasure: The *Philebus* [pages 36–50]

The page numbers in this section refer to the *Philebus* unless another source is given.

1. *Second Letter* 314 c.
2. 19 c.
3. 52 e.
4. 50 d.
5. 11 b.
6. Cicero, *On Ends* 1.31.
7. 15 c. In 11 c, Philebus had "withdrawn" or "grown tired" (*apeireke*). It has been suggested that this verb puns on "infinite" (*apeiron*), which characterizes pleasure (27 e): Jacob Klein, "About Plato's *Philebus*" (1971), in *Lectures and Essays,* ed. Robert B. Williamson and Elliot Zuckerman (Annapolis, Md.: St. John's College Press, 1985), 327.
8. Aristotle, *Metaphysics* 1028 b 3.
9. 15 d.

10. Aristotle, *Nicomachean Ethics* 1172 b 9 ff.
11. Ibid., 1153 b 5, 1104 b 25.
12. 14 c.
13. 16 b.
14. 16 d.
15. 42 d.
16. Aristotle, *Rhetoric* 1369 b 1.
17. Lucretius, *De Rerum Natura,* ed. Cyril Bailey, vol. 1 (Oxford: Clarendon Press, 1963), 61.
18. 20 d.
19. *Apology* 38 a.
20. 22 c.
21. 23 d.
22. 25 d. Socrates' account of One, Many, and Number—how far they are given and how far generated—is too concise for clarification here.
23. 27 e.
24. 28 c.
25. 30 d.
26. 31 b.
27. 31 e.
28. Wordsworth, "Tintern Abbey" (1798).
29. 33 b.
30. 43 a–b.
31. 34 a.
32. *Meno* 81 d.
33. 35 c (my italics).
34. 36 a.
35. 37 e.
36. 38 a.
37. 38 e.
38. *Republic* 382 b.
39. 41 a.
40. 45 e, 11 d.
41. 42 a.
42. 43 c.
43. 44 b.
44. 44 e.
45. 46 a.
46. 47 a.
47. Nietzsche, *Birth of Tragedy,* passim.
48. For example, Euripides, *Bacchae.*
49. 47 e; Philip Fisher, *The Vehement Passions* (Princeton: Princeton Univ. Press, 2002), passim.
50. 48.
51. 50 d.
52. Kant, *Critique of Judgment,* para. 2.
53. 51 b.
54. Erwin Panofsky, *Galileo as a Critic of the Arts* (The Hague: Martinus Nijhoff, 1954), 24 ff.
55. 52 c.
56. 54 e.
57. 55 c.
58. 58 a.
59. 60 b.
60. 61 c.
61. 64 b.
62. 64 e.
63. Klein, "About Plato's *Philebus,*" 312–13, 343.

8. Aristotle on Pleasure and Happiness:
After the *Philebus* [pages 50–58]

For this section, I often consulted Martin Ostwald's annotated translation of Aristotle's *Nicomachean Ethics* (Upper Saddle River, N.J.: Prentice Hall, Library of Liberal Arts, 1999).

1. *On the Soul* 433 a 26.
2. *Nicomachean Ethics* 1153 a 14.
3. Ibid., 1174 b 33.
4. *Rhetoric* 1369 b 33; *Nicomachean Ethics* 1152 b 34.
5. *Nicomachean Ethics* 1370 a 27.
6. Ibid., 1378 a 20.
7. *On the Soul* 431 a 11.
8. Joe Sachs, trans., *Aristotle's "Metaphysics"* (Santa Fe: Green Lion Press, 1999), li, lvii.
9. *Nicomachean Ethics* 1153 a 11.
10. Ibid., 1095 a 14 ff.
11. Ibid., 1097 b 22 ff.
12. Ibid., 1098 a 8.
13. Ibid., 1098 a 17.
14. Stephan Strasser, *Phenomenology of Feeling: An Essay on the Phenomena of the Heart* (1956), trans. Robert E. Wood (Pittsburgh: Duquesne Univ. Press, 1977), 349–75.
15. John Locke, *An Essay on Human Understanding* (1690), bk. 2, chap. 21 ("Of Power"), para. 47. "Pursuit" evidently means "practice" in the Declaration, see Arthur M. Schlesinger, "The Lost Meaning of 'The Pursuit of Happiness,'" in *A Casebook on the Declaration of Independence*, ed. Robert Ginsberg (New York: Thomas Y. Crowell, 1967), 216–18.
16. *Daedalus* 133, no. 2 (Spring 2004), the issue "On Happiness." I should mention here a recent history of happiness in the West from the Greco-Judaean world to our times: Darrin M. McMahon, *Happiness: A History* (New York: Atlantic Monthly Press, 2006). It is full of wonderful detail well told, but as Hegel famously said of the abstract absolute in cognition, that it was a night in which all cows are black, so the concrete history of happiness is perforce a day in which all calves are golden.
17. *Nicomachean Ethics* 1099 a 10.
18. Ibid., 1152 b 7.
19. Ibid., 1072 a 17.
20. Elaine Scarry, *The Body in Pain: The Making and Unmaking of the World* (Oxford: Oxford Univ. Press, 1985), 16, 161; an analysis of pain into eight factors is given on 52–59.
21. *Nicomachean Ethics* 1154 b 12.
22. Ibid., 1154 b 30.
23. Ibid., 1154 b 27.
24. Ibid., 1152 b 3.
25. Joe Sachs, trans., *Nicomachean Ethics* (Newburyport, Mass.: Focus, 2001), 137 n. 216; 180 n. 280.
26. Sarah Broadie, *Ethics with Aristotle* (Oxford: Oxford Univ. Press, 1991), 313 ff.
27. *Nicomachean Ethics* 1174 a 14.
28. Ibid., 1177 a 19.
29. Unless one wished to say that the passions underlie the virtues, and these are indeed activities.
30. *Rhetoric* 1370 a.
31. *Rhetoric* 1370 a–b.
32. *On the Soul* 424 a.

9. Pleasure and Desire Long After [pages 59–67]

1. Sigmund Freud, *Beyond the Pleasure Principle* (*Jenseits des Lustprinzips*, 1920), trans. James Strachey (London: Hogarth Press and the Institute of Psycho-analysis, 1950).
2. Ibid., sec. 6, end.
3. An aggressive attack with citations of the large literature: Frederick Crews, *The Memory Wars: Freud's Legacy in Dispute* (New York: New York Review of Books, 1995).

4. *Beyond the Pleasure Principle,* sec. 1.
5. Bruno Bettelheim, "Reflections: Freud and the Soul," *New Yorker,* 1 March 1982, 84.
6. *Beyond the Pleasure Principle,* sec. 6.
7. Ibid., sec. 2.
8. Ibid., sec. 5.
9. Ibid., sec. 6.
10. Ibid.
11. Thus Freud suggests possibilities of Greek derivativeness from the East. Toward the end of his century such attributions became an academic rage; for example, Far East: Thomas McEvilley, *The Shape of Ancient Thought: Comparative Studies in Greek and Indian Philosophies* (New York: Allworth Press, 2002); Near East: Martin Bernal, *Black Athena: The Afroasiatic Roots of Classical Civilization,* 3 vols. (New Brunswick, N.J.: Rutgers Univ. Press, 1987–2006).
12. *Beyond the Pleasure Principle,* sec. 7.
13. Ibid., near the end (my italics).
14. William Alston, "Pleasure," in *The Encyclopedia of Philosophy,* vol. 6 (New York: Macmillan, 1967), 341–46.
15. Alexandre Kojève, *Introduction to the Reading of Hegel: Lectures on the "Phenomenology of Spirit"* (1933–39), assembled by Raymond Queneau, ed. Allan Bloom, trans. James H. Nichols, Jr. (New York: Basic Books, 1969), chap. 1, especially the exposition of Hegel's chap. 4 A, "Independence and Dependence; Lordship and Bondage"; Peter Kalkavage, *The Logic of Desire: An Introduction to Hegel's "Phenomenology of Spirit"* (Philadelphia: Paul Dry Books, 2007), chap. 7.
16. *Metaphysics* 1072 a 297.
17. Thomas Hobbes, *Leviathan,* pt. 1, chap. 11.
18. Eugene Goodheart, *Desire and Its Discontents* (New York: Columbia Univ. Press, 1991); the authors there discussed are Conrad, Mann, D. H. Lawrence, Ford Maddox Ford, Emily Brontë, Freud, Philip Roth, DeLillo.
19. They are taken from Joel Marks, "On the Need for Theory of Desire," introduction to *The Ways of Desire: New Essays in Philosophical Psychology on the Concept of Wanting,* ed. Joel Marks (Chicago: Precedent Publishing, 1986), 1–15; the articles that follow address the problems marshalled in the Introduction.
20. *Pride and Prejudice,* chap. 26.
21. Philip Pettit, "Desire," in *The Routledge Encyclopedia of Philosophy,* vol. 3 (London: Routledge, 1998), 30.

chapter III
The Passions as Extremes:
Aristotle as the Founder of Passion Studies
[pages 68–105]

In this chapter the chief texts are Aristotle, *Eudemian Ethics, Nicomachean Ethics, Rhetoric,* and *On the Soul.*

[Introduction: page 68]

1. *Eudemian Ethics* 1229 a 2.
2. Ibid., 1235 b 21.
3. *Rhetoric* 1378 a 21.
4. *Eudemian Ethics* 1245 a 24.

1. Why Aristotle Studies the Passions: Ethics and Persuasion
[pages 69–70]

1. Martin Heidegger, *Being and Time,* 138–39.
2. *Eudemian Ethics* 1020 b 11.
3. This information is gleaned from the Introductions to books that will be cited below.

2. The Appetitive Reach of Human Beings: Rational, Reason–Amenable, Natural [pages 70–78]

1. Plato, *Phaedo* 65 c; *Second Letter* 312 e.
2. *On the Soul* 412 a 28 ff.
3. Ibid., 413 b 23 ff.
4. *Nicomachean Ethics* 1102 a 30 ff.
5. See Figure V-A in Ch. V, Sec. 2, herein.
6. *Nicomachean Ethics* 1139 a 4 ff.
7. *On the Soul* 408 b; Aristotle is plainly opposing Socrates, who presents the parts of the soul as moved and the whole as self-moving (*Phaedrus* 245 d).
8. This answer is an exploitation of a brilliant proposal made by Horst Seidl in *Der Begriff des Intellekts (nous) bei Aristoteles* (Meisenheim am Glan: Verlag Anton Hain, 1971), 113 ff: The highest part of the soul is the "active (or making) intellect" (*nous poetikos*); it thinks. It is immortal and undisturbed by affects. In just one place, however, Aristotle introduces a mystery notion, that of a "passive intellect" (*nous pathetikos*; *pathetikos* actually means "impassioned," "feeling-prone"). Aristotle says that this intellect serves as "material" to the maker-intellect's art (*On the Soul* 430 a). It is potential, for it must be informed and activated; it is perishable, for it is movable; and it is passive because it is affected. What Seidl proposes is that this intellect is identical with that part of the soul which loves and hates, and of which Aristotle has said that "love and hate are not passions of that [active intellect] but of that which supports it" (408 a 27), namely the passion-prone intellect. I am persuaded that this is indeed the name for the left side of Figure III-A: *the passive intellect*.
9. Each reference is to the first line of the passage: *On the Soul* 414 b 2, 433 a 8; *Eudemian Ethics* 1223 a 15 ff., 22 ff; *Nicomachean Ethics* 1111 b 11, 1118 b 8, 1139 a 18, b 5, 1149 b 1; *Politics* 1327 b 41; *Rhetoric* 1370 a 17; *Magna Moralia* 1187 b 37.
10. Dorothea Frede, "Mixed Feelings in Aristotle's *Rhetoric*," in *Essays on Aristotle's "Rhetoric*," ed. Amélie Oksenberg Rorty (Berkeley: Univ. of California Press, 1996), 281 n. 24.
11. *On the Soul* 433 a 16.
12. Ibid., 433 a 10.
13. *Metaphysics* 1073 a 23 ff.
14. Dante, *Divine Comedy*, last lines.
15. *Metaphysics* 1072 b 15 ff.
16. Dante, *Paradiso* 24.130–33.
17. Thomas Aquinas, *Summa Theologiae* Pt. I, Q. XX.
18. Ibid., Art. 1, Reply to Obj. 3.
19. *On the Motion of Animals* 701 a 33.
20. *On the Soul* 433 a 10 ff.
21. *On the Motion of Animals* 702 a 18 ff.
22. *Rhetoric* 1369 a 17.
23. *Nicomachean Ethics* 1111 b 7 ff.
24. *Metaphysics* 1072 a 26 ff.
25. *Politics* 1253 a 10.
26. A pretty conclusive argument against speech in animals is to be found in Stephen R. Anderson, *Doctor Dolittle's Delusion: Animals and the Uniqueness of Human Language* (New Haven: Yale Univ. Press, 2004).
27. *Nicomachean Ethics* 1139 a 21 ff.
28. *On the Soul* 431 a 12.
29. *Iliad* XVIII 109, 113; *Rhetoric* 1370 b 1 ff.
30. *Politics* 1327 b 41.
31. *Eudemian Ethics* 1223 a 27, b 27; *Nicomachean Ethics* 1111 b 11.
32. *On the Soul* 432 b 7; apparently and inexplicably to the contrary: *Eudemian Ethics* 1221 b 32. This is already true, though not explicit, in Plato's *Republic*.
33. *Nicomachean Ethics* 1149 b 1 ff.
34. *Rhetoric* 1356 a 14.
35. *On the Soul* 414 b 18.

36. *Rhetoric* 1370 b 28.
37. Euripides, *Andromeda,* frag. 133.
38. Virgil, *Aeneid* 1.203.

3. The Qualities of the Human Soul: Conditions, Powers, Passions [pages 79–80]

1. *On the Motion of Animals* 700 b 22.
2. *Nicomachean Ethics* 1105 b 29 ff.
3. *Categories* 8 b 25 ff.
4. Joe Sachs, trans., *Nicomachean Ethics,* glossary, 201.
5. *Categories* 8 b 25 ff.
6. Ibid., 916 b 18.
7. *Eudemian Ethics* 1221 b 39 ff.

4. The Lists of Passions: *Eudemian Ethics, Nicomachean Ethics, Rhetoric* [pages 81–84]

1. *Eudemian Ethics* 1220 b 33 ff.; *Nicomachean Ethics* 1105 b 19 ff. (there is a similar list in *On the Soul* 403 a 17); *Rhetoric* 1378 a ff.
2. *Nicomachean Ethics* 1138 b 35 ff.
3. Jon Elster, "Aristotle on the Emotions," *The Great Ideas Today* (Chicago: Encyclopedia Britannica, 1998), 233, 237.
4. *Eudemian Ethics* 1222 b 11.
5. *Nicomachean Ethics* 1179 b 36.
6. Marcus Fabius Quintilian, *The Institutes of Oratory* (95 C.E.), bk. 4, chap. 2.
7. *Nicomachean Ethics* 1103 a 17.
8. Ibid., 1105 b 21.
9. Ibid., 1104 b 4.
10. *Rhetoric* bk. II; the list is culled from the description beginning at 1378 a.
11. Ibid., 1389 a 2 ff.

5. The Bracketing Effect: Extreme-Mean-Extreme [pages 85–89]

1. Diels-Kranz, *Fragmente der Vorsokratiker,* I 63, 3; Plato, *Protagoras* 443 a–b; *Nicomachean Ethics* 1040 b 12.
2. *Nicomachean Ethics* 1131 a 29 ff.
3. *Metaphysics* 1048 a 38.
4. Joe Sachs, trans., *Aristotle's "Metaphysics,"* xxix, li.
5. *Nicomachean Ethics* 1106 a 26 ff.
6. *Politics* 1342 a 8.
7. *Nicomachean Ethics* 1006 b 24–25.
8. Ibid., 1106 b 17 ff.
9. *Eudemian Ethics* 1222 a 27.
10. *Nicomachean Ethics* 1117 a 29, 1116 a 3.
11. Leo Tolstoy, *Anna Karenina,* opening sentence.
12. *Nicomachean Ethics* 1108 a 31.
13. This way had been formulated by Plato for magnitudes (*Statesman* 283 e). He says that there are two kinds, those that are relative to each other and those that are relative to a given mean.
14. *Nicomachean Ethics* 1108 b 13, 1106 b 36; Sarah Broadie, *Ethics with Aristotle* (Oxford: Oxford Univ. Press, 1991), 96.
15. *Nicomachean Ethics* 1104 b 24, *Eudemian Ethics* 1222 a 3.
16. *Nicomachean Ethics* 1106 b 8 ff.
17. Ibid., 1107 a 9.
18. *Metaphysics* 986 a 23.
19. *On the Soul* 431 a 9.
20. *On Generation and Decay* 324 b 18, 335 b 30.

6. From Passions to Virtues and Vices [pages 89–91]

1. *Eudemian Ethics* 1221 b 28 ff., 1222 b 11; Aristotle continues to emphasize the close relation of virtue to pleasure and pain in *Nicomachean Ethics* 1104 b 13 ff., where he goes so far as to say that the latter are what the entire ethical enterprise is about.
2. St. Thomas Aquinas, *Commentary on Aristotle's "Physics,"* trans. R. Blackwell, R. Spath, and E. Thirlkel (New Haven: Yale Univ. Press, 1963), 444–45.
3. *Physics* 246 b 19 ff.
4. *Nicomachean Ethics* 1118 b 9.
5. *Physics* 247 a 8 ff.
6. *On the Soul* 403 a 4 ff.
7. Ibid., 25.
8. *Nicomachean Ethics* 1105 a 28.
9. Ibid., 1098 a 17.

7. Passion and Persuasion: The *Art of Rhetoric* [pages 92–98]

For this section I consulted two translations: Aristotle, *The "Art" of Rhetoric,* trans. J. H. Freese, Loeb Classical Library (1959); Aristotle, *On Rhetoric: A Theory of Civil Discourse,* trans. with an introduction and annotations by George A. Kennedy (Oxford: Oxford Univ. Press, 1991). I also consulted these works: E. M. Cope, *An Introduction to Aristotle's "Rhetoric"* (London: Macmillan and Co., 1867, reprint); *Rhetorika: Schriften zur aristotelischen und hellenistischen Rhetorik,* ed. Rudolf Stark (Hildesheim: Georg Olms Verlagsbuchhandlung, 1986); *Essays on Aristotle's "Rhetoric,"* ed. Amélie Oksenberg Rorty (Berkeley: Univ. of California Press, 1996).

1. *Phaedrus* 266 ff.; *Rhetoric* 1354 a.
2. *Phaedrus* 261 b, 271 d.
3. Abraham Lincoln, Temperance Address, Springfield, February 22, 1842.
4. *Rhetoric* 1355 a 4.
5. Ibid., 1355 a 4, 1356 a 2.
6. Ibid., 1377 b 24, 1388 b 28, 1378 a 24.
7. Ibid., 1370 b 19; references to long citations are to the first line.
8. Herodotus, *Persian Wars* 5.55 ff., 6.123; Thucydides, *Peloponnesian Wars* 1.20, 6.54, 57.
9. *Nicomachean Ethics* 1155 a 22.
10. *Rhetoric* 1381 b 27.
11. Ibid., 1380 b 34.
12. *Iliad* I 1.
13. *Rhetoric* 1378 a 31.
14. David Konstan, "Aristotle on Anger and the Emotions," in *Ancient Anger: Perspectives from Homer to Galen,* Yale Classical Studies 33, ed. Susanna Braund and Glenn Most, (Cambridge: Cambridge Univ. Press, 2003), 103 ff.
15. *Rhetoric* 1382 a 21.
16. *On the Soul* 428 b 30.
17. Ibid., 427 b 22.
18. *Nicomachean Ethics* 1115 a–1117 b.
19. Ibid., 1129 b 31, 1130 d 11, 1129 b 31, 1130 a 11, 1131 a 11.
20. *Eudemian Ethics* 1229 a 15; *Nicomachean Ethics* 1116 a 16.
21. Joe Sachs, "Three Little Words," *St. John's Review* XLIV 1 (1997): 15. The "three little words" are *hexis, mesotes,* and *kalon.*
22. *Nicomachean Ethics* 1128 b 10.
23. *Rhetoric* 1383 b 12.
24. Ibid., 1386 b 9; Ronna Burger, "Nemesis," *Graduate Faculty Philosophy Journal* XIII 1 (Fall 1989): 67.
25. Herodotus, *Persian Wars* 1.10; Thucydides, *Peloponnesian War* 1.6. In Sparta even the women trained naked, see Plutarch, "Lycurgus."
26. *Eudemian Ethics* 1221 a.
27. *Human All-Too-Human* vol. 2, 100.
28. David Konstan, "Shame in Ancient Greece," *Social Research* 70, no. 4 (Winter 2003): 1039.

8. Shame after Aristotle [pages 98–105]

Sources:

Ben-Ze'ev, Aaron. *The Subtlety of the Emotions.* Cambridge: M.I.T. Press, 2000. [Addresses Philosophy of Mind, interdisciplinary sources.]

Bowman, James. "The Lost Sense of Honor." *Public Interest*, no. 149 (Fall 2002). [Addresses loss of the language of honor, shame's complement and opposite.]

Darwin, Charles. *The Expression of Emotions in Man and Animals* (1872). Commentaries by Paul Ekman. Oxford: Oxford Univ. Press, 1998.

Dodds, E. R. *The Greeks and the Irrational.* Berkeley: Univ. of California Press, 1966.

Fisher, Philip. *The Vehement Passions.* Princeton: Princeton Univ. Press, 2002.

Heidegger, Martin. *Parmenides* (1942–43). Translated by André Schuwer and Richard Rojcewicz. Bloomington: Indiana Univ. Press, 1998.

Isenberg, Arnold. "Natural Pride and Natural Shame." *Philosophy and Phenomenological Research* X, no. 1 (Sept. 1949): 1–24. [Parallel analyses of pride and shame as feelings involving reflection on self.]

Izard, Carroll E. *Human Emotions* (pp. 385–419). New York: Plenum Press, 1978. [Shame and shyness as part of a system of emotions and their interactions with other emotional aspects, based on psychological research.]

Katz, Jack. *How Emotions Work* (pp. 142–74). Chicago: Univ. of Chicago Press, 1999.

Kundera, Milan. *Immortality* (pp. 298 ff). Translated by Peter Kussi. New York: Harper Perennial, 1992.

Nathanson, Donald L. *Shame and Pride: Affect, Sex, and the Birth of the Self.* New York: Norton, 1992. [Nathanson is a follower of Tomkins.]

Nussbaum, Martha. *Hiding from Humanity: Disgust, Shame and the Law.* Princeton: Princeton Univ. Press, 2004.

Parrott, W. Gerrod, and Rom Harré. "Embarrassment and the Threat to Character." In *The Emotions: Social, Cultural and Biological Dimensions* (pp. 39–56). Edited by Harré and Parrott. London: Sage Publications, 1996.

Riezler, Kurt. "Comment on the Social Psychology of Shame." *American Journal of Sociology* 48 (Jan. 1943): 457–65.

————. "Shame and Awe." In *Man, Mutable and Immutable: The Fundamental Structure of Social Life* (pp. 226–34). Chicago: Henry Regnery Company, 1950.

Scheler, Max. "Über Scham und Schamgefühl" (1912–16). In *Zur Ethik und Erkenntnislehre* (pp. 65–154), vol. 1 of *Schriften aus dem Nachlass.* Edited by Maria Scheler. Bern: Francke Verlag, 1957.

Seeger, Antony and Judith. "Concepts and Methods of Social Control Among the Suyá of Brazil." Draft of a paper delivered at the American Anthropological Society (November 18, 1989). [Shows how the Suyá concept of shame has certain features that parallel Aristotle's.]

Shame: Interpersonal Behavior, Psychopathology and Culture. Edited by Paul Gilbert and Bernice Andrews. Oxford: Oxford Univ. Press, 1998.

Shame, a special issue of *Social Research* edited by Arien Mack. Vol. 70, no. 4 (Winter 2003).

Solomon, Robert C. *The Passions: The Myth and Nature of Human Emotions* (pp. 363–65). Notre Dame, Ind.: Univ. of Indiana Press, 1983. [Contains an inventory of shame features.]

Straus, Erwin. "Shame as a Historiological Problem." In *Phenomenological Psychology: The Selected Papers of Erwin W. Straus* (pp. 217–24). New York: Basic Books, 1966. [Addresses the phenomenology of shame in terms of human engagement with the world through time.]

Williams, Bernard. *Shame and Necessity.* Berkeley: Univ. of California Press, 1993.

1. E.g., Seeger and Seeger.
2. Emily Dickinson, no. 1304.
3. Scheler, 79.
4. Ibid., 80, 86, 149.

5. Kundera, 303.
6. Epictetus, *Discourses* 1.5.
7. Sophocles, *Oedipus at Colonus* 1.1267; Heidegger, 74.
8. Ben-Ze'ev, 3.
9. Ibid., 512.
10. Katz, 148 ff.
11. *Emma* (1816), chap. 43.
12. Nathanson, 139.
13. Recall that for Freud the reduction of affect is the basic drive.
14. Fisher, 64 ff.
15. *Social Research*, vol. 70, introduction.
16. Ibid., 1028, 1087, 1117, 1263 ff. (with reference to Kundera's treatment of shame).
17. Nussbaum, *Hiding from Humanity,* 206.
18. Ibid., 184–85.
19. Ibid., 16.
20. Ibid., 218–19.
21. "Recordare," *Requiem Mass.*
22. Darwin, 33–54, 310–44, 258.
23. Konstan, "Shame in Ancient Greece," *Social Research*, vol. 70, 1031.
24. *Shame,* ed. Gilbert and Andrews, 3 ff.
25. Ibid., 44 ff.
26. Ibid., 71.
27. Ibid., 80.
28. *Social Research*, vol. 70, 99.
29. Erving Goffman, *Stigma: Notes on the Management of a Spoiled Identity* (Englewood Cliffs, N.J.: Prentice-Hall, 1963), 140.
30. *Shame,* ed. Gilbert and Andrews, 126.
31. Frank Henderson Stewart, *Honor* (Chicago: Univ. of Chicago Press, 1994), chaps. 2, 3; *Shame,* ed. Gilbert and Andrews, 275.
32. Aristotle, *Rhetoric* 1382 b.

chapter IV
The Pathology and Therapy of the Passions:
Stoicism through Cicero
[pages 108–147]

The following two sources will be cited throughout this chapter:

Cicero on the Emotions: Tusculan Disputations 3 and 4, trans. and comm. Margaret Graver (Chicago: Univ. of Chicago Press, 2002). Citations are by book and paragraph number (e.g., 4.60), unless a page is indicated.

Stoicorum Veterum Fragmenta, 4 vols., ed. J. von Arnim (1903–5) (New York: Irvington Publishers, 1986). Citations to *Stoicorum Veterum Fragmenta* are by volume and fragment number (e.g., 2.471).

1. Why Study Stoicism? Why through Cicero? [pages 108–110]

1. John M. Cooper, "Posidonius on the Emotions," in *Reason and Emotion: Essays on Ancient Moral Psychology and Ethical Theory* (Princeton: Princeton Univ. Press, 1999), 449 ff.
2. Epictetus, *The Discourses, The Handbook, Fragments* (early 2nd cent. C.E., as reported by Arrian), ed. Christopher Gill, trans. Elizabeth Carter (1758), rev. Robin Hard (London: Everyman, 1995).
3. E.g., Epictetus, *Discourses* 1.4 and 1.17, *Handbook,* n. 49.
4. *Charmides* 166 ff.
5. Julia Annas, *Hellenistic Philosophy of Mind* (Berkeley: Univ. of California Press, 1992), 61.
6. Amélie Rorty, "The Two Faces of Stoicism: Rousseau and Freud," *Journal of the History of Philosophy* XXIV 3 (July 1996): 354 ff.

2. The Stoic Theory of World and Soul [pages 112–124]

1. Annas, 104; *Stoicorum Veterum Fragmenta* 3.378.
2. Still for Epictetus (*Discourses* 1.17), who, however, sidelines physics (*Fragments* 1).
3. Zeno in Diogenes Laertius, *Lives of Eminent Philosophers,* 7.40.
4. *Stoicorum Veterum Fragmenta* 2.471.
5. S. Sambursky, *Physics of the Stoics* (London: Routledge, 1959), 1 ff.
6. F. H. Sandbach, *The Stoics* (Indianapolis: Hackett, 1989), 75.
7. *Stoicorum Veterum Fragmenta* 3, "De Affectibus."
8. Annas, 52; Origen in *Stoicorum Veterum Fragmenta* 2.988.
9. Chrysippus in Annas, 61–62.
10. Annas, 54.
11. As had Aristotle, *On the Soul* 429 a 3.
12. I learned of Stoic representation theory and its importance in a study group convened at St. John's College, Annapolis, in the 1980s and led by Anderson Weekes, a graduate of the college. His thoughts are recorded in a superb unpublished paper on Early Stoic epistemology.
13. Kant, *Critique of Pure Reason,* B 376.
14. *Stoicorum Veterum Fragmenta* 2.54.
15. Annas, 73; Sextus Empiricus in *Stoicorum Veterum Fragmenta* 2.56.
16. *Stoicorum Veterum Fragmenta* 2.61.
17. Diogenes Laertius in *Stoicorum Veterum Fragmenta* 2.52.
18. Annas, 78; *Stoicorum Veterum Fragmenta* 2.73.
19. Kant, *Critique of Pure Reason,* B 75.
20. Cicero, *Academica* 1.11.40.
21. *Phantasmata* play a central though difficult role in knowledge for Aristotle, but this much is clear: For him mental images convey something of the external objects into the soul, namely their sensory looks and their intellectual form (*On the Soul* III 7).
22. Cicero, *Academica* 2.144 in *Stoicorum Veterum Fragmenta* 2.66.
23. Sextus Empiricus in *Stoicorum Veterum Fragmenta* 2.187.
24. *Stoicorum Veterum Fragmenta* 2.322.
25. Annas, 79.
26. Chrysippus in *Stoicorum Veterum Fragmenta* 2.54.
27. Sappho, frag. 2.
28. *Republic* 439 d.
29. Annas, 53; *Stoicorum Veterum Fragmenta* 2.988.
30. Richard Sorabji, *Emotion and Peace of Mind: From Stoic Agitation to Christian Temptation* (Oxford: Oxford Univ. Press, 2000), 57, 336.
31. *Stoicorum Veterum Fragmenta* 2.125.
32. *Tusculan Disputations* 4.60.
33. *Stoicorum Veterum Fragmenta* 3.201.
34. *Tusculan Disputations* 4.61.
35. Ibid., 3.83.
36. Ibid., p. 215 ff.; Cooper, 462 ff.

3. Cicero's Rowing and Sailing [pages 125–126]

1. *Tusculan Disputations* 3.7.
2. Ibid., 3.23.
3. Ibid., p. xiv.
4. Ibid., 3.25.

4. The Foursquare Taxonomy of the Passions
[pages 126–128]

1. *Tusculan Disputations* 4.14.
2. Ibid.
3. Ibid., 3.27.
4. Ibid., p. xiii.

5. The Passions Explained:
Perturbations of Mind
[pages 129–132]

1. These proto-affects or pre-emotions are discussed by Margaret R. Graver (the editor of the Cicero text I have been using) in chapter 7 of her *Stoicism and Emotion* (Chicago: Univ. of Chicago Press, 2007), 85–108. She points out how important they are for understanding Stoic affectivity, since they imply that not all passions are voluntary but only a subset of them (87). For the *propatheiai* are understood as natural, insuppressible, physical reactions to incitements and therefore non-culpable. How far they are already-conceptualized impressions remains a problem, but they are not, at any rate, assented to; thus, though they may be propositions they are not asserted statements.

   Graver thinks that these pre-emotions (i.e., pre-passions) in fact go back to the Early Stoa. If so, my supposition, that the originators were appealingly radical in regarding *all* affects as false judgments and that the purity of their doctrine was compromised by the later addition of *propatheiai*, is weakened.

   The Stoic notion of *propatheiai* proved useful in Christology. The question there is how humanly passionate Jesus could be without losing his divine passionlessness. The pre-passions, as incipient emotions, are a necessary experience of any incarnate, embodied being, but they do not reach the level of willed and thus sinful passion. To that latter perturbation Jesus, conceived either as God who is above passion or as a human being of exemplary rationality, does not succumb. Thus his humanity and his divinity are both at once explicated (106–7).
2. Thomas Aquinas, *Summa Theologiae* I, Q. 59, Art. 4.
3. Augustine, *City of God* 9.5.
4. *Tusculan Disputations* 4.14.
5. Ibid., 4.12.
6. Ibid., 4.62.
7. Ibid., 4.34.
8. Kant, *Foundations of the Metaphysics of Morals*, secs. 1, 2.
9. *Tusculan Disputations* 4.14.
10. Ibid., 3.52.
11. Ibid., 4.22.
12. Ibid., 3.28.
13. Ibid., 4.29.
14. Ibid., 4.9.
15. Ibid., 4.57.

6. The Cure for Dis-ease:
Therapeutic Philosophy
[pages 132–135]

1. Peter Gay, *The Enlightenment: An Interpretation*, vol. 1 (New York: Norton, 1977), 50, 288–89.
2. Epictetus, *Handbook* 3.
3. Marcus Aurelius, *Meditations* 3.11.
4. Ibid., 7.29, 8.29.
5. Ibid., 3.2.
6. Epictetus, *Handbook* 1.
7. *Tusculan Disputations* 3.59.
8. Ibid., 3.61; the Latin is *ad officium pertinere*, "to be proper to one's station." "Appropriate," the going translation, is in line with the current propensity not to condemn behavior candidly, as in nursery school you don't say to your two-year-olds "That's bad," but "That's inappropriate"; of course they know that that's just a polysyllabic weasel-word for "bad."
9. *Tusculan Disputations* 4.62.
10. Rorty, "Two Faces," 353 ff.

7. The Close but Lesser Adversary: The Epicureans
[pages 136–140]

1. Montaigne says it is the common practice but wrong ("Of Cruelty").
2. Isaac Newton, *Philosophiae Naturalis Principia Mathematica,* bk. 3, "Rules of Reasoning in Philosophy," rule 3.
3. Lucretius, *De Rerum Natura* 6.1138 ff.; text used: *Titi Lucreti Cari De Rerum Natura Libri Sex,* 3 vols., ed. Cyril Bailey (Oxford: Oxford Univ. Press, 1963).
4. *De Rerum Natura* 4.1153 ff.
5. Cicero, *Letters to his Brother Quintus* 2.9, 3.
6. Milton, *Paradise Lost* 6.459–61.
7. *De Rerum Natura* 5.706 ff., 1.155, 2.251 ff.
8. Ibid., 3.91.
9. Ibid., 4.482, 4.426.
10. Diogenes Laertius, *Lives of Eminent Philosophers,* "Epicurus," 10.63. The main extant works of Epicurus come to us through Diogenes.
11. Ibid., 10.48.
12. For example, Annas, 189 ff.; Solomon, *The Passions,* 157 ff.; Ben-Ze'ev, *The Subtlety of Emotions,* 45–46.
13. Diogenes Laertius 10.6; Cicero, *On Ends* 1.30.
14. Diogenes Laertius 10.129, 10.131, 10.136, 10.78.
15. Ibid., 10.132.
16. An emergent property is a qualitatively novel one that arises from a combination of elements, as when hydrogen and oxygen together form water, or—in some theories—when brain cells and circuits cooperate to let mind emerge. It is not yet a perfectly lucid notion; see Ch. X, Sec. 4, note 5, herein.

8. A List of Some Stoic Preformations of Modernity Relating to the Passions [pages 142–144]

1. Diogenes Laertius 10.78.
2. Kant, *Critique of Pure Reason,* B 376.
3. E.g., Richard Rorty, *Philosophy and the Mirror of Nature* (Princeton: Princeton Univ. Press, 1979).
4. *Stoicorum Veterum Fragmenta* 2.187.
5. Alexius Meinong, "The Theory of Objects," in *Realism and the Background of Phenomenology,* ed. Roderick Chisholm (Atascadero, Calif.: Ridgeview Publishing Co., 1960), 76–117.
6. *Stoicorum Veterum Fragmenta* 2.83.
7. John Locke, *An Essay Concerning Human Understanding* (1690), bk. 4, chap. 3, para. 6.
8. *Stoicorum Veterum Fragmenta* 2.83.
9. *Posterior Analytics* 100 a.

9. The Neostoics of Our Day [pages 144–147]

1. Martha Nussbaum, "Emotions as Judgments of Value and Importance," in *Thinking about Feeling: Contemporary Philosophers on Emotions,* ed. Robert C. Solomon (Oxford: Oxford Univ. Press, 2004); Nussbaum, *Upheavals of Thought: The Intelligence of Emotions* (Cambridge: Cambridge Univ. Press, 2001).
2. Solomon, *The Passions,* xiv.
3. This description of reason is from an early summary, announced in 1993, of the Neostoic theory. It is, to be sure, omitted in the revised account in *Upheavals of Thought* (19–64). However, since this description was reprinted in *Thinking about Feeling* (194), which was published after *Upheavals of Thought,* I take it as not superseded, though perhaps suppressed in that book.
4. *Upheavals of Thought,* 62.
5. Ibid., 129; workers in the field tend to be cognitivist neostoics, but, Nussbaum observes, they have interpretational trouble with the language-less cognition they ascribe to animals; I think a pertinent revisal of Stoic doctrine would modify it beyond recognition, for the Stoics think that cognition is *essentially* language-like, and so linguistically expressible.
6. Ibid., 65.

chapter V
The Passions Sited:
Thomas Aquinas and the Soul in Sum
[pages 148–192]

The main texts for this chapter are:

"Treatise on the Passions": St. Thomas Aquinas, *Summa Theologiae*, vols. 19–21 (New York: Blackfriars in conjunction with McGraw Hill, 1965–75), vol. 19: *The Emotions* and vol. 20: *Pleasure*, ed. Eric D'Arcy, vol. 21: *Fear and Anger*, ed. John Patrick Reid. Here cited as "Treatise," followed by Question, Article, Objection, On the Contrary, Reply, Reply to Objections (e.g., Q. 22, Art. 1, Obj. 1, etc.).

The First Part of the Second Part (*Prima Secundae*: Ia IIae) of the *Summa Theologiae* contains the whole Treatise (Qq. 22–48), and is cited here as *Summa*. Other parts of the *Summa: Basic Writings of Saint Thomas*, 2 vols., ed. and ann. by Anton C. Pegis (New York: Random House, 1945). The *Summa* is cited here by Part, Part of Part (i.e., I, II i, II ii), but otherwise similarly to the Treatise: Question, Article, Objection, etc., as seems required. The first volume contains the First Part of the *Summa*, which has no sub-parts (Qq. 1–119).

[Introduction: page 148]

1. *Summa*, Prologue.

1. Why Read Thomas on the Passions?
[page 149]

1. Thomas Aquinas, *Questions on the Soul*, trans. James H. Robb (Milwaukee: Marquette Univ. Press, 2005), 13 ff.

2. The Soul Situated, the Passions Sited
[pages 151–159]

1. *Summa*, Qq. 75–89.
2. *Thomas Aquinas on Human Nature*, ed. Thomas S. Hibbs (Indianapolis: Hackett, 1999), 17, 28, 33.
3. It is not, however, a Platonic soul of three parts as set out in the dialogue *Timaeus* (69 c), which is critically interpreted by Thomas as really three separate souls, because each part is seated in its own organ whence it moves the body (*Summa* I, Q. 76, Art. 3, Reply); recall, however, that in the *Republic* (435 b 1) the soul is *not* located in the body.
4. *Summa* I, Q. 75; *On the Soul* 412 a–b; Hibbs, 17.
5. *On Being and Beingness*, chap. 3.
6. *Summa* I, Q. 75, Art. 1, Reply.
7. *Commentary on Aristotle's "De Anima,"* Lectio XIII on b. III 8.
8. *Summa* I, Q. 76, Art. 2.
9. "Treatise," Q. 22, Art. 3, Reply; *Summa* I, Q. 89, Art. 1, Reply; *Thomas Aquinas: A Summary of Philosophy*, trans. and ed. Richard Regan (Indianapolis: Hackett, 2003), 108.
10. *Summa* I, Q. 77, Art. 8.
11. Ibid., I, Q. 77, Art. 3, Reply.
12. Ibid., I, Q.78 ff.
13. "Treatise," Q. 30.
14. *Summa* I, Q. 84, Art. 6 ff.; Aristotle, *On the Soul* III 3.
15. Hibbs, 43, 117, 148, 156, 160; *Summa* I, Q. 79, Art. 9.
16. *Summa* I, Q. 37, Art. 1, Reply; "Treatise," Q. 22, Art. 2; *Summa* I, Q. 79, Art. 3, Reply to Obj. 2.
17. *On the Soul* 429 b.
18. *Summa* I, Q. 79, Art. 2, Reply; for quite a different understanding of the passive intellect, see Ch. III, Sec. 2, note 8, herein.
19. Ibid., I, Qq. 79–83.
20. Ibid., II i, Qq. 8–21; "Treatise," Qq. 22–48.

21. Ibid., II ɪ, Q. 6, Arts. 6, 7.
22. Ibid., II ɪ, Q. 11, Art. 4.
23. *Nichomachean Ethics* 1111 b 23.
24. *On the Soul* 413 b 12, 432 b 3, 8, 433 a 24, 411 a 29, 434 a 13.
25. Hannah Arendt, "Augustine, the First Philosopher of the Will" in *Willing*, vol. 2 of *The Life of the Mind* (New York: Harcourt Brace Jovanovich, 1978), 84 ff.
26. Richard Sorabji, *Emotion and Peace of Mind*, 335 ff. This will is unmistakably pre-figured in Plotinus, e.g., *Enneads* 6.8.
27. *Summa* I, Q. 81, Art. 1, On the contrary.
28. Ibid., I, Q. 78, Art. 3; Hibbs, 33.
29. Ibid., I, Q. 78, Art. 4.
30. Ibid., I, Q. 81, Art. 3, Reply.
31. Ibid., I, Q. 77, Art. 4.
32. Ibid., II ɪ, Q. 55, Art. 1, Reply.
33. Ibid., II ɪ, Q. 71, Art. 4, Reply.

3. How Are the Passions Passive?
[pages 160–161]

1. Timothy McDermott, trans., Thomas Aquinas, *Selected Philosophical Writings* (Oxford: Oxford Univ. Press, 1993), 327; *Summa Contra Gentiles*, chap. 26, in Pegis, 2:48–49.
2. "Treatise," Q. 22, Art. 1, Reply.
3. See Ch. X, Sec. 4, herein.

4. The Ordering and Enumeration of the Passions
[pages 162–165]

1. *Summa* I, Q. 81, Art. 2.
2. "Treatise," Q. 23, Art. 3.
3. Ibid., Q. 35, Art. 6.
4. D'Arcy, *The Emotions*, p. xxv f.
5. "Treatise," Q. 23, Reply.
6. *On the Soul* 408 b.
7. "Treatise," Q. 25, Art. 3.
8. Ibid., Q. 25, Art. 4.

5. The Particular Passions: Simple Desires
[pages 165–176]

1. "Treatise," Qq. 26–48.
2. Ibid., Q. 30. Art. 2, Reply, no. 3; Q. 23, Art. 4, Reply.
3. See Ch. X, Sec. 1, Subsec. B, herein; *Summa* II ɪ, Q. 71, Art. 2, Reply.
4. Augustine, *Confessions* 2.8.
5. "Treatise," Qq. 26–28.
6. Ibid., Q. 27, Art. 3.
7. Ibid., Q. 41, Reply, 1.
8. Ibid., Q. 30.
9. *Physics* 206 a 14.
10. "Treatise," Qq. 31–34.
11. Ibid., Q. 31.
12. Ibid., Q. 31, Reply.
13. Ibid., Q. 32.
14. *Nichomachean Ethics* 1153 a 14.
15. Keats, "Ode on a Grecian Urn" (1819).
16. "Treatise," Q. 33, Art. 1.
17. Ibid., Q. 34.
18. Ibid., Qq. 35–39.
19. Ibid., Qq. 36–37.
20. Ibid., Q. 38.

6. The Particular Passions: Spirited Desires
[pages 178–181]

1. "Treatise," Q. 40, Art. 1.
2. Ibid., Q. 46, Art. 8, 3; Q. 47, "On the contrary."
3. Ibid., Qq. 41–44.
4. Ibid., Q. 41, Art. 1, Reply.
5. First Inaugural, 1933.
6. "Treatise," Q. 45.
7. Ibid., Qq. 46–48.
8. Ibid., Q. 47.
9. Ibid., Q. 48.

7. Virtuous Passions, Passionate Vices— and Sin [pages 182–184]

1. "Treatise," Q. 40, Reply; *Summa* II II, Q. 35.
2. *Summa* II I, Q. 49 ff.; II II, Q. 1 ff., passim.
3. Ibid., II II, Qq. 17–18.
4. Ibid., II I, Q. 49, Art. 1, Q. 55.
5. Ibid., II I, Q. 59, Art. 1, Reply.
6. "Treatise," Q. 45, Art. 1, Reply.
7. *Summa* II II, Q. 21, Art. 2, Reply; Q. 75, Art. 2, Reply.
8. Ibid., II I, Q. 77, Art. 1.
9. Ibid., II I, Qq. 3–4.

8. The Leap from Thomas to Descartes
[pages 185–192]

1. Stephen Jay Gould, *Hen's Teeth and Horse's Toes* (New York: Norton, 1983), 259–60.
2. Jacob Klein, *Greek Mathematical Thought and the Origin of Algebra* (1936), trans. Eva Brann (New York: Dover, 1992), 19 ff.
3. Etienne Gilson, *The Christian Philosophy of Thomas Aquinas* (New York: Random House, 1956), 221.
4. *Republic*, 508–9; Regan, 78, 83; Descartes, *Meditations on First Philosophy*, "Synopsis" of Fourth Meditation.
5. *Summa* I, Q. 3, Art. 5, Reply to Obj. 1.
6. Ibid., I, Q. 76, Art. 8, Reply.
7. Descartes, *Discourse on Method*, pt. 6, end.
8. *Summa* I, Q. 76, Art. 3, Reply.
9. Descartes, *Discourse on Method*, pt. 5; *Treatise on Man*.
10. *Republic* 580; *Summa* I, Q. 75, Art. 3; Descartes, Sixth Meditation.
11. *Summa* I, Q. 82, Art. 4; II I, Q. 9, Art. 1; Gilson, 255.
12. Descartes, *Discourse on Method*, pt. 5; Descartes, *Principles of Philosophy*, pt. 1, 35.
13. Gilson, 229; Dennis Sepper, *Descartes's Imagination: Proportion, Images, and the Activity of Thinking* (Berkeley: Univ. of California Press, 1996), 244 ff.; Descartes, *Rules for the Direction of the Mind*, rule 12.
14. Descartes, *Principles of Philosophy*, pt. 2, 23.
15. Descartes, *The Passions of the Soul*, art. 30 ff.
16. "Treatise," Q. 23, Art. 1, Reply.
17. Descartes, *Passions*, art. 68.
18. Ibid., art. 52.
19. To Hyperaspistes, Aug. 1641; Descartes, *Passions*, passim.
20. "Treatise," Q. 26, Art. 2, Reply; Descartes, *Passions*, art. 80.
21. Descartes, *Passions*, art. 87.
22. McDermott, 135–36; Descartes, *Passions*, arts. 6, 16.
23. "Treatise," Q. 40, Art. 3, Reply; *Summa* I, Q. 78, Art. 4, Reply; Descartes, *Passions*, art. 50.

chapter VI
The Passions of the Soul as Actions of the Body:
Descartes and the Obscurity of Clear and Distinct Ideas
[pages 193–229]

The chief text for this chapter is:

René Descartes, *The Passions of the Soul,* trans. and ann. Stephen Voss (Indianapolis: Hackett, 1989), cited here as *Passions,* followed by Descartes' own article numbers (1–212); if reference is to the Voss edition in particular, the page number is given.

Almost all the other texts are cited from:

The Philosophical Writings of Descartes, 3 vols. (Cambridge: Cambridge Univ. Press, 1984–91), vol. 1 and 2, trans. John Cottingham, Robert Stoothoff, and Dugald Murdoch, vol. 3: *The Correspondence,* trans. Cottingham, Stoothoff, and Anthony Kenny. This edition is cited as "Cottingham" plus volume and page number, but wherever feasible reference is to the work itself and Descartes' own divisions or the standard pagination (cited without "p."), referring to the twelve-volume edition *Oeuvres de Descartes,* ed. C. Adam and P. Tannery (1964–76).

1. Descartes' Title: Cunning Candor [pages 193–195]

1. *Passions* 138.
2. Ibid., pp. xxi, 17.
3. Ibid., p. 1, n. 1; p. 2; *Principles of Philosophy,* Preface to the French edition, 17.
4. *Passions,* p. 112, n. 18; [Art.] 144.
5. Cottingham, 2:183, 275.
6. Richard Kennington, "The 'Teaching of Nature' in Descartes' Soul Doctrine," *Review of Metaphysics* XXVI 1 (1972): 86–117; *Principles of Philosophy,* pt. 4, para. 200.

2. Method, Metaphysics, Man [pages 195–202]

1. Dennis Sepper, *Descartes's Imagination,* 91 ff.
2. *Principles of Philosophy,* pt. 1, para. 1.
3. Ibid., pt. 1, para. 7.
4. G. Chr. Lichtenberg, *Aphorismen und Schriften,* ed. Ernst Vincent (Leipzig: Alfred Kröner Verlag, 1931), 151, on Kant. Later, Nietzsche will write in *Beyond Good and Evil:* "It is a falsification of the state of affairs to say: the subject 'I' is the condition of the predicate 'think.' It thinks: but that this 'it' has to be just this famous old 'I' is, speaking mildly, only an assumption, an assertion, above all no 'immediate certainty'" ("Of the Prejudices of the Philosophers," no. 17).

    We can be sure that the "I" has not just insinuated itself into the conclusion of Descartes' Latin argument through our common pronoun-using "analytic" language, for the thinking thing is ego-istic in the French texts: "*je suis, moi qui sois certain que je sois*" (Second Meditation, 25).
5. Fifth Meditation, 67.
6. *Principles of Philosophy,* pt. 1, para. 9.
7. Second Meditation, 28.
8. *Principles of Philosophy,* pt. 1, para. 32; Sepper, *Descartes's Imagination,* 272 ff.
9. *Principles of Philosophy,* pt. 1, para. 52.
10. Sepper, *Descartes's Imagination,* 259 ff.
11. The unity (Averroes) or plurality (Thomas) of the active intellect is debated in the *Summa Theologiae* I, Q. 79, Art. 5.
12. *Pace* Rousseau's invention of a "general will."
13. Fourth Meditation, 57.
14. *Principles of Philosophy,* pt. 1, para. 43.
15. Sixth Meditation, 79.
16. Second Meditation, 31.

17. Sixth Meditation, 78.
18. Ibid., 73.
19. Fifth Meditation, 63.
20. Sixth Meditation, 71.
21. *Principles of Philosophy*, pt. 2, para. 1–14.
22. Ibid., pt. 2, para. 3.
23. Sixth Meditation, 71.
24. Ibid., 79.
25. Ibid., 85–86.
26. Ibid., 83; "Author's Replies to the Second Set of Objections," Cottingham, 2:119, prop. 4; "Replies to the Fourth Set of Objections," para. 228–29.
27. *Rules for the Direction of the Mind*, Rule 14, 447.

3. Why Study Descartes on the Passions? [pages 202–206]

1. *Passions* 30.
2. Sepper, *Descartes's Imagination*, 243, and Cottingham, 3:138; *Passions*, p. 16, n. 25.
3. *The World*, chap. 7.
4. *Principles of Philosophy*, pt. 4, para. 197.
5. Letter to Elizabeth, June 28, 1643, Cottingham, 3:228.
6. Sixth Meditation, "Reply to Fourth Set of Objections," 222.
7. *Passions* 31.
8. Ibid., 43.
9. Ibid., 39.
10. Aristotle, *On the Soul* 403 a 28.
11. *Passions* 1.
12. *Principles of Philosophy*, pt. 4, para. 199.
13. Ibid., Preface to the French Edition, 18.

4. Actions of the Body: Passions of the Soul (First Part) [pages 207–213]

1. Aristotle, *Metaphysics* 1020 b 31; see also Plato, *Sophist* 248 b.
2. Aristotle, *On the Soul* 430 a 24; Thomas Aquinas, *Summa Theologiae* I, Q. 79.
3. *Passions* 2.
4. *Principles of Philosophy*, pt. 1, para. 69.
5. *Passions*, p. 83, n. 46.
6. Ibid., p. 45, n. 47.
7. Ibid., 147, 68, 17.
8. Ibid., 4.
9. Ibid., p. 20, n. 6; [Art.] 5.
10. Ibid., 47.
11. Ibid., 30.
12. Ibid., 4 ff.; 96 ff.
13. Ibid., 13 ff.; *The World*, chap. 1; *Principles of Philosophy*, pt. 4, para. 191; *Optics*, 134.
14. *Passions* 17.
15. Third Meditation, 37–38; *Passions* 212.
16. *Passions* 25–29.
17. Ibid., 18; 41.
18. Ibid., 62.
19. Ibid., 19.
20. Ibid., p. 57, n. 14.
21. Sepper, *Descartes's Imagination*, 175 ff.
22. *Passions* 35.
23. Ibid., 40.
24. Ibid., 46–47.
25. Ibid., 49, 63.

5. The Order and Enumeration of the Passions
(Second Part) [pages 213–224]

1. *Discourse on Method,* 18–19; *Passions,* p. 18, n. 1; *Rules,* rule 5; *Passions,* p. 50, n. 1.
2. To Princess Elizabeth, Oct. 3, 6, and Nov. 3, 1645.
3. *Passions* 52.
4. Ibid., 53.
5. Philip Fisher, *Wonder, the Rainbow, and the Aesthetics of Rare Experiences* (Cambridge: Harvard Univ. Press, 1998), 47.
6. *Passions* 71.
7. Ibid., 70; 75–77.
8. Edmund Burke, *A Philosophical Enquiry into the Origin of Our Ideas of the Sublime and Beautiful* (1757), pt. 1, sec. 1.
9. *Passions* 69.
10. Ibid., 68.
11. Ibid., 102.
12. Ibid., 79.
13. *Principles of Philosophy,* para. 32 ff.; Fourth Meditation, 56 ff.
14. Cottingham, vol. 2, e.g., 376 ff., 416.
15. *Passions* 81.
16. Ibid., 82.
17. Ibid., 90.
18. Ibid., 84.
19. Ibid., 89.
20. Ibid., 91.
21. Ibid., 85, 93.
22. Ibid., 93; p. 70, n. 30.
23. Ibid., 94.
24. Ibid., 96–136.
25. Ibid., 102.
26. Ibid., 79–80.
27. Ibid., 176.
28. Ibid., 177 ff.
29. Ibid., 143.
30. Ibid., 144.
31. Ibid., 145.
32. *Discourse on the Method* (1637), pt. 3; *Passions,* p. 97, n. 70.
33. *Discourse on the Method,* pt. 3, Third Maxim.
34. To Chanut, Nov. 1, 1646.
35. *Passions* 147.
36. Ibid.
37. Ibid., 82.
38. Ibid., 148.

6. Particular Passions: The Turn to Virtue
(Third Part) [pages 224–227]

1. *Passions* 160.
2. Ibid., 160, 161.
3. *Principles of Philosophy,* Dedicatory letter to Elizabeth.
4. *Passions* 152.
5. Ibid., 67, 210.
6. Ibid., 63, 190–91.
7. Ibid., 190.
8. Ibid., 153–161.
9. Kant, *Groundwork of the Metaphysic of Morals* (1785), sec. 1.

10. *Passions* 161, p. 109, n. 12.
11. Ibid., 156.
12. Ibid., 161.
13. Ibid., 156.
14. Ibid., 147.
15. Ibid., 212.

7. Transition: Descartes to Spinoza [pages 228–229]

1. *Principles of Philosophy*, para. 56.
2. Sixth Meditation, 80.
3. *Principles of Philosophy*, para. 41.
4. *Passions* 28.
5. Ibid., p. xx.
6. Ibid., 82; 88.

chapter VII

Human Affect as Our Body's Vitality:
Spinoza and the Price We Pay for Resolving All Oppositions
[pages 233–285]

All Spinoza references are to the *Ethics, Proved in Geometrical Order* (*Ethica ordine geometrico demonstrata*) unless otherwise stated. The roman numerals at the beginning of a citation refer to part numbers of the *Ethics*. Additional abbreviations: Def. = Definition; Ax. = Axiom; Prop. = Proposition; Post. = Postulate; Dem. = Demonstration; Cor. = Corollary; Sch. = Scholium (Note). Thus "I Prop. XIV Cor. II" = Part I, Proposition XIV, Corollary II.

2. Why It Is Very Fruitful to Come to Grips with Spinoza [pages 233–234]

1. Hegel, *History of Philosophy*, vol. 3, pt. 3, sec. 2, chap. 1, A 2.
2. *Albert Einstein: Philosopher Scientist*, vol. 1, ed. Paul Schilpp (La Salle, Ill.: Open Court, 1969), 103.

3. Hopes and Helps [page 234]

1. An analysis of the meaning of such a question, asked about consciousness, is in Thomas Nagel's "What Is It Like to Be a Bat?" in *The Nature of Consciousness: Philosophical Debates*, ed. Ned Block, Owen Flanagan, and Güven Güzeldere (Cambridge: M.I.T. Press, 1998), 519–27.

4. An Interlude to Throw the Way of the *Ethics* into Relief: Adam Smith's *Theory of Moral Sentiments* [pages 235–238]

1. Adam Smith, *The Theory of Moral Sentiments*, ed. D. D. Raphael and A. L. Macfie (Indianapolis: Liberty Fund, 1982).
2. Ibid., 31.
3. Ibid., 16.
4. Ibid., 158, 131, 126.
5. Ibid., 138, 130.
6. Ibid., 294.
7. Rousseau, *Second Discourse*, pt. 1.
8. Smith, 270 ff.

5. Spinoza's *Ethics*: The Alpha That Is the Omega [pages 239–244]

1. Hegel, *History of Philosophy*, vol. 3, pt. 3, sec. 2, chap. 1, A 2.
2. Euclid, *Elements* 1.5.
3. Thomas Aquinas, *Summa Theologiae* I, Q. 88, Art. 3.
4. I Prop. XI, I Def. II, IV Preface, IV Prop. IV Dem.
5. Spinoza, *Theologico-Political Treatise* (1670), IV, on God conceived as law-giver.

6. Parmenides, frags. 4 and 3.
7. V Prop. XXXIII, Prop. XXXV.
8. Hegel, *Phenomenology of Spirit*, Preface, para. 16.

6. Attributes: The Discernible Aspects of God [pages 244–246]

1. I Prop. XX.
2. Thomas Aquinas, *Summa Theologiae* I, Q. 4, Art. 3, Reply 1.
3. Errol E. Harris, *Spinoza's Philosophy: An Outline* (Atlantic Highlands, N.J.: Humanities Press, 1992), 28.
4. Jonathan Bennett, *A Study of Spinoza's "Ethics"* (Indianapolis: Hackett, 1984), 92.
5. I Appendix.

7. Human Beings as Two Ways of God: A Mystery [page 246]

1. Harris, 39.

8. Dual Humanity: Body and Mind [pages 247–248]

1. III Preface.
2. II Prop. XV.
3. I Ax. VI.
4. II Prop. XI.
5. II after Prop. XIII, Ax. I ff. Lemmas.
6. III General Def., Explanation.
7. V Prop. I.
8. II Prop. XIII Sch.
9. Michael Della Rocca, *Representation and the Mind-Body Problem in Spinoza* (Oxford: Oxford Univ. Press, 1996), 11–12.
10. II Prop. XVII Sch.

9. Thought vs. Extension: The Parallelism of Dissimilars [pages 249–250]

1. Bennett (153 ff.) puts this in analytic terms.
2. Aristotle, *On the Soul* 430 a 14.
3. Della Rocca, 129–40.

10. Interlude: Once More the Question in Question [page 251]

1. II Ax. II–III.

11. Affections and Affects: Motions and Emotions [pages 252–253]

1. Robert C. Solomon, "Emotions, Thoughts and Feelings: Emotions as Engagements with the World" in *Thinking about Feeling*, 84 f. (see Ch. IV, Sec. 9, note 1, herein); Peter Goldie, *The Emotions: A Philosophical Exploration* (Oxford: Oxford Univ. Press, 2000), chap. 3.
2. III Def. III.
3. III General Def. of the Affects.
4. III Ax. I.
5. Rousseau, *Reveries of the Solitary Walker* (1782), Fifth Walk.
6. Thomas Hobbes, *Leviathan* (1651), chap. 6, appropriated by Leibniz, e.g., in the "Specimen of Dynamics," pt. 1.
7. Goethe, *Faust* 2.11936–7. He also, infamously, has Faust revise the first sentence of the Gospel of St. John: "In the beginning was the Word (*logos*)." Faust first tries "power" (*Kraft*) for "word," then sets down "deed" (*Tat*) as a translation (1.1224, 1237).

12. Thinking Thing: The Human Being as a Mind That Is an Idea [page 254]

1. II Def. III.
2. Spinoza, *The Principles of Descartes' "Philosophy"* (1663), Pt. 1, Def. I.
3. II Def. IV; Descartes, *Meditations*, Third Meditation, para. 37.

13. Interlude: Emotions as Bodily Feels
[page 255]

1. William James, "What Is an Emotion?" in *Collected Essays and Reviews* (New York: Longmans, Green and Co., 1920), 247.
2. G. Dennis Rains, *Principles of Human Neuropsychology* (Boston: McGraw-Hill, 2000), 305.
3. Floyd E. Bloom et al., *Brain, Mind, and Behavior* (New York: W. H. Freeman and Co., 1985), 147.
4. III Prop. LIX Sch.

14. Inadequacy : Adequacy—Passions : Actions
[pages 256–258]

1. III Prop. XII.
2. III Post. I.
3. Thomas Aquinas, *On Truth,* Q. 1, Art. 1, Reply.
4. III Prop. II.
5. I Ax. VI.
6. IV Prop. LXVIII.
7. II Prop. XXXV, XLIII Sch.
8. III Def. III Explanation.
9. II Prop. XLVIII Sch.
10. II Prop. XL Sch. II.
11. Letter to E. W. Tschirnhaus, July 29, 1675. Tschirnhaus first brought Leibniz news of Spinoza's *Ethics*: Leibniz, *Philosophical Papers and Letters,* vol. 1, ed. Leroy E. Loemker (Chicago: Univ. of Chicago Press, 1956), 567.

15. Physics and Physiology: The Prerequisites for Blessedness
[pages 258–259]

1. II Prop. XIII Sch.
2. II Ax. I ff.
3. III Prop. II Sch.
4. David R. Lachterman, "The Physics of Spinoza's *Ethics,*" *Southwestern Journal of Philosophy* III 3 (1977): 71 ff.
5. Kant, "Refutation of Idealism," *Critique of Pure Reason,* B 277.

16. Interlude: Spinoza and Neuroscience
[pages 260–262]

1. Antonio Damasio, *Looking For Spinoza: Joy, Sorrow, and the Feeling Brain* (Orlando: Harcourt Books, 2003), 208.
2. Ibid., 29, 88.
3. Ibid., 198.
4. Ibid., 104; R. Tootell et al., "Functional Anatomy of Macaque Striate Cortex, II. Retinotopic Organization," *Journal of Neuroscience* VIII 5 (May 1988): 1536–37; more brain depictions have been observed since: Stephen M. Kosslyn, William L. Thompson, and Giorgio Ganis, *The Case for Mental Imagery* (Oxford: Oxford Univ. Press, 2006), chap. 4; a recognition of the problem: Arnold H. Modell, *Imagination and the Meaningful Brain* (Cambridge: M.I.T. Press, 2006), 108–9, 195 ff.
5. Damasio, 213–14; Spinoza, *Ethics* I Appendix.
6. Damasio, 209.
7. Ibid., 39–40.

17. Impulse: The Proto-Affect [pages 262–263]

1. III Prop. VII Sch.
2. Thomas Aquinas, *Disputed Questions on Spiritual Creatures,* Art. 11, Reply.
3. III Prop. LVII.
4. III Prop. IX Sch., Def. of the Affects I.
5. III Prop. IX Sch.

18. A Return to Negativity and the Partial Spectator
[page 264]

1. Augustine, *Confessions* 7.12.
2. I Prop. XVII Sch.

19. The Specificity of Passion: Its Object
[pages 264–265]

1. III Prop. LVI Dem.
2. Thomas Aquinas, *Summa Theologiae,* Q. 22, Art. 1.
3. Elizabeth Barrett Browning, *Sonnets from the Portuguese* 43; Shakespeare, Sonnet 53.
4. III Prop. LVII Sch.

20. The Passionate Affects: Preliminaries
[page 266]

1. III Prop. XXVIII.
2. III Prop. LIX.
3. II Prop. XLIV Sch., III Prop. XVII Sch., Prop. LVI.

21. The Passions [pages 267–271]

1. Isaiah 66:10.
2. III Def. of the Affects, Explanation.
3. III Prop. I.
4. III Prop. LVII Sch.
5. Leibniz, *Monadology,* para. 20.
6. III Prop. LIX Dem.
7. Thomas Hobbes, *Leviathan* (1651), pt. 1, chap. 6.
8. III Def. of the Affects IV.
9. III Prop. XXIV.
10. III Def. of the Affects XLVIII Explanation.
11. IV Appendix XXX, Prop. XLV Sch.
12. IV Prop. XLII Dem.
13. IV Prop. L.
14. IV Prop. LIV, III Def. of the Affects XVII.
15. IV Prop. XVIII.

22. Of the Degrees of Knowledge: Imagination, Reason, Intuition [pages 271–273]

1. II Prop. XL Sch. II.
2. One reason why the *whole* of Nature, a complex of existences and their ineractions, is *the* object of intuition, rather than, as for Plato, ideal individual beings with qualitative essences (the forms), seems to be precisely that Spinoza's individual existences (which incidentally, all have a physical mode) have no knowable essences apart from the—quantitative—degree of their vitality, that is their persisting existence itself. Such existences are therefore, though radically individual, qualitatively homogeneous—as individuals not suited to physical sciences. For that science studies such elements in *complexes* ruled by universal laws.
3. II Prop. XVII Sch.
4. II Prop. XLIV Sch.
5. V Prop. XXXIV Dem.
6. II Prop. XL Sch. II.
7. III Prop. XII.
8. IV Prop. LXII Dem.

23. From Passions to Virtues
[page 274]

1. III Def. III Explanation.

24. Passion Pitted against Passion: Practical Advice
[page 274]

1. IV Prop. II Dem.
2. IV Prop. III.
3. IV Prop. VII.

25. Good and Bad: Joy and Sadness [page 275]

1. III Prop. IX Sch.
2. Plato, *Euthyphro* 11 ff.
3. IV Preface.

27. Insoluble Problems [pages 276–278]

1. Kant, "What Does It Mean to Orient Oneself In Thinking?," sixth note.
2. Kant, *Critique of Pure Reason,* B 584.
3. III Prop. XII.
4. II Prop. XVII Sch.
5. Bennett, 299.

28. The Social Virtues of an Impulsive Being [pages 278–279]

1. Spinoza, *Theologico-Political Treatise* (1670), XVI.
2. III Def. of the Affects XLIII.
3. IV Prop. XXXV.
4. IV Prop. XXXVI Sch.
5. IV Prop. XXXVII Sch. I.
6. IV Prop. XXXVII Sch. II.
7. IV Prop. XVIII Sch., Prop. XXXV Sch., Appendix IX.
8. V Prop. LXXI Dem.

29. The Individual Virtues [pages 280–281]

1. IV Def. VIII.
2. IV Prop. XX.
3. IV Prop. XXIV.
4. III Prop. LIX Sch.
5. V Preface.
6. IV Prop. XXXVIII–XXXIX.
7. II Prop. XXVII, XXIX.

30. Freedom as Necessity [pages 281–282]

1. IV Prop. LXXIII.
2. IV Prop. LXVII.
3. III Prop. II Sch.
4. I Def. VII.
5. To G. H. Schaller, October 1674.

31. Freeing the Imagination [pages 282–283]

1. V Preface.
2. V Prop. III–IV.
3. V Prop. V ff.
4. V Prop. VII ff.
5. V Prop. X Sch.

32. The Intellect's Body [pages 283–284]

1. V Prop. XIV Dem., Prop. XVI.
2. V Props. XV, XLII Sch.
3. III Prop. XVIII Dem., V Prop. XXI Dem.

4. V Prop. XXIV.
5. To Tschirnhaus, July 29, 1675.
6. V Prop. XXI Dem., Prop. XXV–XXIX.

33. The Ultimate Affect: The Love of God [page 285]

1. V Prop. XXVI.
2. V Prop. XXXV; God is thus described by Plotinus, *Enneads* 6.8, 15: He loves himself, is his own cause, his being is desire.
3. V Prop. XXVII Dem.
4. III Def. of the Affect XXV.

chapter VIII

The Passions as Reflective Impressions:
Hume and the Price We Pay for Scepticism
[pages 288–317]

The main text for this chapter is:

David Hume, *A Treatise of Human Nature* (1739–40), ed. L. A. Shelby-Bigge (Oxford: Clarendon Press, 1960), here cited as *Treatise* plus page number.

1. Spinoza as Hume's Predecessor [pages 288–289]

1. Thomas Dixon, *From Passions to Emotions: The Creation of a Secular Psychological Category* (Cambridge: Cambridge Univ. Press, 2003), chap. 3.
2. *Treatise* 240–44.
3. Ibid., 248.

2. Why Study Hume's *Treatise*? [pages 289–291]

1. Alasdair MacIntire, *Whose Justice? Which Rationality?* (Notre Dame, Ind.: Univ. of Notre Dame Press, 1988), 284.
2. Adela Pinch, *Strange Fits of Passion: Epistemologies of Emotion, Hume to Austen* (Stanford: Stanford Univ. Press, 1996), 32.
3. Dixon, 101, 104.
4. *Treatise* 276.
5. Ibid., 540.
6. Ibid., 470.
7. Dixon, 3.
8. *Treatise* 272.

4. Problems and Griefs: Perceptions of the Mind
[pages 293–295]

1. *Treatise* 276.
2. Ibid., 1–2.
3. Ibid., 84.
4. Ibid., 89.
5. Ibid., 269.
6. Ibid., 623.
7. Ibid., 269–70.
8. Ibid., 252–53.
9. Ibid., 262.

5. Pride in the Tradition: The Morally Ambiguous Passion [page 295]

1. *Treatise* 297.
2. Ibid., 596.

6. The True System of the Passions: The Double Relation [pages 296–306]

1. *Treatise* 276.
2. Ibid., 7, 276.
3. Ibid., 385.
4. Ibid., 277.
5. Ibid., 367.
6. Ibid., 458.
7. Ibid., 278.
8. Ibid., 277.
9. Ibid., 279.
10. Ibid., 278.
11. *Iliad* IV 145.
12. *Treatise* 279.
13. Ibid., 280.
14. Ibid., 283.
15. Ibid.
16. Ibid., 10.
17. Ibid., 675.
18. Ibid., 60.
19. Ibid., 239.
20. Ibid., 168–69.
21. Ibid., 106.
22. Ibid., 343, 283.
23. Ibid., 70.
24. Ibid., 4–5, 19.
25. Ibid., 283.
26. Ibid., 284.
27. Ibid., 286.
28. Ibid.
29. Ibid., 289.

7. The Afterlife of the System: Reconsiderations and Retentions [pages 307–308]

1. Hume, "On the Delicacy of Taste and Passion" (1742) in *Essays Moral, Political, and Literary,* ed. Eugene F. Miller (Indianapolis: Liberty Fund, 1987), 3–8.
2. Hume, "On the Passions," in *"Four Dissertations" and "Essays on Suicide and the Immortality of the Soul"* (South Bend, Ind.: St. Augustine's Press, 1995), 119–81, particularly 143.
3. Ibid., 130.
4. Ibid., 173.
5. Ibid., 181.
6. *Treatise* 366.
7. "Of Tragedy," in *Four Dissertations,* 185–200.
8. Ibid., 200.

8. What Is Engaging about the True System? [page 309]

1. *Treatise* 634.
2. Ibid., 367.
3. Ibid., 277, 329, 259.

9. Limitations and Expansions of the System [pages 310–311]

1. *Treatise,* secs. 6–12.
2. Ibid., 325, 327.

3. Ibid., 328.
4. Ibid., 458.
5. Ibid., 415.

10. Love and Hatred: The System without the Self
[pages 311–314]

1. *Treatise* 330–31.
2. Ibid., 397.
3. Ibid., 176.
4. Ibid., 177.
5. John Locke, *The Second Treatise of Government* (1690), chap. 15, para. 173.
6. *Treatise* 333.
7. Ibid., 369, 577.
8. Ibid., 372.
9. Ibid., 394.

11. Pleasure/Good, Pain/Evil, Virtue/Vice, Loose Necessity
[pages 314–316]

1. *Treatise* 399, 439.
2. Ibid., 574.
3. Ibid., 409.
4. Ibid., 414–15.
5. Ibid., 294.
6. Ibid., 295–96.
7. Ibid., 470.
8. Ibid., 575, 473.
9. Ibid., 439.

12. Philosophy as Hunting [pages 316–317]

1. Plato, *Republic* 475 d.
2. *Treatise* 451.
3. Ibid., 453.
4. Ibid., 274.

chapter IX
Mood as News from Nothing:
Kierkegaard, Heidegger, and the Age of Anxiety
[pages 318–371]

1. Mood Situated and Delineated [pages 318–322]

1. Thomas Aquinas, *Summa Theologiae* II i, Q. 35, Art. 8; Helmut Flashar, *Melancholie und Melancholiker in den medizinischen Theorien der Antike* (Berlin: Walter de Gruyter, 1966), 91 n. 27.
2. Sorabji, *Emotion and Peace of Mind,* 151, 211 (see Ch. IV, Sec. 2, note 30, herein).
3. Aristotle or a follower, *Problems* XXX, 945 b 16, 955 a 39; also quoted in *The Nature of Melancholy from Aristotle to Kristeva,* ed. Jennifer Radden (Oxford: Oxford Univ. Press, 2000), 49–50; 55–60.
4. Quoted in Doris Kearns Goodwin, *Team of Rivals: The Political Genius of Abraham Lincoln* (New York: Simon and Schuster, 2005), 102.
5. Kay Redfield Jamison, *Touched With Fire: Manic-Depressive Illness and the Artistic Temperament* (New York: Free Press, 1993), 17, on the classification of melancholia; Sigmund Freud, "Mourning and Melancholia" (1917), in *General Psychological Theory,* ed. Paul Rieff (New York: Collier Books, 1963), 167–68.
6. Robert Burton, *The Anatomy of Melancholy* (1624), pt. 1, sec. 2, subsec. 4.

7. Erwin Panofsky, *The Life and Art of Albrecht Dürer* (Princeton: Princeton Univ. Press, 1955), fig. 209 and pp. 156–71.

8. A book dealing with certain dominating dualisms of Western modernity: Antonio J. Quinones, *Dualisms: Agons of the Modern World* (Toronto: Univ. of Toronto Press, 2008).

9. W. H. Auden, "The Age of Anxiety: A Baroque Eclogue" (1947), *Collected Poems,* ed. Edward Mendelson (New York: Vintage Books, 1991): "Malin sang," pt. 5, 526; Prologue, 449; "Malin suggested," pt. 1, 463–64. Leonard Bernstein's "Age of Anxiety" is a musical rendition of Auden's poem in jazz rhythms for piano and orchestra (1949).

10. Mrs. Oliphant, *The Perpetual Curate* (1864), a wonderful, very long novel; I found the quotation in Penelope Fitzgerald, *The Afterlife: Essays and Criticism* (New York: Counterpoint, 2003), 49.

2. Between Hume and Kierkegaard [pages 323–340]

1. Pinch, *Strange Fits of Passion,* 47 (see Ch. VIII, Sec. 2, note 2, herein); this section relies heavily on her study.

2. For example, in the chapters "Journal," "I find the Print of a Man's Foot," and "I Seldom Go from My Cell."

3. Ricarda Huch, *Die Romantik: Ausbreitung, Blütezeit und Verfall* (Tübingen: Rainer Wunderlich Verlag, 1979), 270.

4. Augustine, *Confessions* 6.3.

5. Hume, *A Treatise of Human Nature,* bk. 2, sec. 11; bk. 3, sec. 3.

6. James Russell Lowell, "Rousseau and the Sentimentalists," in *Among My Books* (Boston: Houghton Mifflin, 1884), 366.

7. Pinch, 45.

8. Virginia Woolf, introduction to *A Sentimental Journey through France and Italy,* by Lawrence Sterne (Oxford: Oxford Univ. Press, 1960), xii. (The two Italian volumes never appeared.)

9. Pinch, 4.

10. Ann Hartle, *The Modern Self in Rousseau's "Confessions": A Reply to St. Augustine* (Notre Dame, Ind.: Univ. of Notre Dame Press, 1983), 10, 33, 156; Jeffrey Smith, "Pity and Rousseau's Three Stages," unpublished paper (2006), 3, 15.

11. Rousseau, *Second Discourse* (1755), Preface.

12. Ibid., pt. 1; Rousseau, *Reveries of the Solitary Walker* (finished in 1778), Fifth Walk.

13. Goethe, *Faust* 1.1711.

14. Friedrich Schlegel in Huch, *Die Romantik,* 270.

15. Rousseau, *Reveries,* Fifth Walk; Hartle, 174 n. 36.

16. Huch, *Die Romantik,* "Romantische Lebensläufe," 467.

17. Carl Schmitt, *Political Romanticism,* trans. Guy Oakes (Cambridge: M.I.T. Press, 1968), 51, 73.

18. This interpretation and the quotations come from Paul de Man, "The Image of Rousseau in the Poetry of Hölderlin," chap. 2 of *The Rhetoric of Romanticism* (New York: Columbia Univ. Press, 1984), 37–45. I am reporting here what I myself see neither in Rousseau's reverie nor in Hölderlin's poem, though I recognize it as essential Romanticism.

19. Heinrich Heine, *Die Romantische Schule* (1835), *Werke* II, ed. Stuart Atkins (Munich: C. H. Beck Verlag, 1978), bk. 2, 178 and passim.

20. Frederick Copleston, S.J., *Modern Philosophy,* vol. 7 of *A History of Philosophy* (Garden City, N.Y.: Image Books, 1963), 29.

21. Quoted in M. H. Abrams, *Natural Supernaturalism: Tradition and Revolution in Romantic Literature* (New York: Norton, 1973), 195.

22. Kalkavage, *The Logic of Desire,* chap. 7 (see Ch. II, Sec. 9, note 15, herein).

23. Quoted in Lawrence S. Lockridge, *The Ethics of Romanticism* (Cambridge: Cambridge Univ. Press, 1989), 76.

24. Kant, *Critique of Judgment,* bk. 2, para. 29, Akademie edition, 272.

25. Ibid., bk. 3, Introduction, Akademie edition, 177.

26. Kant, *Anthropology from a Pragmatic Point of View,* Preface.

27. Kant, *Critique of Judgment,* trans. Werner S. Pluhar (Indianapolis: Hackett, 1987), First Introduction, 232.

28. Schopenhauer, *The World as Will and Representation* (*Vorstellung* in German; 1st ed. 1819, 2d ed. 1844), bk. 4, para. 57.

29. Nietzsche, *The Will to Power: Attempt at a Revaluation of all Values* (posthumous), bk. 1, sec. 2 a, "The Modern Darkening," no. 84; bk. 3, sec. 1, "Thing in itself and Appearance," no. 569.

30. Ibid., bk. 4, no. 1023.

31. Nietzsche, *Human All-too-Human* (1890), vol. 2, sec. 1, no. 408.

32. *Will to Power*, bk. 4, sec. 3, "Theory of Will to Power and Values," para. 688–704.

33. Ibid., bk. 4, sec. 2, "My five 'nos'," no. 1021.

34. Nietzsche, *Beyond Good and Evil* (1886), chap. 2, no. 36.

35. *Human All-too-Human*, sec. 9, no. 606.

36. *Will to Power*, bk. 2, sec. 2, no. 296, 383; bk. 4, sec. 1, no. 933; bk. 3, sec. 3, no. 778.

37. *Human All-too-Human*, vol. 2, sec. 2, no. 37.

38. Ibid., vol. 1, sec. 9, no. 584; Nietzsche, *The Gay Science* (1882), bk. 1, no. 47; *Human All-too-Human*, vol. 1, sec. 9, no. 637.

39. Nietzsche, *Genealogy of Morals* (1887), Essay 3, nos. 14–15; First Essay, "Good and Evil, Good and Bad," no. 10.

40. *Beyond Good and Evil*, chap. 9, "What is Noble?" no. 260.

41. Ibid., chap. 5, no. 202; chap. 7, no. 225; *Will to Power*, bk. 2, sec. 2, nos. 367–68.

42. *Human All-too-Human*, vol. 2, sec. 2, no. 68.

43. Ibid., vol. 2, sec. 1, no. 202.

44. *Beyond Good and Evil*, chap. 9, no. 284; *Genealogy of Morals*, Essay 3, no. 15.

45. *Will to Power*, bk. 4, no. 670.

46. *Beyond Good and Evil*, chap. 2, no. 36.

47. *Will to Power*, bk. 4, sec. 3, nos. 1066–67.

48. Rousseau, *Second Discourse*, pt. 2.

49. Kant, *Education* (from lectures), trans. Annette Chorton (Ann Arbor: Univ. of Michigan Press, 1964).

50. Kant, *Critique of Judgment*, Introduction, III, 177 ff.

51. Diogenes Laertius, "Epicurus," 10.34.

52. Kant, *Critique of Practical Reason*, Introduction, note 4.

53. An exposition of the complexities of "moral feeling": Susan Meld Shell, *The Embodiment of Reason: Kant on Spirit, Generation, and Community* (Chicago: Univ. of Chicago Press, 1996), 97 ff.

54. Kant, *Groundwork of the Metaphysics of Morals*, Introduction, note 1; 211.

55. Käte Hamburger, "Novalis und die Mathematik" in *Philosophie der Dichter: Novalis, Schiller, Rilke* (Stuttgart: W. Kohlhammer Verlag, 1966), 16–19.

56. Huch, *Die Romantik*, 110, 426 ff.

57. Johannes Kepler discovered the elliptical orbit of the planets in his study of Mars, *Astronomia Nova* (1609).

58. Hannah Gardner Creamer's *Delia's Doctors or a Glance Behind the Scenes* (1852) is a knowing exposé of the moody hypochondriac bred by idleness in the American middle class and its ridiculous but unfunny therapies.

59. For an overview, see Maurice Cranston, "The Romantic Imagination," in *The Great Ideas Today* (Chicago: Encyclopedia Britannica, 1992), 249 ff.

60. Quoted in Lockridge, 88.

61. Helmut Prang, *Die Romantische Ironie* (Darmstadt: Wissenschaftliche Buchgesellschaft, 1980), 78–84, 9.

62. Søren Kierkegaard, "For Orientation," pt. 2 of *The Concept of Irony With Constant Reference to Socrates*.

3. Anxious about Nothing: Kierkegaard and the Mood of Freedom [pages 342–349]

1. Blaise Pascal, *Pensées* (posthumously published in 1669), trans. A. J. Krailsheimer (New York: Penguin, 1987), no. 24, p. 36; no. 136, pp. 67–68; no. 418, p. 149; no. 414, p. 148; no. 424, p. 154; no. 143, p. 73.

2. Søren Kierkegaard, *The Concept of Anxiety: A Simple Psychologically Orienting Deliberation on the Dogmatic Issue of Hereditary Sin,* trans. Reidar Thomte with Albert B. Anderson (Princeton: Princeton Univ. Press, 1980), 43; references are to the pages of this edition rather than to the Danish edition cited in the margins.

3. Kierkegaard, "The Ancient Tragical Motif as Reflected in the Modern," vol. 1 of *Either/Or.*

4. *Concept of Anxiety,* intro., 14.

5. Ibid., chap. 1, para. 2, p. 31.

6. Ibid., intro., 16–20.

7. Ibid., intro., 21–24.

8. Ibid., chap. 1, para. 2, pp. 28–29.

9. Ibid., chap. 1, para. 4, p. 41.

10. I must say here that this is my interpretation of Kierkegaard's phrase the "difference between myself and my other" which describes what is posited; it is usually taken to be the difference, not between Adam's soul and body, but between Adam and the world.

11. *Concept of Anxiety,* chap. 1, para. 5, p. 41.

12. Ibid., chap. 1, para. 5, p. 42.

13. Ibid., chap. 3, p. 82, n. 1; Aristotle, *Physics* 2001 a 10 ff.

14. Genesis 2:17.

15. *Concept of Anxiety,* chap. 1, para. 5, p. 45.

16. Ibid., chap. 3, para. 2, pp. 64–66.

17. Ibid., chap. 1, para. 6, p. 49; chap. 2, p. 52, para. 1, p. 57; chap. 3, para. 1, p. 93.

18. Ibid., chap. 2, para. 2, p. 68.

19. Ibid., chap. 2, para. 2, p. 61; chap. 2, para. 2, p. 73.

20. Ibid., chap. 2, para. 1, p. 59, n. 1.

21. Ibid., chap. 5, p. 159; chap. 3, para. 2.

22. Aristotle, *Poetics* 1453 a 10.

23. Ibid., 1459 a 24.

24. *Concept of Anxiety,* chap. 5, p. 155.

25. Quoted in Gertrude Himmelfarb, *The Moral Imagination from Edmund Burke to Lionel Trilling* (Chicago: Ivan R. Dee, 2006), 111–12. In the last edition of the *Principles of Political Economy* (1852) Mill, under the influence of Harriet Taylor, reversed himself and accepted socialism's claim to cure anxiety.

4. Anxiety as the Openness to Nothing: Heidegger's Metaphysical Mood [pages 349–362]

1. These three texts—"Was ist Metaphysik?" (1929), "Nachwort zu 'Was ist Metaphysik?'" (1943), and "Einleitung zu 'Was ist Metaphysik?'" (1949)—come from Heidegger, *Wegmarken* (Frankfurt am Main: Vittorio Klostermann, 1976). Translations can be found in *Pathmarks,* ed. William McNeill, translation of the essay by David Krell and William McNeill (Cambridge: Cambridge Univ. Press, 1998), 82–86; also, without Postscript or Introduction, in *Basic Writings: From "Being and Time" (1927) to "The Task of Thinking" (1964),* ed. David Farrell Krell (San Francisco: Harper Collins, 1993).

2. Herman Philipse, *Heidegger's Philosophy of Being: A Critical Interpretation* (Princeton: Princeton Univ. Press, 1998), 275.

3. *Wegmarken,* 30.

4. Heidegger, *Sein und Zeit* (here *Being and Time*) (Tübingen: Max Niemeyer Verlag, 1963, 10th printing); the English translations are keyed to this edition, and I will cite passages from *Being and Time* by Heidegger's paragraphs and its paging.

5. Philipse, 246–76 and passim; Robert Denoon Cumming's *Phenomenology and Deconstruction* (Chicago: Univ. of Chicago Press, 2001) reveals Heidegger's tainted relations to his contemporaries.

6. *Being and Time,* 190 n. 1.

7. Philipse, 10.

8. *Being and Time,* Introduction, end.

9. Plato, *Timaeus* 290 e; Thomas Aquinas, *Summa Theologiae* I, Q. 44, Art. 4.

10. Aristotle, *Physics* 193 a 3 ff.
11. A lucid explication of the whole which emphasizes "Nothing" is given by Thomas Sheehan in "Reading Heidegger's 'What Is Metaphysics?'" *New Yearbook for Phenomenology and Phenomenological Philosophy* 1 (2001): 181–201.
12. *Wegmarken*, 105 n.
13. Friedrich Kluge, *Etymologisches Wörterbuch der deutschen Sprache* (Berlin: Walter de Gruyter, 1963), see under *stimmen*.
14. *Wegmarken*, 110.
15. Ibid., 110–11.
16. Ibid., 112.
17. *King Lear* 3.4.103.
18. *Wegmarken*, 114.
19. *Being and Time*, 6.
20. *Wegmarken*, 118.
21. Ibid.
22. *Being and Time*, para. 29: Condition-in-which-one-finds-oneself-existing; para. 30: Fear; para. 39–41: Care; para. 40: Anxiety; para. 53: Anxiety and Death; para. 68: Anxiety and Nothingness.
23. Sheehan, 182.
24. *Being and Time*, para. 29.
25. Ibid., 137.
26. Ibid.
27. Ibid., 136.
28. Ibid., 138.
29. Ibid., 185–86.
30. Ibid., 184.
31. Ibid., para. 41.
32. Ibid., 180.
33. Ibid., 187.
34. Ibid., 190.
35. Ibid., 344.
36. Ibid., para. 53, p. 266.
37. Ibid., 266.
38. Heidegger, *History of the Concept of Time: Prolegomena* (1925), trans. Theodore Kiesel (Bloomington: Indiana Univ. Press, 1985), para. 30, p. 291.
39. *Being and Time*, 138.

5. Anxiety as the Repression of Instinctual Impulses: Freud's Mythological Mood [pages 363–368]

1. Sigmund Freud, *Hysterie und Angst* (1926), ed. Alexander Mitscherlich, Angela Richards, and James Strachey (Frankfurt a.M.: S. Fischer-Verlag, 1971). This study edition has a much-needed summary of the development of Freud's anxiety-theory, 229–32. My references are to "Hemmung, Symptom und Angst," chaps. 9–11, pp. 284–308. English: *The Problem of Anxiety*, trans. Henry Alden Bunker (New York: Norton, 1936). Main text: "Anxiety and Instinctual Life," Lecture 32, *New Introductory Lectures on Psychoanalysis* (1932), trans. James Strachey (New York: Norton, 1965).
2. *Interpretation of Dreams* (1900), note toward end of chap. 6 E.
3. *Hysterie und Angst*, 289, 302.
4. Ibid., 230.
5. *New Introductory Lectures*, Lecture 31, p. 72.
6. Ibid., 58.
7. Heidegger, *The Basic Problems of Phenomenology* (1927), trans. Albert Hofstadter (Bloomington: Indiana Univ. Press, 1982), 170.
8. *New Introductory Lectures*, 70–71.
9. Plato, *Phaedrus* 230 a.

10. *New Introductory Lectures,* 95 (my italics).
11. Ibid., 76.
12. Ibid., 78–79.
13. Ibid., 78.
14. Ibid., Lecture 32, 85–86.
15. Ibid., 88.
16. Ibid., 93.
17. Ibid., 94–95.
18. *Being and Time,* 136.

6. In a Better Mood: Bollnow's Rehabilitation of Happiness [pages 368–371]

1. Otto Friedrich Bollnow, *Das Wesen der Stimmungen* (Frankfurt: Vittorio Klostermann, 1968).
2. Ibid., 26–29.
3. Heidegger, *Fundamental Concepts of Metaphysics: World, Finitude, Solitude,* trans. William McNeill and Nicholas Walker (Bloomington: Indiana Univ. Press, 1995), para. 18–38, pp. 69–167.
4. Ibid., 115.
5. Ibid., 40–43.
6. Ibid., para. 33, p. 153; "What is Metaphysics?" 110.
7. Bollnow, 78.
8. *Being and Time,* 134.
9. Bollnow, chaps. 5–7.
10. Ibid., 37, quoting Lersch.
11. Strasser, *Phenomenology of Feeling,* 182 (see Ch. II, Sec. 8, note 14, herein).
12. Bollnow, 57.
13. *Being and Time,* 217.

chapter X
Our Times: *Theorizing*
[pages 372–439]

[Introduction: pages 372–373]

1. Overview: James Hillman, "The Various Denials," chap. 1 of *Emotion: A Comprehensive Phenomenology of Theories and Their Meanings for Therapy* (London: Routledge & Kegan Paul, 1962), 37–39.
2. Alfred Jules Ayer, *Language, Truth and Logic,* 2d ed. (New York: Dover, 1946), chap. 6, p. 107 ff. and chap. 2, p. 57.
3. Overviews: Ronald de Sousa, *The Rationality of Emotion* (Cambridge: M.I.T. Press, 2001), 36 ff.; Ira J. Roseman and Craig A. Smith, "Appraisal Theory: Overview, Assumptions, Varieties, Controversies," in *Appraisal Processes in Emotion: Theory, Methods, Research,* ed. Klaus R. Scherer, Angela Schorr, and Tom Johnstone (Oxford: Oxford Univ. Press, 2001), 3–19. Invaluable: Christiane Voss, *Narrative Emotionen: Eine Untersuchung über Möglichkeiten und Grenzen philosophischer Emotionstheorien* (Berlin: Walter de Gruyter, 2004).

1. Experienced Emotion: The Continent [pages 373–385]

1. Jean-Paul Sartre, *The Emotions: Outline of a Theory* (1939), trans. Bernard Frechtman (Secaucus, N.J.: Citadel Press, 1972); *Being and Nothingness: A Phenomenological Essay on Ontology* (*L'être et le néant,* 1943), pt. 1, chap. 2, sec. 2; also, Glen A. Mazis, "A New Approach to Sartre's Theory of Emotions," and Hazel Barnes, "Sartre on Emotions," both in *Sartre and Existentialism: Existentialist Ontology and Human Consciousness,* ed. William McBride (New York: Garland Publishing, 1997), 117–47.
2. A way to get at the chief terms of Phenomenology is through its founder's, Edmund Husserl's, *Ideas for a Pure Phenomenology and Phenomenological Philosophy* (1913).

3. *The Emotions,* chap. 3, pp. 50–57.

4. See Ludwig Wittgenstein, *Philosophical Investigations* (1947–49), 193 ff.

5. *The Emotions,* chap. 3, p. 61.

6. Ibid., 77.

7. Ibid., 91, 70, 76.

8. Ibid., 71.

9. This problem is central to Jerome Kagan's book, *What is Emotion?: History, Measures, and Meanings* (New Haven: Yale Univ. Press, 2007), though to be sure, with disquieting consequences. Kagan adopts experimental results which analyze an emotion as a "cascade of events," beginning with the brain's response to a feeling-changing event and proceeding through our unconscious appraisal, motor response, and conscious interpretation to overt behavior. Each of these stages, he comments, may be "incommensurable," that is, non-analogous with the others. "At the moment, therefore, the hope of finding a well-defined biological pattern that always accompanies a particular emotion has not been realized" (82). He thinks that the above-mentioned inexactitude of emotion-terminology is to blame and recommends a brand-new terminology to identify not so much the emotion as its stimulus; this vocabulary would, however, not be a refined emotion-terminology, since we "need to use biological names, not psychological ones." Then "*fear, sad* and *happy* would be relegated to the ash heap of history" (196)—where, to be sure, much of humanity now lies buried. What would these terms mean in the world of feeling folk? Would identical neurological events have the same emotive meaning by fiat, when they don't by observation?

10. *The Emotions,* 72.

11. In the language of behavioral science: "[E]motions show signs of being goal-directed processes that are ultimately selected by their consequences not just their antecedents." (George Ainslee, "Précis of *Breakdown of the Will,*" *Behavioral and Brain Sciences* 28 [2005]: 639.

12. *The Emotions,* 78–79.

13. Joseph S. Catalano, *A Commentary on Jean-Paul Sartre's "Being and Nothingness"* (Chicago: Univ. of Chicago Press, 1980); the commentary on pt. 1, chap. 1, on negation (53 ff.), is the helpful ontological setting for chap. 2, sec. 2, "Patterns of Bad Faith," where the magical theory reappears.

14. *Being and Nothingness,* pt. 1, chap. 1, sec. 3.

15. Catalano, 61 n. 5.

16. *Being and Nothingness,* pt. 1, chap. 1, sec. 1, "Bad Faith and Falsehood."

17. Ibid., pt. 1, chap. 2, sec. 2, "Patterns of Bad Faith."

18. Ibid., pt. 3, chap. 3, sec. 1 and 2.

19. Roger Shattuck, *Forbidden Knowledge: From Prometheus to Pornography* (New York: Harcourt, Brace and Company, 1996), chap. 8, p. 301 ff.

20. Patricia Meyer Spacks, *Boredom: The Literary History of a State of Mind* (Chicago: Univ. of Chicago Press, 1995): epidemic boredom and the "Age of Boredom," 3; postmodern boredom, 243 ff.; introduction of term, 13; "psychic anorexia," 14; "atrophy of desire" (the self-described condition of a quarter of modern Frenchwomen making love), 3.

21. Sartre, *Nausea* (1938), trans. Lloyd Alexander, introduction by Hayden Carruth (New York: New Directions, 1964).

22. *Being and Nothingness,* pt. 3, chap. 2, sec. 1, "The Body As Being-for-itself: Facticity."

23. Catalano, 4.

24. *Nausea,* 128; "*de trop*" is sometimes translated as "in the way," but of what?—perhaps "one thing too many."

25. Ibid., 131, 134.

26. Ibid., 103.

27. J. S. Bach, Cantata No. 81.

28. *Nausea,* 122.

29. *Being and Nothingness,* pt. 3, chap. 2, sec. 3.

30. J.-K. Huysmans, *Against Nature* (1884, *À Rebours,* literally, "Against the grain" or "Backwards"), trans. Robert Baldick (London: Penguin, 1959), 169.

31. Aurel Kolnai, *On Disgust* (1927), ed. and introduced by Barry Smith and Carolyn Kornmeyer (Chicago: Open Court, 2004).

32. Kolnai, 53. Recall the Stoic Marcus Aurelius's preference for the "off."

33. Jonathan Swift, *Gulliver's Travels* (1726), pt. 2, chap. 5; Kolnai, 60.

34. Otto Weininger in Kolnai, 62.

35. Kolnai, 77, 72; also Sianne Ngai, "Afterword: On Disgust," in *Ugly Feelings* (Cambridge: Harvard Univ. Press, 2005).

36. Kolnai, 70–71.

37. Spacks, *Boredom*, 12–14; this compendious review of boredom, for example, makes no reference to Heidegger's one hundred plus pages on the mood.

38. John Berryman, "The Dream Songs, 14" (1964).

39. Reinhard Kuhn, *The Demon of Noontide: Ennui in Western Literature* (Princeton: Princeton Univ. Press, 1976).

40. Ibid., 12–13.

41. Baudelaire in Kuhn, 310.

42. Jacques Prévert in Kuhn, 338.

43. Paul Valéry, *Soul and Dance*, a Socratic dialogue, quoted in Kuhn, 339.

44. Kuhn, 43–44.

2. Externalized Emotion: Ryle [pages 385–390]

1. Reductionism, which I am using somewhat casually as the propensity for explaining fairly elusive psychological effects in terms of more hard-edged physicalistic elements, is, in fact, a well-defined epistemological theory. Its pertinent characteristic is that a higher-level situation is reduced to, that is, explained in, the terms of a lower one; here higher level concepts stand to lower ones as, for example "gases, lightening, life" stand to "molecules, electrons, and physiological systems." (Carl F. Craver, "Beyond Reduction: Mechanisms, Multifield Integration and the Unity of Neuroscience," *Studies in History and Philosophy of Biological and Biomechanical Science* 36 [2005]: 376.) The notion of "emergence" is introduced to save the reality of objects intended by higher level theory by showing how the lower-level elements in conjunction give rise to a new kind of existence; see Ch. X, Sec. 4, note 5, herein.

2. Gilbert Ryle, *The Concept of Mind* (New York: Barnes and Noble Books, 1949), chap. 4, "Emotion."

3. *The Oxford Companion to the Mind*, ed. Richard L. Gregory (Oxford: Oxford Univ. Press, 1987), "Gilbert Ryle."

4. *Concept of Mind*, 7.

5. Diogenes Laertius, *Lives of Eminent Philosophers*, "Plato," bk. 3, 59.

6. John Dewey, "The Theory of Emotion" in *What Is an Emotion?* ed. Cheshire Calhoun and Robert C. Solomon (New York: Oxford Univ. Press, 1984), 154–71.

7. Ibid., 164.

8. Ibid.

9. *Concept of Mind,* chap. 1, "Descartes' Myth."

10. Ibid., chap. 2, sec. 1.

11. Ibid., chap. 4, sec. 2.

12. Voss, *Narrative Emotionen*, 66.

13. *Concept of Mind,* chap. 4, sec. 1; chap. 4, sec. 5; chap. 4, sec. 4.

14. Ibid., chap. 5, sec. 3, "Mental Capacities and Tendencies."

15. Ibid.

16. Plato, *Phaedrus* 230 a.

17. *Concept of Mind,* chap. 10, sec. 2.

3. Empirically-Based Conceptualization: Tomkins
[pages 390–394]

1. Carroll E. Izard, *Human Emotions* (New York: Plenum Press, 1977), 13–18. Izard said then that the science of emotions was not yet ready to resolve broad philosophical issues (2)—nor does it seem to be now.

2. Such lists are to be found in Izard, 29, 35, 46; also Joseph LeDoux, *The Emotional Brain: The Mysterious Underpinnings of the Emotional Life* (New York: Simon and Schuster, 1998), 112–14.

3. Report of work on facial recognition of emotion, including the difficulty of establishing identifying indices: Keith Oatley and Jennifer Jenkins, *Understanding Emotions* (Malden, Mass.: Blackwell, 2006), 62–70, especially on C. E. Izard and P. Eckman.

4. Silvan S. Tomkins, *Affect, Imagery, Consciousness*, 4 vols. (New York: Springer Publishing, 1962–92), vol. 1: *The Positive Affects*, vol. 2: *The Negative Affects*, vol. 3: *The Negative Affects: Anger and Fear*, vol. 4: *Cognition: Duplication and Transformation of Information*; *Shame and Its Sisters: A Silvan Tomkins Reader*, ed. Eve Kosofsky Sedgwick and Adam Frank (Durham: Duke Univ. Press, 1995). Tomkins's work has been revived by Donald Nathanson in *Shame and Pride: Affect, Sex, and the Birth of Self* (New York: Norton, 1992). Dr. Brian Lynch, a St. John's alumnus, is making it accessible to the public for practical use.

5. Nathanson, 48–51.

6. Tomkins, *Affect, Imagery, Consciousness*, 1:337, 339; description: chap. 10.

7. Oxford Latin Dictionary: *intersum*.

8. Albert O. Hirschman, *The Passions and the Interests: Political Arguments for Capitalism Before Its Triumph* (1977) (Princeton: Princeton Univ. Press, 1997), 32 ff.

9. Spacks, *Boredom*, 113 ff.

10. Heidegger, "Was heisst Denken?" in *Vorträge und Aufsätze* (Pfullingen: Verlag Günther Neske, 1954), 131.

11. Tomkins, *Affect, Imagery, Consciousness*, 1:342–44. The organizing Image seems to be only metaphorically visual.

12. Ibid., 1:345, 362–363.

13. Heidegger, *Being and Time*, 347.

14. Plato, *Republic* 475 c.

15. Augustine, *Confessions* 10.35.

16. Hobbes, *Leviathan* 6; both passages are cited in Shattuck, *Forbidden Knowledge*, 46.

17. Patricia Meyer Spacks, *Gossip* (Chicago: Univ. of Chicago Press, 1986), 151.

4. Emotion and Knowledge: Cognitivism [pages 394–423]

1. Surveys: Ronald de Sousa, *The Rationality of Emotion* (Cambridge: M.I.T. Press, 2001), 36–46; Voss, *Narrative Emotionen*, 45–180.

2. LeDoux, 1996; Antonio Damasio, *The Feeling of What Happens: Body and the Making of Consciousness* (New York: Harcourt, 1999).

3. Augustine, *Confessions* 4.14.

4. Daniel M. Wegner, *The Illusion of Conscious Will* (Cambridge: M.I.T. Press, 2002), 50–55.

5. *The Oxford Companion to Mind* (1987), 217: "'Emergence' and 'Reduction' in Explanation."

Twenty years later emergence has become a vibrantly controversial issue in philosophy and science (*Emergence: Contemporary Readings in Philosophy and Science*, ed. Mark A. Bedau and Paul Humphreys [Cambridge: M.I.T. Press, 2008]).

The phenomenon itself was well known to the ancients, though not thematized as such. The ontologically most significant case I know is Plato's theory of *arithmoi*, the counting-numbers, which he regards as composed of units. Thus he says of the first number, two, that in it, "each is one, but both are two" (*Republic* 524 b); hence the units are the basic elements from which emerges a new, higher-level structure with a character not found in its constituent elements. Plato regarded this "arithmological" structure as offering a solution to the problem of the participation of lower-level forms in a hyper-form; for example, Motion and Rest, two— albeit irreducibly dissimilar—units are thrown together to yield Being, an emergent higher-lever entity (Klein, *Greek Mathematical Thought*, 82 ff.; see Ch. V, Sec. 8, note 2, herein).

The politically most important example is the emergent relation of citizens to their *polis* (political community), an implicit theme of both Plato's *Republic* and Aristotle's *Politics*. Aristotle, however, notices emergence explicitly on a much smaller scale: "Since that which is composed in such a way that the whole is one, and not as an aggregate but like a syllable, [we must observe that] a syllable is not [just] its elements: BA is not the same as B and A, nor is flesh [just] fire and earth. For, once dissolved, the whole no longer exists ... but the elements do exist ..." (*Metaphysics* 1041 b).

That description contains some of the features nowadays attributed to emergence after much analysis: the irreducibility of the emergent to the basic phenomena, the unpredictability of the emergent features, the unexplainability of the higher level merely in terms of the lower, the emergence of conceptual and perhaps ontological (real) novelty, and the holism of the emergent level (*Emergence*, 11).

The notion of emergence itself has several degrees. There is a strong emergence verging on reductionism in which the emergent entity pretty nearly results, fully determined, from the elements and their relations, so that its dependence on them is fairly transparent. Strong emergence is sometimes called "supervenience"; the term is actually traceable to the Latin translation of Aristotle's most appealing definition of pleasure as a "certain supervening perfection" upon good work being done (Ch. II, Sec. 8, Subsec. A, herein; also *Emergence*, 96, 411 ff.).

Weak emergence is, in fact, more interesting for present purposes. All practitioners of neuroscience whose works I have read are committed either to radically reductive physicalism (mind *is* brain) or to a range of degrees of emergence. For consciousness, strong emergence appears to me to be a mere hope; the inventory of conscious and unconscious mental states and events that is needed to relate intellectual and *affective* consciousness strongly to brain structures and events is simply—and perhaps in principle—not available, nor have bridging rules between the two phenomenal realms yet been articulated.

Weak emergence too is full of difficulties. It is unclear that it applies to anything *but* consciousness (which the editors of *Emergence* refer to as an "exotic phenomenon," 12, 338), that it is not terminally mysterious, and that it does not involve some strange causal relations, among them "downward causation," that is, a possible back-causation of the emergent on the elemental realm, namely consciousness causing brain events (*Emergence*, 141 ff.).

John Searle has addressed the problem head on (*Emergence*, 69 ff.). He supports a strong emergence which assumes that physical elements and their interactions *cause* consciousness and that its capabilities are strictly congruent with the physical system: "macro mental phenomena are all caused by lower-level micro-phenomena" (79). However, this causation is only sufficient, not necessary; the same mental phenomena need not have—and this is in accord with observation—identical neurophysiological antecedents (78). To me, there seems to be an unsettling loose joint here.

Searle gives the following neatly dismissive description of the weakest emergence: "The naïve idea here is that conciousness gets squirted out by the behavior of neurons in the brain, but . . . then it has a life of its own" (70).

No one, I think, who grapples with affectivity can fail to come to grips with emergence, but so far it is an elusive shade. The relation of soul to body is an unsolved mystery; I omit the usual qualifier "so far."

6. LeDoux, 37.
7. Voss, *Narrative Emotionen*, 12.
8. Robert C. Solomon, "Emotions, Thoughts and Feelings: What Is a 'Cognitive Theory' of the Emotions and Does It Neglect Affectivity?," in *Philosophy and the Emotions*, ed. Anthony Hatzimoysis (Cambridge: Cambridge Univ. Press, 2003), 15.
9. Anthony Kenny, *Action, Emotion, Will* (London: Routledge & Kegan Paul, 1963).
10. Solomon, *The Passions*, xvi ff. (see notes to Ch. III, Sec. 8, "Sources," herein).
11. W. B. Yeats, "The Second Coming" (1920).
12. Hegel, *Logic (Encyclopaedia)*, para. 90, 99.
13. Richard Rorty, *The Linguistic Turn: Recent Essays in Philosophic Method* (Chicago: Univ. of Chicago Press, 1967), 1–3.
14. E.g., Richard D. Winfield, *Overcoming Foundations: Studies in Systematic Philosophy* (New York: Columbia Univ. Press, 1989); James R. Mensch, *Postfoundational Phenomenology: Husserlian Reflections on Presence and Embodiment* (University Park: Pennsylvania State Univ. Press, 2001).
15. Latin *re*, "again," and *bellum*, "war," Locke, *Second Treatise of Civil Government*, chap. 9.
16. E.g., Nicolaus Copernicus, *On the Revolutions of the Heavenly Spheres* (1453), bk. 1.4; *orbis* is used by Copernicus for the great circle, the "orbit," in which the planet is located on its spherical shell.
17. Of course, modernity too has its absorbers and preservers, especially Leibniz and Hegel.
18. E.g.: Kant, *The Contest of the Faculties* (1798) I, i, 2; F. W. J. Schelling, *On University Studies* (1803), trans. E. S. Morgan (Athens: Ohio Univ. Press, 1966), 48 ff.; Bruce A. Kimball, *Ora-*

tors and Philosophers: A History of the Idea of Liberal Education (New York: Teachers College, Columbia Univ., 1986), 58 ff. For America, Frederick Rudolph, *The American College and University: A History* (New York: Random House, 1962), chap. 13, "The Emerging University."

19. Amélie Rorty, "Enough Already with Theories of Emotion," in *Thinking about Feeling*, ed. Solomon, 269–78 (see Ch. IV, Sec. 9, note 1, herein).

20. Accordingly, Paul E. Griffiths asks "Is Emotion a Natural Kind?" (*Thinking About Feeling*, 235), and supports his negative answer with an operational definition: A "natural" kind is one that allows reliable predictions in a large domain of its properties; emotional responses to identical stimuli vary greatly in their properties. One might object that emotions may not be natural kinds as responses but may be such intrinsically, as affects.

21. V. C. Chappell, Preface to *The Philosophy of Mind*, ed. Chappell (New York: Dover, 1981), vii–ix.

22. Errol Bedford, "Emotions," *Aristotelian Society Proceedings* LVII (1956–57): 281–304; also in Chapell, *Philosophy of Mind*, 110–26; and in *What Is an Emotion?* 265–78 (incomplete).

23. Keats, "Ode on a Grecian Urn" (1819).

24. Oatley and Jenkins, 115 ff.

25. James Whitley, *Style and Society in Dark Age Greece: The Changing Face of a Pre-Literate Society 1100–700 B.C.* (Cambridge: Cambridge Univ. Press, 1991), 137 ff.

26. *Iliad* XVIII 27.

27. La Rochefoucauld, *Maxims*, trans. Stuart D. Warner and Stéphane Douard (South Bend, Ind.: St. Augustine Press, 2001), no. 136.

28. Daniel M. Gross, *The Secret History of Emotion: From Aristotle's "Rhetoric" to Brain Science* (Chicago: Univ. of Chicago Press, 2006).

29. Ibid., 15.

30. Ibid., 50; he claims that this economicized rhetorical analysis is thus more meaningful than brain science with its emphasis on individual cases and universal applications.

31. Ibid., 179.

32. Bedford, in Chappell, *Philosophy of Mind*, 119.

33. Kenny, *Action, Emotion, Will*, 1.

34. Rorty, *Linguistic Turn*, passim.

35. De Sousa, *The Rationality of Emotion*, 52.

36. Paul E. Griffiths, *What Emotions Really Are: The Problem of Psychological Categories* (Chicago: Univ. of Chicago Press, 1997): conceptual analysis, 23, 21–43; Schachter and Singer's ANS experiments, 24–25, 80–84; also LeDoux, *The Emotional Brain*: appraisal in cognitive and brain science, 49–53; Damasio, *The Feeling of What Happens*: emotions involved in reasoning, 40–42.

37. Kenny, 296; he writes "intensional," but in this country the Continental spelling "intention" is used, while "intension," opposed to "extension," refers to the set of defining attributes of a class versus the collection of its members. The advantage of using the "s" version is that it preserves "intention" for its common use, as in "I have the intention, I mean it in my heart." Nonetheless, I will stick with the American usage.

38. Kenny, chap. 9, "Objects"; Thomas Aquinas, *Summa Theologiae* I, Q. 77, Art. 3; II I, Q. 18, Art. 2; "Treatise on the Passions," Q. 18, Art. 2; Aristotle, *On the Soul* 415 a 19 ff.

39. W. B. Yeats, "Among School Children" (1928).

40. *Iliad* II 16.

41. There are, however, philosophic schools that deny that a mental image is an object, e.g., Jean-Paul Sartre, *The Psychology of the Imagination* (1940), pt. 1, sec. 1.

42. Job 6:6–7.

43. Shakespeare, Sonnet 150.

44. Milton, *Paradise Lost*, 4.110.

45. Kenny, 194–95.

46. Ibid., 196.

47. Ibid., 219.

48. Euripides, *Hippolytus* l.612.

49. Kenny, 100.

50. Solomon: *The Passions*, 185; "Emotions and Choice" (1973), in *What Is an Emotion?* 305–26; "Emotions, Thoughts and Feelings," 1–18.

51. Solomon, *The Passions,* 188 ff.; "Emotions and Choice," 306, 325; "Emotions, Thoughts and Feelings," 18.
52. Solomon, "Emotions, Thoughts and Feelings," 15, 11, 6.
53. Blaise Pascal, *"Pensées" and "Provincial Letters"* (New York: Modern Library, 1941), Pensées nos. 277, 282. The numberings differ in different editions; the Modern Library edition, from which some later editions derive, has the advantage of keeping the Thoughts relevant to this topic together.
54. Patricia S. Greenspan, *Emotions and Reasons: An Inquiry into Emotional Justification* (New York: Routledge, 1988); Paul Redding, *The Logic of Affect* (Ithaca: Cornell Univ. Press, 1999); de Sousa, *The Rationality of Emotion.* Solomon, the early American proponent of this movement, had already spoken of "the rationality of the emotions" and "the logic of emotion" (*The Passions,* chap. 9, 4 and chap. 10).
55. The old version of the physical uncertainty relation, as formulated by its discoverer, is this: To "see" an electron we must bounce a light particle (a photon) off it. But then the electron recoils and alters its motion. So the act of observation itself renders its object, the electron's orbit, uncertain—in principle: Werner Heisenberg, *Das Naturbild der heutigen Physik* (1955), chap. 2, sec. 3.
56. Solomon, *The Passions,* 253 n.
57. Greenspan, 14, 175, 167–73.
58. Redding, chap. 3, "Freud, Affect, and Logic of the Unconscious."
59. Freud, *The Interpretation of Dreams* (1900), chap. 6, sec. C, "The Means of Representation in Dreams."
60. Susan Haack, *Deviant Logic, Fuzzy Logic: Beyond the Formalism* (Chicago: Univ. of Chicago Press, 1996), pt. 1, especially chap. 1, "'Alternative' in 'Alternative logic'"; chap. 2, "Reasons for Deviance," 1–46.
61. Stephan Strasser, *Phenomenology of Feeling,* 259 ff.
62. Robert M. Gordon, *The Structure of Emotions: Investigations in Cognitive Philosophy* (Cambridge: Cambridge Univ. Press, 1987), 117–27.
63. Ibid., 125.
64. De Sousa, *The Rationality of Emotion,* chap. 5–7, 107–203; also "The Rationality of the Emotions" in *Explaining the Emotions,* ed. Amélie Rorty (Berkeley: Univ. of California Press, 1980), 127–51; Aaron Ben-Ze'ev, "The Logic of Emotions," in *Philosophy and the Emotions,* 147–62.
65. De Sousa, 114 ff.; 137 f.
66. Ibid., 126.
67. Ibid., 153; he doesn't, of course, mean that there are no subservient brain centers.
68. Ibid., 163.
69. Ibid.
70. Virgil, *Aeneid* 4.622–23, trans. Rolfe Humphries.
71. John Searle, *Intentionality: An Essay on Philosophy of Mind* (Cambridge: Cambridge Univ. Press, 1983), 33.
72. De Sousa, 166, 167–70.
73. Ibid., 122, 286.
74. Ibid., 182.
75. Ibid., 189.
76. Letter to Karl Kerényi, Feb. 18, 1941.
77. De Sousa, 183.
78. Ibid., 201.
79. Voss, *Narrative Emotionen,* 121 ff.
80. Ben-Ze'ev, *The Subtlety of the Emotions,* 153–54.

5. The Role of the Imagination in the Passions: Few Take It Up [pages 424–439]

Some of the few emotion studies with thematic references to the imagination:

Ben-Ze'ev, Aaron. *The Subtlety of the Emotions.* Cambridge: M.I.T. Press, 2000. Chap. 7, "Emotions and Imagination."

Goldie, Peter. *The Emotions: A Philosophical Exploration*. Oxford: Clarendon Press, 2000. Chap. 7, "How We Think of Others' Emotions."

Hillman, James. *Emotion: A Comprehensive Phenomenology of Theories and Their Meanings for Therapy*. London: Routledge & Kegan Paul, 1962. Chap. 14, "Emotion and Representation."

Levinson, Jerrold. "Emotion in Response to Art." In *Routledge Encyclopedia of Philosophy*. London and New York: Routledge, 1998.

Moran, Richard. "The Expression of Feelings in the Imagination." *Philosophical Review* 103: 75–106.

Opdahl, Keith M. *Emotion as Meaning: A Literary Case for How We Imagine*. Lewisburg: Bucknell Univ. Press, 2002. Pt. 1, "The Mental Construction of Meaning."

Terada, Rei. *Feeling in Theory: Emotion after the Death of the Subject*. Cambridge: Harvard Univ. Press, 2001.

Voss, Christiane. *Narrative Emotionen*. Berlin: Walter de Gruyter, 2004. Pt. 3, "Die Narrativität der Emotionen."

1. Wallace Stevens, "Final Soliloquy of the Interior Paramour" (1950).
2. Arthur Schopenhauer, *The World As Will and Representation*, bk. 3, para. 52: on the metaphysics of music.
3. Suzanne K. Langer, *Philosophy in a New Key: A Study in the Symbolism of Reason, Rite, and Art*, 3d ed. (Cambridge: Harvard Univ. Press, 1978), chap. 8; Terada, 92 ff.
4. Jenefer Robinson's *Deeper than Reason: Emotion and Its Role in Literature, Music and Art* (Oxford: Clarendon Press, 2005) presents a critical review of expression in the arts, especially for music. Expression theories, with their emphasis on subjectivity, came to the fore in the Romantic era; she contributes her own, neuroscientific-inspired revision.
5. E.g., Kendall Walton, *Mimesis As Make-Believe* (Cambridge: Harvard Univ. Press, 1990); Jerome Neu, *A Tear Is an Intellectual Thing: The Meanings of Emotion* (Oxford: Oxford Univ. Press, 2000), 29–32; Moran, 75 ff.
6. Keats, "Ode on a Grecian Urn" (1819).
7. In this, as in other respects, cognitive scientists are sometimes at odds with academic philosophers. Thus this long-standing "imagery debate" is definitively summarized from the scientific point of view and presumed resolved in favor of mental imagery by Stephen M. Kosslyn, William L. Thompson, and Giorgio Ganis in *The Case for Mental Imagery* (Oxford: Oxford Univ. Press, 2006). The hard-edged framing of the question "Are there mental images or are they mere epiphenomena of introspection?" is whether there is neuroscientific data supporting their occurrence and whether "depictive [mental] representations can in fact function effectively within a plausible information-processing system" (134). The defeated counterclaim was that no spatial images are used in cognitive mental processing but only propositional-verbal type representations. Thus in brief: Is there evidence in the brain for quasi-visual events, and are they cognitively engaged? Kosslyn's answer seems to be yes for both criteria (chap. 5), though the opposition has not conceded.

    What is of interest in my context is that the case for emotions is different from that of images. Depictions, be they external or internal, are overt. I mean that they are extended and are patent not only before the sensory eye without but also in the perceptual "space" within, where they can be made to reveal measurable dimensions (Kosslyn, chap. 2); most remarkably, mental images may even be depictively represented in the brain, as pictures visible in brain scans (ibid., chap. 4). Emotions, on the other hand, are ultimately interior, inherently nonfigural, and often descriptively equivocal. Of the two issues analogous to those of the mental imagery debate, whether there *are* emotions and whether they are *functional*, the first has gone a little out of fashion (perhaps because it is hard to feel strongly in behalf of the non-existence of feelings), and the second has been resolved positively by the evolutionists. Thus the great residual problem in the neuroscience of emotions appears to be how to particularize the correlation of emotion and brain events. Here no closure seems in sight.
8. Aristotle, *On Memory and Recollection* 449 b 32.
9. Eva T. H. Brann, *The World of the Imagination: Sum and Substance* (Lanham, Md.: Rowman and Littlefield, 1991), 237, 785, 620; see passim for imagery topics mentioned above.

10. Thomas Aquinas, *Summa Theologiae* II, Q. 91, Art. 6.

11. Goethe, *Elective Affinities* (1809), pt. 2, chap. 8.

12. Shakespeare, Sonnet 53.

13. Susanne Langer, *Mind: An Essay on Human Feeling* (1967) (Baltimore: Johns Hopkins Univ. Press, 1988), 276.

14. William James, *Psychology* (abridged, 1892), chap. 11, "The Stream of Consciousness."

15. John Dryden, "A Song for St. Cecilia's Day, 1687," later set to music by Handel.

16. There is in fact a book that shows how great a freight of affectivity graphs can convey; its most moving image is a graphical tracing of the size of Napolean's army marching on Moscow and returning thence, a mighty stream moving east and a failing trickle marching west: Edward R. Tufte, *The Visual Display of Quantitative Information* (Cheshire, Conn.: Graphics Press, 1983), 40–41.

17. Basic for images and thinking: P. N. Johnson-Laird, *Mental Models: Towards a Cognitive Science of Language, Inference, and Consciousness* (Cambridge: Harvard Univ. Press, 1983), chap. 7, "Images, propositions, and models," 146 ff.; for images and emotions, a lay presentation: Damasio, *The Feeling of What Happens*, passim.

18. E.g., LeDoux, 23 and chap. 7; Damasio, 11–12, appendix, and passim.

19. However, a recent theory denies that the brain functions representationally but without giving up talk of mental images: Gerald M. Edelman and Giulio Tononi, *The Universe of Consciousness: How Matter Becomes Imagination* (New York: Basic Books, 2000), 94.

20. Rita Carter, *Exploring Consciousness* (Berkeley: Univ. of California Press, 2002), 255. The amygdala and hypothalamus are chiefly involved; early work was done by Magda B. Arnold, *Memory and the Brain* (Hillsdale, N.J.: Lawrence Erlbaum Associates, 1984), chap. 23, 340 ff.; Dennis Rains, *Principles of Human Neuropsychology* (Boston: McGraw Hill, 2002), 294.

21. Augustine, *Confessions* 10.14.

22. Goldie, 195, 199, 209.

23. Ibid., 209.

24. Ben-Ze'ev, *The Subtlety of the Emotions*, 205, 219.

25. Hillman, 182.

26. For controlled experiments establishing the imagery code, see Stephen Kosslyn, *Image and Mind* (Cambridge: Harvard Univ. Press, 1980), 29 ff.

27. Opdahl, 60–66.

28. Ibid., 45.

29. Voss, *Narrative Emotionen*, 184.

30. This very God-usurping "creativity" we admire so indiscriminately is damned in some Bible-derived religions: "Islam tells us that on the unappealable Day of Judgment, all who have perpetrated images of living things will reawaken with their works, and will be ordered to blow life into them, and they will fail, and they and their works will be cast into the fires of punishment" (From J. L. Borges' story "Covered Mirrors," in *The Maker* [1960]).

31. Proclus, *A Commentary on the First Book of Euclid's Elements* (c. 450 C.E.), trans. Glenn R. Morrow (Princeton: Princeton Univ. Press, 1970), Prologue, pt. 2, p. 44; Kant, *Prolegomena to Any Future Metaphysics* (1783), para. 10.

32. Mother Goose: "Sing a Song of Sixpence."

33. From Boccaccio's *Life of Dante*, quoted in the introduction to Dante, *The New Life: La Vita Nuova*, introduced and trans. by William Anderson (Baltimore: Penguin, 1964), 10–11 and para. 1.

34. The superposition of sensation and images, the recovery of lost time, and the attendant "moments of felicity" experienced by Proust, the connoisseur of the recalled image, is the subject of Roger Shattuck's *Proust's Binoculars: A Study of Memory, Time and Recognition in "À la recherche du temps perdu"* (Princeton: Princeton Univ. Press, 1962).

35. Thomas Wright, *The Passions of the Minde in Generall* (1604) (Urbana: Univ. of Illinois Press, 1971), 51–52.

36. Aristotle, *On the Soul* 427 b 24.

37. Shakespeare, Sonnet 30.

38. E.g. Rains, chap. 10, "Memory Systems," 255 ff.

39. Though there are, to be sure, those who deny this piece of "folk psychology," e.g., Nelson Goodman, *Languages of Art* (Indianapolis: Hackett, 1976), 5–9.
40. *Midsummer Night's Dream* 5.1.17.

By Way of a Conclusion: *On the Questions*
[pages 441–469]

1. Proclus as quoted in Thomas L. Heath, *The Thirteen Books of Euclid's Elements,* vol. 1 (New York: Dover, 1956), 125, and bk. 1, props. 1 and 5.
2. Kant, *Critique of Pure Reason* (1787), B 295.
3. Plato, *Timaeus* 29 d.
4. David Pye, *The Nature and Art of Workmanship* (London: Studio Vista, 1971), 7 ff.
5. Jane Austen, *Pride and Prejudice* I ix; *Hegel's "Philosophy of Mind": Being Part Three of the "Encyclopedia of Philosophical Sciences"* (1830), trans. William Wallace, together with *Zusätze* (1845), trans. A. V. Miller (Oxford: Clarendon Press, 1976), 87–88; Heinrich Heine, "Lyrisches Intermezzo" 36, from *Buch der Lieder* (1822–23): *"Aus meinen grossen Schmerzen mach ich die kleinen Lieder."* I am quoting from memory.
6. Shakespeare, Sonnet 18.
7. Song of Solomon 3:1. Nicholas Ayo, *Sacred Marriage: The Wisdom of the Song of Songs* (New York: Continuum, 1997).
8. Paul Valéry, "The Angel," *Poems in the Rough,* trans. Hilary Corke in *The Collected Works,* Bollingen Series XIV 2 (Princeton: Princeton Univ. Press, 1969), 14–16. Valéry reworked his draft of 1921 in 1945 for his last poem.
9. Milton, *Paradise Lost* 8.530.
10. Two books on emotion in the great apes: Jane Goodall, *The Chimpanzees of Gombe: Patterns of Behavior* (Cambridge: Harvard Univ. Press, 1986); Frans de Waal, *Good Natured: The Origins of Right and Wrong in Humans and Other Animals* (Cambridge: Harvard Univ. Press, 1996).
11. Species dissolved: Massimo Pigliucci and Jonathan Kaplan, *Making Sense of Evolution: The Conceptual Foundations of Evolutionary Biology* (Chicago: Univ. of Chicago Press, 2006), chap. 9, "Species as Family Resemblance Concepts: The Dis-Solution of the Species-Problem?" 207 ff. Human nature become flexible: Edward O. Wilson, *Consilience: The Unity of Knowledge* (New York: Knopf, 1998), on the Protean character of humanity (a notion traceable to the early Renaissance, for example in Giovanni Pico della Mirandola's "Oration on the Dignity of Man" [1487]: "Who then will not look with awe upon this our chameleon . . . this creature man . . . this nature capable of transforming itself . . . symbolized in the figure of Proteus"; Wilson emphasizes the notion of "volitional evolution" that replaces natural evolution as a "prosthetic" environment replaces the natural environment and thus natural selection: *Homo sapiens* has become a new species, the indeterminately flexible *Homo proteus* [276, 278, 289]). Emotion not a natural kind: Paul E. Griffiths, *What Emotions Really Are: The Problem of Psychological Categories* (Chicago: Univ. of Chicago Press, 1997), chap. 9, 228 ff.
12. Pigliucci and Kaplan, 162 ff.
13. Griffiths, 247.
14. Kant, *Untersuchung über die Deutlichkeit der Grundsätze der natürlichen Theologie und der Moral* (1764) 1, para. 3.
15. Hegel, *Philosophy of Mind,* sec. 1 (Mind Subjective), subsec. A (Anthropology, the Soul), para. 400–403, p. 73. This sense of ownness can be dissociated from one's memories in traumatic brain injury, with a loss of "warmth and immediacy" (Daniel M. Wegner, *The Illusion of Conscious Will* [Cambridge: M.I.T. Press, 2002], 234 n. 5, quoted from Stuss).
16. Moreover, my availing myself of the term subjectivity itself might need justification (as -isms, -ologies, and -ivities generally do). I mean by it here just an attribute of a middle realm of the human soul, the region of affect, reachable by introspection. It must be distinguished from the *Subject,* the Ego, which is in some great philosophical frameworks the ultimate ground and bearer of self-consciousness and world-cognition. As such, the latter is beyond, it "transcends," even inner experience and observation and requires a deeper inquiry than I am engaged in

here. Husserl formulates my meaning: "I myself, as transcendental ego 'constitute' the world, and at the same time, *as soul* [my italics] I am a human ego in the world"—a soul which is amenable to study in "a natural and naïve manner of being directed toward the 'inwardness' of men" (Edmund Husserl, *The Crisis of European Sciences and Transcendental Phenomenology: An Introduction to Phenomenological Philosophy* [Evanston, Ill.: Northwestern Univ. Press, 1970], 202, 244). It is this inwardness that can be thought about naturally and naively, that has "subjectivity," and that is the focus of this Conclusion.

17. Richard Dien Winfield, *Systematic Aesthetics* (Gainesville: Univ. Press of Florida, 1995), 79.

18. I here take it that self-consciousness is to self-awareness as looking *at myself* is to *being my*self. My colleague Robert Druecker's lecture "'You are that': The *Upanishads* Read Through Western Eyes," to appear in the *St. John's Review,* contains a meditation on an analogous distinction in the Indian context.

19. Hegel, *Philosophy of Mind,* 85.

20. I stay away here from, and have merely touched on earlier, the vexed question of identifying facial expressions: how it is done for non-articulate species, whether expressions are universal in humans, and what their origin is in general and in particular. These are Darwin's great questions.

   Species-specific facial expressions in chimpanzees seem to be established in the sense that it is possible to inventory a variety that go with situations and behavior reasonably interpreted as specifically emotional: Jane Goodall, *In the Shadow of Man* (Boston: Houghton Mifflin, 1971), appendix B, 272 ff; a similar inventory of culture-specific facial, gestural—and linguistic—expressions for Frenchmen: Lawrence Wylie and Rick Stafford, *Beaux Gestes: A Guide to French Body Talk* (New York: E. P. Dutton, 1977). What makes this topic fascinating is that such expressions are so telling an externalization of affects in their double nature of being at once type and token. Doesn't every tale of love hang on recognizing one person's repertoire of expressions as the ideal representation of a human type while at the same time seeing it as an utterly unique singularity?

21. Hegel, *Philosophy of Mind,* 92–93.

22. *Odyssey* XX 18; Antonio Damasio, *Descartes' Error: Emotion, Reason, and the Human Brain* (Berkeley: Putnam, 1994), chaps. 1 and 2.

23. Adam Smith, *The Theory of Moral Sentiments,* 320.

24. Shakespeare, Sonnet 116.

25. Aristotle, *On the Soul* 430 a.

26. Tolstoy, *War and Peace* III 25, said of the governor of Moscow who, in his panic, is about to incite a lynching.

27. Lewis Carroll, *Alice in Wonderland,* chap. 12.

28. For both: Plato, *Sophist* 236 d ff.

29. Deuteronomy 6:5.

30. LeDoux, *The Emotional Brain,* 284 ff. Here is the physical mirror of the old problem of emotional control, of the difficult mastery of the affects by will or intellect. It has a very recent version, whose popularity preceded the complete conceptualization of its construal in theory and the corroboration of its existence by research, namely "emotional intelligence": "EI refers to the competence to identify and express emotions, understanding emotions, assimilate emotions in thought, and regulate both positive and negative emotions in the self and others." (Gerald Matthews, Moshe Zeidner, and Richard D. Roberts, *Emotional Intelligence: Science and Myth* [Cambridge: M.I.T. Press, 2002], 3.) EI is intended to have practical application as a teachable technique for the management of emotions. Thus the construct reconceives moral reasoning as a technical skill—at least implicitly: The seven-hundred-page book here cited has no index entry for ethics or morality. The efficacy of the program is so far unconfirmed (466). As so often in these conceptual ventures it is hard to tell whether the call for corroborating research is a beginning or the end.

31. George Eliot, *Middlemarch,* chap. 34; Aristotle, *On the Soul* 433 b 29.

32. *Much Ado about Nothing* 1.1 (my italics).

33. Pascal, *Pensées,* no. 410 in Penguin edition.

34. Plato, *Phaedrus* 230 a.

35. Aaron Sloman, "How Many Separately Evolved Emotional Beasties Live Within Us?" in *Emotions in Humans and Artifacts*, ed. Robert Trappl, Paolo Petta, and Sabine Payr (Cambridge: M.I.T. Press, 2002), 35–114.

36. Aristotle, *Nichomachean Ethics* 1166 a 17.

37. Spinoza, *Ethics* III, Def. of the Emotions, 1.

38. Oatley and Jenkins, *Understanding Emotions,* 166 ff.

39. Keith Baines' translation of Malory's *Morte d'Arthur* (New York: Mentor Classics, 1962), 458.

40. Aeschylus, *Agamemnon* 1.177.

41. I put culture in scare quotes because it has literally upward of a hundred definitions, listed in A. L. Kroeber and Clyde Kluckhohn, *Culture: A Critical Review of Concepts and Definitions* (New York: Vintage Books, 1963), 77–142.

42. *Iliad* II 212 ff.

43. G. S. Kirk and J. E. Raven, *The Presocratic Philosophers* (Cambridge: Cambridge Univ. Press, 1963), 424, no. 418; Empedocles was born c. 495 B.C.E.

44. Aristotle, *Metaphysics* 1072 b 3; Dante, *Paradiso* 33, where, however, the divinity not only attracts love but *is* love and emanates it.

45. Mark Johnson, *The Body in the Mind: The Bodily Basis of Meaning, Imagination, and Reason* (Chicago: Univ. of Chicago Press, 1987), examples: 7 ff.

46. The term Pathetic Fallacy was coined by John Ruskin, *Modern Painters* (1856) III iv; the quotation is from Babette Deutsch, *Poetry Handbook: A Dictionary of Terms* (New York: Grosset and Dunlap, 1962), 106.

47. Alexander Baumgarten, *Reflections on Poetry* (1735).

48. Walter Benjamin, *Das Kunstwerk im Zeitalter seiner technischen Reproduzierbarkeit* (1936).

49. Lennard J. Davis, *Factual Fictions: The Origins of the English Novel* (New York: Columbia Univ. Press, 1983), 45 ff.

50. Stephen Miller, *Conversation: A History of a Declining Art* (New Haven: Yale Univ. Press, 2006), 284.

51. *Twelfth Night* 1.1.1.

52. On the relation of mathematics and music: Edward Rothstein, *Emblems of Mind: The Inner Life of Music and Mathematics* (New York: Random House, 1995); on movement in music: Victor Zuckerkandl, *Man the Musician: Sound and Symbol II,* Bollingen Series XIV 2 (Princeton: Princeton Univ. Press, 1973).

53. Hegel, *Aesthetik,* pt. 3, sec. 3, chap. 2, 1; Hegel quotes Schlegel's saying that architecture is "frozen music" (sec. 2, chap. 2), because like music it embodies a mathematical structure.

54. Oatley and Jenkins, *Understanding Emotions,* chap. 3.

55. For example, the notorious "precursors of warfare," carried on by a male gang of chimpanzees for no evident adaptive good but out of sheer xenophobic passion, reported by Jane Goodall, *The Chimpanzees of Gombe,* chap. 17, especially 523, 530.

56. Oatley and Jenkins, 62–63; Pigliucci and Kaplan, chaps. 5 and 6; evolutionists seem to be in perpetual danger of telling "just so stories," named by scientists after Rudyard Kipling's children's book of 1902, which gives cute etiologies of the way animals came to be the way they are.

57. Rains, *Principles of Human Neuropsychology,* 323 ff., 347 ff.

58. Karen Blau, quoted in Thomas Bertonneau and Kim Paffenroth, *The Truth is Out There: Christian Faith and the Classics of TV Science Fiction* (Grand Rapids: Brazos Press, 2006), 71 ff., and n. 22. If the screenplay was written without conscious reference to Plato, the parallelism pointed out by the authors is even more gratifying.

59. Valéry, *The Angel,* 180.

60. Note well: By "our own mode" I don't mean the unconscious cognitive constructions that shape our knowledge below the threshold of our conscious desire.

61. Magda B. Arnold (1945), a pioneer in brain science and one of the scientific initiators of the appraisal theory of emotions, quoted in Oatley and Jenkins, 26.

62. As opposed to thoughtless, that is, rationalistic, reason.

63. Shakespeare, Sonnet 57.

Index